CW01655990

500 PORTRAITS

BP PORTRAIT AWARD

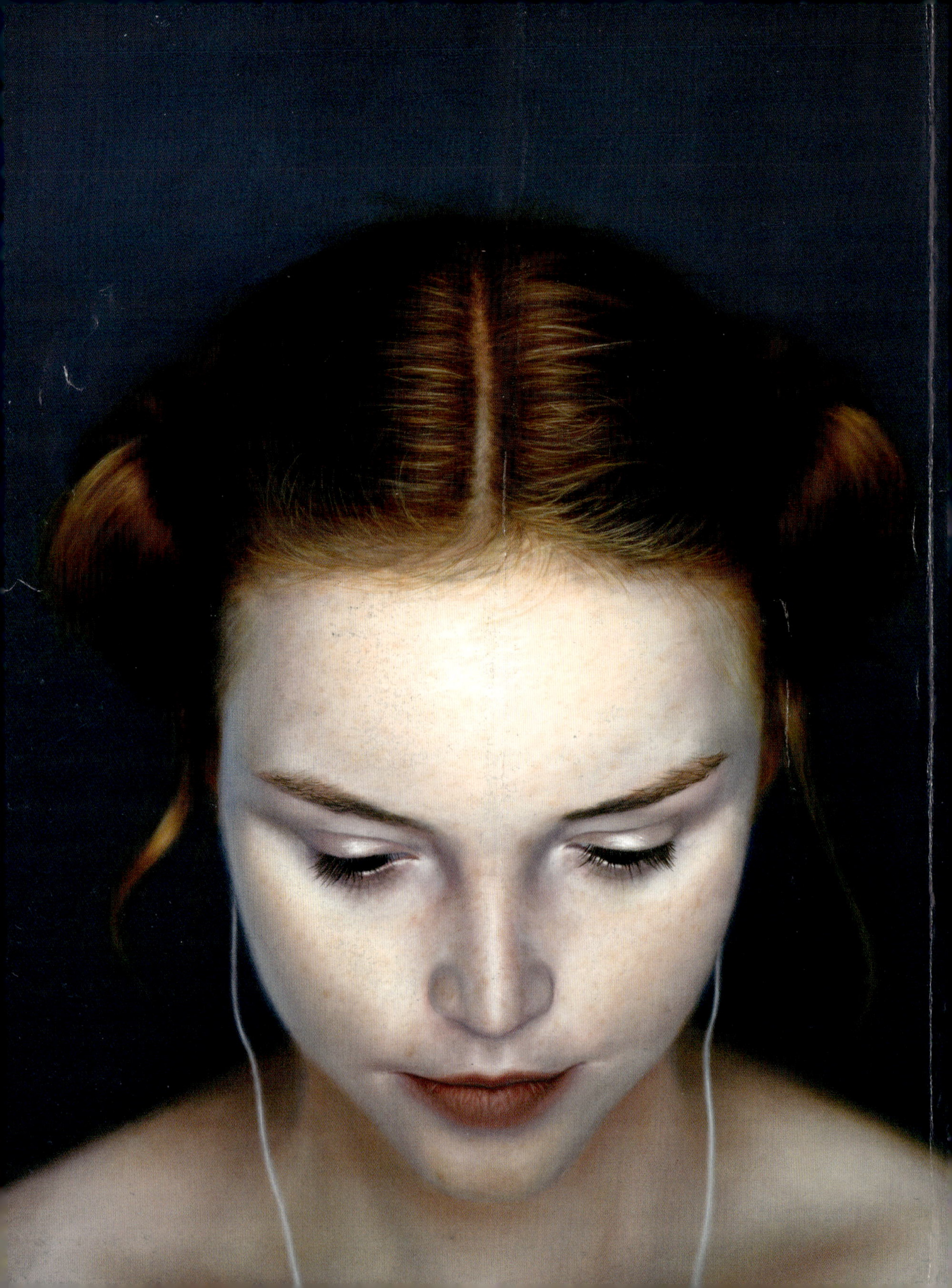

500 PORTRAITS

BP PORTRAIT AWARD

NATIONAL PORTRAIT GALLERY, LONDON

Published in Great Britain by
National Portrait Gallery Publications
National Portrait Gallery
St Martin's Place, London WC2H 0HE

For a complete catalogue of current publications please write to the address above, or visit our website at www.npg.org.uk/publications

Copyright © 2011 National Portrait Gallery, London

Images on pages 14–31 and 317–19 copyright © National Portrait Gallery, London. All other images copyright © the artists. Every effort has been made to contact copyright holders. We apologise for any inadvertent omissions, which will be corrected in future editions if the publisher is notified in writing.

The moral rights of the authors have been asserted. All rights reserved. No part of this publication may be reproduced, stored in a retrieval system or transmitted in any form or by any means, whether electronic or mechanical, including photocopying, recording or otherwise, without the prior permission in writing of the publisher.

ISBN 978 1 85514 448 4

A catalogue record for this book is available from the British Library.

10 9 8 7 6 5 4 3 2 1

Head of Publications: Celia Joicey
Managing Editor: Christopher Tinker
Editorial: Robert Davies, Susie Foster
Art Direction: October
Design: Toni Din
Production: Ruth Müller-Wirth
Printed and bound in Italy

MIX
Paper from responsible sources
FSC
www.fsc.org
FSC® C015829

Caption texts to prizewinning works have been drawn from various sources, including biography forms submitted for the BP Portrait Award, more recent communications with the National Portrait Gallery, catalogues, press releases and, in some cases, artists' websites. Every effort has been made to ensure that the information is correct at the time of going to press. Should any artist wish to supply updated information about their current status, the National Portrait Gallery would be pleased to hear from them: bpaward@npg.org.uk

Front cover: *Erin* (2005)
by Jonathan Yeo (see page 211).

Back cover (left to right): *Tom* (2009, detail) by Michael Gaskell (see page 275); *Sarah* (2006, detail) by Darvish Fakhr (see page 218); *Konjit* (2008) by Maryam Foroozanfar (see page 264).

Page 2: *iDeath* (2010, detail)
by Michal Ožibko (see page 308).

Page 6: *Don't Be Too Serious* (2010, detail)
by Elizabeth McDonald (see page 291).

Page 8: *Blue Coco* (2010, detail)
by Shaun Downey (see page 297).

Page 10: *Harry* (2010, detail)
by Michael Gaskell (see page 289).

Page 13: *Fiona Shaw* (2002, detail)
by Victoria Russell (see page 25).

Page 35: *Giulietta Coates* (2005, detail)
by Dean Marsh (see page 51).

Page 60: *Blue in Yellow* (1990, detail)
by Sara Rossberg (see page 65).

The portrait of Thomas Adès by Phil Hale reproduced on page 318 was commissioned with help from the Jerwood Charitable Foundation through the Jerwood Portrait Commission, 2002.

Quotations are taken from BP Portrait Award catalogue essays by William Packer (2002), A.S. Byatt (2003), Blake Morrison (2004), Philip Hensher (2005), Margaret Forster (2006), Lynne Truss (2007), Alexander McCall Smith (2008), Sarah Dunant (2009) and Rose

CONTENTS

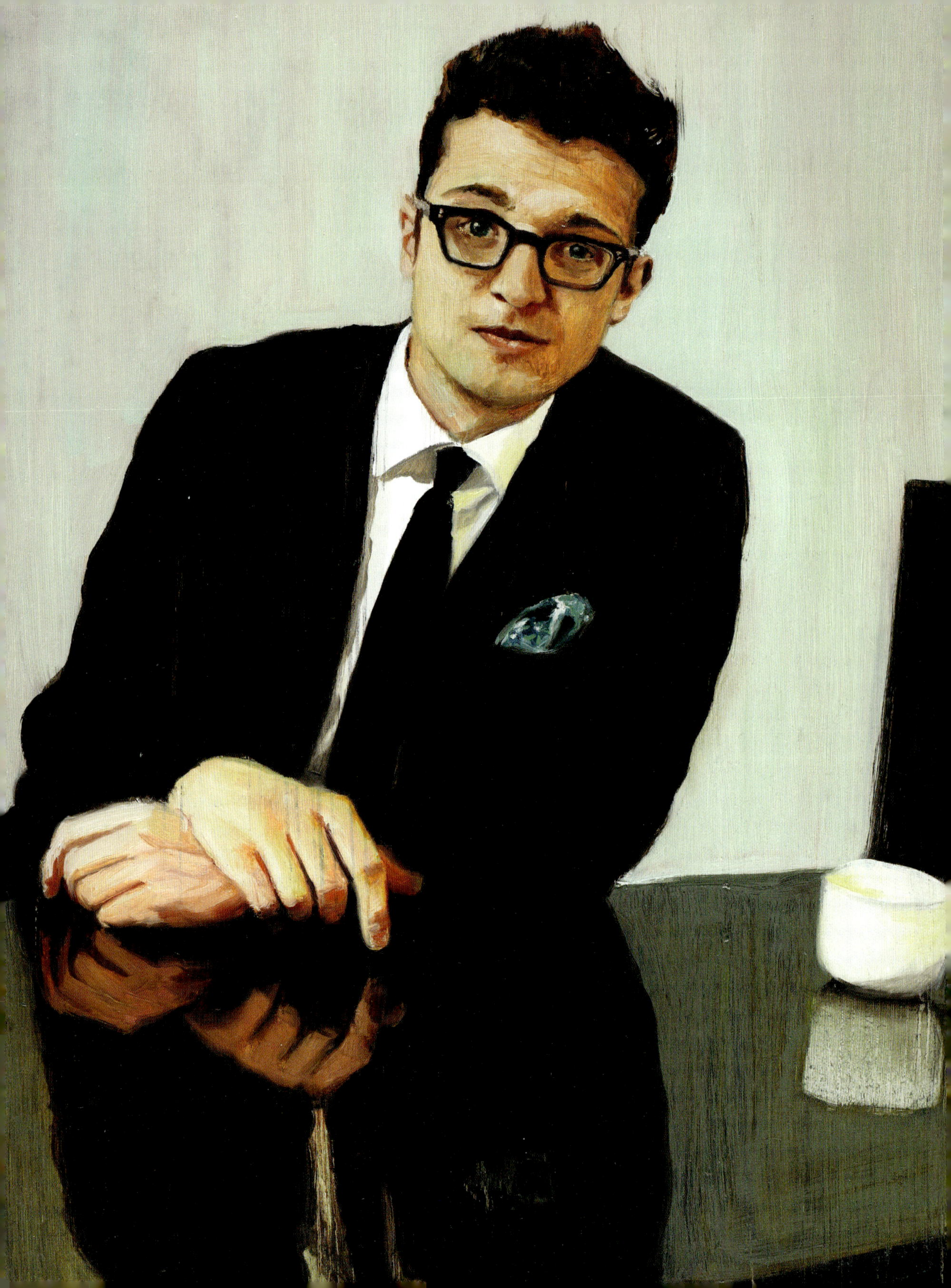

FOREWORD
PETER MATHER

Group Regional Vice President, Europe
BP plc

BP has supported the Portrait Award since 1990. The programme has evolved over the past twenty years and seen a number of developments including the popular Travel Award, which encourages portrait artists to experience working in a different environment. In 2007 the Award was opened up to a wider age range and, as a result, there has been a significant increase in entries. Most recently, we extended the programme with the BP Portrait Award: Next Generation project, enabling young people to work with some of the many talented artists who have been past winners of the Award.

One of the highlights over the years has been the commissions that form part of the prize for each year's overall winner, some of which can be seen in this book. The annual exhibition of winners and selected work is held at the National Portrait Gallery, London. Taking the exhibition on tour has also been an important aspect of the partnership and has helped to establish strong connections with both the Aberdeen Art Gallery and the Scottish National Portrait Gallery.

The exhibition is a testament to the great talent that the BP Portrait Award attracts from around the world, and this book clearly demonstrates the range, creativity and enthusiasm of the artists – not only those who have been selected for the exhibition, but also the many others who, over the years, have responded to the call for entries.

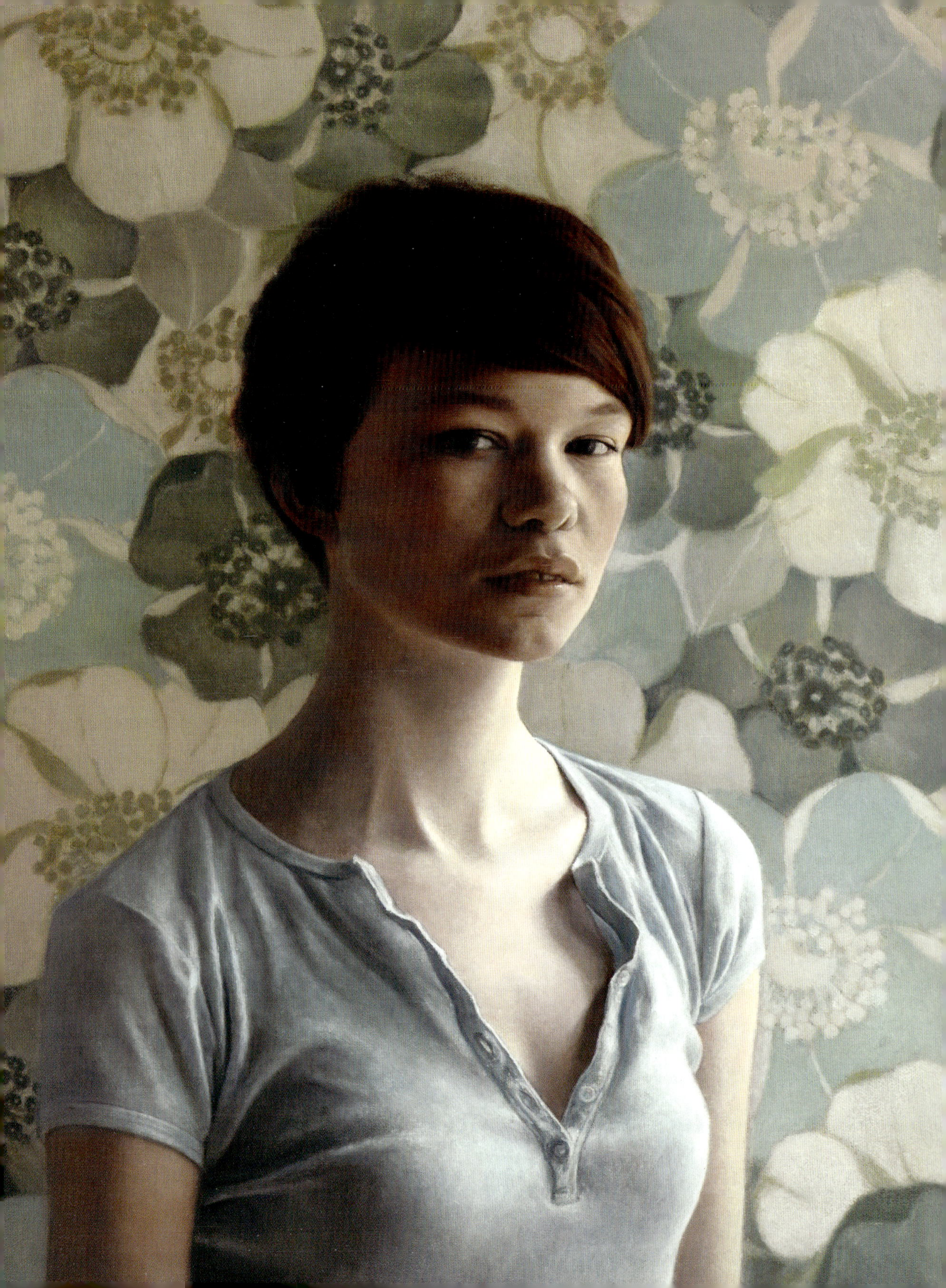

PAINTING PEOPLE: RENEWING TRADITION AND MAKING NEW

SANDY NAIRNE
Director,
National Portrait Gallery, London

In the history of the National Portrait Gallery, the founding of the Portrait Award in 1980 counts as one of the most significant events. Under the leadership of its then Director, John Hayes, the Gallery moved away from simply displaying and collecting contemporary painted portraits to become an active agent in the renewal of portrait traditions and the promotion of new generations of younger painters attracted to portraiture. This was at a time when abstract, conceptual or more political strands held sway in art-critical circles. It was a bold move.

When, after a decade, BP became involved as the sponsor of the Portrait Award, a certain momentum was gathering. With renewed support, the competition has become increasingly popular, and the exhibition a key event in London's cultural calendar, asserting the continuing international significance of painted portraiture within an increasingly media-driven world. The Award is currently one of the longest-running arts sponsorships, and such dedicated partnership has allowed it not only to grow, but also to respond to changing priorities. With twenty years of continuous support, BP has therefore raised the bar in terms of commitment for a corporate sponsor. This book tells the story of that development, and provides an overview of the achievements of more than 400 talented artists whose skills and creative abilities are celebrated.

The BP Portrait Award is a competition open to artists from around the world, based on the submission of a single portrait, which should be completed during the previous year and painted from life. Each painting is considered directly, not through a reproduction, and is judged anonymously so that the judges have no idea which artist's work is in front of them. Originally targeted at younger artists – deliberately to nurture new talent – the competition has since 2007 been open to all artists over the age of eighteen. In recent years we have received annual entries from more than 2,000 artists, and around sixty works have been selected for the exhibition each year. Prizewinners are chosen and the overall winner is invited to undertake a commissioned portrait of a public figure for the Gallery's Collection.

The exhibition travels in England, Scotland and Wales, and is now seen by more than 350,000 people each year. The BP Travel Award has become an important element of the project, with an artist given the chance each year to pursue their work in a different environment. Assignments have included Darvish Fakhr capturing subjects chosen from the streets of Tehran,

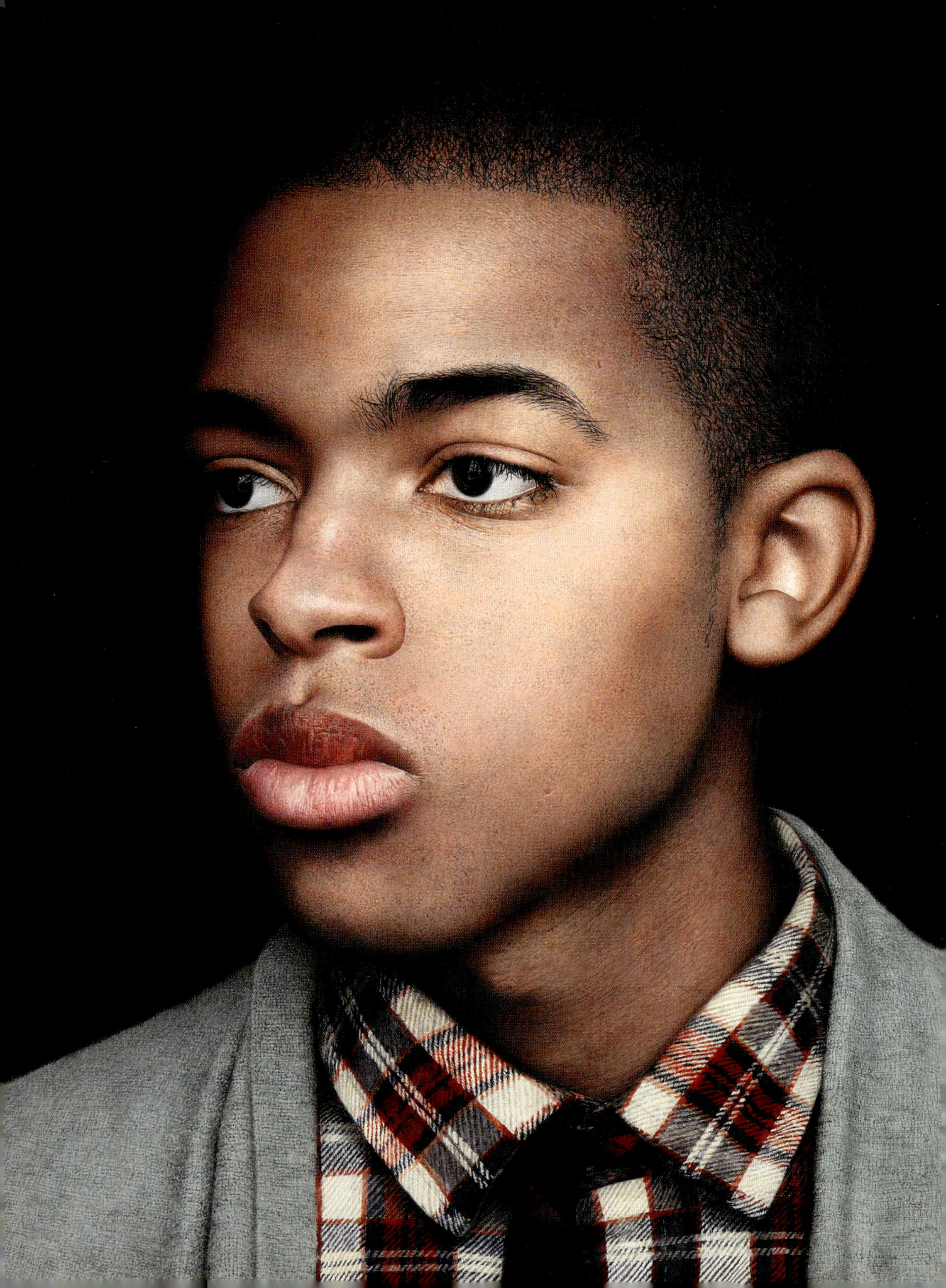

Joel Ely portraying the commitment of Basque people renewing their cooking traditions, and Isobel Peachey tracking the characters involved in re-enacting historical battles. In addition, since 2010, the BP Portrait Award: Next Generation project has sought to offer talented young people the chance to be tutored in portrait painting by BP prizewinners, spreading the word to fourteen to nineteen year olds that these are skills worth honing over the years ahead.

The Award has gradually attracted more entrants – and from an ever-larger number of countries. This broadening submission has been matched by the growing number of visitors. Perhaps even more important is the role of the Award in offering wider recognition for talented artists, acting as a springboard for Charlotte Harris, Stephen Shankland, Stuart Pearson Wright, Craig Wylie and many others. The prize money provides the recipient with a period of financial stability, but also leads to commissions and critical recognition.

The BP commissions are an admired feature of the Gallery's contemporary collection. They range from the powerful figure of Fiona Shaw as rendered by Victoria Russell, to Catherine Goodman's intense evocation of Dame Cicely Saunders and to the wonderful winter portrait of V.S. Naipaul by Paul Emsley. These works are a lasting testament to the skills of contemporary portrait painters. Yet matching the most suitable artist to the chosen subject for a successful commission also involves the particular skills of the Gallery's curators.

The choice of portraits in each exhibition is made by the judges, who include artists, critics and curators. As the Chair of the panel I am conscious of the need for proper process: first, to guarantee that each artist's work is examined appropriately, and secondly, to ensure that the breadth of the judges' views is translated into the final selection. Interestingly, the annual debates often anticipate the public discussion of the exhibition that inevitably follows – about, for instance, the relative merits of more realist or more painterly styles, the place of group portraits and the various choices of subject and pose. Indeed, many visitors are prepared to challenge the views of the judges through the exhibition's Visitors' Choice process.

Since 2002 the BP Portrait Award catalogue has provided a record of all the chosen works and, equally importantly, it has encouraged critical debate around the role of contemporary painted portraiture. Whether A.S. Byatt, Blake Morrison, Sarah Dunant or Rose Tremain, each essayist has excited readers by sharing their personal engagement with portraiture, often revealing how it interacts with their own thinking and writing.

The Portrait Award has a vital part to play in the contemporary visual arts scene in Britain and, given the interest of artists and the attentiveness of viewers, a very bright future.

WINNERS' COMMISSIONS

The National Portrait Gallery commissions about six works a year as part of its commitment to collecting portraits of those who have made an important contribution to British history and culture. Part of the First Prize for winning the BP Portrait Award is a commission to paint a well-known figure, and the resulting work subsequently enters the Gallery's Collection. This section highlights those portraits that have been commissioned from artists who won First Prize in the Portrait Award.

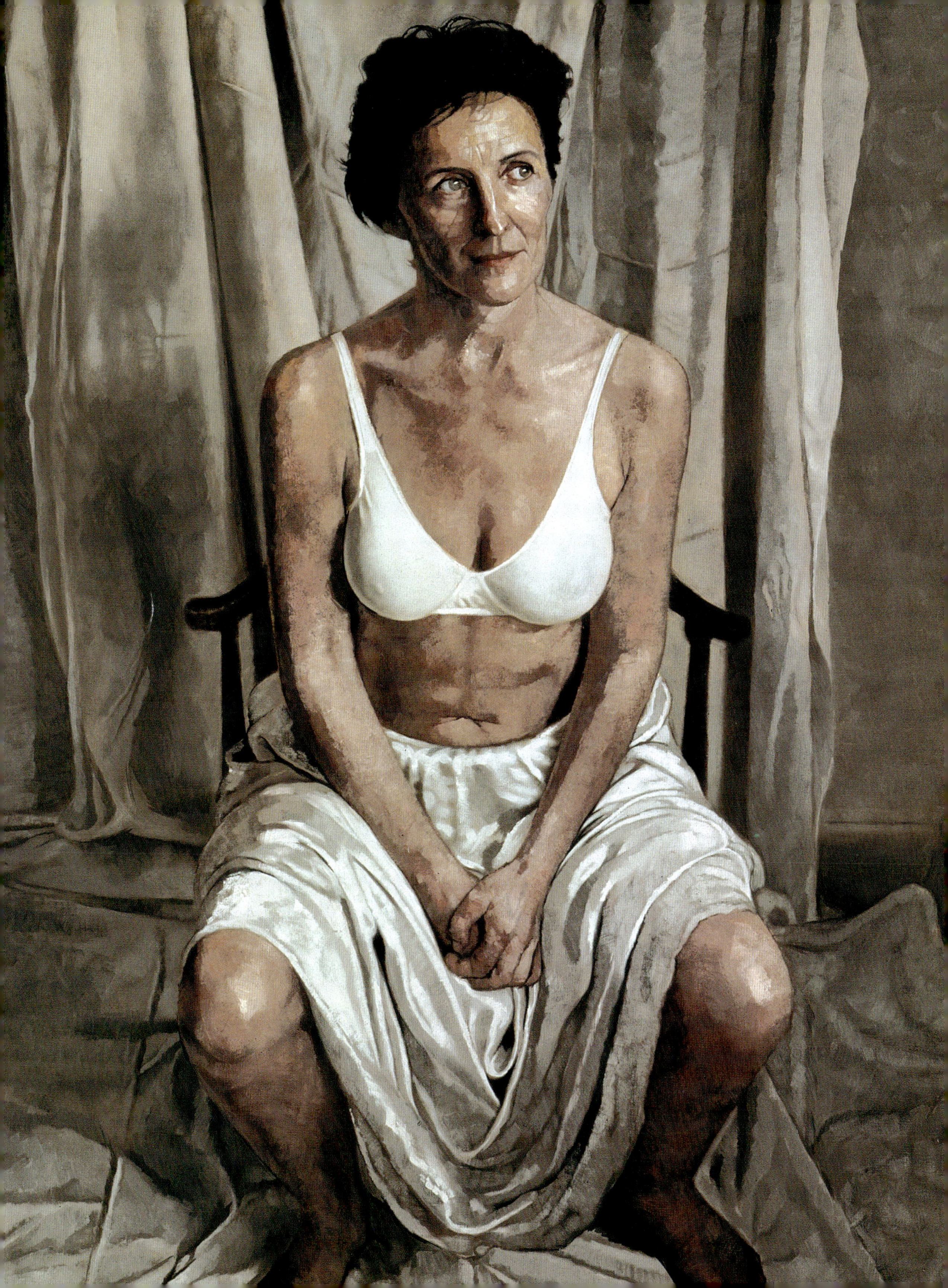

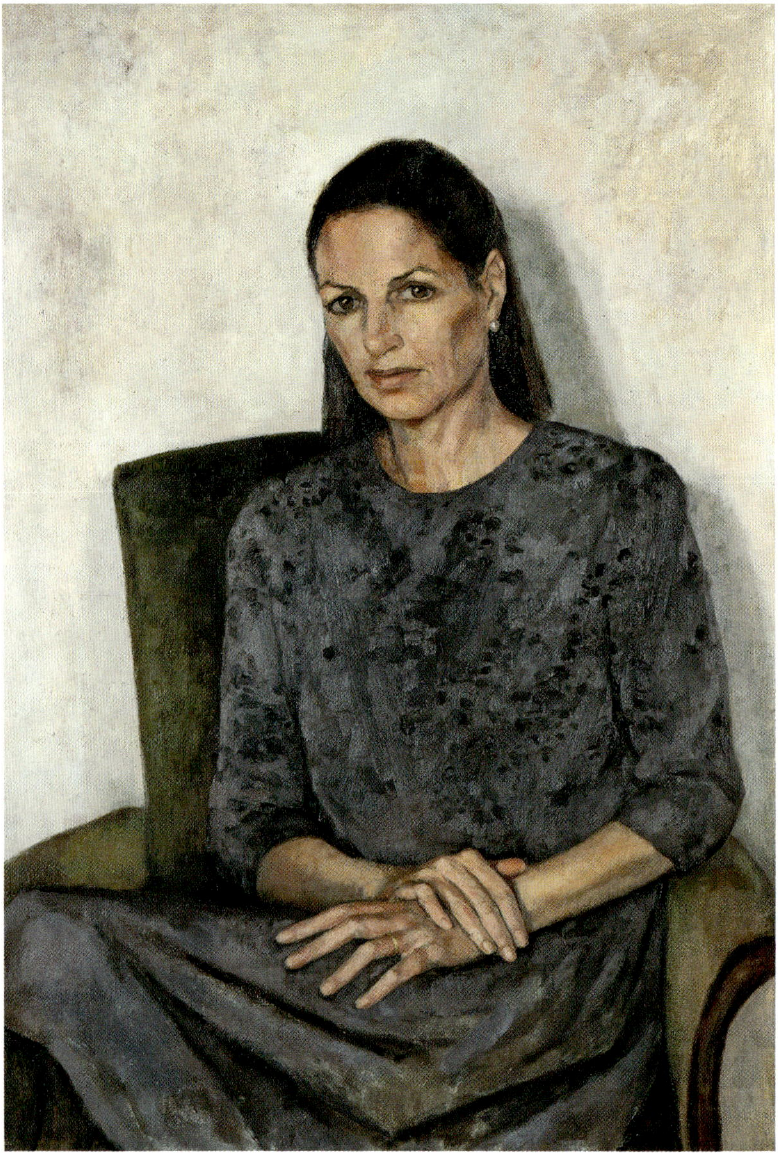

TESSA BLACKSTONE, BARONESS BLACKSTONE
ANNABEL CULLEN

Oil on canvas
1991
914 x 607mm
NPG 6157

Academic, educationalist and politician, Baroness Blackstone (b.1942) has been Vice-Chancellor of the University of Greenwich since 2004. As part of the Labour government, she was Minister of State for the Arts (2001–3) and Minister of State for Education and Employment (1997–2001). For a decade from 1987 she was Master of Birkbeck College, University of London and Chair of the BBC's General Advisory Council (1987–91). Awarded a life peerage in 1987, Baroness Blackstone has published many books on education and social policy issues. Annabel Cullen's portrait was painted following around eight sittings which took place over a period of three months, at Baroness Blackstone's flat in London.

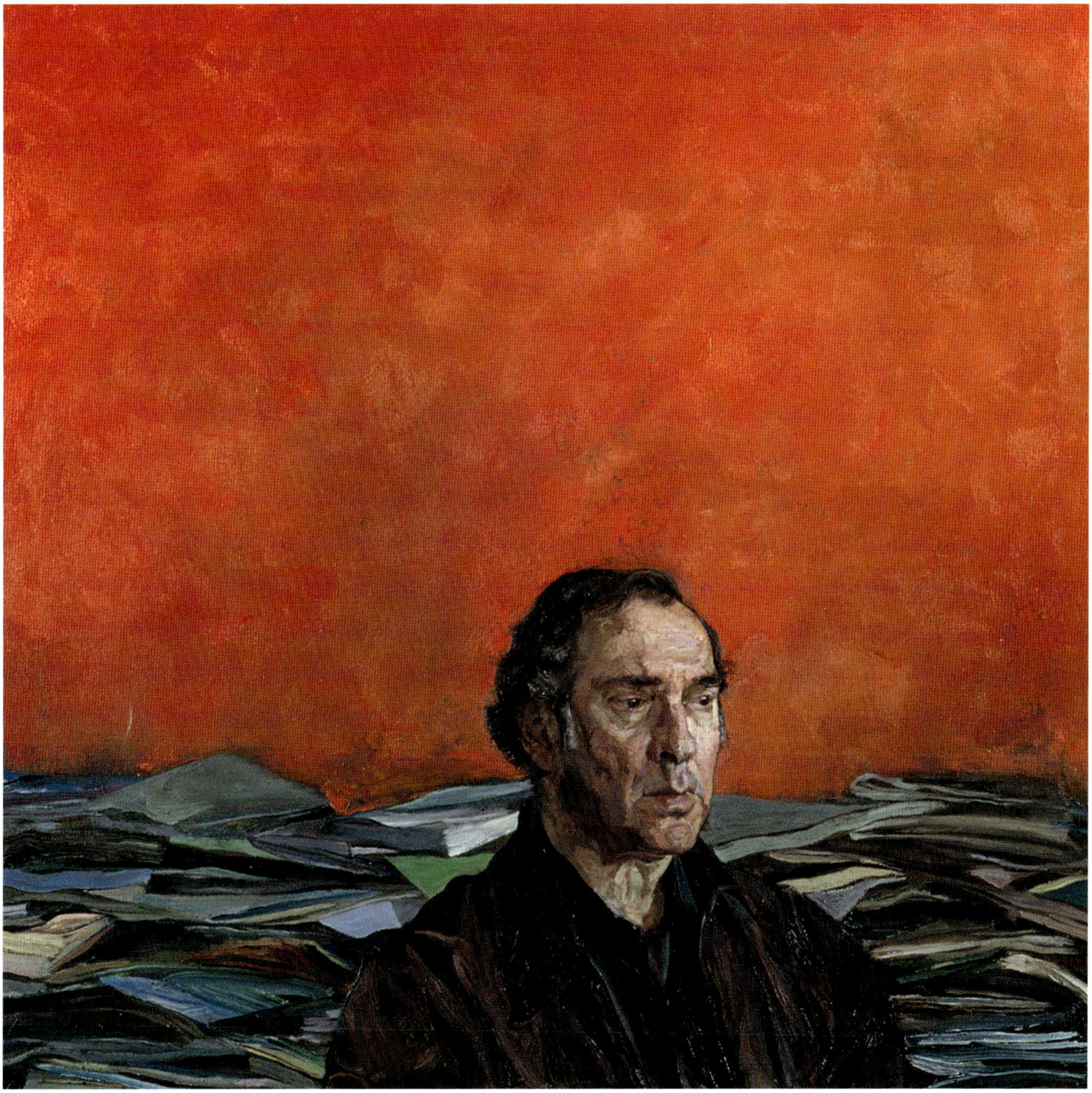

HAROLD PINTER
JUSTIN MORTIMER

Oil on canvas
1992
910 x 910mm
NPG 6185

Harold Pinter (1930–2008) was a playwright, director, actor and writer. During a career spanning over fifty years, he produced such memorable plays as *The Birthday Party* (1957), *The Caretaker* (1960) and *The Homecoming* (1965), as well as screenplays including *The Servant* (1962) and *The French Lieutenant's Woman* (1981). He also wrote several volumes of poetry and was awarded the Nobel Prize for Literature in 2005. Despite frail health in later life, he continued to act until 2006. Justin Mortimer's vivid portrait depicts Pinter in front of a huge pile of books and scripts, an appropriate symbol of his prolific output during a long and influential career.

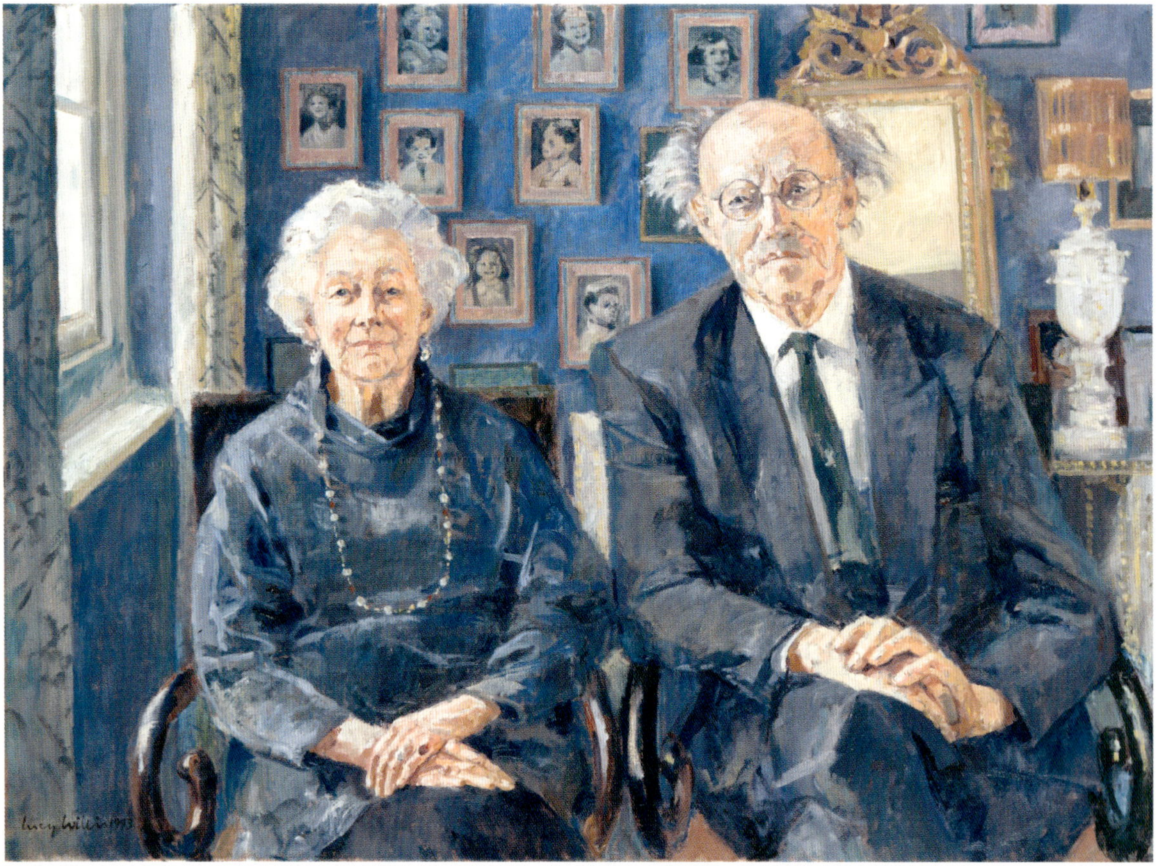

ELIZABETH, COUNTESS OF LONGFORD; FRANCIS, 7TH EARL OF LONGFORD

LUCY WILLIS

Oil on canvas
1993
762 x 1011mm
NPG 6210

Author, publisher, politician and penal reform campaigner, Francis Pakenham, Lord Longford (1905–2001), served as Labour Leader of the House of Lords (1964–8), Lord Privy Seal (1966–8) and Secretary of State for the Colonies (1965–6). Chairman of the publishing firm Sidgwick and Jackson, his publications include *The Idea of Punishment* (1961) and two volumes of autobiography. Lord Longford's wife, Elizabeth (1906–2002), was a biographer and historian. She wrote authoritative biographies on Joseph Chamberlain, the Duke of Wellington and Queen Victoria. This double portrait was painted in the bedroom of the Longfords' flat in Chelsea, and includes photographs of their children on the wall in the background.

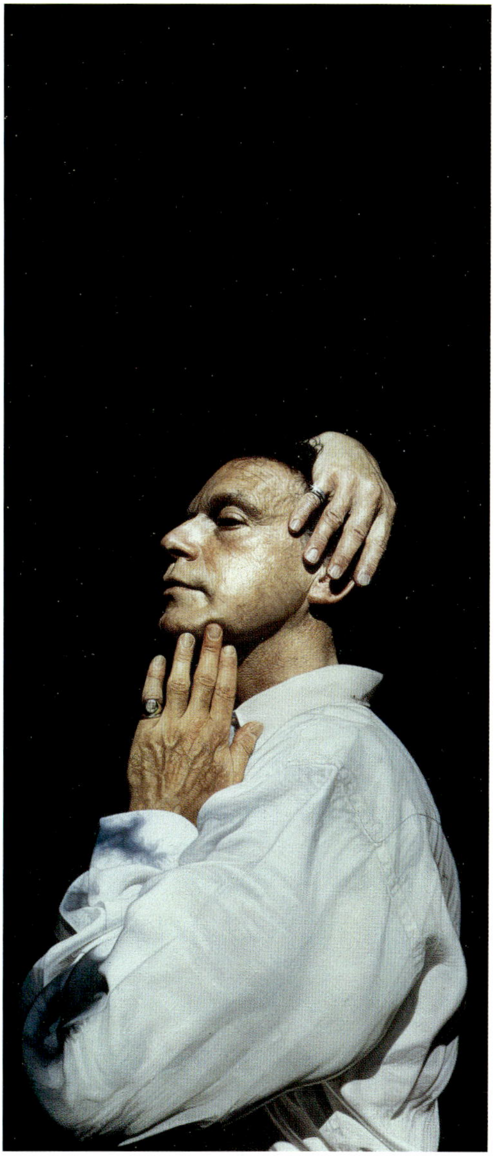

SIR ANTHONY DOWELL
PHILIP HARRIS

Oil on canvas
1995
959 x 406mm
NPG 6331

One of the foremost dancers of his generation, Anthony Dowell (b.1943) joined the Royal Ballet in 1961. Promoted to principal dancer in 1966, he later became artistic director of the Royal Ballet (1986–2001). Among the most notable roles he has created are Oberon in *The Dream* (1964), Troyte in *Enigma Variations* (1968) and Beliaev in *A Month in the Country* (1976). Philip Harris based his portrait on a series of photographs taken in the sitter's garden in strong sunlight. Dowell, so often directed by choreographers, was posed in an attitude to portray a sense of dance.

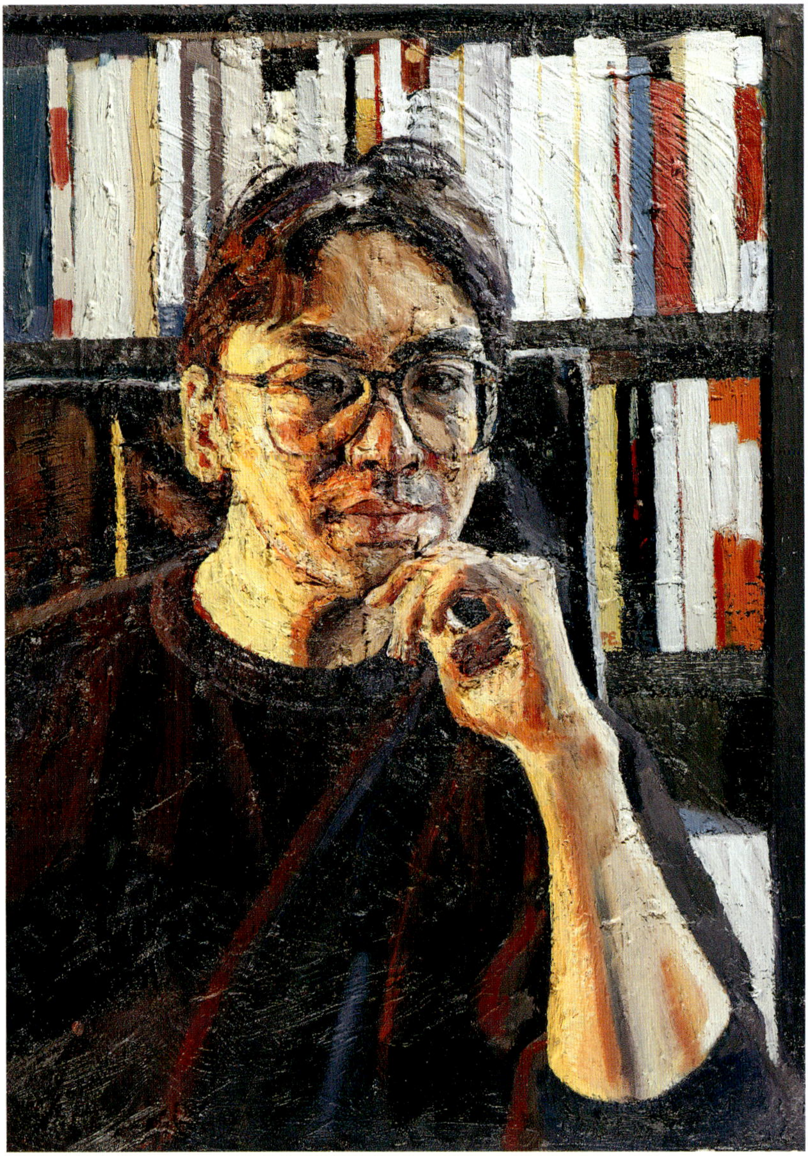

KAZUO ISHIGURO
PETER EDWARDS

Oil on canvas
1995
749 x 556mm
NPG 6332

Kazuo Ishiguro was born in Nagasaki, Japan, in 1954 and came to England at the age of six. After studying creative writing at the University of East Anglia he became a community worker in Glasgow before writing his first novel, *A Pale View of Hills* (1982), a highly personal view of Japanese history and society. His third novel, *The Remains of the Day* (1989), won the Booker Prize and was made into an award-winning film in 1993. Other works include *When We Were Orphans* (2000) and *Never Let Me Go* (2005), which was also made into a film in 2010.

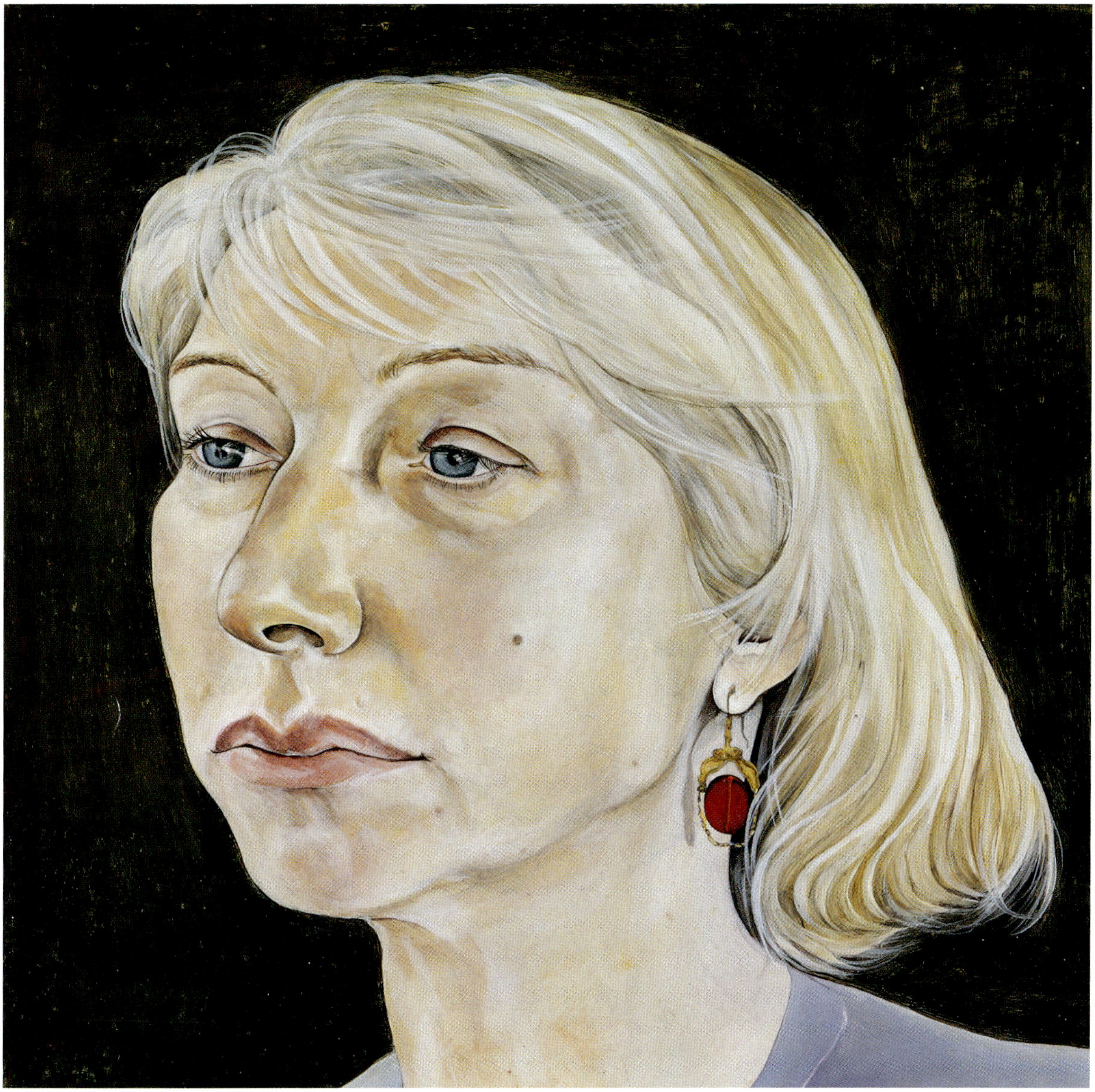

DAME HELEN MIRREN
ISHBEL MYERSCOUGH

Oil on board
1997
351 x 348mm
NPG 6415

From acting with the Royal Shakespeare Company to starring in Hollywood films, the actress Helen Mirren (b.1945) has taken on a wide range of roles for both stage and screen during her distinguished career. Her film performances include Robert Altman's *Gosford Park* (2001) and *The Queen* (2006), for which she won an Oscar for Best Actress. Mirren has been vocal in human rights issues, particularly for women in developing countries. She was made a Dame of the British Empire in 2003. Completed in just one week at Mirren's Los Angeles home, this portrait's small scale reflects Ishbel Myerscough's solution to capturing a busy sitter.

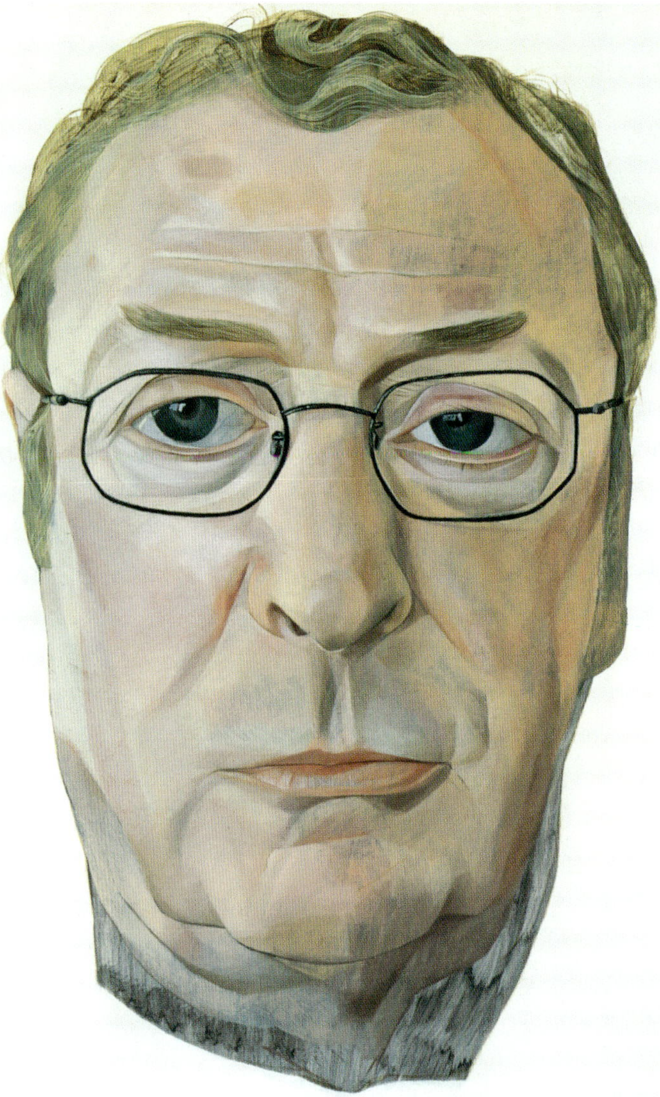

SIR MICHAEL CAINE
JAMES HAGUE

Oil on board
1998
356 x 279mm
NPG 6411

Born Maurice Micklewhite in London in 1933, Michael Caine came to prominence as an actor in 1964 as Lieutenant Bromhead in *Zulu* and, with his trademark glasses and Cockney accent, went on to star in many hit films of the 1960s and 1970s. His most memorable roles include the spy Harry Palmer in *The Ipcress File* (1965), the title role in *Alfie* (1966) and Charlie Croker in *The Italian Job* (1969). Caine has won two Oscars and was knighted in 2000. This work by James Hague was painted in the sitter's London flat and was the result of five sittings totalling about twelve hours.

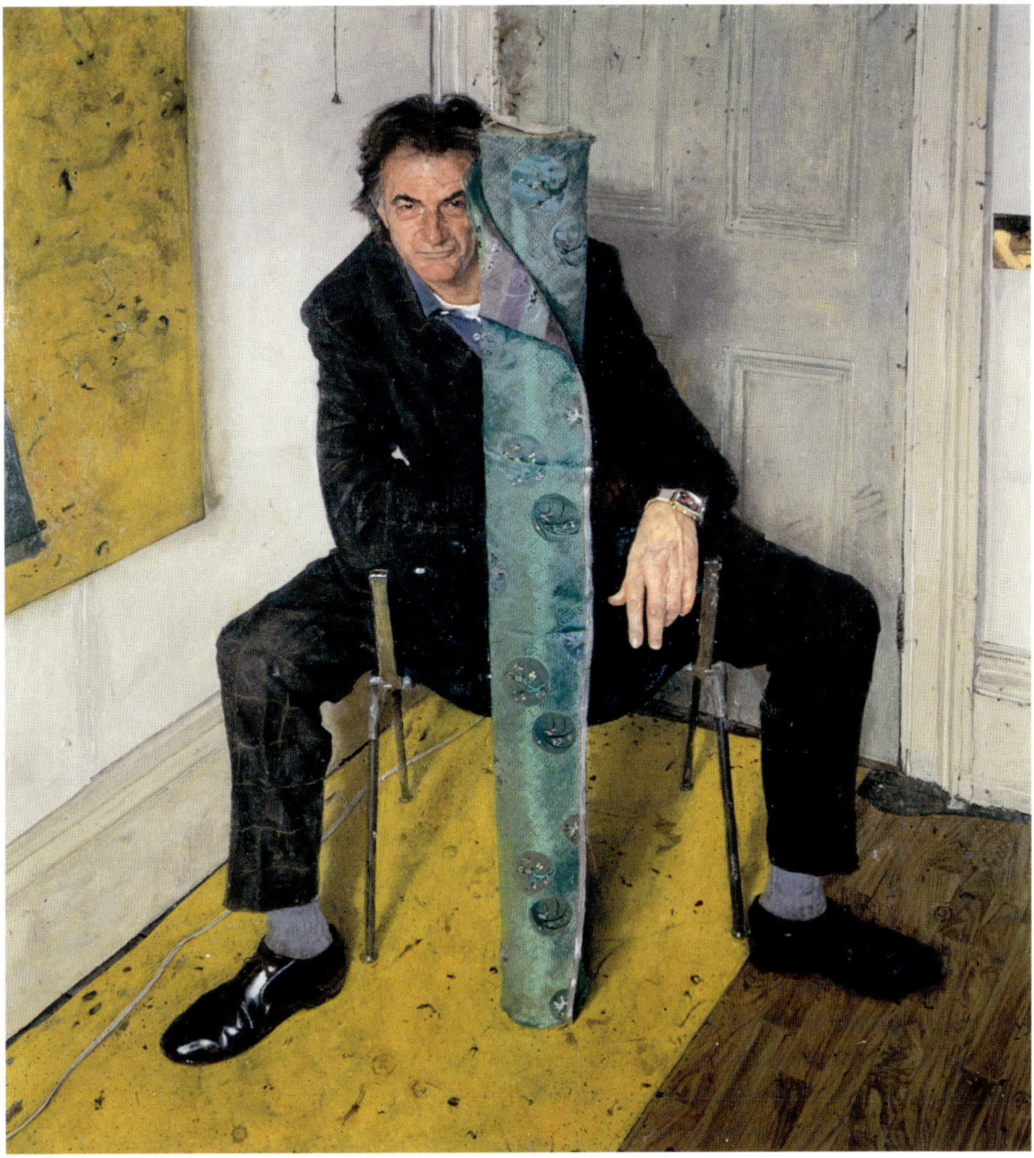

SIR PAUL SMITH
JAMES LLOYD

Oil on canvas
1998
1624 x 1451mm
NPG 6441

At the age of sixteen, Paul Smith (b.1946) was introduced to fashion through working at a clothing warehouse in his home town of Nottingham. After taking evening classes in tailoring, he was offered a job in Savile Row and in 1970 opened his first shop back in Nottingham. He now has twelve collections that are sold worldwide and was knighted in 2000. James Lloyd held the Paul Smith Scholarship at the Slade School of Art (1994–6). Painted in the artist's studio, this portrait includes part of an earlier painting by Lloyd (back left), which is now in Smith's collection.

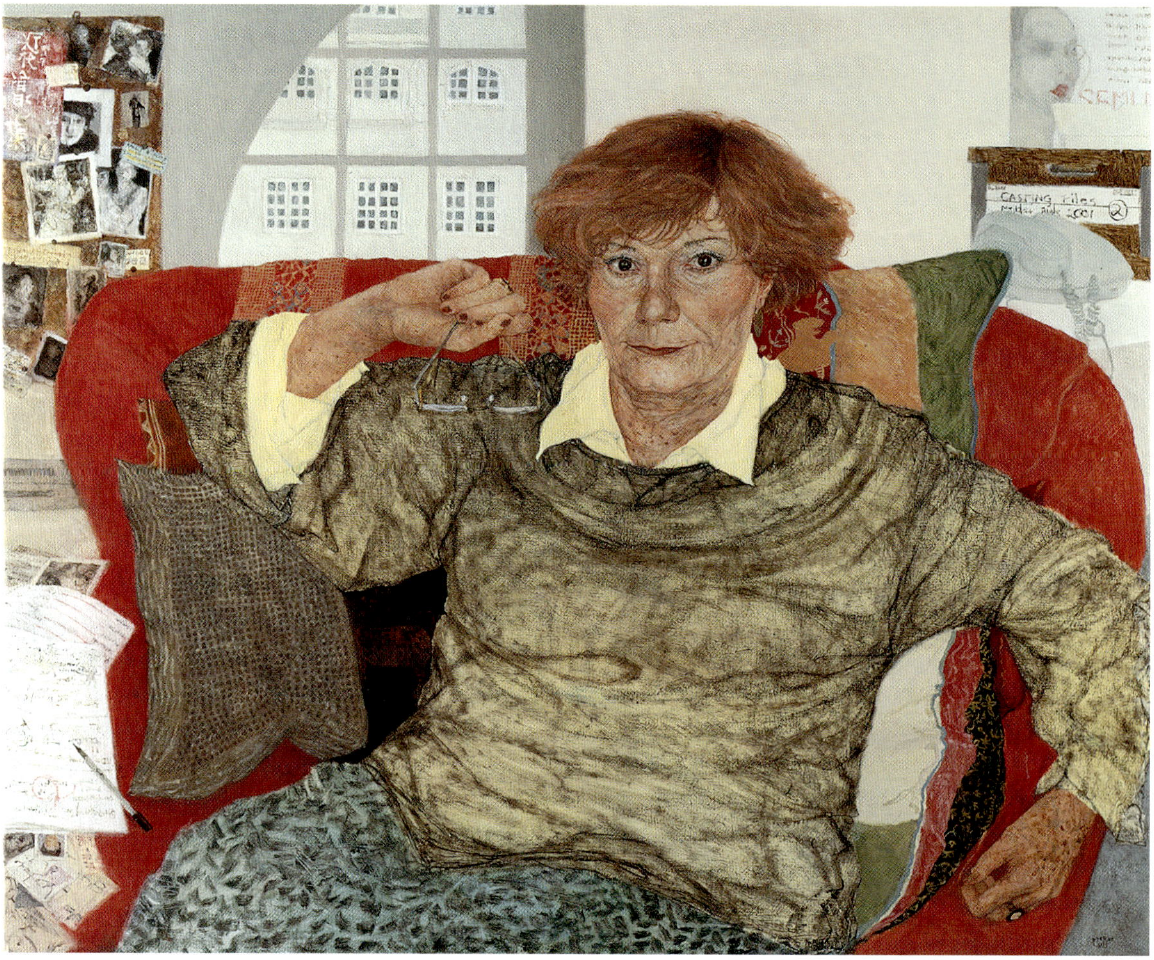

THELMA HOLT
JENNIFER MCRAE

Oil on canvas
2001
737 x 864mm
NPG 6608

Theatre producer Thelma Holt (b.1932) is known for her visionary and daring productions. After studying at the Royal Academy of Dramatic Art, she embarked on an acting career, most memorably appearing as Lady Macbeth in an avant-garde production of 1969. Holt co-founded London's Open Space Theatre in 1965 and was Artistic and Executive Director of the Roundhouse Theatre from 1977 to 1983. In 1990 she formed Thelma Holt Ltd, with notable productions including Chekhov's *Three Sisters* (1990) and Ibsen's *A Doll's House* (1996). She co-produced *Musashi* at the Barbican in 2010. Jennifer McRae's portrait depicts Holt in her office in the heart of the London theatre world, and is the result of numerous sittings, which took place over a four-month period.

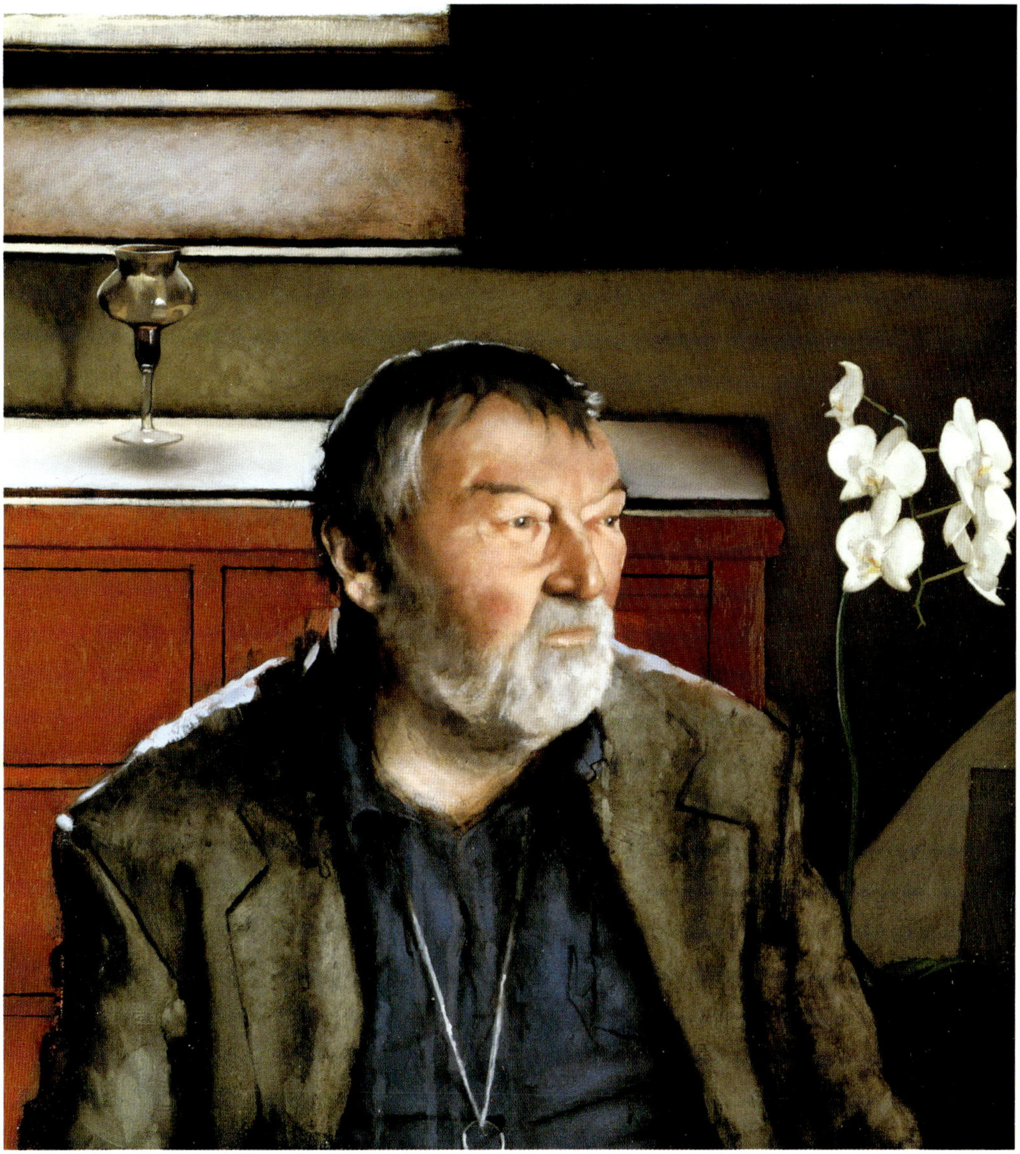

JOHN FOWLES
TOMAS WATSON

Oil on linen
2001
712 x 614mm
NPG 6584

Writer John Fowles (1926–2005) was born in Leigh-on-Sea in Essex and educated at the University of Edinburgh and New College, Oxford. A master of layered story-telling, illusionism and ambiguous endings, Fowles worked in a variety of genres from psychological thriller (*The Collector*, 1963) to mythological magic realism (*The Magus*, 1966). His semi-historical novel *The French Lieutenant's Woman* (1969) was made into a film in 1981. This portrait was painted in a flat owned by the sitter near his home in Lyme Regis, where the artist stayed. Tomas Watson had thirteen sittings and worked for over 100 hours on the portrait. Fowles sat looking out of a window at the Cobb, a sea wall that is featured in *The French Lieutenant's Woman.*

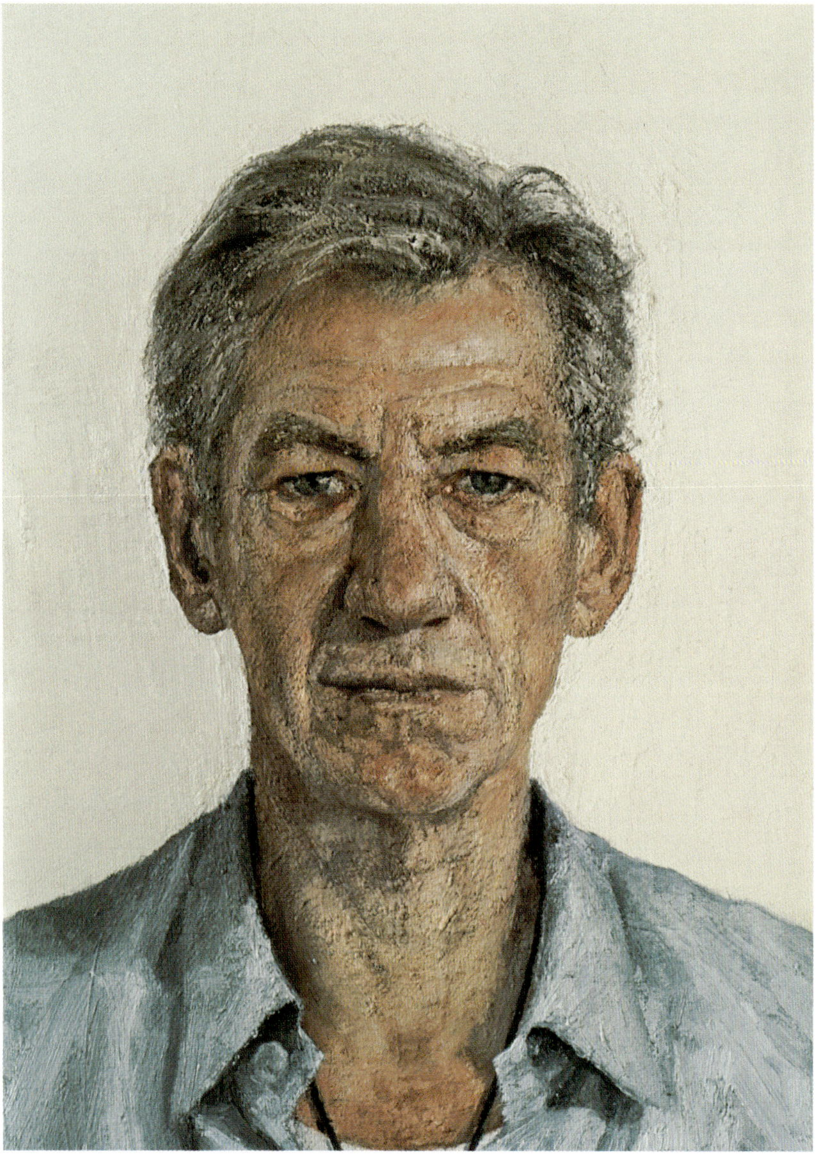

SIR IAN MCKELLEN
CLIVE SMITH

Oil on canvas
2002
336 x 206mm
NPG 6610

Ian McKellen (b.1939) is widely regarded as one of the greatest stage and screen actors of his generation. Born in Burnley in Lancashire and educated at Cambridge University, he made his London debut in *A Scent of Flowers* (1964). His stage performances include the title roles in *Richard II* (1968–70) and *Macbeth* (1976–7). McKellen has been nominated for Oscars for his performances in *Gods and Monsters* (1998) and as Gandalf in the *Lord of the Rings* film trilogy (2001–3). This portrait was painted entirely from life in the actor's New York apartment during his appearance in Strindberg's *Dance of Death* with Helen Mirren.

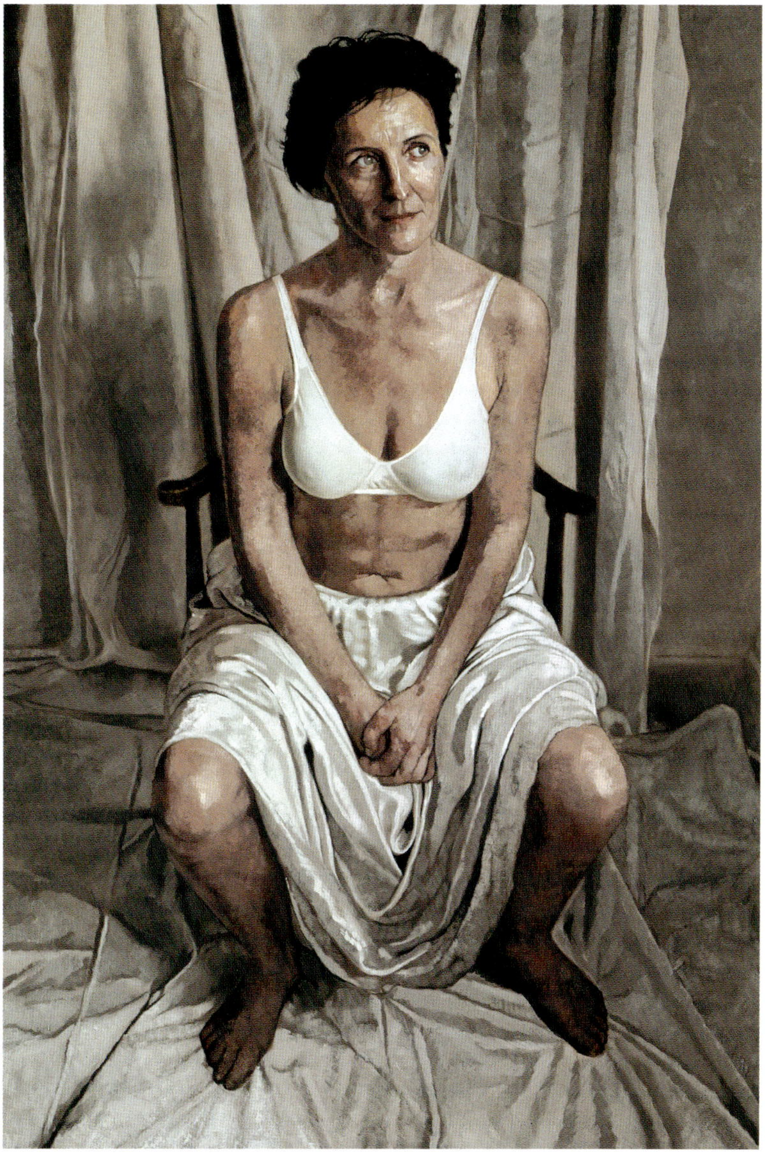

FIONA SHAW
VICTORIA RUSSELL

Oil on canvas
2002
1828 x 1220mm
NPG 6609

Irish-born actress Fiona Shaw (b.1958) graduated from the Royal Academy of Dramatic Art in 1982 and is often hailed as one of Britain's finest classical performers. Her stage appearances are controversial and powerful, notably her title roles in *Electra* (1988), *Richard II* (1995) and *Medea* (2000), all collaborations with the director Deborah Warner. Shaw has won the Laurence Olivier Award for Best Actress three times. Victoria Russell painted the actress in her London home, where sittings took place two to three times a week over a period of three months.

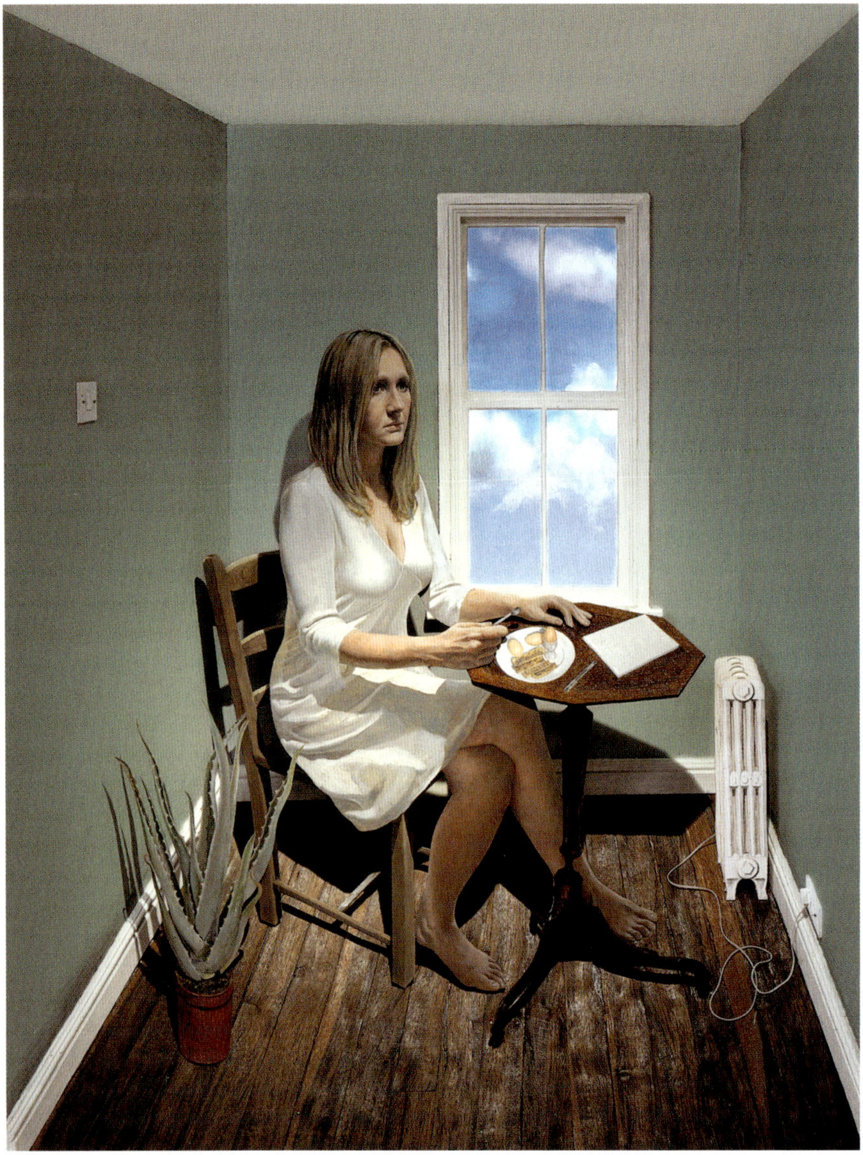

J.K. ROWLING
STUART PEARSON WRIGHT

Oil on board construction with coloured pencil on paper
2005
972 x 720mm
NPG 6723

The phenomenally successful Harry Potter novels of J.K. Rowling (b.1965) have captivated children and adults alike. Stuart Pearson Wright began this portrait of the author in early 2004, when he paid several visits to her Scottish home. The artist observed his subject, making sketches, sometimes while the author was at work, and taking photographs for reference. Rowling is seated at a table, suggestive of the café where she famously wrote her first novel. The narrative alludes to Rowling's public and private self, both as a writer who has made an enormous impact on children's imaginations the world over, and as a mother – the eggs represent her own three children.

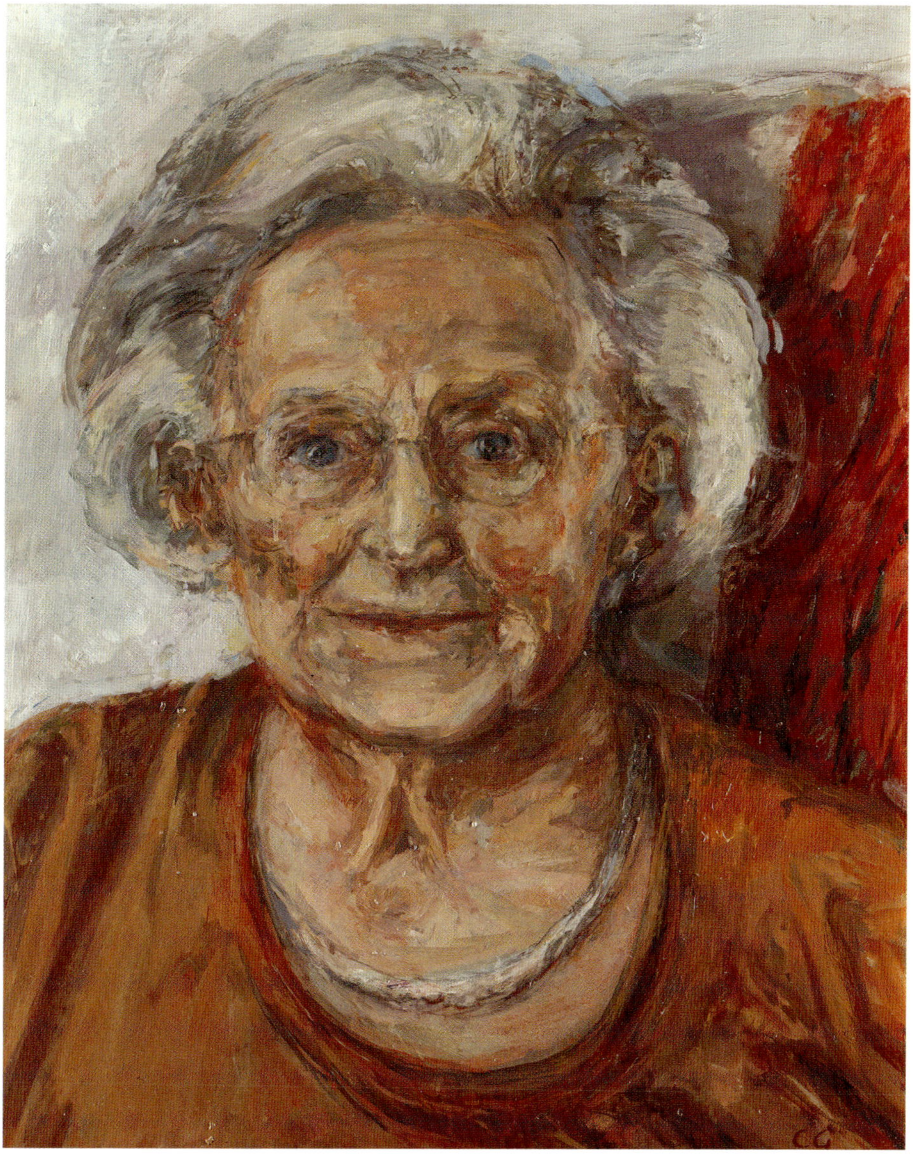

DAME CICELY SAUNDERS
CATHERINE GOODMAN

Oil on canvas
2005
912 x 707mm
NPG 6704

A pioneer of modern palliative care, particularly for the terminally ill, Cicely Saunders (1918–2005) established St Christopher's Hospice in 1967 as the first research and teaching hospice with the aim of providing relief from 'total pain' through physical, psychological, social and spiritual care linked with clinical treatment. She later became a founder trustee and President of Cicely Saunders International, a charity set up in 2002 to improve the care of the dying, whether in a hospice, hospital or at home. This portrait is a poignant record of Dame Cicely's own battle with pain, having undergone surgery for cancer during the sittings. Dame Cicely became fascinated by the collaborative nature of the process, saying to Catherine Goodman on the portrait's completion: 'I see this as much my work as yours.'

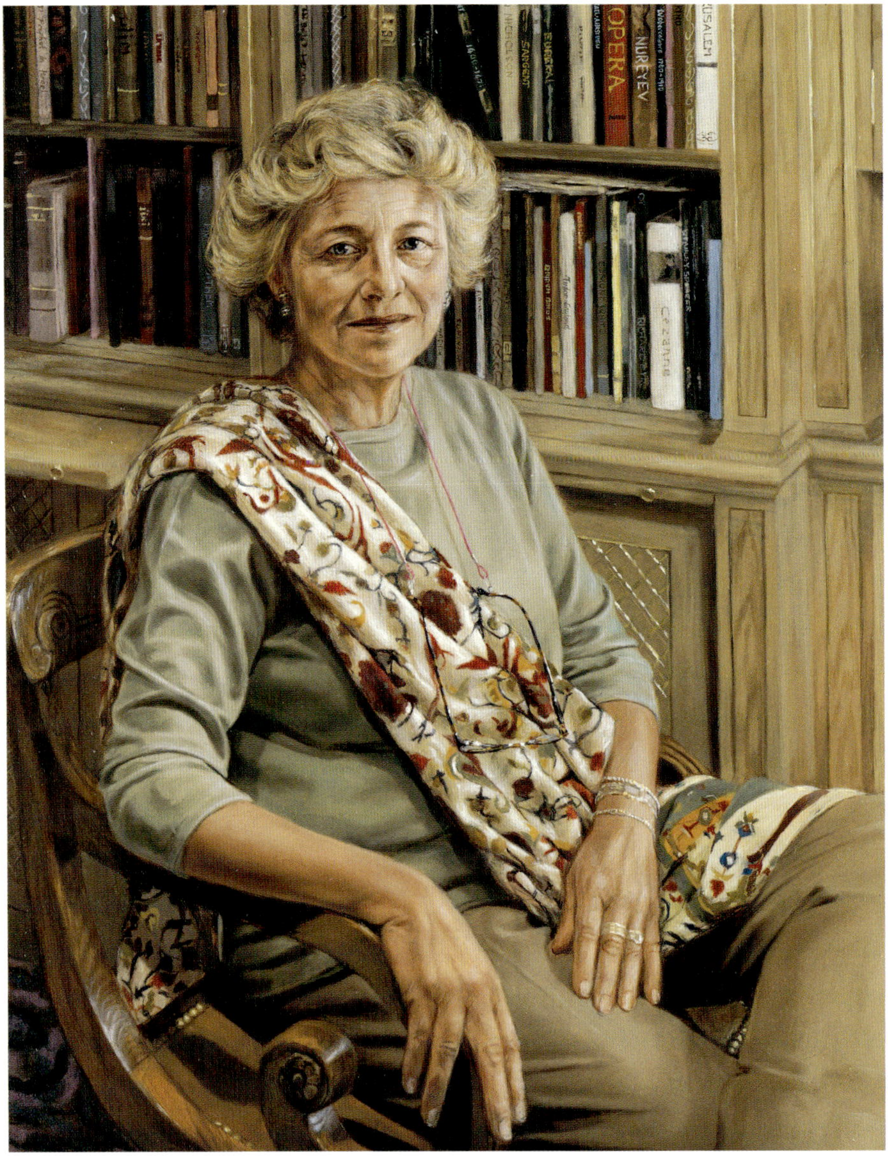

DAME VIVIEN DUFFIELD
CHARLOTTE HARRIS

Oil on canvas
2005
970 x 728mm
NPG 6765

Vivien Duffield (b.1946) is a philanthropist and charitable giver who heads the Clore Duffield Foundation. Her achievements include raising the funds for the £100 million redevelopment of the Royal Opera House and leading the campaign to raise £20 million for the South Bank Centre. Together with the former Culture Secretary, Chris Smith, she set up the Clore Leadership Programme, which aims to strengthen leadership within a range of cultural activities.

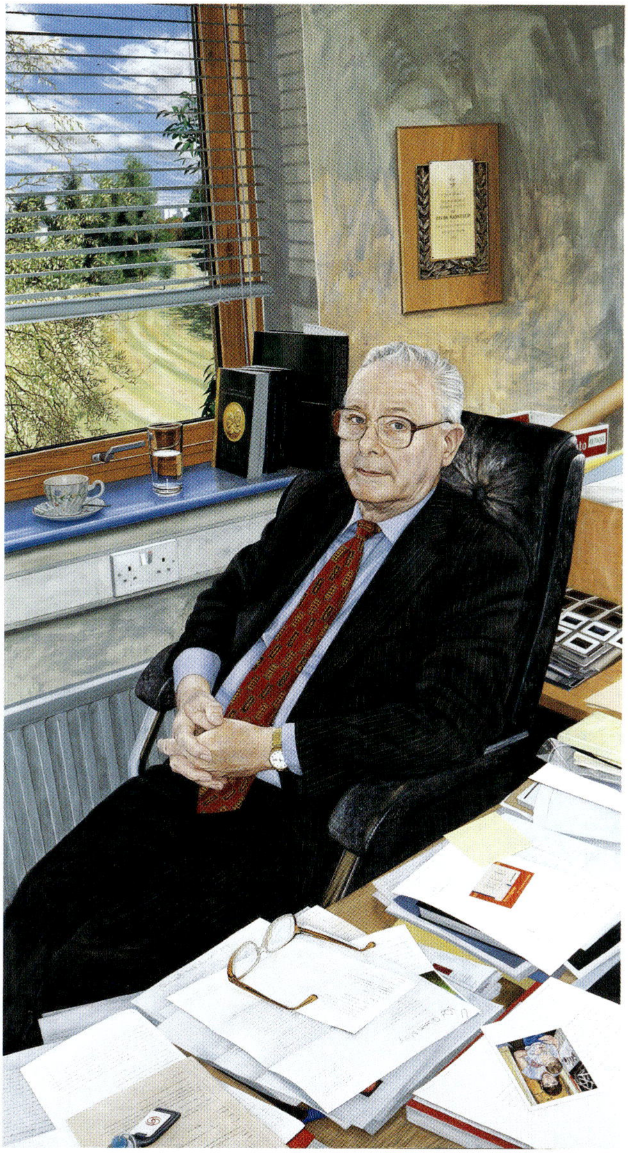

SIR PETER MANSFIELD
STEPHEN SHANKLAND

Oil on board
2008
1470 x 790mm
NPG 6836

Peter Mansfield (b.1933) was awarded the Nobel Prize for Medicine in 2003 for his contribution to the invention of magnetic resonance imaging (MRI). His vision and research have made widespread clinical use of the technique a reality. MRI scanners are now used in hospitals all over the world, and it is estimated that over 60 million investigations with MRI are carried out every year. Here Mansfield is shown in his office at the University of Nottingham, where he is Emeritus Professor of Physics. A postcard of Stephen Shankland's portrait *The Miracle*, which won the BP Portrait Award in 2004, can be seen on Mansfield's desk. It shows the artist's wife and son, who underwent MRI scans due to a life-threatening condition when he was born.

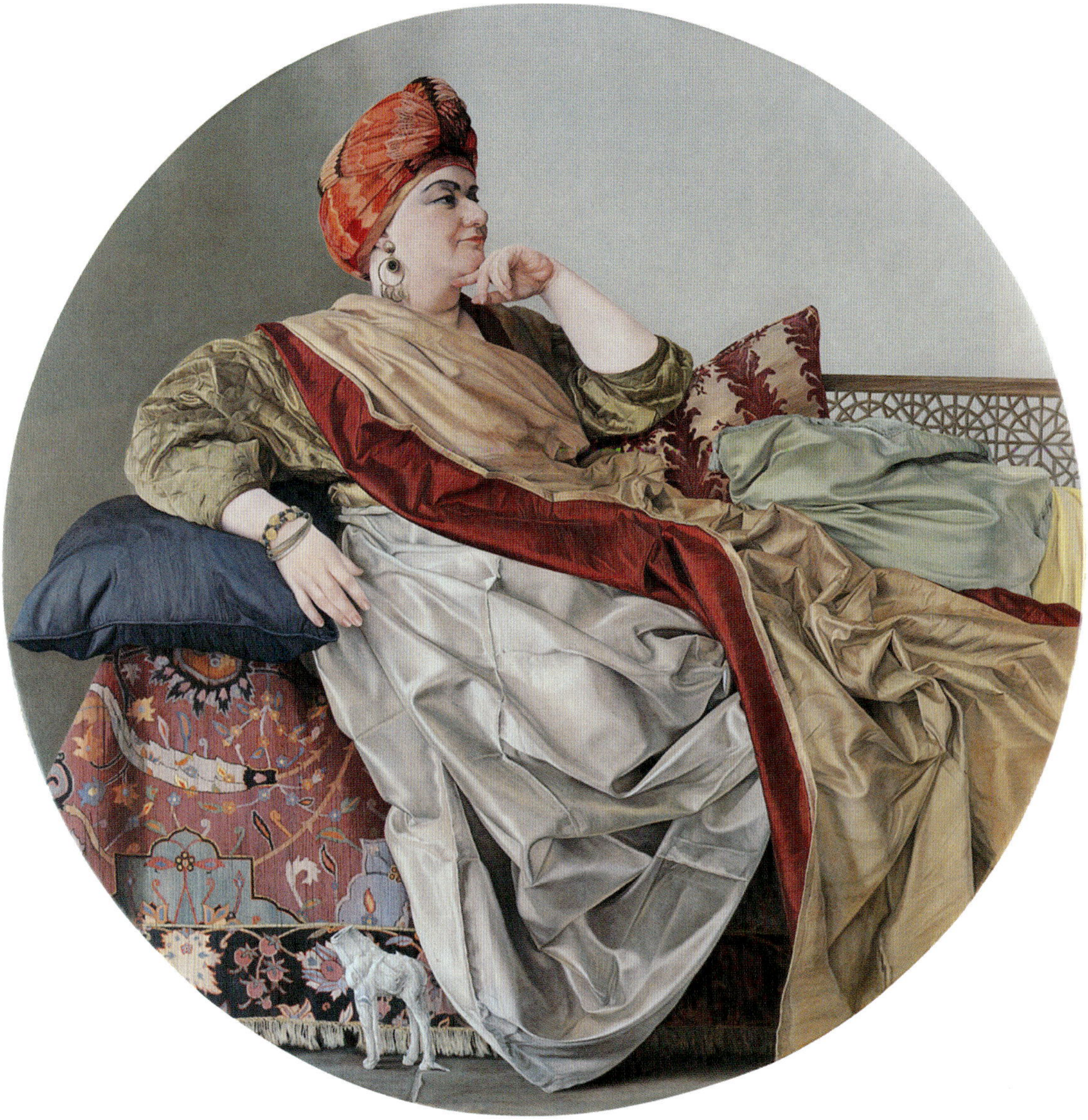

CAMILA BATMANGHELIDJH
DEAN MARSH

Oil on plywood panel
2008
763mm diameter
NPG 6845

Iranian-born psychotherapist Camila Batmanghelidjh (b.1963) founded the charity Kids Company, which provides practical, emotional and educational support to vulnerable inner-city children and young people. The charity reaches 12,000 children a year and has raised £40 million since its beginnings in a disused railway arch in Camberwell, south London, in 1996. Batmanghelidjh is also the founder of The Place2Be, a charity that offers school-based counselling services. Dean Marsh was drawn to the sitter's distinctive style of dress and found inspiration in the portraits of the nineteenth-century French artist Jean-Auguste-Dominique Ingres.

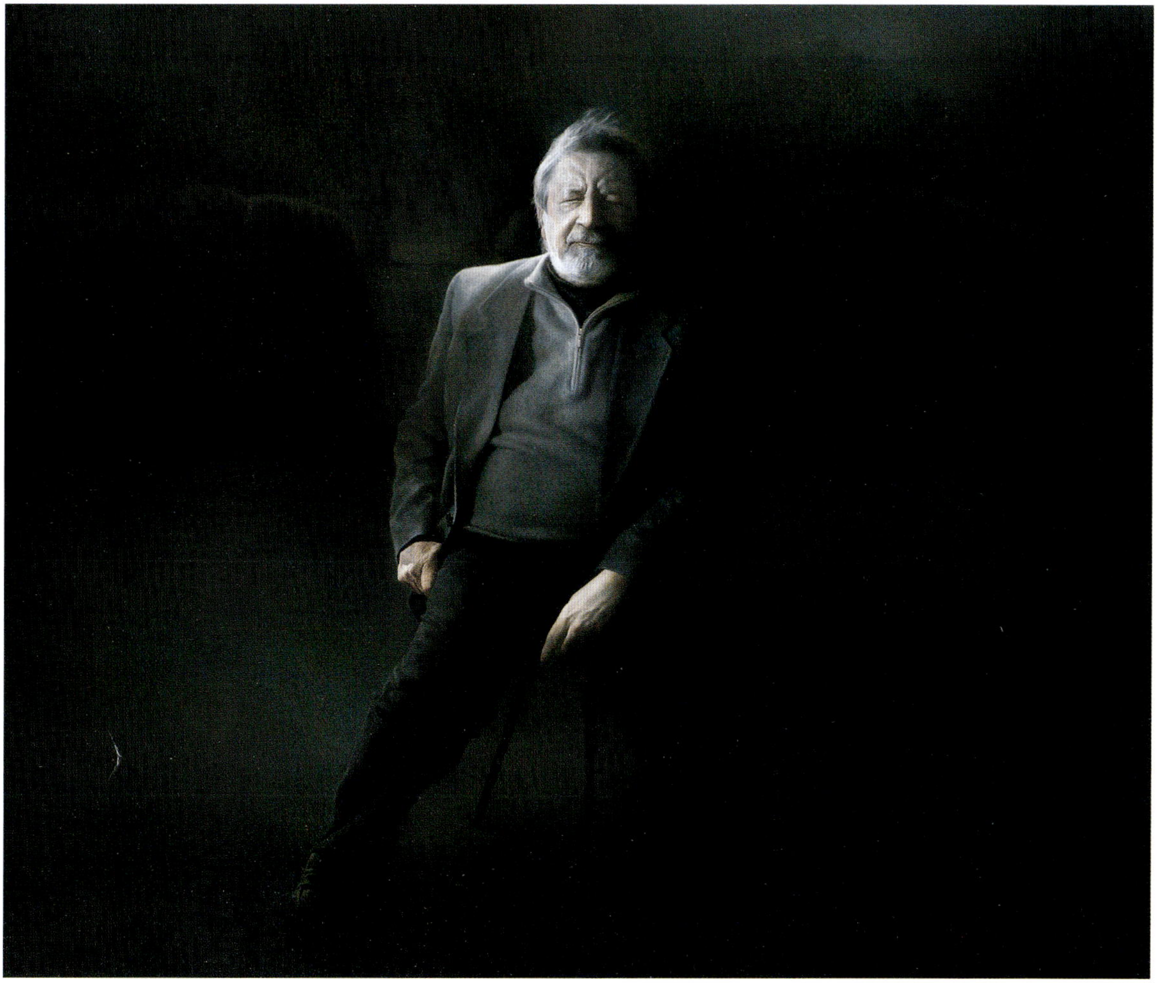

SIR VIDIADHAR SURAJPRASAD NAIPAUL
PAUL EMSLEY

Oil on canvas
2009
962 x 1120mm
NPG 6875

The Trinidadian-born novelist V.S. Naipaul (b.1932) left the Caribbean for England in 1950 to study at Oxford University. His first novel, *The Mystic Masseur* (1957), was followed by his critical success *A House for Mr Biswas* (1961). Naipaul's literary themes include exile and displacement, and in 1971 he won the Booker Prize with *In a Free State*. He was knighted in 1990 and in 2001 was awarded the Nobel Prize for Literature. Paul Emsley is interested in emphasising the way in which light and shade fall across the subject through a careful balancing of tones to evoke the singularity of silence and form. Here, he depicts the writer in his Wiltshire garden.

We've arrived at one definition of the portrait painter's prime aspiration: to record without words the internal life of the individual.

Rose Tremain

A real face, as the raw material of art, is limitless in its potential.

Lynne Truss

Contemporary portrait painters are in pursuit of deeper, more subversive kinds of beauty.
Sarah Dunant

Flattery, like visual analysis, erotic pleasure or disgust, is part of the cultural atmosphere in which portraits are made.
A.S. Byatt

FIRST PRIZEWINNING WORKS

Over time, the prize money available to winners of the Award has increased significantly. What has not changed is the stature of the Award: it remains one of the most important prizes for excellence in figurative painting in the world. Each year the choice of First Prizewinner provokes intense debate in the national media, and this section shows the wide range of styles and approaches that have been rewarded over the years.

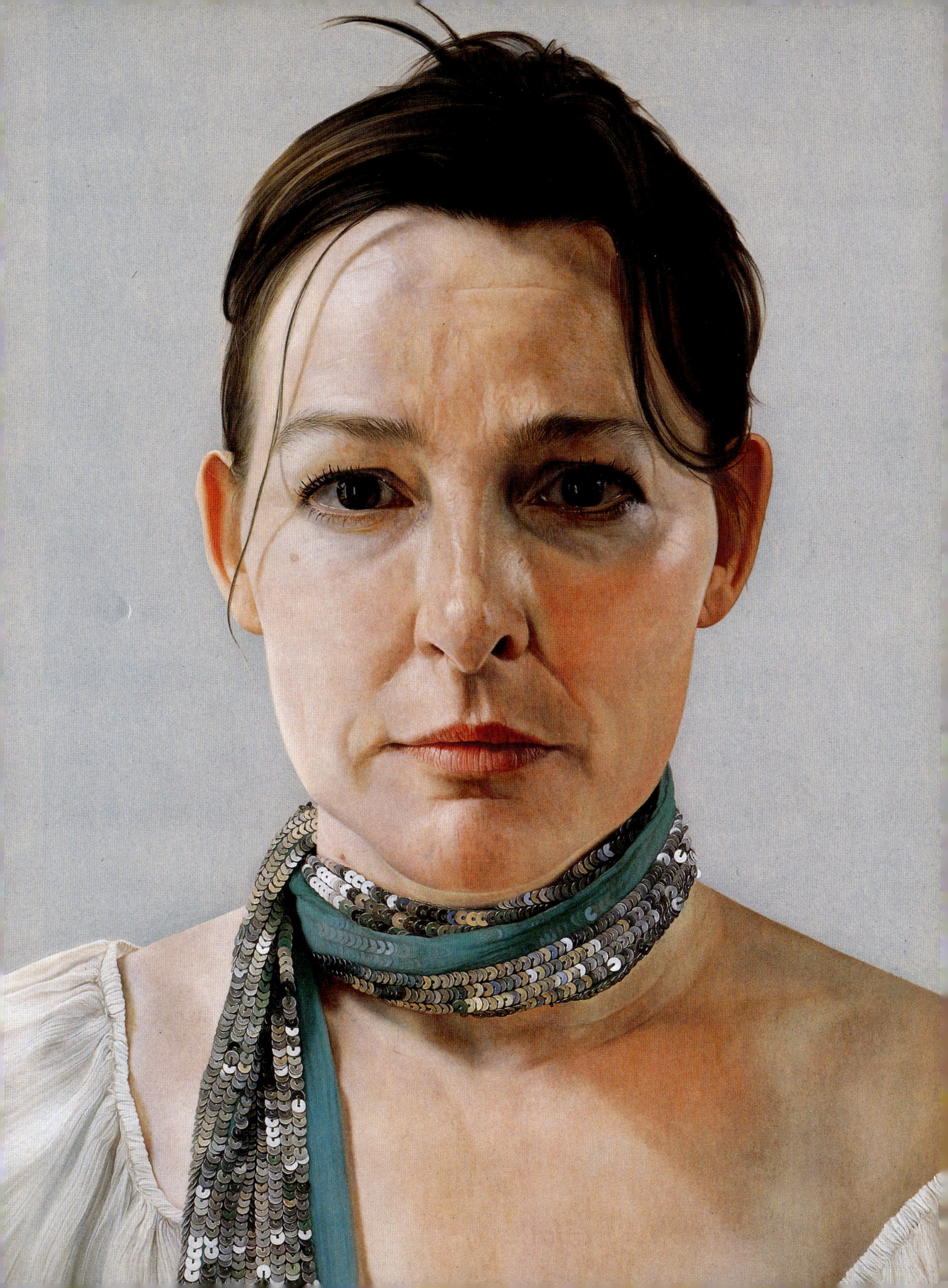

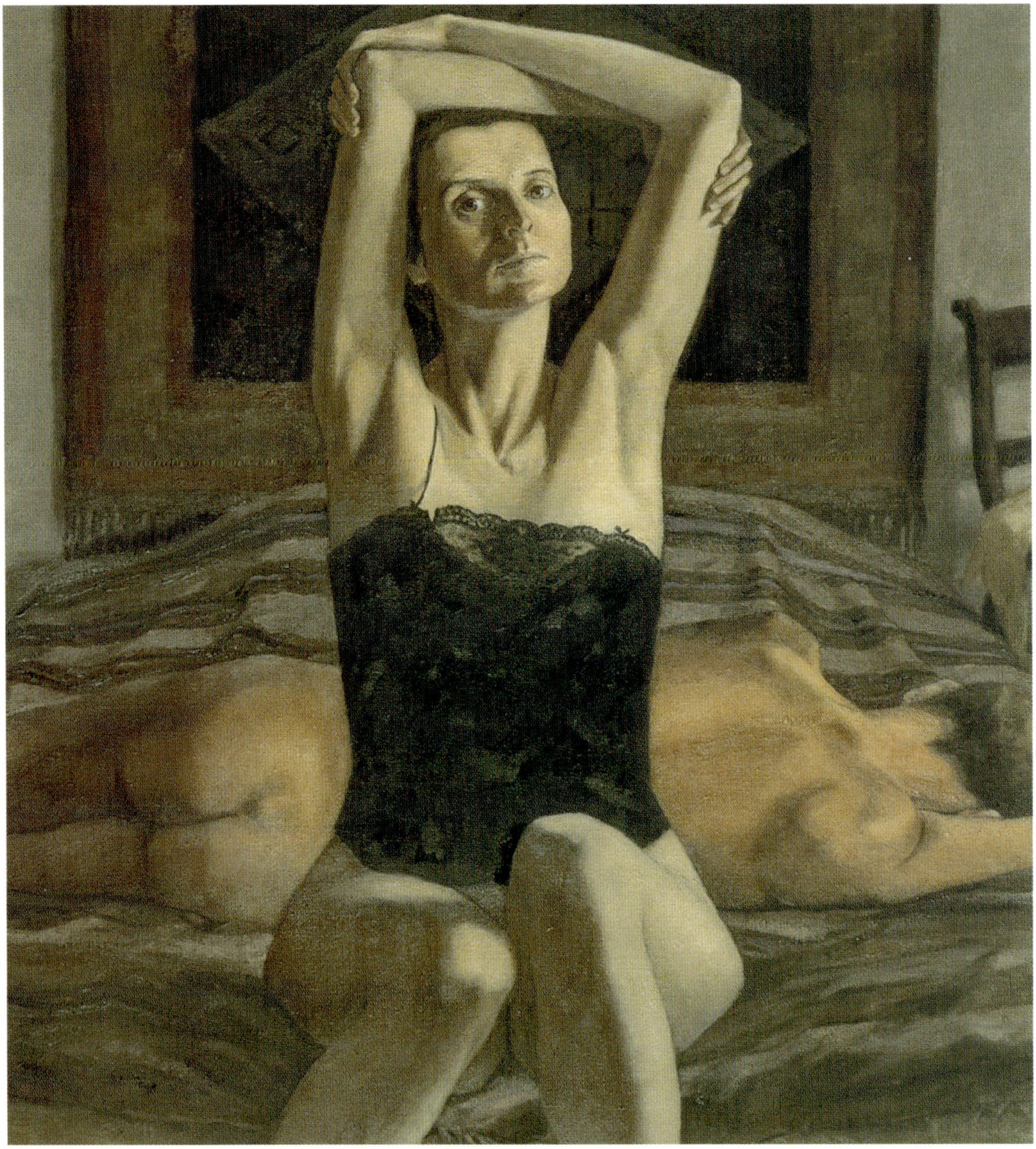

SELF-PORTRAIT
ANNABEL CULLEN

Oil on canvas
1990
1220 x 1070mm

Born in Surrey, Annabel Cullen studied at Camberwell College of Arts and Crafts and the Royal College of Art. She had previously been selected for exhibition in 1984. Cullen has exhibited widely and has undertaken many commissions, including that of writer Nina Bawden in 2002. She currently teaches drawing at Putney School of Art and Design in London. This self-portrait was the last in a series made between 1982 and 1990, which was about a particular relationship. Cullen was pregnant with her first child at the time.

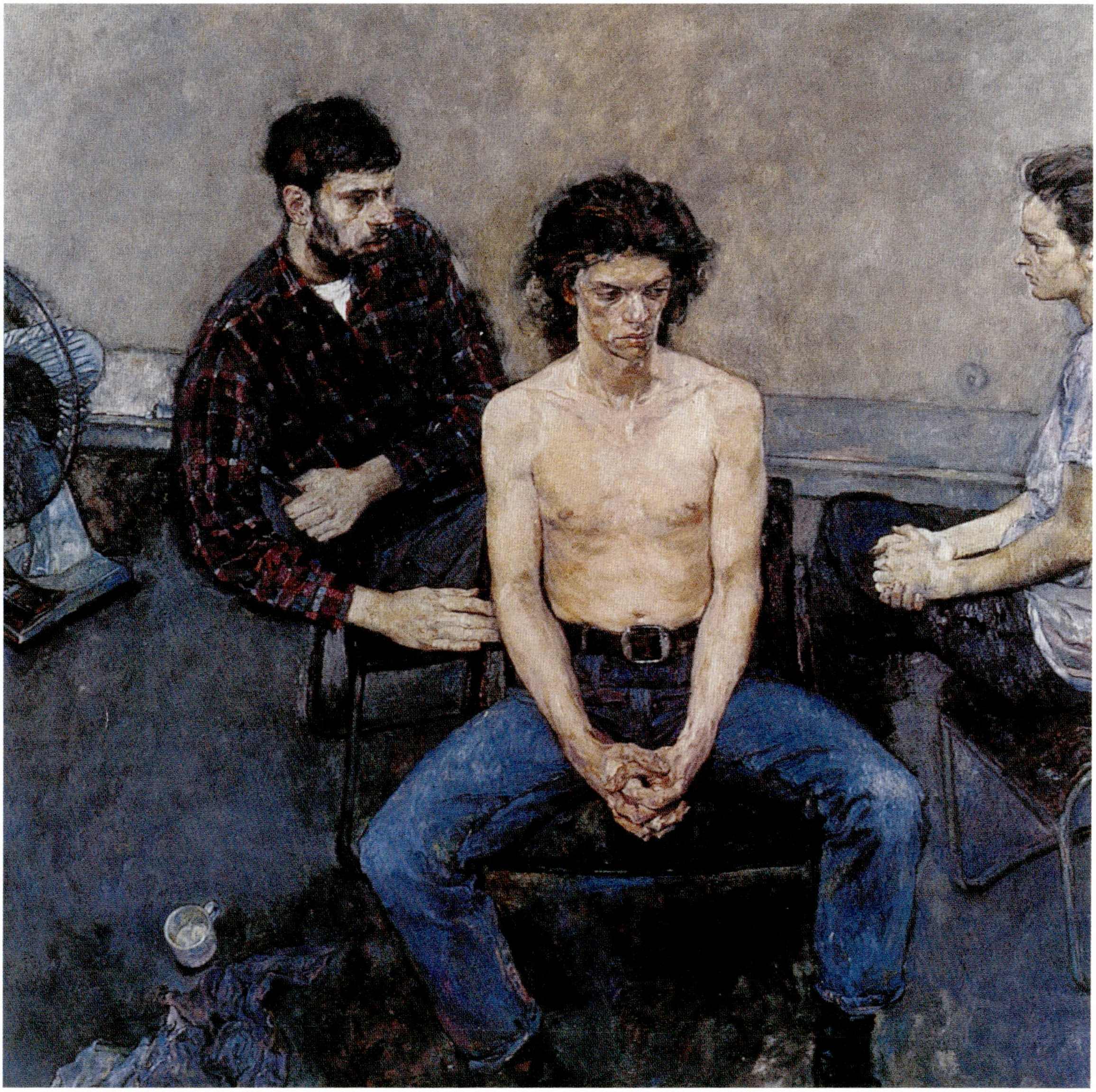

THREE SEATED FIGURES
JUSTIN MORTIMER

Oil on canvas
1991
1827 x 1827mm

At the time he painted this portrait of three of his friends, Justin Mortimer was a third-year student at the Slade School of Fine Art. Since then, he has undertaken a number of important commissions, including portraits of HM The Queen, Sir Steven Redgrave and, at the National Portrait Gallery, three directors of the Royal Court Theatre. Mortimer currently lives and works in London, and has works in private and public collections around the world.

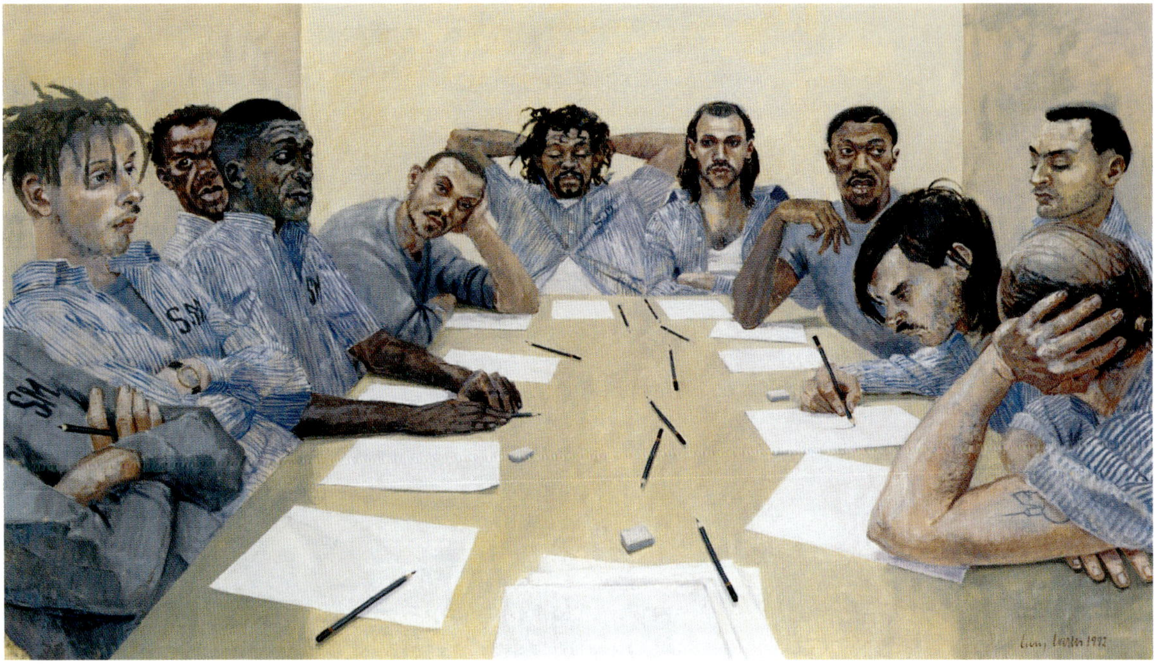

HER MAJESTY'S PLEASURE
LUCY WILLIS

Oil on canvas
1992
1020 x 1705mm

Lucy Willis graduated from the Ruskin School of Drawing and Fine Art in Oxford in 1975. In the late 1970s she established an etching studio on the Greek island of Syros, before returning to Britain to open and teach at the Moorland House Workshop in Somerset, a centre for residential courses in painting and printmaking (1980–6). Willis has exhibited her paintings and prints widely, and has been involved in many art-based projects both in Britain and abroad.

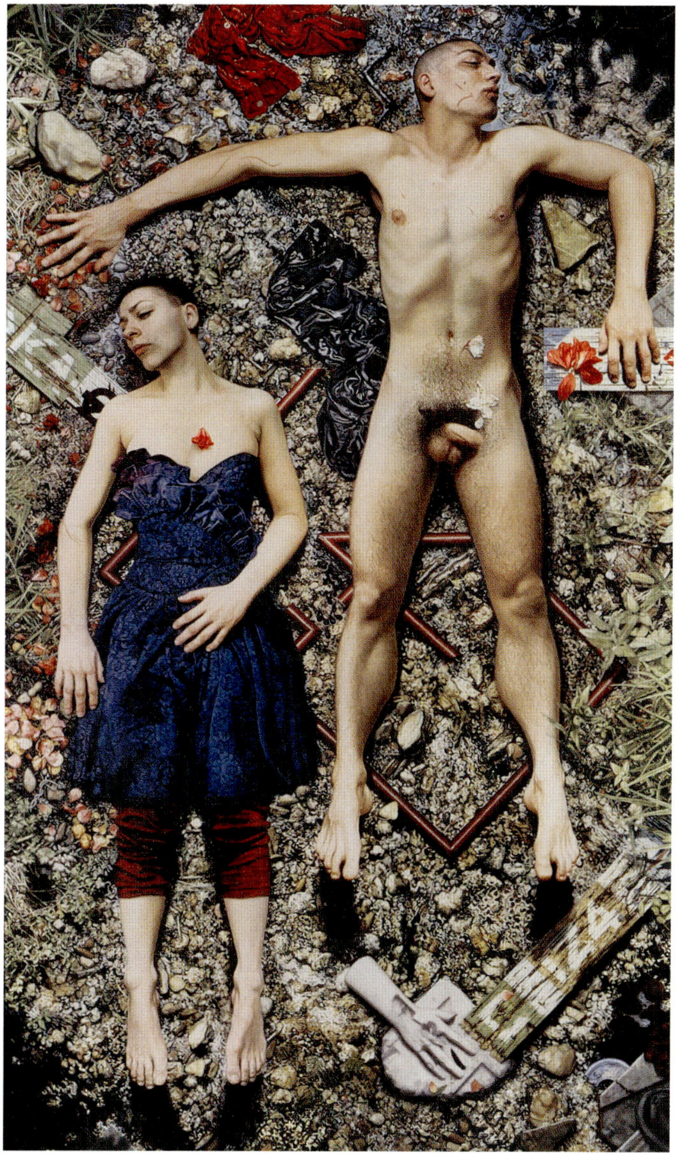

TWO FIGURES LYING IN A SHALLOW STREAM
PHILIP HARRIS

Oil on canvas
1993
1825 x 1070mm

Philip Harris specialises in photorealistic figurative painting and portraiture. He was born in Yorkshire and studied at Mansfield College of Art and Design, and Bradford College of Art and Design. Before winning the BP Portrait Award, his work had been included in various exhibitions, including several solo shows in London and Belgium. Harris has since continued to exhibit internationally and has undertaken private commissions. This painting combines a self-portrait with a depiction of his girlfriend, Louise.

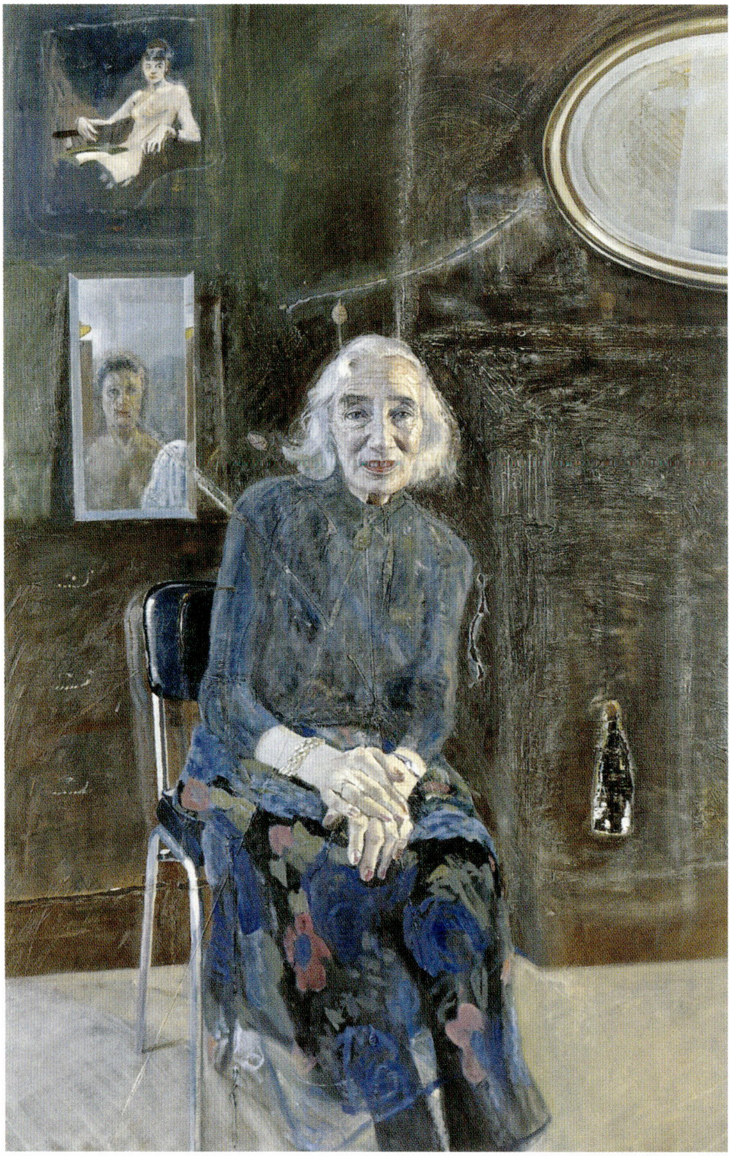

PORTRAIT OF AN ARTIST'S MODEL

PETER EDWARDS

Oil on canvas
1994
2070 x 1358mm

Born in Wales, Peter Edwards studied at Gloucestershire College of Art and Design. Having been selected for the Portrait Award five times in the 1980s, he was a prizewinner three times before receiving First Prize for this painting of Marguerite Kelsey, a celebrated professional artists' model of the 1920s and 1930s. Edwards has works in many private and public collections, such as the Metropolitan Museum of Art in New York, and the National Portrait Gallery now holds six of his paintings, including his popular portrait of footballer Sir Bobby Charlton and writers Seamus Heaney and Kazuo Ishiguro.

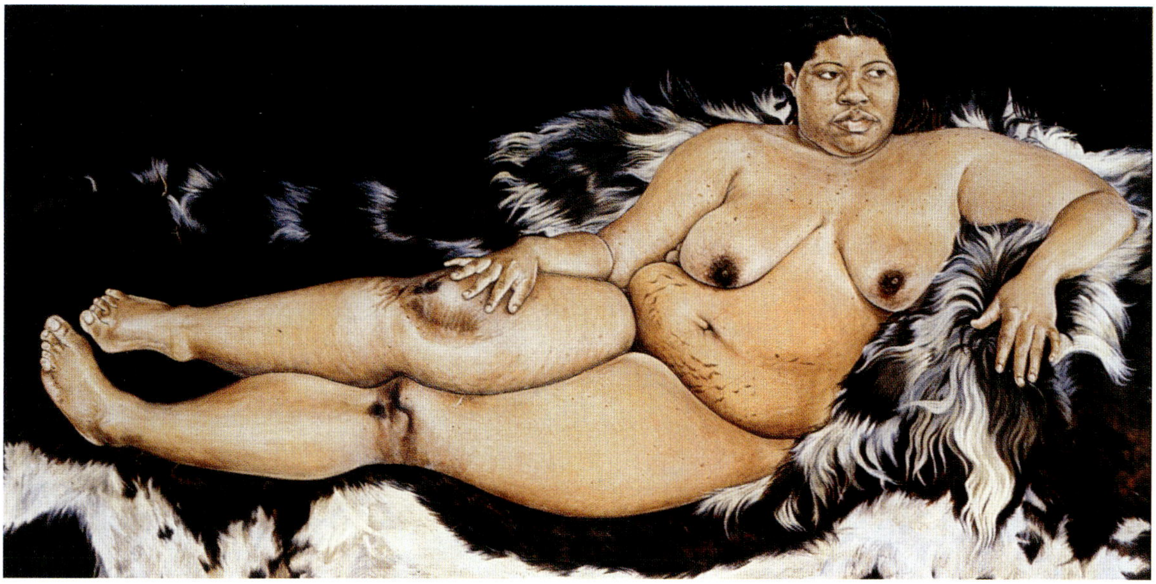

KRISHENDA
ISHBEL MYERSCOUGH

Oil on canvas
1995
860 x 1840mm

Having studied at the Glasgow School of Art and the Slade School of Fine Art, Ishbel Myerscough was a minor prizewinner of the BP Portrait Awards three times before winning First Prize in 1995 with her portrait of Krishenda, a stranger whom she had met in Glasgow and asked to sit for her. Myerscough paints entirely from life and usually has numerous sittings with her subjects. In 2009 she completed a portrait commission for the National Portrait Gallery of the opera singer Sir Willard White.

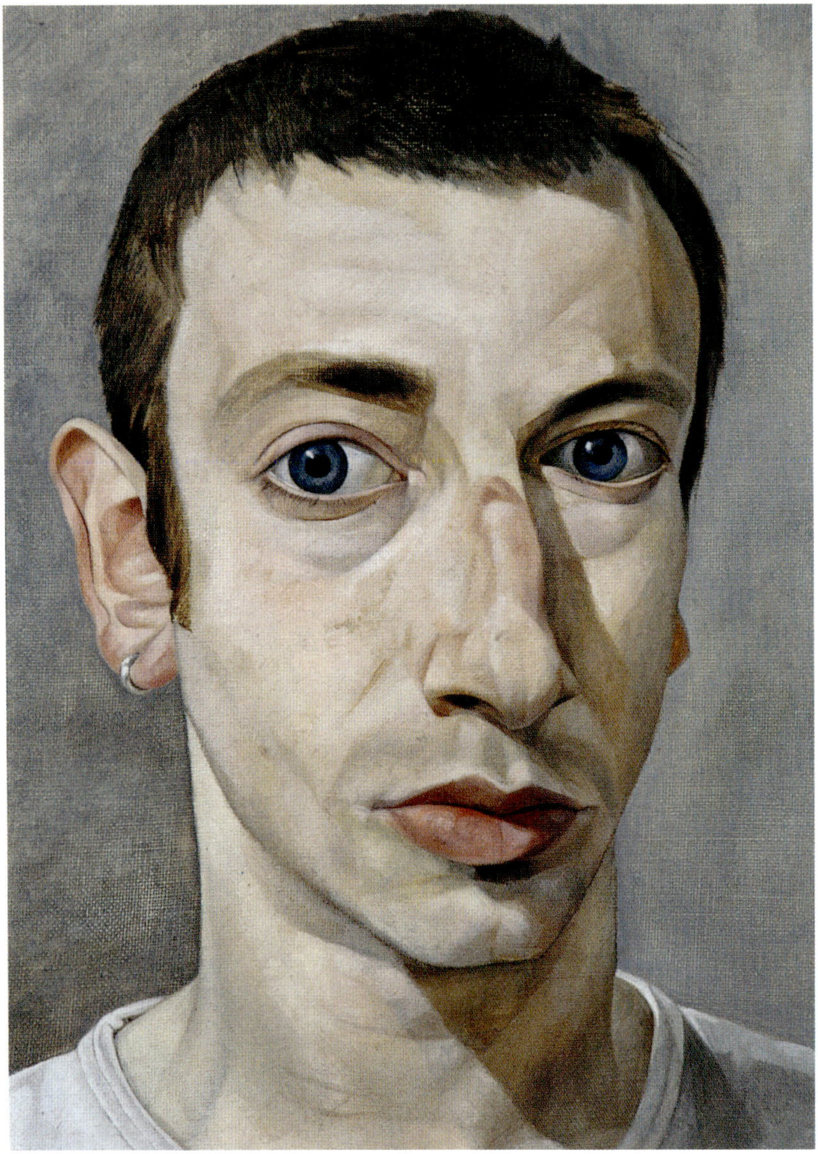

SELF-PORTRAIT
JAMES HAGUE

Oil on canvas
1996
330 x 245mm

Nottingham-born James Hague studied at the Fine Art University of Northumbria and holds a Master of Arts in painting from the Royal College of Art. He has exhibited at the Royal Academy Summer Exhibition, the Interim Show at the Royal College of Art and with the Royal Society of Portrait Painters. He was awarded the Stanley Smith Scholarship in 2004 and the Amlin Painting Prize in 2005. Hague is currently working on a series exploring the relationship between subject and object through the media of painting, sculpture and photography.

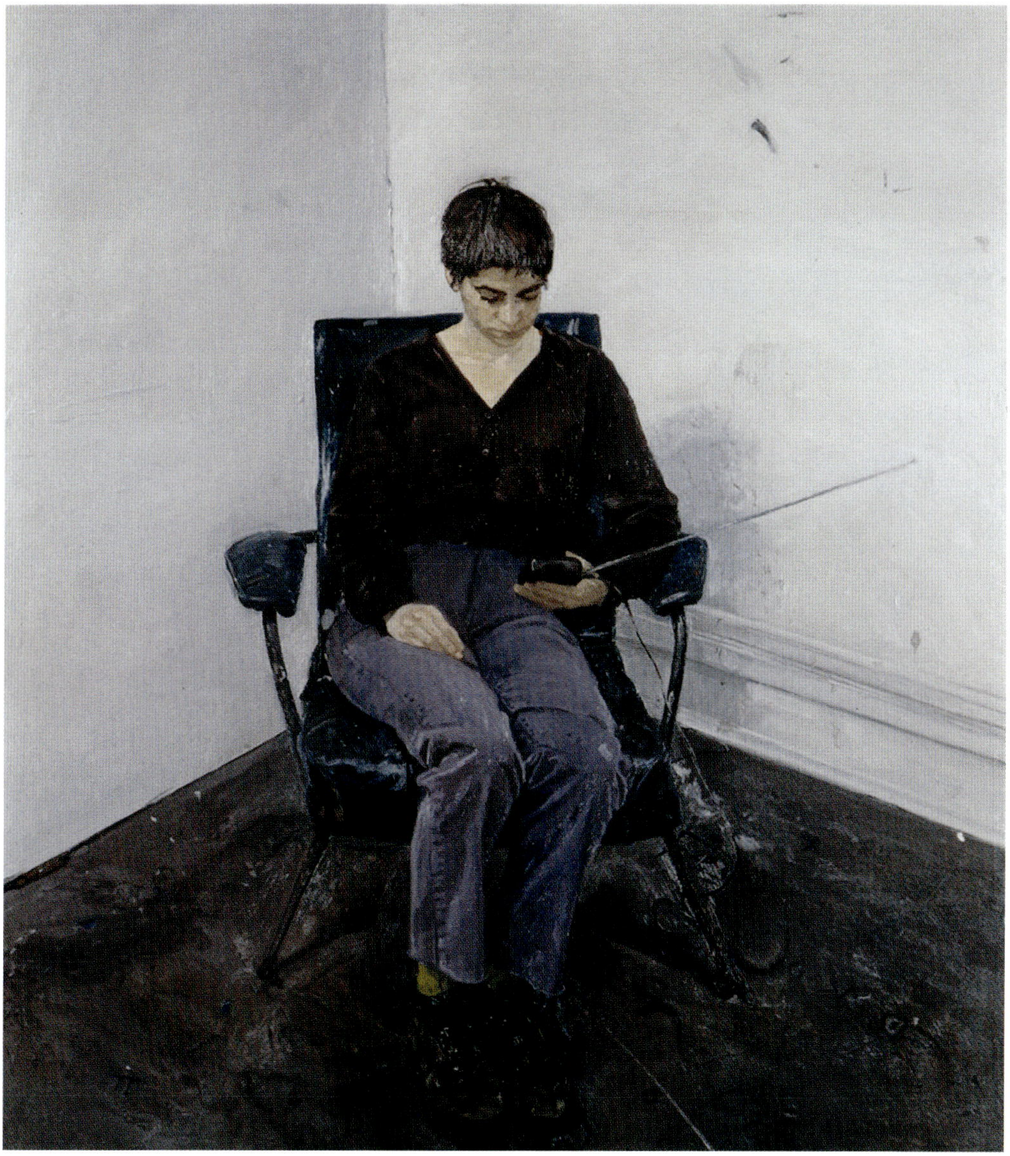

PENELOPE WATCHING TV
JAMES LLOYD

Oil on canvas
1997
1880 x 1625mm

London-based artist James Lloyd had recently graduated from the Slade School of Fine Art when he won First Prize for this painting. By that time Lloyd had received various accolades, including an Elizabeth Greenshields Foundation Award (1996) and second prize in the Winsor & Newton Young Artists Award (1997). In 2008 he won the Ondaatje Prize at the Royal Society of Portrait Painters annual exhibition.

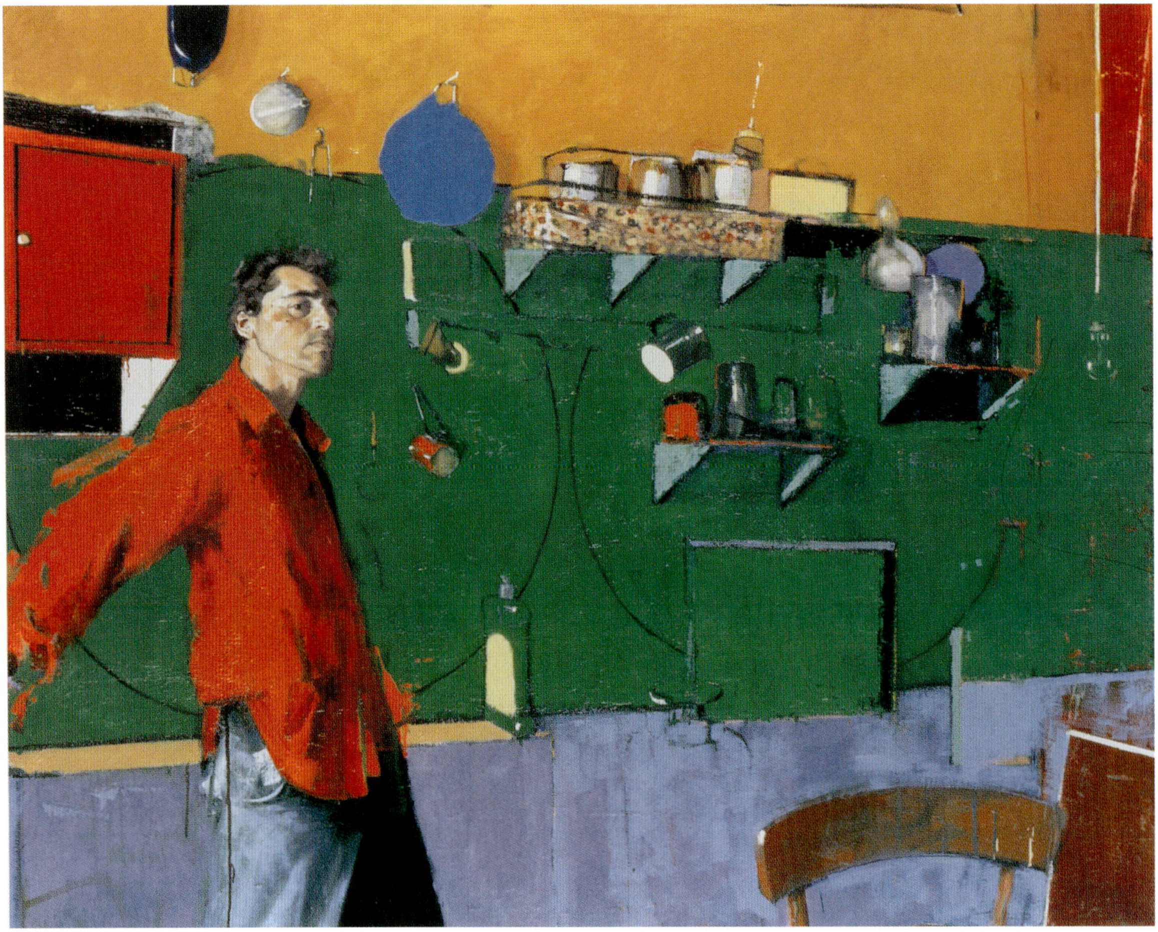

JUDE
TOMAS WATSON

Oil on canvas
1998
1253 x 1525mm

Sussex-born Tomas Watson graduated from the Slade School of Fine Art in 1994. In that same year he received the Robert Ross Scholarship and the first of two awards from the Greek Government, the second being in 1995. Since then, Watson has lived and worked in Greece. He had exhibited at the BP Portrait Award in 1997 and has had several solo exhibitions in London and Greece.

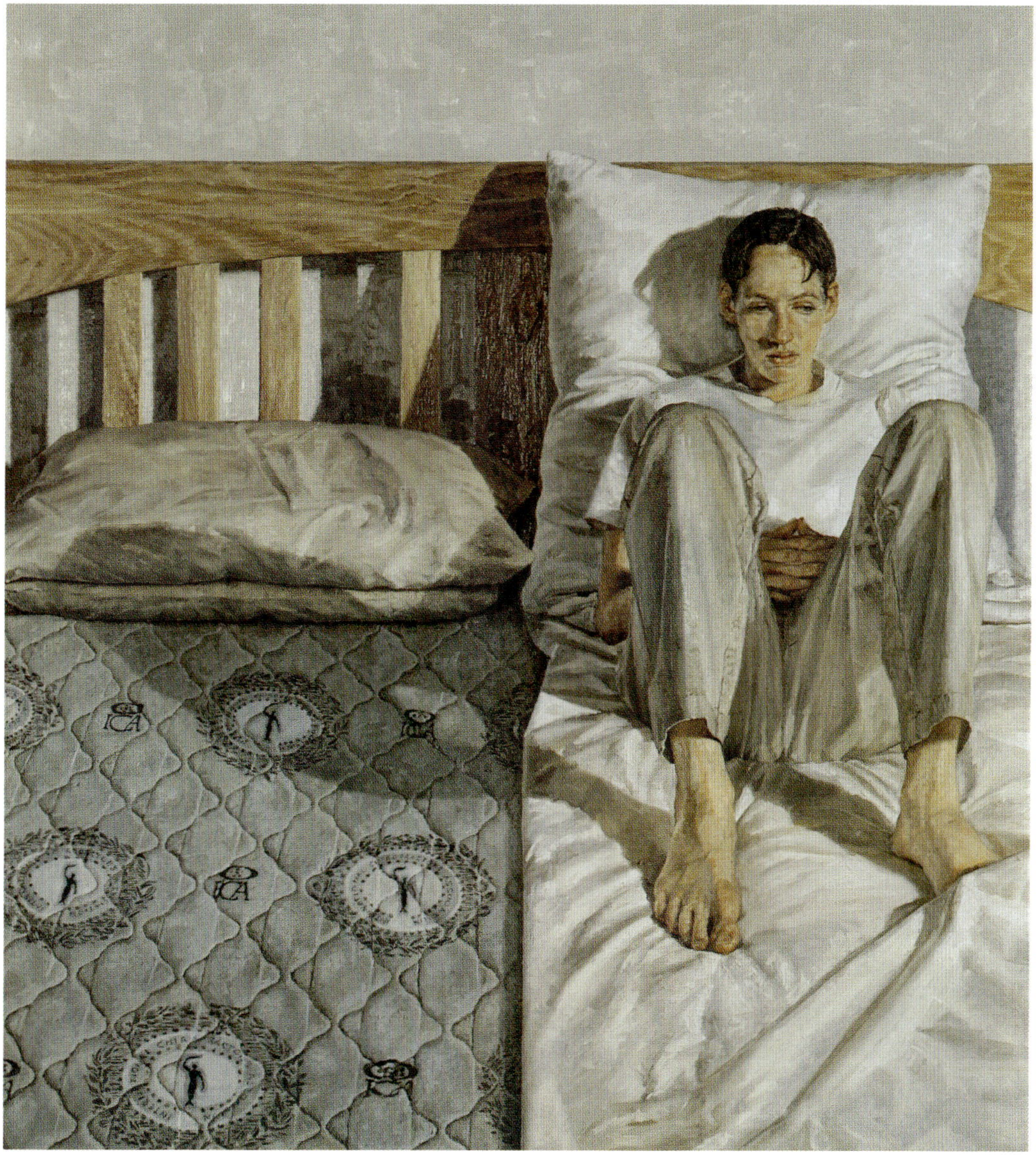

DOUBLE SINGLE
CLIVE SMITH

Oil on canvas
1999
1186 x 1060mm

Clive Smith was born in St Albans and initially studied Fashion Design at Kingston Polytechnic. After a short career in the fashion industry, between 1995 and 1997 he studied drawing and painting under Peter Cox in New York. He won Third Prize in the BP Portrait Award in 1998. Smith has had a number of solo exhibitions in London, New York and Montreal, and he currently lives and works in New York.

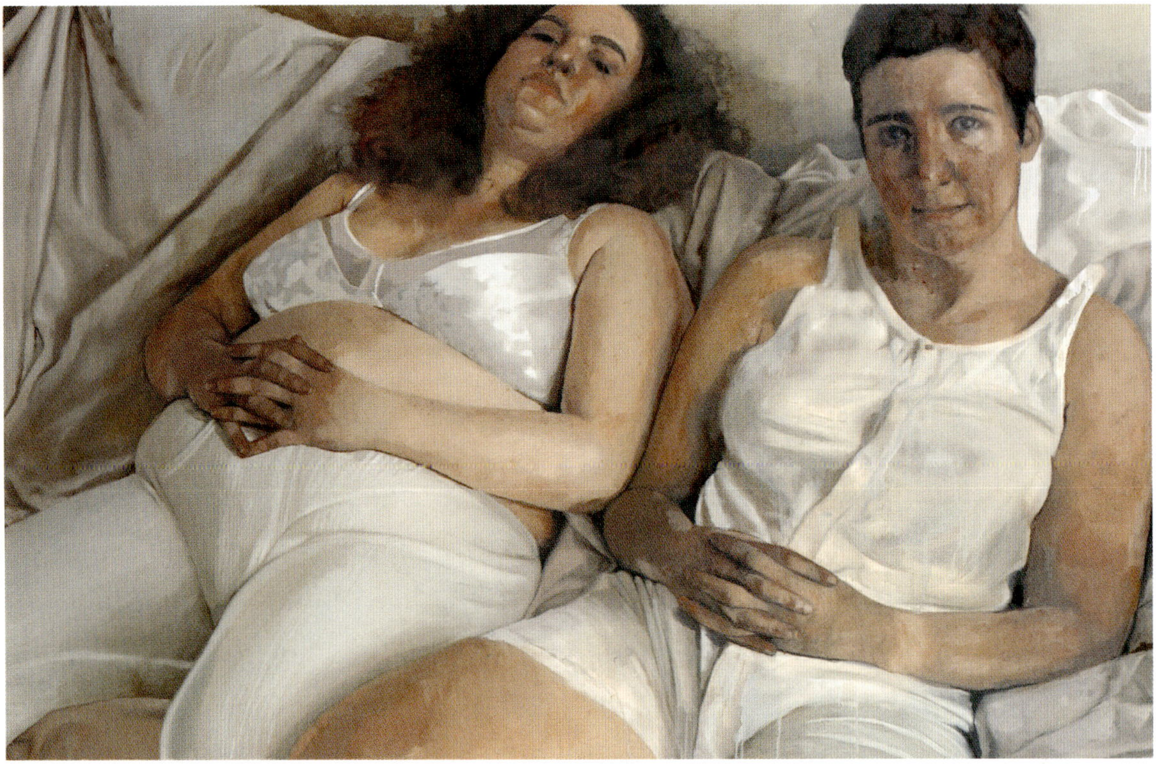

TWO WOMEN IN WHITE
VICTORIA RUSSELL

Oil on canvas
2000
1203 x 1803mm

London-based artist Victoria Russell graduated from Central St Martin's College of Art and Design with a First-class Honours Degree in Fine Art in 1994 before undertaking a diploma at the Royal Academy Schools. She had previously been selected for exhibition in the BP Portrait Award in 1998 and went on to have many exhibitions and commissions, including portraits of philosopher, writer and academic Onora O'Neill, Baroness O'Neill of Bengarve (for the National Portrait Gallery, 2004) and the Archbishop of Canterbury, Rowan Williams (2007).

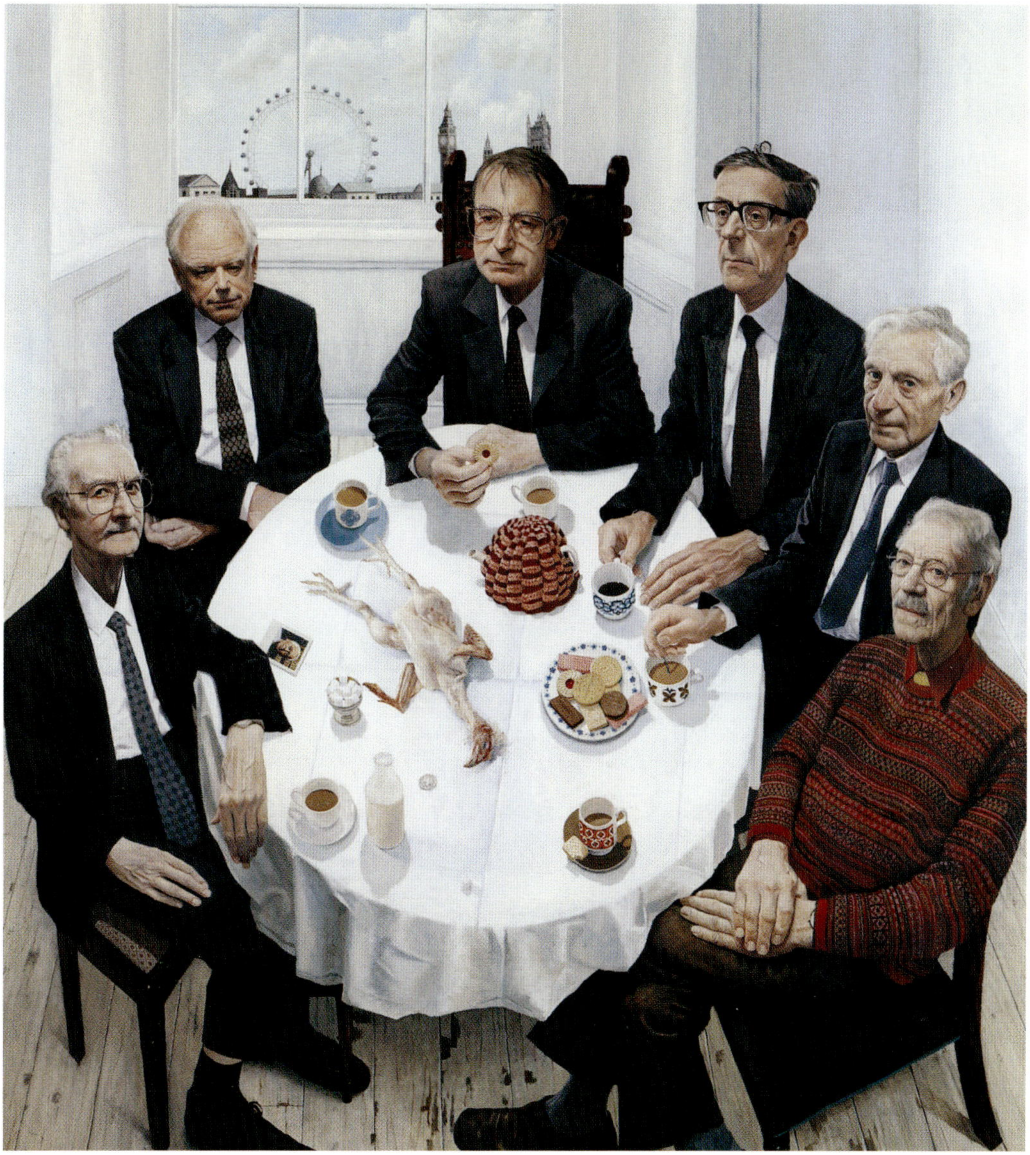

THE SIX PRESIDENTS OF THE BRITISH ACADEMY
STUART PEARSON WRIGHT

Oil on linen
2001
1915 x 1715mm

Best known for his irreverent and detailed figurative portraits, Stuart Pearson Wright, originally from Eastbourne, currently works and lives in London. He graduated from the Slade School of Fine Art in 1999. In 1998, while still a student, he won the BP Travel Award and subsequently produced the series of work *From Eastbourne to Edinburgh: A Painter's Odyssey*, which was exhibited at the National Portrait Gallery the following year. Pearson Wright has exhibited widely and undertaken several high-profile commissions.

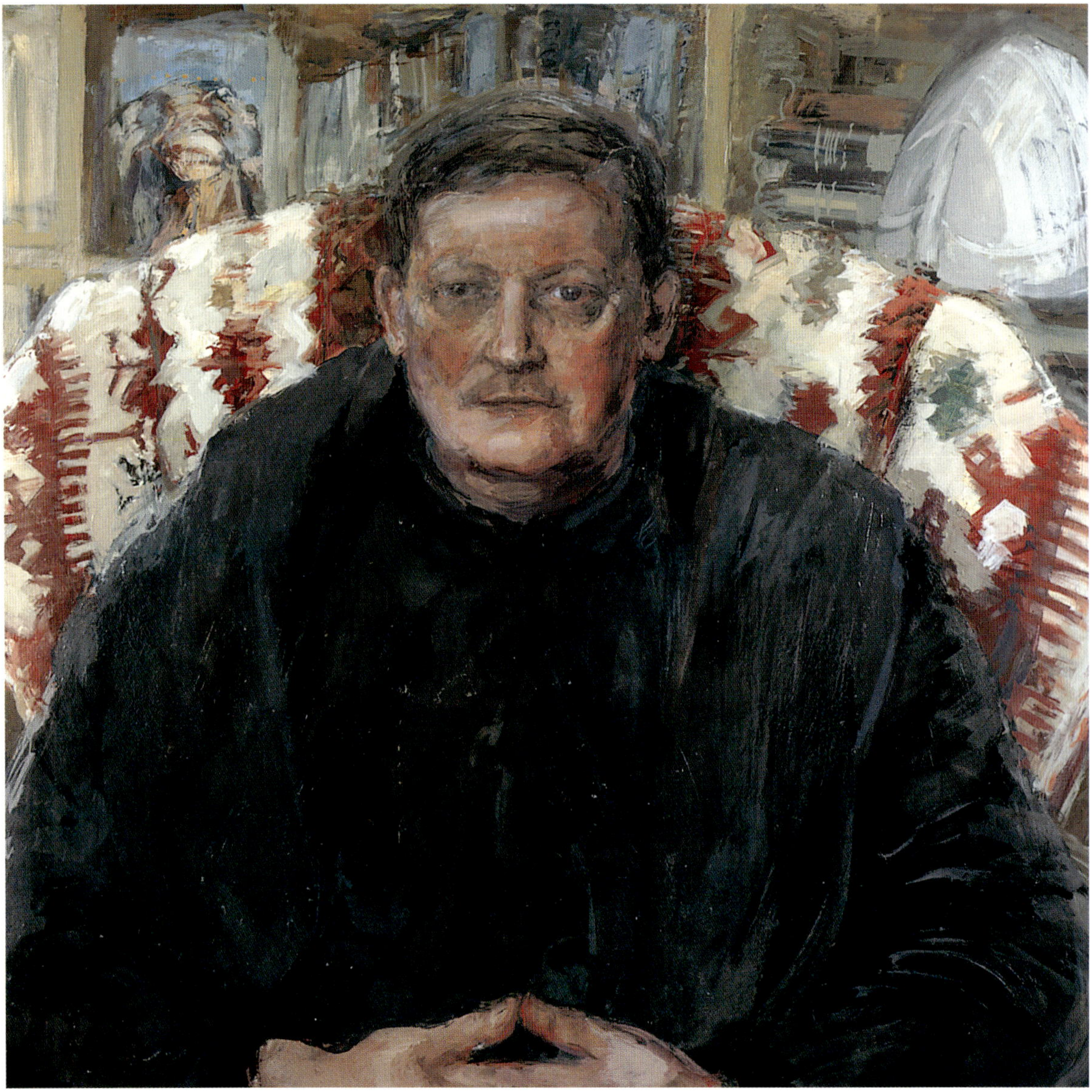

ANTONY
CATHERINE GOODMAN

Oil on canvas
2002
1265 x 1265mm

Catherine Goodman was born in London and studied at Camberwell School of Art and Crafts and the Royal Academy Schools. In 1987 she was awarded the Royal Academy Gold Medal. She helped establish the Prince's Drawing School, founded by the Prince of Wales, in London in 2000, where she is now Artistic Director. Her portrait of Dame Cicely Saunders, commissioned by the National Portrait Gallery in 2005 as a result of winning the BP Portrait Award, was reproduced as a Royal Mail stamp in 2006.

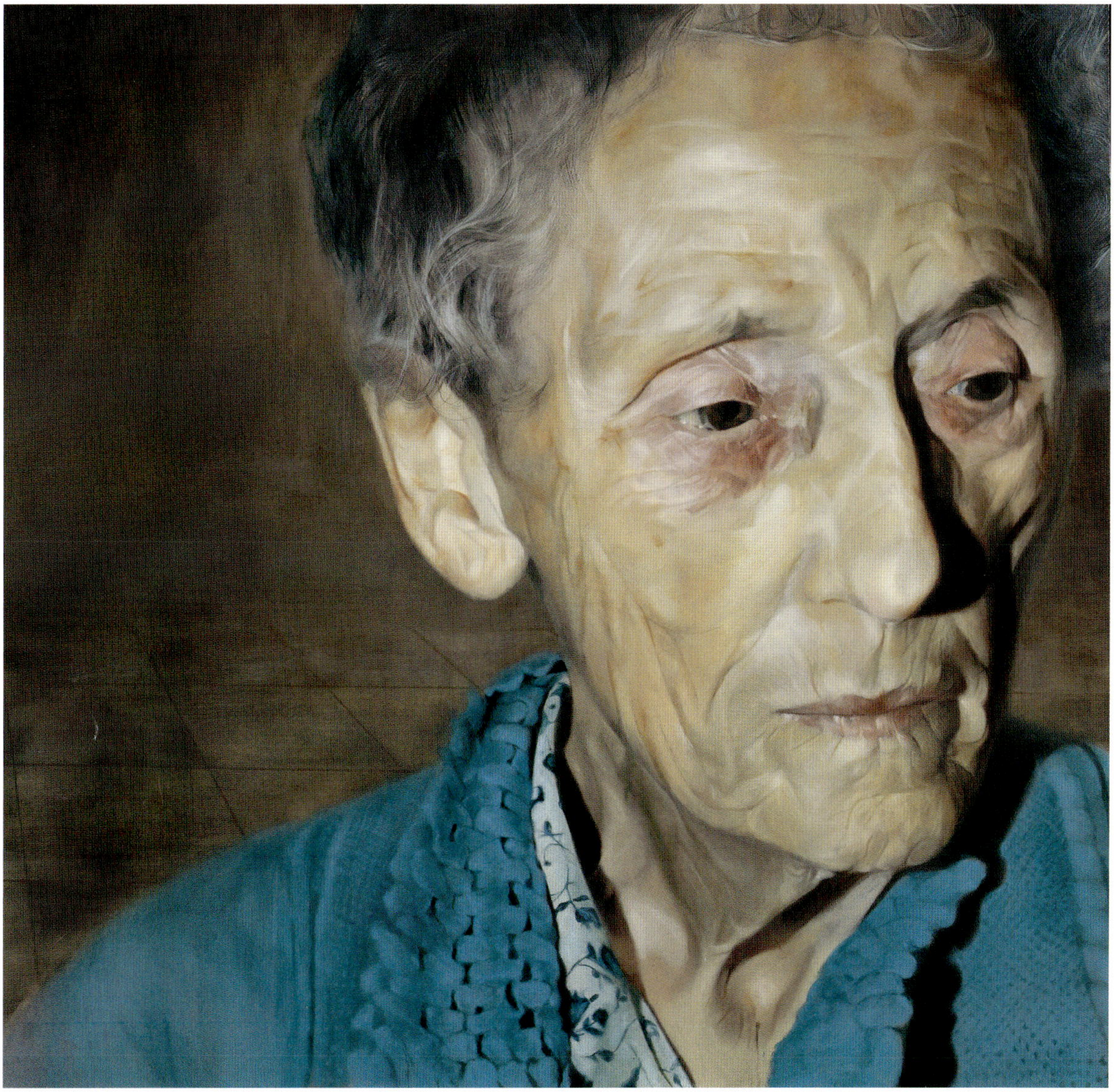

UNTITLED
CHARLOTTE HARRIS

Oil on canvas
2003
1220 x 1225mm

Charlotte Harris was born in Ashford, Kent, in 1981 and currently works from her studio in Folkestone. While a student she worked as a studio assistant for the artist Tom Wood. She was still studying at Leeds Metropolitan University when she won the BP Portrait Award with this painting of her grandmother, and graduated with a First-class Honours Degree in Fine Art later that same year. Harris has exhibited throughout the United Kingdom. Her recent commissions include portraits of Welsh politician Lord David Rowe-Bedoe and ophthalmic surgeon Brenda Billington.

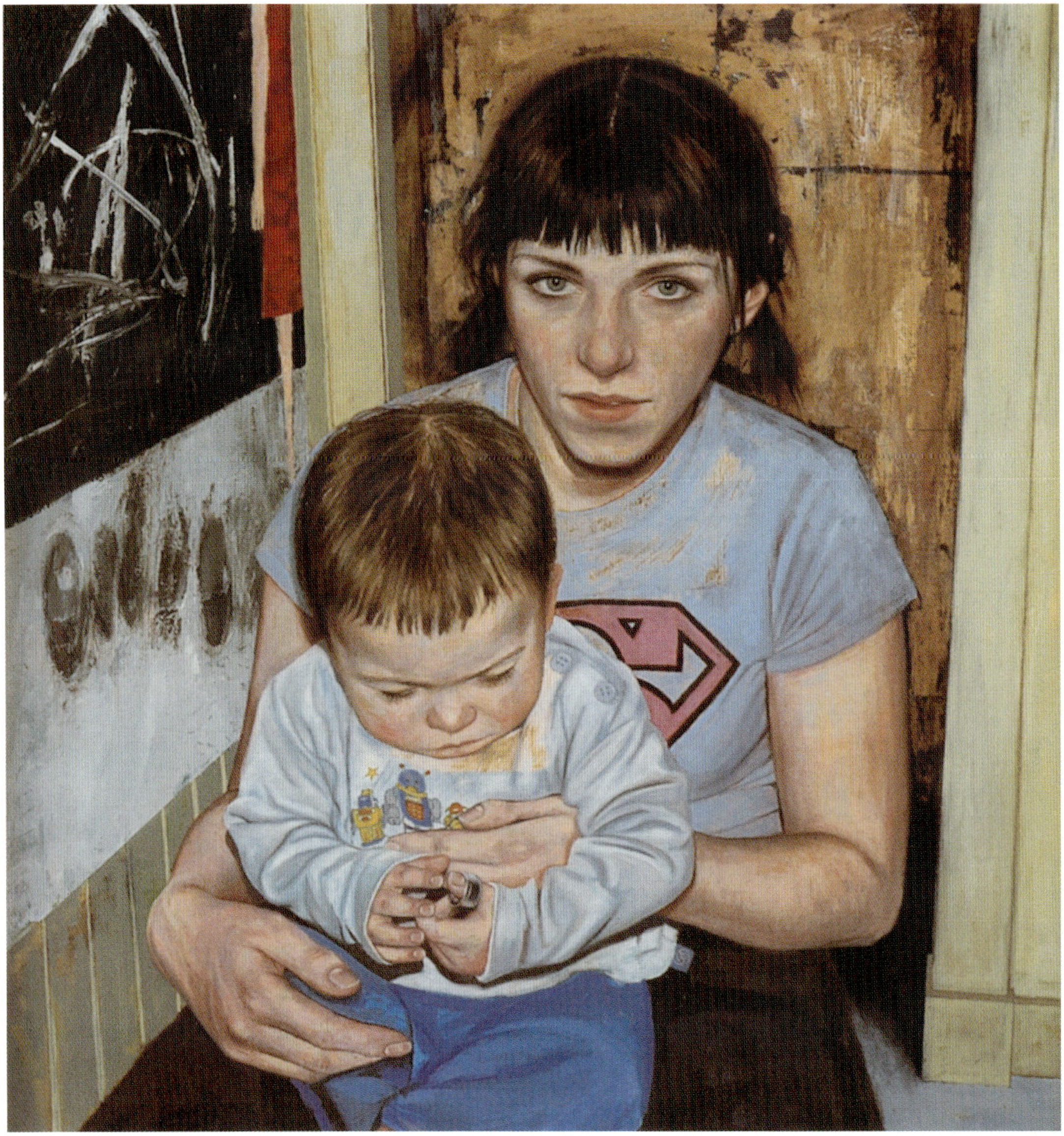

THE MIRACLE
STEPHEN SHANKLAND

Oil on board
2004
662 x 612mm

Scottish artist Stephen Shankland studied Design at Gray's School of Art in Aberdeen and now lives and works in Aberdeenshire. He has works in many collections, both private and public, including Aberdeen Art Gallery and Heriot-Watt University. Having previously been an exhibitor in the BP Portrait Award of 1999, Shankland won First Prize with this portrait depicting his wife Kelly and their son Connor, who was born prematurely. Shankland described the painting as a tribute to the strength and courage of his wife and his son's strong will to survive. The title refers to the nickname given to Connor by his doctors: 'the little miracle'.

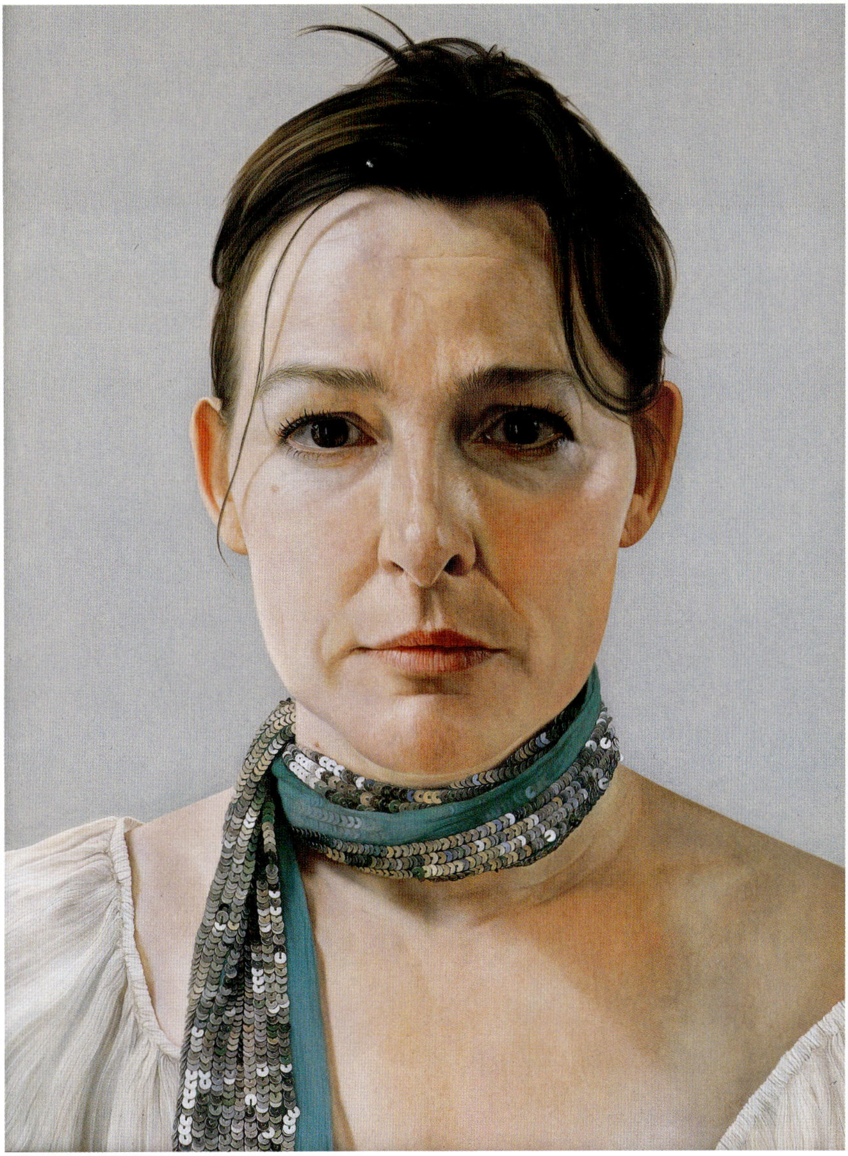

GIULIETTA COATES
DEAN MARSH

Oil on board
2005
731 x 575mm

Dean Marsh had exhibited several times in the BP Portrait Award, being commended in 2002 for his portrait of Dame Rosalind Savill before winning Fourth Prize in 2003. Marsh won First Prize in 2005 with the second of two paintings of his then girlfriend, Giulietta. His largest painting to date, it took almost six months to complete. Marsh is interested in realism and describes himself as having an honest approach to portraiture in that he tries to create intimate pictures without flattering the sitter.

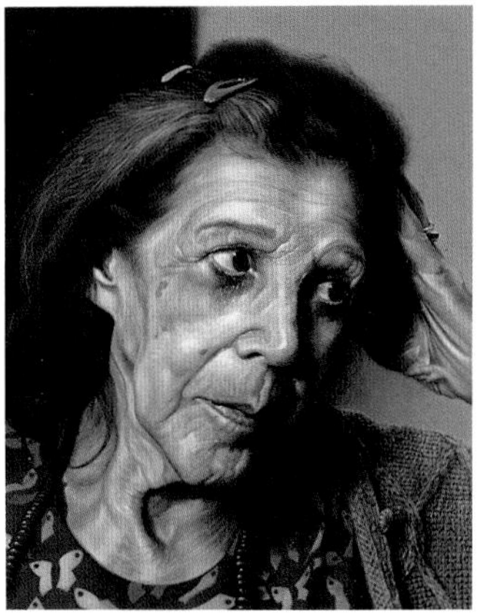 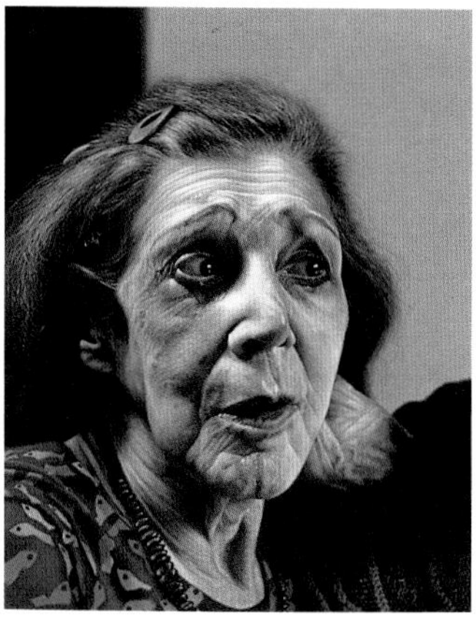 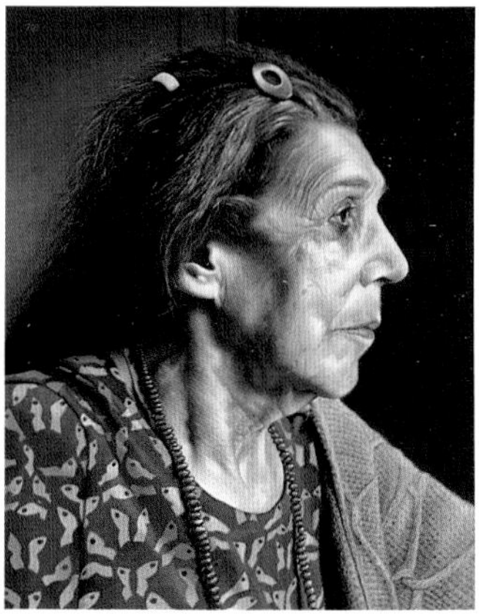

KITTY
ANDREW TIFT

Acrylic on board
2006
Triptych, each 350 x 250mm

Andrew Tift studied at the University of Central England, where he obtained a First-class Honours Degree and a Master of Arts in Illustration. Having exhibited in the BP Portrait Award ten times before, received the Travel Award and been on the judges' shortlist for First Prize on four previous occasions, Tift finally won in 2006 with this triptych of Kitty Garman, first wife of the painter Lucian Freud. Tift has described himself as a figurative realistic painter whose aim is to achieve a pure and objective likeness. His previous commissions include Neil and Glenys Kinnock for the National Portrait Gallery in 2001.

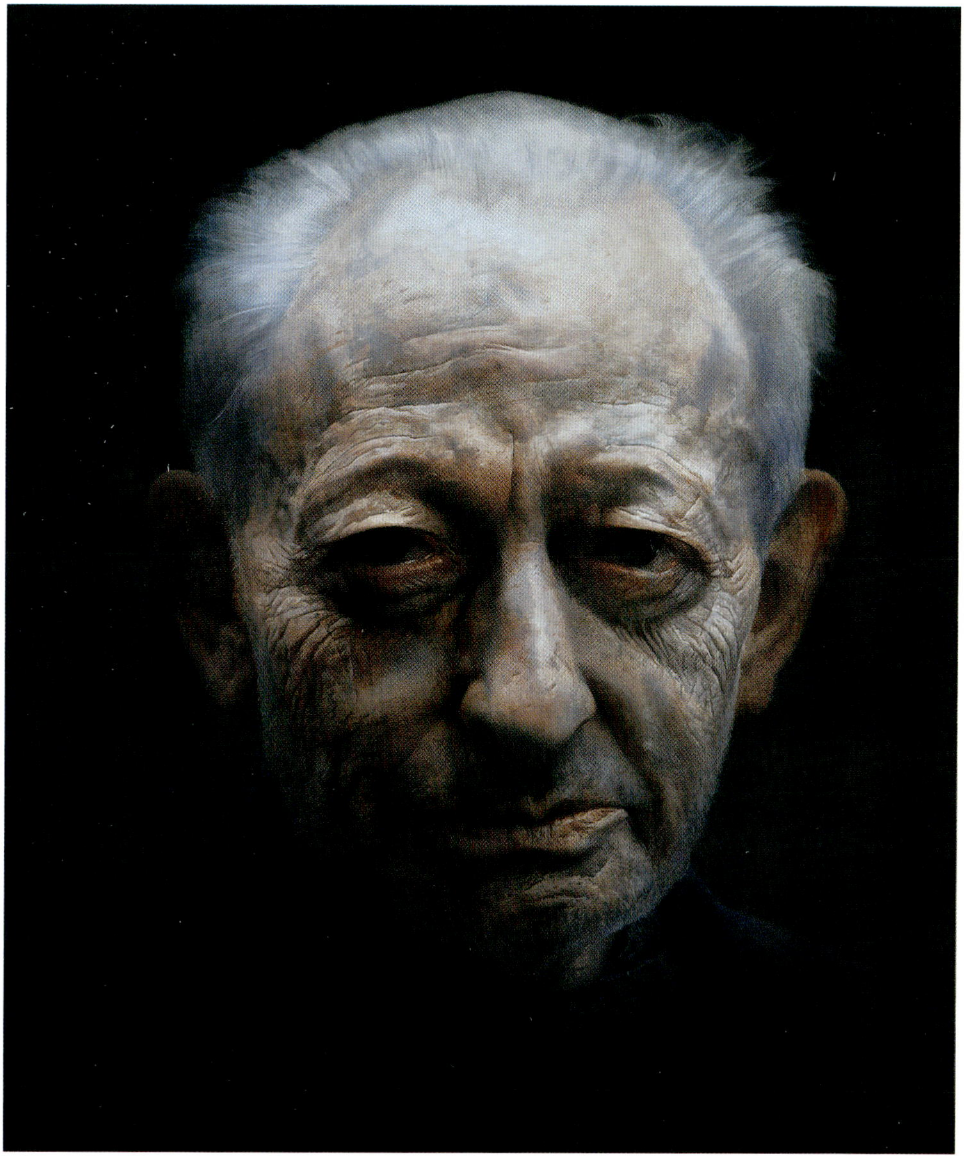

MICHAEL SIMPSON
PAUL EMSLEY

Oil on canvas
2007
1370 x 1120mm

Paul Emsley won First Prize when aged fifty-nine, in the first year the Award did not have an upper age limit. His winning painting is a large-scale study of Michael Simpson, a 67-year-old artist whom Emsley often met by chance in his local area near Bath in Somerset. He was drawn to the strong presence of Simpson's face, which he felt reflected something of the history of Eastern Europe (Simpson has Russian ancestry). Emsley has exhibited widely in Britain and South Africa, and completed a portrait of Nelson Mandela in 2011.

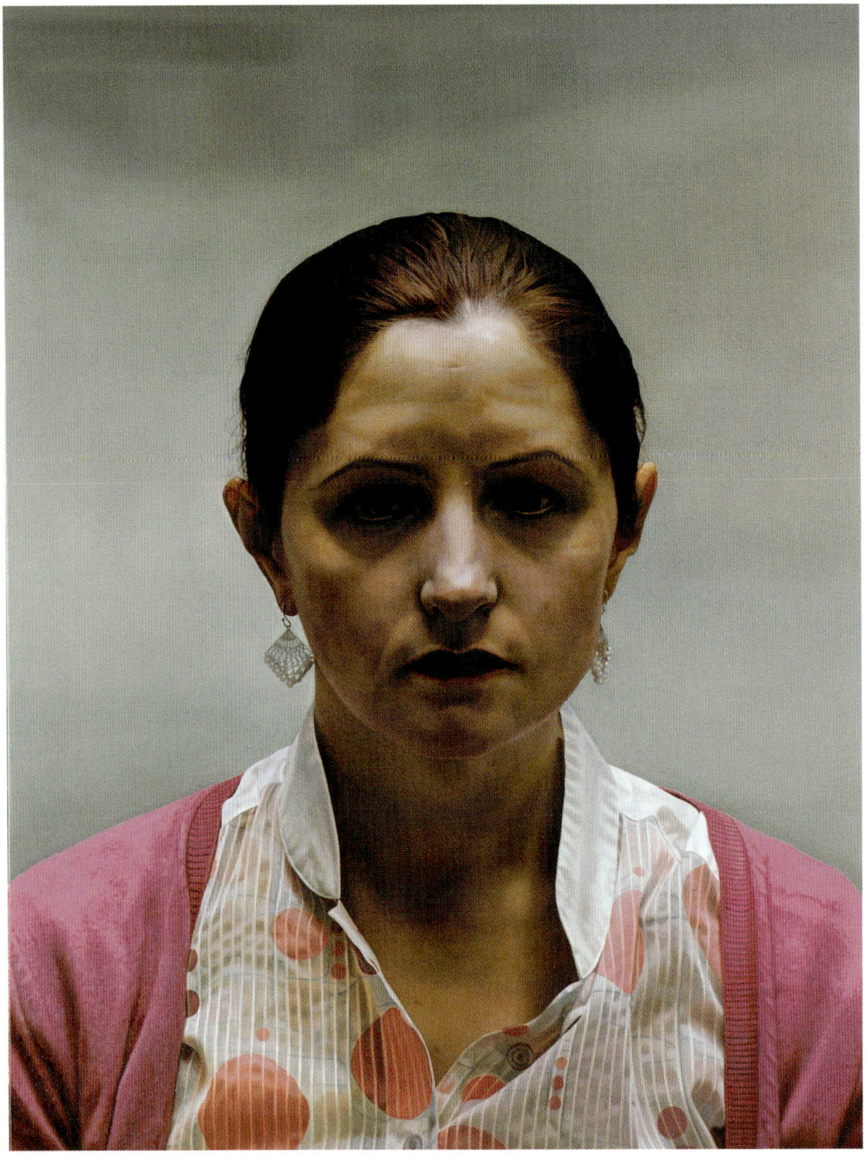

K
CRAIG WYLIE

Oil on canvas
2008
2100 x 1650mm

After exhibiting as part of the BP Portrait Award for three successive years, Craig Wylie won First Prize at the age of thirty-five with a portrait of his girlfriend, Katherine Raw. Based on sittings at Wylie's studio in Hackney Wick, east London, in 2005, the final painting was his third attempt at capturing his subject. Wylie has said of this work that while on one level the viewer's intrusion into the sitter's emotional state is tacitly accepted, on another level it is positively rebuffed. He studied at Rhodes University, Grahamstown, South Africa, before moving to London in 1998. His work has been widely exhibited around the world.

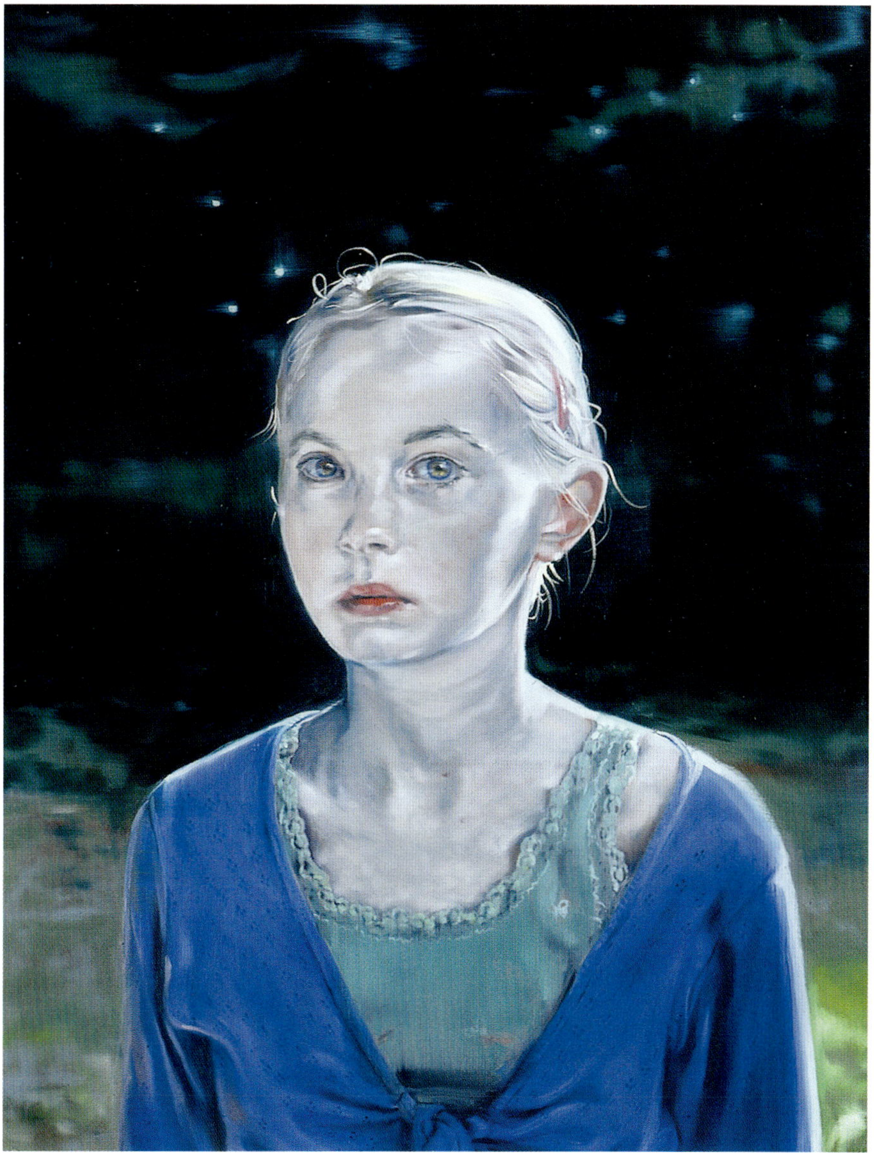

CHANGELING 2
PETER MONKMAN

Oil on canvas
2009
1220 x 900mm

Currently Director of Art at Charterhouse School, Surrey, Peter Monkman studied at Lancaster University, Liverpool John Moores University and the University of London. His work featured in the BP Portrait Award exhibitions of 1999, 2001 and 2003. *Changeling 2* is part of a series of portraits of Monkman's daughter Anna, exploring the concept of the changeling, a child substituted for another by stealth. Monkman sought to challenge idealised notions of childhood and to replace them with more unsettling and complex representations. The initial idea for this portrait came from photographic studies of Anna playing in woods in Brittany, France, where the artist felt the light had a magical quality.

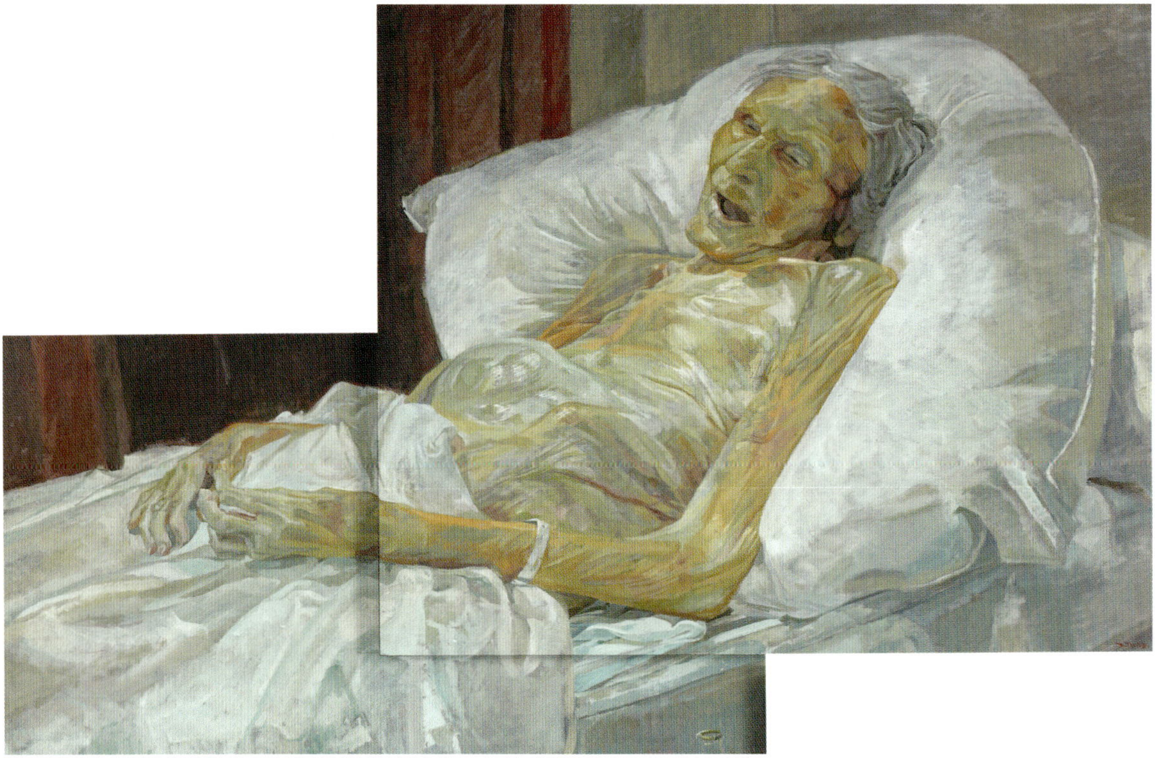

LAST PORTRAIT OF MOTHER
DAPHNE TODD

Oil on wooden panels
2010
650 x 920mm

Daphne Todd attended the Slade School of Fine Art and was the first woman president of the Royal Society of Portrait Painters (1994–2000). Todd's prizewinning painting was the third that she had exhibited as part of the BP Portrait Award, although she had previously won Second Prize in the Gallery's Portrait Award of 1984. Todd chose to portray her mother, Annie Mary Todd, on her deathbed and thereby create a devotional study. Todd's mother had lived with the artist for the last fourteen years of her life before dying at the age of 100. Todd has won many awards and has works in numerous private and public collections, including four paintings in the National Portrait Gallery.

Intimacy and mystery are present in many portraits: often, we feel like intruders on a private relationship.

Philip Hensher

Painted portraiture … helps us, I believe, to be more appreciative, more forgiving, and ultimately kinder.

Alexander McCall Smith

There is, to the true portrait, always something more than the mere business of a likeness, and indeed true portraiture is never about likenesses, but about an essence and a spirit and a deeper truth.

William Packer

Portraits – especially painted portraits – are essential to any biography. They are the beginning.

Margaret Forster

Portraits have to make an impact at a glance but also repay closer examination, so that even at a hundredth look they're inexhaustible.

Blake Morrison

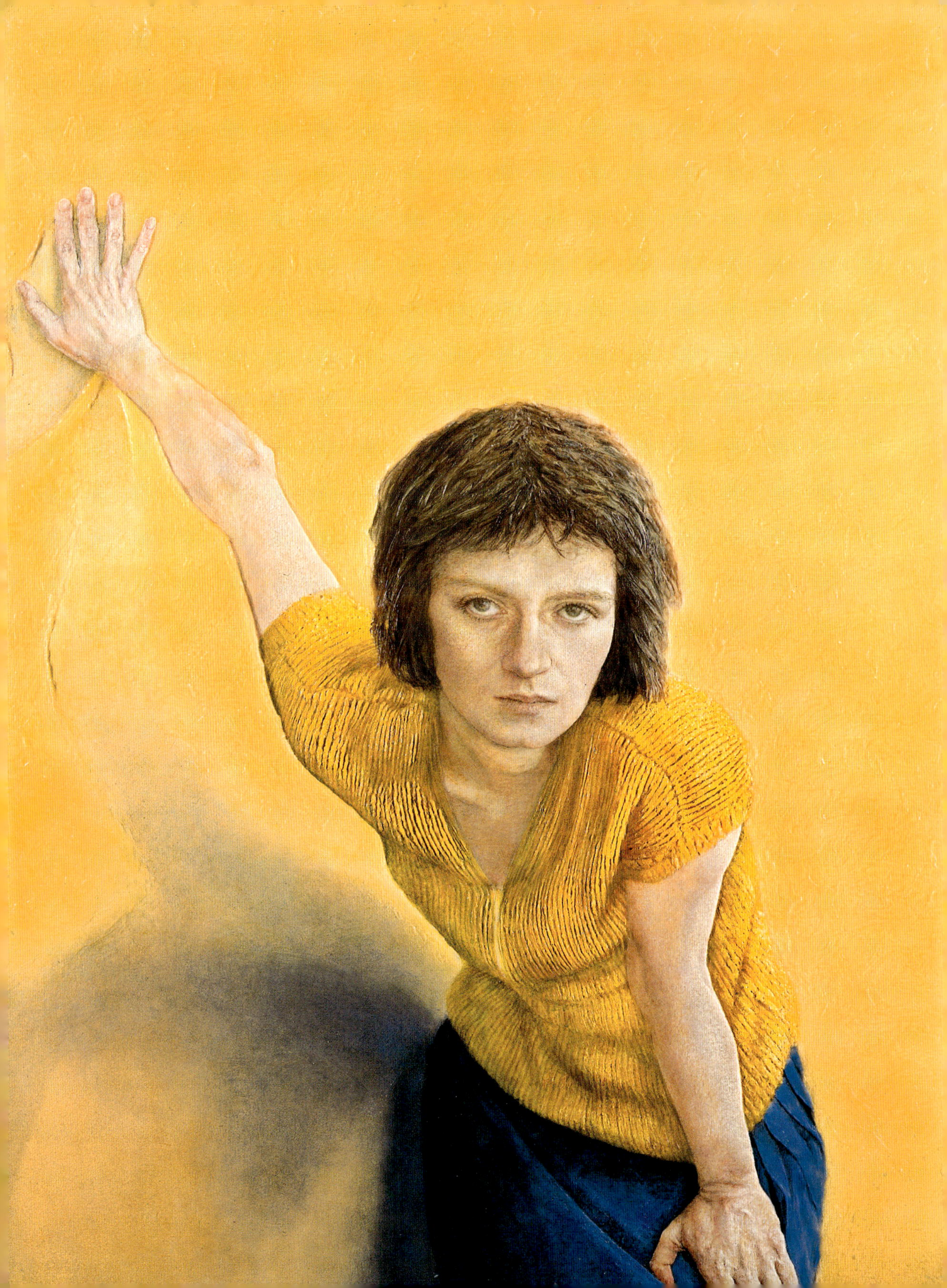

SELECTED WORKS

1990–2010

1990

ARTISTS WHOSE PORTRAITS WERE EXHIBITED

Lesley Banks / Mark Barnett / Lynn Bates / Nicholas Bernstein / Alexandra Boardman / Nick Botting / Paul Brason / Rima Bray / Sharon Brindle / Michael Checketts / Martin Churchill / Terence Clarke / David Cooper / Michael Corkrey / Haydn Cottam / Annabel Cullen / Saied Dai / Pedro Diablo / Alasdair Duncan / Helen Elwes / David Gleeson / Sarah Godsill / Nicolas Granger-Taylor / David Hamilton / Philip Harris / Matilda Harrison / Ross Henriksen / Andrew Ignarski / Gavin Jones / Margaret Levittoux / Jane Lewis / Binny Mathews / Fergus Mayhew / Donna McLean / Lawrence Merrifield / Margaret Milne / Ishbel Myerscough / Janie Nicoll / John Notter / Chris Ofili / Clive Pates / Johannes Phokela / Simon Redington / Raymond Richardson / Anthony John Robson / Sara Rossberg / Jenny Saville / Eric Seeley / Brian Shields / David James Smith / Chris Stevens / Martin Stevenson / Caroline Waller / Sarah Webb / Steven Williams

SECOND PRIZE
PORTRAIT OF MARIA CHEVSKA
MARTIN CHURCHILL

Oil on canvas
1420 x 1120mm

Born in Glasgow, Martin Churchill studied at Edinburgh College of Art during the 1970s. He has shown at solo and group exhibitions throughout his career, predominantly in London and Scotland, including the Royal Academy Summer Exhibitions and the Royal Scottish Academy. This prizewinning portrait depicts the painter Maria Chevska. Churchill currently works on a diverse range of subject matter, from racing scenes to large-scale industrial studies and sculpture.

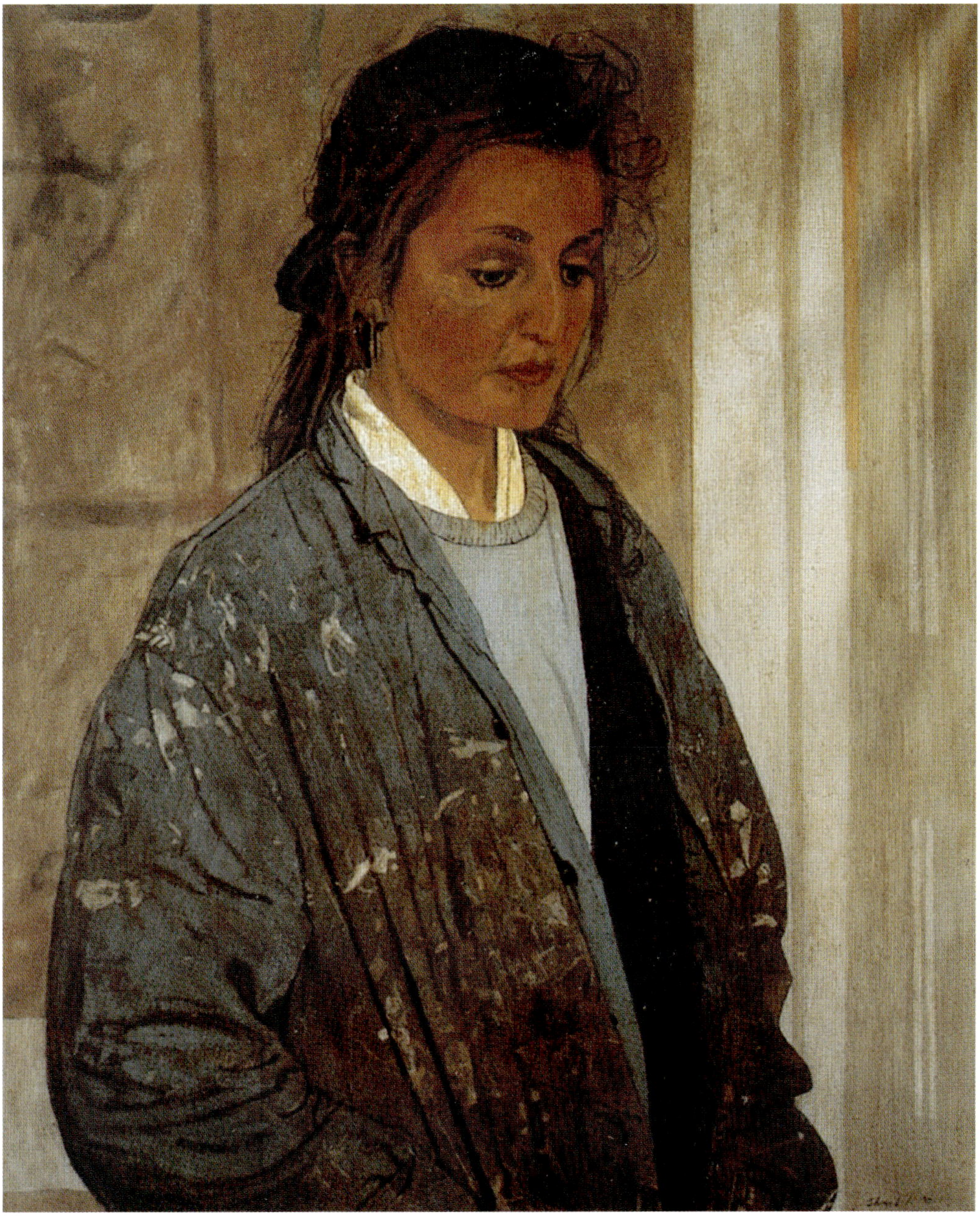

THIRD PRIZE
SELF-PORTRAIT
PHILIP HARRIS

Oil on canvas
355 x 305mm

Having graduated from Bradford College of Art and Design in 1986, Philip Harris was working as a full-time artist when he submitted this self-portrait for the first year of the BP Portrait Award. Harris has received significant critical acclaim for his figurative work and he has paintings in the Metropolitan Museum of Art, New York, and the Jersey Museum in St Helier. He went on to win the BP Portrait Award in 1993.

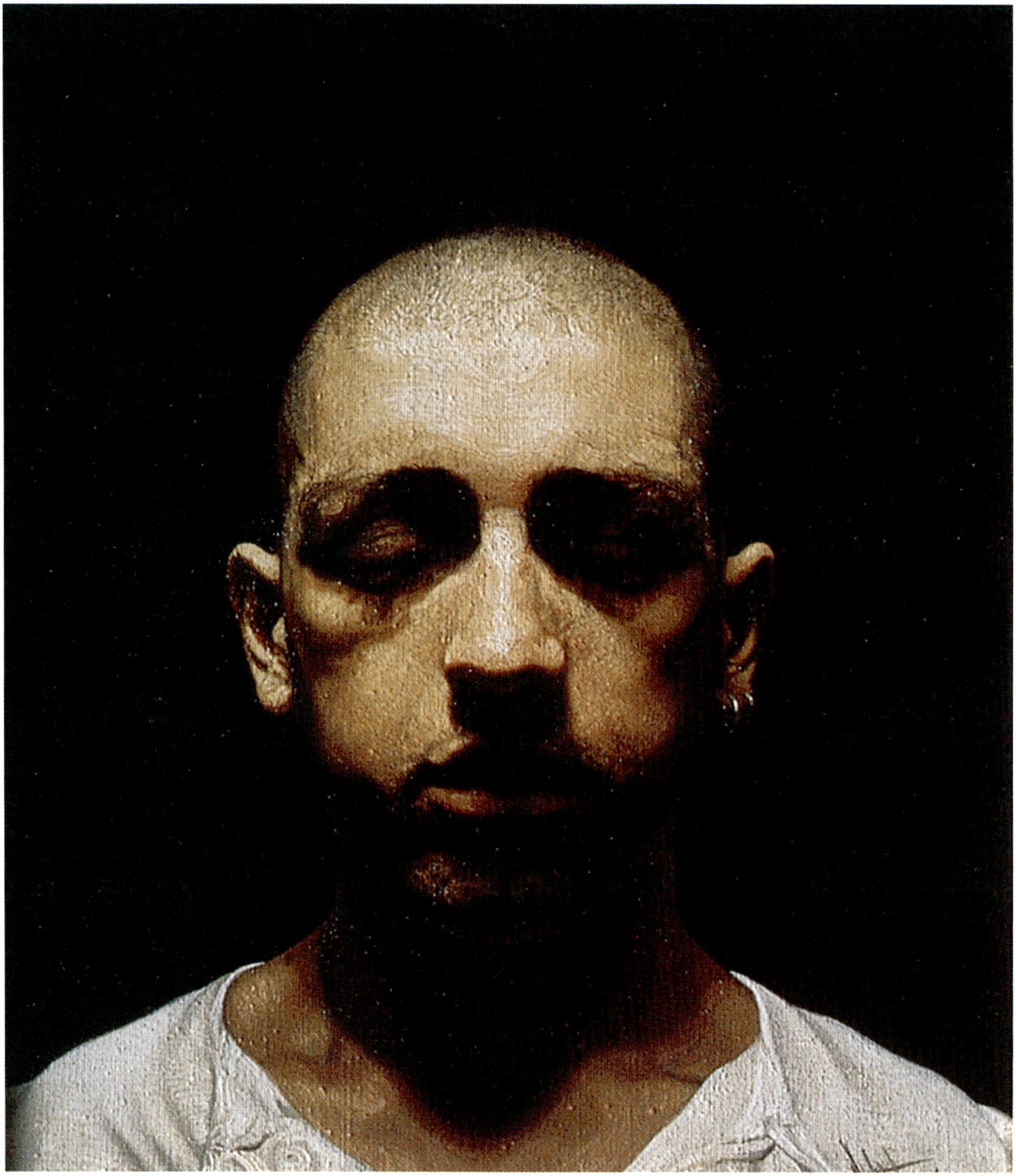

Commended
Blue in Yellow
Sara Rossberg
Acrylic on canvas
1830 x 1525mm

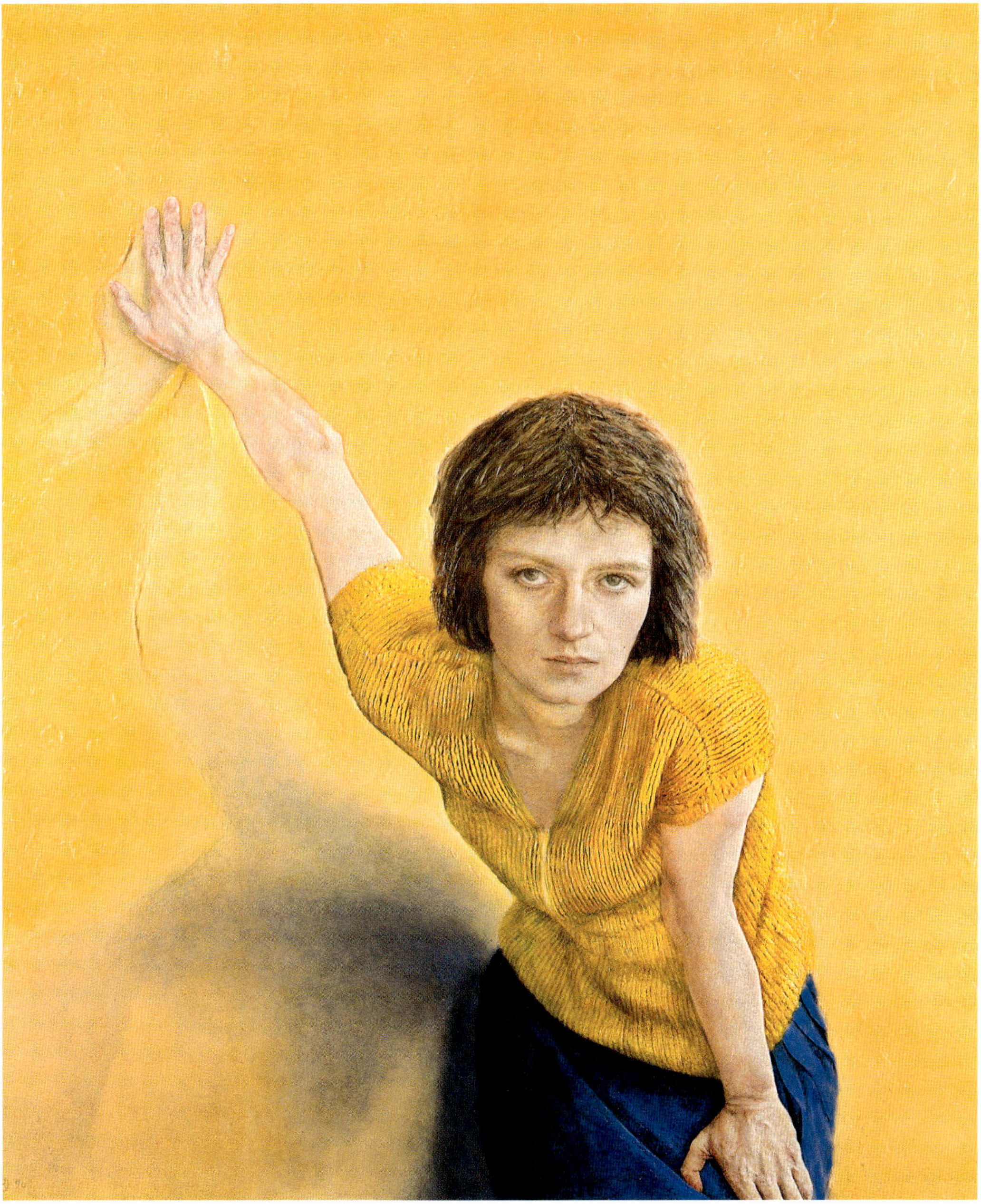

Commended
Alison
Haydn Cottam
Oil on canvas
2430 x 1800mm

Commended
Sandy & Child
Johannes Phokela
Oil on canvas
1930 x 1320mm

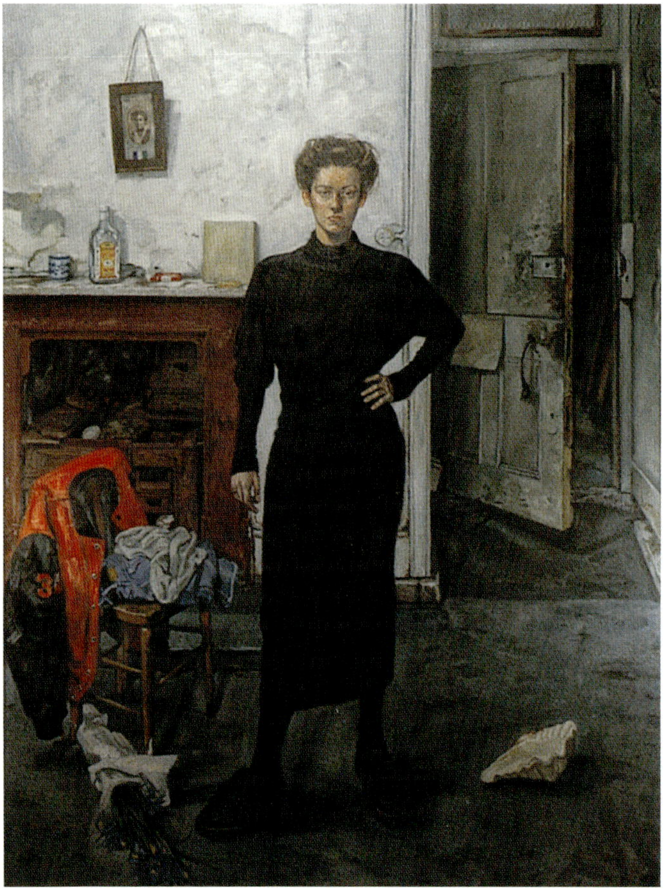

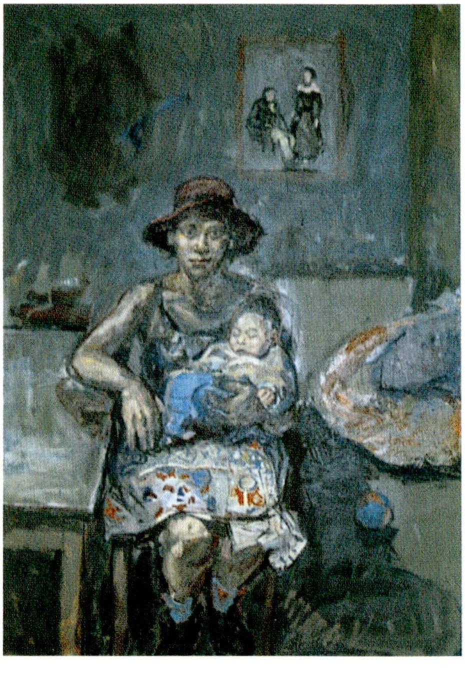

Commended
The Untouchables
Raymond Richardson
Oil on canvas
1425 x 1730mm

Commended
Regents Park
Chris Stevens
Oil on canvas
1525 x 1830mm

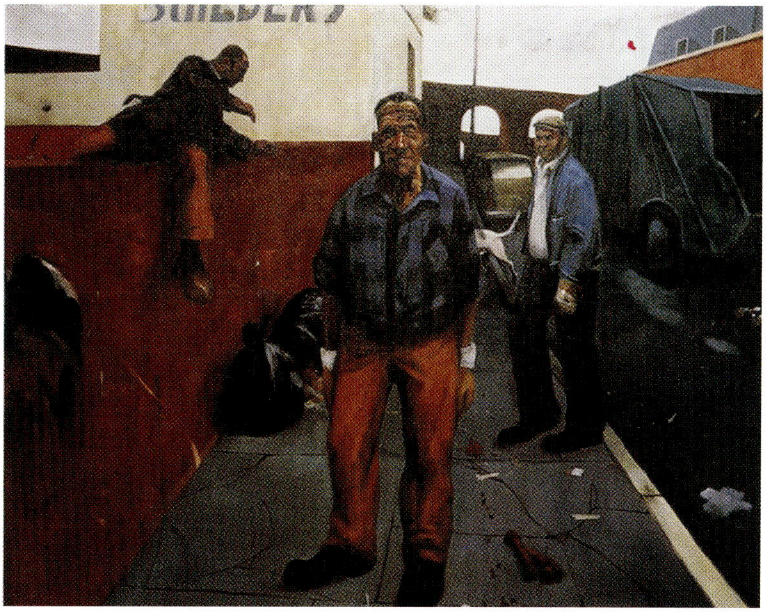

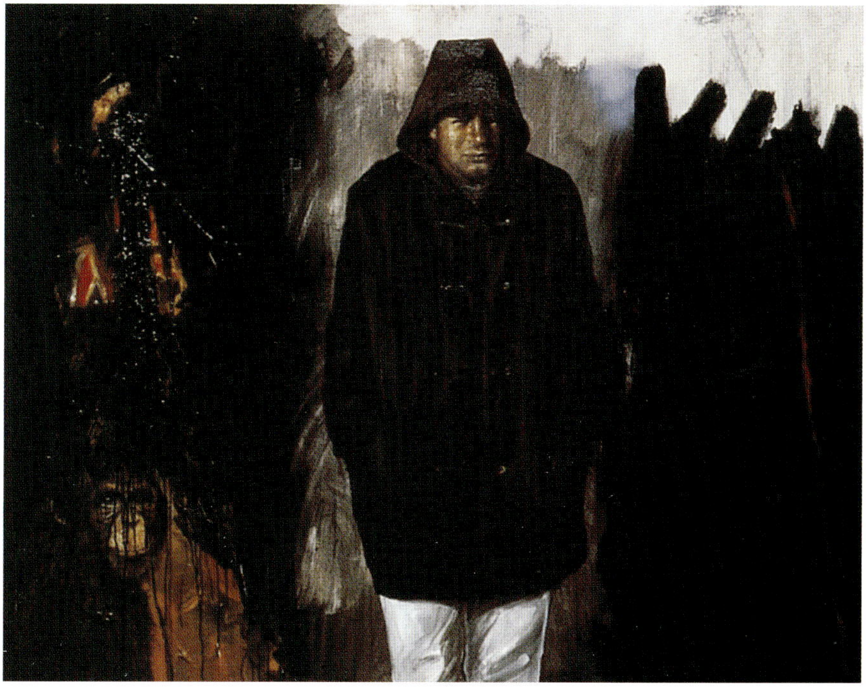

1991

ARTISTS WHOSE PORTRAITS WERE EXHIBITED

Crawfurd Adamson / Peter Amachree / Warren Baldwin / Mark Barnett / Peter Batchelor / Nicholas Bernstein / Carey Blundun / Alexandra Boardman / Robert Bound / Paul Brason / Michael Clark / Edward Clarke / Paul Cook / Michael Corkrey / Haydn Cottam / Louise Courtnell / Amanda Danicic / Lucy Edkine / Susannah Fiennes / Alan Flood / Jane Ford / Robin-Lee Hall / Sarah Hall-Craggs / Philip Harris / Lucy Higgins / Steven Hubbard / Duncan Hulme / Valda Jackson / Chantal Joffe / Brendan Kelly / Alexander Macdonald / Hugh McKay / Donna McLean / Peter McNiven / Justin Mortimer / Ishbel Myerscough / Adele Neave / Angus Northeas / John Notter / Chris Ofili / Stephen Palmer / Shanti Panchal / Roderic Read / Andrew Rollo / David Rycroft / Jenny Saville / Fiona Scott / Louise Soloway / Stephen St Angelo / Jason Sullivan / Phillip Swarbrick / Sadie Tomlinson / Bob Tulloch / Colin Watson / Gavin Watson / Michael B. White

SECOND PRIZE
MARIA CABANAS AND MAGGIE MAGUIRE
JASON SULLIVAN

Oil on canvas
462 x 360mm

Born in Dorset, Jason Sullivan trained at Grimsby College of Technology and Sheffield Polytechnic in the 1970s. His work had been selected for the Gallery's Portrait Award of 1986 prior to being awarded Second Prize in 1991, and has been widely exhibited since. In 2003 Sullivan became an elected member of the Royal Society of Portrait Painters.

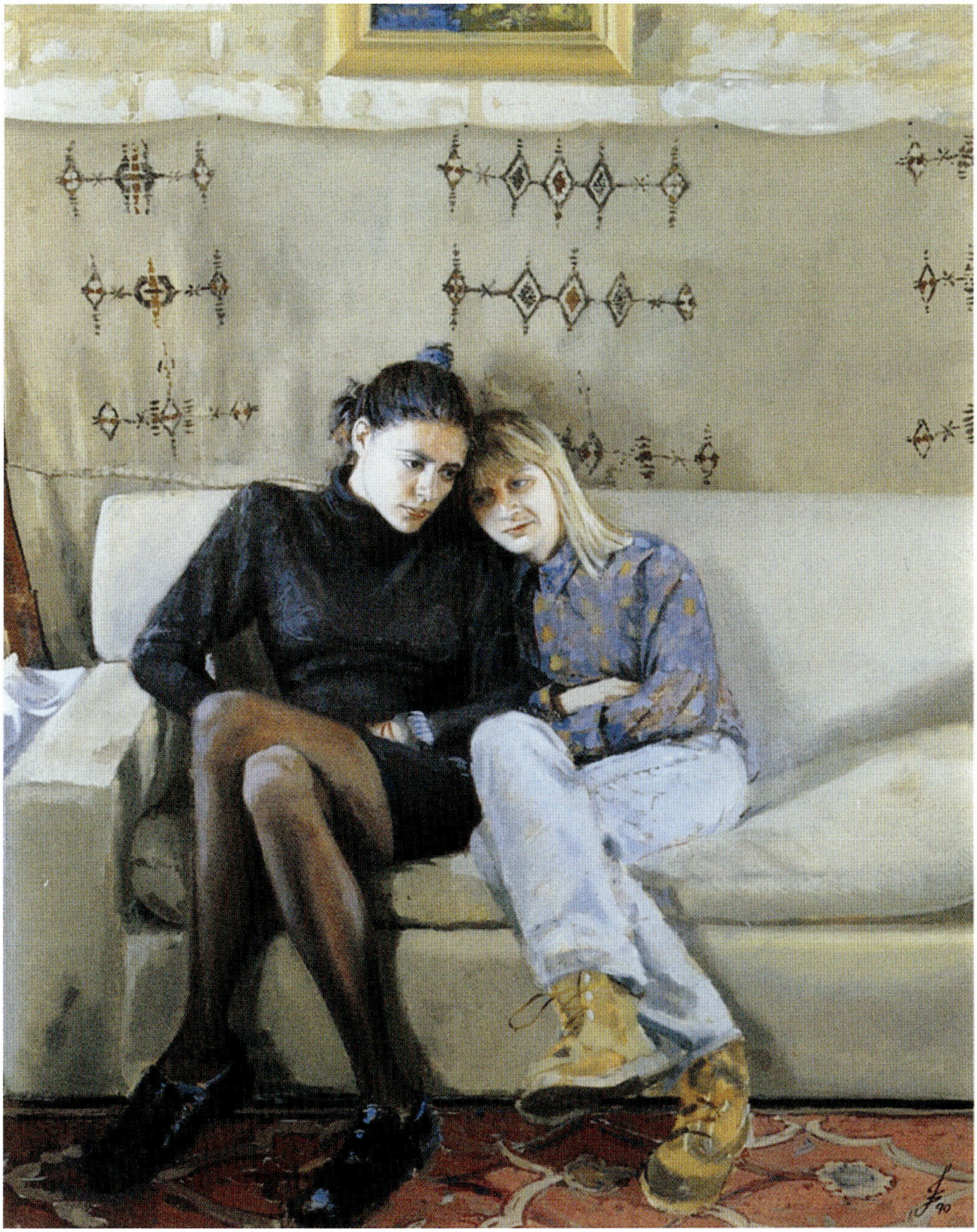

THIRD PRIZE
LETTER FROM INDIA
SHANTI PANCHAL

Acrylic
1713 x 1220mm

Born in Gujarat, Shanti Panchal studied at the J.J. School of Art in Bombay and, with the help of a British Council scholarship, at the Byam Shaw School of Art in London. Based in Britain since 1980, he has exhibited widely in both India and Europe, and has won and been shortlisted for many awards. Having initially worked primarily in oils and acrylics, Panchal now specialises in watercolour paintings.

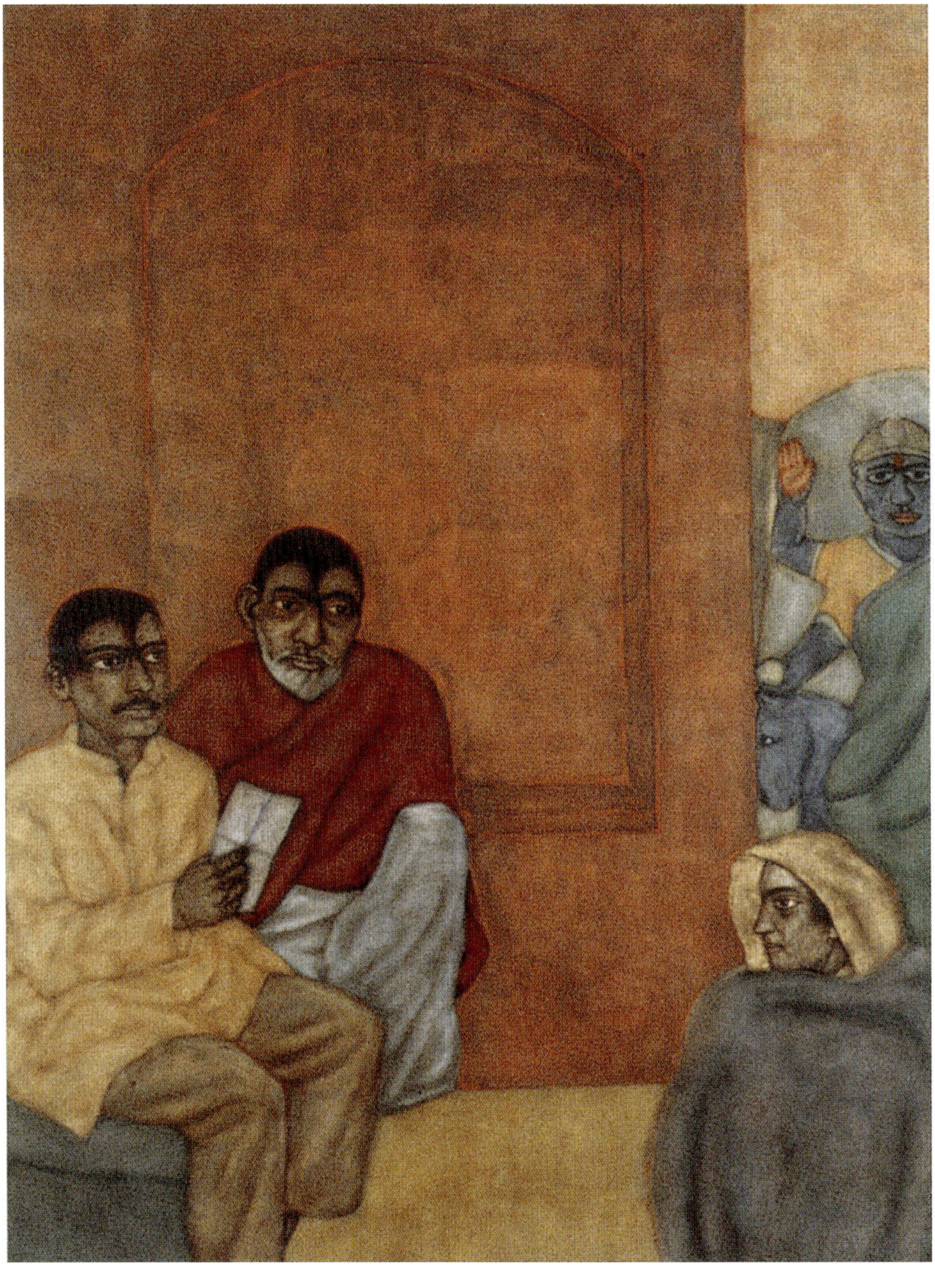

Commended
My Mother
Amanda Danicic
Oil on canvas
1525 x 1220mm

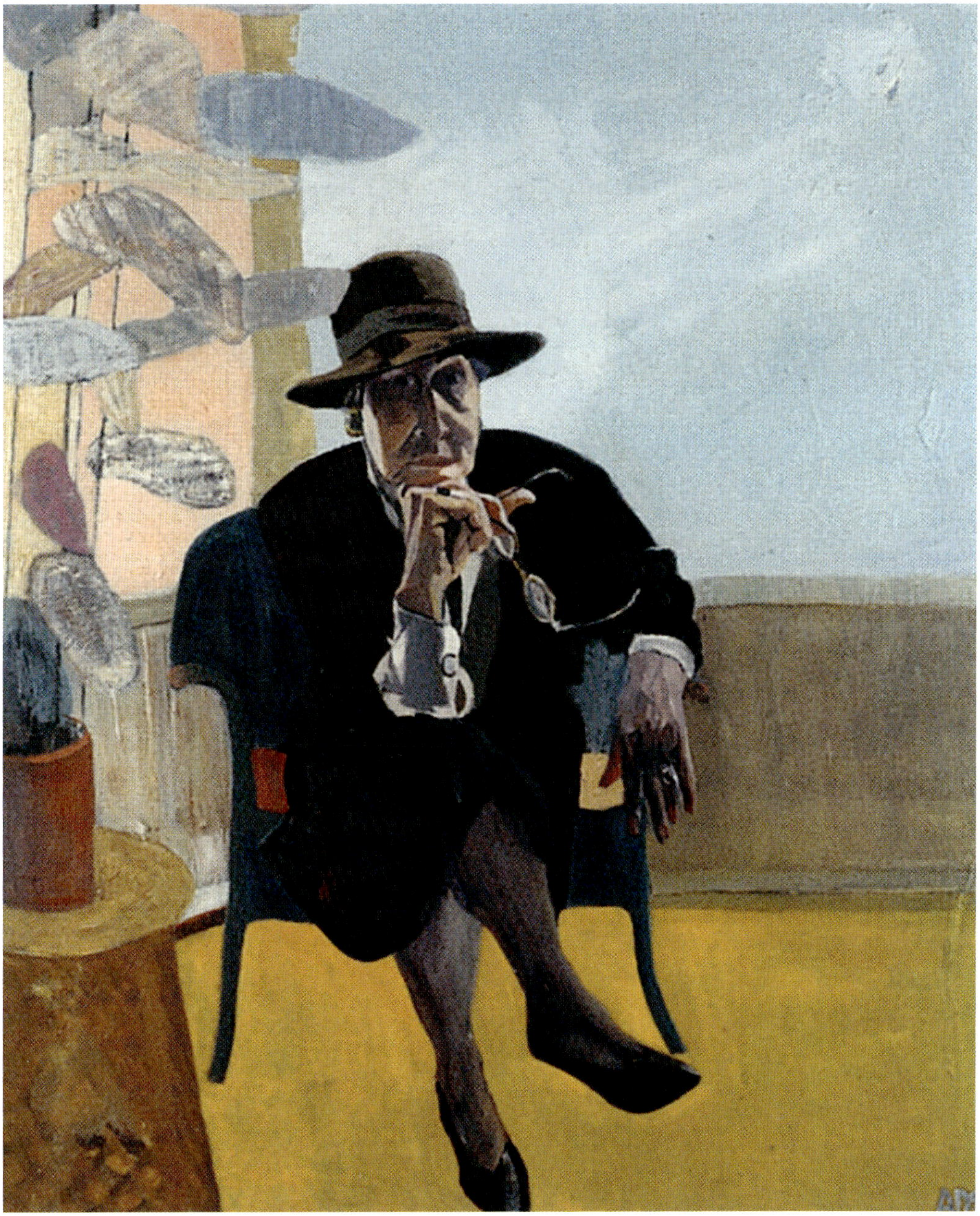

Commended
Self-portrait
Nicholas Bernstein
Oil on canvas
1010 x 760mm

Commended
Self-portrait
Louise Courtnell
Oil on canvas
305 x 255mm

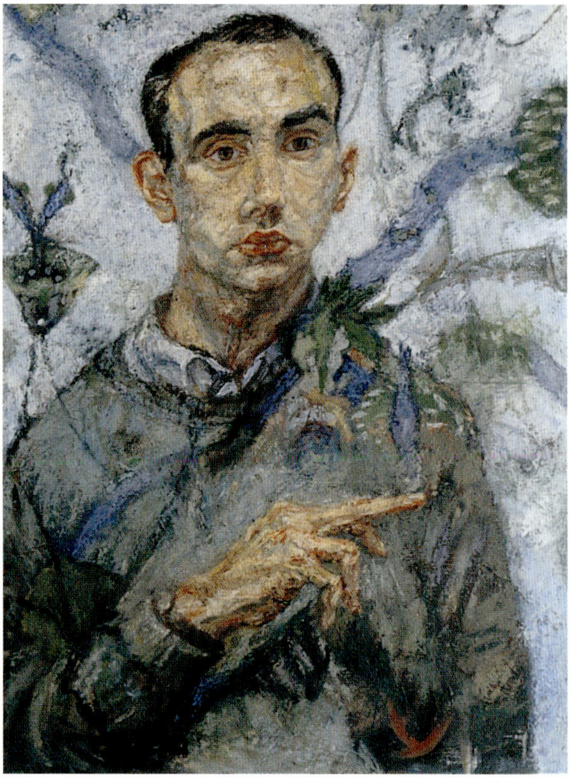

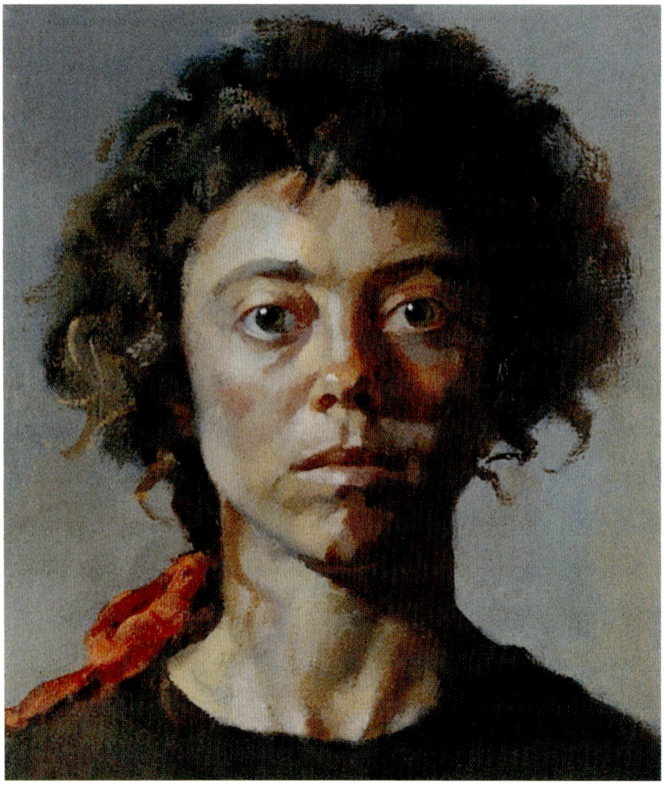

Commended
Self-portrait with Knitted Tie
Peter McNiven
Oil on board
608 x 595mm

Commended
Portrait
Ishbel Myerscough
Oil on canvas
680 x 406mm

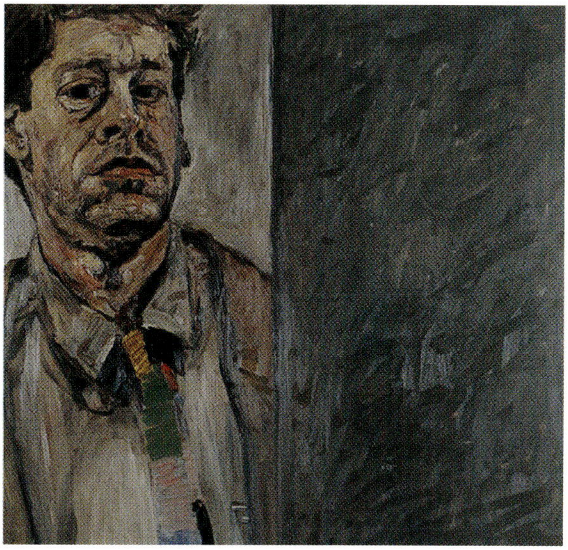

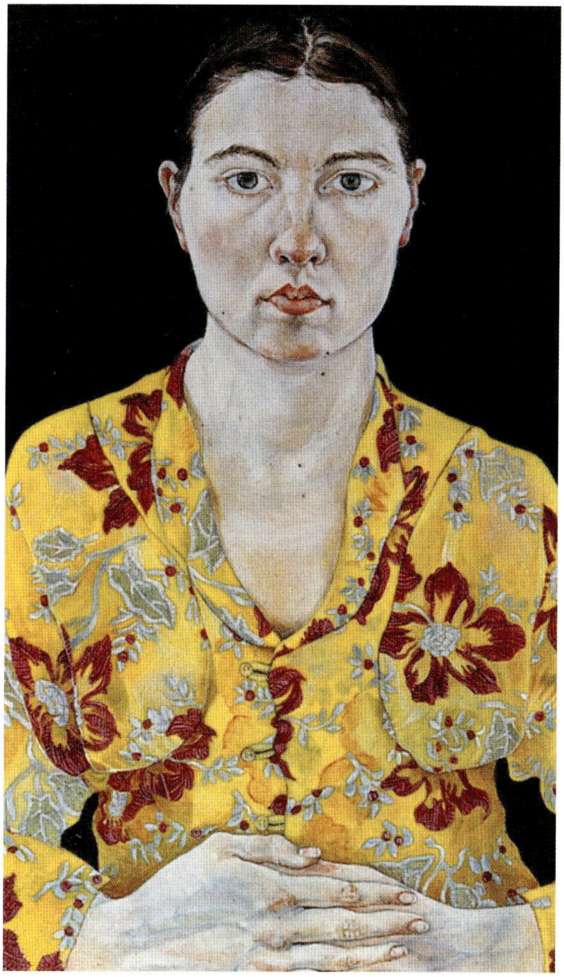

1992

ARTISTS WHOSE PORTRAITS WERE EXHIBITED

Jane Allison / Nicholas Bernstein / Nick Botting / Paul Brason / Isobel Brigham / Betty Brown / Claire Bushe / Alec Chanda / Paul Charles-Cook / Martin Churchill / Michael Clark / Rachel Clark / Michael Corkrey / Louise Courtnell / Oliver Deney / Daniel Eghan / Emily Feaver / Penny Francis / Ann Gardner / Christopher Greene / Mary Griffiths / Robin-Lee Hall / Ross Hall / Desmond Healy / Chantal Joffe / Gavin Jones / Brendan Kelly / Paul Lake / Jane Lewis / Brian Martin / Brian McLaughlin / Craig Mulholland / Ishbel Myerscough / Patricia Napier / Roger Nobs / John Notter / Alison Rylands / Melissa Scott-Miller / Steve Sharples / Michael Shaw / Matthew Sibley / Renee Spierdijk / Christopher Stevens / Jason Sullivan / Andrew Tift / Helen Tipper / Anthea Toorchen / Helen Vicat / Lyndon Volney / Lucy Willis / Barry Wilson / Neale Worley / Robert Wraith / Patricia Wright

SECOND PRIZE
MINNIE WITH MAX
ALEC CHANDA

Oil on canvas
2090 x 1895mm

After studying at Camberwell School of Art and Crafts, Alec Chanda spent a period travelling in Australia, Indonesia and India before becoming a part-time art tutor in Twickenham. This portrait of Chanda's mother was painted while he was working as a self-employed picture framer. Chanda had previously exhibited in the Portrait Award in 1988 as well as at the Whitechapel Open, and had won second prize in the Hunting Group Art Prizes in 1990. His first solo exhibition was in 2003.

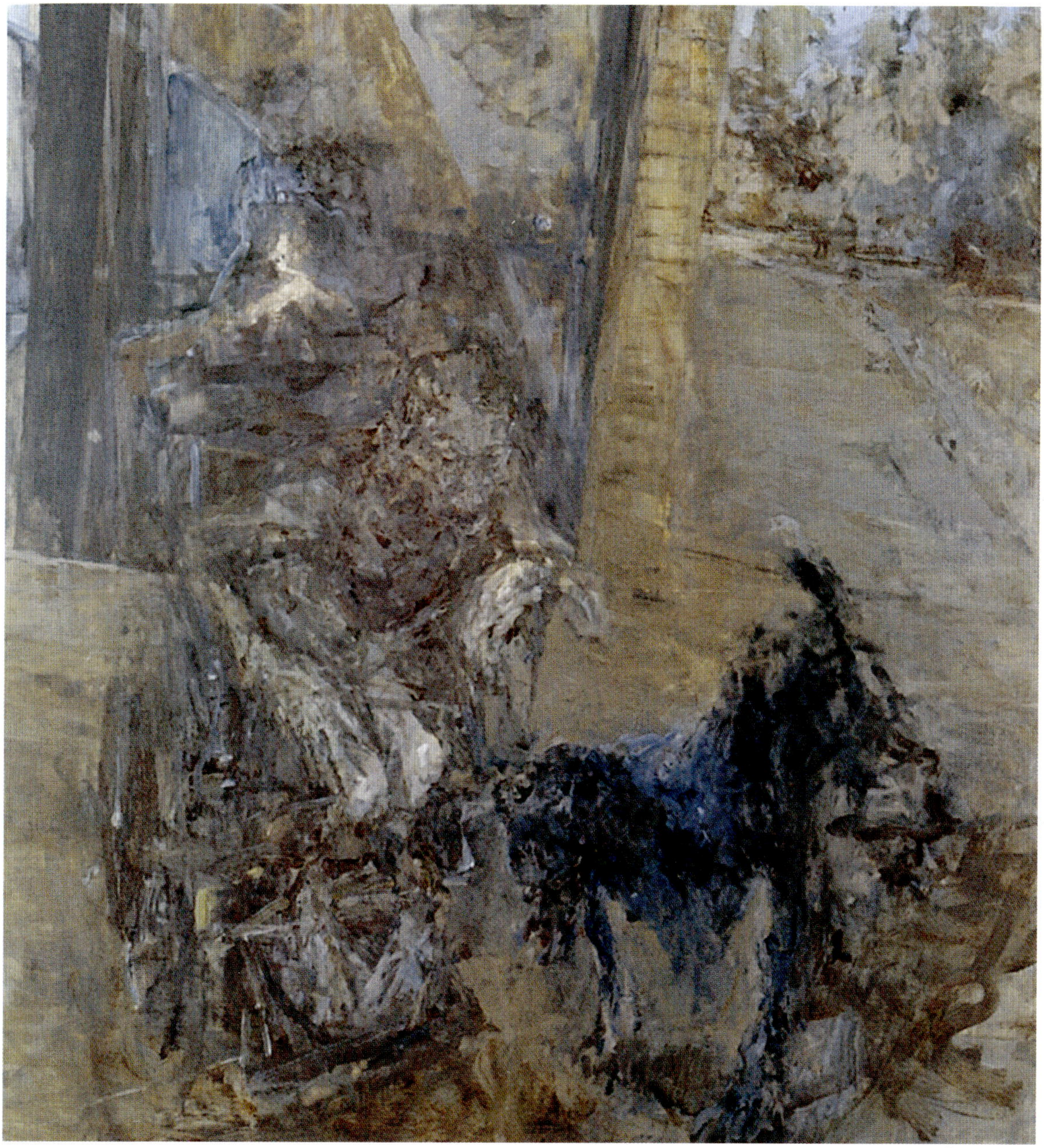

THIRD PRIZE
RICHARD (HAIRY MAN)
ISHBEL MYERSCOUGH

Oil on board
640 x 430mm

Ishbel Myerscough was twenty-four when she painted this portrait of a friend, by which time her work was in the collections of NatWest and Barings Banks, as well as in private collections in Britain and Germany. She had also completed several commissions. Myerscough went on to win First Prize in the BP Portrait Award in 1995.

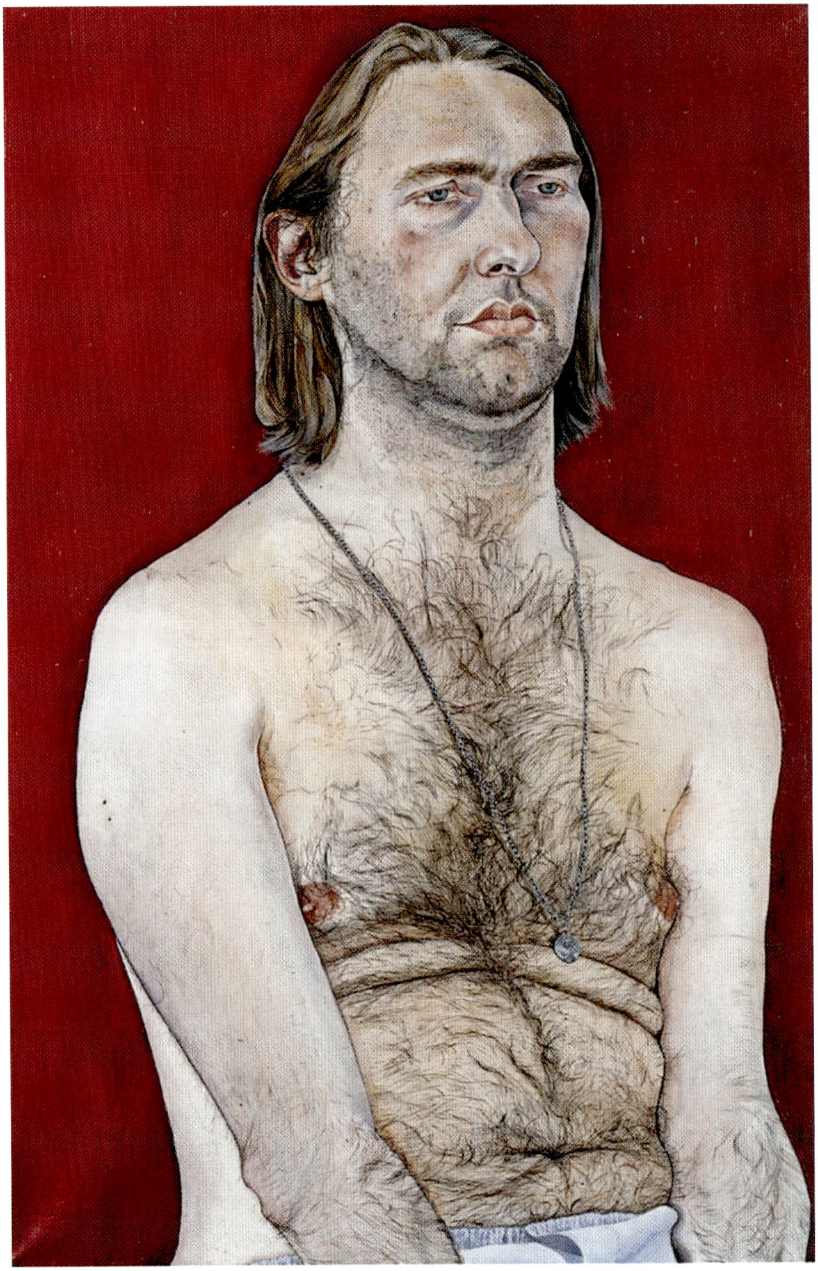

Commended
Me and My Family
Ross Hall
Oil on board
905 x 1220mm

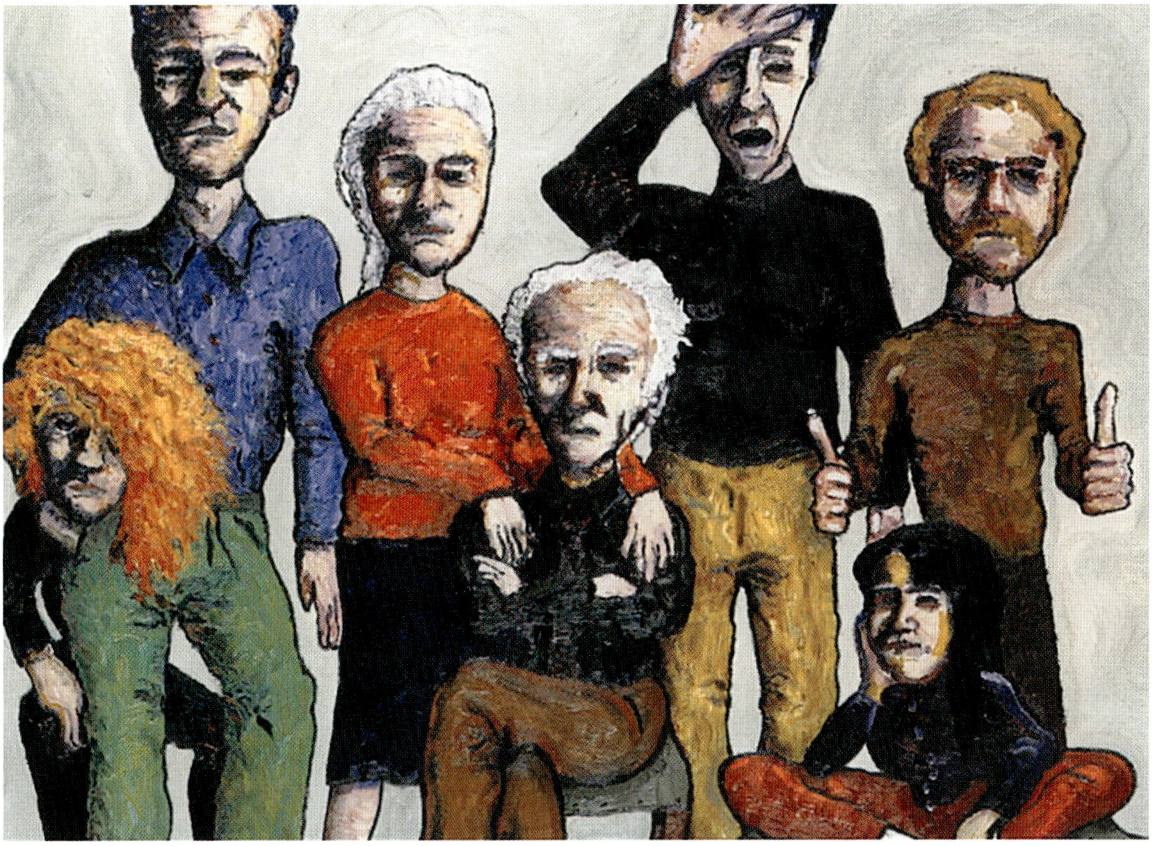

Commended
The Slaughtermen
Martin Churchill
Oil on canvas
1660 x 1160mm

Commended
Head of Marguerite Kelsey
Michael Clark
Oil on canvas
460 x 410mm

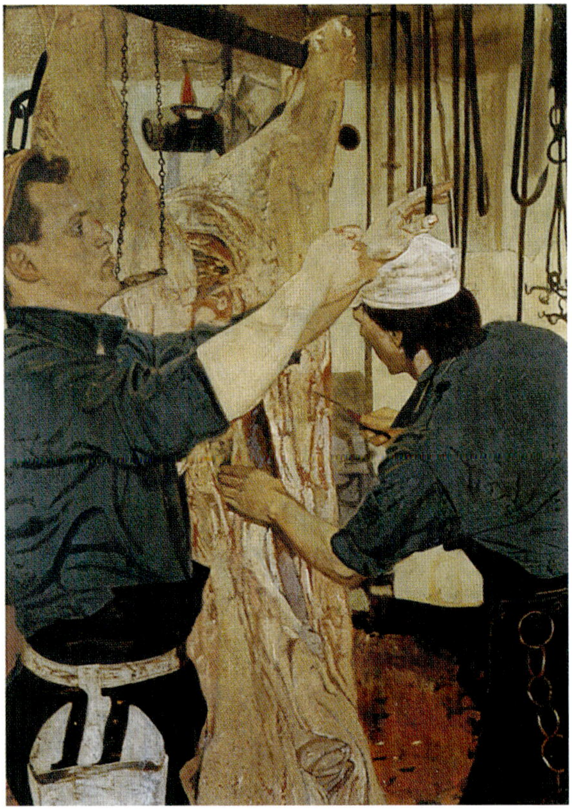

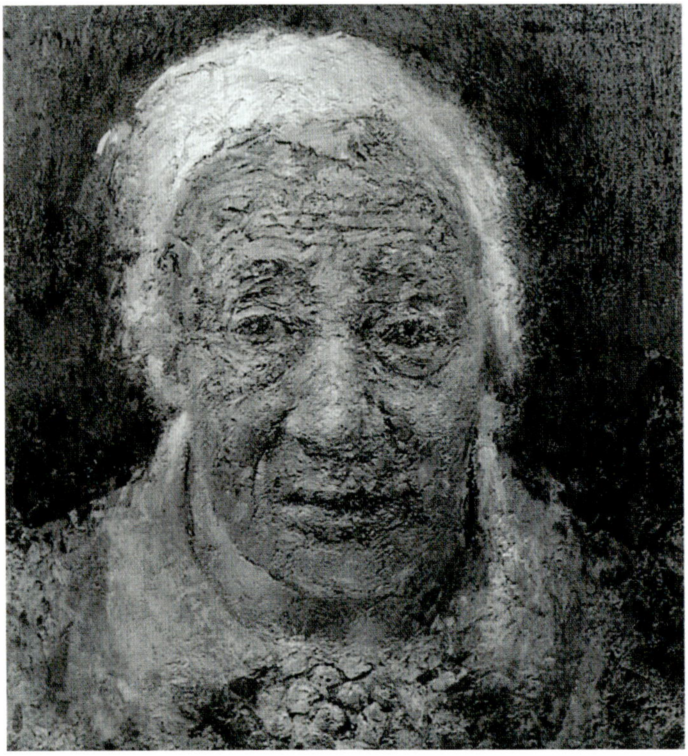

Commended
Diptych
Gavin Jones
Oil on canvas
each panel 995 x 610mm

Commended
The Doorway
Brendan Kelly
Oil on canvas
2130 x 1830mm

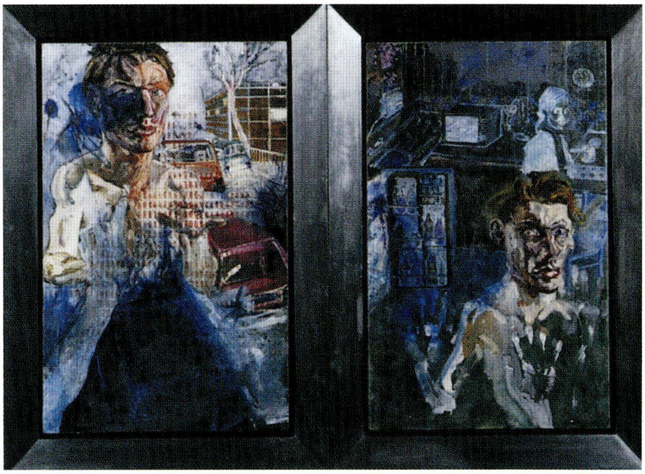

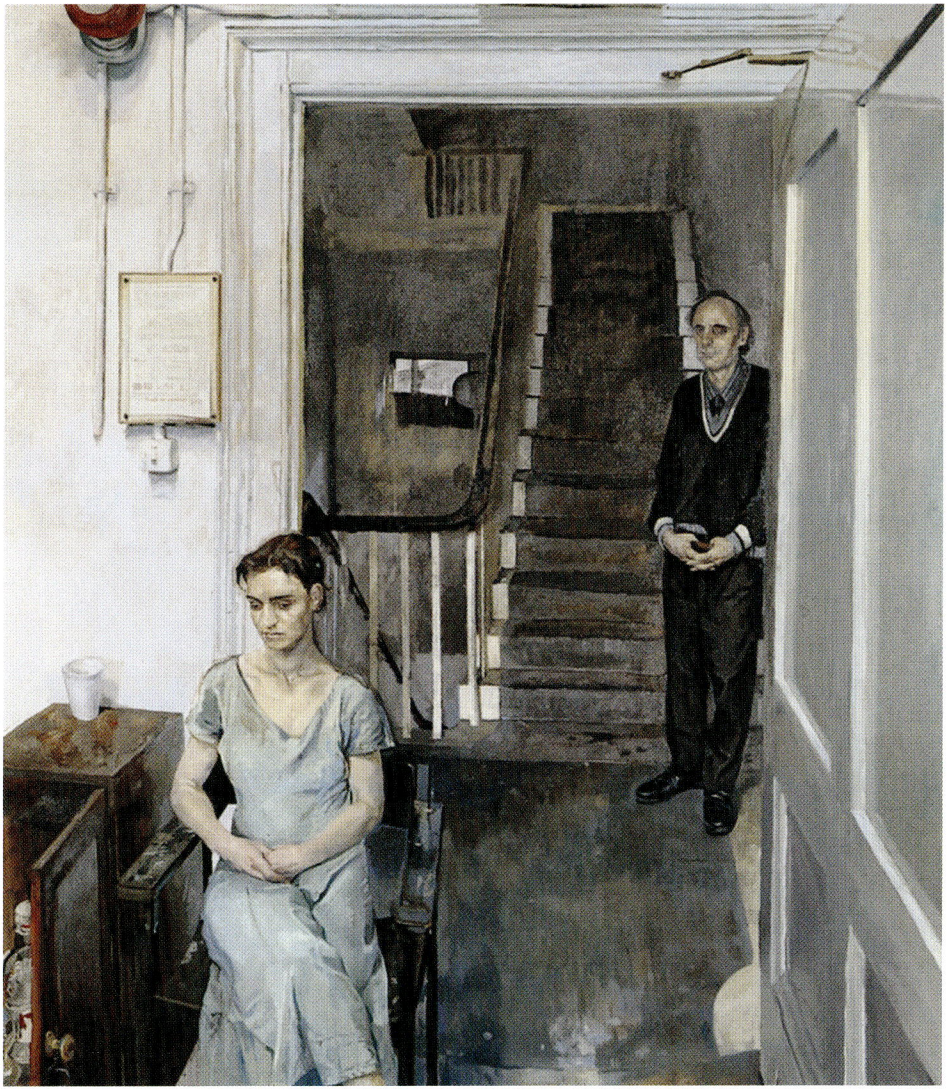

1993

ARTISTS WHOSE PORTRAITS WERE EXHIBITED

Jane Allison / Lesley Banks / Tess Barnes / Stephen Bishop / Ben Blant / Paul Brason / Michael Browne / Edmund Chamberlain / Lewis Chamberlain / Martin Churchill / Rachel Clark / Louise Courtnell / Antony Crossfield / Ian Dawes / Arturo Di Stefano / Katherine Downes / Susan Faux / Susannah Fiennes / Mark Gilbert / Stephen Goddard / Tom Hallifax / Linda Hardwicke / Alison Harper / Heather Harrigan / Philip Harris / Guy Harrison / Geoffrey Hayzer / Sophie Herxheimer / Patrick Holley / Steven Hubbard / Chantal Joffe / Brendan Kelly / Caroline Lam / Sadie Lee / Kee Levi / Mandy Lindsay / Polly Lister / David Lynch / Dean Marsh / Binny Mathews / Brian McLaughlin / Annabel Mednick / Hamish Moyle / Ishbel Myerscough / Isis Nassar / Joanna Painter / Angela Panays / Phil Parry / Emily Patrick / Christopher Prewett / Raymond Richardson / Sara Rossberg / Craig Shirley / Nahem Shoa / Jason Sullivan / Christopher Thompson / Andrew Tift / Michael Tomlinson / Gavin Watson / Michael B. White / Nigel Wood / William Wood / Neale Worley

SECOND PRIZE
SELF-PORTRAIT
CHRISTOPHER PREWETT

Oil on canvas
1170 x 910mm

Christopher Prewett studied at Canterbury College of Art. His paintings have been widely exhibited since the 1970s in both group and solo exhibitions throughout Britain and in Europe. He had been selected for the Portrait Award in 1984 and 1988 before winning Second Prize with this self-portrait. His recent work includes a series of portrait heads painted from life and memory.

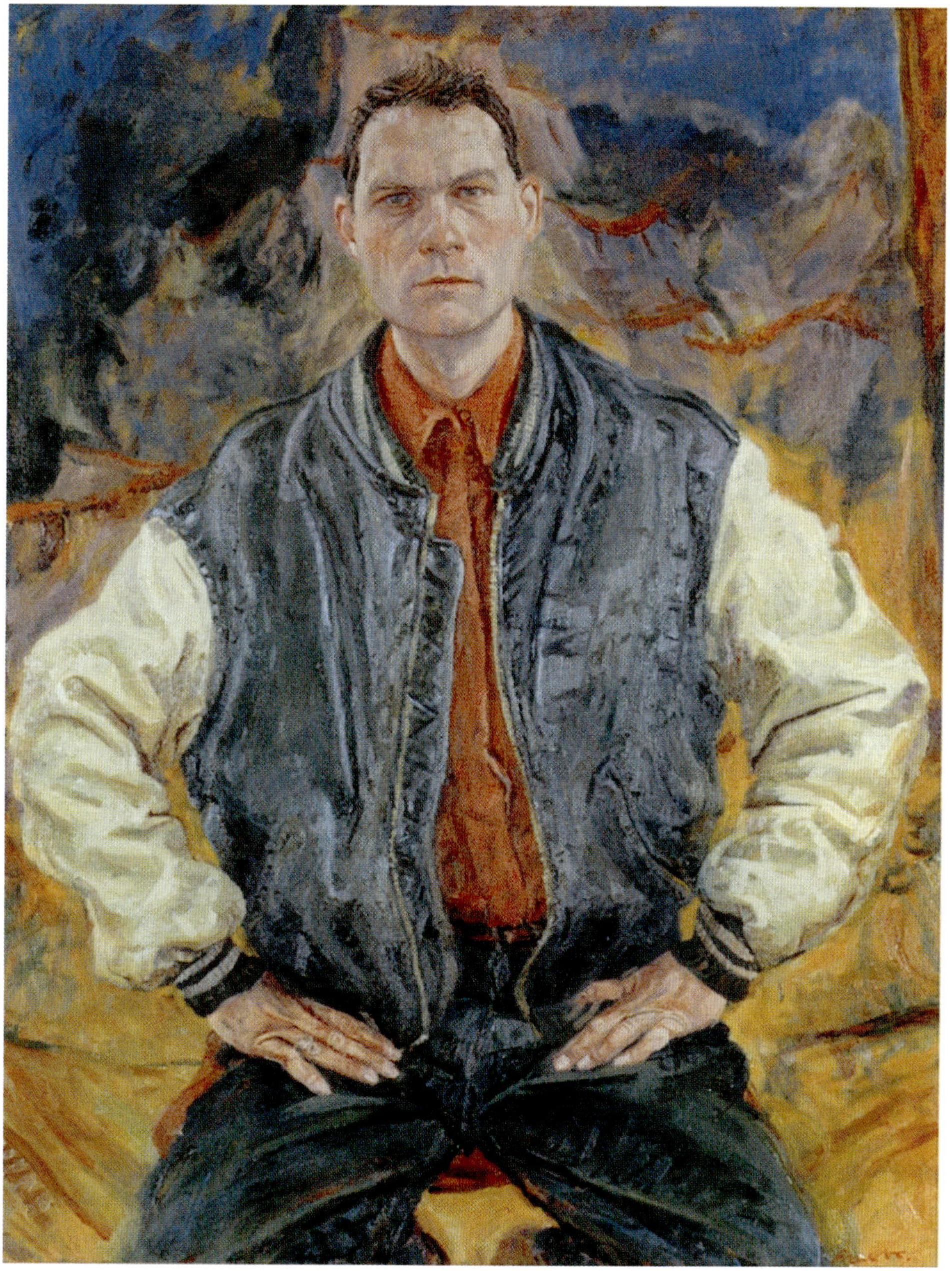

THIRD PRIZE
IOLO BACH
MICHAEL TOMLINSON

Oil on canvas
385 x 385mm

Michael Tomlinson studied Archaeology and Geology at the University of Manchester. At the time this portrait of his infant son Iolo was painted, he was working as an artist at the Centre for Alternative Technology co-operative in Wales.

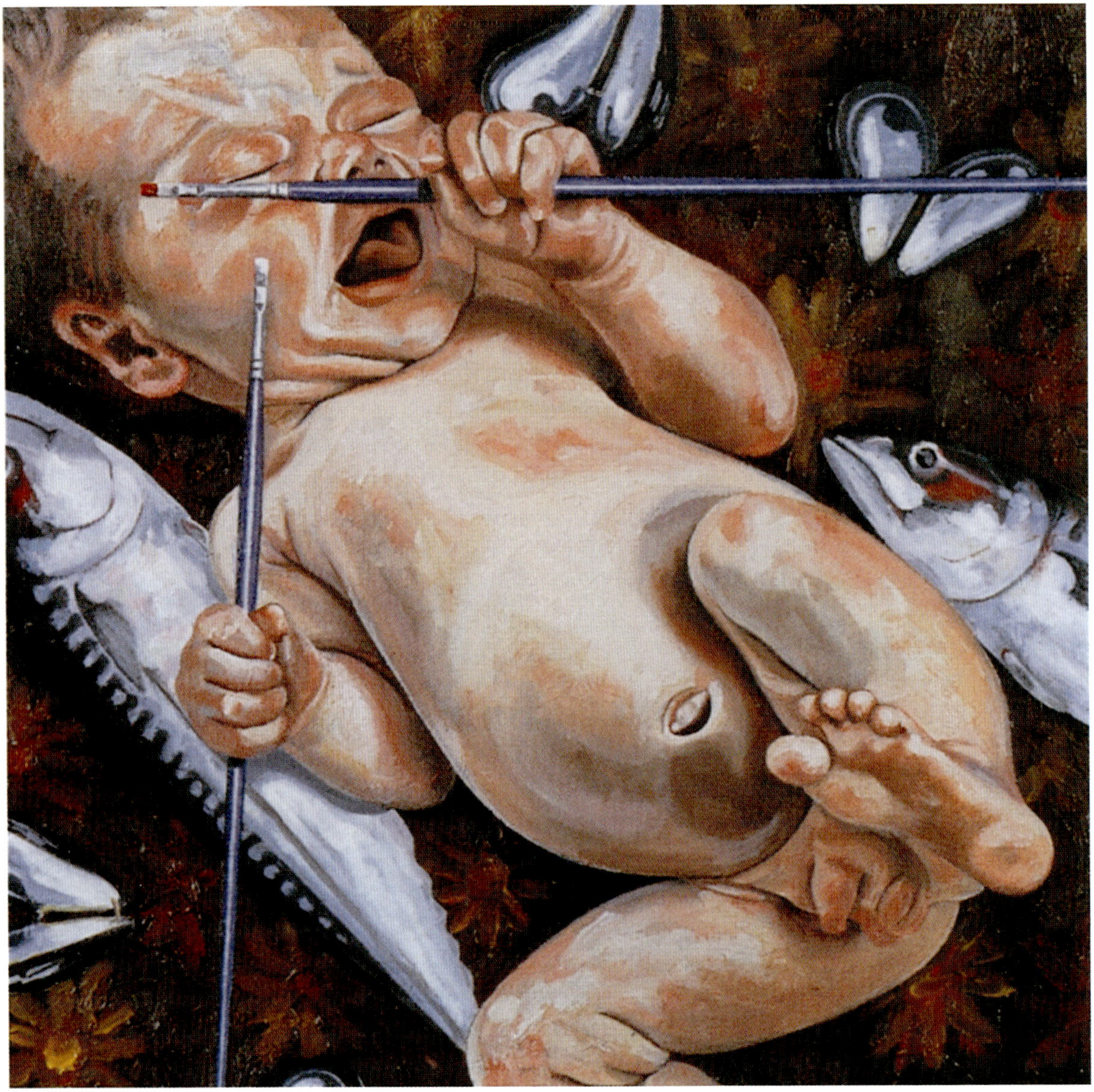

Commended
Rivermede County Middle School
Jane Allison
Oil on canvas
910 x 1225mm

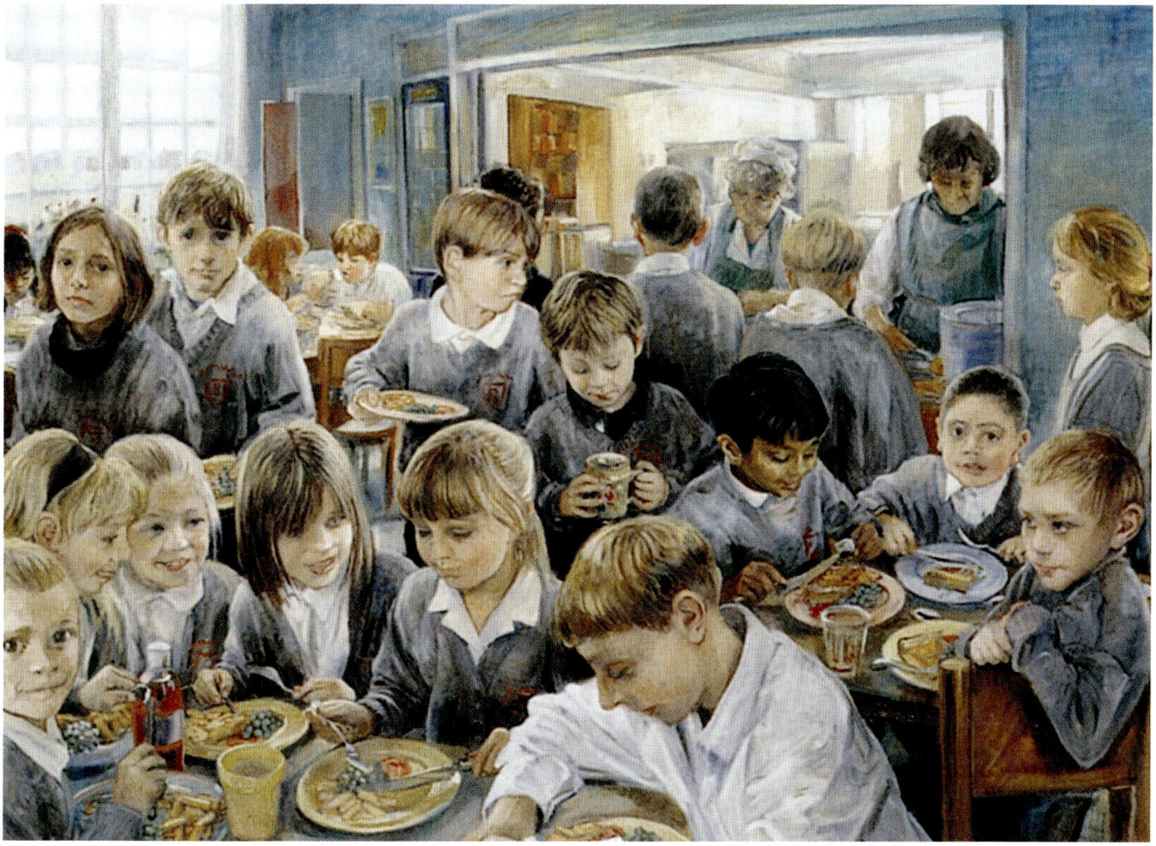

Commended
UV and the Red Lights
Brendan Kelly
Oil on canvas
2120 x 1820mm

Commended
Bill Philby
Annabel Mednick
Oil on canvas
915 x 610mm

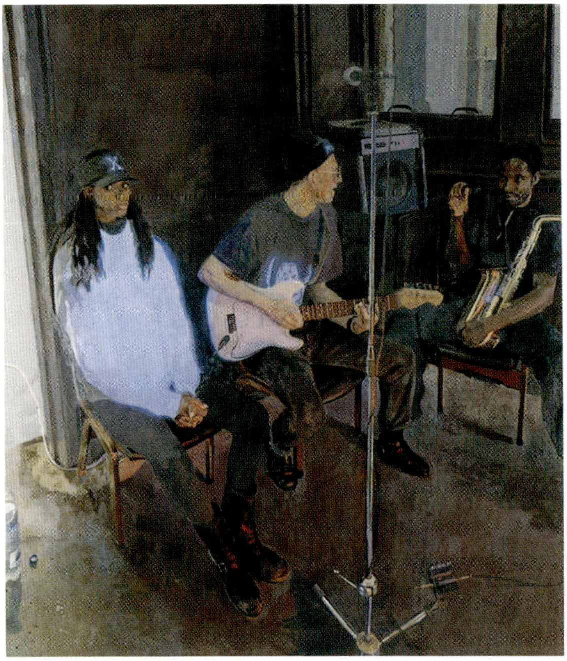

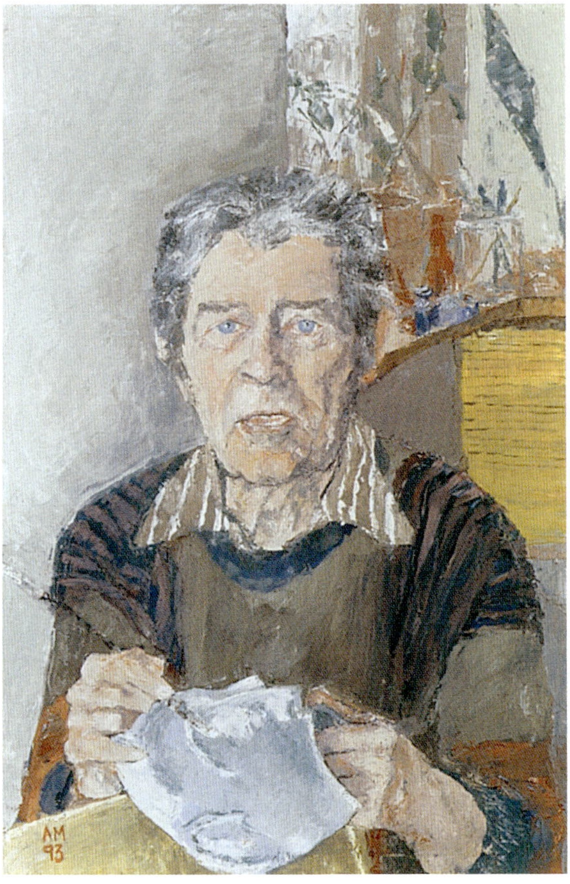

Commended
Miss Shelley Thakral
Ishbel Myerscough
Oil on canvas
1415 x 408mm

Commended
Boozers
William Wood
Oil on canvas
1510 x 2140mm

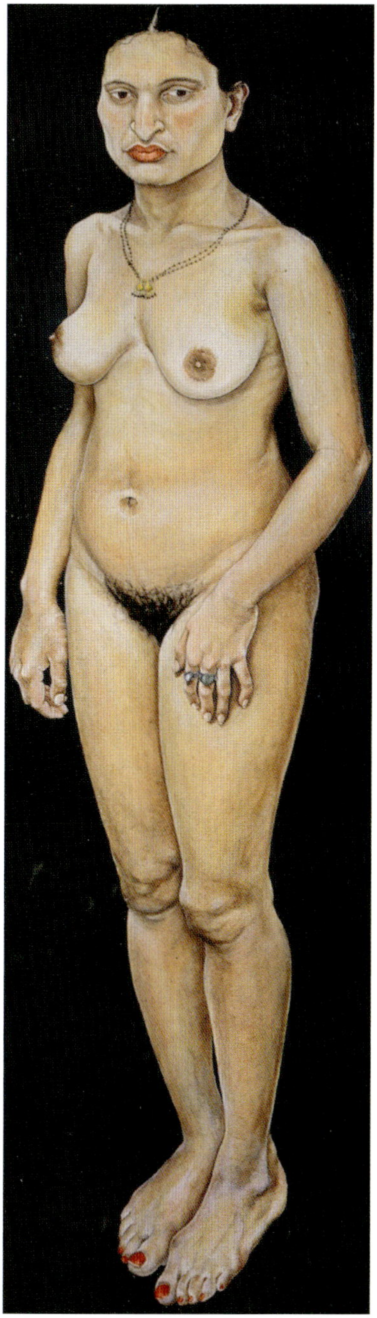

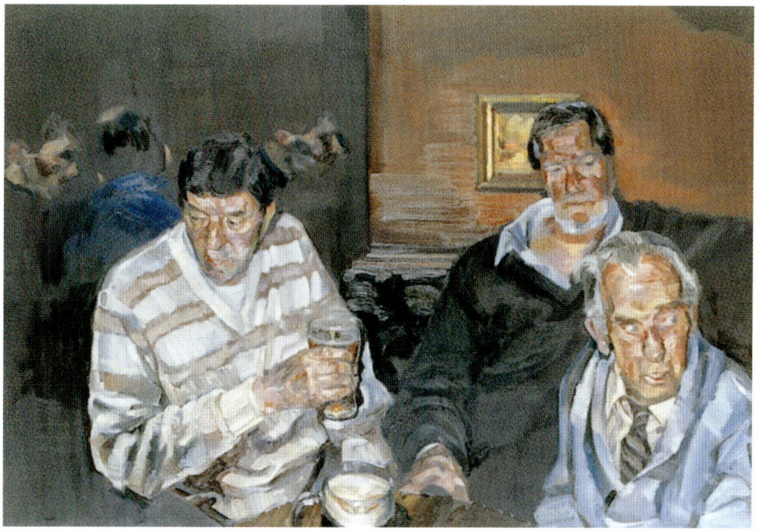

1994

ARTISTS WHOSE PORTRAITS WERE EXHIBITED

Jane Allison / Maryanne Aytoun-Ellis / Lesley Banks / Carey Blundun / Jennie Boulter / Edmund Chamberlain / Louise Courtnell / Kevin M.A. Cunningham / Peter Edwards / Eden Endfield / Susan Faux / Cathy Fenwick / Mark Gilbert / Euan Gray / Roxana Halls / Desmond Haughton / Ben Henriques / William Hold / Ceri House / David Jacques / Gavin Jones / Emma Kay / Mandy Lindsay / Jason Line / Dean Marsh / Brian Martin / Lawrence Mynott / Isis Nassar / Stephen Oliver / Joanna Painter / David Quirke / Shani Rhys-James / Melissa Scott-Miller / Mark Shields / Nahem Shoa / Matthew Sibley / Richard Smith / Christopher Stevens / Lisa Stokes / Jason Sullivan / David Thomas / Peter Thomson / Minna Thornton / Andrew Tift / Simon Turvey / Colin Watson / Clive Wilkins / Craig Withers / Paul Woods

SECOND PRIZE
SELF-PORTRAIT WITH SHADOWS
SHANI RHYS-JAMES

Oil on canvas
1728 x 1223mm

After graduating from St Martin's School of Art in 1976, Shani Rhys-James went on to win numerous awards for her work, including the Gold Medal for Fine Art at the National Eisteddfod of Wales in 1992 and the Jerwood Painting Prize in 2003. Her prizewinning self-portrait of 1994 shows the artist in her studio, standing in front of her painting *Morning Shave*, which depicts her parents. In 2006, Rhys James was made an MBE for services to art.

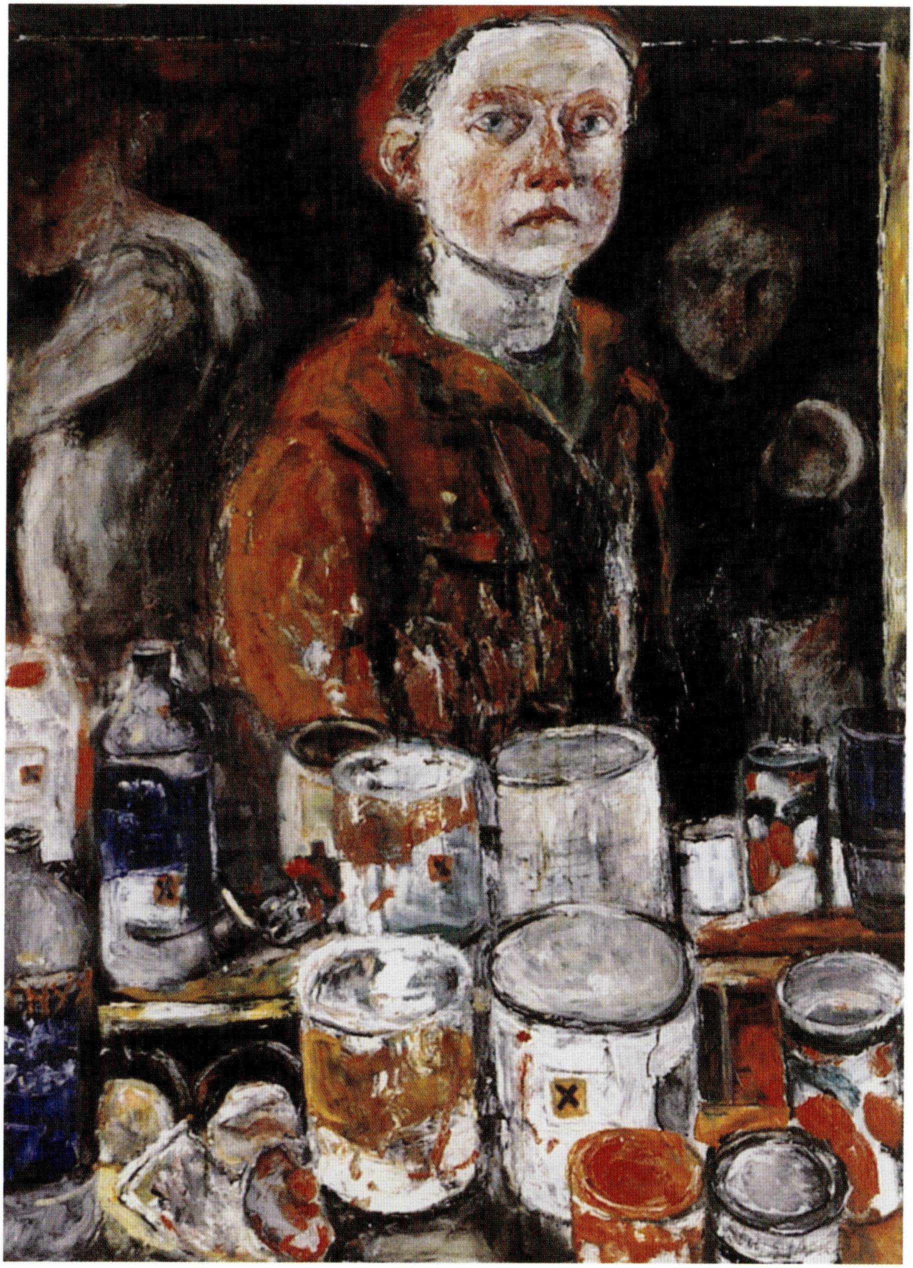

THIRD PRIZE
DON AND LYNNE AND ME EATING FISH AND CHIPS IN THE PARK
STEPHEN OLIVER

Oil on canvas
1018 x 850mm

The first work that Stephen Oliver had exhibited at the BP Portrait Award, this painting portrays Oliver's partner Lynne and his friend Donald Lowe. Oliver's artwork has often been reproduced by fine art publishers as prints and posters, and his commissions include portraits of Neil Kinnock for the National Library of Wales and the late Sir Alistair Pilkington for the University of Liverpool.

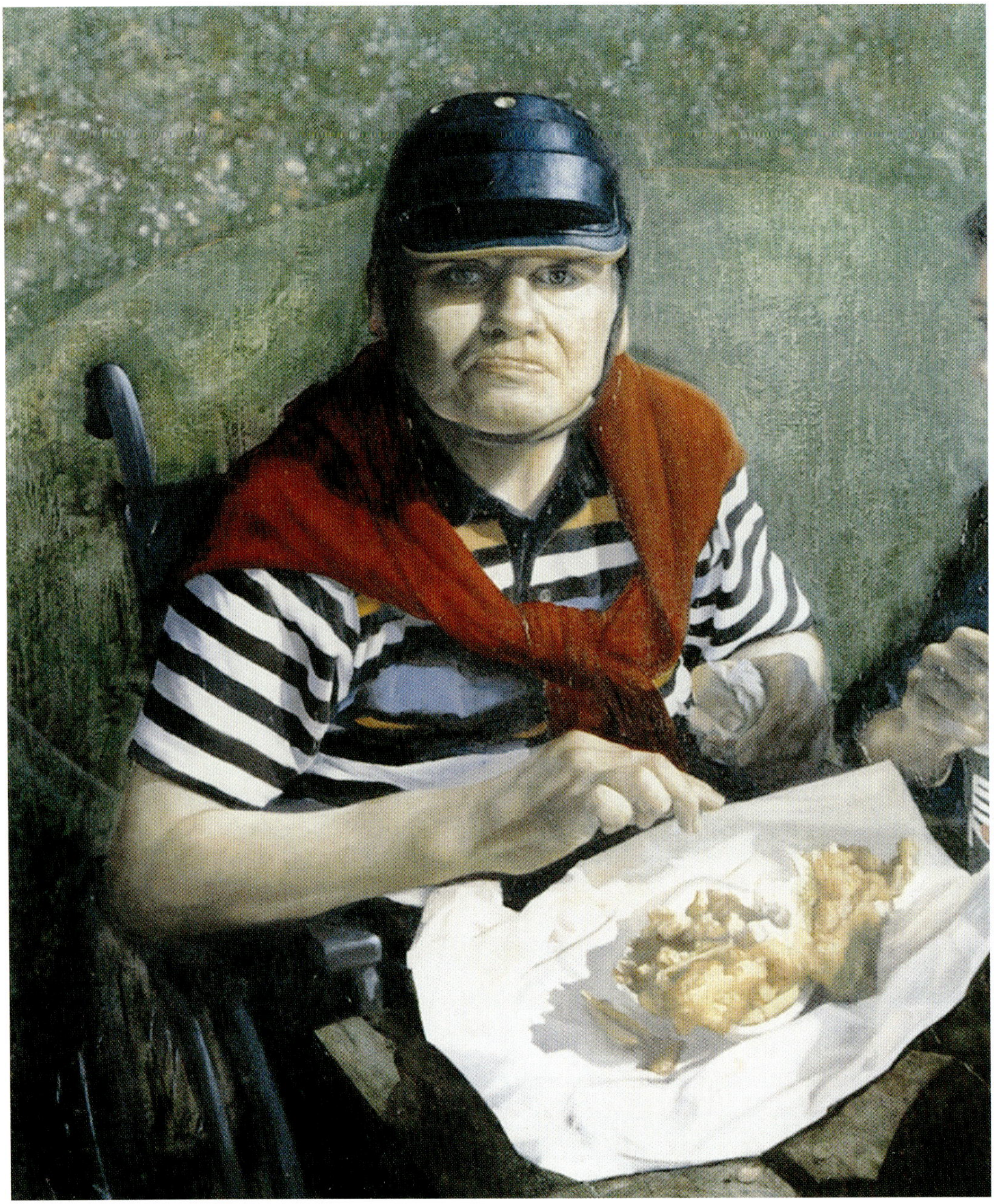

Commended
Twins I
Emma Kay
Oil on canvas
914 x 1320mm

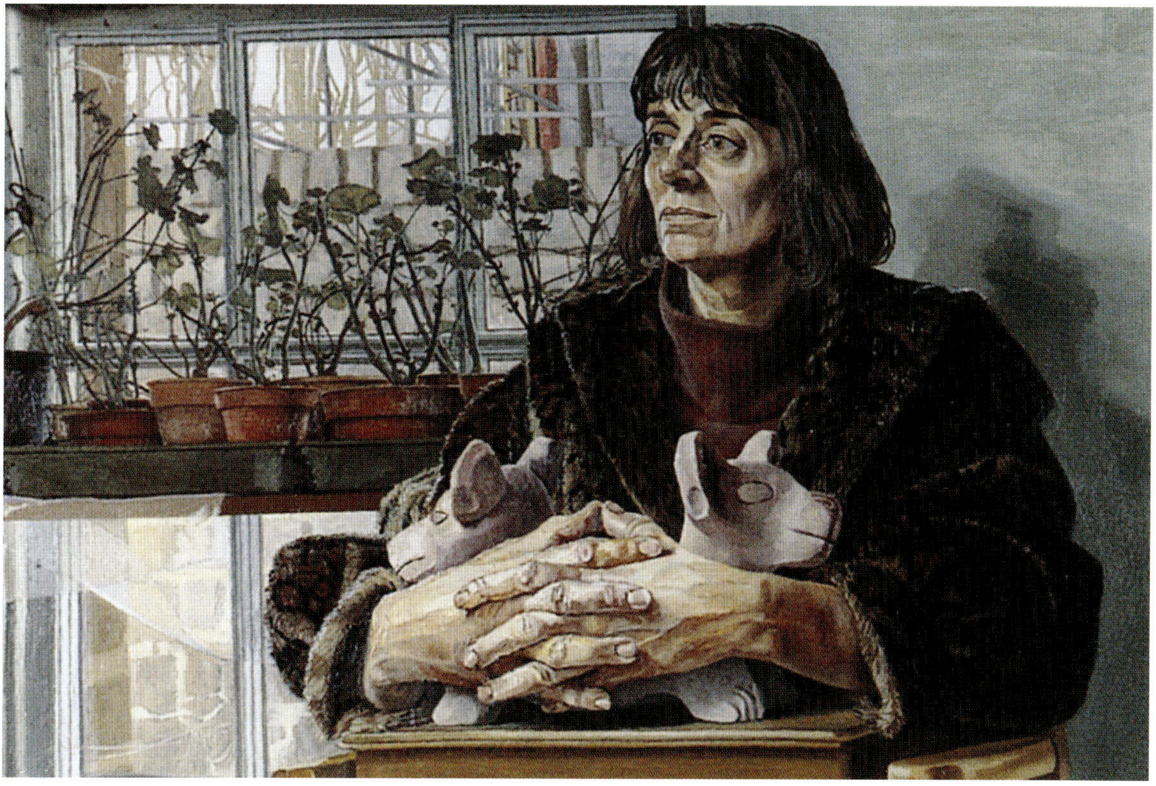

Commended
Self-portrait – Nude Study
Louise Courtnell
Oil on canvas
660 x 510mm

Commended
Fresh Ripe Fruit at West Kilbride Nursing Home
Kevin M.A. Cunningham
Oil on canvas
1380 x 1840mm

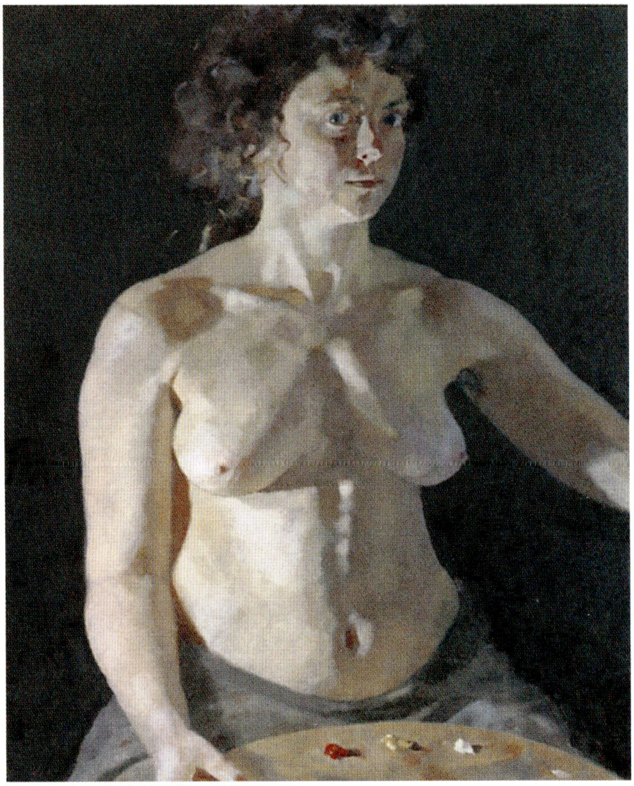

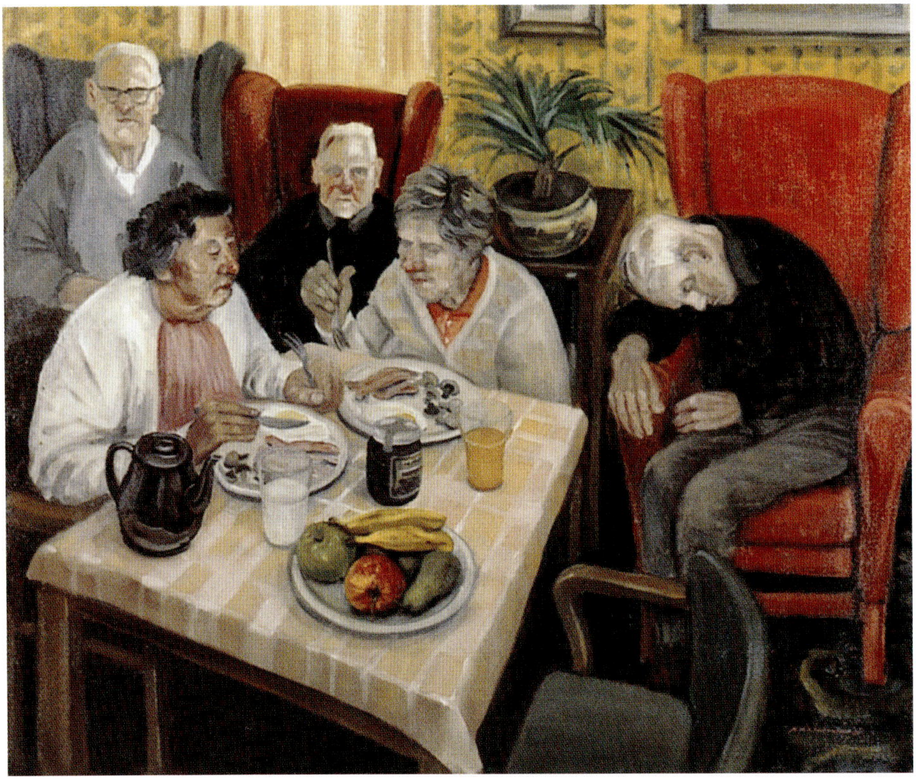

Commended
Figure on Carpet
Mark Gilbert
Oil on canvas
1525 x 1835mm

Commended
The Obscurity and Revelation of Andrew
Andrew Tift
Oil on canvas
Diptych, each panel
625 x 635mm

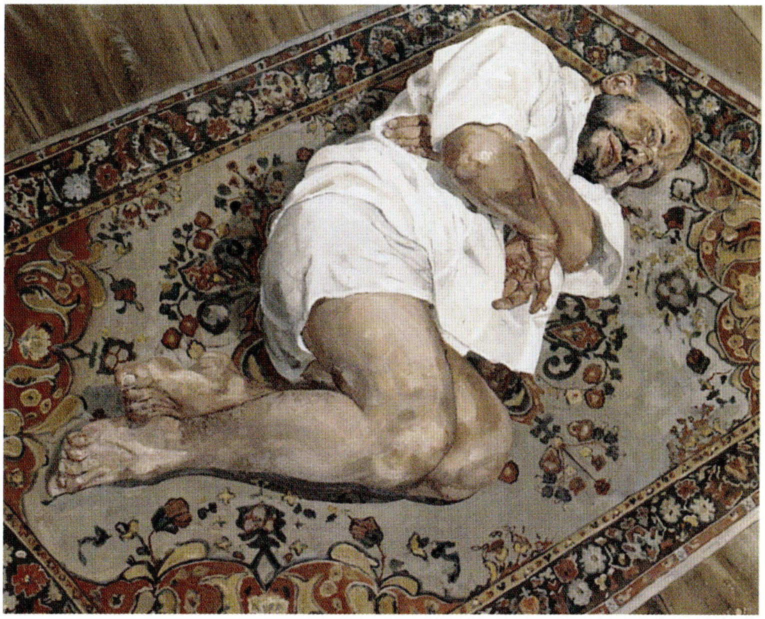

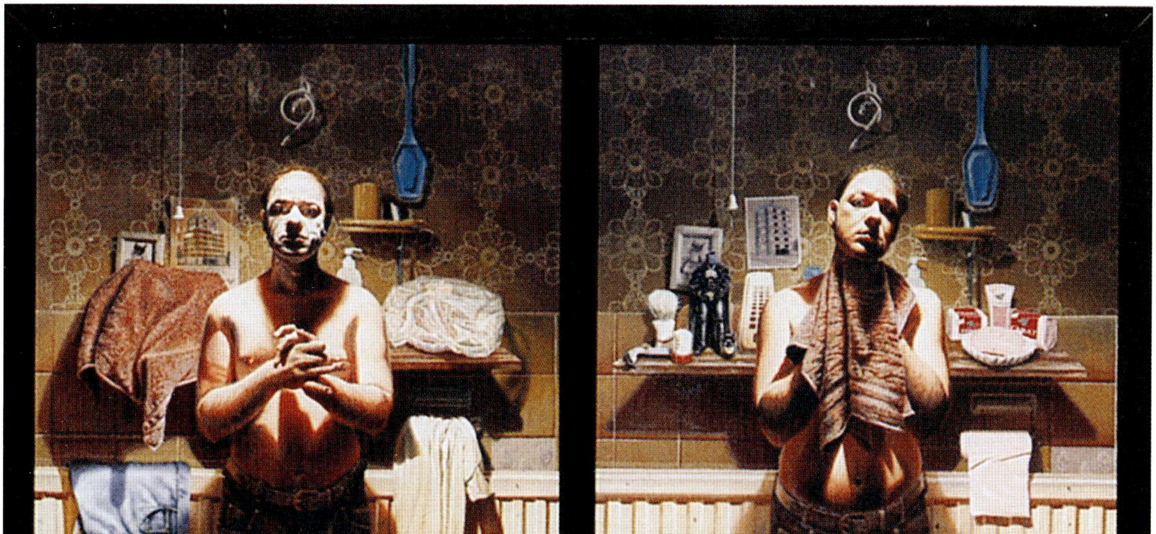

1995

ARTISTS WHOSE PORTRAITS WERE EXHIBITED

Alastair Adams / Jane Allison / Nicola Bealing / Paul Benney / Liberty Blake / Carey Blundun / Karl Bourke / Paul Brewster / Isobel Brigham / Stuart Buchanan / Melanie Carvalho / David Cobley / Kevin M.A. Cunningham / Claire Curran / Gareth Davies / Leonard Dayle / John Devane / Susan Faux / Daniel Fooks / Mark Gilbert / Des Gorman / Nicolas Granger-Taylor / Teresa Grealish / Roxana Halls / Guy Haring / Heidi Harrington / Desmond Haughton / Geoffrey Hayzer / Andrew Hunt / David Jacques / Thomas Daniel Jones / Kate Jordan / Diarmuid Kelley / Brendan Kelly / Amanda Lee / Sadie Lee / Mandy Lindsay / Yuen-Ching (Lisa) Ling / Jincheng Liu / Fergus Mayhew / Abigail McLellan / Shaun McNally / Jennifer McRae / Ishbel Myerscough / Mark Newton / Anthony O'Keeffe / Stephen Oliver / Alan Parker / Jane Patterson / Victoria Rees / Irene Riddell / Stephen Rose / Gordon Scott / Melissa Scott-Miller / Mark Shields / Rabindra Singh / Gary Sollars / Chris Stevens / Christopher Stevens / David Thomas / Minna Thornton / Sophie Tute / Colin Watson / Gavin Watson / Russell Webb / Clive Wilkins / Antony Williams / Charles Williams / Craig Withers

SECOND PRIZE
DOMINIC RAMOS
ISOBEL BRIGHAM

Oil on canvas
465 x 358mm

Isobel Brigham studied at Chelsea College of Art and Design, and the Slade School of Fine Art. She had already won the NatWest Prize for Art in 1991 and exhibited in the BP Portrait Award of 1992 before winning Second Prize. Brigham was awarded a Prince of Wales Drawing School Bursary in 2001.

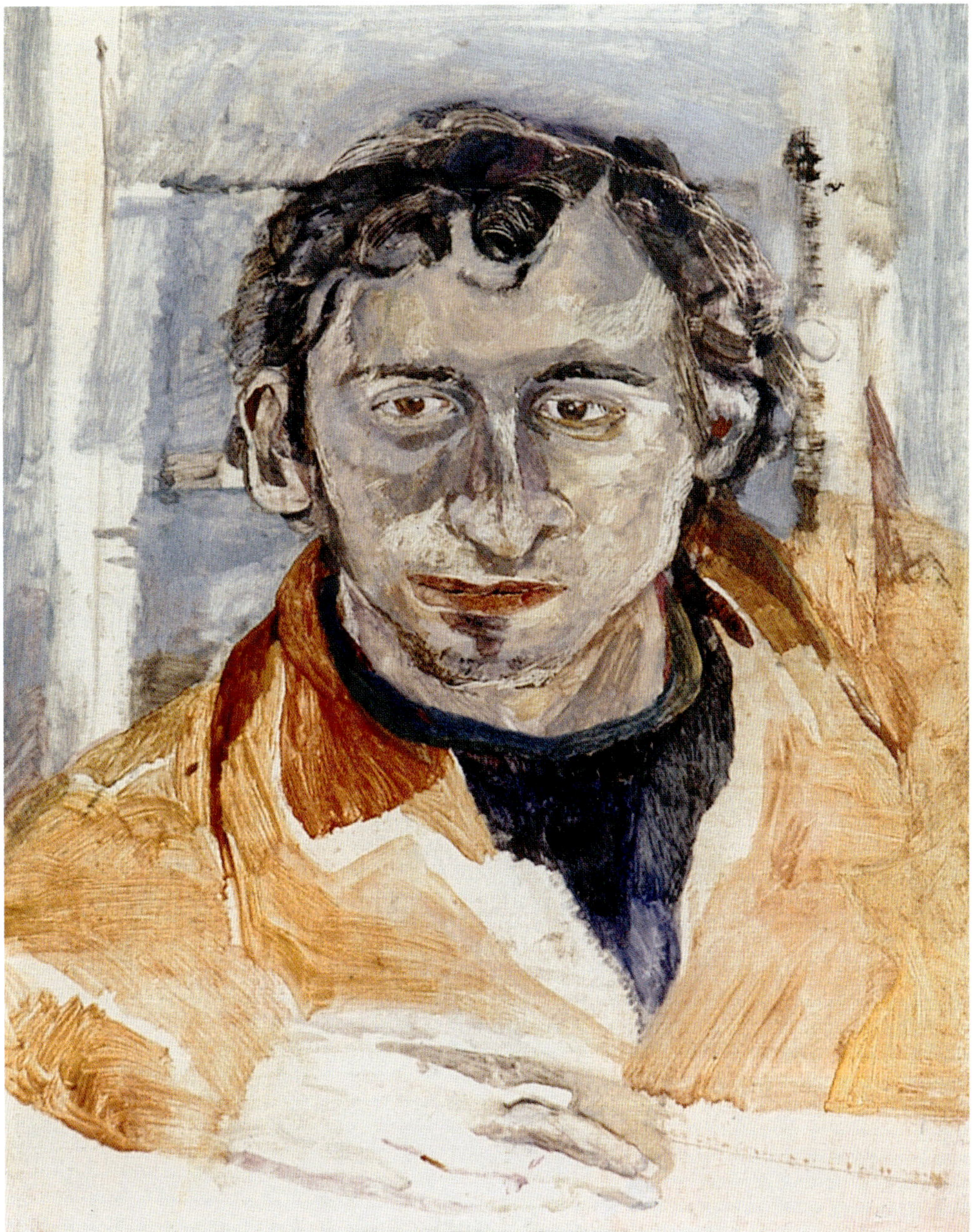

THIRD PRIZE
RAPHAEL
JANE PATTERSON

Oil on canvas
795 x 600mm

After graduating from the Slade School of Fine Art, Jane Patterson was awarded a travelling scholarship enabling her to spend a year in Sri Lanka. She continues to work from the model and still life. Patterson has taught at the Slade School of Fine Art and has exhibited at Browse & Darby gallery in London. She is a Visiting Lecturer at West Dean College in Sussex.

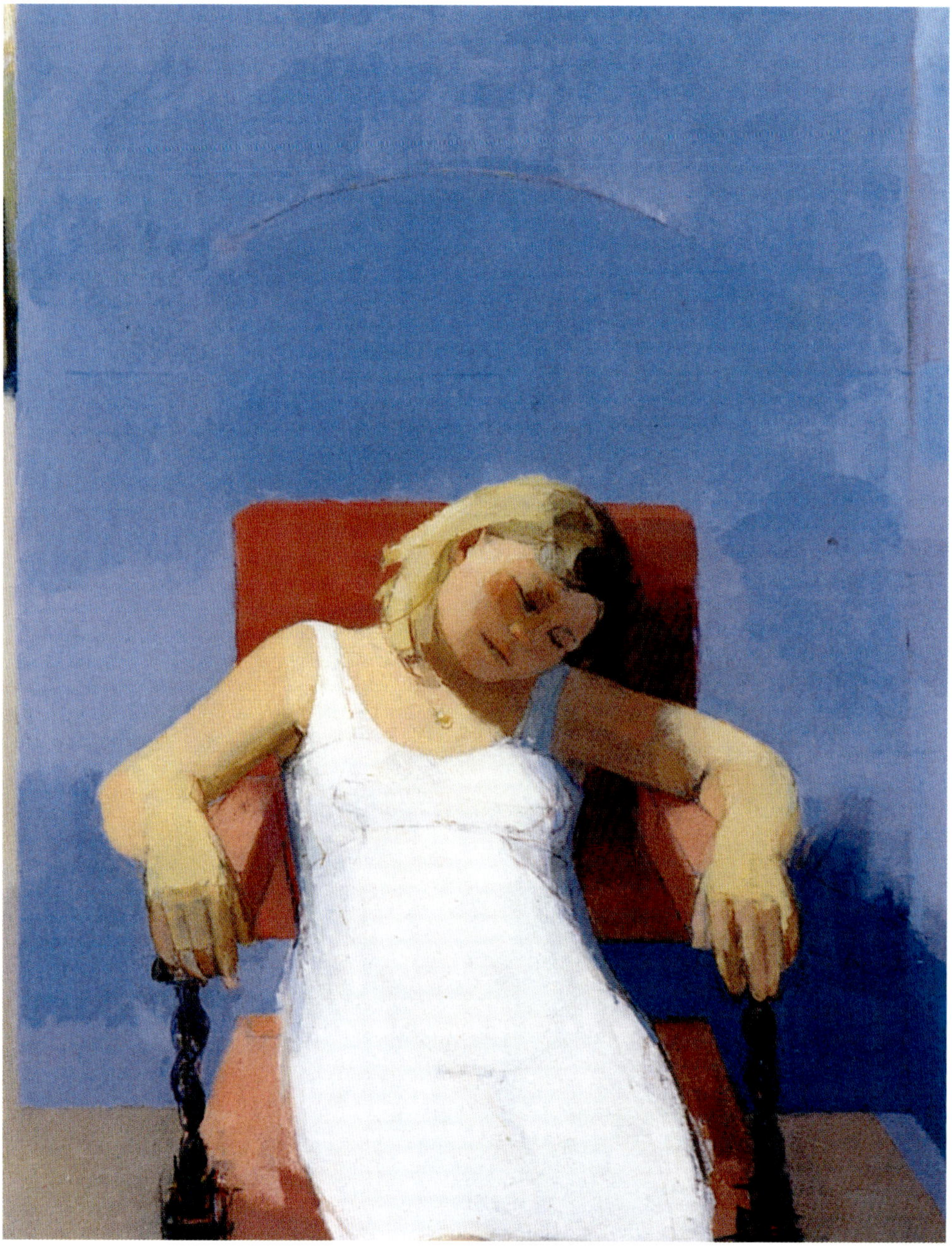

Commended
Porthleven Pier (Self-portrait)
Nicola Bealing
Oil on canvas
220 x 460mm

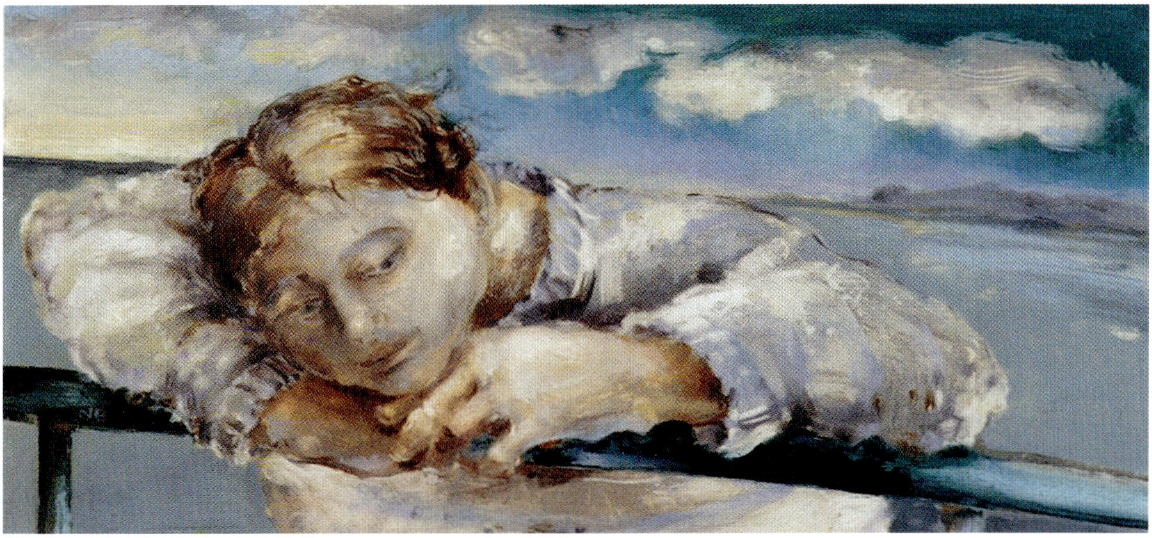

Commended
Elisa Francesca
Paul Brewster
Acrylic on canvas
1235 x 1080mm

Commended
Priest and Undertaker (Waiting for Death)
Kevin M.A. Cunningham
Oil on canvas
1140 x 1000mm

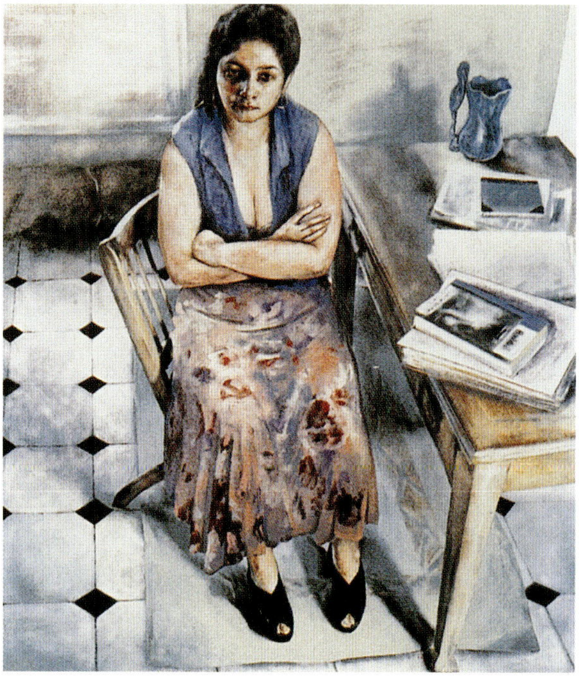

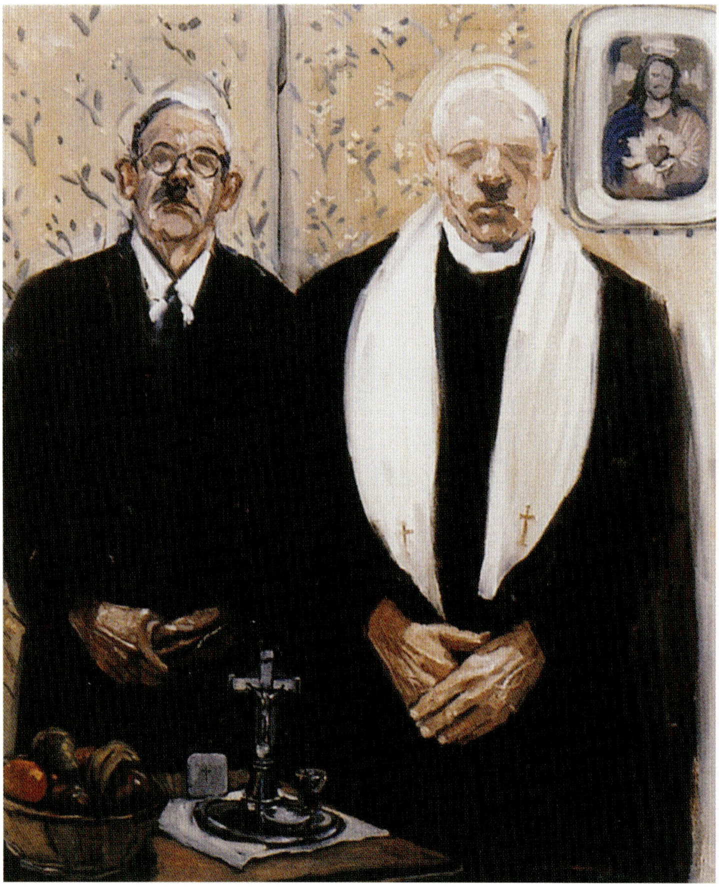

Commended
Ennui
Mark Gilbert
Oil on canvas
1835 x 1835mm

Commended
Jubilee Road
Diarmuid Kelley
Oil on canvas
1065 x 760mm

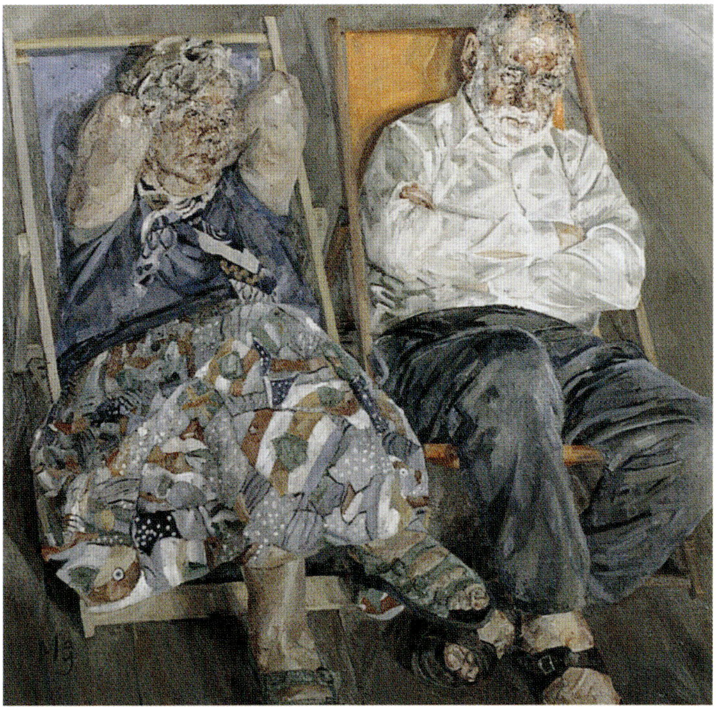

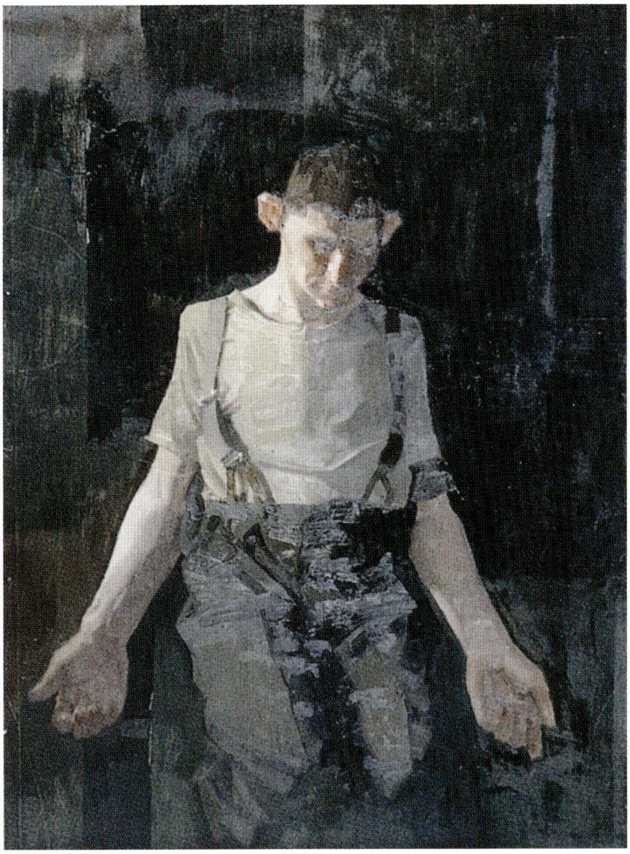

1996

ARTISTS WHOSE PORTRAITS WERE EXHIBITED

Michael Alan-Kidd / Peter Andersen / Martyn Baldwin / Nicola Bealing / Paul Benney / Frances Borden / Nick Botting / Keith Breeden / William Brennen / Paul Brewster / Laura Buxton / Nicola Clark / R.A. Combes / Anthony Connolly / Andrew Crocker / Kevin M.A. Cunningham / Claire Curran / Sarah Florence / Michael Fullerton / Jarrod Gabbitas / Bridget Garrett / Mark Gilbert / Andrew Griffiths / James Hague / Tom Hallifax / Roxana Halls / Guy Haring / Heidi Harrington / James Hart Dyke / Ross Henriksen / David Hosie / Sonja Howick / Amanda Lee / Sadie Lee / Sophie Levi / Jason Line / Dean Marsh / Gerald McCauley / Donna McGlynn / Audrey McGuire / Lorna McIntosh / Abigail McLellan / Mark McPadden / Steve McQueen / Jennifer McRae / James Meiklejohn / Simon Moore / Noel Paine / Alan Parker / Margaret Theresa Reddy / Melissa Scott-Miller / Mark Shields / Charlotte Sorapure / Chris Stevens / David Thomas / Andrew Tift / Yana Trevail / Frances Turner / Christina Ure / Charles Williams / Steve Wilson / Nigel Wood / William Wood

SECOND PRIZE
FAMILY
PETER ANDERSEN

Oil on canvas
1525 x 1827mm

Peter Andersen graduated with a Master of Arts in Art and Design Education at the University of Warwick in 1995, having previously studied English and Related Literature. He had been producing street paintings, copies of old masters and portraits in York, Paris and Munich since 1990. This painting depicts the artist's cousin with his partner and child, and echoes Holbein's *The Ambassadors* (1533) with the inclusion of placed objects that were important to the family.

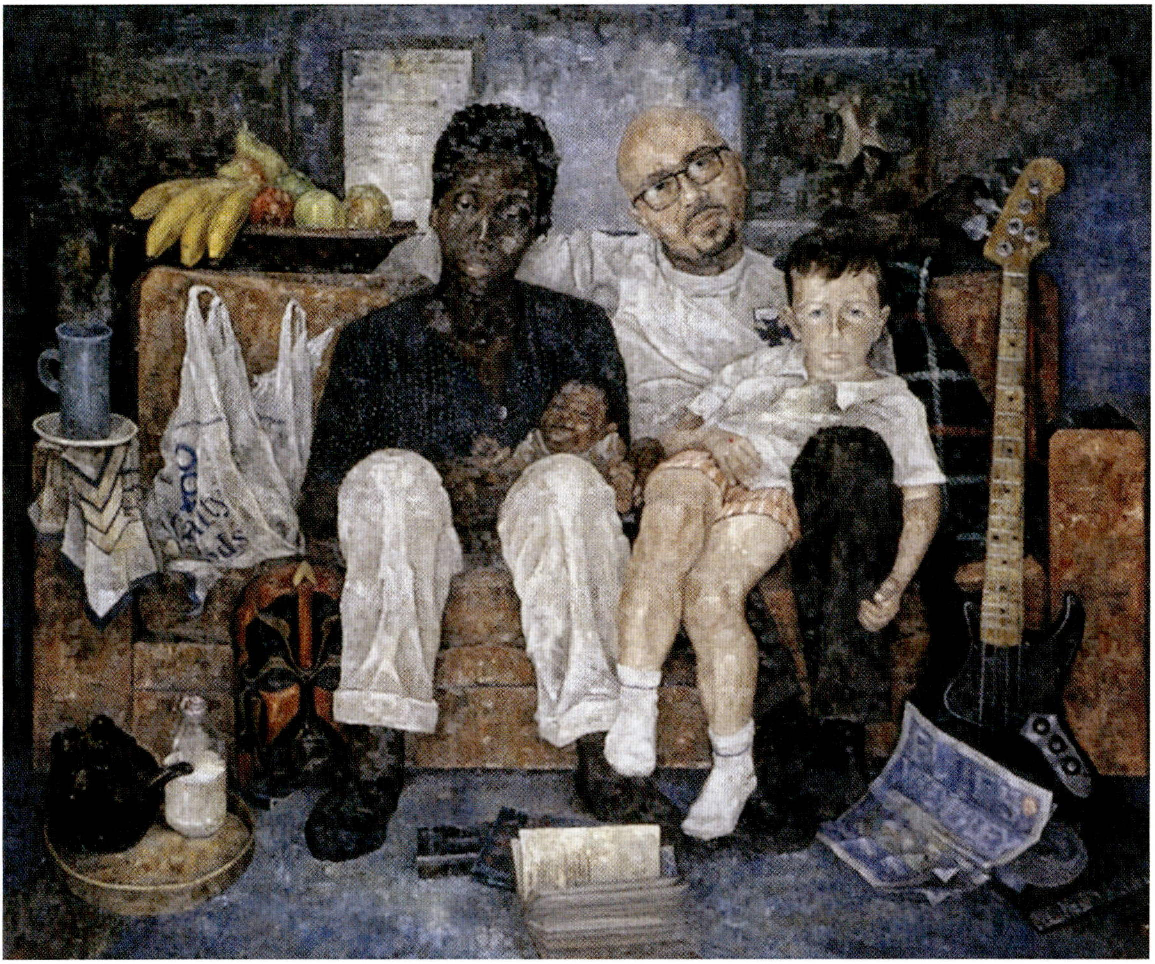

THIRD PRIZE
IL PAPA
MARK MCPADDEN

Oil on canvas
2000 x 1840mm

Shortly after graduating from the Glasgow School of Art in 1994, Mark McPadden was awarded the Elizabeth Greenshields Scholarship. In 1999 McPadden moved to Italy, where he studied at the Florence Academy of Art. With a keen interest in the techniques and working methods of the old masters, McPadden works only from life, and grinds his own paint, following traditional recipes in the preparation of his own varnishes and media. He currently lives and works in Budapest in Hungary.

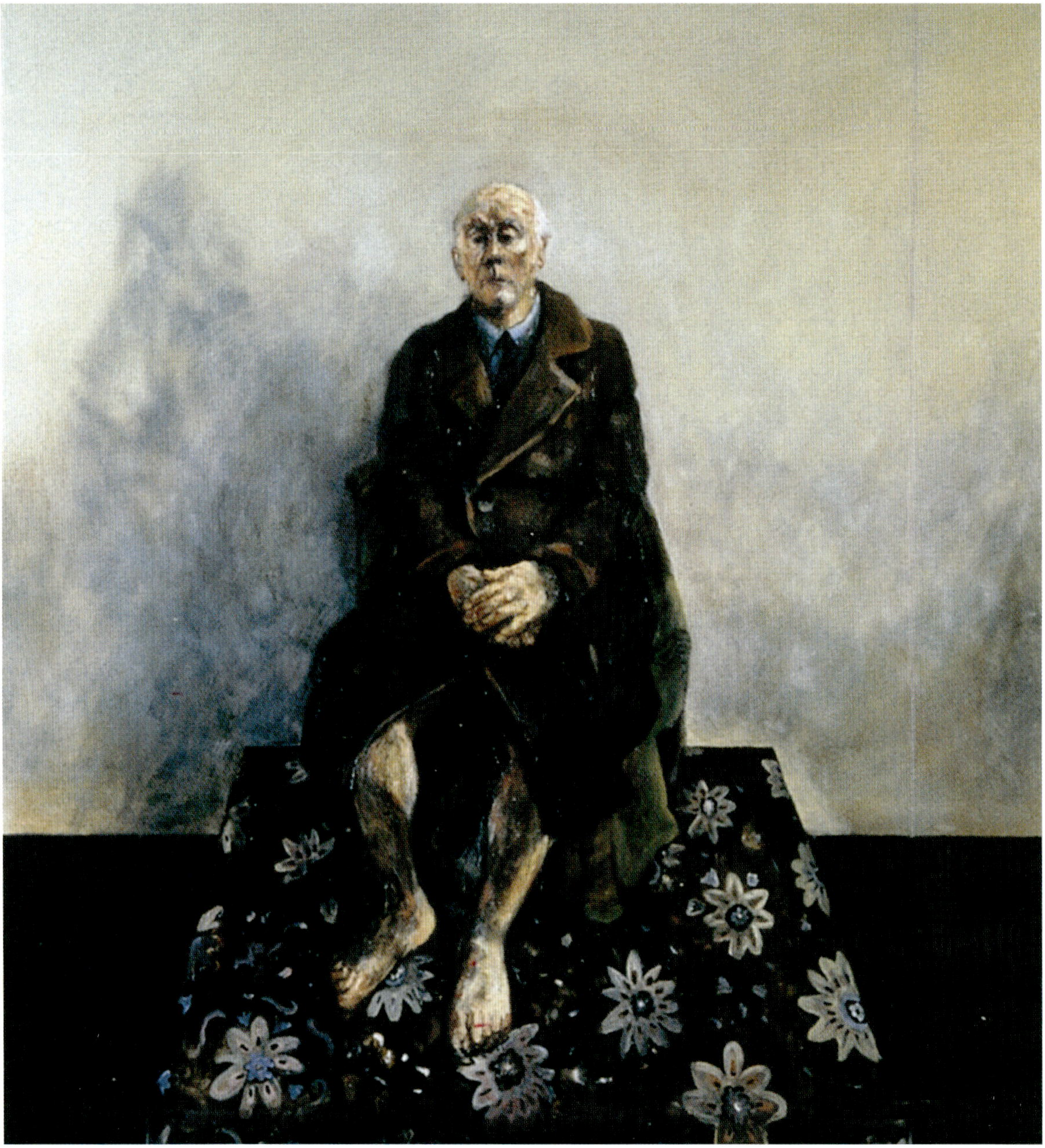

Commended
Here No Evil
Martyn Baldwin
Oil on board
305 x 250mm

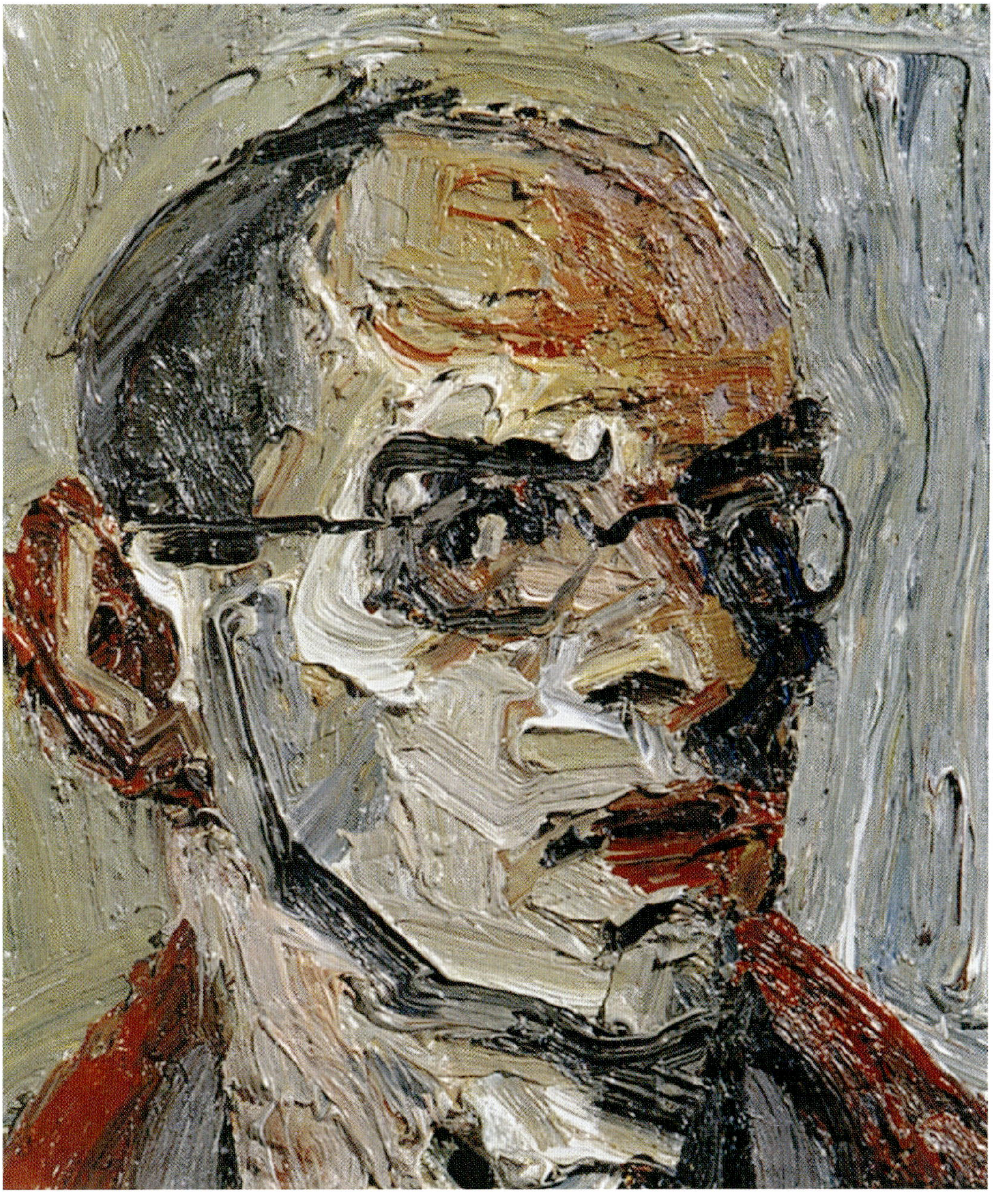

Commended
Self-portrait
Frances Borden
Oil on board
300 x 250mm

Commended
Figure in Black
Mark Gilbert
Oil on canvas
1515 x 1515mm

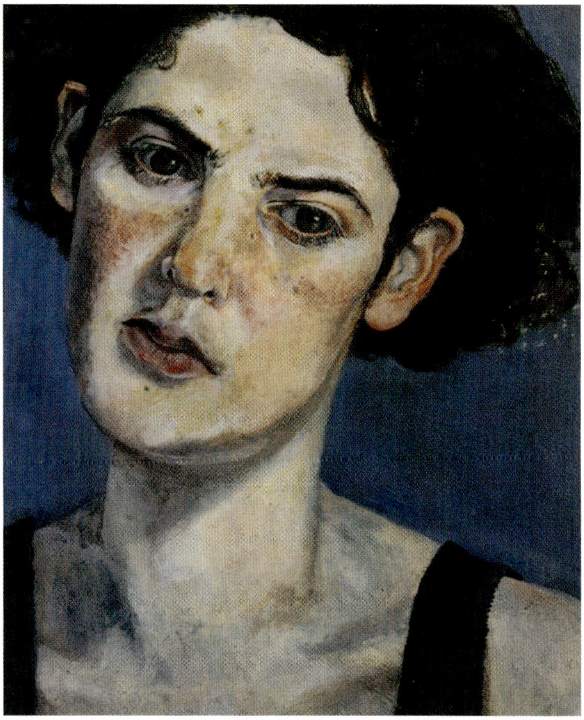

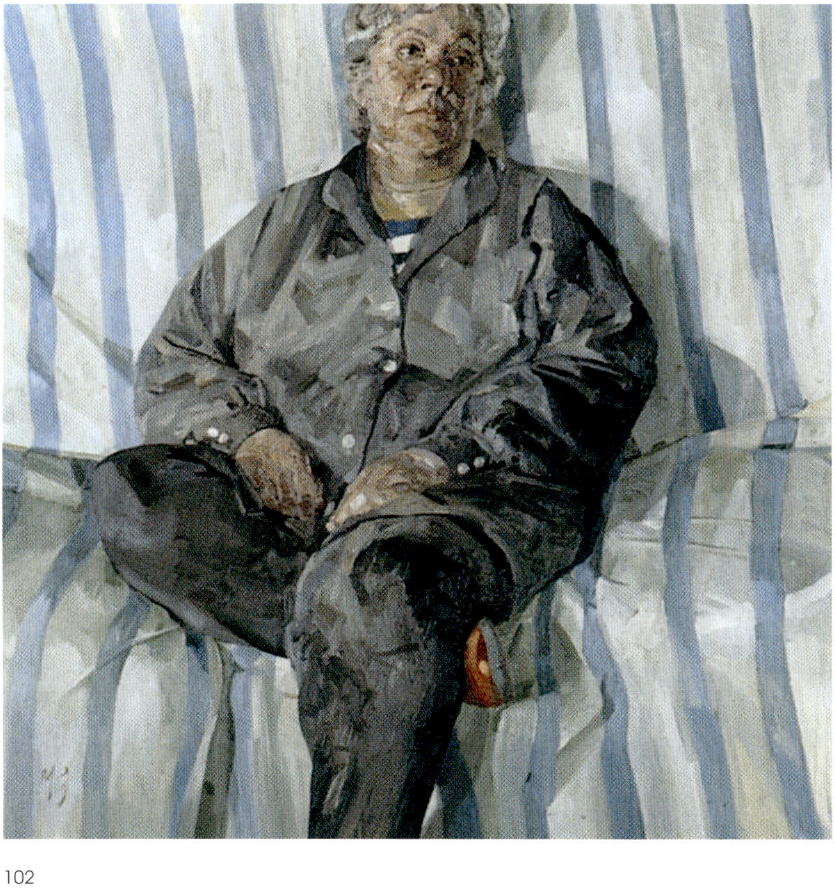

Commended
Victor and Mitzi – Security
Tom Hallifax
Oil on board
1220 x 915mm

Commended
Man with Flowers
David Hosie
Oil on board
1070 x 256mm

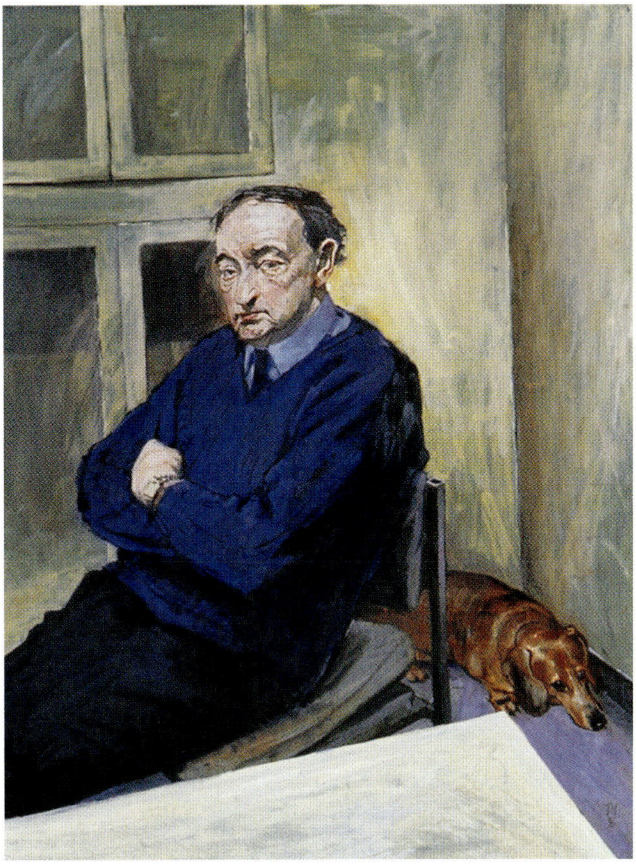

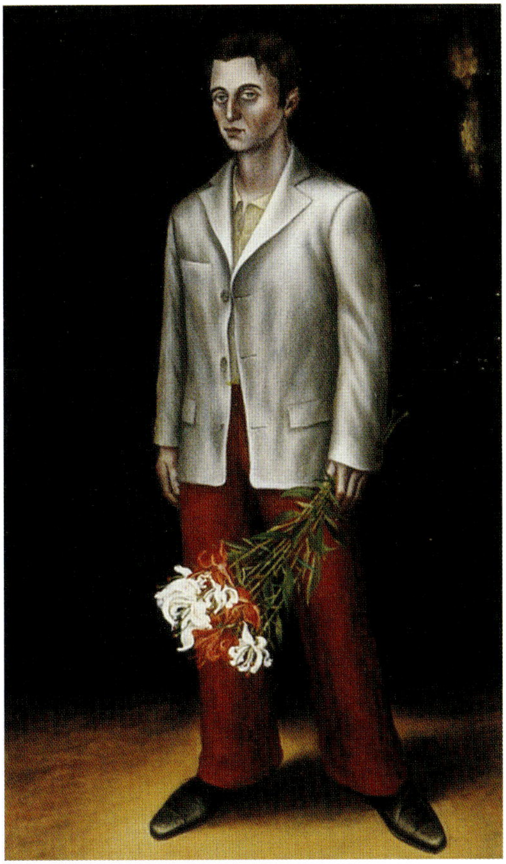

1997

ARTISTS WHOSE PORTRAITS WERE EXHIBITED

Jane Allison / Michelle Anderson / Matthew Baker / James Baylay / Paul Benney / Akash Bhatt / Frances Borden / Richard Brazier / Paul Brewster / Sharon Brindle / Lucy Burscough / Damian Callan / Nicola Clark / Marina Cooper / Louise Courtnell / Kevin M.A. Cunningham / Saied Dai / Joseph Davie / Julian Day / Joe Dunne / Robert Durkin / Andrew Gadd / Paul Rudolph Gildea / Andrew Gizauskas / Gary Goodman / Brian Gorst / Steve Haigh / Heather Harrigan / Heidi Harrington / Geoffrey Hayzer / Pamela Hewetson / Susan Holpin / Sheldon Hutchinson / Nicholas Jolly / Michael Jones / Neal Jones / Robin Jones / Gwyneth Leech / Tim Lenathen / Sophie Levi / Yuen-Ching (Lisa) Ling / James Lloyd / Maeve McCarthy / Gerald McCauley / Abigail McLellan / Orlando Mostyn Owen / Craig Mulholland / Elizabeth Mulholland / Blanca Muñoz de Baena / John Notter / John O'Neill / Ian Palmer / Irene Riddell / Boris Röhrl / Heath Rosselli / Duncan Shoosmith / Christopher Stevens / Michael Tomlinson / Yana Trevail / Frances Turner / Colin Watson / Lucy Watson / Thomas Watson / Jago Williams / Andrew Zucchi

SECOND PRIZE
PHILIP KNIGHTLEY (SPY WRITER WITH INDIAN WIFE)
KEVIN M.A. CUNNINGHAM

Oil on canvas
1605 x 1280mm

Born in Ayrshire, Scotland, Kevin M.A. Cunningham obtained a First-class Honours Degree in Illustration at Duncan of Jordanstone College of Art and Design, Dundee, before embarking on a successful career as an illustrator in London. He exhibited with the Royal Society of Portrait Painters in 1994, and since then he has practised as a full-time portrait painter. Cunningham's numerous portrait commissions include Peter and Autumn Phillips in 2008.

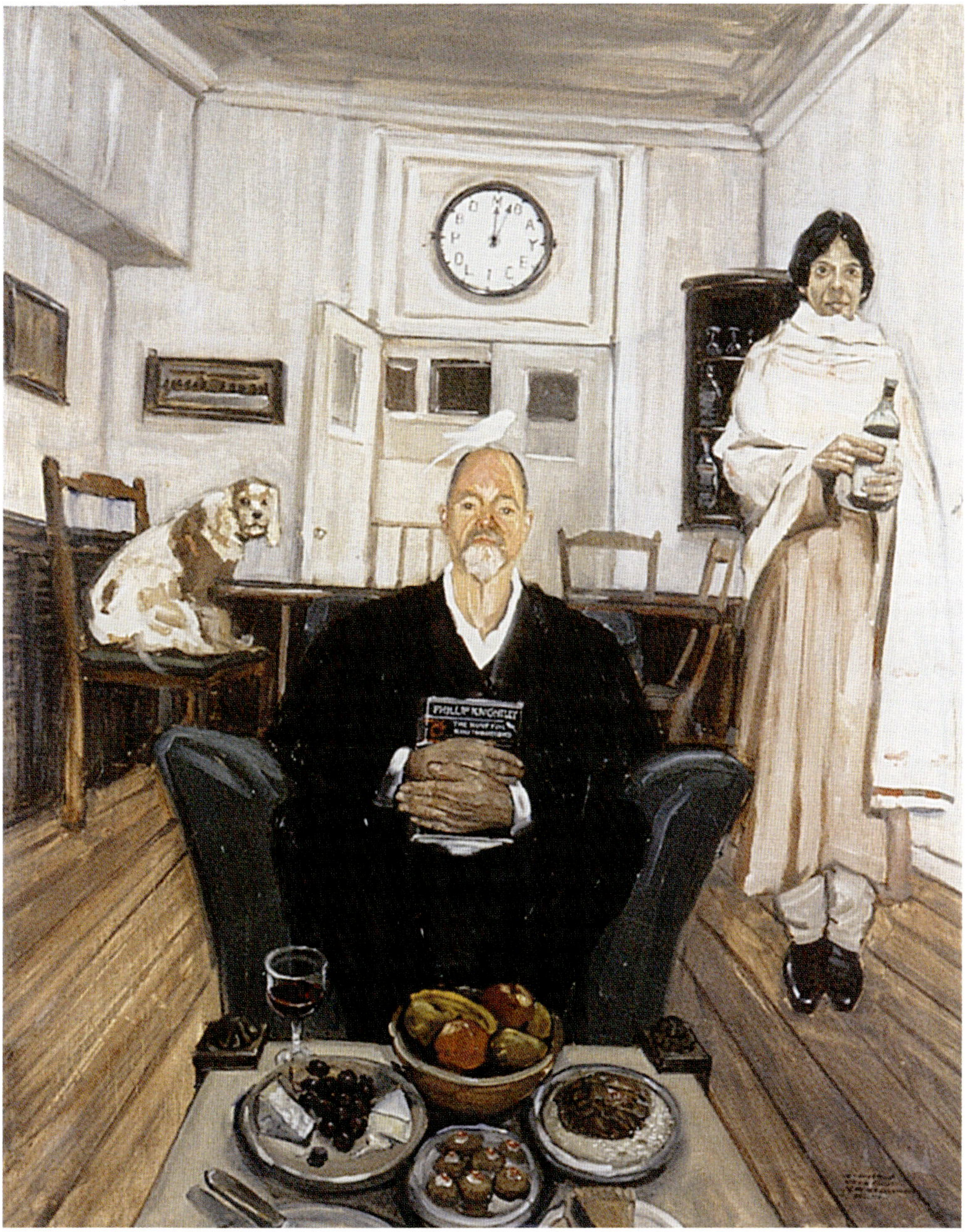

THIRD PRIZE
MR & MRS PANCHAL AT HOME?
NICOLA CLARK

Oil on canvas
910 x 1220mm

A graduate of Central St Martin's School of Art and Design, Nicola Clark worked in a variety of disciplines and travelled extensively, living in Germany and India, before returning to Britain to practice as a portrait painter. She had exhibited in the BP Portrait Award in 1996 before winning Third Prize with this double portrait. Clark currently lives in St Ives, Cornwall, where she works as a painter and illustrator and as a singer-songwriter, performing at music festivals throughout the country.

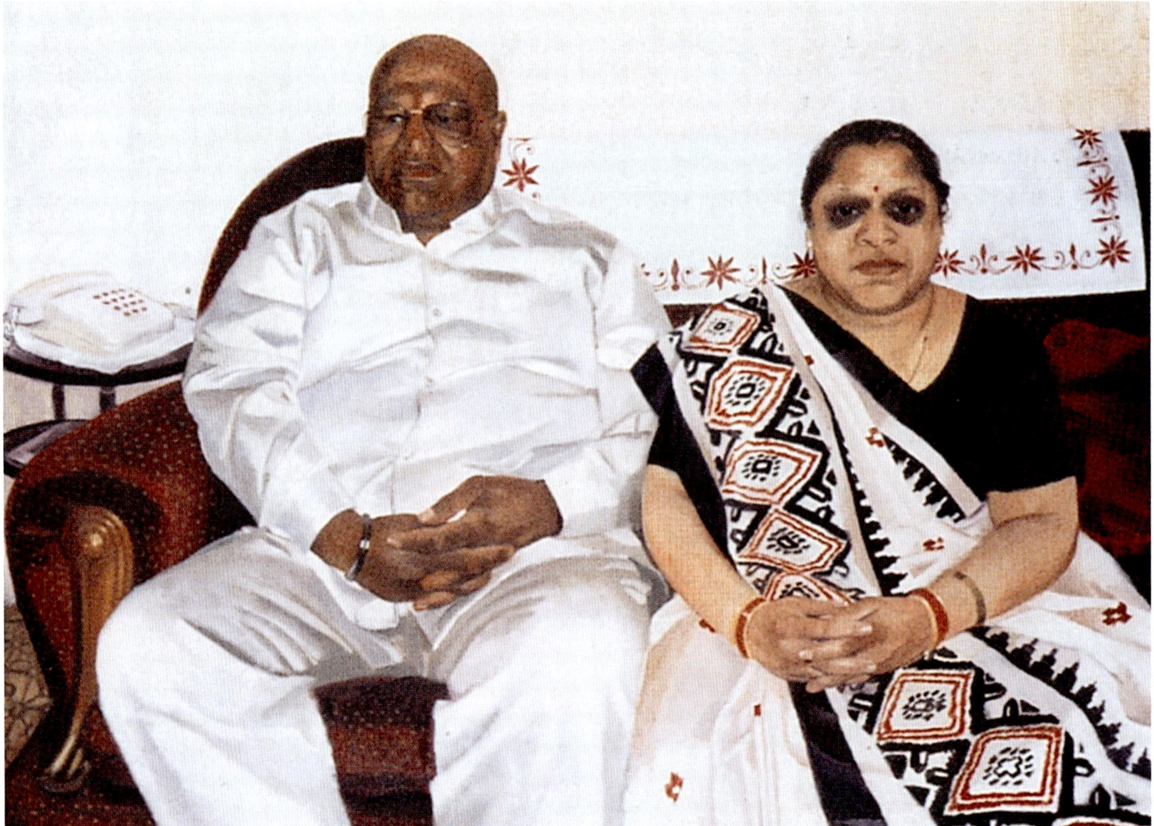

Commended
Still Life
Jago Williams
Oil on canvas
1835 x 1530mm

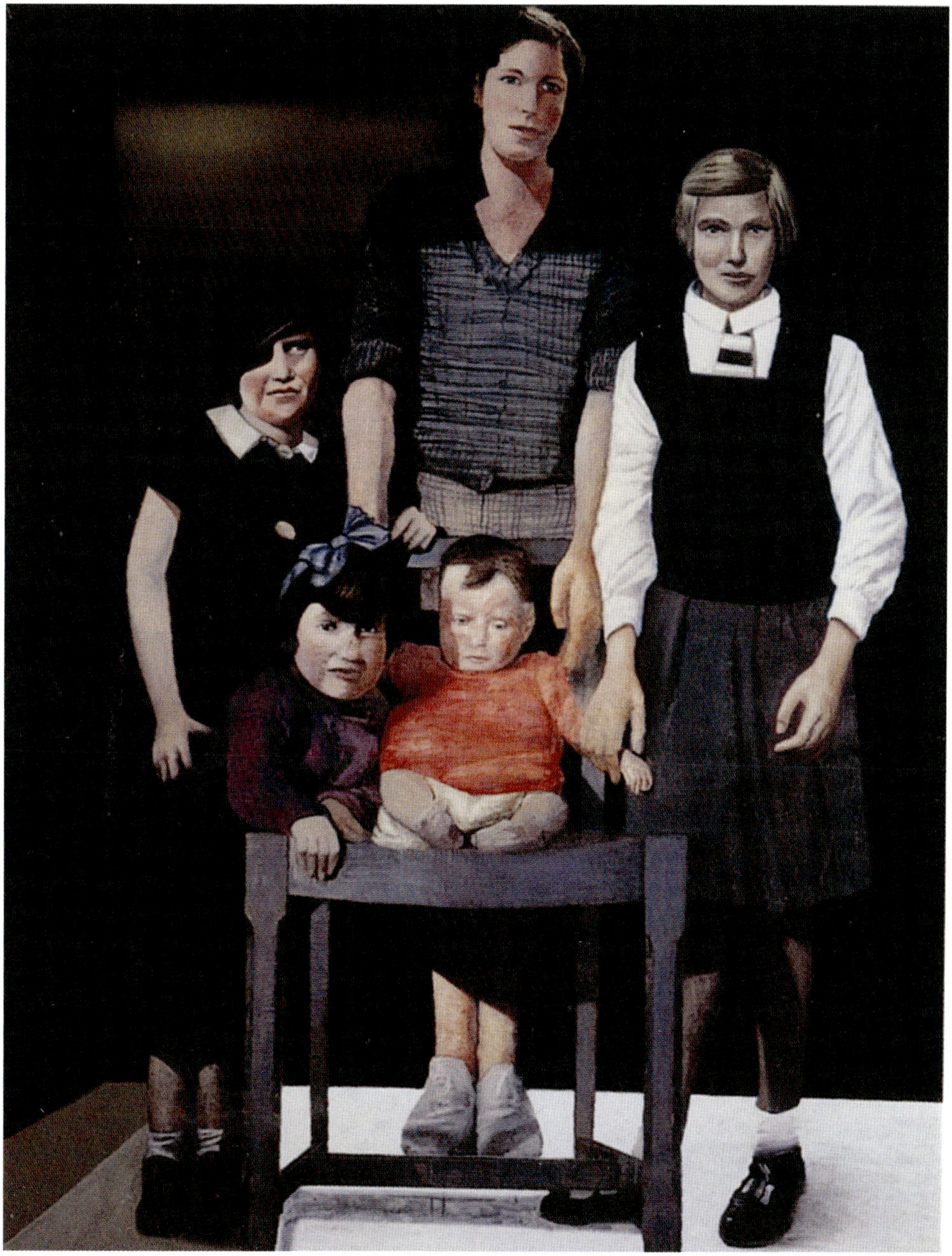

Commended
Spitz
Paul Benney
Oil on canvas
1980 x 1320mm

Commended
Christina Kirk
Paul Brewster
Acrylic on canvas
1705 x 1610mm

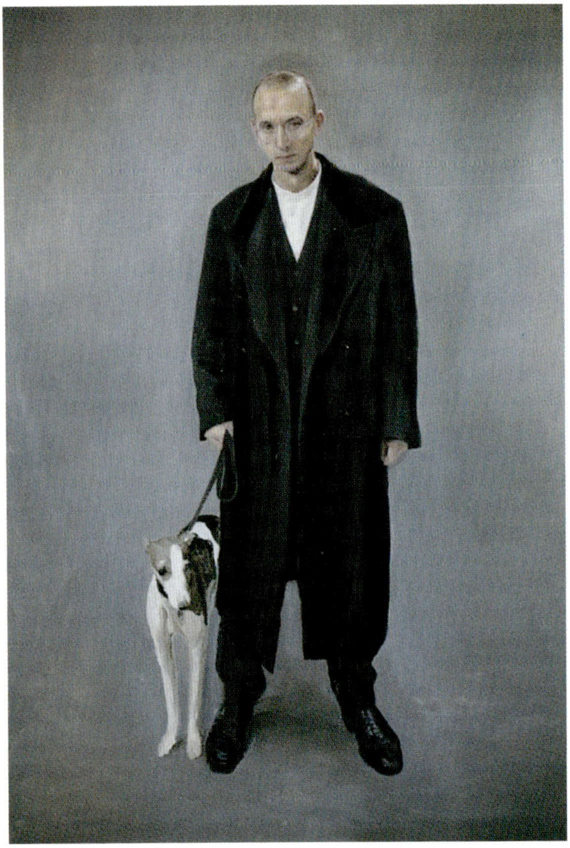

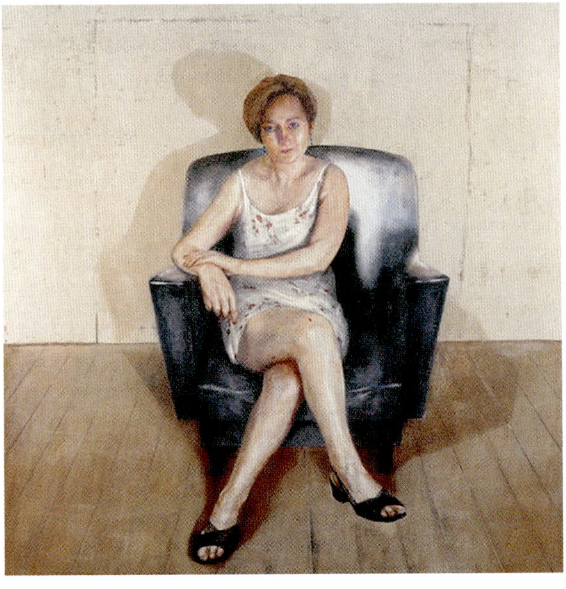

Commended
Lia
Sharon Brindle
Oil on canvas
405 x 305mm

Commended
Enrica at Blackpatch
John Notter
Oil on canvas
1115 x 1370mm

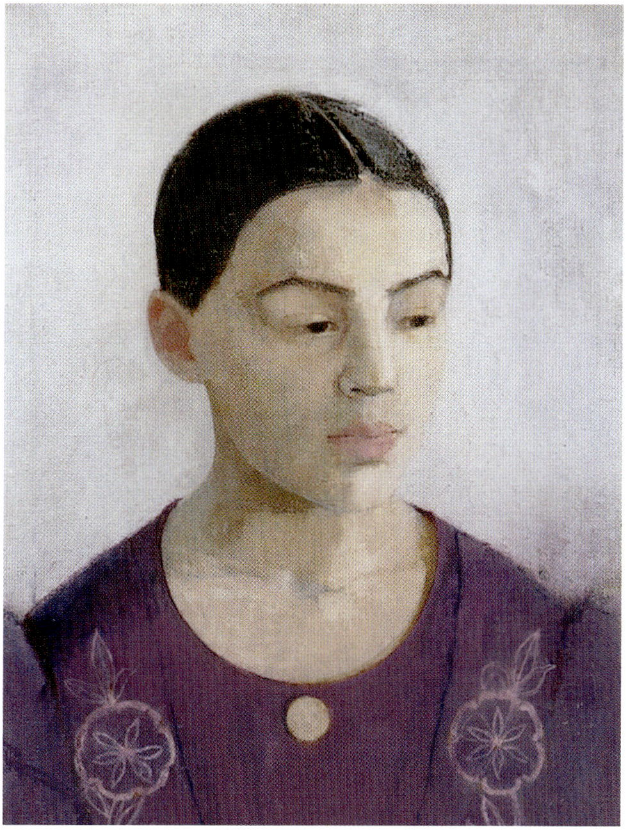

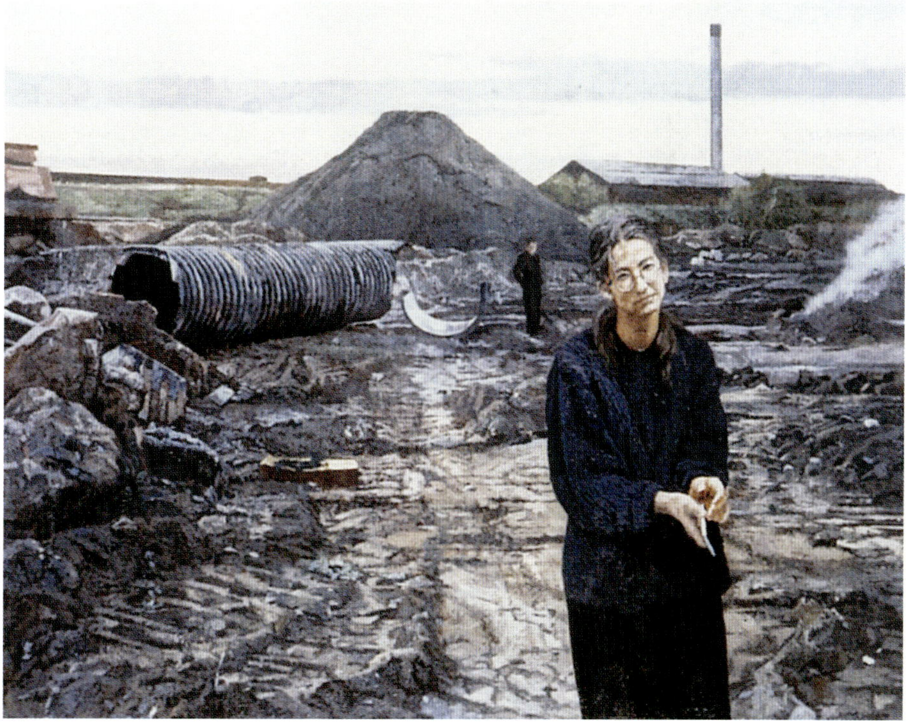

1998

ARTISTS WHOSE PORTRAITS WERE EXHIBITED

Paul Abbott / Nicholas Archer / Richard Atkinson / Matthew Batt / Nicola Bealing / Paul Benney / Akash Bhatt / Stephanie Bithell / Frances Borden / Nick Botting / Richard Brazier / Paul Brewster / Lucy Burscough / Lewis Chamberlain / Michael Checketts / Marina Cooper / Louise Courtnell / Leigh Curtis / Lisa Dixon / Darvish Fakhr / Julian Figg / Andrea Fortina / Jane Frederick / Bridget Garrett / Michael Gaskell / Roxana Halls / Alexander Hanna / Ross Hansen / Desmond Haughton / Geoffrey Hayzer / Nadia Hebson / Ben Henriques / Robert Henson / David Hosie / Ciaran Hughes / Juliet Kac / Diarmuid Kelley / Sadie Lee / Ann Edmonds McCay / Jennifer McRae / Tim O'Keeffe / Joe Painter / Gareth Reid / Mark Roscoe / Victoria Russell / Duncan Shoosmith / Clive Smith / Matthew Smith / Gary Sollars / Louise Sturgis / Eleanor Taylor / Francis Terry / Tony Threadgold / Yana Trevail / Frances Turner / Tomas Watson / Amanda Webster / Robert White / Antony Williams / Julia Wilson / Stuart Pearson Wright

SECOND PRIZE
SELF-PORTRAIT
FRANCES BORDEN

Oil on board
450 x 375mm

Frances Borden studied at Chelsea College of Art and Design. She had previously exhibited in the BP Portrait Award in 1996 and 1997. After winning Second Prize in 1998 with one of the many self-portraits that she had been concentrating on at that time, she was again selected for exhibition in 2000. Borden has been awarded a number of prizes and has exhibited widely in Britain and, in 2005, in California.

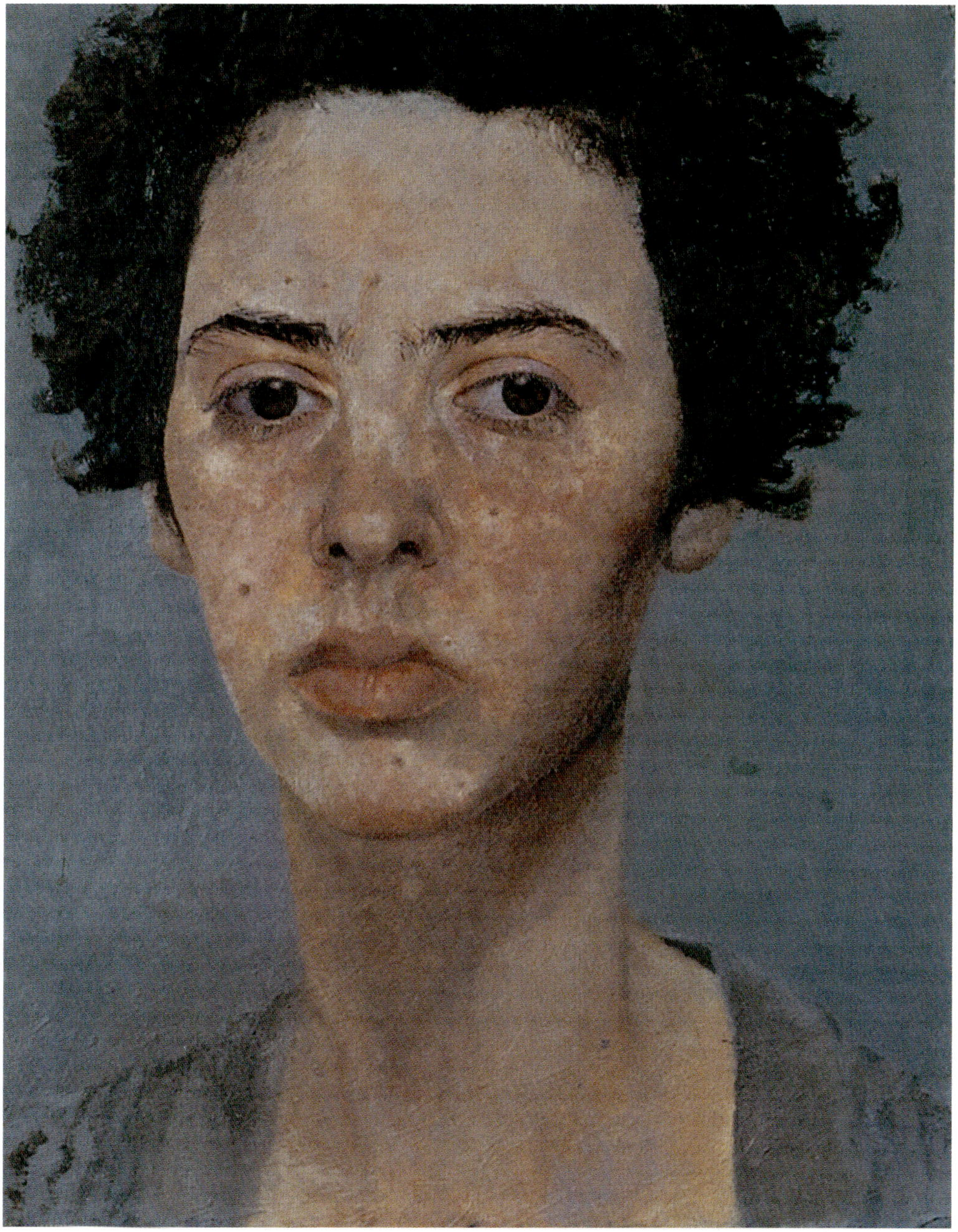

THIRD PRIZE
A SPACE
CLIVE SMITH

Oil on canvas
1436 x 1057mm

The year before this portrait was painted, Clive Smith completed his studies at the Art Students League in New York, an independent art school established by artists for artists. He went on to win the BP Portrait Award in 1999. Smith's works can now be found in collections around the world, including the Arnot Art Museum in New York, and the Frissiras Museum in Athens.

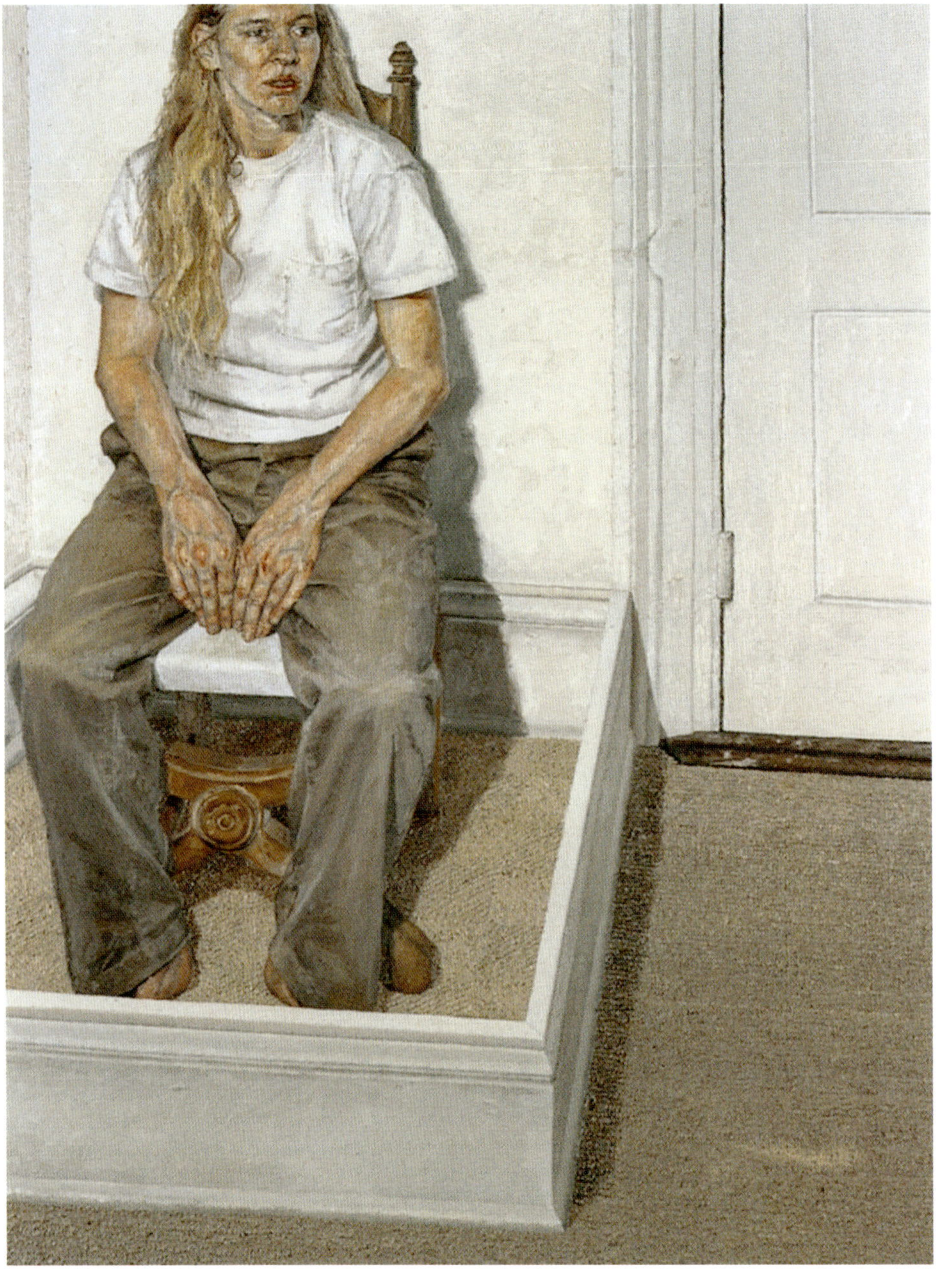

Commended
Pinky
Sadie Lee
Oil on canvas
2050 x 1370mm

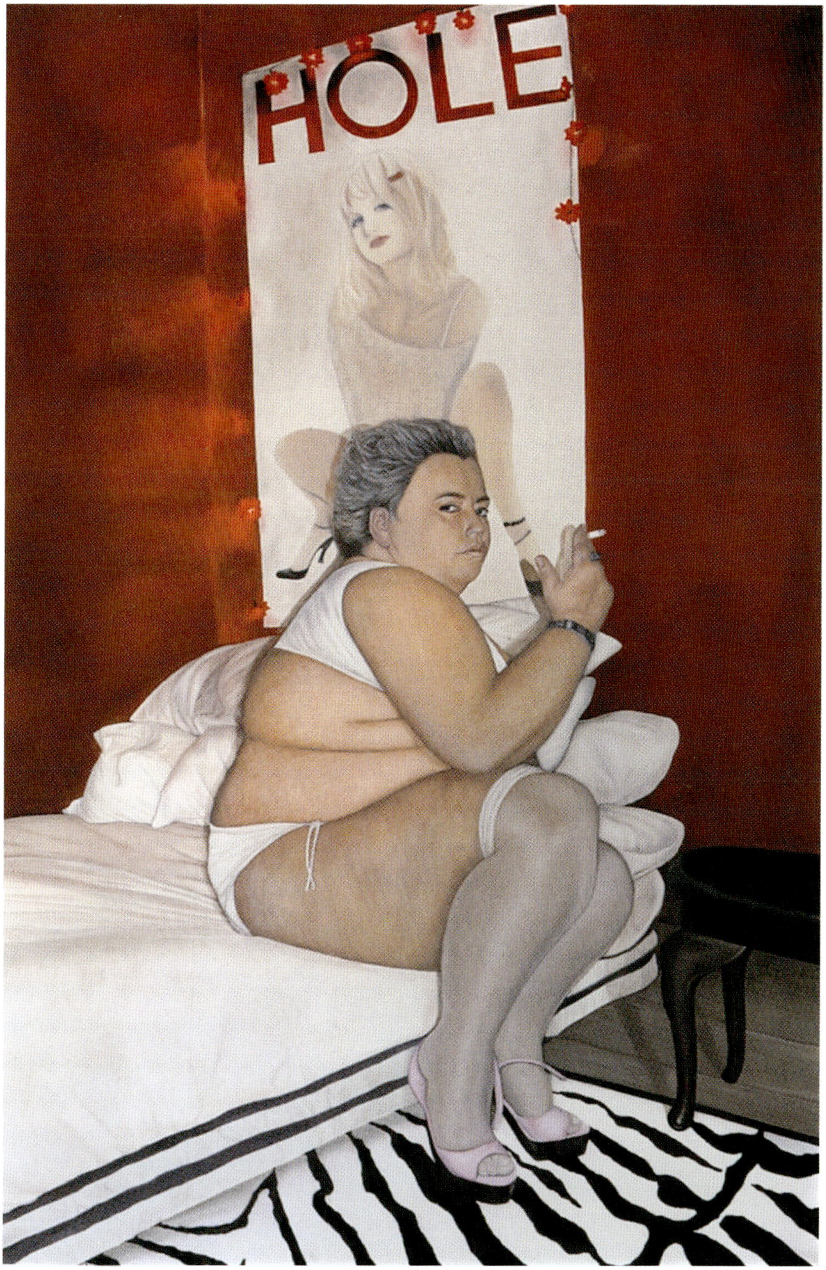

Commended
Kim in her hat
Nicholas Archer
Oil on canvas
515 x 420mm

Commended
Interior with Seated Figure
Lewis Chamberlain
Oil on canvas
515 x 465mm

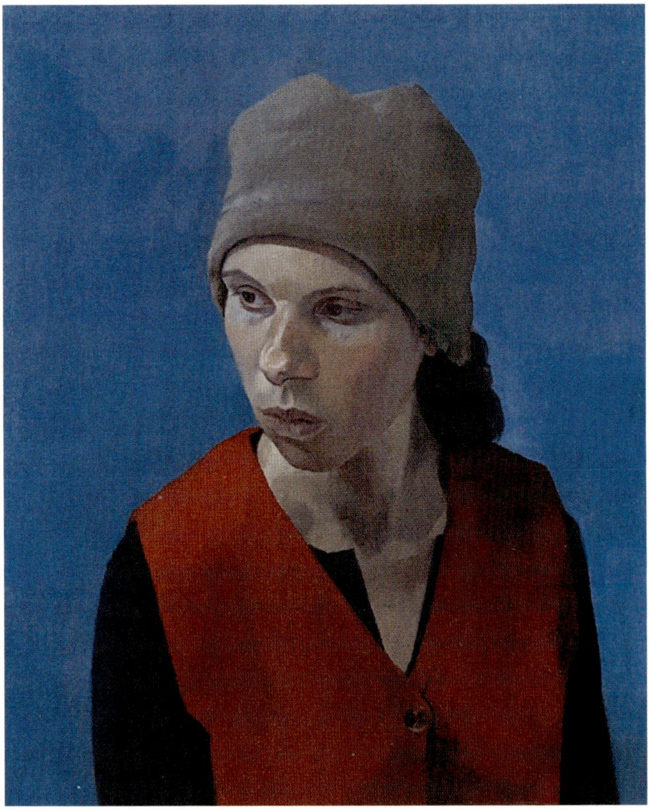

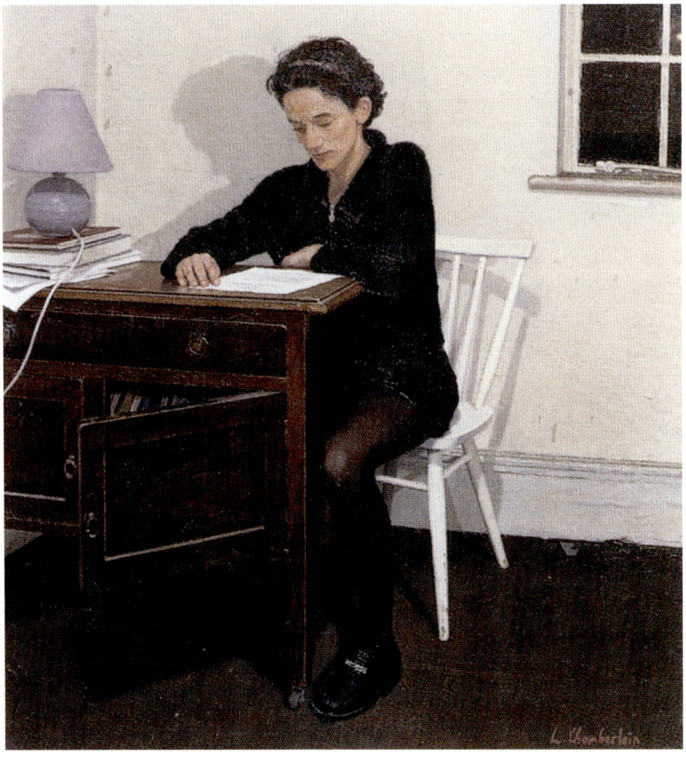

Commended
Double Portrait: Mother & Daughter
Marina Cooper
Oil on canvas
1270 x 965mm

Commended
Self-portrait
Julia Wilson
Acrylic on canvas
1000 x 540mm

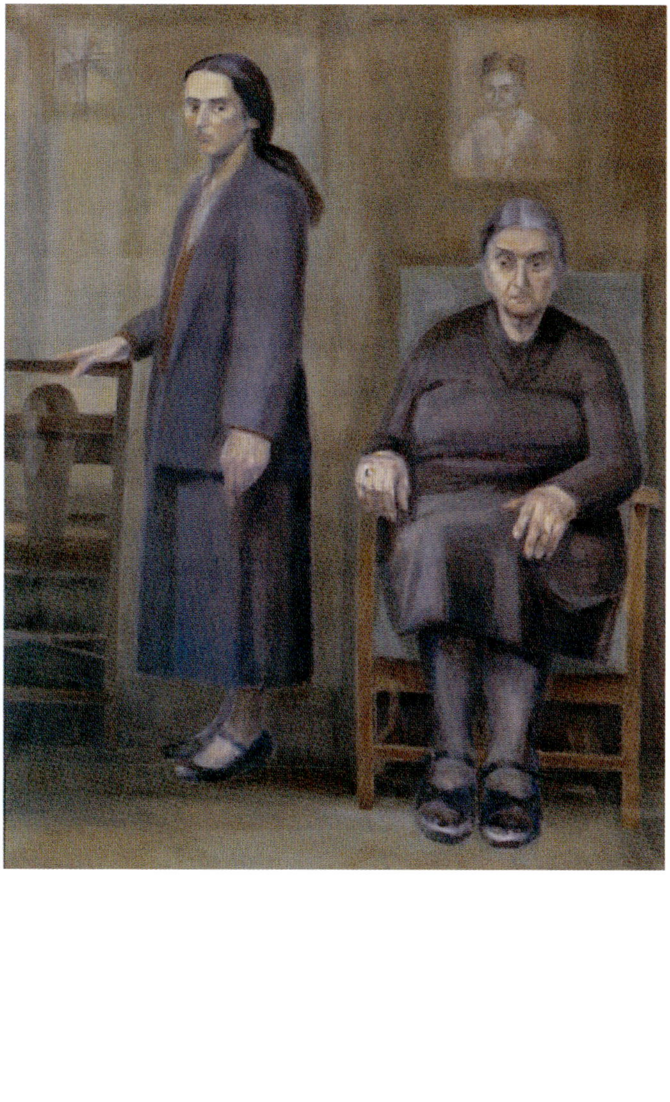

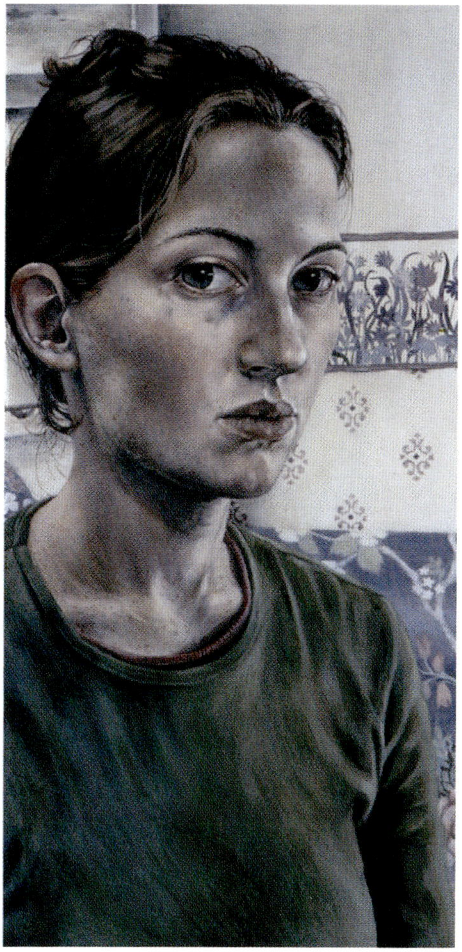

1999

ARTISTS WHOSE PORTRAITS WERE EXHIBITED

Nicolas Archer / Arwen Banning / Paul Benney / Akash Bhatt / Nick Botting / Merrilees Brown / Kelly-Anne Cairns / Lewis Chamberlain / Zara Chancellor / Rebecca Driffield / Susan Eaton / Tom Ellis / Darvish Fakhr / Jane Frederick / Christian Furr / Michael Gaskell / Ulyana Gumeniuk / Desmond Haughton / Ben Henriques / Ashley Hold / Ciaran Hughes / Diarmuid Kelley / Clare Lee / Sara Lee / Jason Line / Georgina Ludlow / John McCarthy / Clive McDonald / Jennifer McRae / Julian Merrow-Smith / Julian Mitchell / Peter Monkman / Julia Offord / Alan Parker / Robert Priseman / Gareth Reid / Aaron Robinson / Mark Roscoe / Stephen Shankland / Mark Shields / Clive Smith / Arran Steen / Lee Stewart / Lisa Stokes / Simeon Stout / Sarah Taylor / David Thomas / Andrew Tift / Frances Turner / Nigel Turner / Stuart Pearson Wright

SECOND PRIZE
BOYISH BOO
REBECCA DRIFFIELD

Oil on canvas
1177 x 749mm

Australian artist Rebecca Driffield studied in Melbourne. Her work has been exhibited internationally, including shows in Athens, Sydney and Paris. A figurative painter, predominantly concerned with the portrayal of the human face, Driffield appeared in the BBC television series *Star Portraits* in 2003, hosted by Rolf Harris.

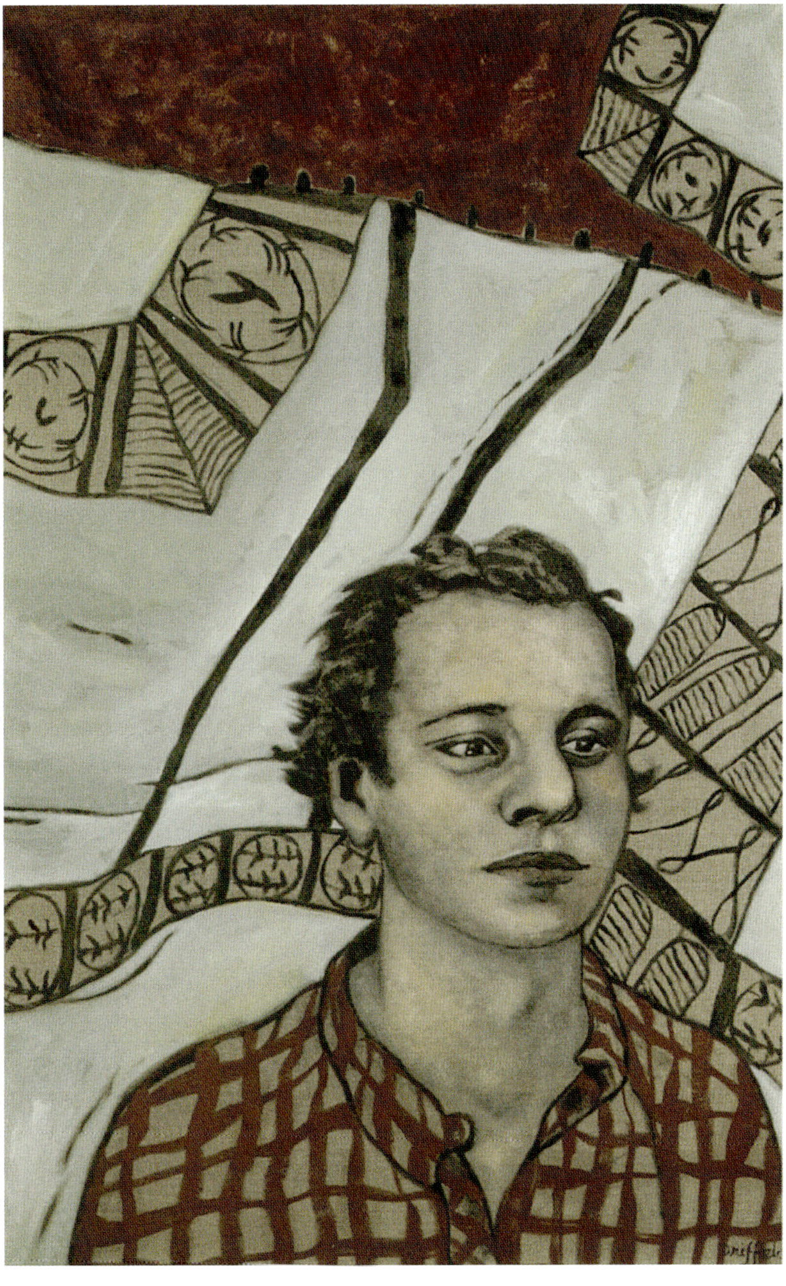

THIRD PRIZE
TONY BENN MP
ANDREW TIFT

Acrylic on canvas
1678 x 1582mm

Andrew Tift regards the environment and surrounding narrative objects as important elements of his portraits, as they can help to reflect and reinforce the sitter's identity. In this portrait, commissioned by the House of Commons, Labour politician Tony Benn is seated on a chair that was once owned by Scottish socialist and former Labour leader Keir Hardie. Tift was commissioned to paint Neil and Glenys Kinnock for the National Portrait Gallery in 2001, and went on to win the BP Portrait Award in 2006.

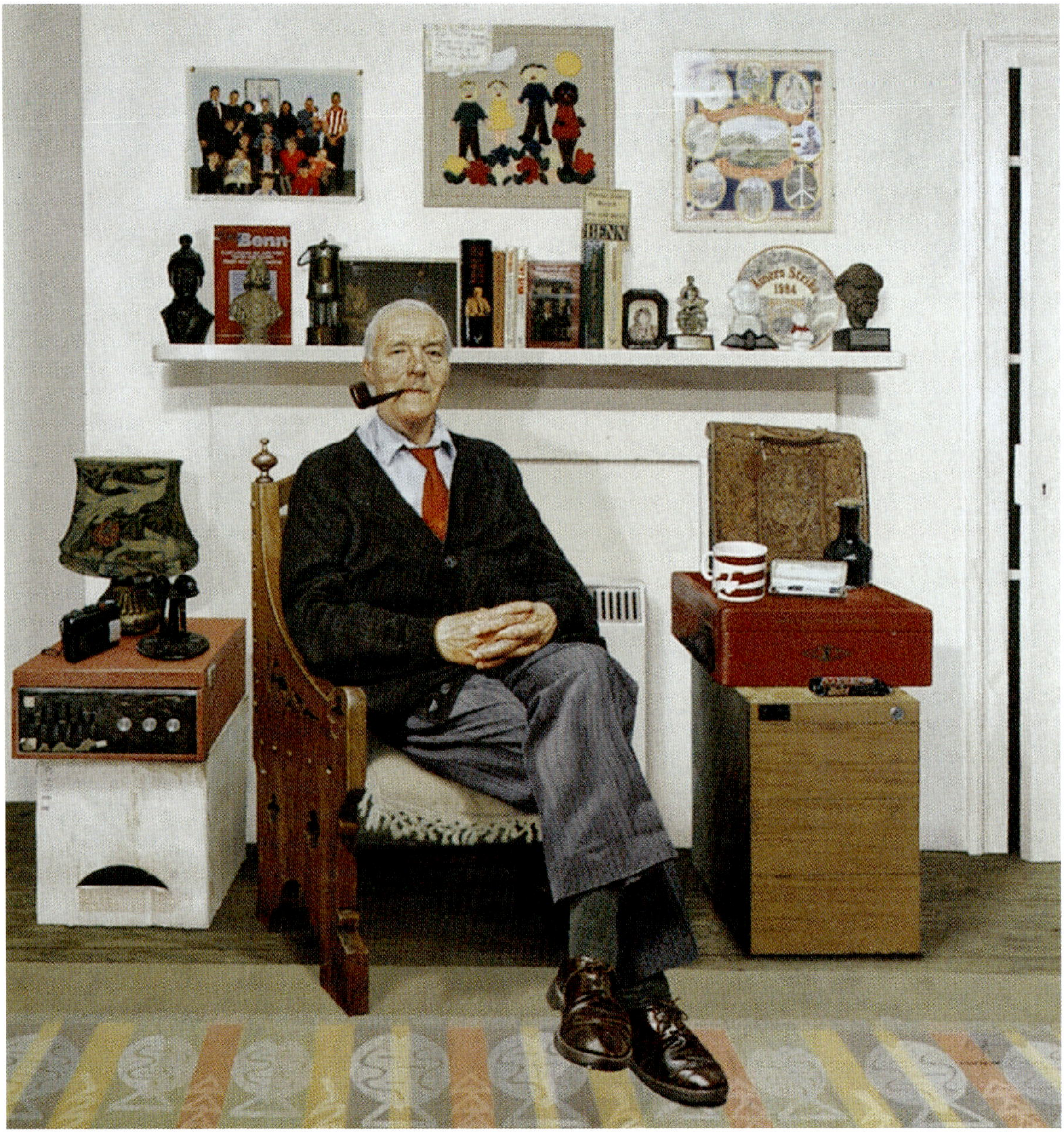

Commended
My Daughters, Nell and Lucca
Paul Benney
Oil on canvas
1439 x 1087mm

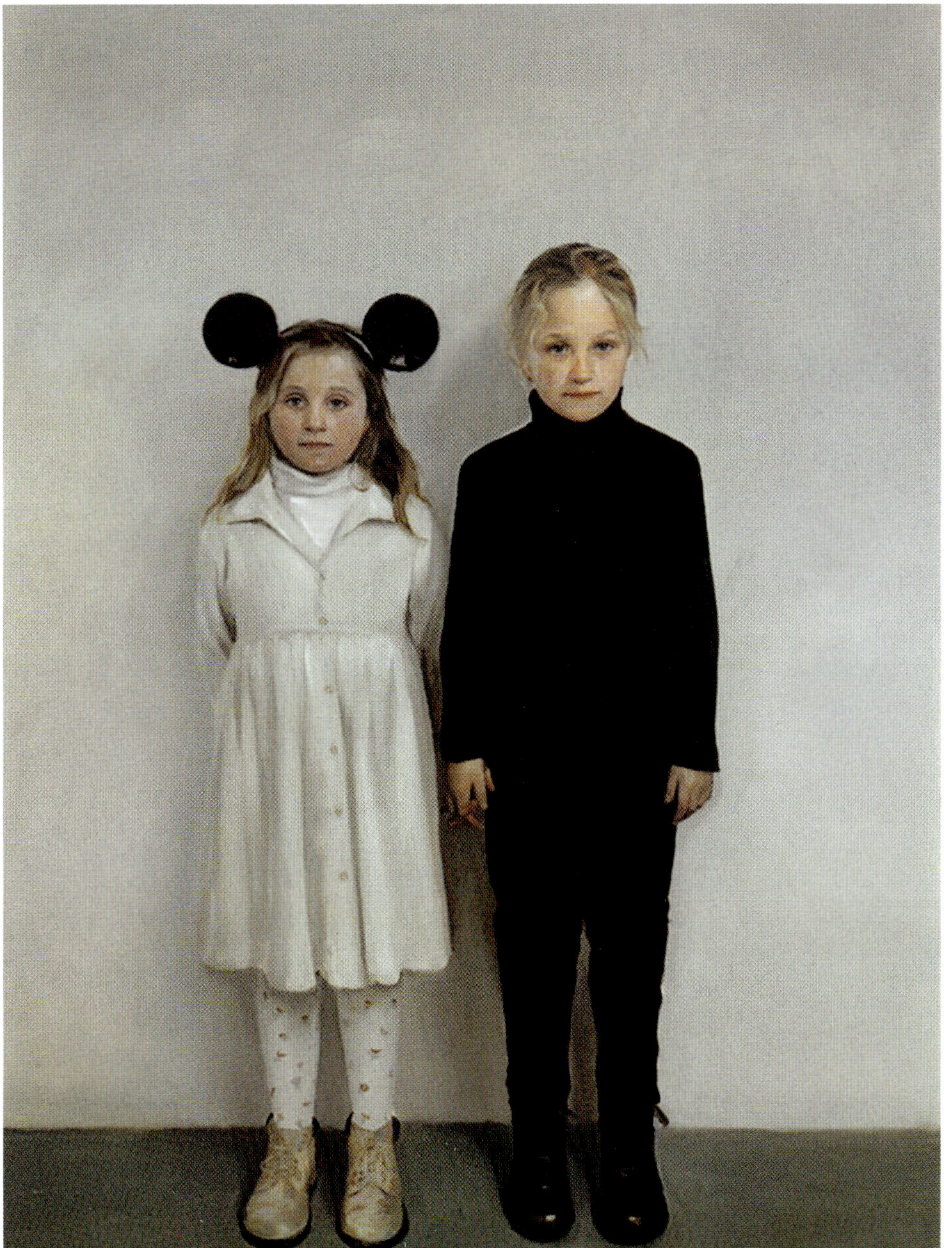

Commended
Custer's Last Stand
Akash Bhatt
Oil on canvas
1182 x 1182mm

Commended
Reflection in the Heat of the Outback
Nick Botting
Oil on canvas
1412 x 1376mm

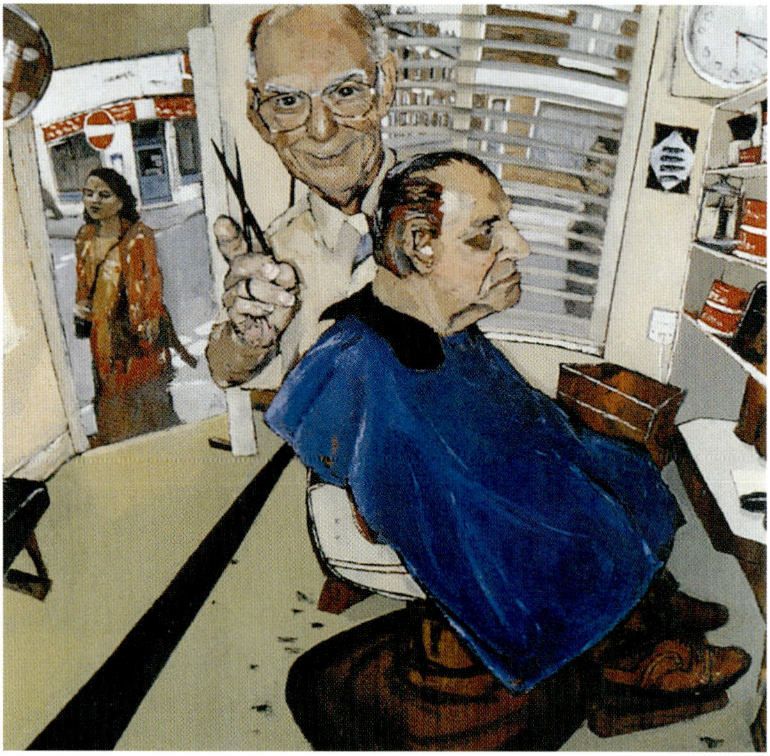

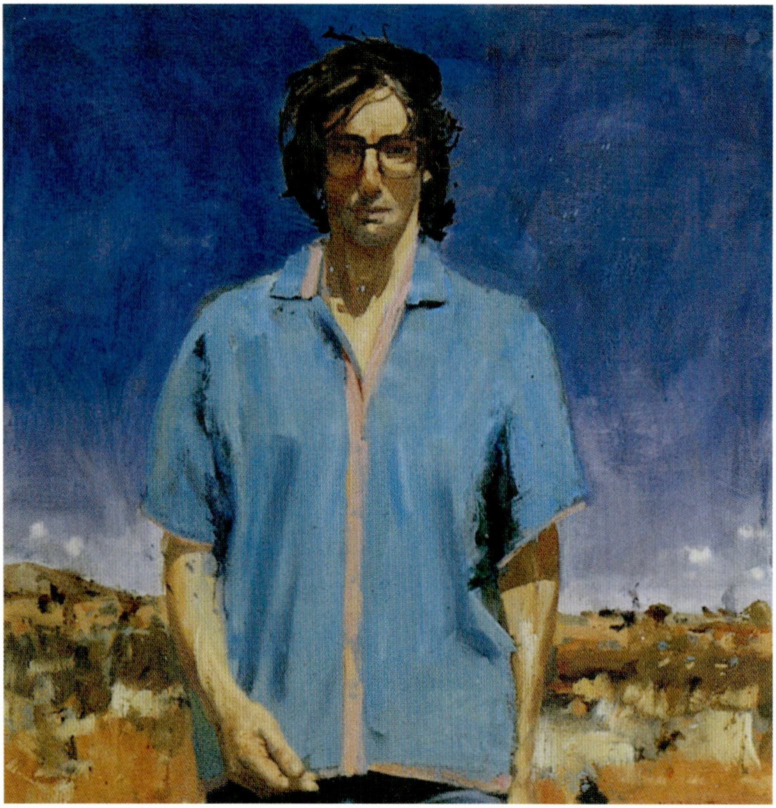

Commended
Night Painting
Lewis Chamberlain
Oil on canvas
716 x 716mm

Commended
Jonathan
Michael Gaskell
Tempera on board
604 x 403mm

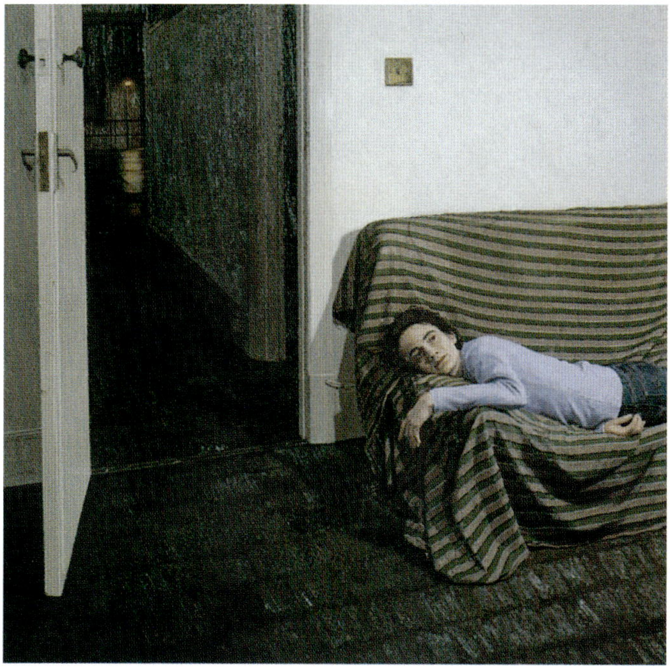

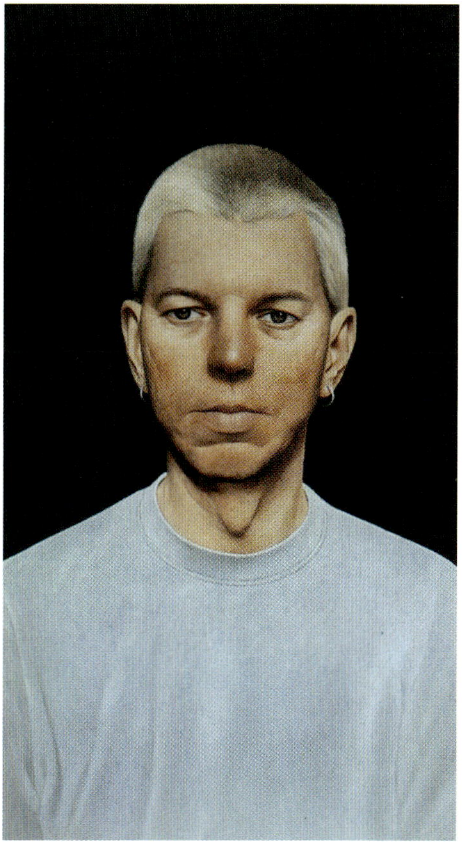

2000

ARTISTS WHOSE PORTRAITS WERE EXHIBITED

Paul Abbott / Aldo Balding / Arwen Banning / Paul Bartlett / Paul Benney / Akash Bhatt / Stephen Booth / Frances Borden / Greame Brooks / John Caple / Francisco Centofanti / Lewis Chamberlain / Louise Courtnell / Rosie Creer / Jonathan Cusick / Juno Doran / Mark Entwisle / Darvish Fakhr / Nathan Ford / Amando Garcia-Seijo / Ann Gardner / Adam Hahn / Phil Hale / Roxana Halls / David Hancock / James Hart Dyke / Martin Huxter / David Lawton / Sadie Lee / Ricardo Leite / Thomas Leveritt / Norman Long / Dean Marsh / Fergus Mayhew / Josie McCoy / Jennifer McRae / Antony Micallef / Chloe Needham / Colin Poole / Gareth Reid / Victoria Russell / Si Sapsford / Amy Smith / Bennedict Smyth / Lee Stewart / Edward Sutcliffe / David Thomas / Andrew Tift / Andrew Ullman / Christina Ure / Leigh D. Walker / Stuart Pearson Wright

SECOND PRIZE
GLAMOUR PUSSY TOKYO
ANTONY MICALLEF

Oil on canvas
1304 x 1101mm

Antony Micallef studied Fine Art at the University of Plymouth. Since winning Second Prize in 2000, he has been widely exhibited throughout the world, and recently appeared in group shows at the Royal Academy of Arts and Tate Britain. His work has been described as 'critical pop', combining draughtsmanship with a form of contemporary expressionism to expose the dark side of consumerism and pop art.

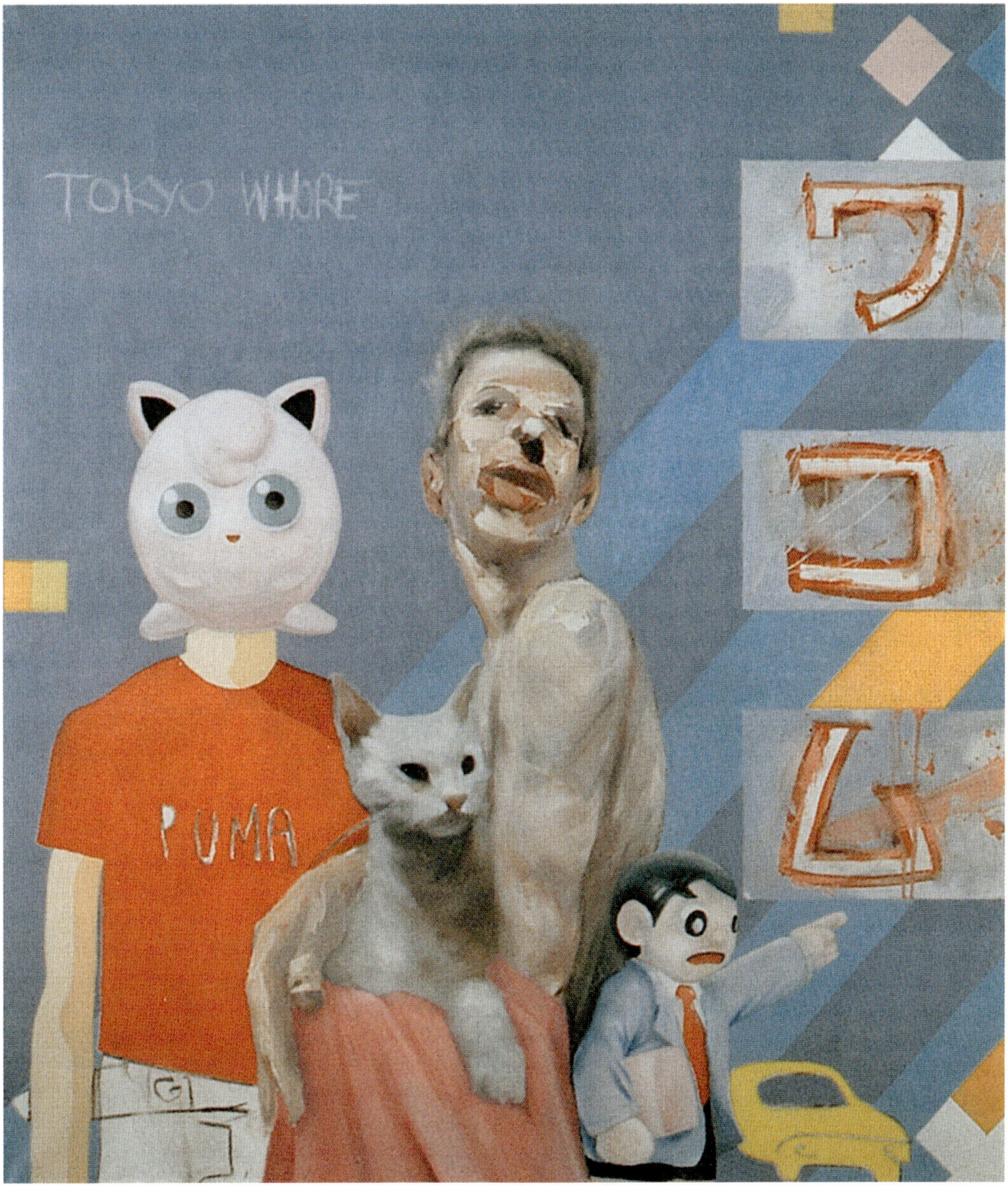

THIRD PRIZE
DR ROWLANDS AT 45
PHIL HALE

Oil on canvas
1703 x 2209mm

Born in Boston, United States, Phil Hale now resides in London. He trained as an apprentice under the American painter Richard Berry, and cites John Singer Sargent as being one of his influences. Prior to becoming a painter, Hale worked as an illustrator and was awarded a Gold Medal by the Society of Illustrators in 1999.

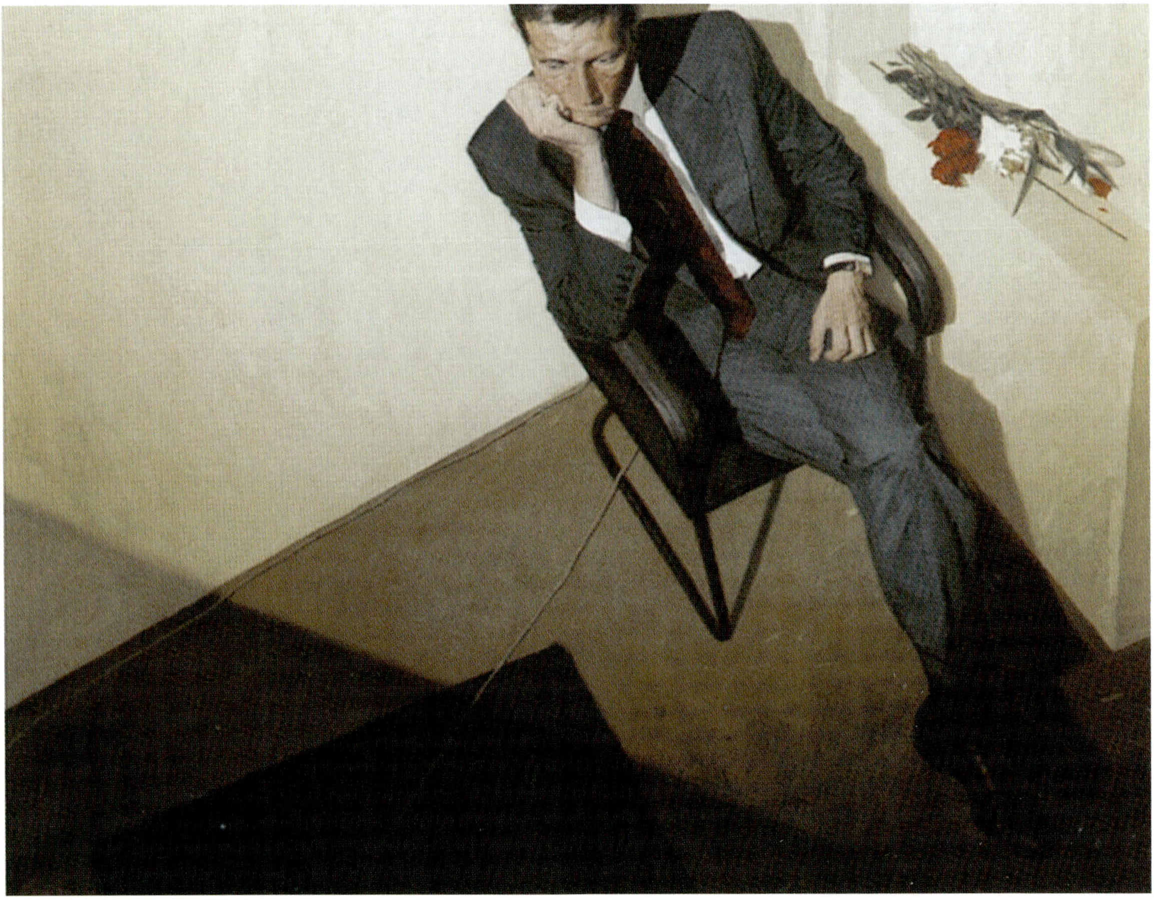

Commended
You Know Not the Day
Nor the Hour (Harry Coleman)
Andrew Tift
Acrylic on canvas
306 x 505mm

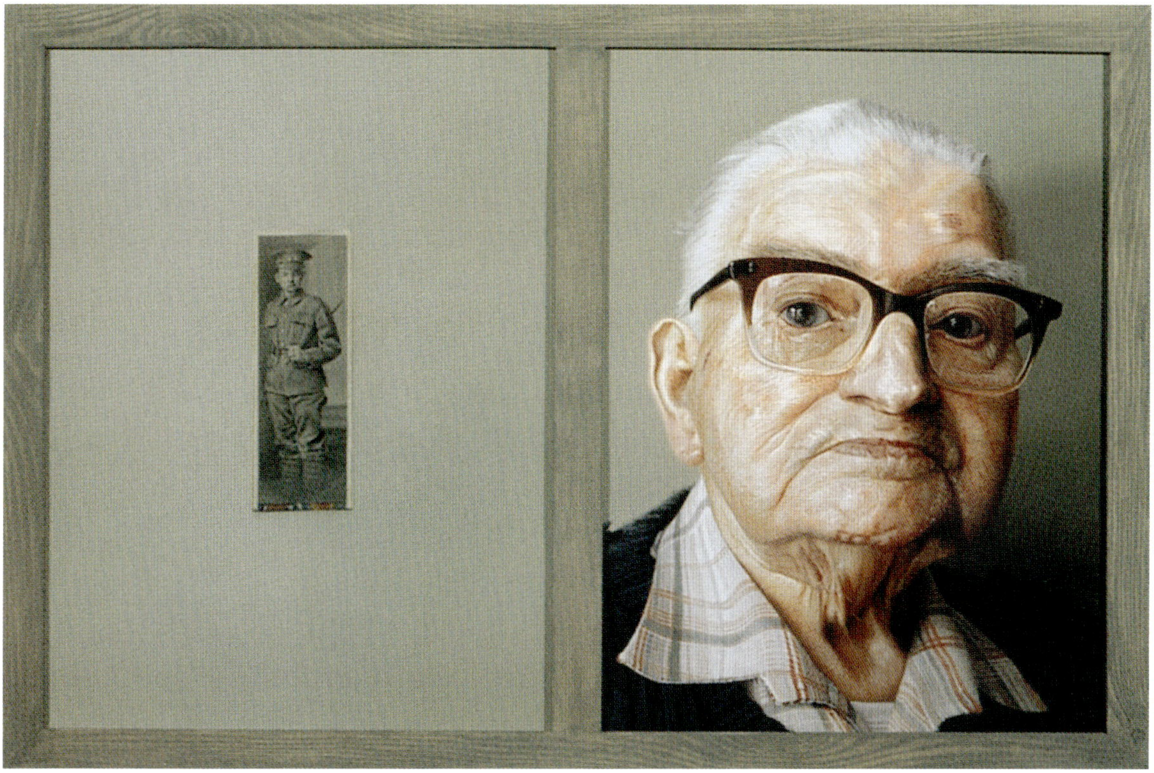

Commended
Juggler
Paul Abbott
Oil on canvas
2404 x 1301mm

Commended
Self-portrait
Frances Borden
Oil on canvas
405 x 305mm

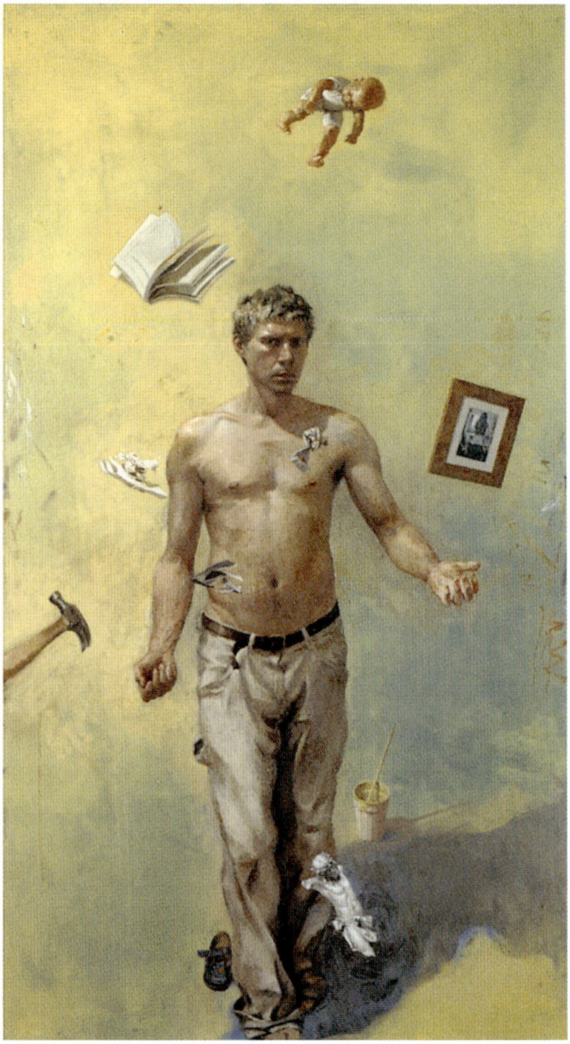

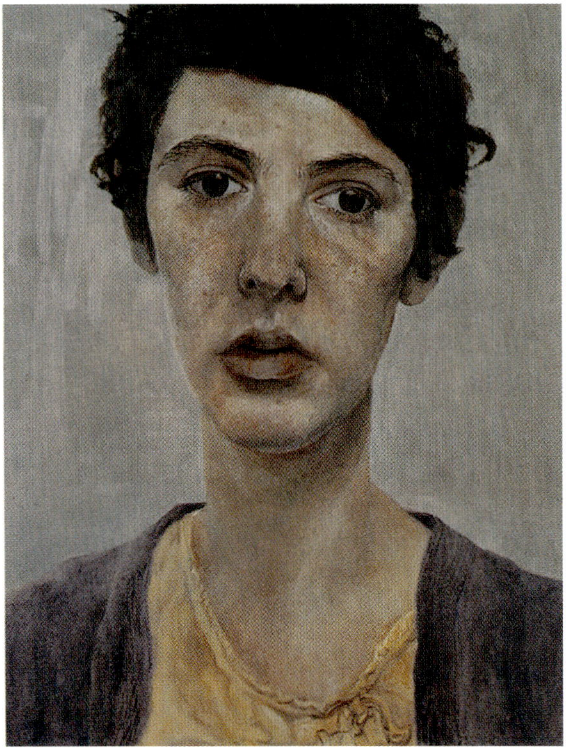

Commended
Black Painting #6
Juno Doran
Oil on canvas
1092 x 1092mm

Commended
Reloj AC
Thomas Leveritt
Oil and acrylic on canvas
1001 x 1001mm

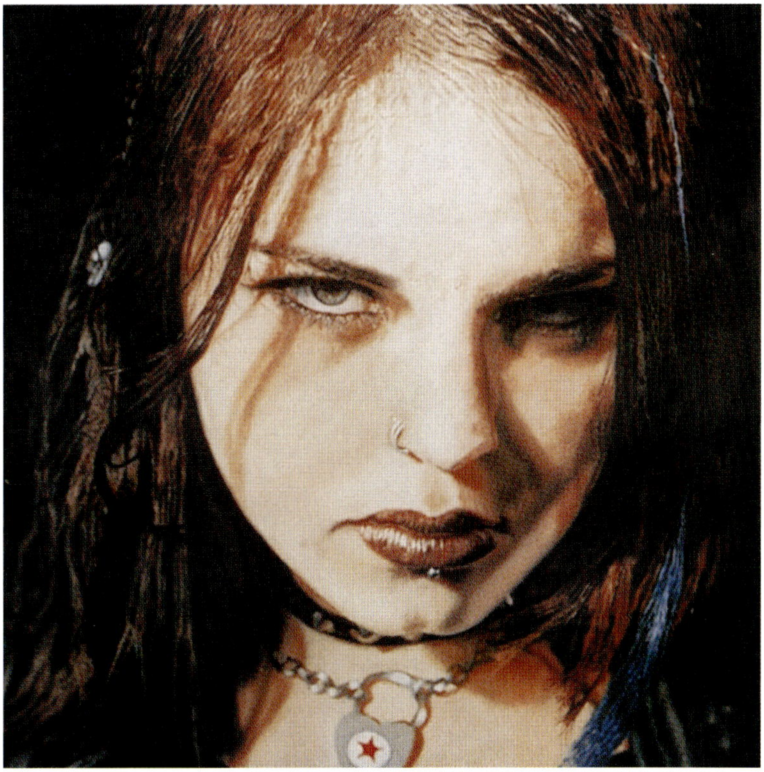

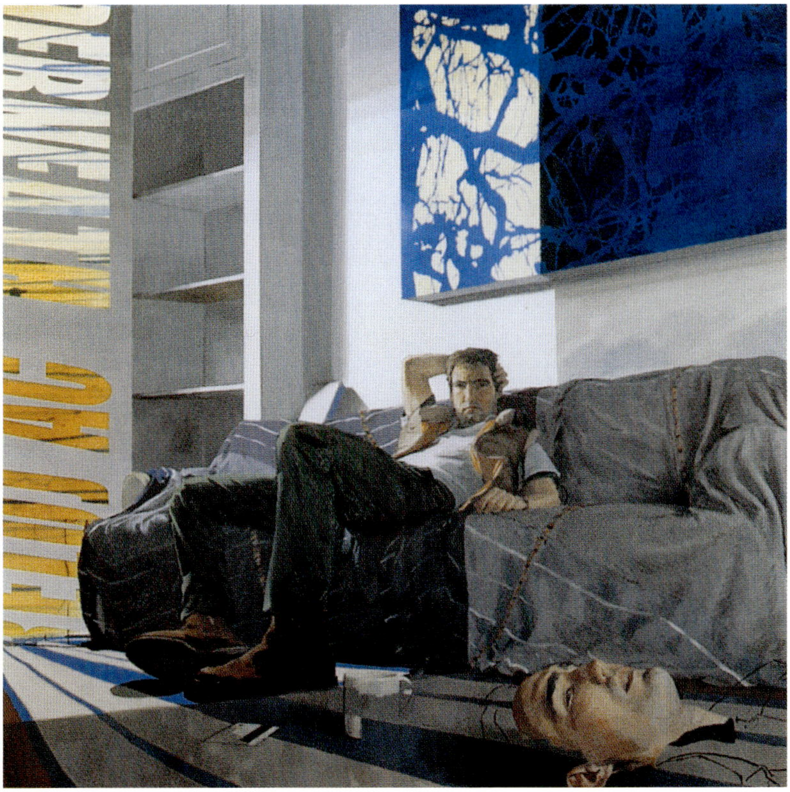

2001

ARTISTS WHOSE PORTRAITS WERE EXHIBITED

Paul Abbott / Jakob Avenius Anckarsvard / Jennifer Anderson / Jeremy Andrews / Maryanne Aytoun-Ellis / Stefan Badham / Marcus Bartlett / Ivan Bray / Richard Brazier / Paul Brewster / Stuart Buchanan / Mark Cazalet / Lewis Chamberlain / Daniel Cimmermann / Louise Courtnell / Rossen Daskalov / David Dipré / Mark Entwisle / Michael Gaskell / Mitch Griffiths / Ulyana Gumeniuk / Phil Hale / David Hancock / H. Craig Hanna / Craig Hawker / Martin Huxter / Natacha Ivanova / Marc Jennings / Diarmuid Kelley / Brendan Kelly / Thomas Leveritt / Jason Line / Constandinos Lytrides / Catherine MacDiarmid / Marielle MacLeman / Josie McCoy / Lee Maelzer / Peter Monkman / Tim Okamura / Alan Parker / Andrew Paterson / Daisy Richardson / Stephen Rogers / James Schneider / Mark Shields / Matthew Small / Alan Stewart / Lee Stewart / Lisa Stokes / Matthew Stradling / Helen Sykes / Christopher Thompson / Frances Turner / Simon Wainwright / Leigh Walker / Gavin Watson / Stuart Pearson Wright

JOINT SECOND PRIZE
SOURCE X
PHIL HALE

Oil on linen
2290 x 1340mm

Phil Hale was awarded joint Second Prize, having won Third Prize in the preceding year, and went on to be selected for the Award in the following three years. Hale has since exhibited widely, and has undertaken private and public commissions, including a portrait of composer Thomas Adès for the National Portrait Gallery in 2002. In 2008, his portrait of Tony Blair, which had been painted during the former Prime Minister's last months in office during 2007, was unveiled in Westminster.

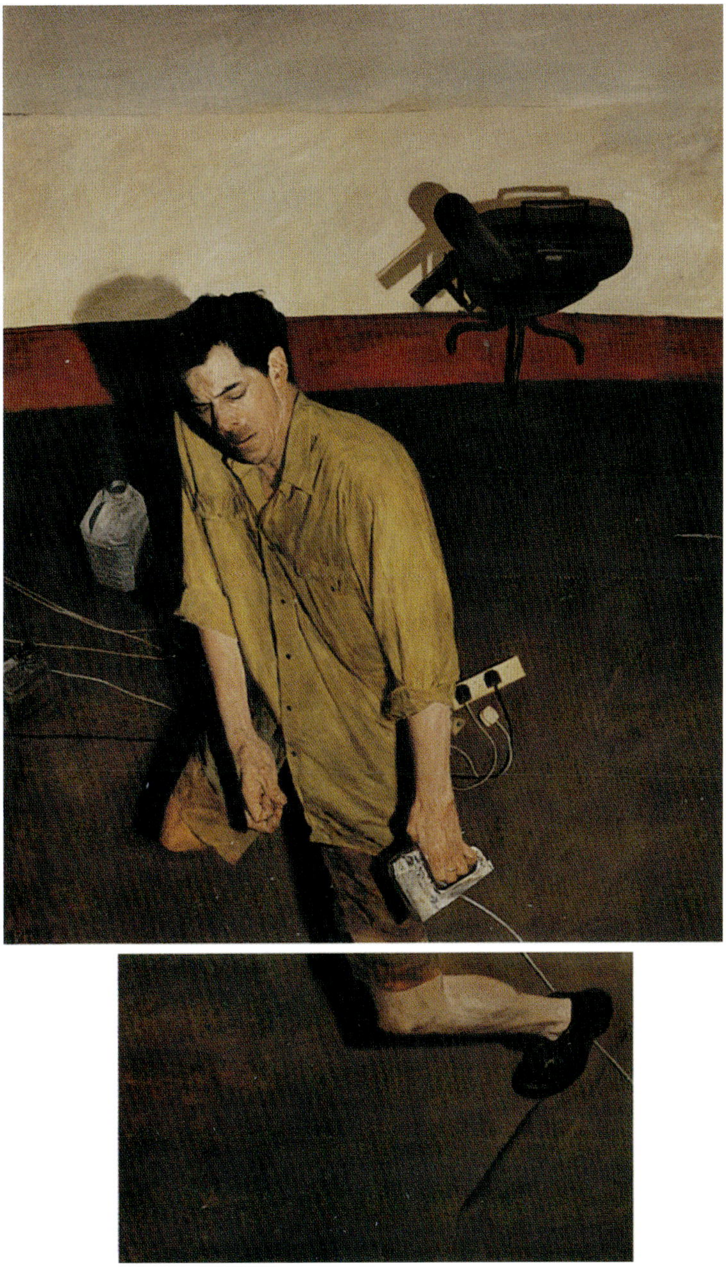

JOINT SECOND PRIZE
NUDE IN A NIGHTCLUB
BRENDAN KELLY

Oil on canvas
1220 x 2440mm

Edinburgh-born Brendan Kelly studied at Camberwell College of Arts and the Slade School of Fine Art, London. He has won a number of national art awards, including the De Laszlo Prize for the best portrait by a young artist at the Royal Society of Portrait Painters. In 2006, Kelly spent time in Afghanistan working as a war artist. He is currently Head of Drawing at London's Art Academy and was recently elected a member of the Royal Society of Portrait Painters. He has undertaken a number of commissions, including a portrait of General Sir Mike Jackson for the National Portrait Gallery, unveiled in 2009.

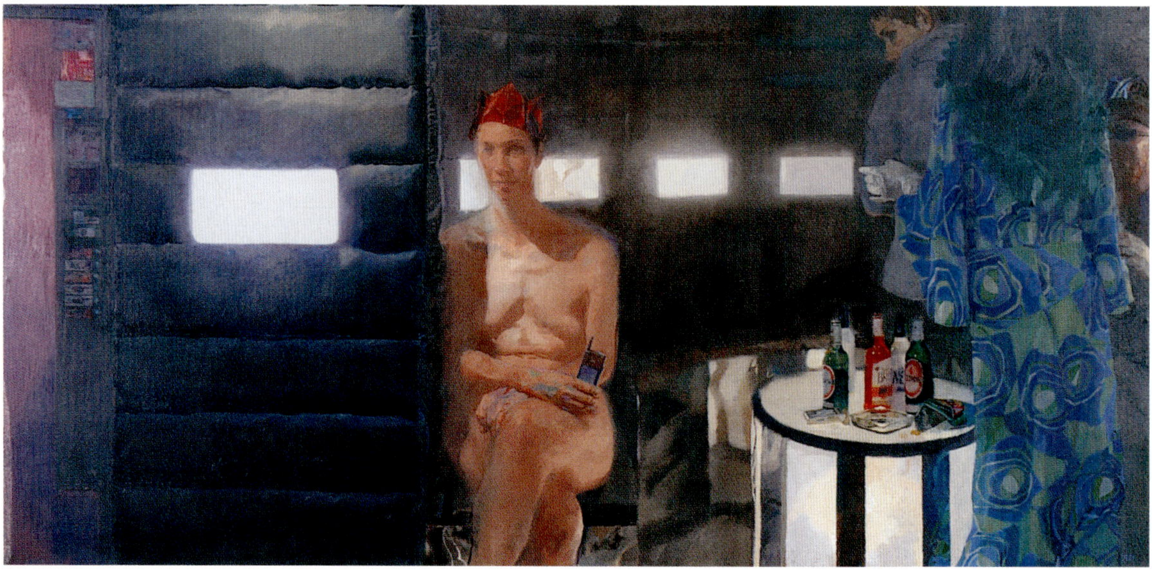

Commended
Carlos Sitting on a Clear Plastic Chair
H. Craig Hanna
Oil and hammerite on board
1873 x 1873mm

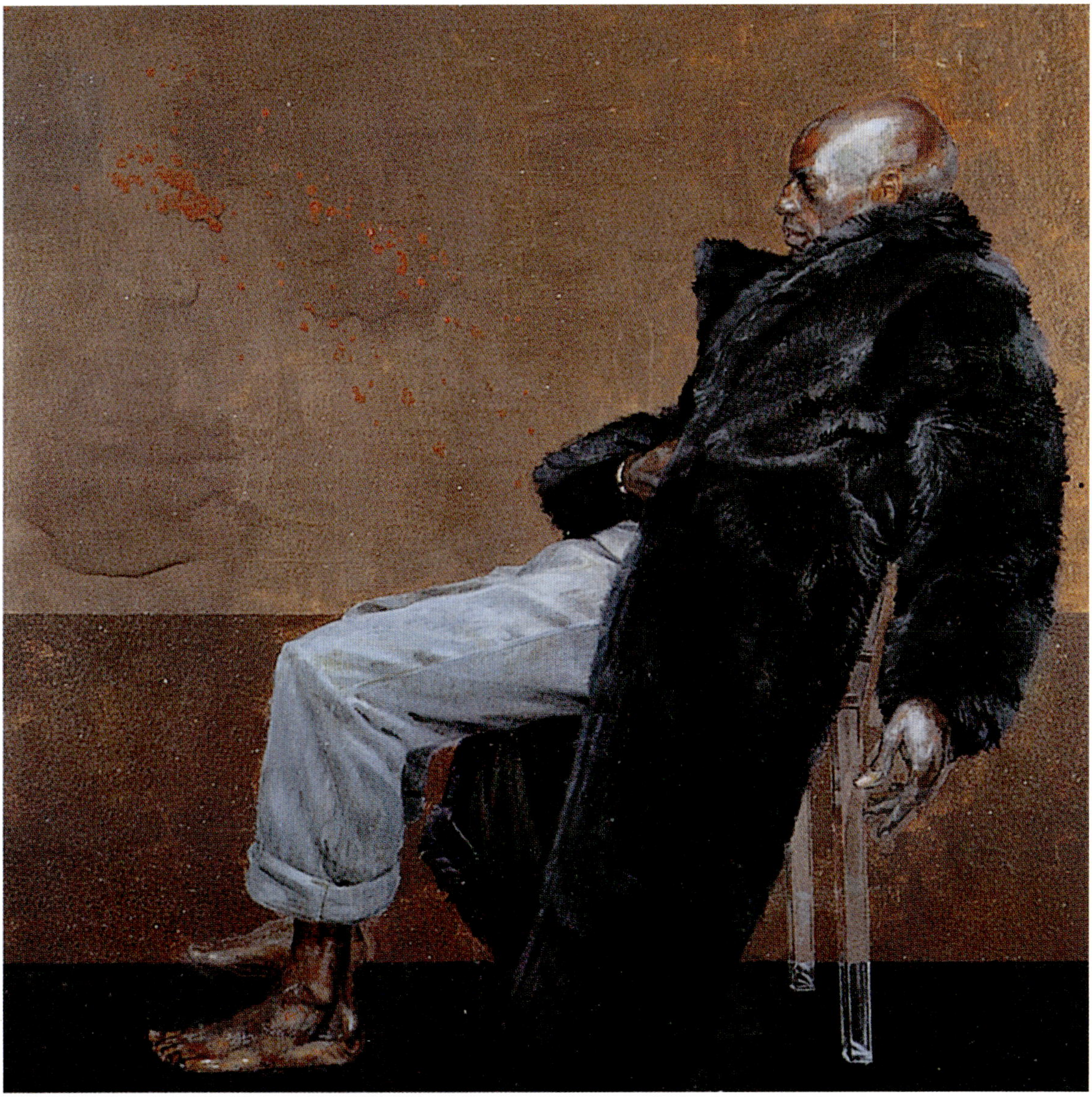

Commended
John Patrick
Michael Gaskell
Tempera on board
440 x 375mm

Commended
U look well intresting
David Hancock
Acrylic on canvas
1220 x 2440mm

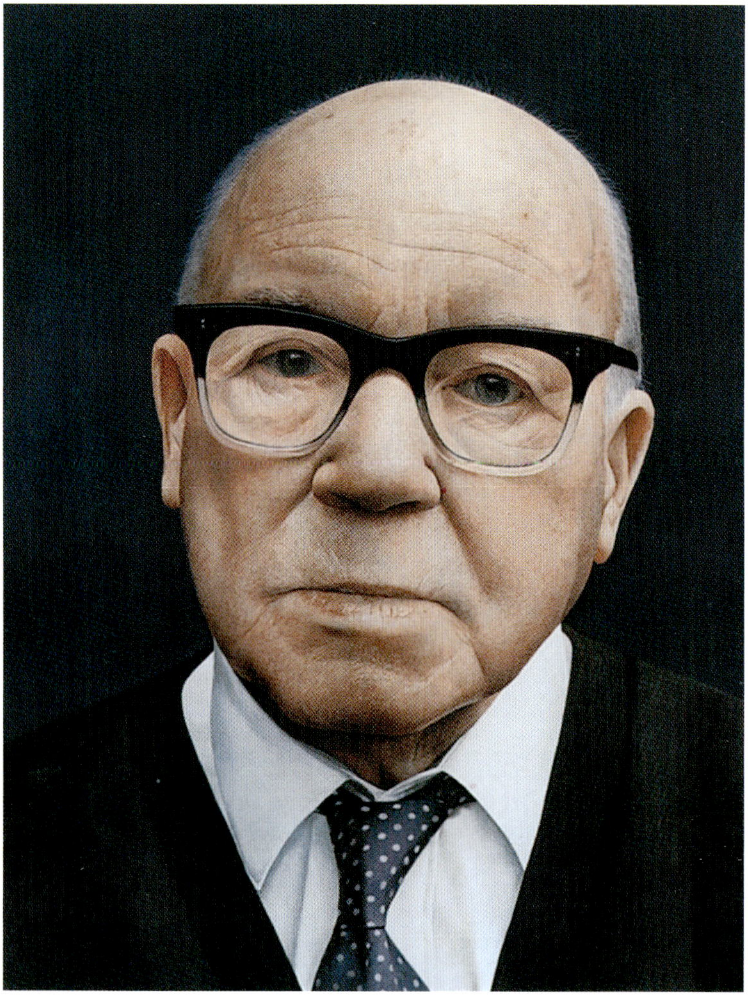

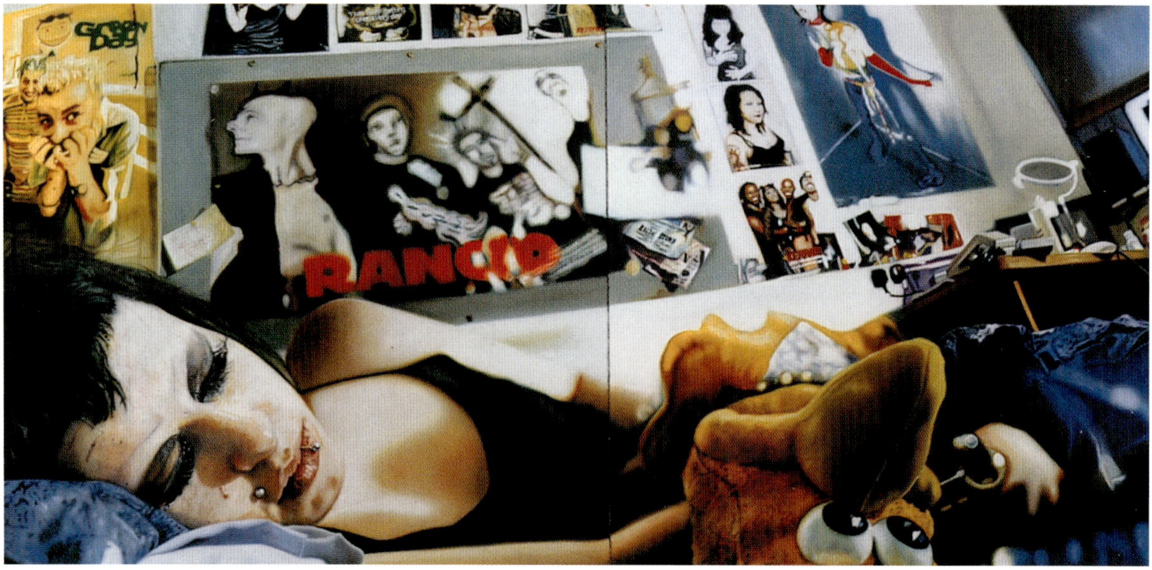

Commended
Malerie's Painting
Thomas Leveritt
Oil and acrylic on canvas
1820 x 3340mm

Commended
Separation
Andrew Paterson
Oil on canvas
1800 x 2700mm

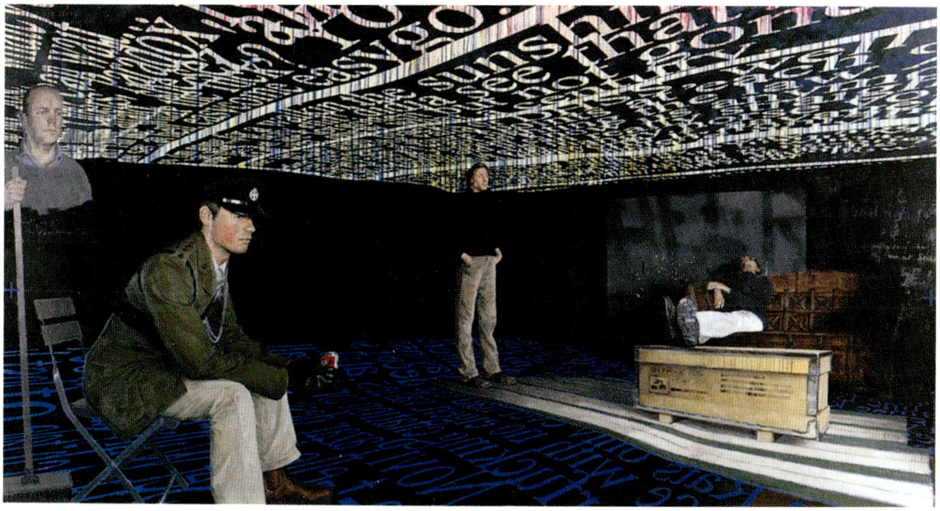

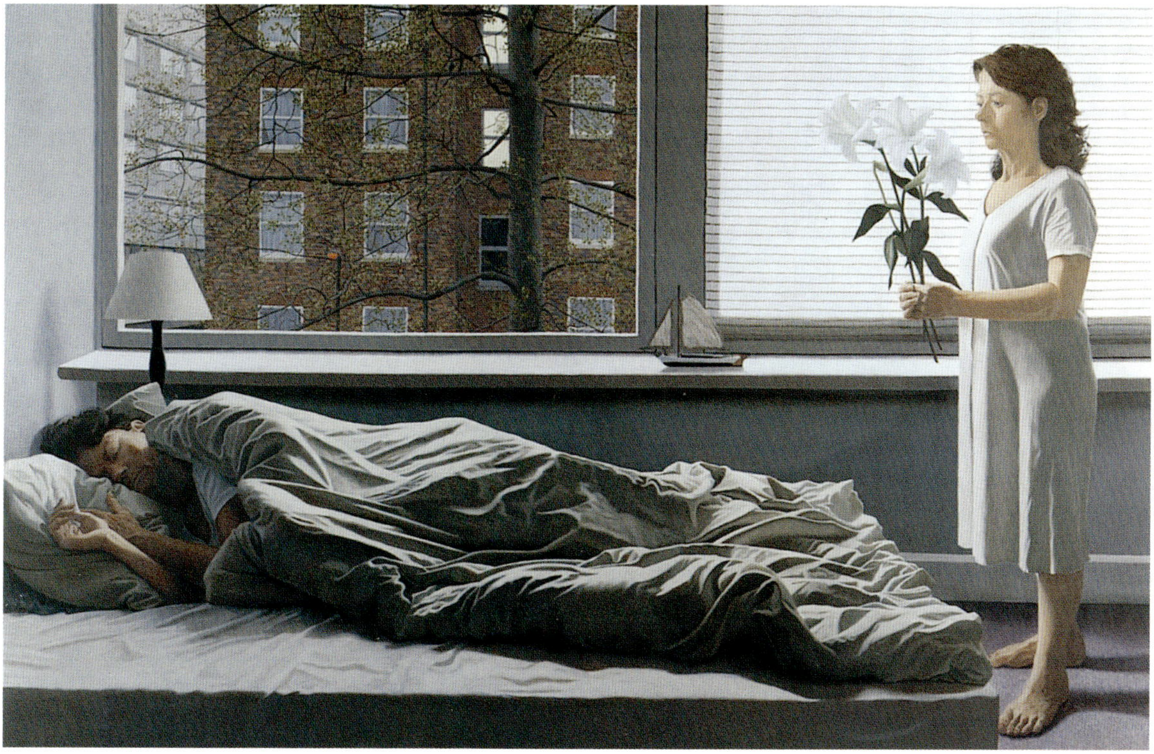

2002

ARTISTS WHOSE PORTRAITS WERE EXHIBITED

Jackie Anderson / Jennifer Anderson / Esao Andrews / Nicholas Archer / Žygimantas Augustinas / Maryanne Aytoun-Ellis / Tomás Baleztena / Matthew Batt / Noah Buchanan / Jason Butler / Comhghall Casey / Anton Cataldo / Daniel Cimmermann / David Dipré / Timur D'Vatz / Gavin Edmonds / Mark Entwisle / Massimo Franco / Vasiliki Gkotsi / Hannah Glickstein / Catherine Goodman / Adam Hahn / Phil Hale / Toby Hunt / Josie Jammet / Diarmuid Kelley / Sadie Lee / Diana Leslie / Brian Love / Oliver Lovley / Sarah McConkey / Josie McCoy / Catherine MacDiarmid / Susan McFarlane / Dean Marsh / Fergus Mayhew / Anastassios Missouras / Ilona Niemi / Adrian O'Donnell / Kristina O'Donnell / Tim Okamura / Carl Randall / Daisy Richardson / Lorna Robertson / Stephen Rogers / Gideon Rubin / Daniel Shadbolt / Mark Shields / Rupert Shrive / Lisa Stokes / Benjamin Sullivan / Christopher Thompson / Andrew Tift / Stergios Tzelepis / Jessica Wolfson

SECOND PRIZE
MAN WITH UTENSIL (OSCAR)
ŽYGIMANTAS AUGUSTINAS

Oil on canvas
1175 x 590mm

Lithuanian artist Žygimantas Augustinas studied at the Vilnius Academy of Art and the Florence Academy of Art in Italy. He became a member of the Lithuanian Artists' Society in 2000. This portrait, modelled on the artist's own body, depicts Oscar, the hero in Günter Grass's book *The Tin Drum*, published in 1959.

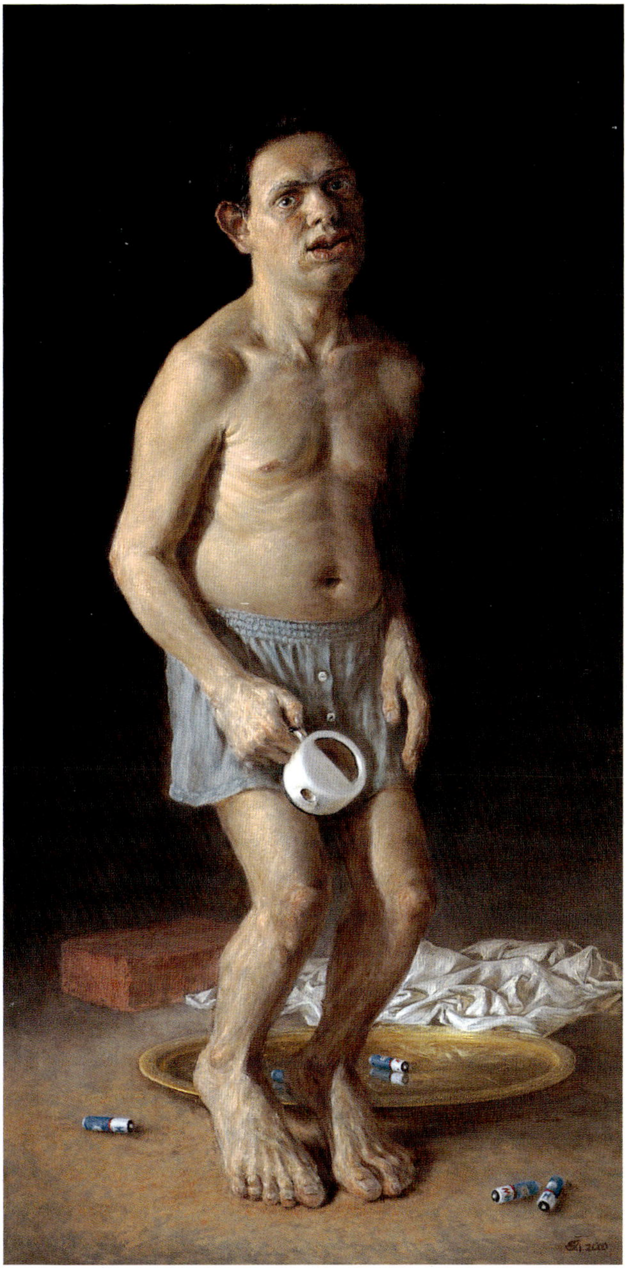

THIRD PRIZE
SEATED WOMAN
MARK SHIELDS

Acrylic on board
1200 x 880mm

Irish artist Mark Shields studied at the University of Ulster. He had been an exhibitor at the BP Portrait Award several times before winning Third Prize with this portrait of his wife. Shields has exhibited at the Royal Academy of Arts, the Royal Ulster Academy and the National Gallery of Ireland, and has works in the Arts Council for Northern Ireland and the National Self-portrait Collection of Ireland. He has painted the Prince of Wales for the headquarters of the Royal Gurka Regiment.

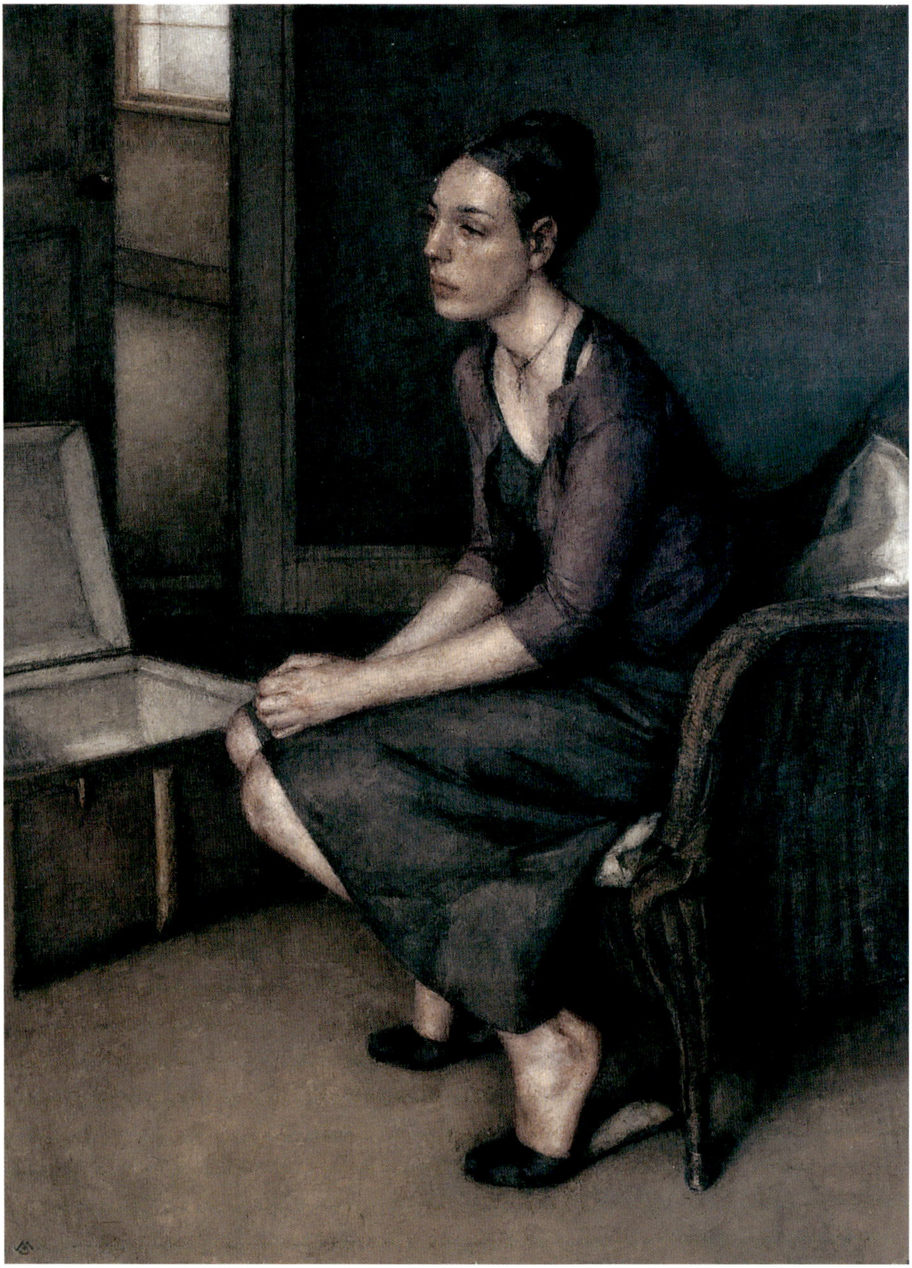

Commended
Mária
Mark Entwisle
Oil on canvas
660 x 610mm

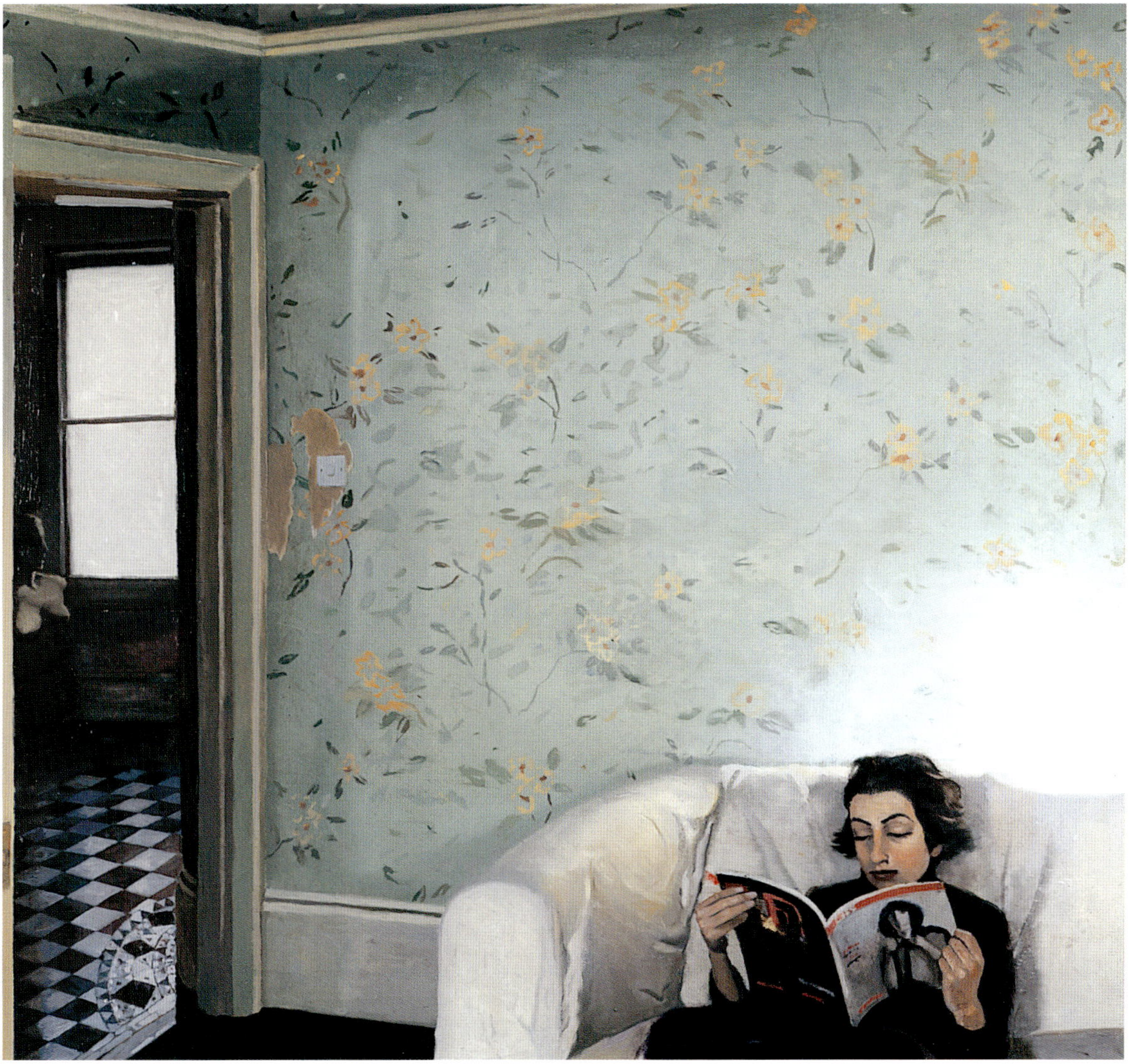

Commended
Self-portrait
Massimo Franco
Oil on board
330 x 310mm

Commended
Same Face 1
Vasiliki Gkotsi
Oil on canvas
1630 x 1630mm

Commended
Rosalind Savill CBE
Dean Marsh
Oil on panel
365 x 255mm

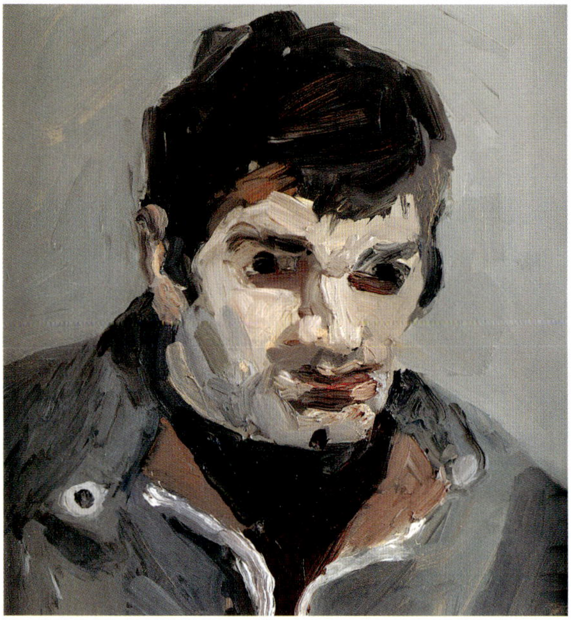

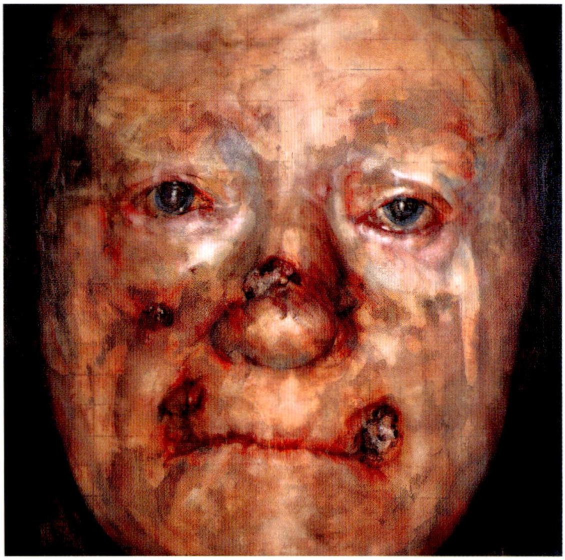

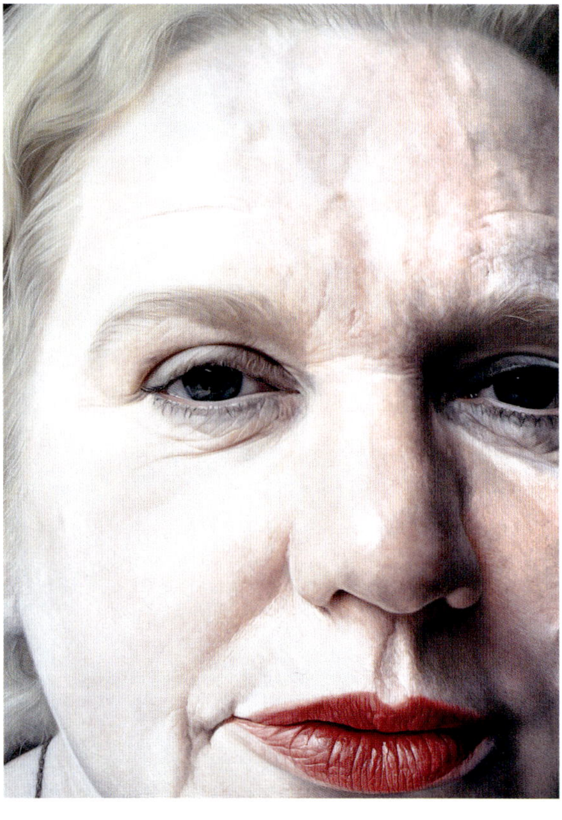

Commended
Self-portrait
Kristina O'Donnell
Oil on canvas
380 x 250mm

Andy
Jackie Anderson
Oil on canvas
1140 x 830mm

Fayette Middle School
Esao Andrews
Oil on board
770 x 920mm

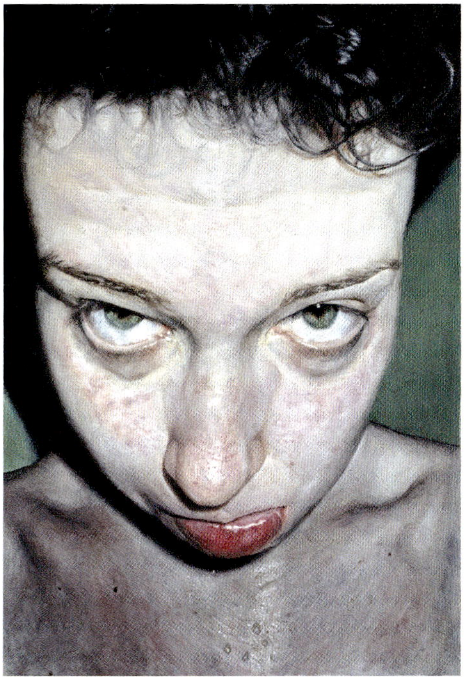

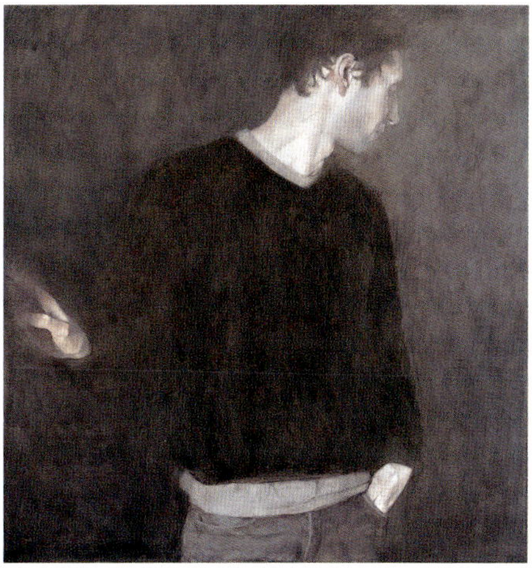

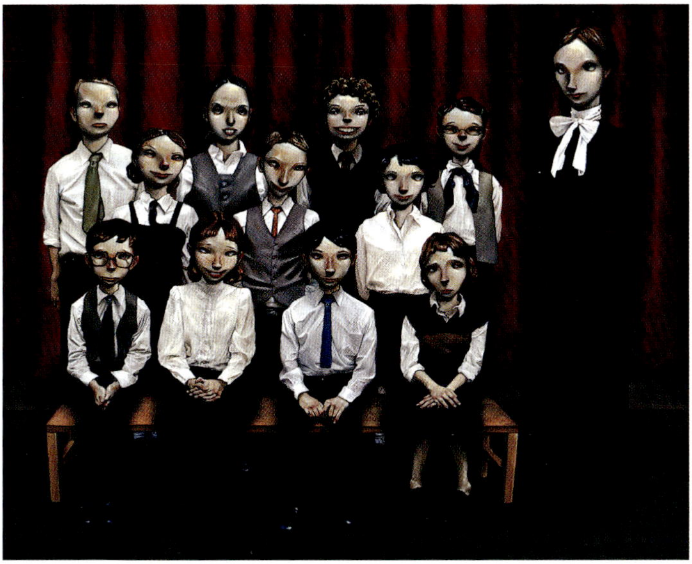

Mother
Maryanne Aytoun-Ellis
Tempera on linen
760 x 540mm

Self-portrait
Tomás Baleztena
Oil on canvas
1040 x 850mm

The Bird Keeper's Daughter
Matthew Batt
Acrylic on canvas
300 x 250mm

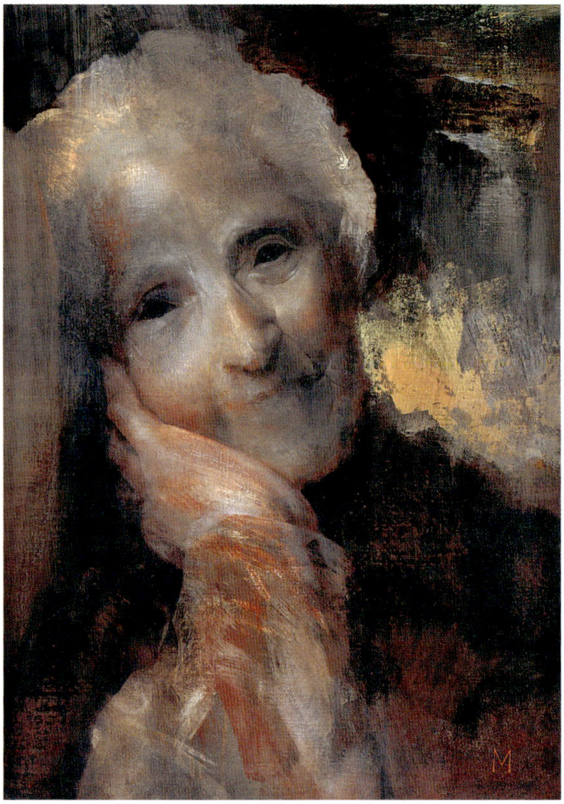

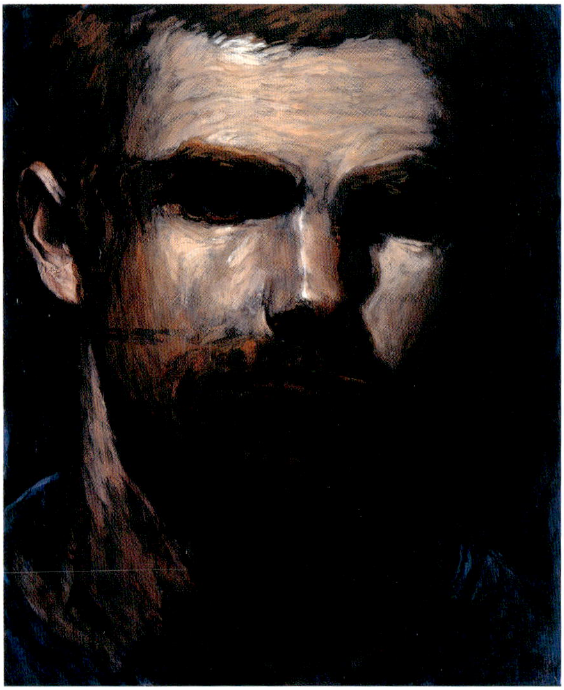

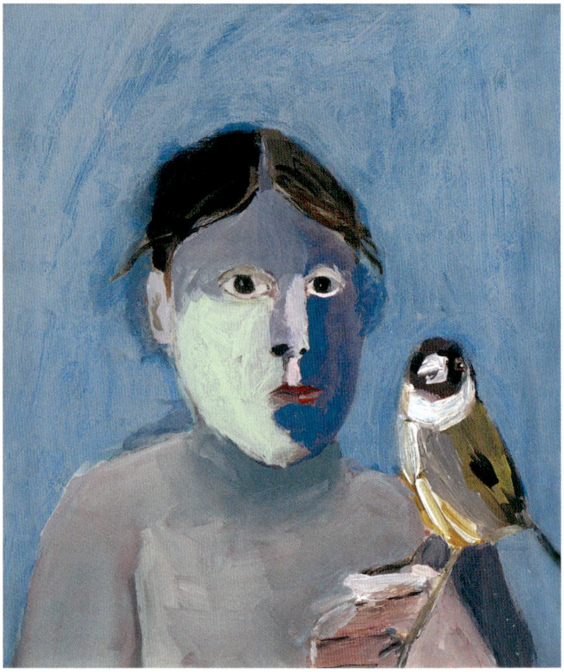

Woman with Headwrap
Noah Buchanan
Oil on panel
406 x 305mm

Eddie
Jason Butler
Oil on canvas
1560 x 1260mm

Self-portrait in Blue Jumper
Comhghall Casey
Oil on linen
840 x 740mm

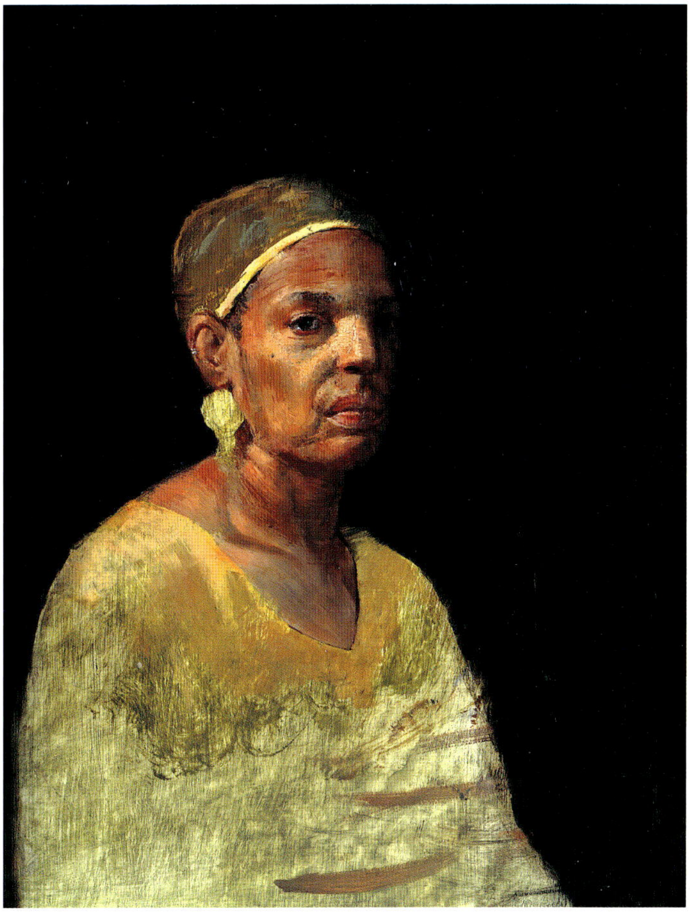

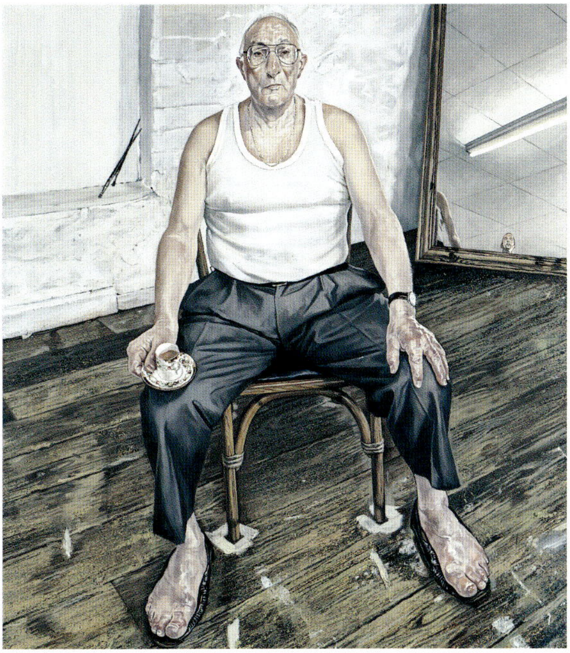

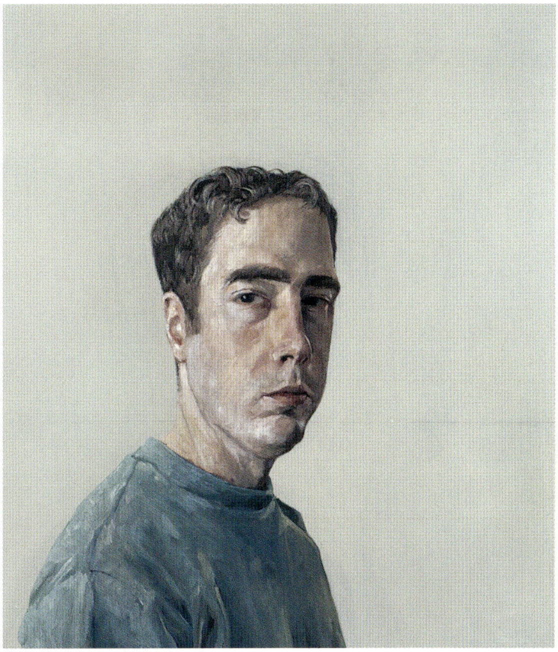

Pete Seated
Anton Cataldo
Oil on board
610 x 460mm

Paranoid Android
Daniel Cimmermann
Oil and encaustic on canvas
610 x 460mm

Portrait of A.D.
David Dipré
Oil on canvas
1780 x 1095mm

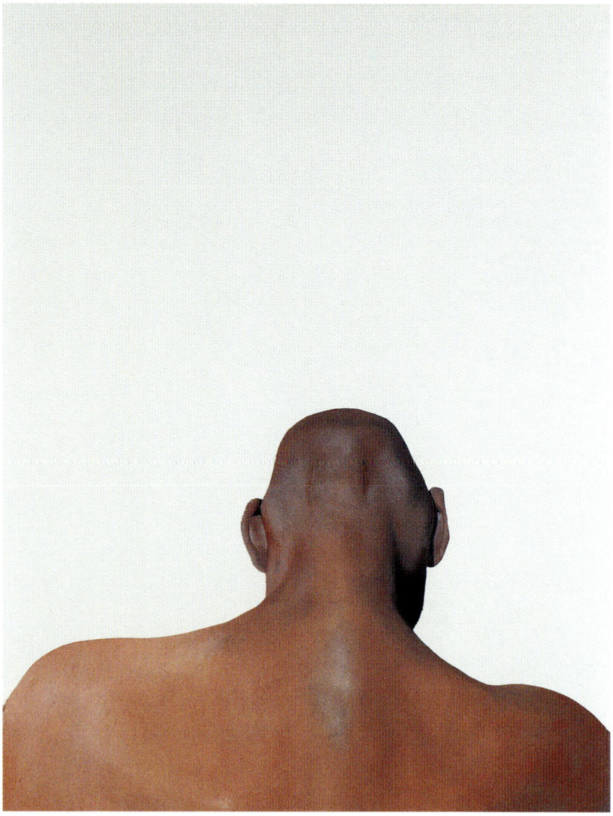

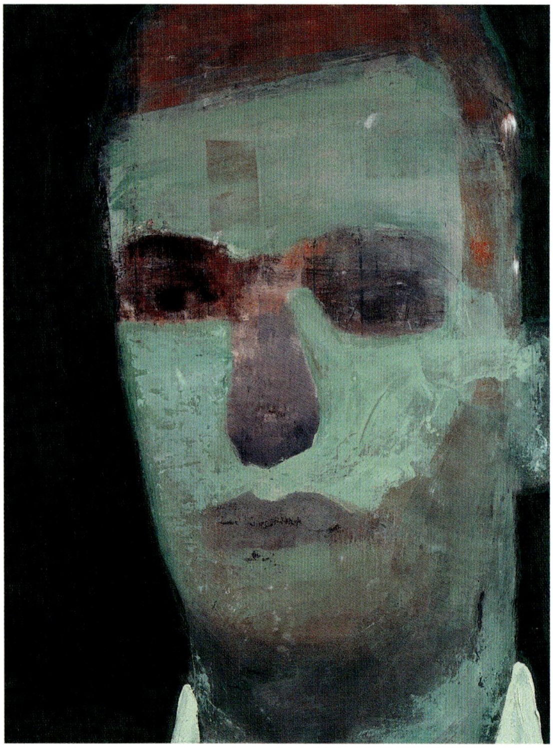

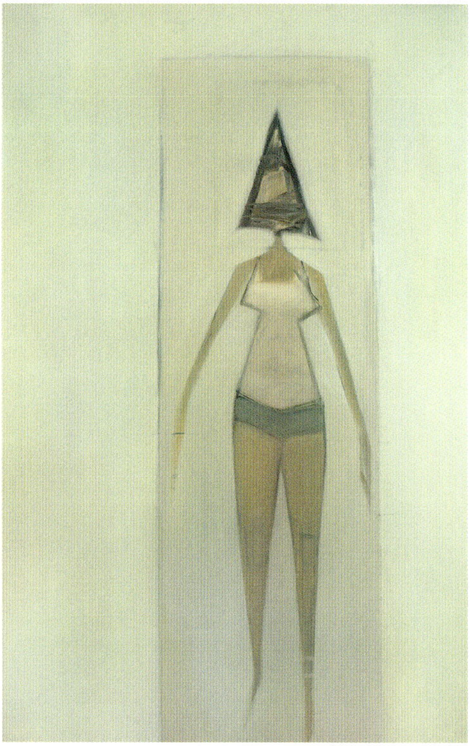

Mr David Frankel and Miss Grace Ayson
Gavin Edmonds
Oil on canvas
1575 x 1168mm

Me
Hannah Glickstein
Acrylic on canvas
1020 x 670mm

Ruth
Adam Hahn
Oil on canvas
1210 x 1300mm

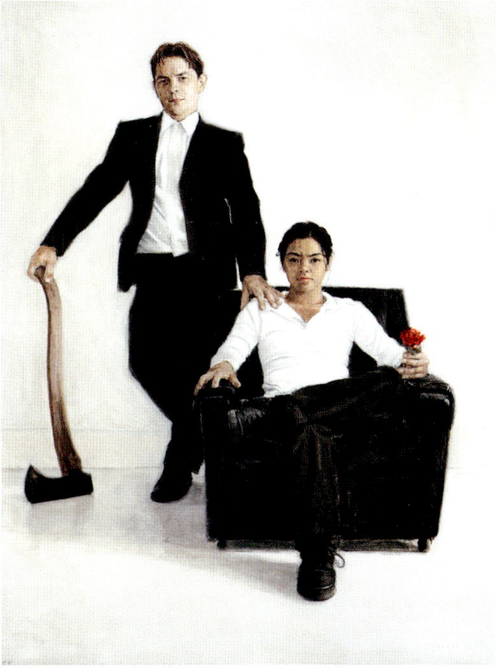

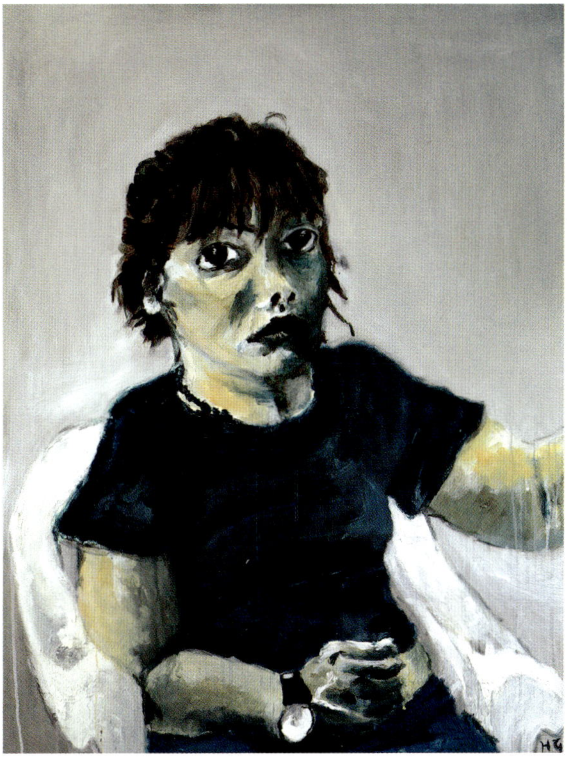

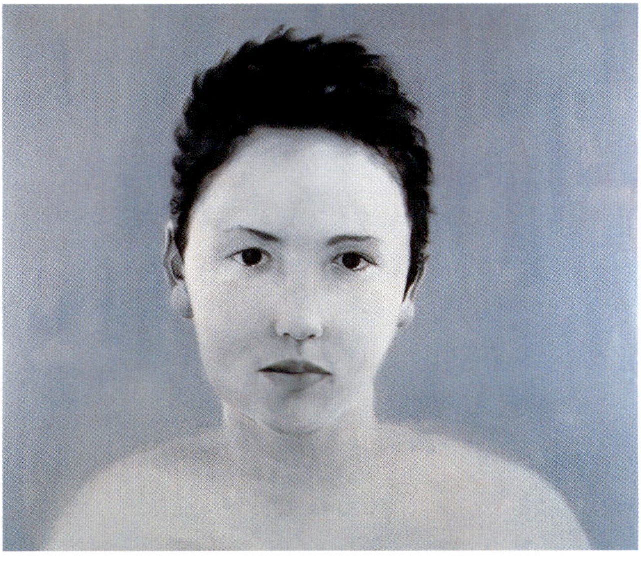

Reaching for Bottles
Toby Hunt
Oil on canvas
950 x 900mm

Molly
Josie Jammet
Acrylic on board
350 x 250mm

Pictures of Lily
Sadie Lee
Oil on canvas
1010 x 455mm

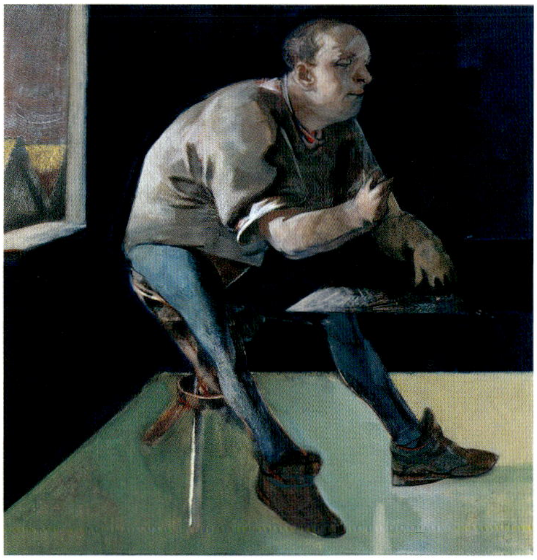

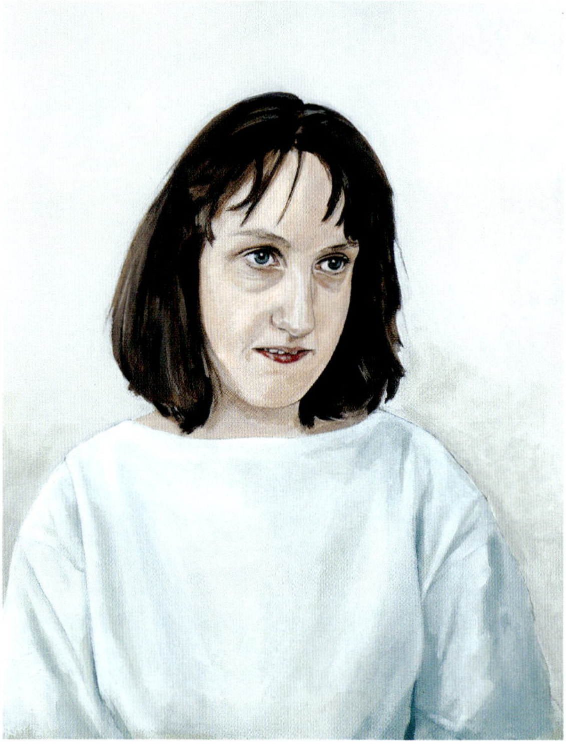

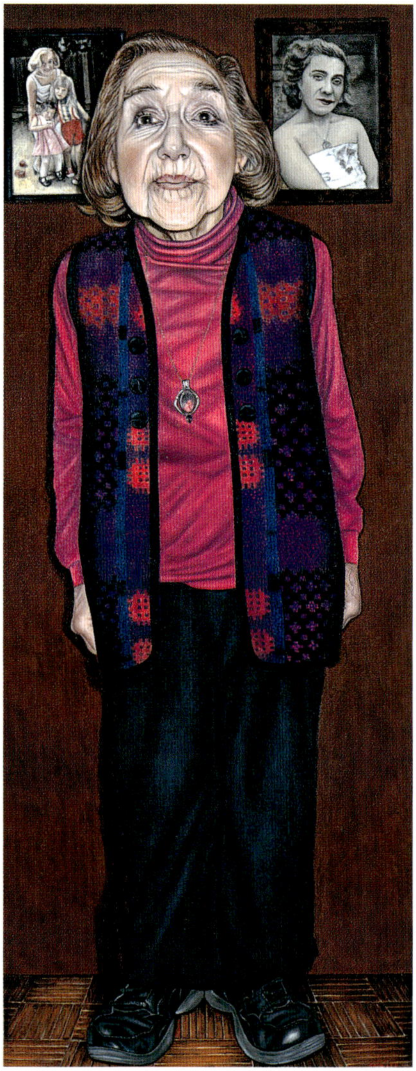

Marco Polo's Responsibility
Diana Leslie
Oil on canvas
980 x 850mm

Windows to the Soul
Brian Love
Oil on linen
590 x 510mm

Mick Lovley
Oliver Lovley
Acrylic on canvas
1016 x 813mm

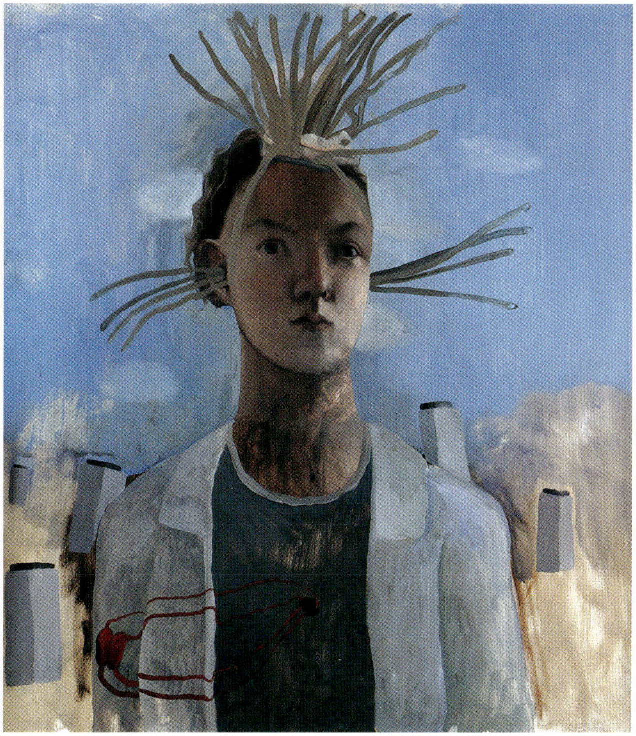

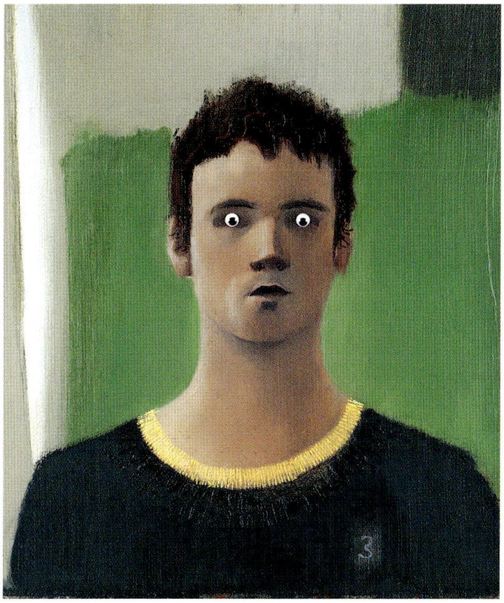

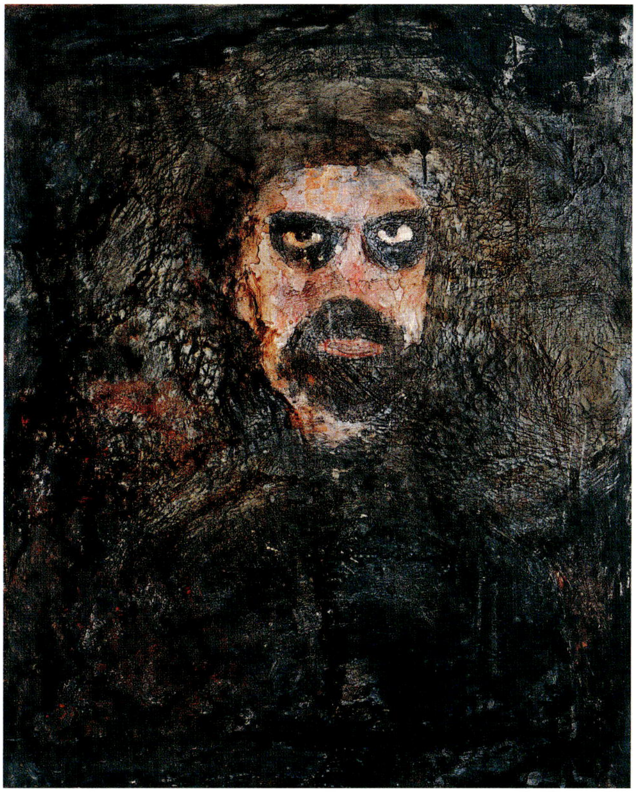

Mug Shot
Catherine MacDiarmid
Oil on canvas
560 x 560mm

This Strange New Fellow
Fergus Mayhew
Oil on board
950 x 840mm

Paint it Black
Sarah McConkey
Oil on canvas
715 x 715mm

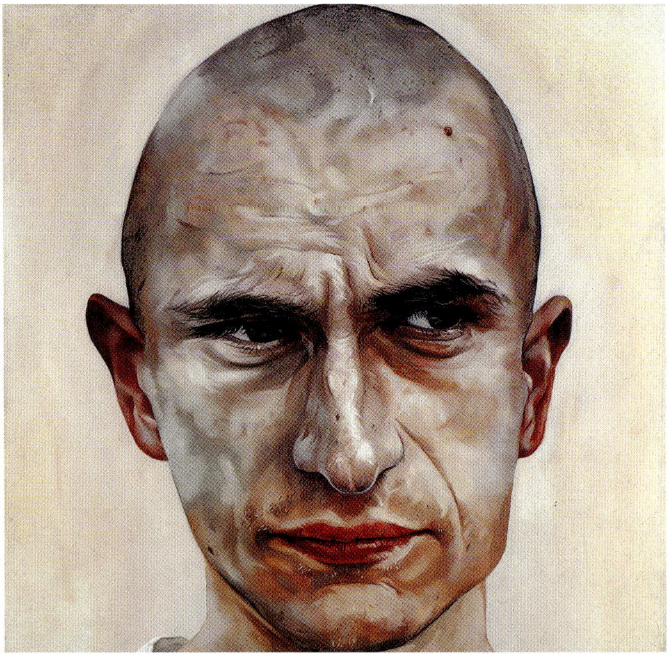

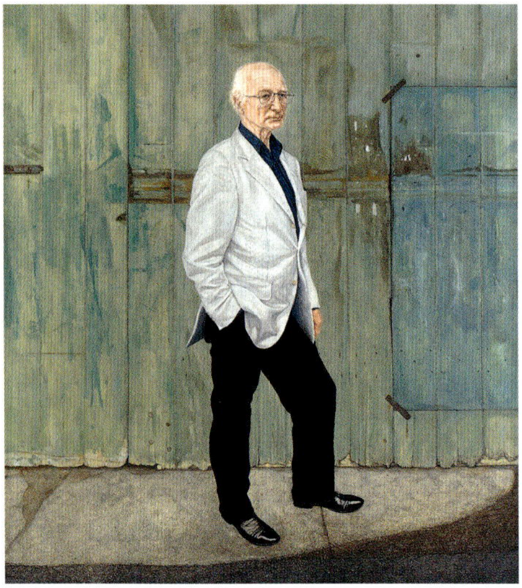

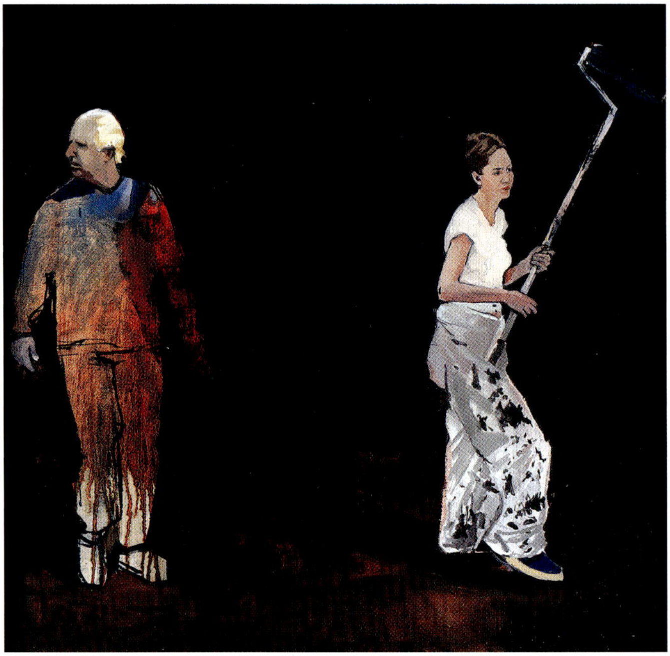

Self-portrait
Susan McFarlane
Oil on canvas
280 x 280mm

Eleonora M
Anastassios Missouras
Oil on board
691 x 673mm

Ilonatic
Ilona Niemi
Oil and mixed media
on board
600 x 400mm

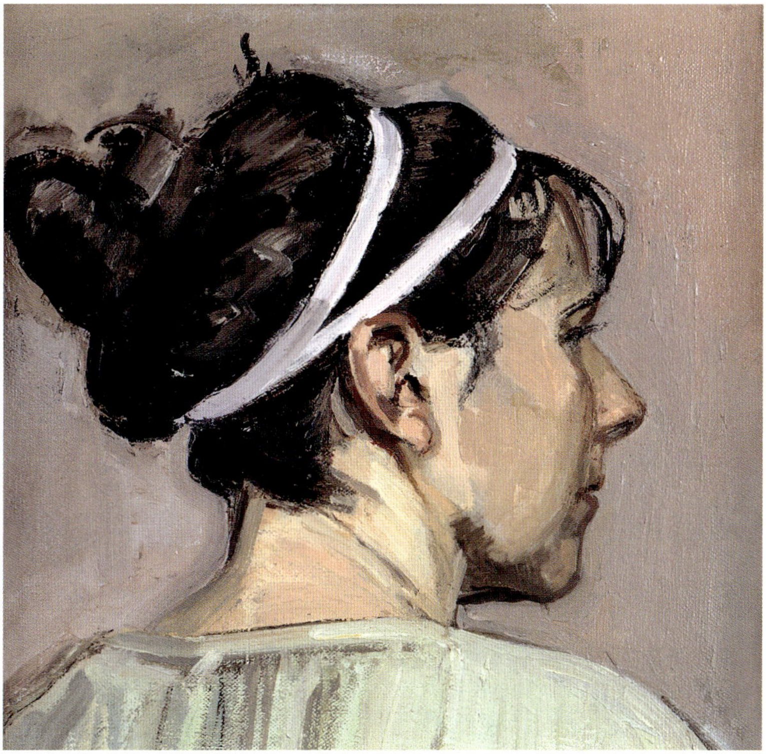

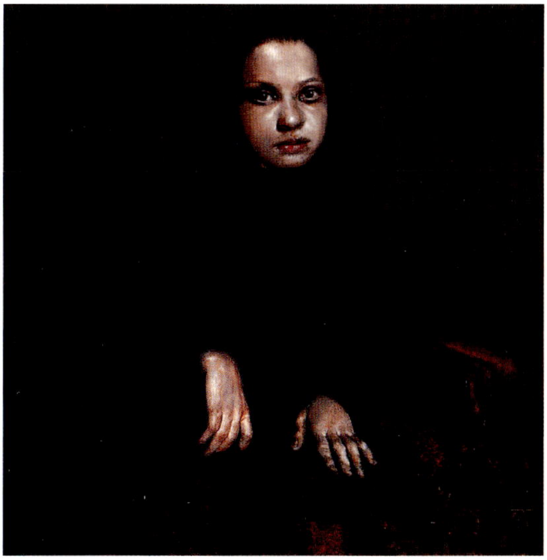

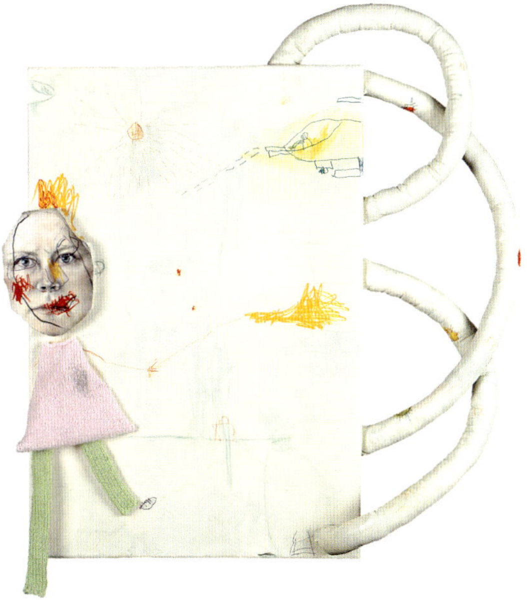

Jeggs
Adrian O'Donnell
Oil on canvas
855 x 700mm

Triptych
Carl Randall
Oil on canvas
250 x 457mm

Double Portrait with Small Bones
Daisy Richardson
Oil on canvas
612 x 612mm

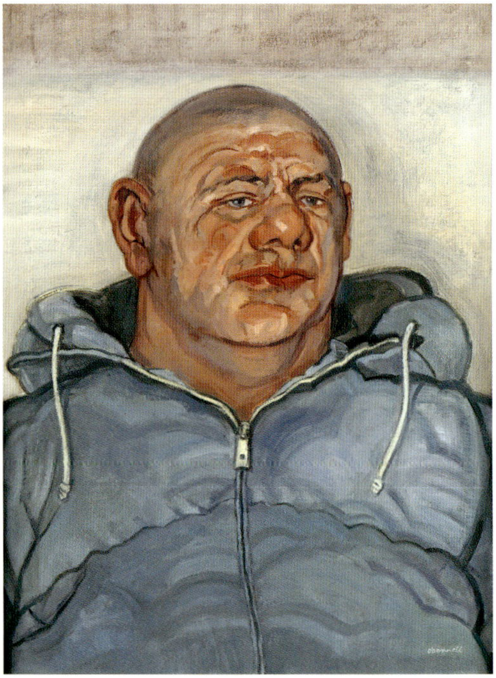

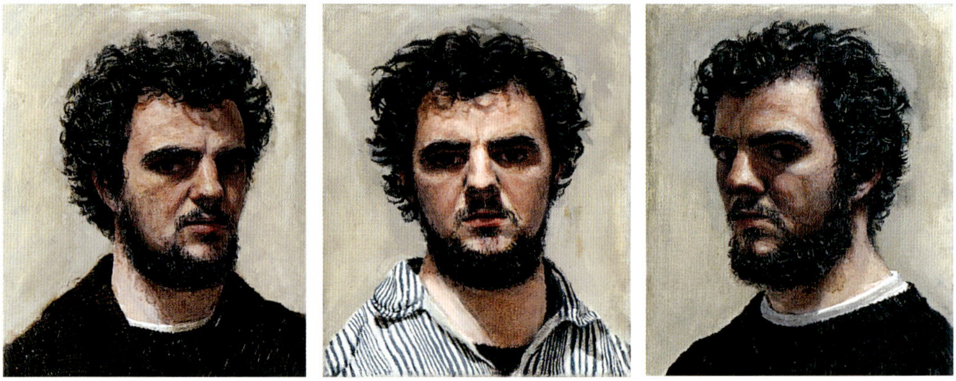

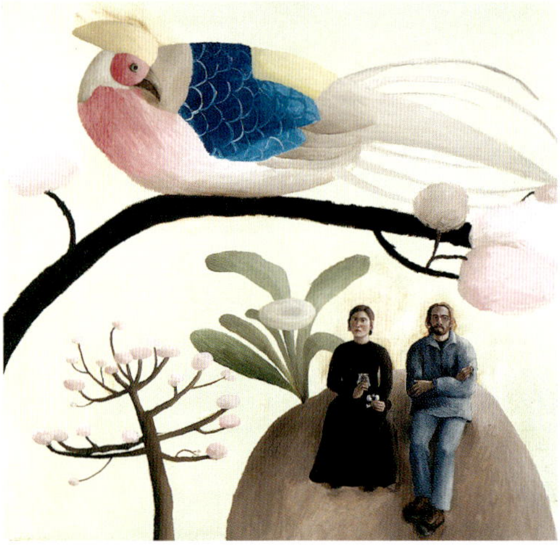

Andy Cranston
Lorna Robertson
Oil on canvas
780 x 1160mm

Royal Guard
Gideon Rubin
Oil on canvas
1930 x 915mm

Alec Leaving
Daniel Shadbolt
Oil on linen
950 x 600mm

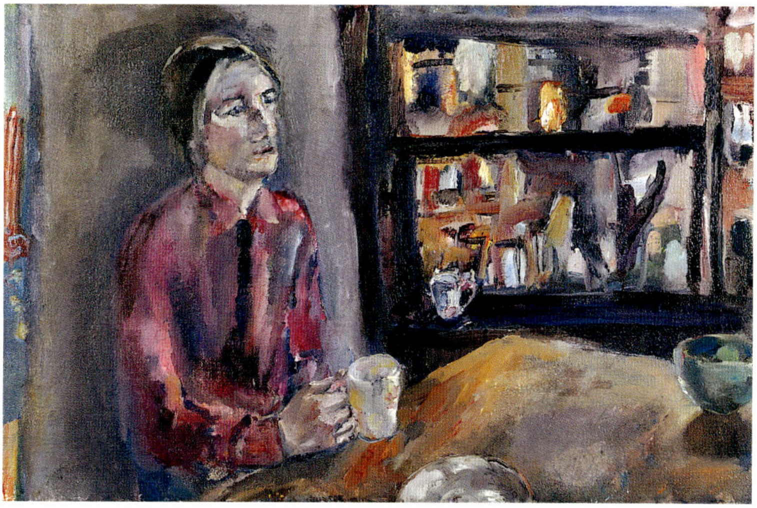

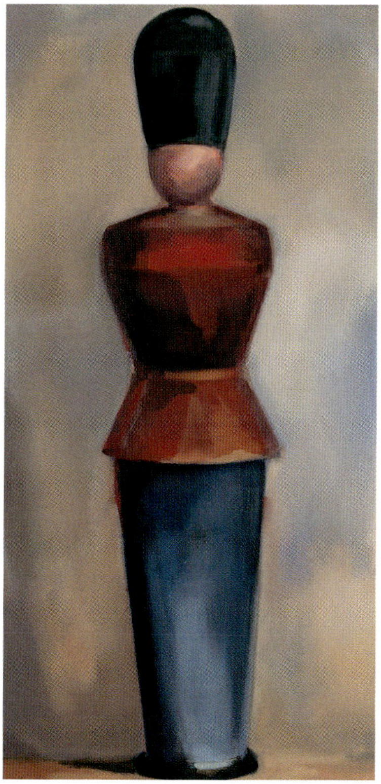

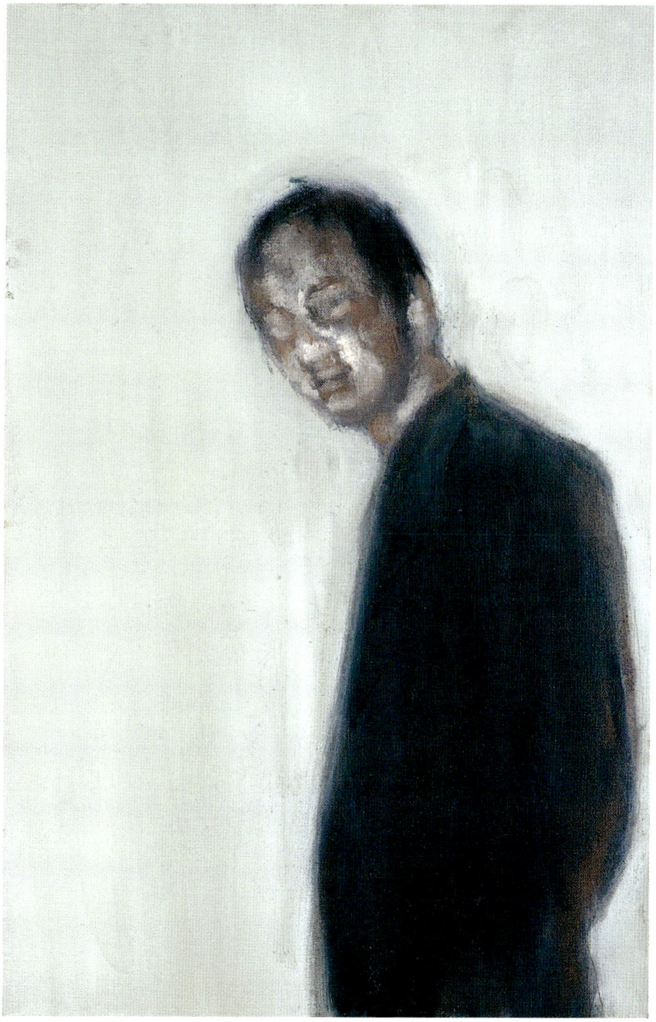

Patrick Procktor
Rupert Shrive
Oil on linen
250 x 200mm

Memento
Lisa Stokes
Oil on canvas
1050 x 940mm

Mum
Benjamin Sullivan
Oil on canvas
1180 x 880mm

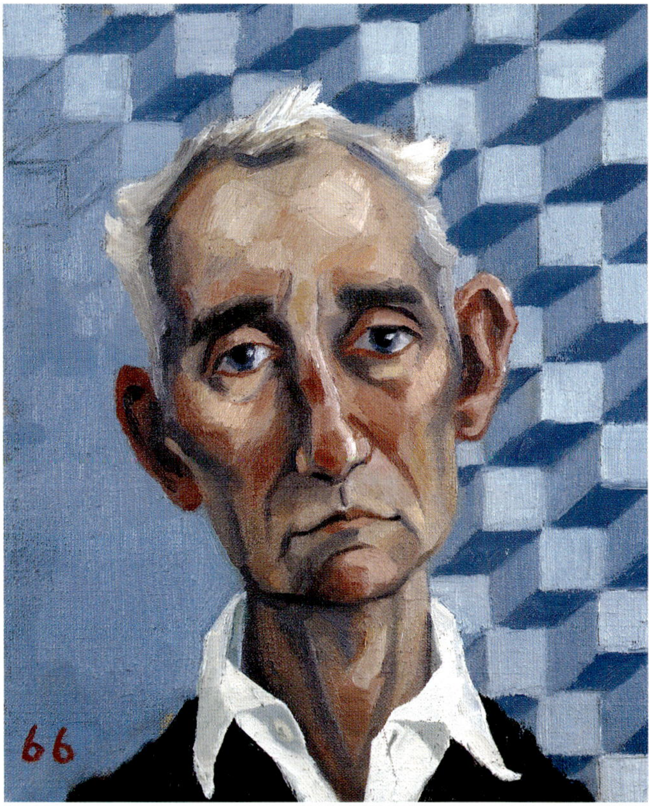

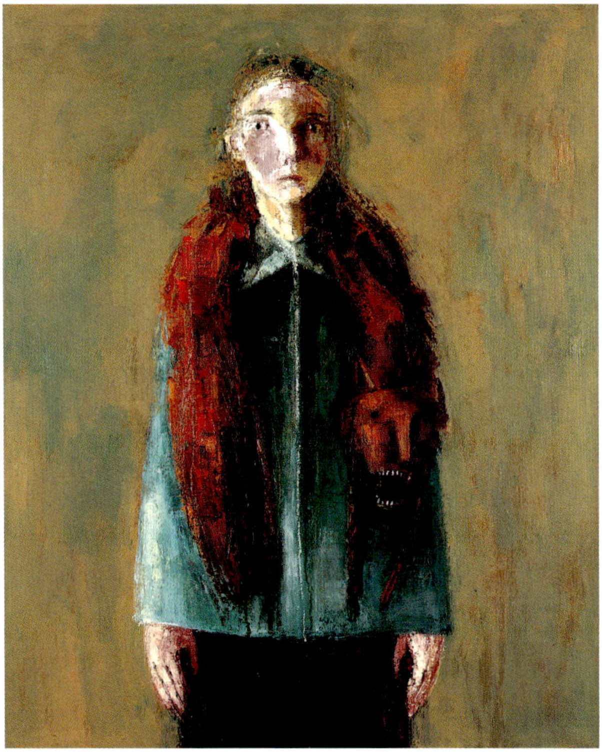

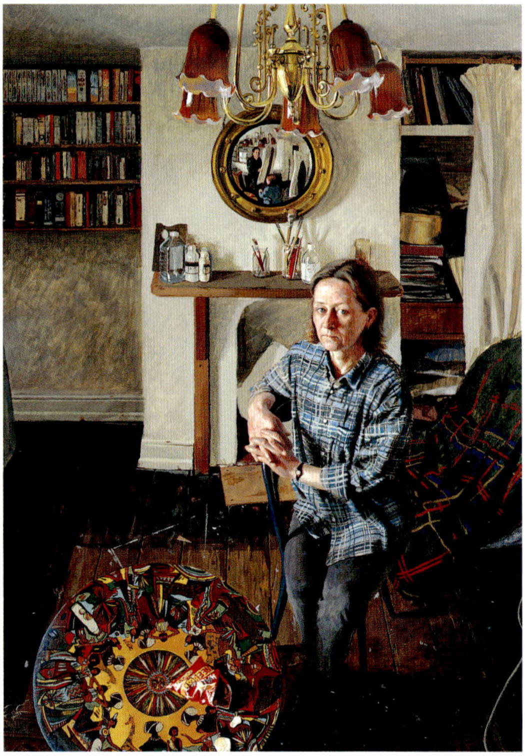

Pete Postlethwaite
Christopher Thompson
Oil on canvas
1380 x 1080mm

Lilith
Stergios Tzelepis
Acrylic on canvas
665 x 570mm

Self-portrait
Jessica Wolfson
Oil on canvas
450 x 400mm

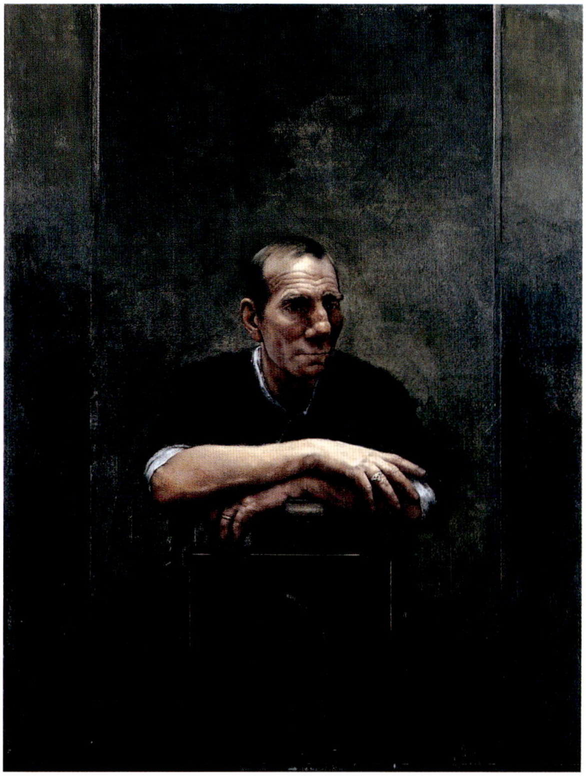

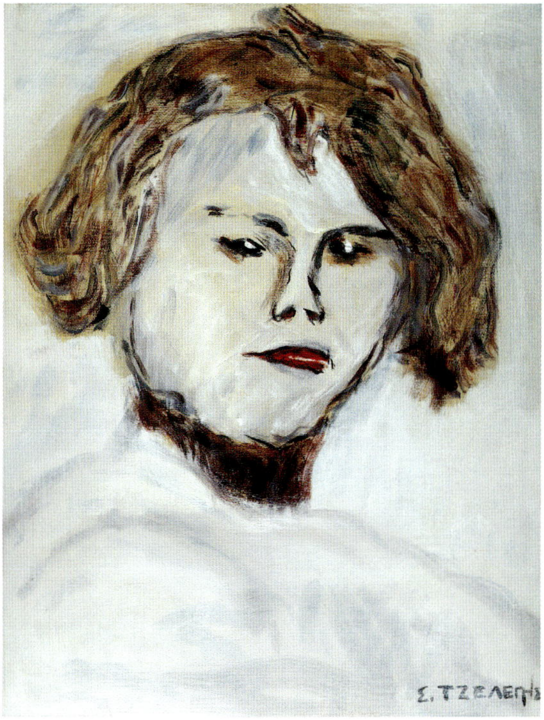

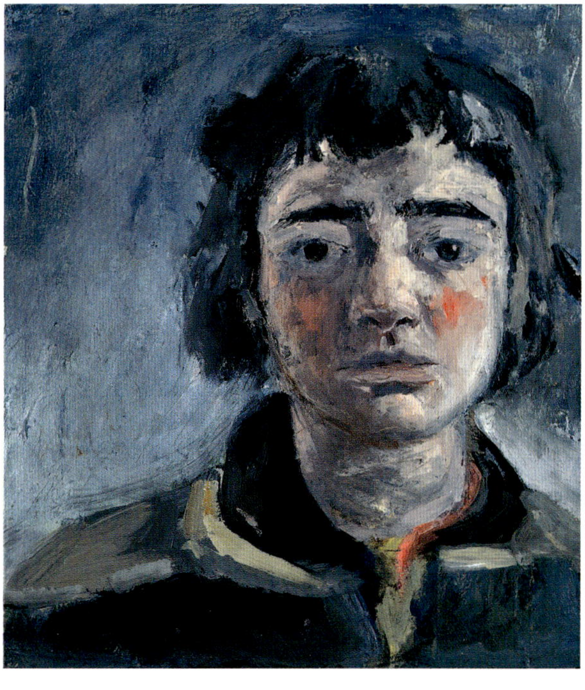

2003

ARTISTS WHOSE PORTRAITS WERE EXHIBITED

Jackie Anderson / Daniel Barry / Graeme Brooks / David Caldwell / Darren Coffield / R.A. Combes / Mark Cook / Gabriel Corcuera-Zubillaga / Kevin M.A. Cunningham / Samuel Dalby / Kelly-Anne Davitt / Paul Denton / Juno Doran / Joe Fan / Graham Flack / Frank Föckler / Michael Gaskell / Vasiliki Gkotsi / Mitch Griffiths / Ulyana Gumeniuk / Phil Hale / Caspar Hall / Jaemi Hardy / Charlotte Harris / Craig Hawker / Laurence Kell / Brendan Kelly / Matthew Usmar Lauder / Josie McCoy / Jane MacNeill / Dean Marsh / Tim Millen / Peter Monkman / Nanne Nyander / Yuka Omura / Anna Hyunsook Paik / Anne-Laure Ponsin / Emily Porter-Salmon / Michael Roberts / Laura Sian Russell / Kim Scouller / Blaise Smith / Lorna Wadsworth / Jason Walker / Emma Wesley / Ian Whitfield / Toby Wiggins / John Worthington / Cindy Wright / Victoria Wright / Paul Wuensche

SECOND PRIZE
NOURA
MICHAEL GASKELL

Tempera on board
450 x 380mm

Sheffield-born artist Michael Gaskell studied at St Helens College of Art and Design, and Coventry Polytechnic. At the time of this painting of Noura Sakaff, Gaskell had already been exhibiting his work for over fifteen years and had won a number of prizes in international painting competitions. He went on to win Second Prize in the BP Portrait Award twice more, in 2009 and 2010. Working in egg tempera, Gaskell has said that he aims to achieve heightened realism in his paintings, whilst conveying a sense of stillness and contemplation.

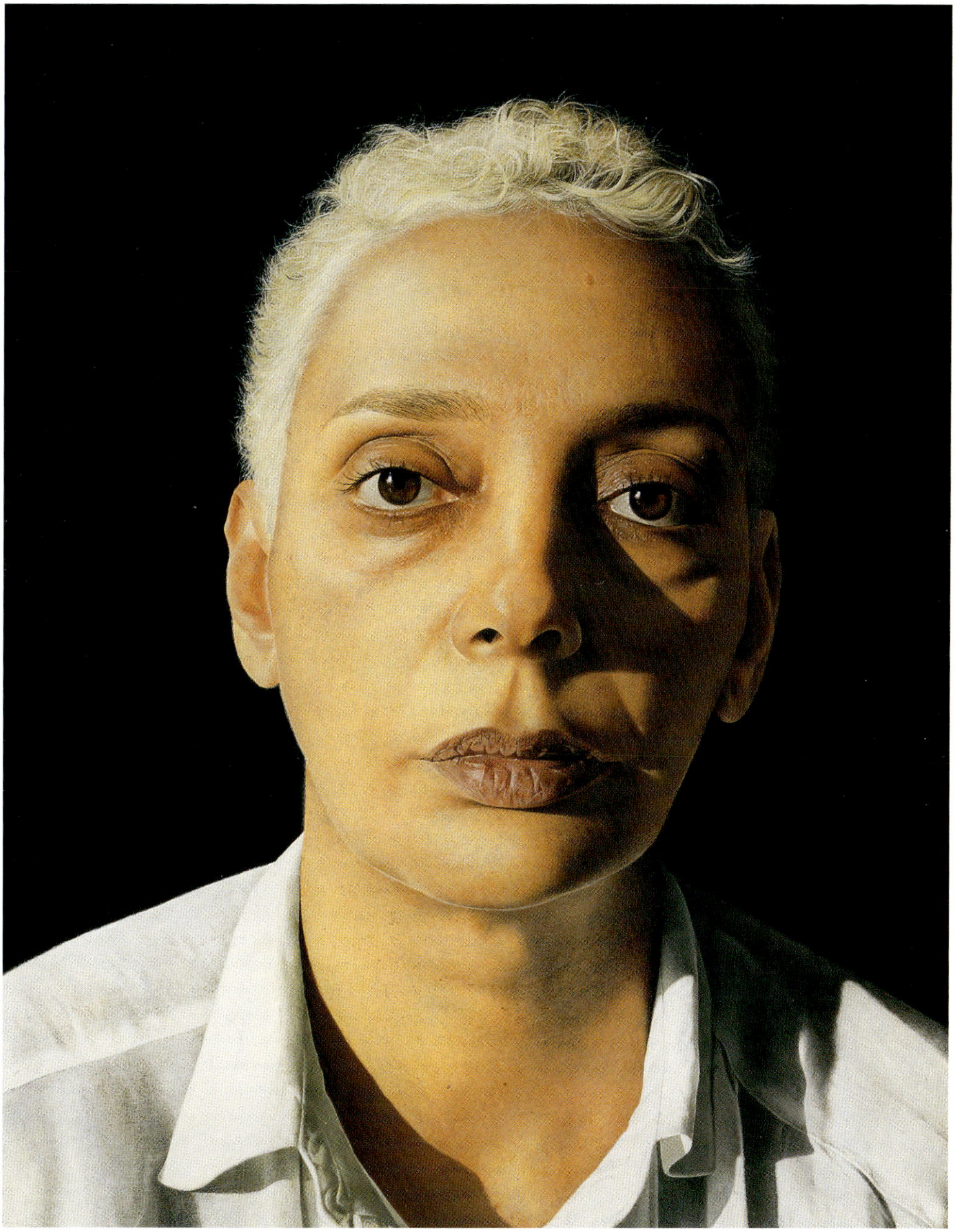

THIRD PRIZE
ELLIOT II
GRAHAM FLACK

Oil on canvas
1560 x 1560mm

Born in Northern Ireland, Graham Flack studied at the Edinburgh College of Art and received the Andrew Grant Postgraduate Scholarship in 2000 and 2001. The subject of this portrait is an American friend of the artist's sister, who Flack had met in Paris. Flack uses a combination of drawing and painting, and has described his interest in developing tension between the head and the space around it, which gives a sculptural strength to his portraits.

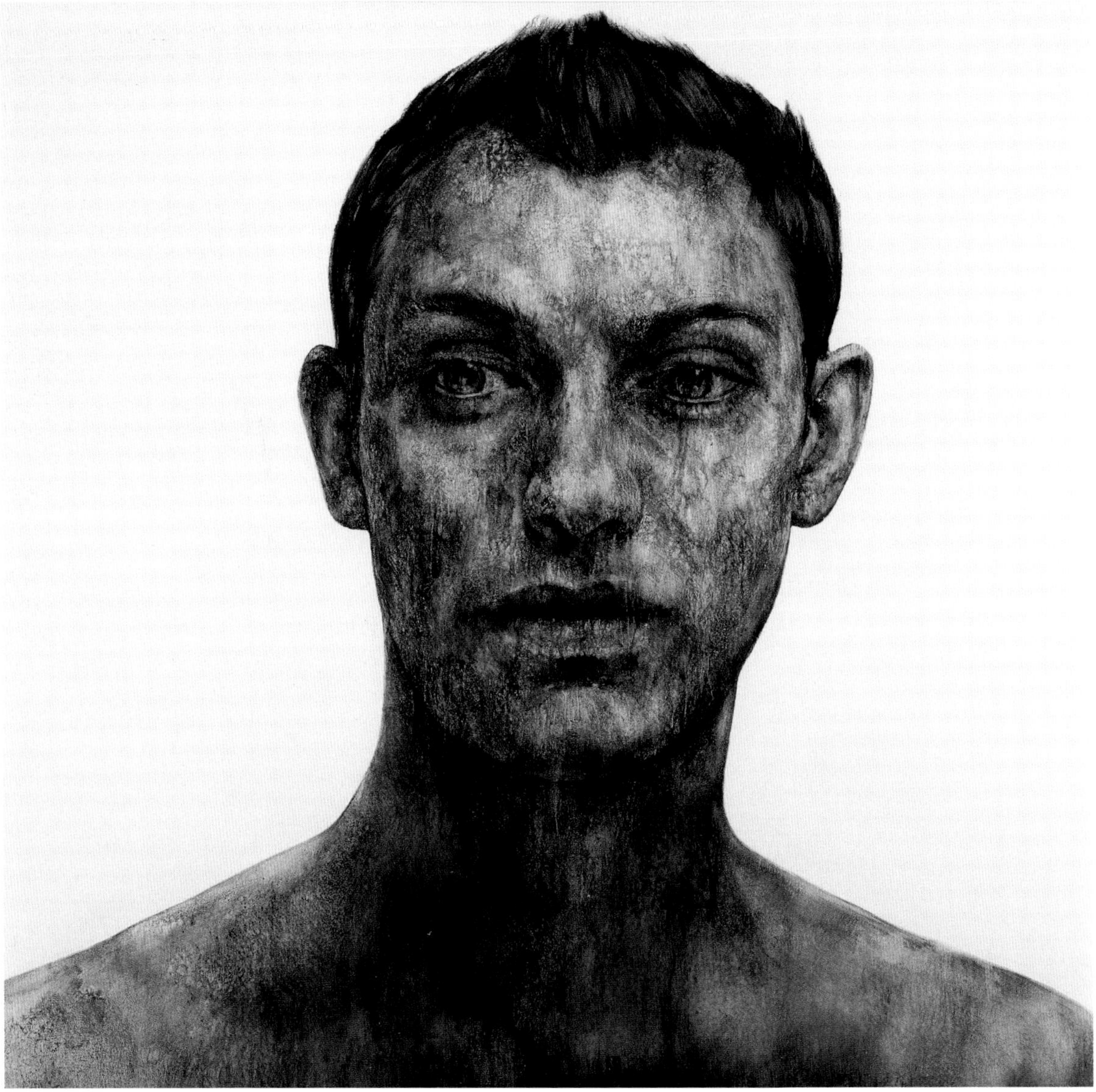

FOURTH PRIZE
MAN WITH GREY SCARF
DEAN MARSH

Oil on board
335 x 285mm

London-based Dean Marsh studied at Ravensbourne College of Design and Communication, and has exhibited internationally. This portrait is of his former colleague John Burns. Marsh had previously exhibited a portrait of Dame Rosalind Savill, Director of the Wallace Collection, at the BP Portrait Award in 2002 and went on to win First Prize in 2005.

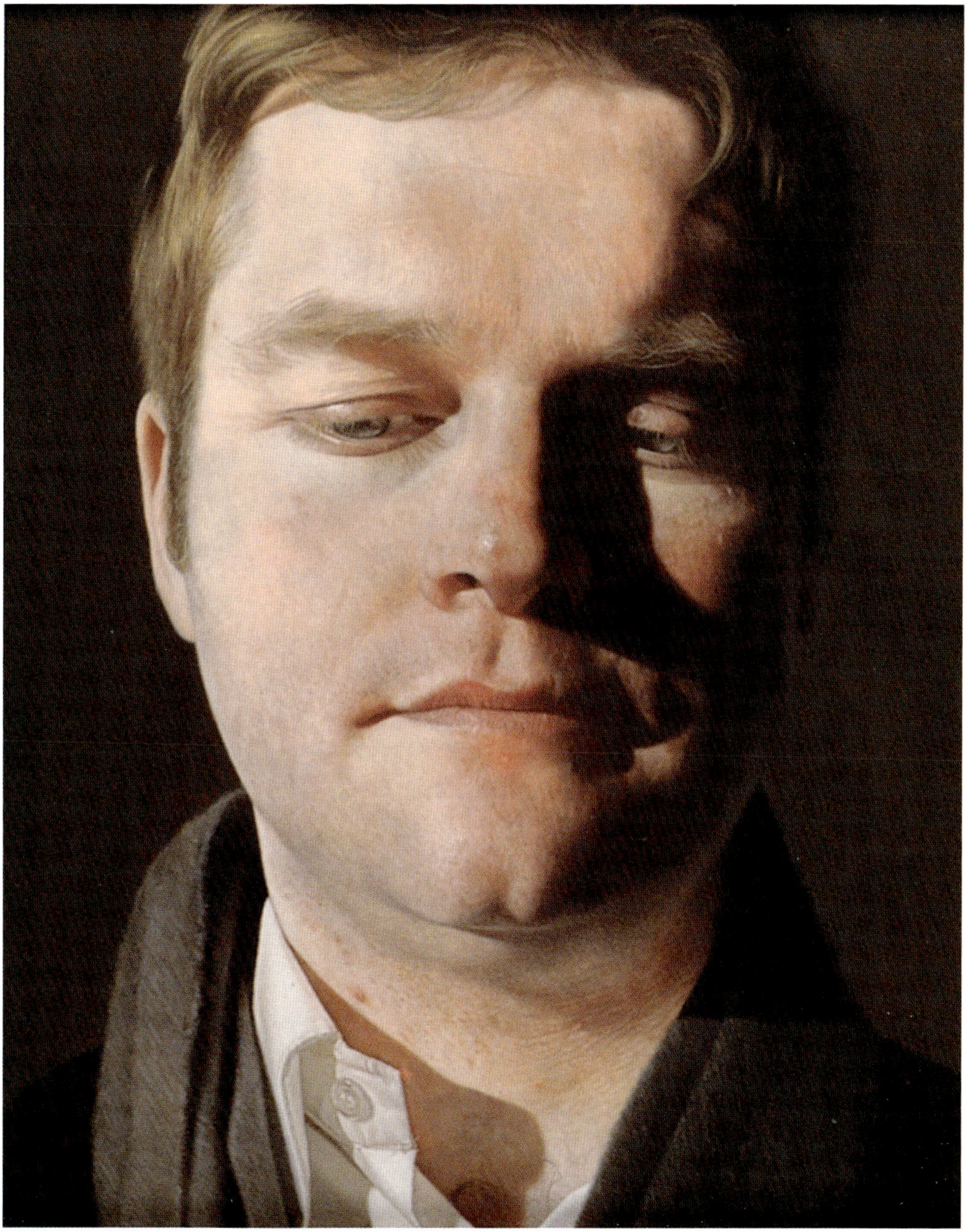

Kyle's Reflection
Jackie Anderson
Oil on canvas
1070 x 905mm

Portrait of my Father
Daniel Barry
Oil on board
400 x 349mm

Frank/Alice
Graeme Brooks
Oil on canvas
1884 x 1348mm

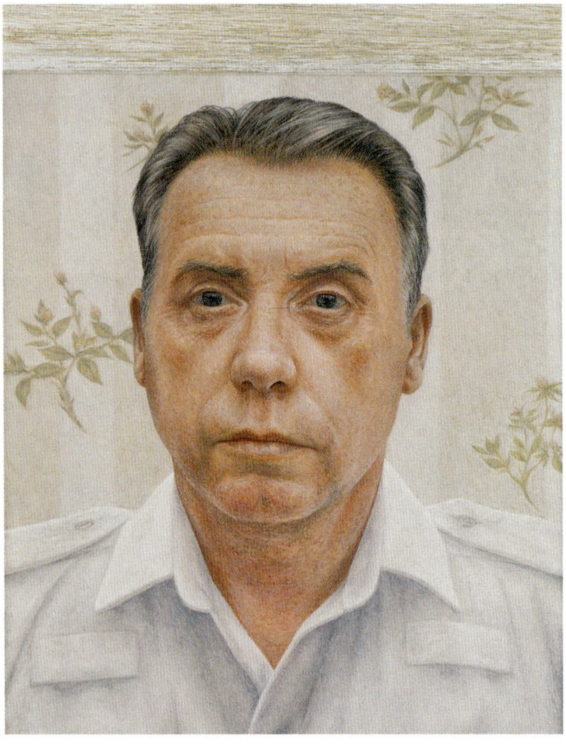

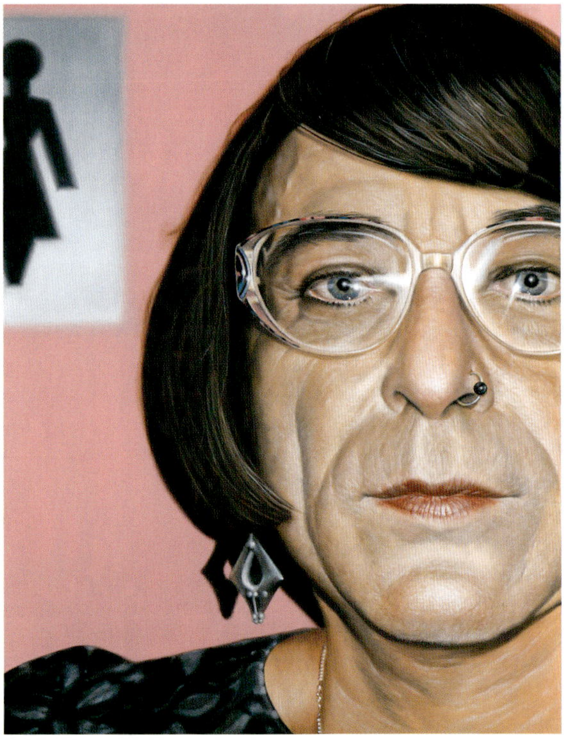

Self-portrait
David Caldwell
Oil on canvas
540 x 500mm

Untitled
(Portrait of Ivan Massow)
Darren Coffield
Acrylic on linen
1530 x 1230mm

Craig leaving Studio
R.A. Combes
Oil on canvas
1415 x 1160mm

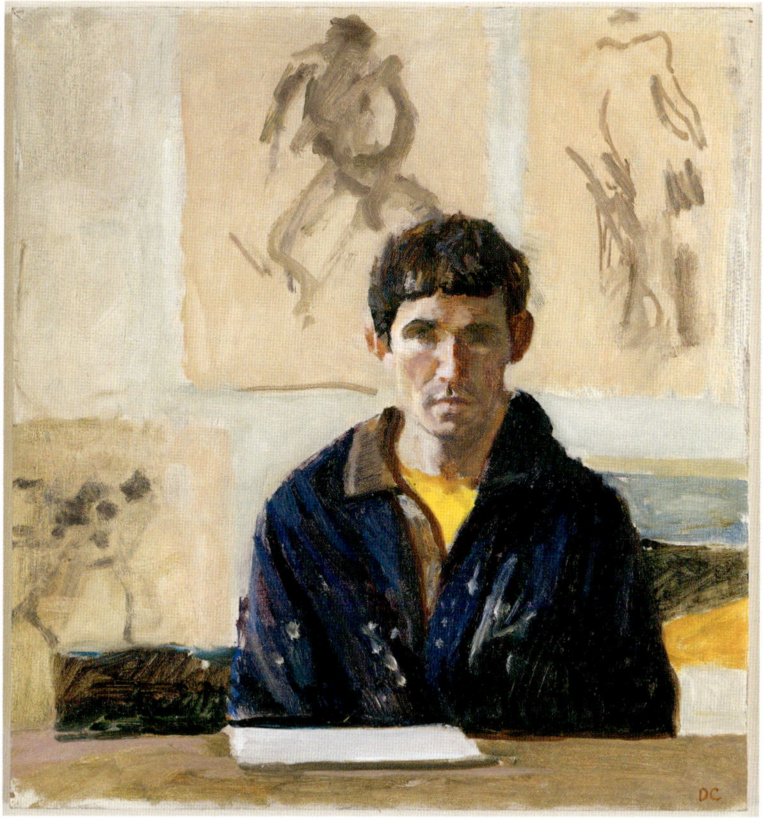

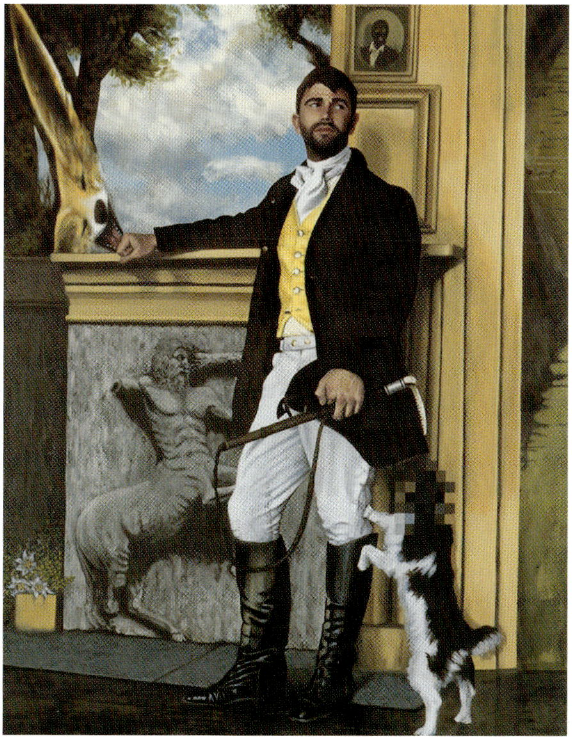

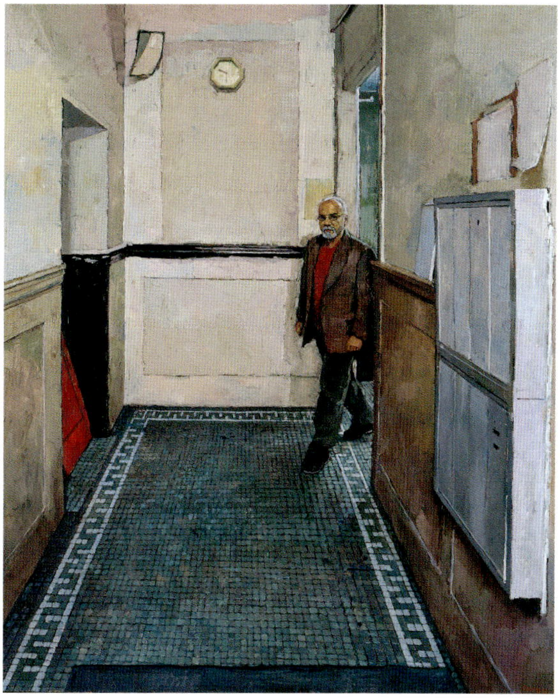

Female Line
Mark Cook
Oil on board
1015 x 1320mm

Self-portrait
Gabriel Corcuera-Zubillaga
Oil and acrylic on canvas
410 x 405mm

Self-portrait
Samuel Dalby
Oil on canvas
635 x 532mm

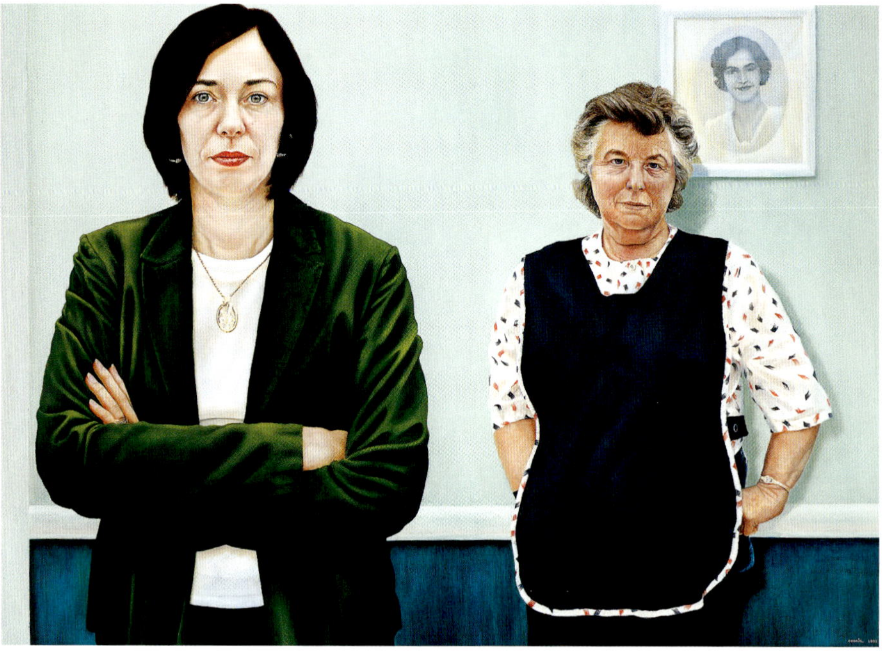

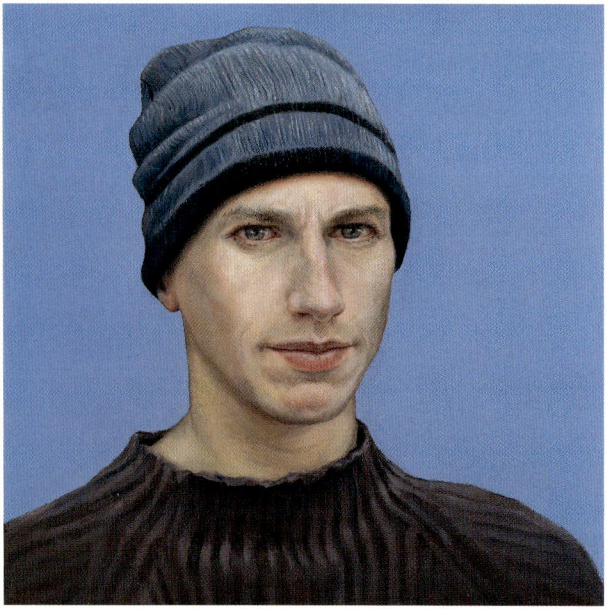

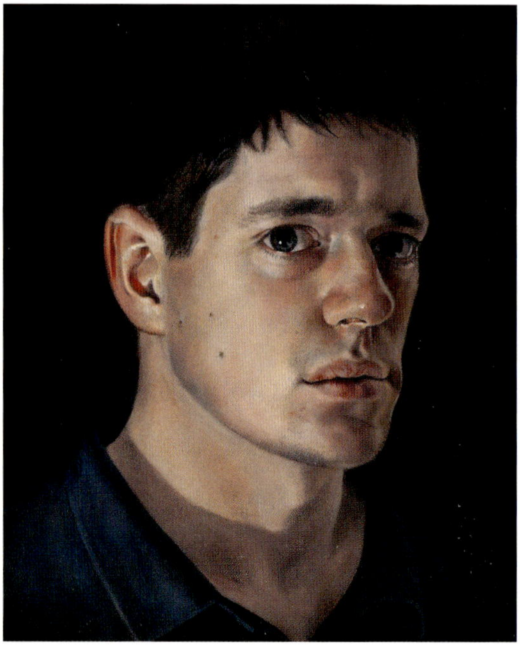

Kate
Paul Denton
Oil on canvas
1000 x 1100mm

Self-portrait
Kelly-Anne Davitt
Oil on canvas
1200 x 900mm

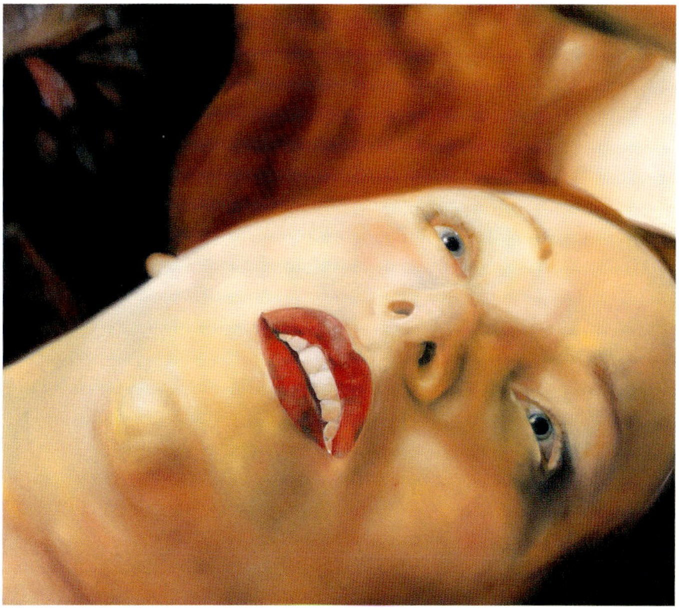

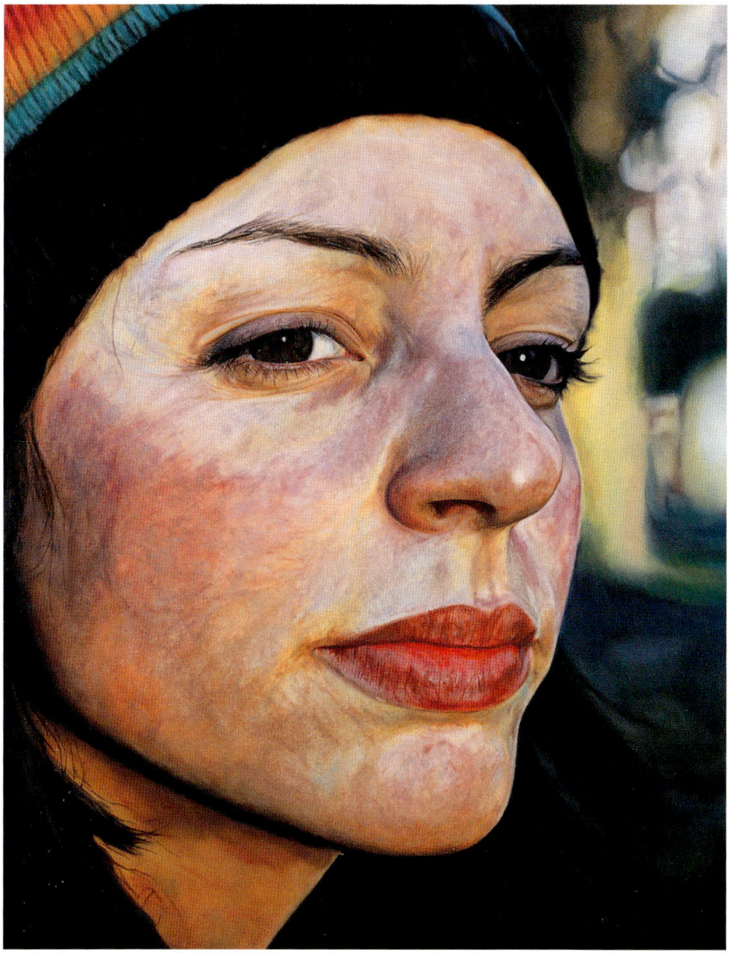

#4 (Self-portrait after a Week's Sleep Deprivation Finishing a Painting for the BP Award)
Juno Doran
Oil on canvas
1840 x 1220mm

Maisy
Joe Fan
Oil on canvas
1600 x 1370mm

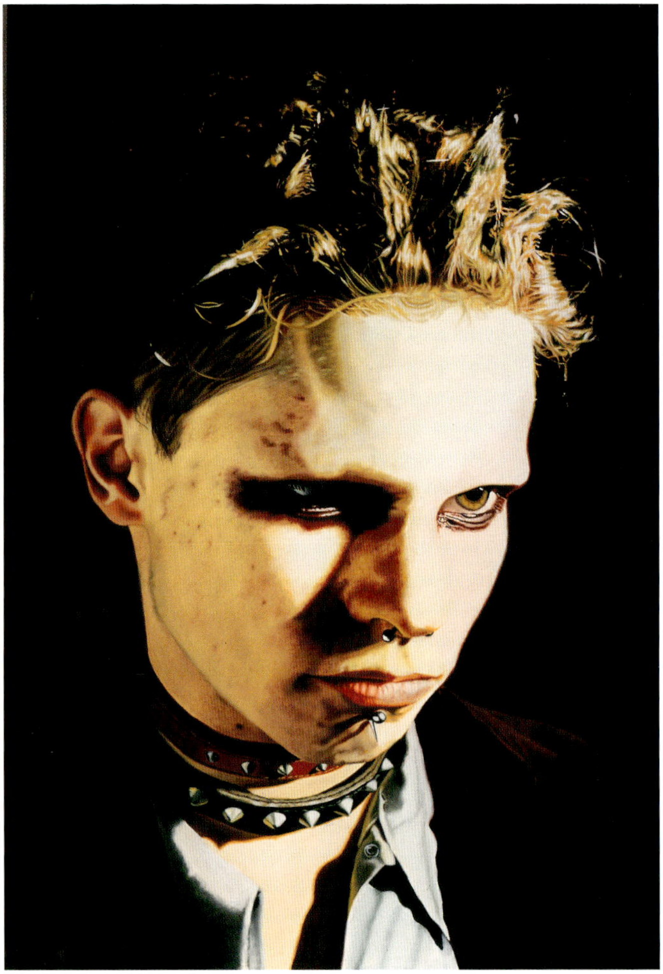

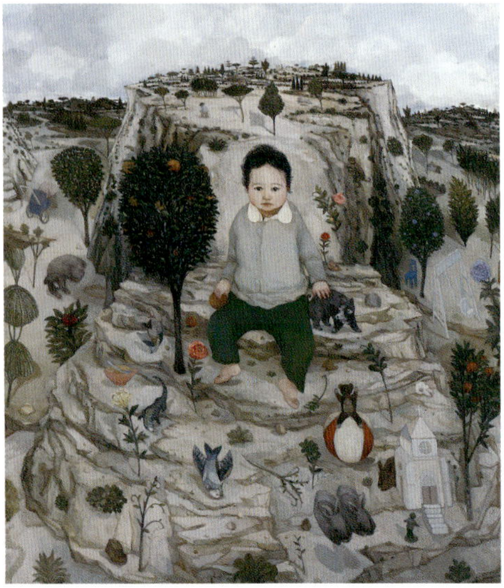

Peter
Frank Föckler
Acrylic on canvas
1100 x 1250mm

Freddy
Ulyana Gumeniuk
Oil on canvas
980 x 1035mm

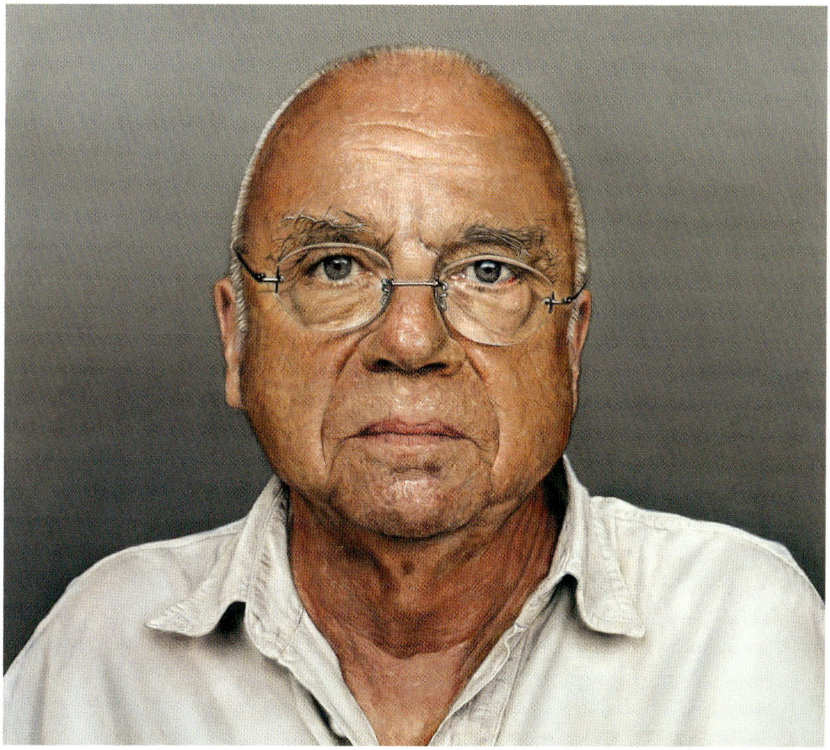

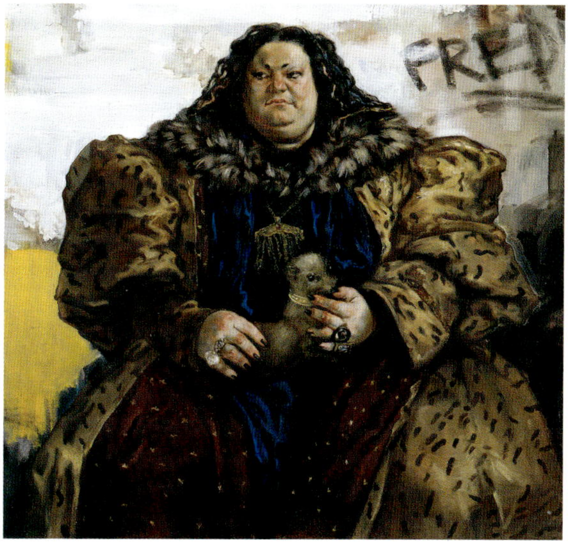

D & G (Diptych)
Caspar Hall
Oil on board
325 x 323mm each

Bête Noire
Craig Hawker
Acrylic on board
430 x 730mm

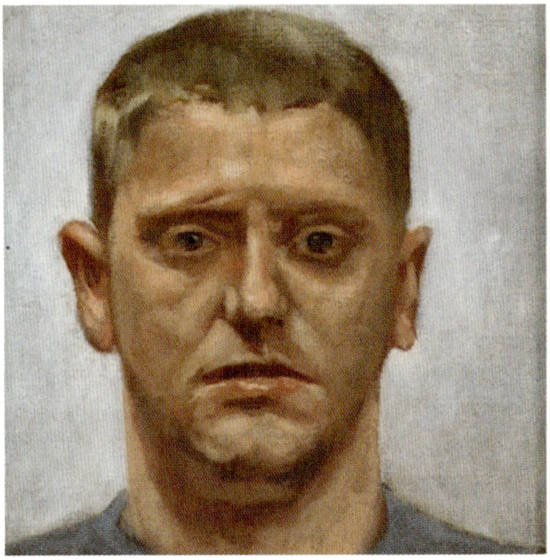

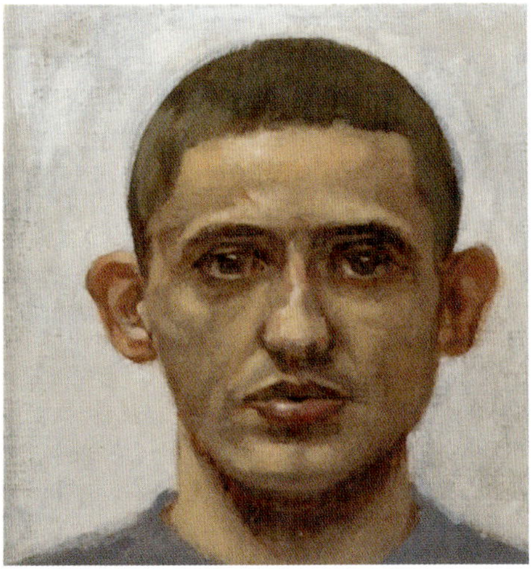

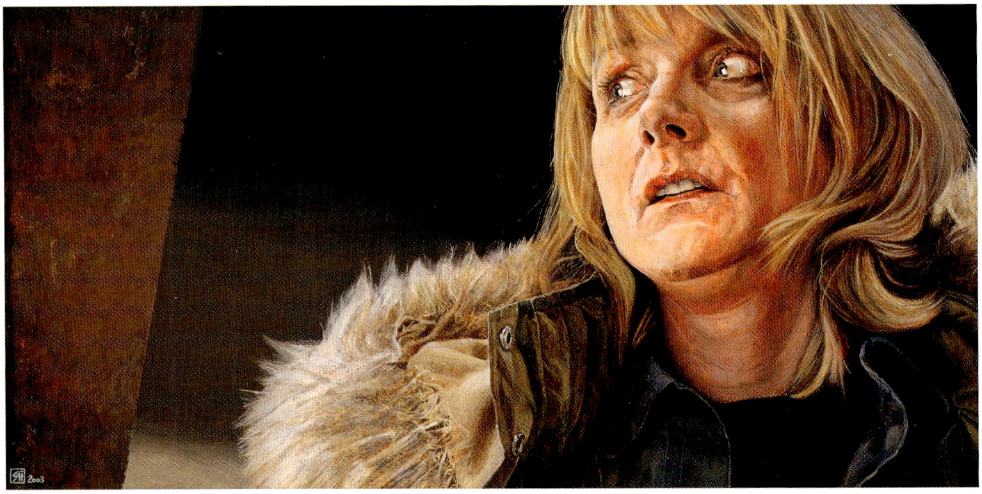

Andrew the Chef
Laurence Kell
Acrylic on board
590 x 600mm

Untitled
(Tom Conran)
Matthew Usmar Lauder
Acrylic on board
857 x 610mm

Ellen
Jane MacNeill
Oil on board
332 x 330mm

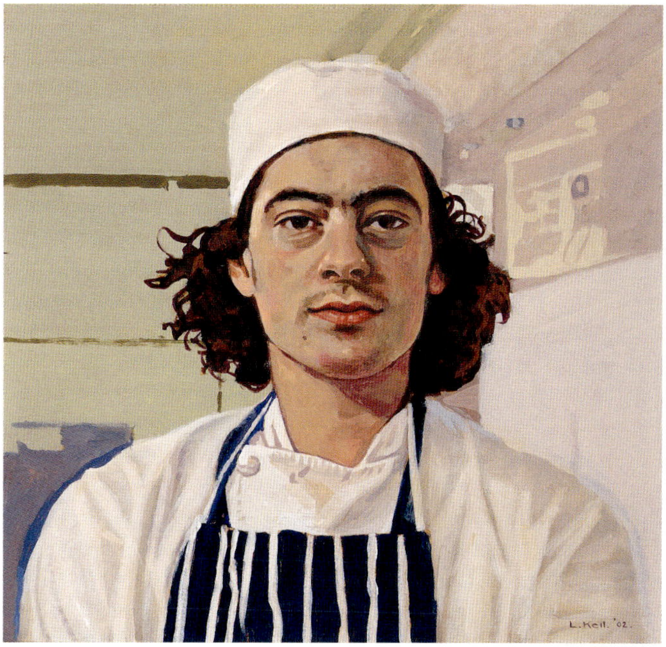

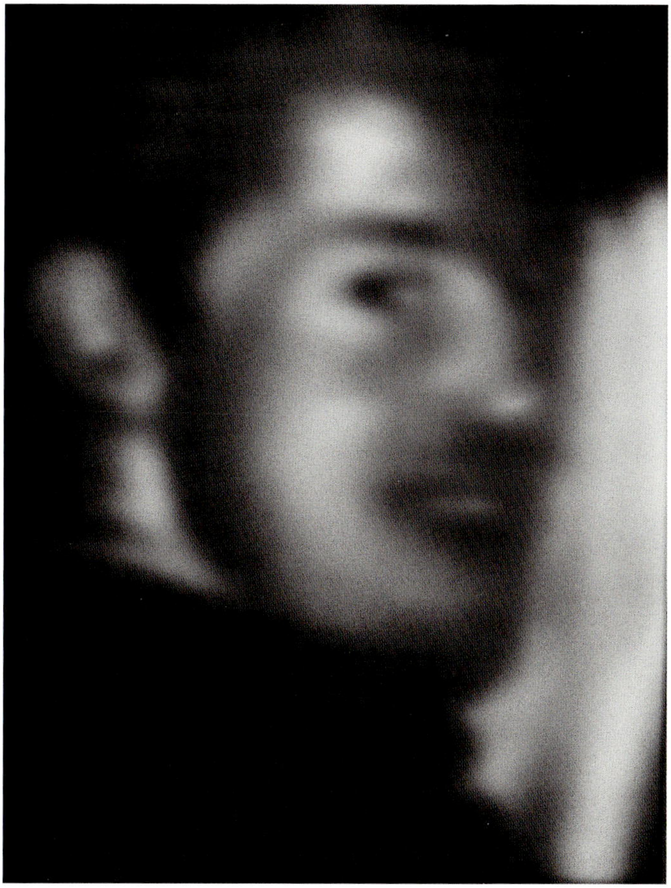

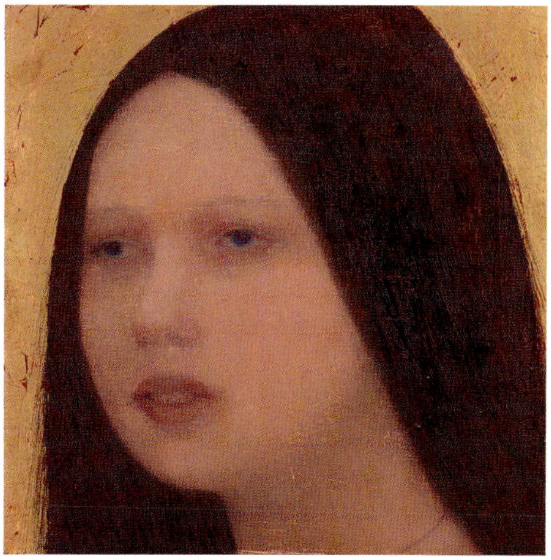

Sarah Pilmer
Josie McCoy
Oil on canvas
600 x 600mm

Below the Window
Tim Millen
Oil on canvas
549 x 488mm

Dayne: Yr. 8
(Wrenn Portrait No. 9)
Peter Monkman
Oil on canvas
310 x 258mm

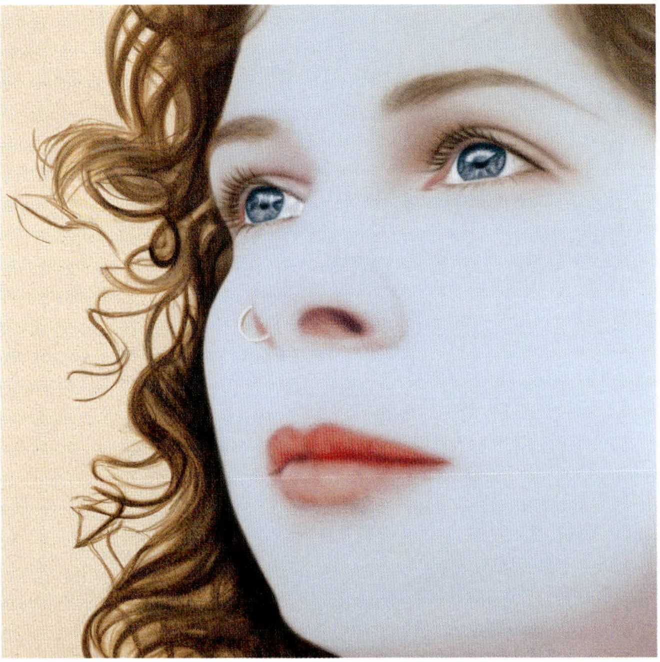

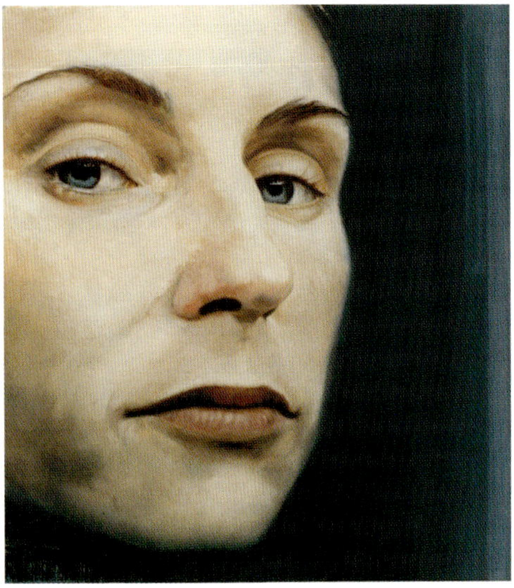

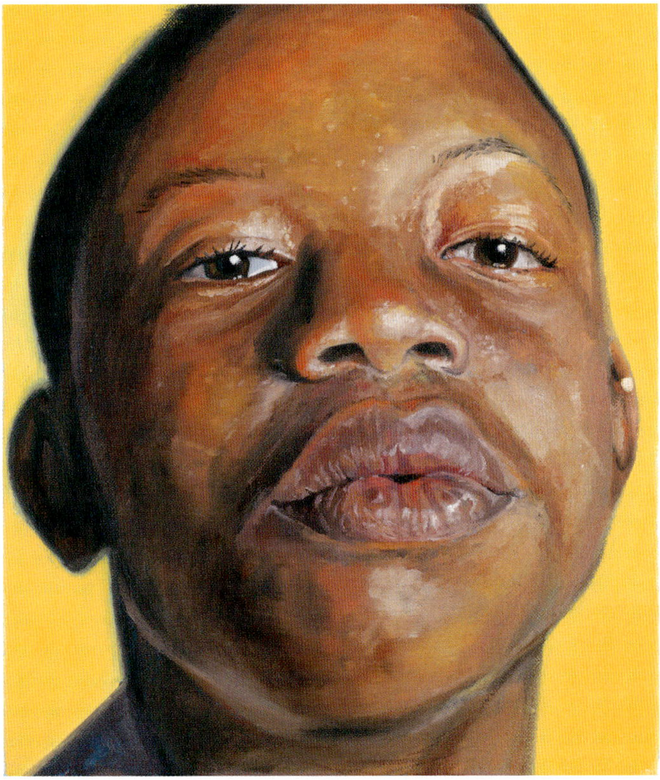

Golden Turban
Nanne Nyander
Oil on board
575 x 455mm

Self-portrait
Yuka Omura
Oil on canvas
610 x 455mm

Self-portrait
(My Inheritance)
Anna Hyunsook Paik
Oil on canvas
1070 x 970mm

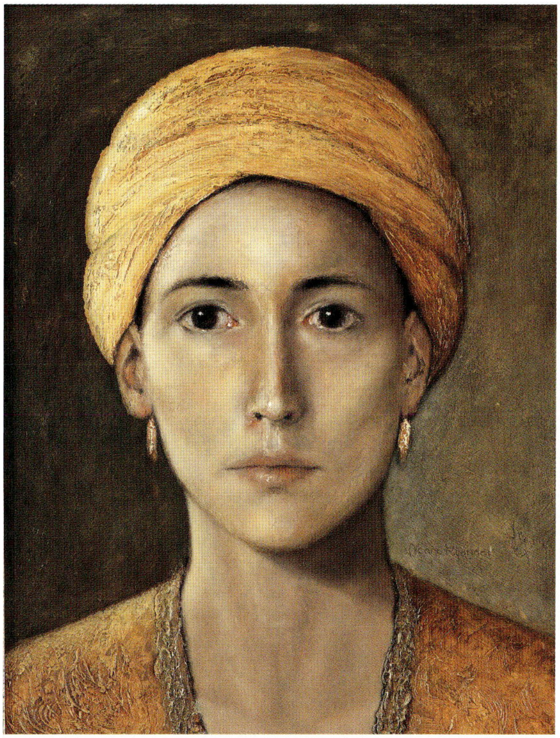

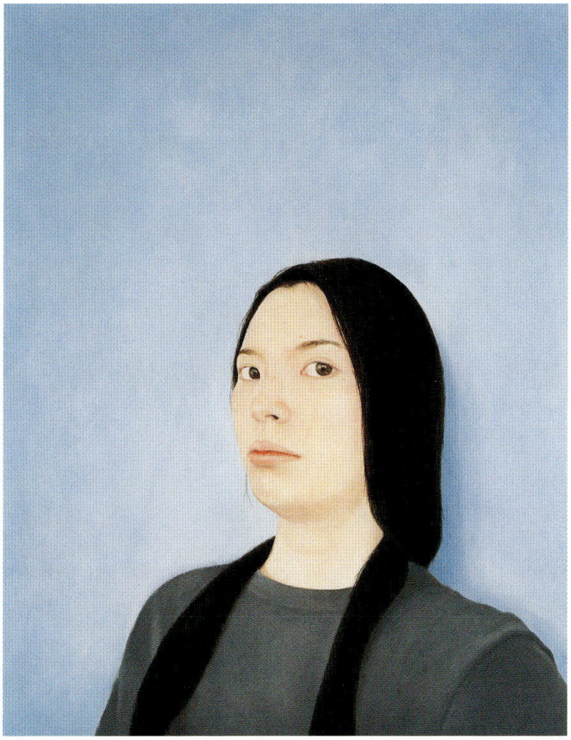

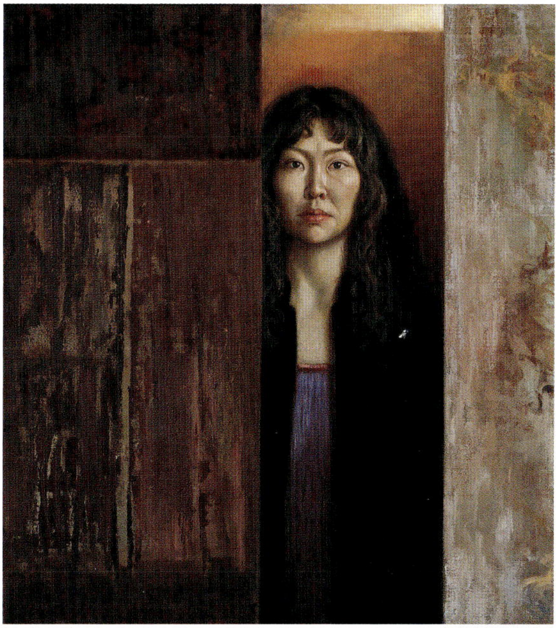

Untitled
Anne-Laure Ponsin
Acrylic on canvas
1190 x 850mm

Taffy TV
Emily Porter-Salmon
Acrylic on canvas
500 x 700mm

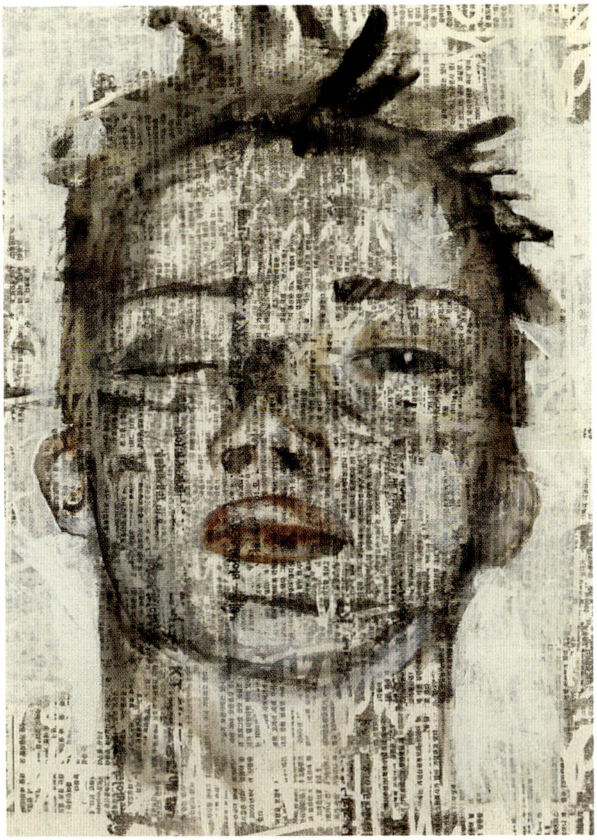

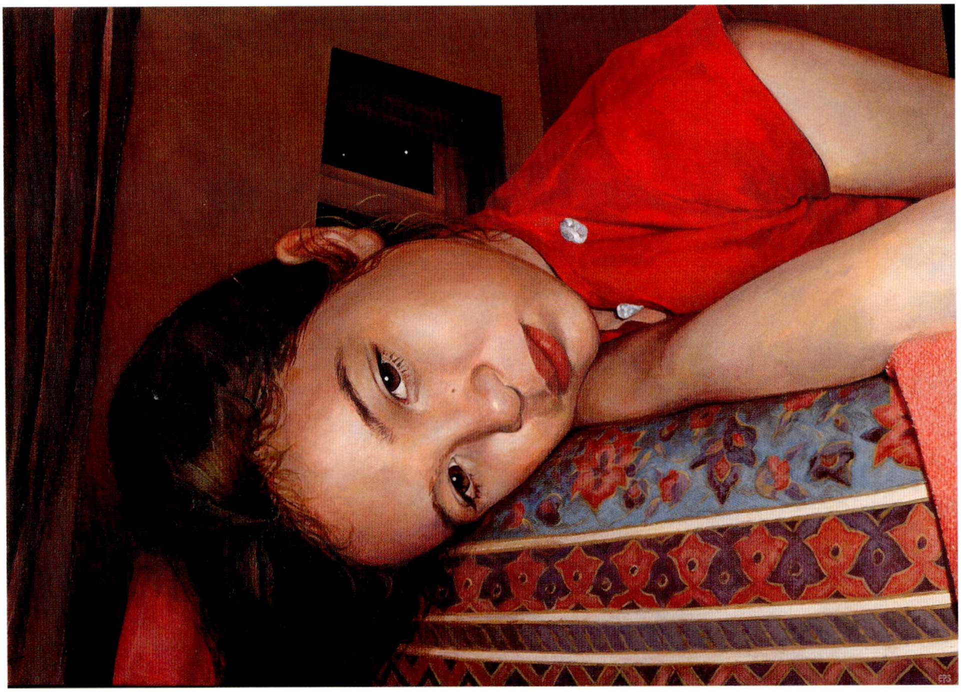

Vicky
Michael Roberts
Acrylic on canvas
1200 x 900mm

Yes
Laura Sian Russell
Acrylic on board
455 x 253mm

Eddie
Kim Scouller
Oil on board
470 x 420mm

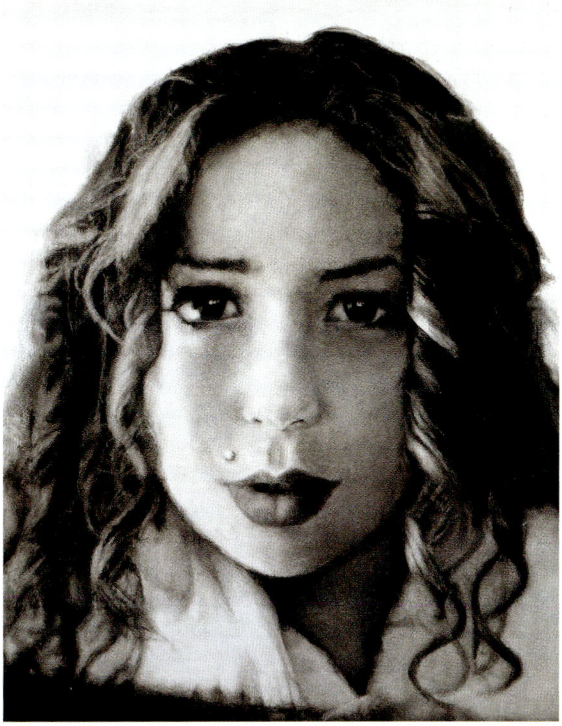

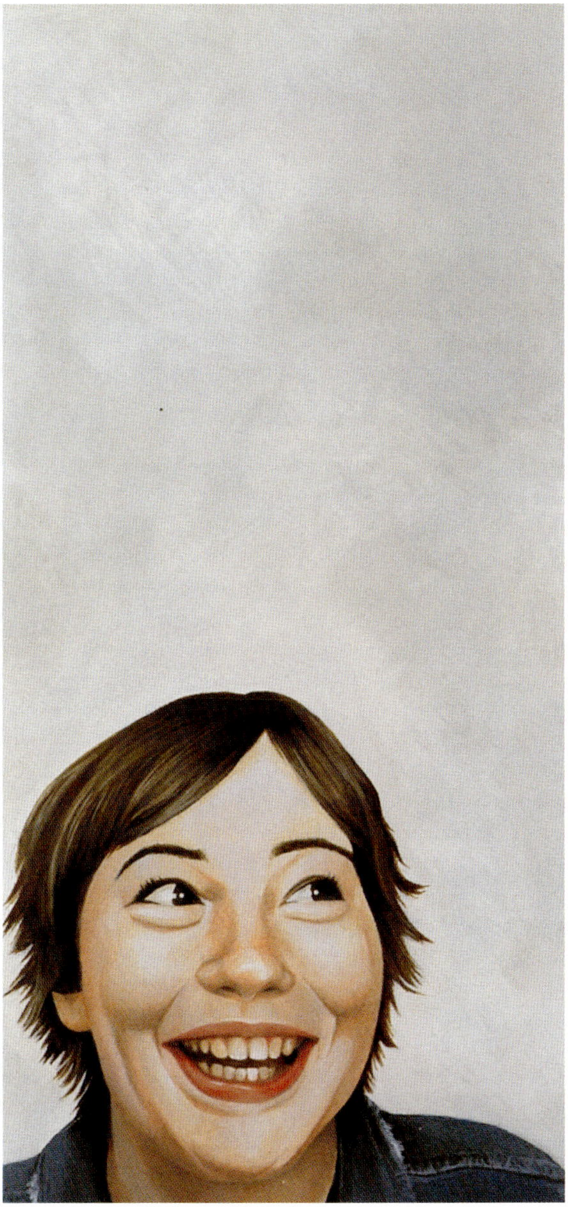

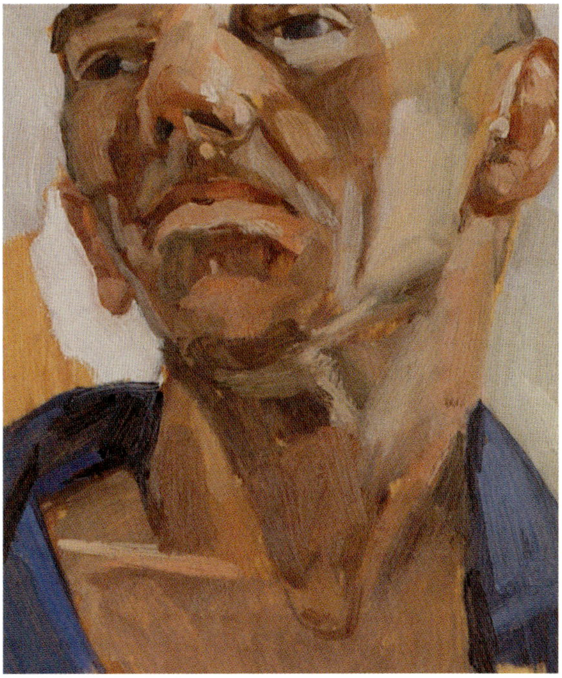

Morgan Kelly
Blaise Smith
Oil on panel
910 x 1210mm

The Rt. Hon. David Blunkett
Lorna Wadsworth
Oil on canvas
870 x 1200mm

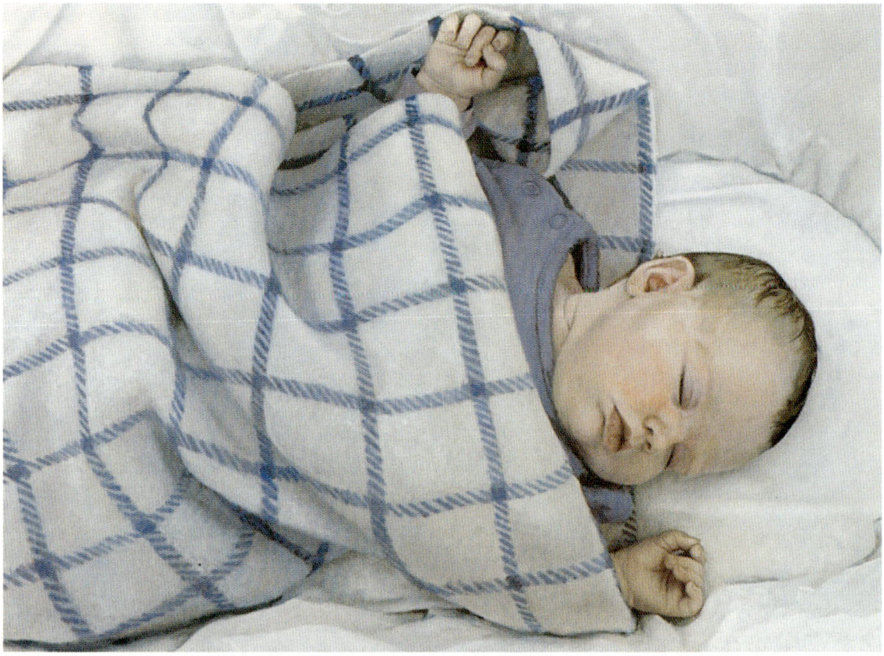

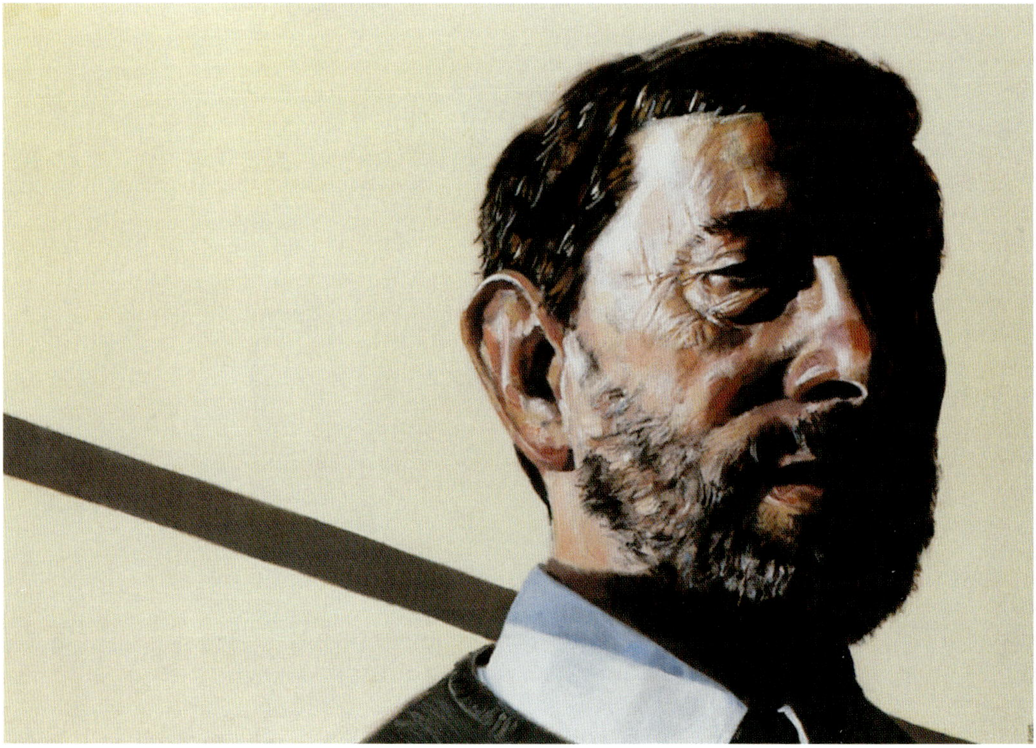

Self-portrait, Postman
Jason Walker
Oil on canvas
1050 x 1050mm

Libby Sheldon
Emma Wesley
Acrylic on board
1210 x 755mm

Dan in my Studio
Ian Whitfield
Acrylic on canvas
797 x 645mm

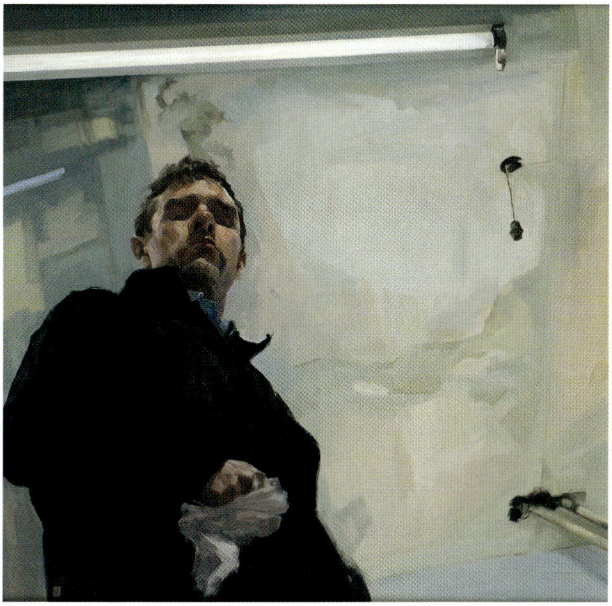

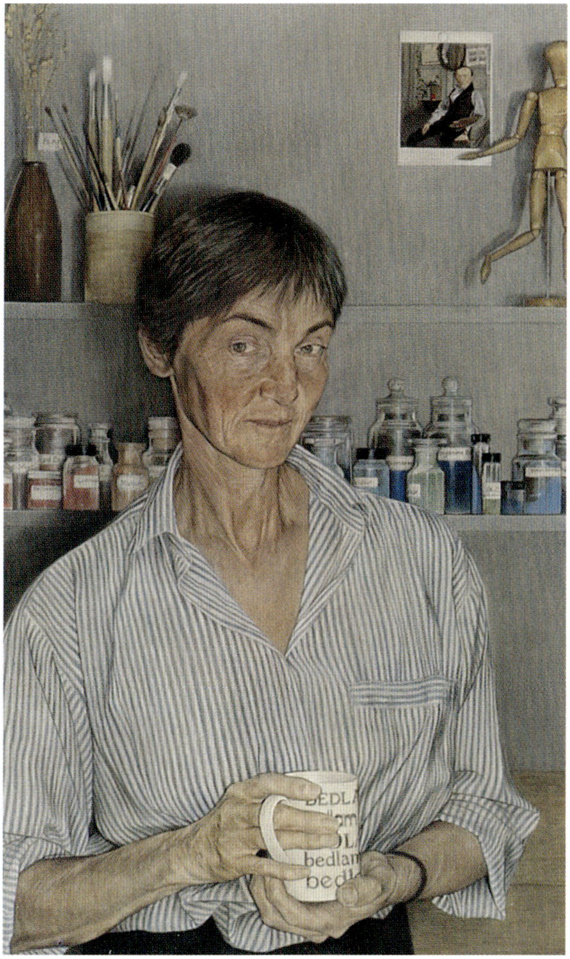

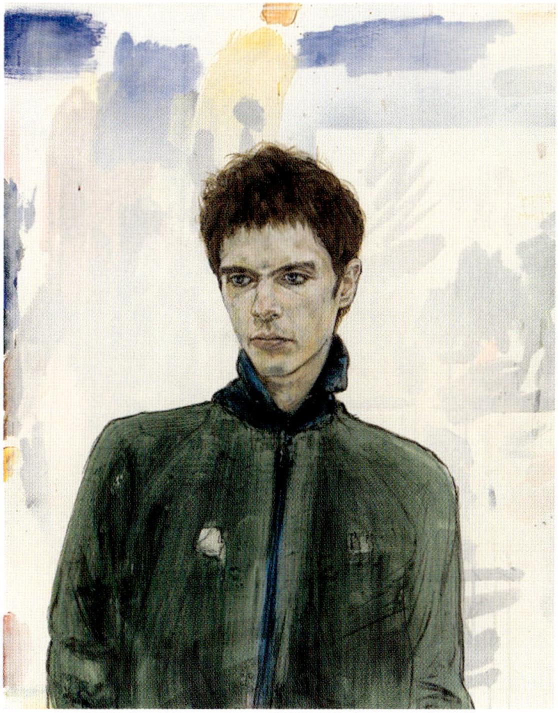

Milo
John Worthington
Oil on canvas
390 x 435mm

Untitled
Cindy Wright
Oil on canvas
1705 x 1280mm

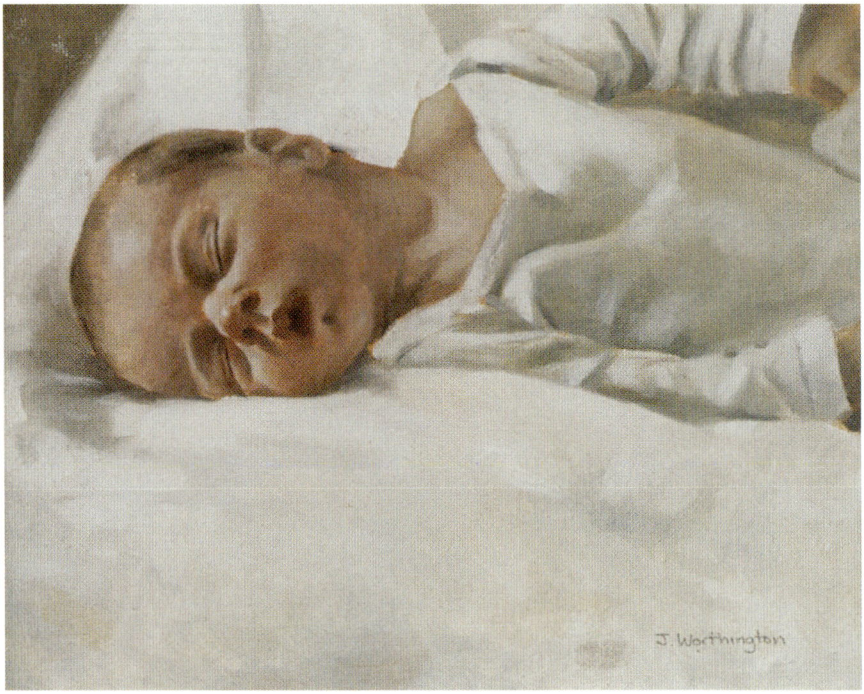

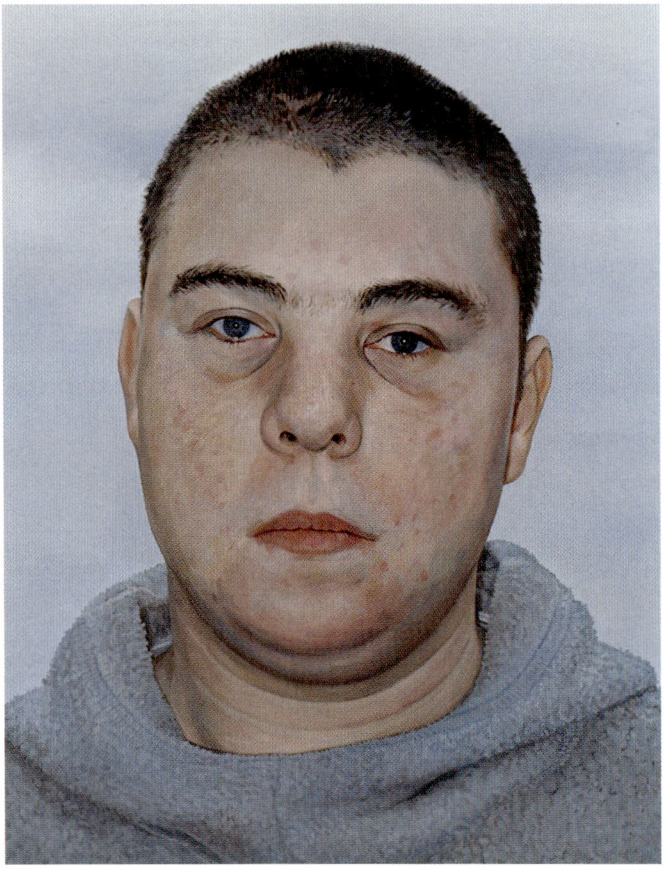

Dawn (Portrait of Mary)
Victoria Wright
Acrylic on canvas
610 x 460mm

George
Paul Wuensche
Oil on canvas
1075 x 875mm

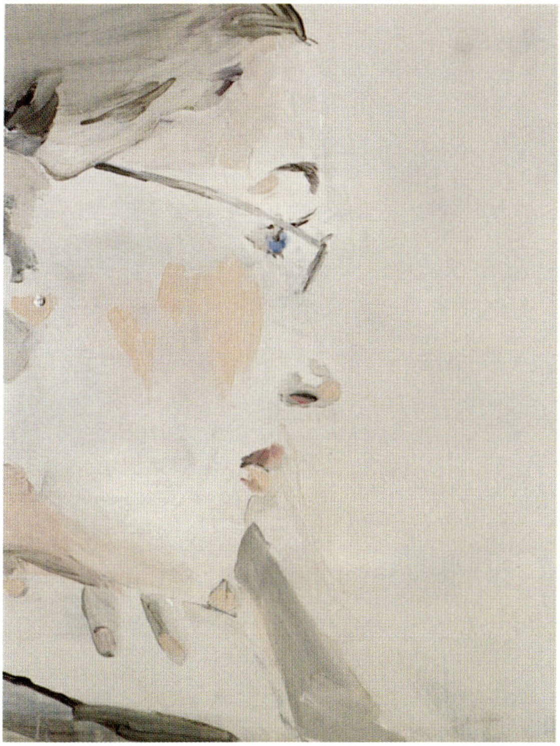

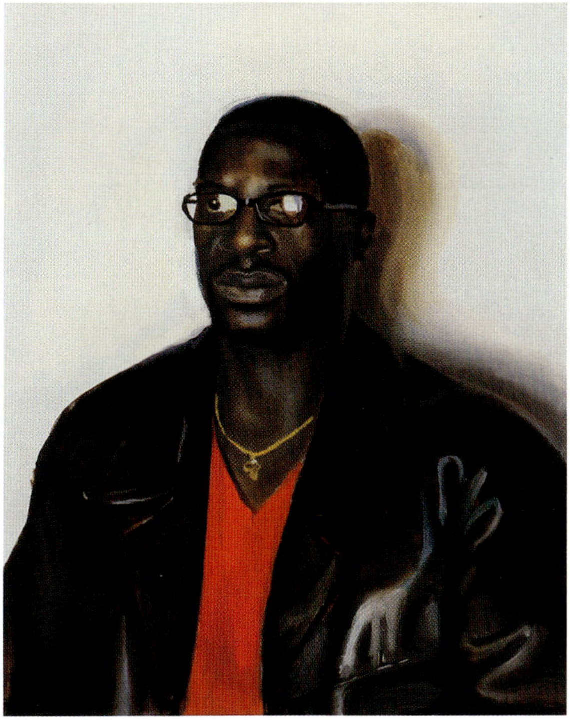

2004

ARTISTS WHOSE PORTRAITS WERE EXHIBITED

Jackie Anderson / Mary Jane Ansell / Nicholas Archer / Bianca Alice Berends / Lanceford Brown / Paul Brown / Vincent Brown / Jason Butler / Gary Colclough / Georgia Cox / James Crowther / Sebastian Dacey / Joel Ely / Darvish Fakhr / Maryam Foroozanfar / Savas Georgiadis / Dominique Grantham / Mitch Griffiths / Phil Hale / Paul Harris / Gemma Harwood / Ralph Heimans / Jon Jones / Paul Lisak / Maeve McCarthy / Marco Marini / Helen Masacz / Fergus Mayhew / Nicholas Middleton / Tim Okamura / Anna Orchard / Alan Parker / Imogen Paton / Freya Payne / Robert Proudfoot / Patrick Redmond / Philippa Robbins / Stephen Rogers / Mark Roscoe / Gideon Rubin / Teri Sanders / Adria Sartore / Nathalie Scott / Sara Shamma / Stephen Shankland / Sarah Simpson / Blaise Smith / Nigel Spong / James Stewart / Andrew Tift / Emma Wesley / Toby Wiggins / Craig Wylie / Jonathan Yeo

SECOND PRIZE
LOUISE TIPLADY
PAUL HARRIS

Oil on canvas
408 x 310mm

Paul Harris studied Fine Art at Camberwell College of Arts before taking an Advanced Diploma in architectural masonry and carving at Weymouth College. After working as a stonemason on Hereford Cathedral, he set up his own stone carving and masonry business in Leominster. This painting depicts his then business partner, Louise Tiplady. Harris now works as a painter and printmaker.

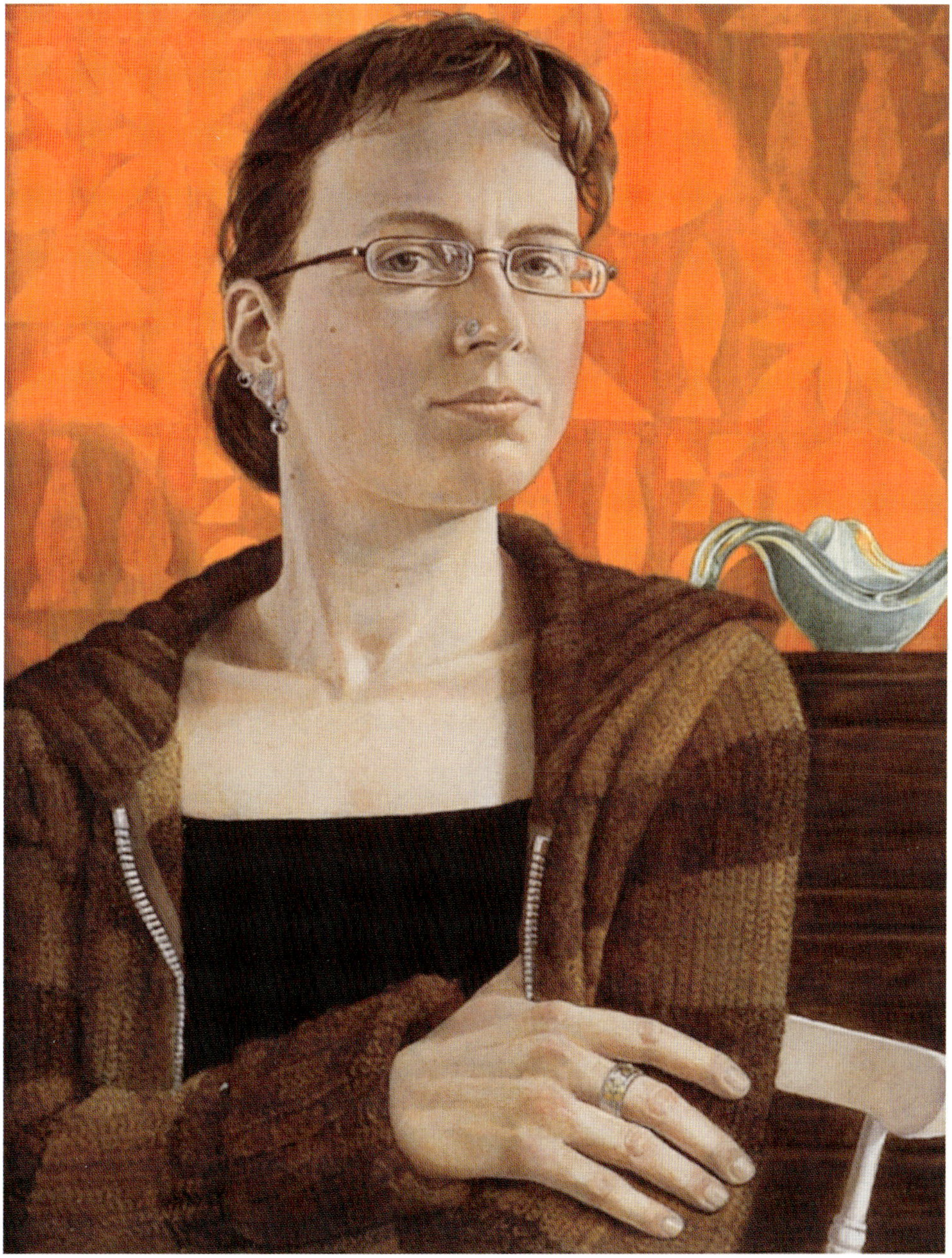

THIRD PRIZE
HEAD FULL OF SMILES
FERGUS MAYHEW

Acrylic and oil on board
468 x 382mm

At the time of painting this portrait of his mother, Bunty, Fergus Mayhew was a full-time father living in Totnes, Devon. Having studied at the Royal Academy Schools, Mayhew had already exhibited in the BP Portrait Award several times before. In 2005, he appeared in the BBC television series *Star Portraits*, painting Cilla Black.

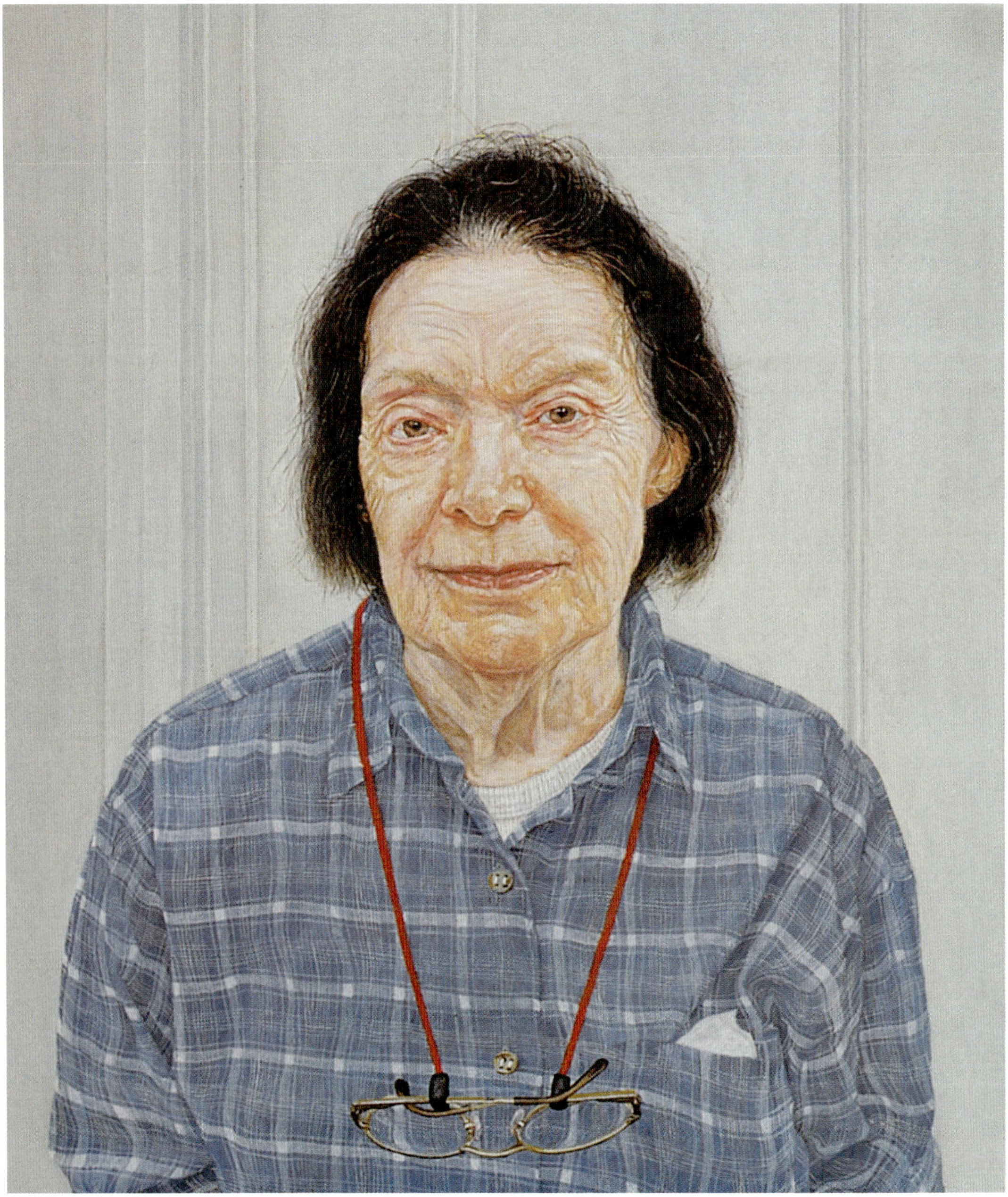

FOURTH PRIZE
SELF-PORTRAIT
SARA SHAMMA

Oil on canvas
1474 x 1152mm

Born in Damascus, where she still lives and works, Sara Shamma is a graduate of the Adham Ismail Fine Arts Institute and Damascus University, where she studied fine art. She has exhibited and won awards in Syria and has contributed to group shows in Europe, Canada and the Middle East. This portrait was painted as one of an ongoing series of self-portraits.

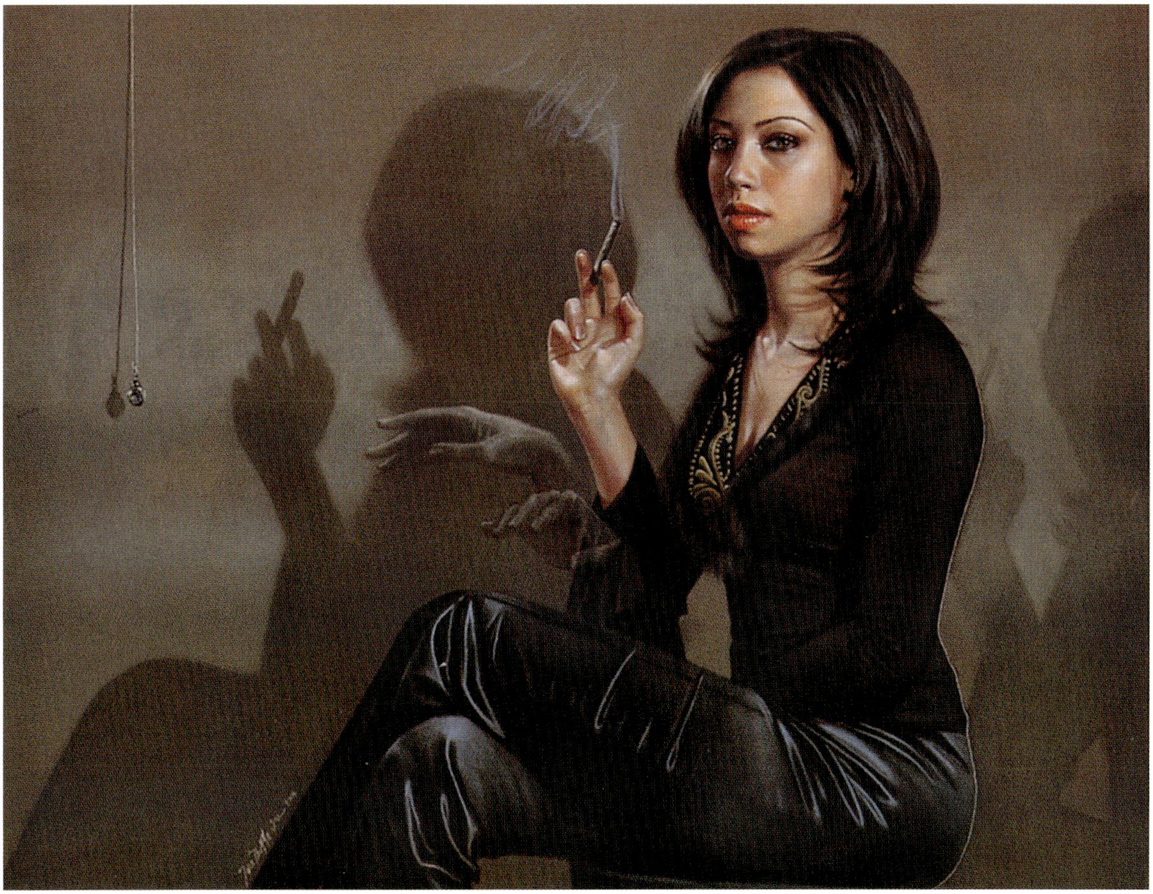

Portrait of Josie
Mary Jane Ansell
Oil on board
393 x 292mm

Bompa
(Grandad)
Bianca Alice Berends
Oil on canvas
1504 x 1000mm

Redeye Jack Jones
Lanceford Brown
Acrylic on board
588 x 390mm

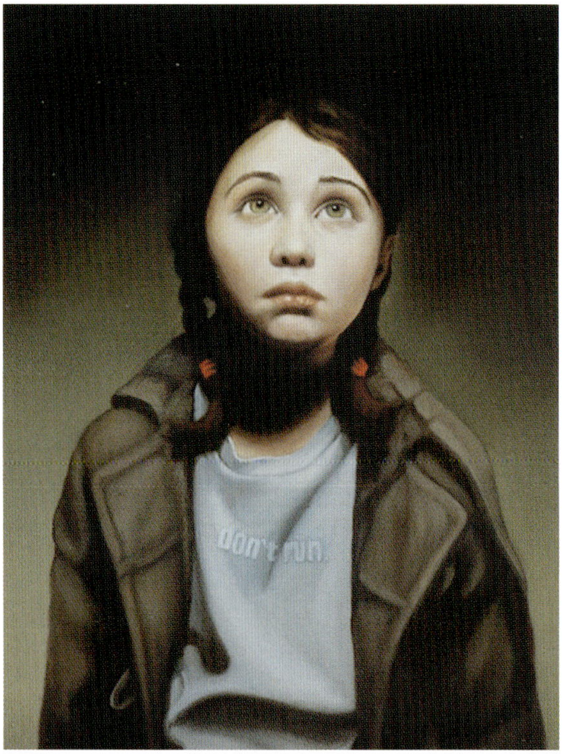

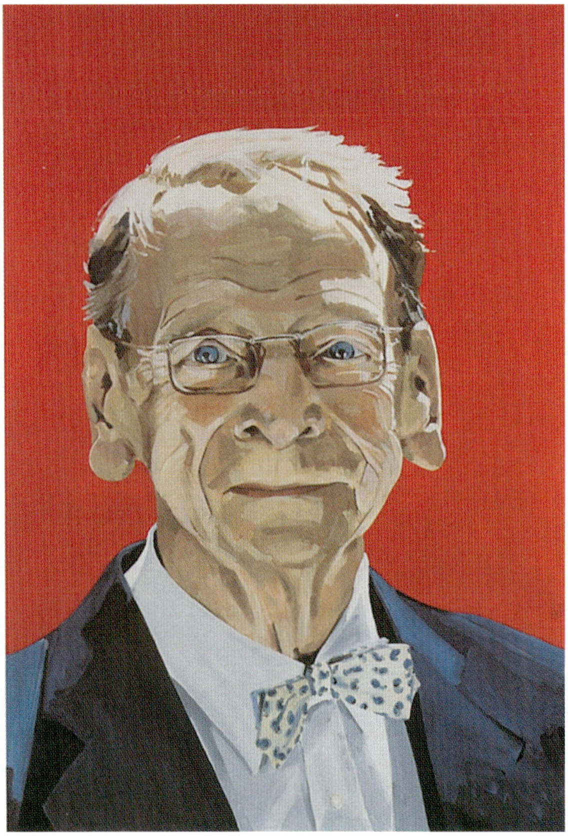

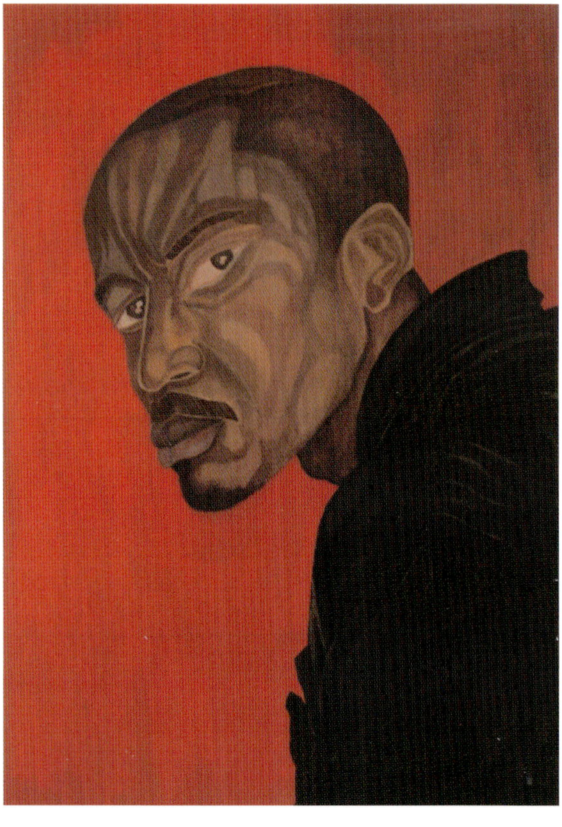

Self-portrait
Paul Brown
Oil on panel
368 x 368mm

Untitled
(Artist's Father)
Vincent Brown
Acrylic on board
1210 x 368mm

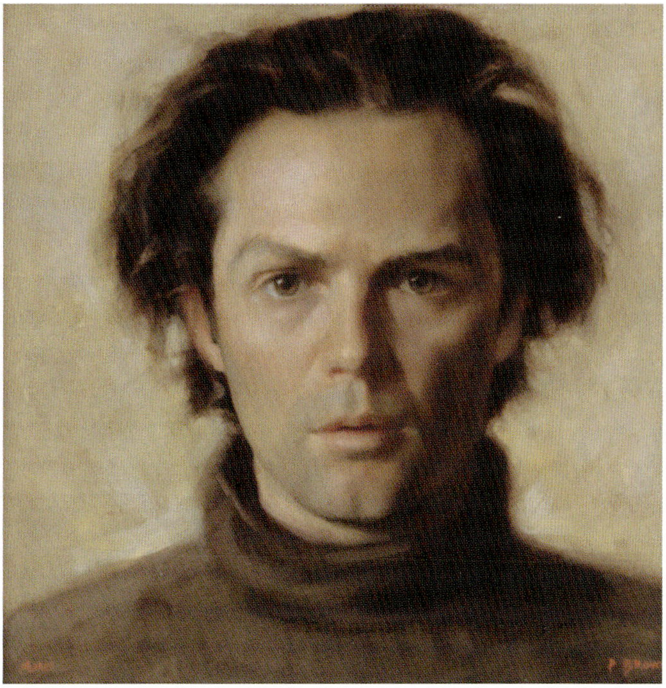

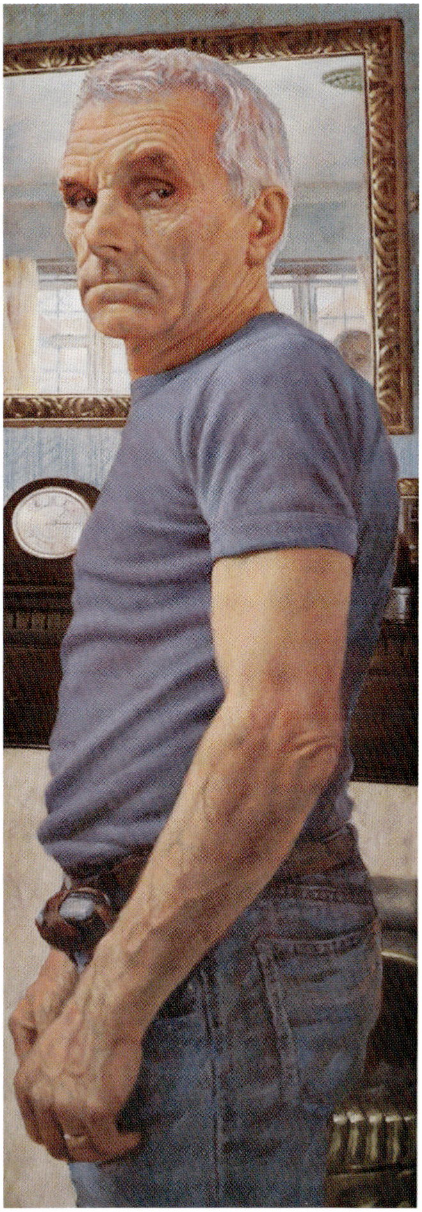

H
Gary Colclough
Oil on canvas
1494 x 1487mm

Self-portrait
Georgia Cox
Oil on canvas
598 x 598mm

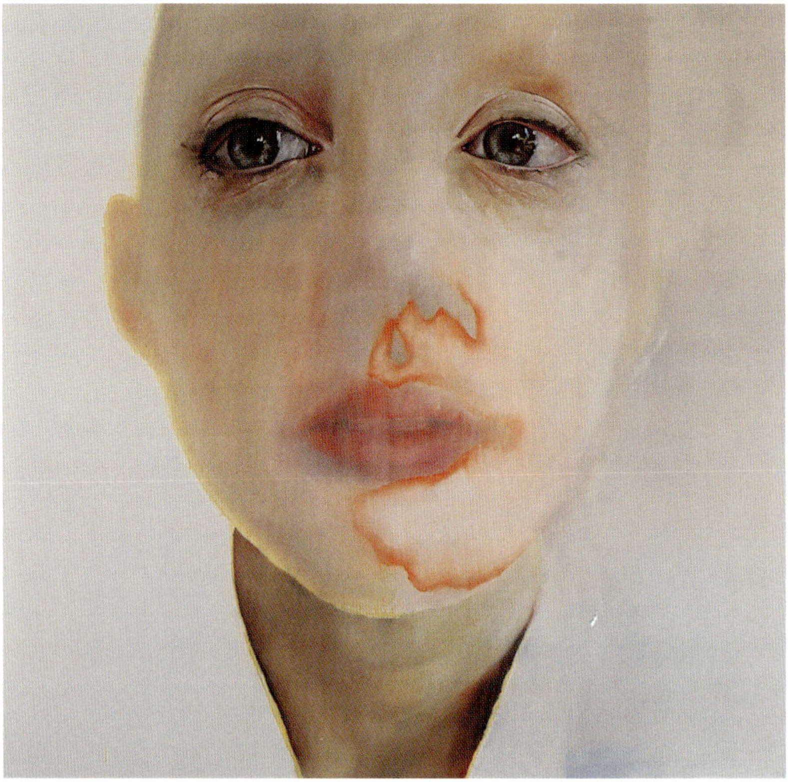

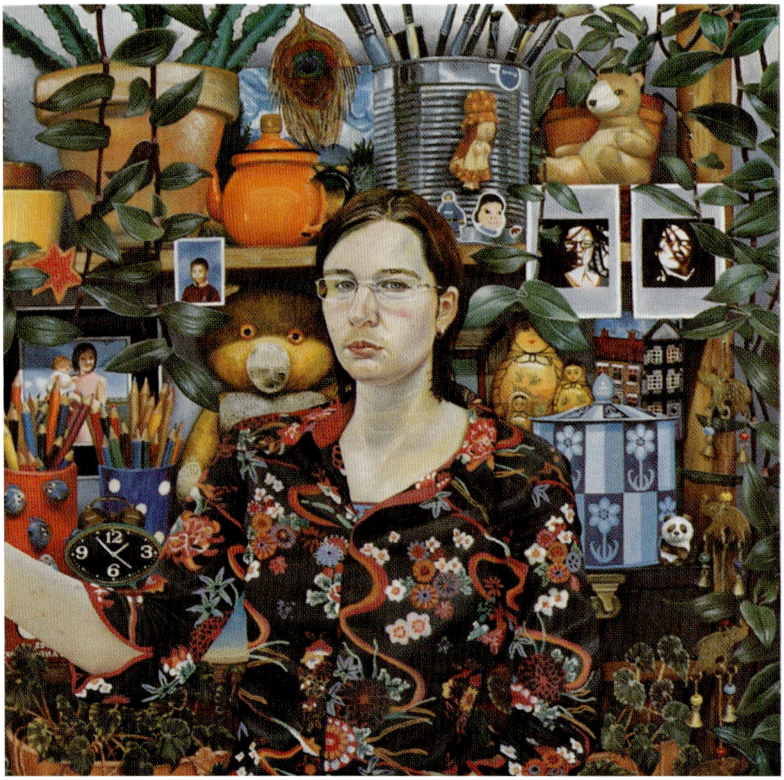

Caroline
James Crowther
Oil on canvas
409 x 307mm

Untitled
Sebastian Dacey
Oil on panel
396 x 204mm

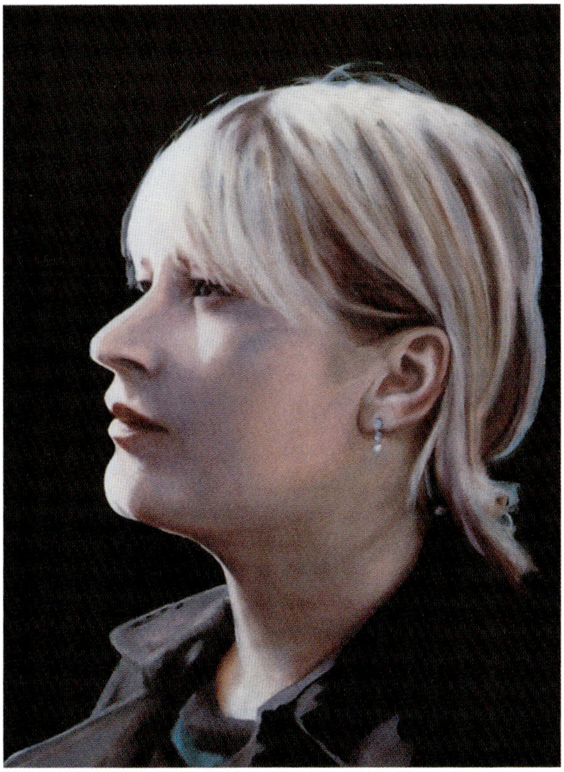

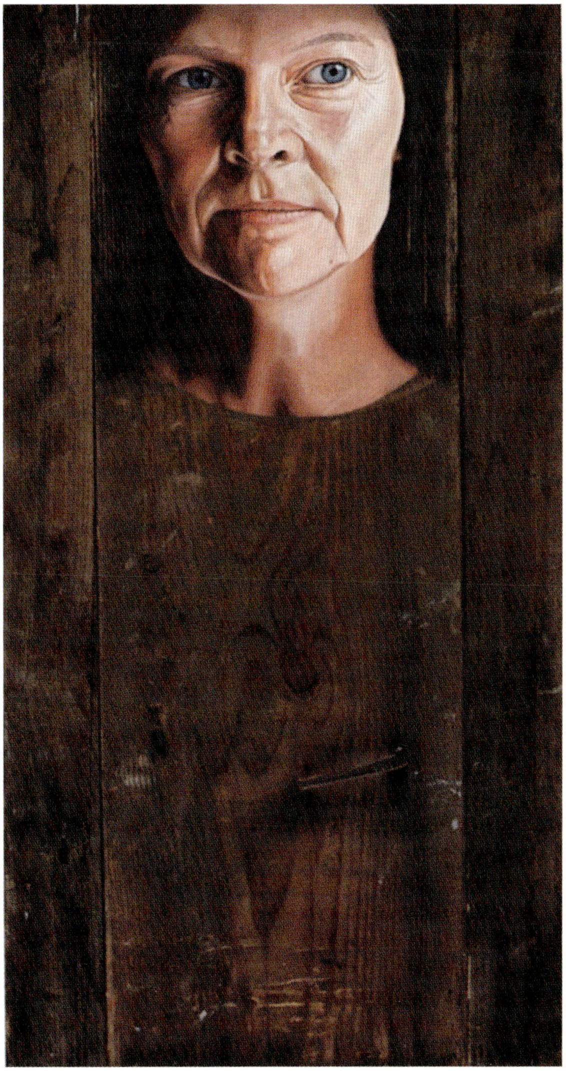

Nicola with Octopus
Joel Ely
Oil on linen
762 x 762mm

Three Men Named Ian
Darvish Fakhr
Oil on board
152 x 457mm

Twenty-eight Days of Veiled Sorrow
Savas Georgiadis
Oil on canvas
1204 x 1002mm

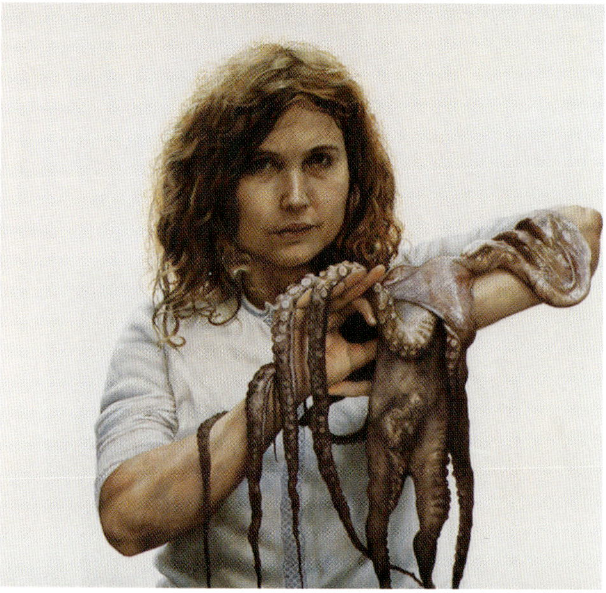

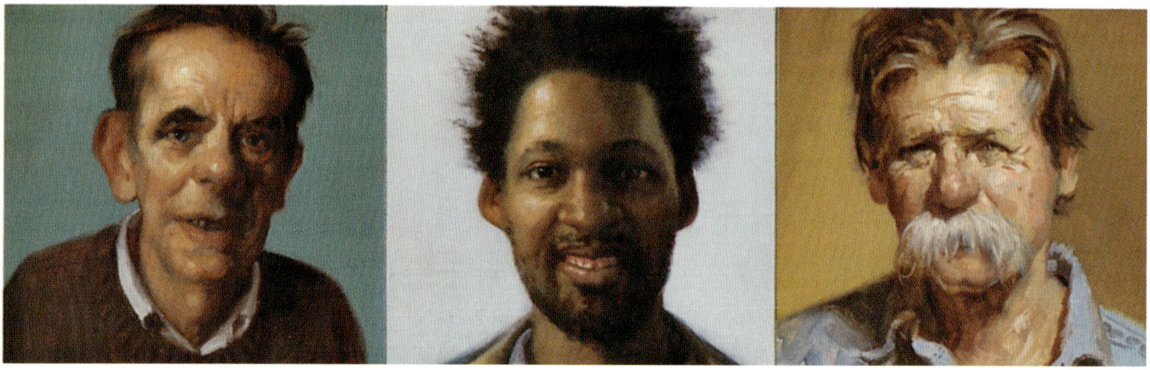

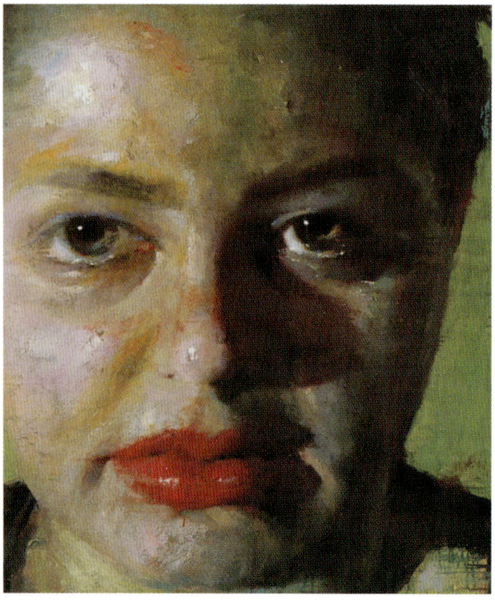

Flora and Betty
Dominique Grantham
Oil on canvas
560 x 760mm

The Artist, the Model and the Critic
Mitch Griffiths
Oil on canvas
1897 x 1239mm

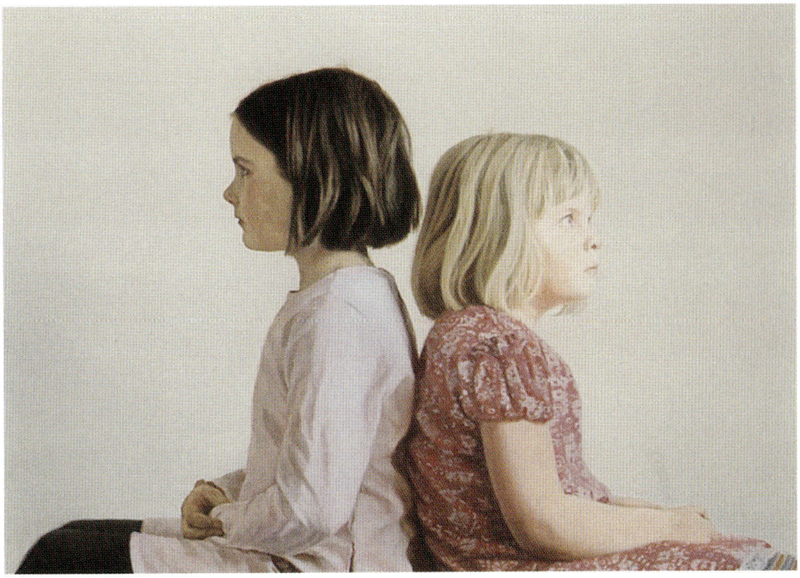

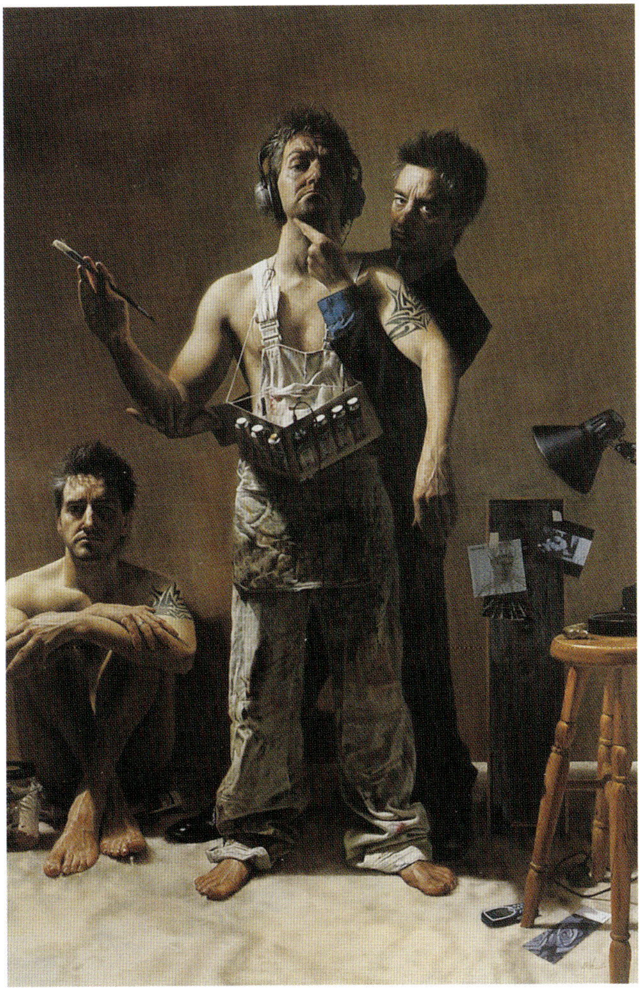

Thomas Fairfax and Father
Gemma Harwood
Oil on canvas
615 x 458mm

Self-portrait in the Metro
Ralph Heimans
Oil on canvas
849 x 1697mm

Matt
Jon Jones
Oil on board
419 x 422mm

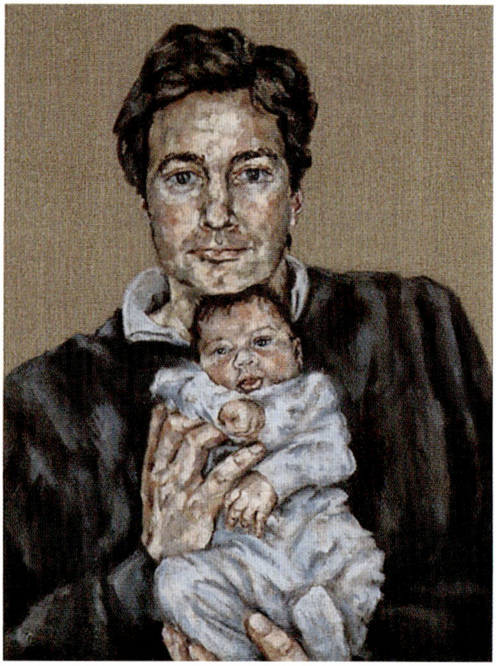

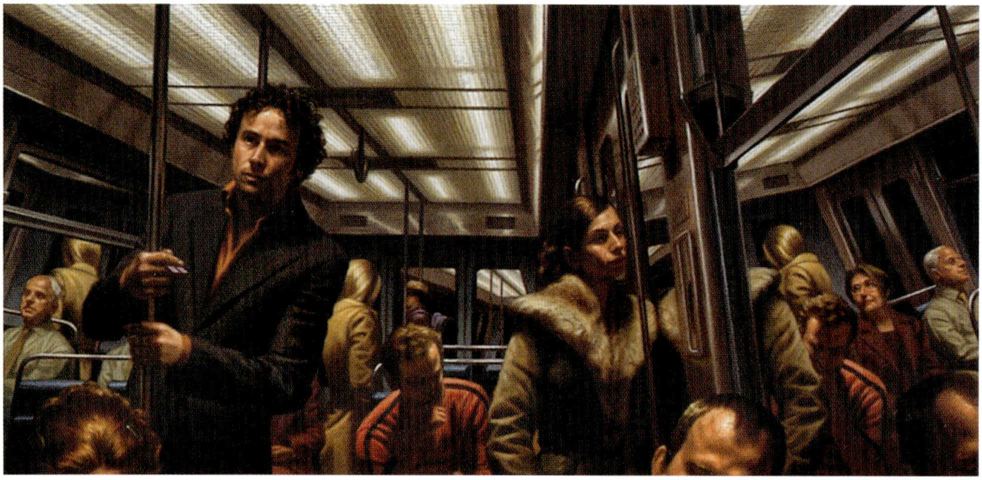

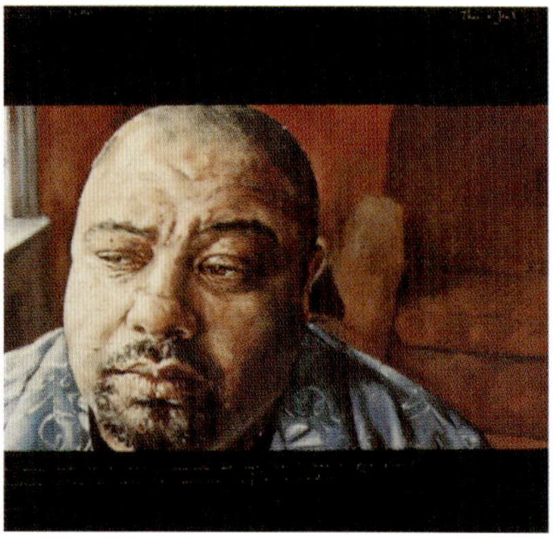

Father Nicholas Cranfield
Paul Lisak
Oil on canvas
1002 x 813mm

The Uncle Rino
Marco Marini
Oil on canvas
550 x 399mm

Self-portrait
Maeve McCarthy
Oil on panel
376 x 380mm

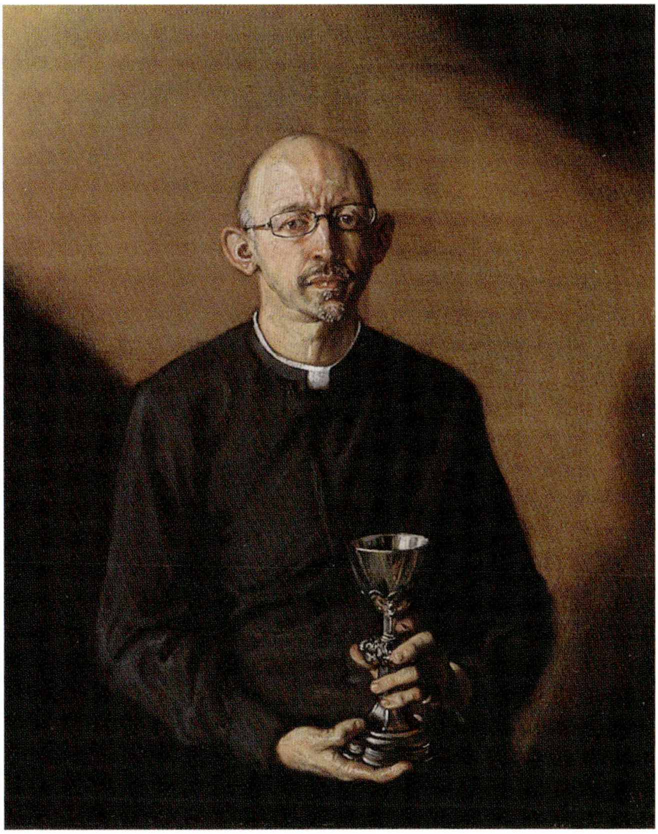

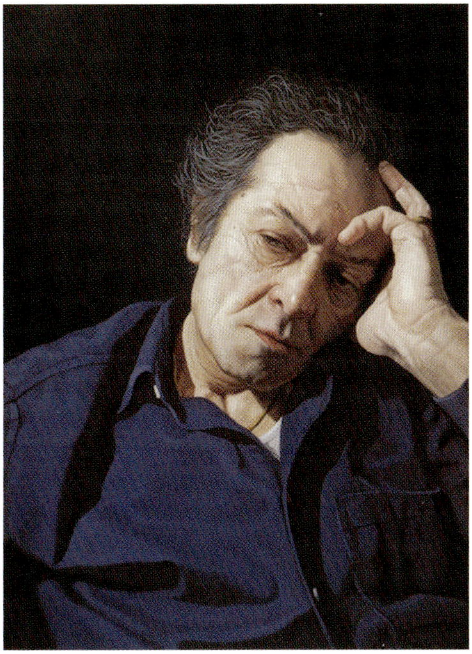

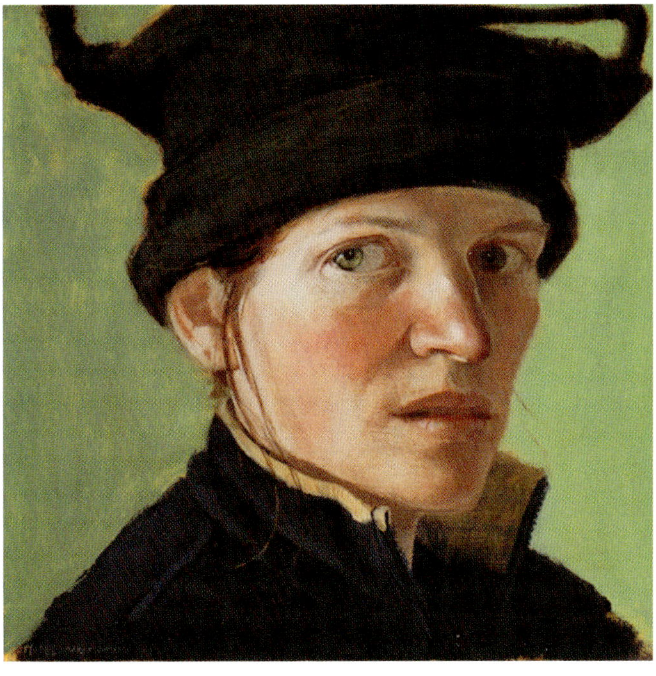

Dr Martin Skittles, Architectural Historian
Nicholas Middleton
Oil on canvas
811 x 812mm

The Elevator
Tim Okamura
Oil on canvas
1268 x 1730mm

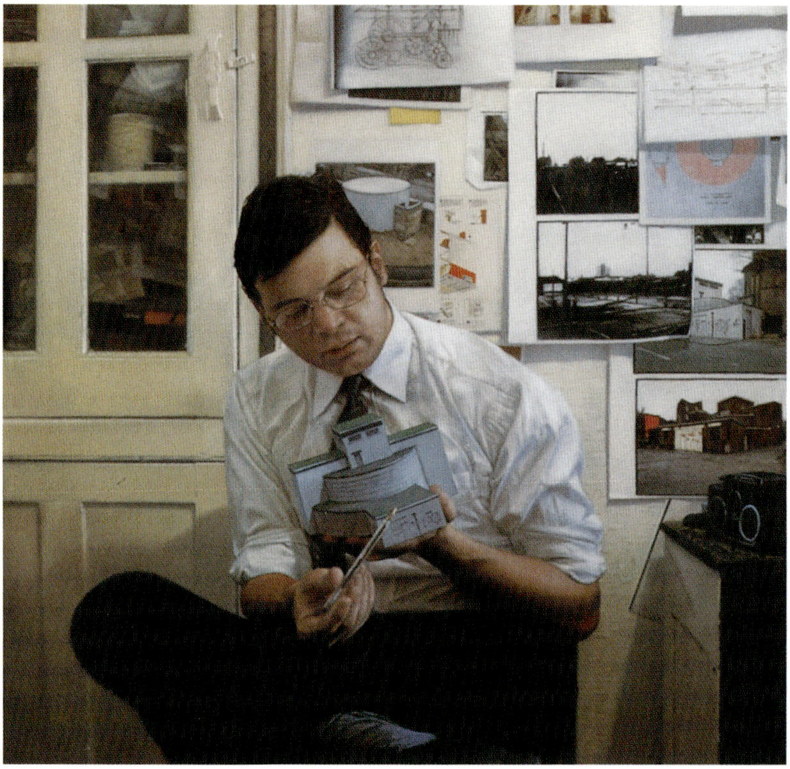

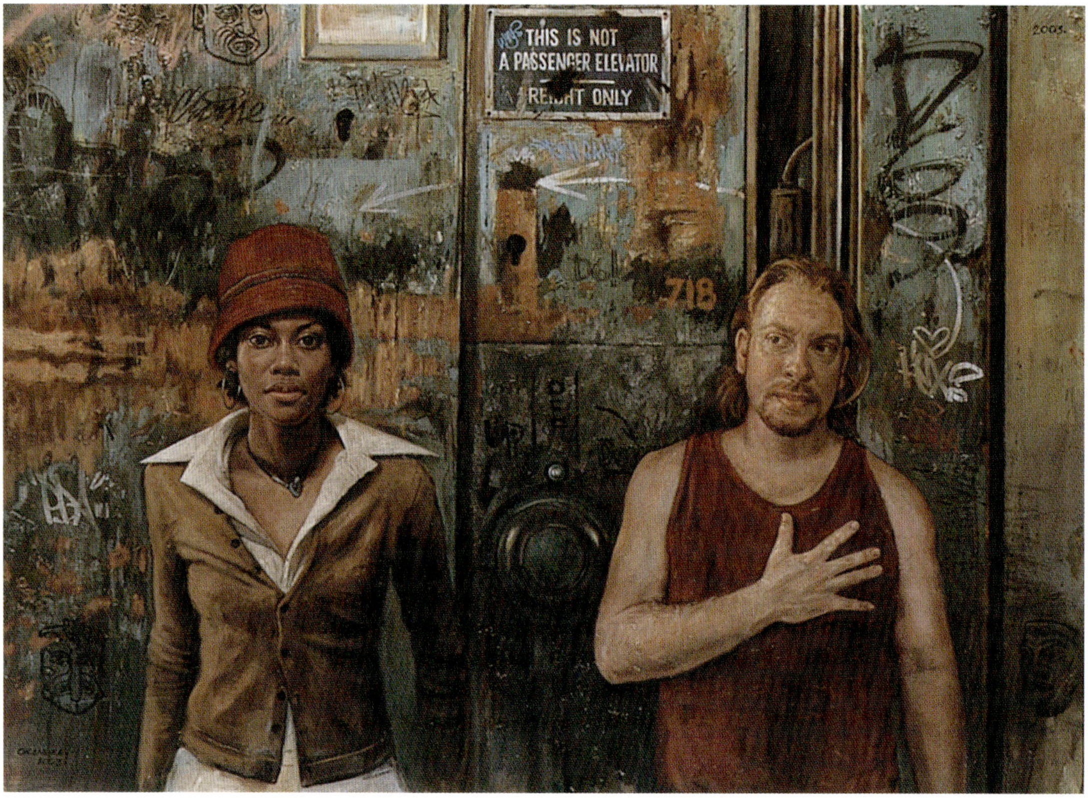

This is Me –
Self-portrait
Anna Orchard
Oil and acrylic on canvas
1219 x 916mm

The Optics Lesson of
Doctor Turner
Alan Parker
Mixed media
1219 x 1219mm

Some Wild, Some Tame
Imogen Paton
Oil on board
1943 x 1440mm

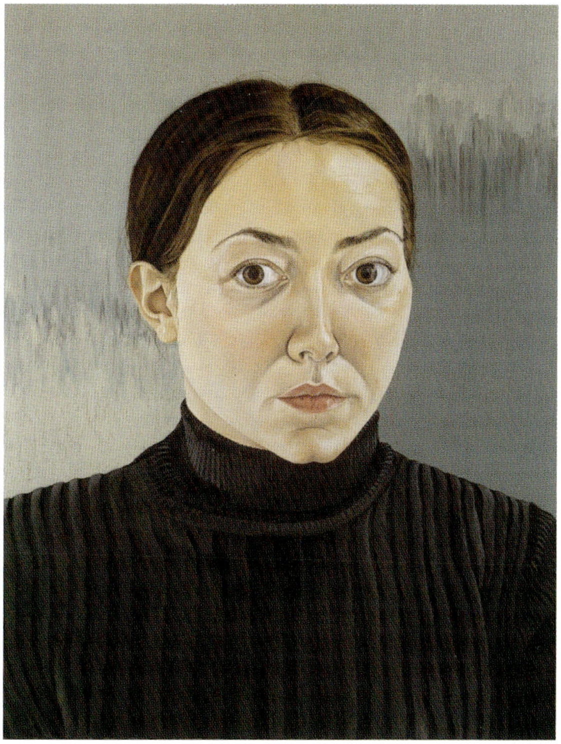

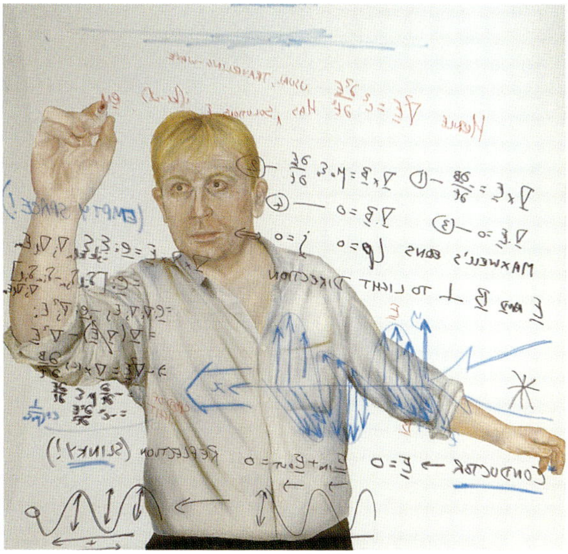

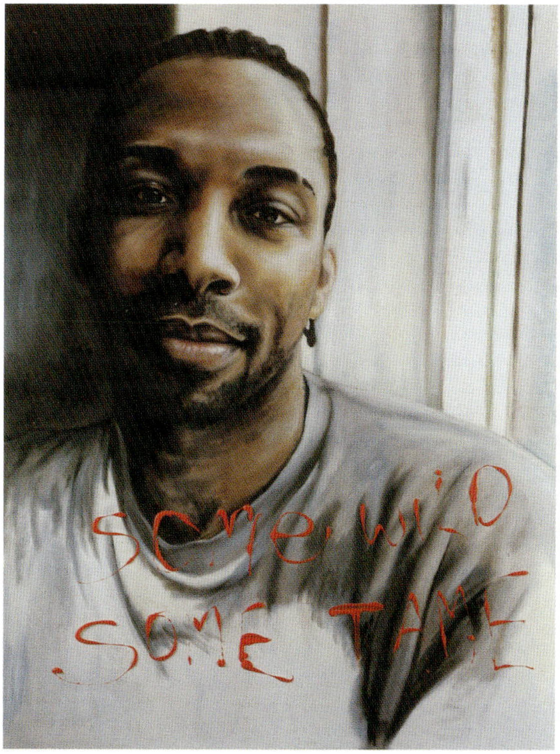

Witness
Freya Payne
Oil on canvas
493 x 493mm

Olivia
Robert Proudfoot
Acrylic on board
387 x 336mm

Raymond
Patrick Redmond
Oil on canvas
505 x 442mm

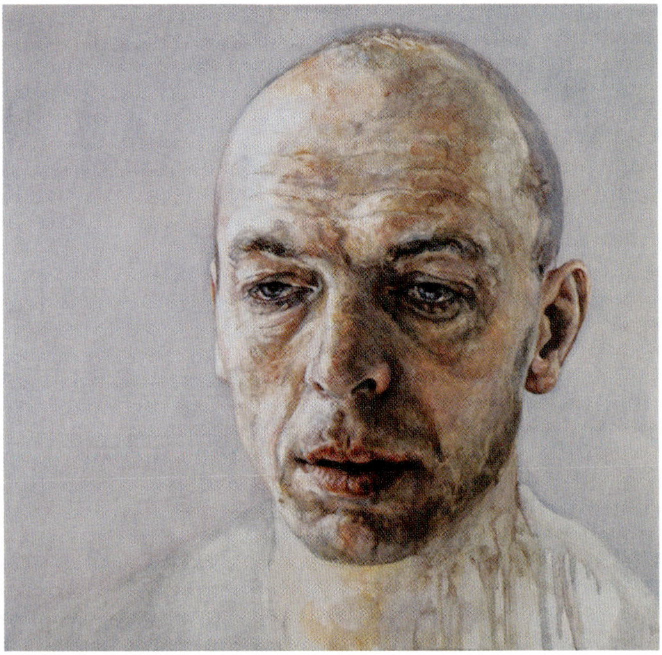

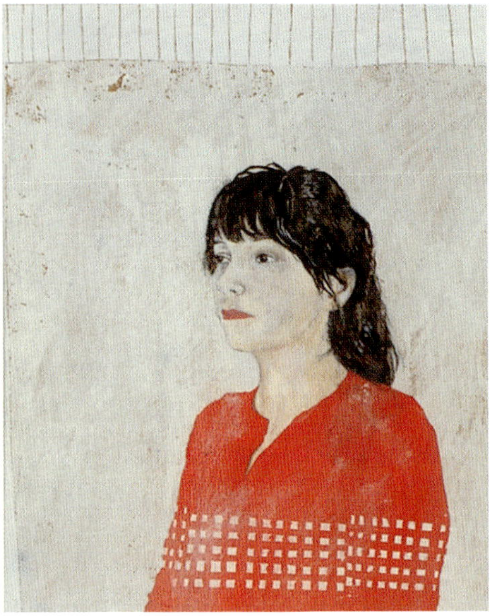

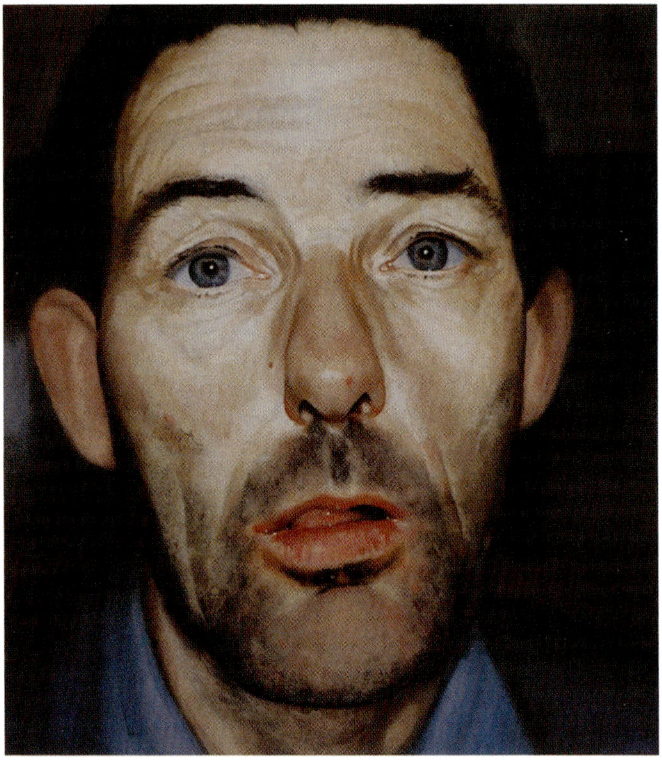

Gaze
Philippa Robbins
Oil on board
190 x 568mm

Self-portrait
Mark Roscoe
Oil on canvas
904 x 703mm

Tiff my Boi
Teri Sanders
Oil on canvas
457 x 305mm

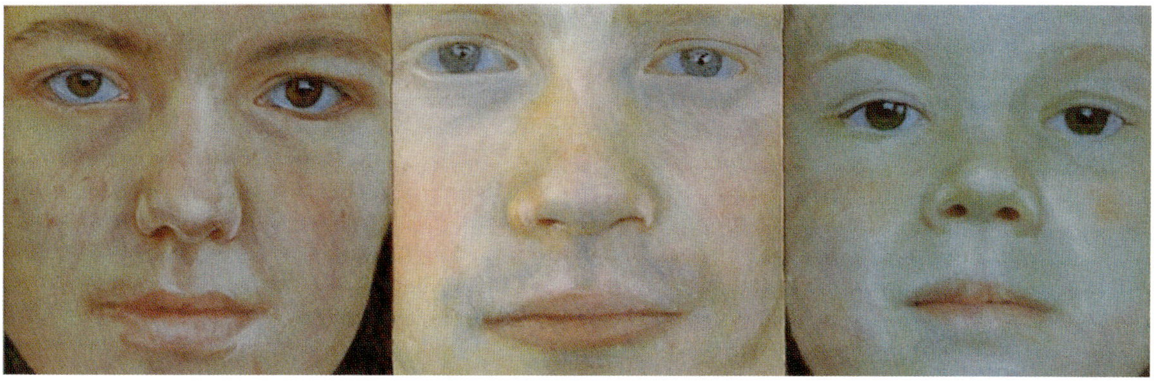

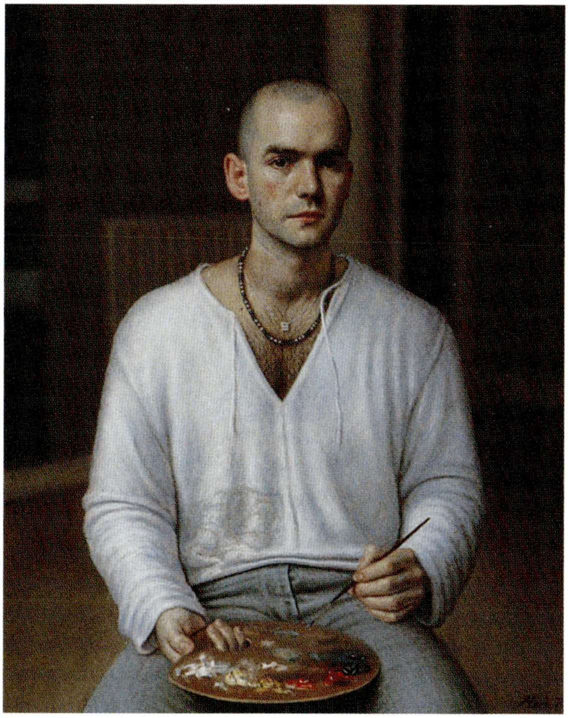

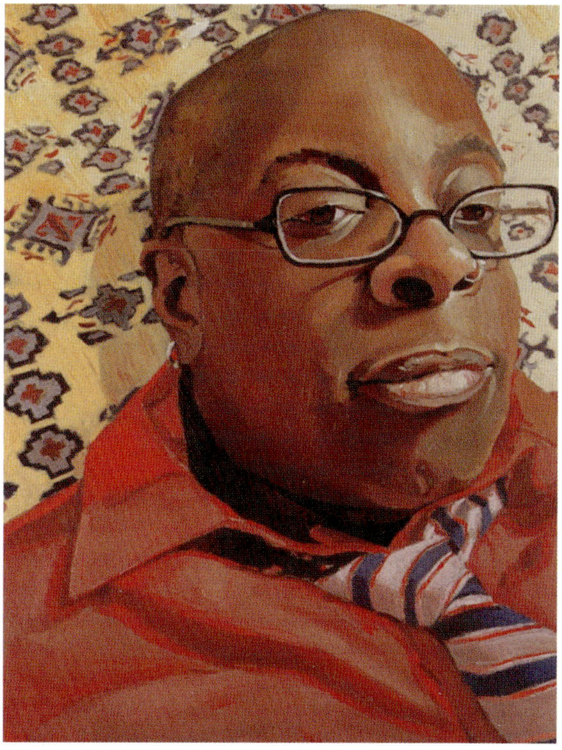

Ellen
Adria Sartore
Oil on canvas
298 x 349mm

Norma
Sarah Simpson
Acrylic on canvas
914 x 915mm

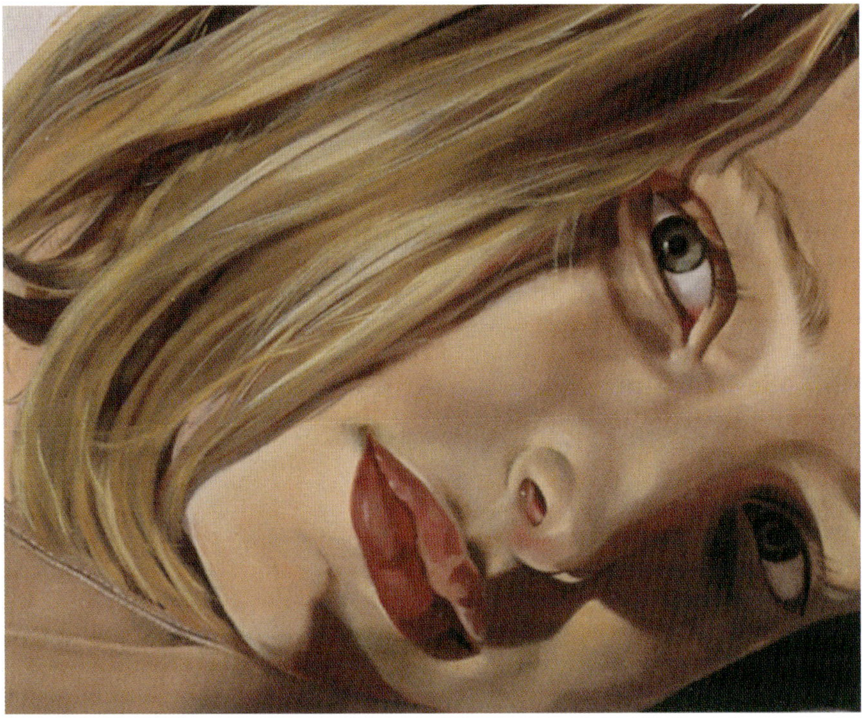

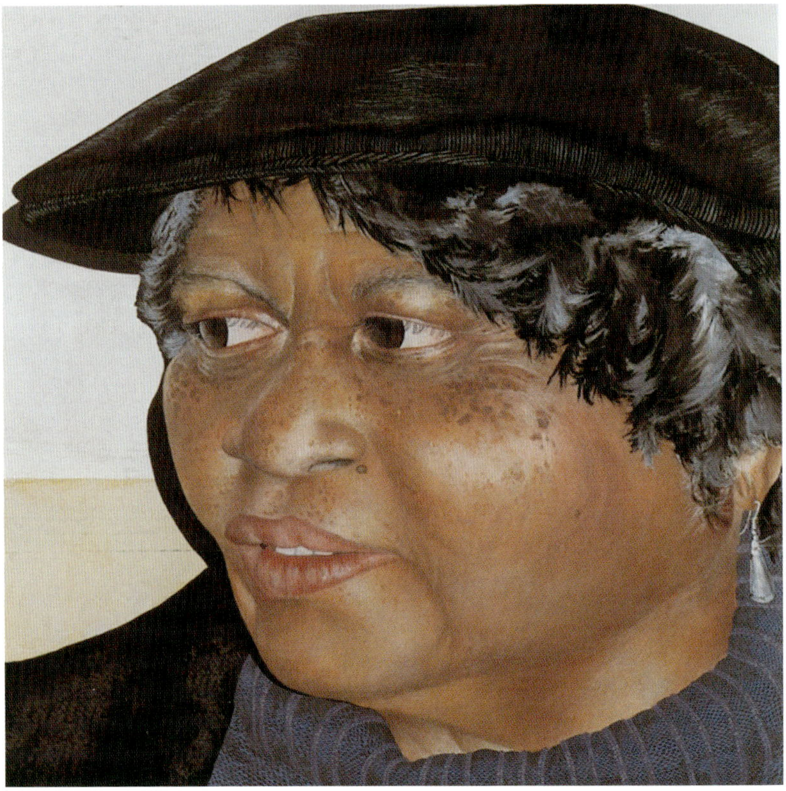

Orla Kelly and Sparky Kelly (in Scart, in the 'New Home')
Blaise Smith
Oil on panel
851 x 603mm

Thomas
Nigel Spong
Acrylic on canvas
816 x 559mm

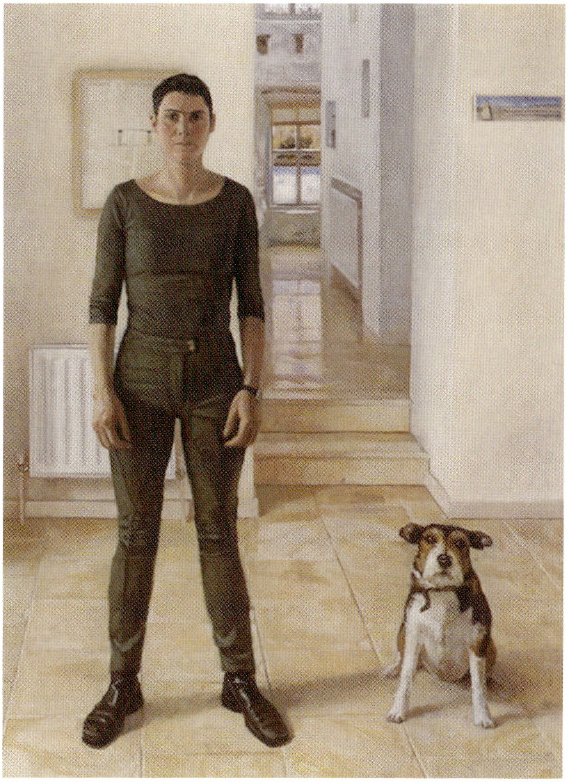

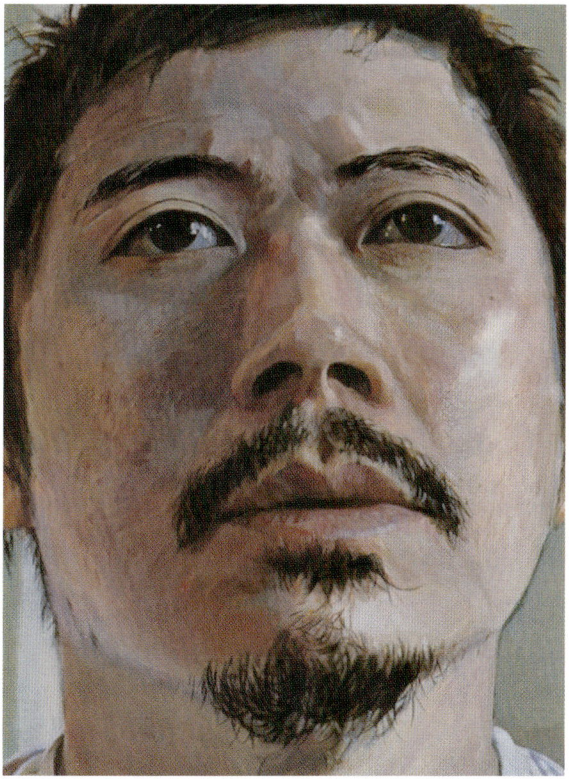

Self-portrait
James Stewart
Oil on board
494 x 1250mm

Mary Spencer-Watson, Sculptor
Toby Wiggins
Oil on canvas
1452 x 917mm

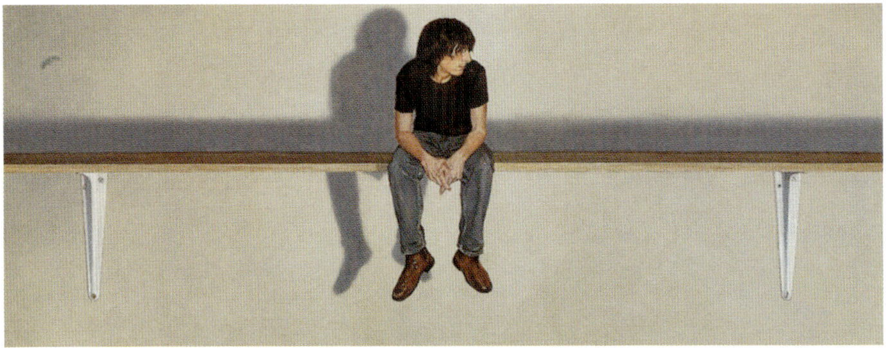

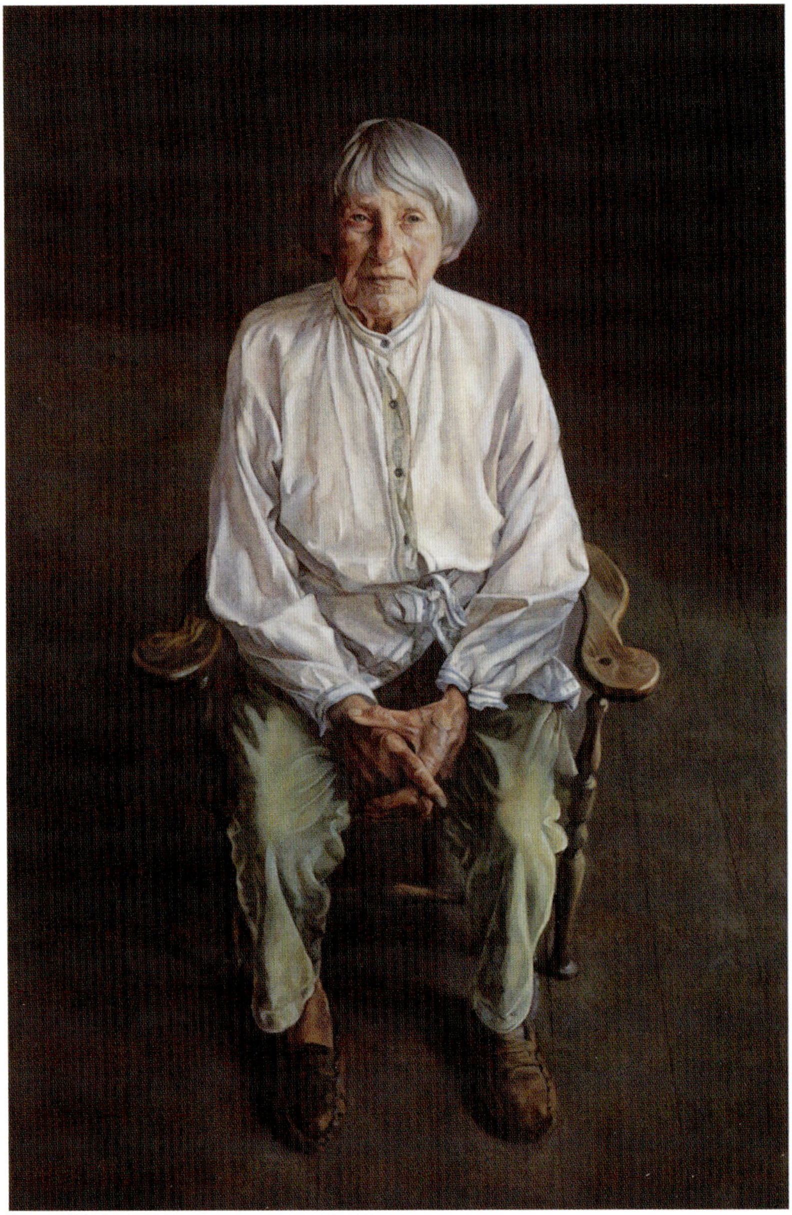

Doug
Craig Wylie
Oil on canvas
889 x 1190mm

Rt. Hon. Paul Boateng
Jonathan Yeo
Oil on canvas
764 x 764mm

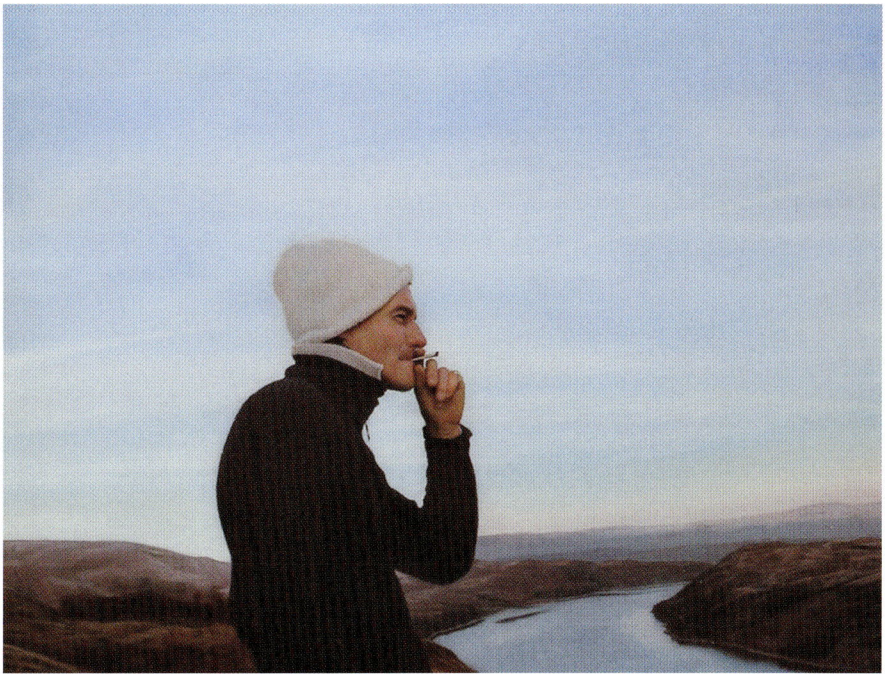

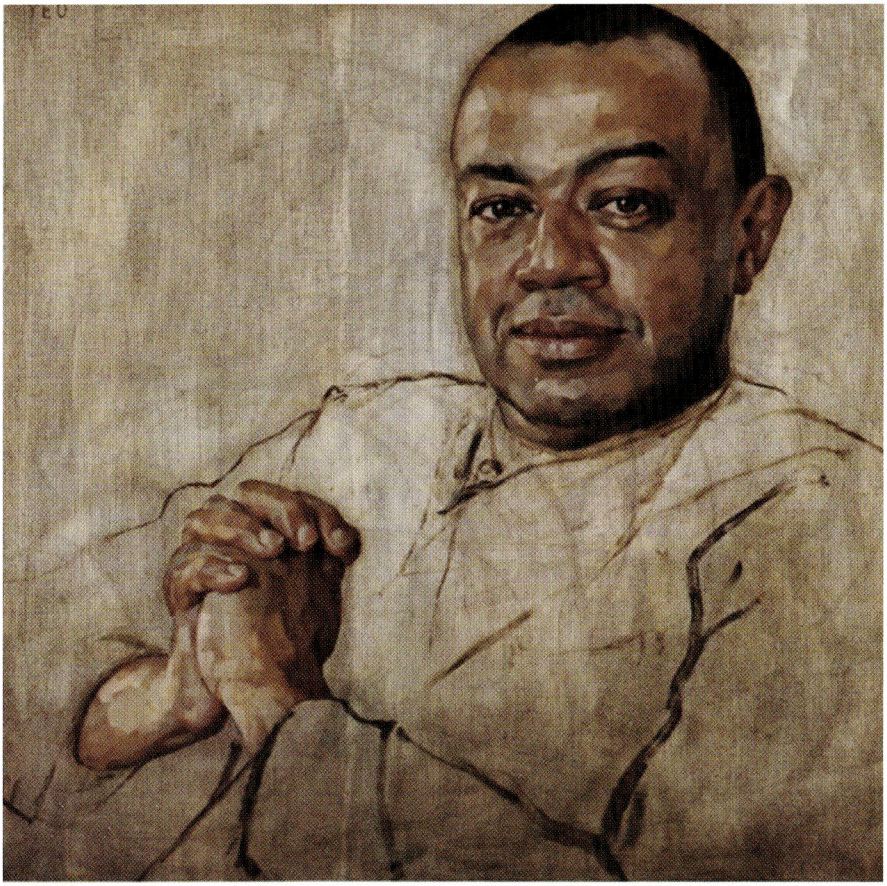

2005

ARTISTS WHOSE PORTRAITS WERE EXHIBITED

Jackie Anderson / Jennifer Anderson / Paul Birdsall / Annemarie Busschers / Davide Castronova / Sean Cheetham / Sylvie Clarke / Gregory Cumins / Megan Davies / Roy Eastland / Joel Ely / Eneko Fraile-Ugalde / James Hart Dyke / Daniel Hughes / Helena Hugo / Sheldon Hutchinson / Shaun James Nielsen / Duncan Joseph / Brendan Kelly / Jack Kettlewell / Ian Lamont / Dean Marsh / David Martin / Maeve McCarthy / Jay McInerney / Cian McLoughlin / Nicholas Middleton / Graham Milton / Daniel Munday / John Murphy-Woolford / Tim Okamura / Paul Oxborough / Andy Pankhurst / Nicky Philipps / Alex Rennie / Saul Robertson / Stephen Earl Rogers / Konstantin Sheiko / Paul Smith / Charlotte Steel / Bonnie Thompson / Andrew Tift / Stefan Towler / Thierry Louis Tremas / Jason Walker / Conor Walton / David Webb / Emma Wesley / Antony Williams / Hugo Wilson / Daniel Wray / Craig Wylie / Jonathan Yeo / Gavin Young

SECOND PRIZE
THE UNIVERSE
SAUL ROBERTSON

Oil on linen
1511 x 770mm

Saul Robertson studied at Duncan of Jordanstone College of Art and Design in Dundee, and now lives and works in Glasgow. He has exhibited extensively throughout Britain and, in the two years before winning Second Prize in the BP Portrait Award, had won both the David Cargill Award, in 2003, and the David Cargill Senior Award, in 2004, at the Royal Glasgow Institute of the Fine Arts. Robertson was also voted Young Artist of the Year at the Hunting Art Prizes in 2001. *The Universe* is a self-portrait of the artist in his studio.

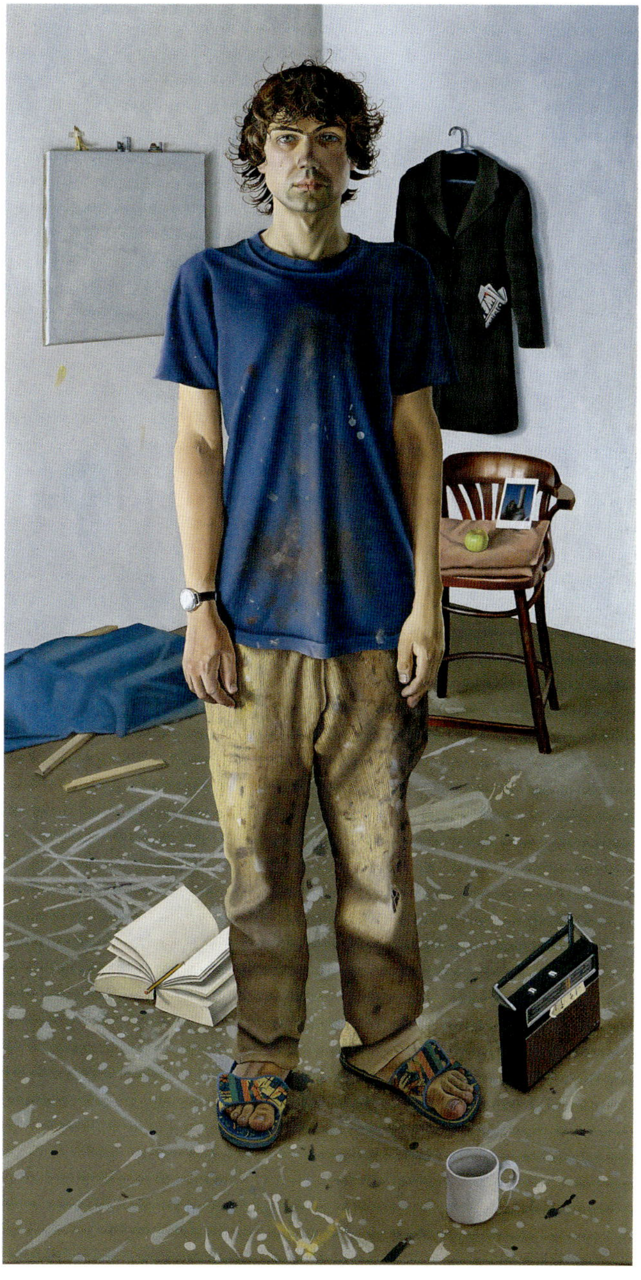

THIRD PRIZE
RICHARD DEACON
GREGORY CUMINS

Mixed media
1500 x 1510mm

French artist Gregory Cumins graduated in sculpture in 1999 from the École Nationale Supérieure des Beaux-Arts in Paris, where he was taught by British sculptor Richard Deacon, the subject of this prizewinning portrait. After finishing his studies, Cumins worked for a website agency as a graphic designer and web designer. He started painting in 2003 and now lives and works in Berlin.

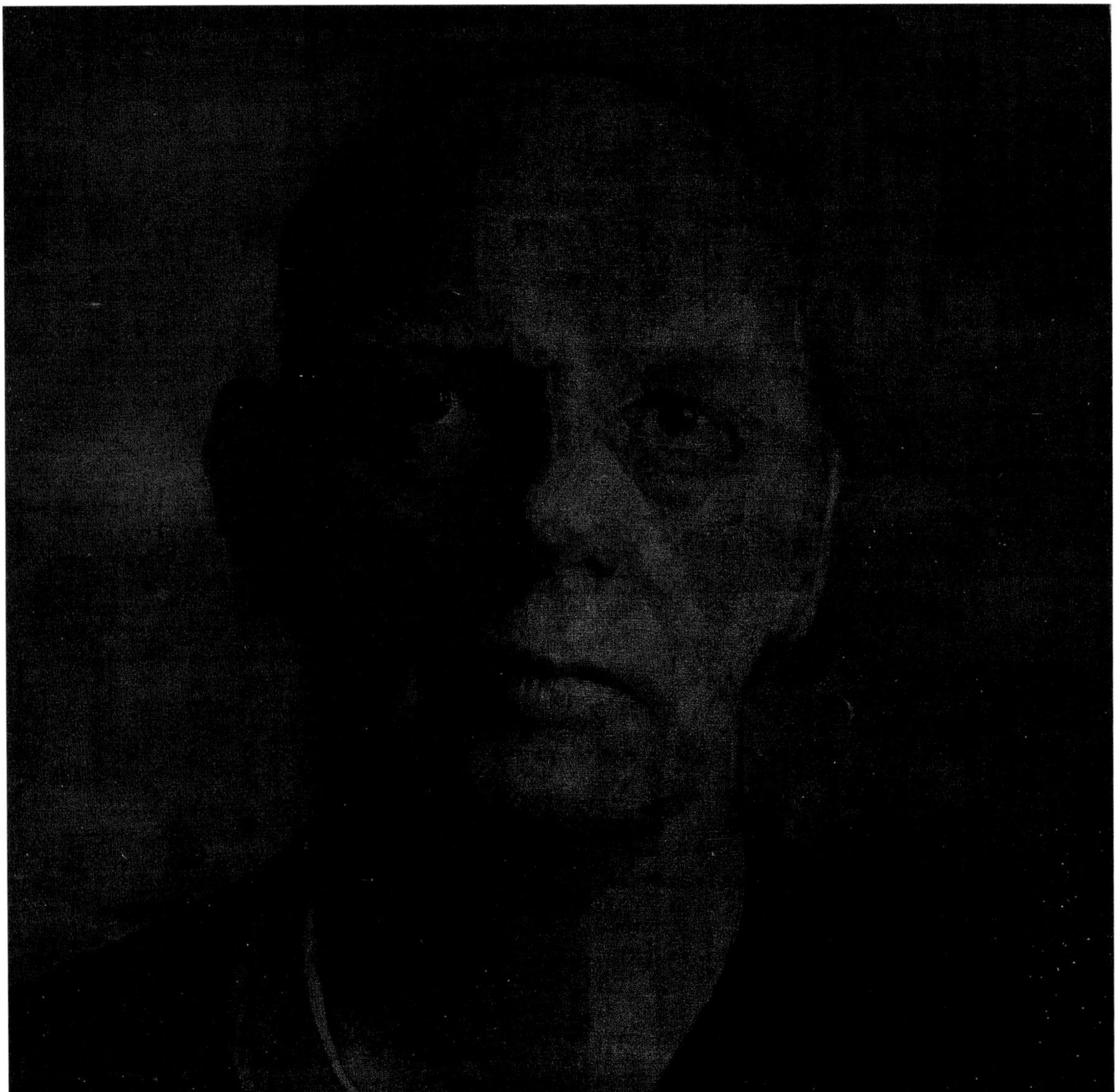

FOURTH PRIZE
MONKEY PAINTING
CONOR WALTON

Oil on panel
775 x 620mm

Born in Dublin, Conor Walton studied at the National College of Art and Design. Following his Master of Arts in Art History and Theory at the University of Essex, he went to Florence in Italy to study painting and old master techniques. He returned to Ireland in 1996 and now lives and works in County Wicklow. Walton has described this painting as an homage to seventeenth-century portraiture, and to the human aesthetic that underlies it, as well as an exercise in the genre of *singerie*, or 'monkey painting'.

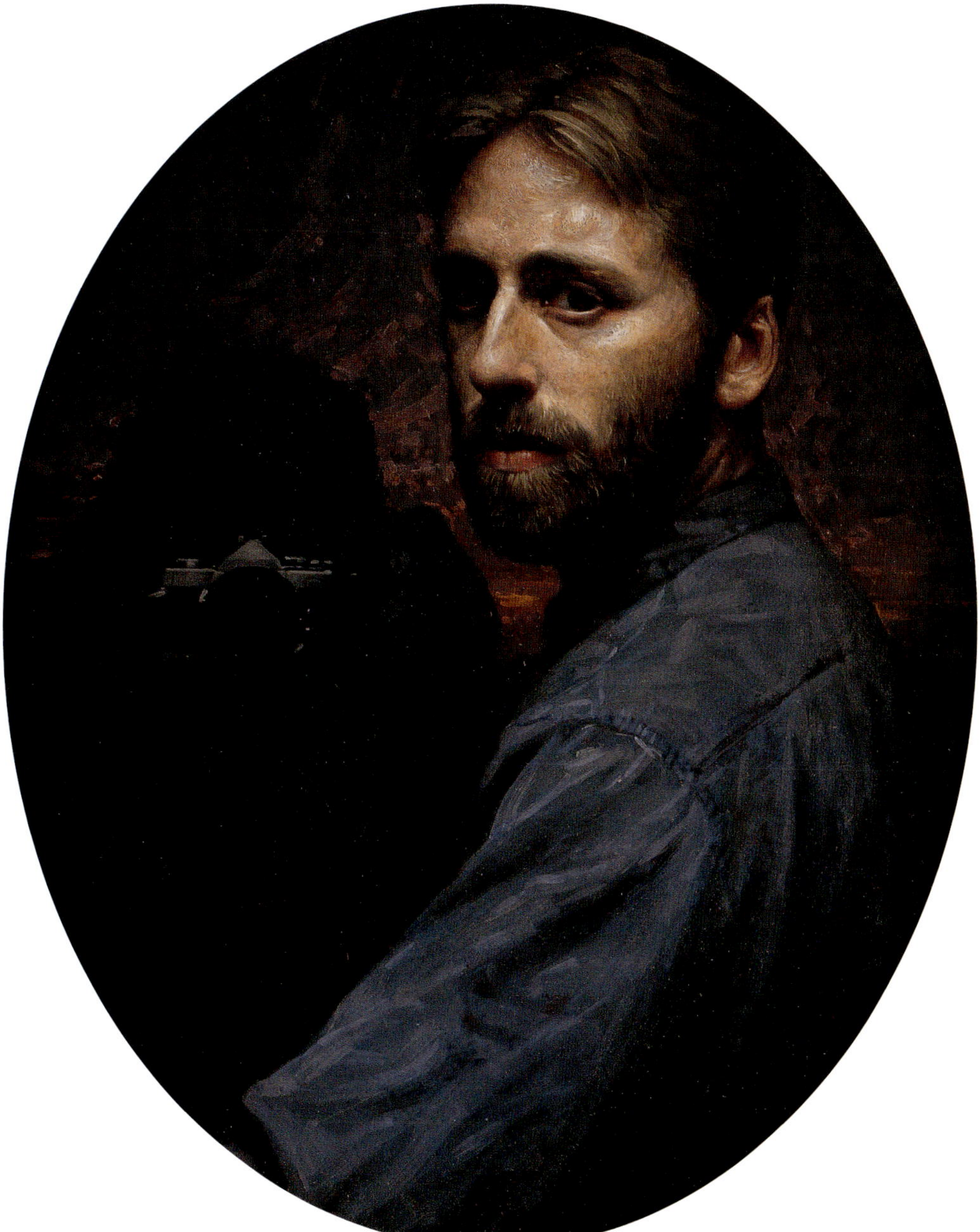

Falling
Jennifer Anderson
Oil on canvas
1030 x 1680mm

Waiting for Margaret
Paul Birdsall
Oil on canvas
715 x 922mm

Domanda e Risposta
Davide Castronova
Oil on board
Diptych, each
326 x 280mm

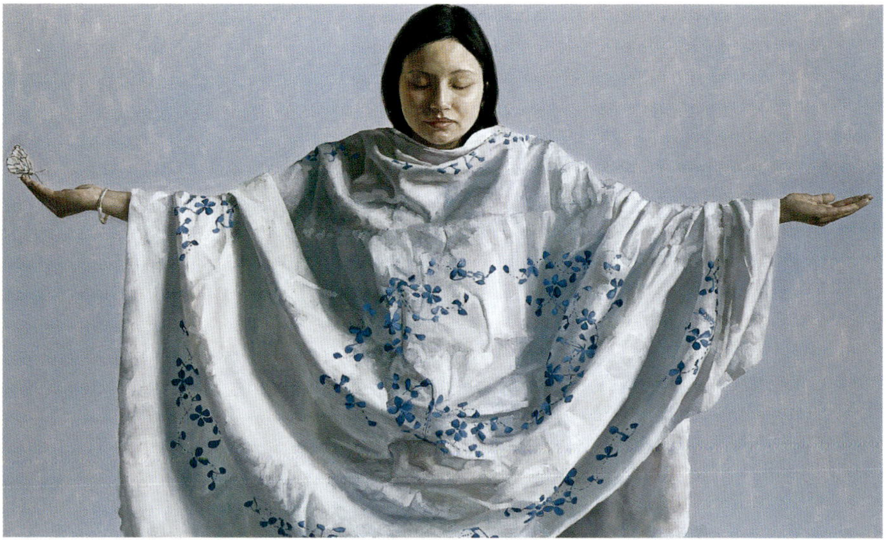

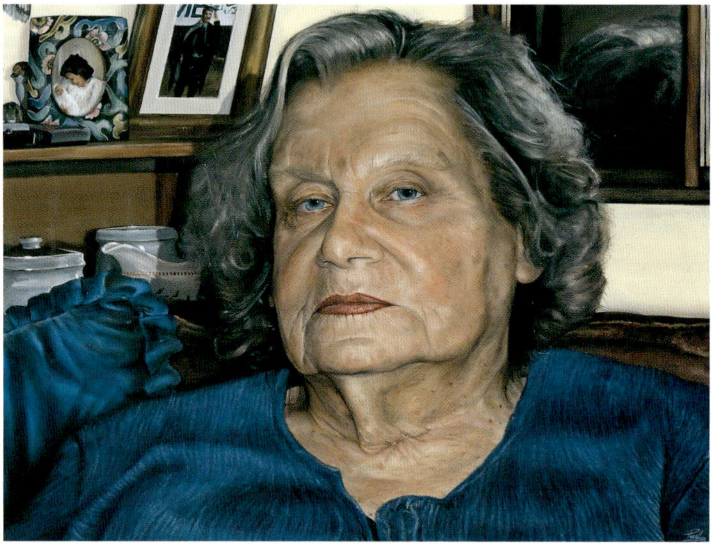

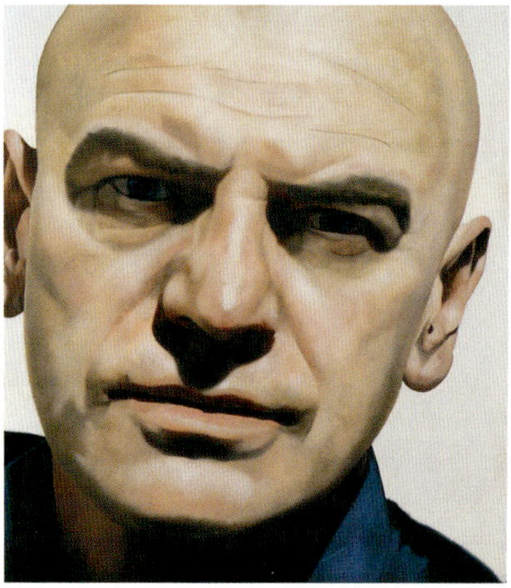

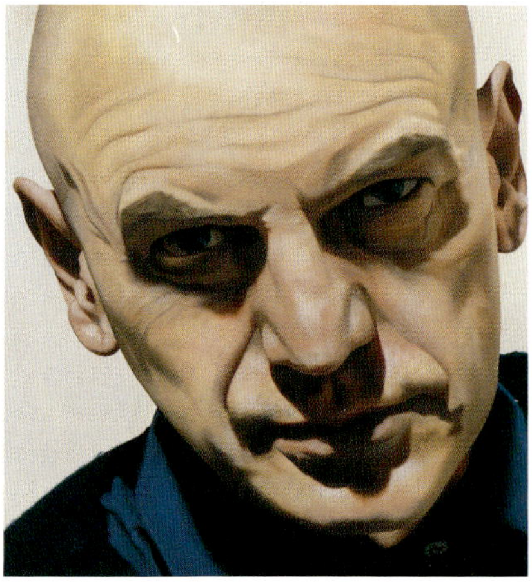

Portrait of Chantal Menard
Sean Cheetham
Oil on panel
354 x 304mm

Paul
Sylvie Clarke
Oil on canvas
920 x 920mm

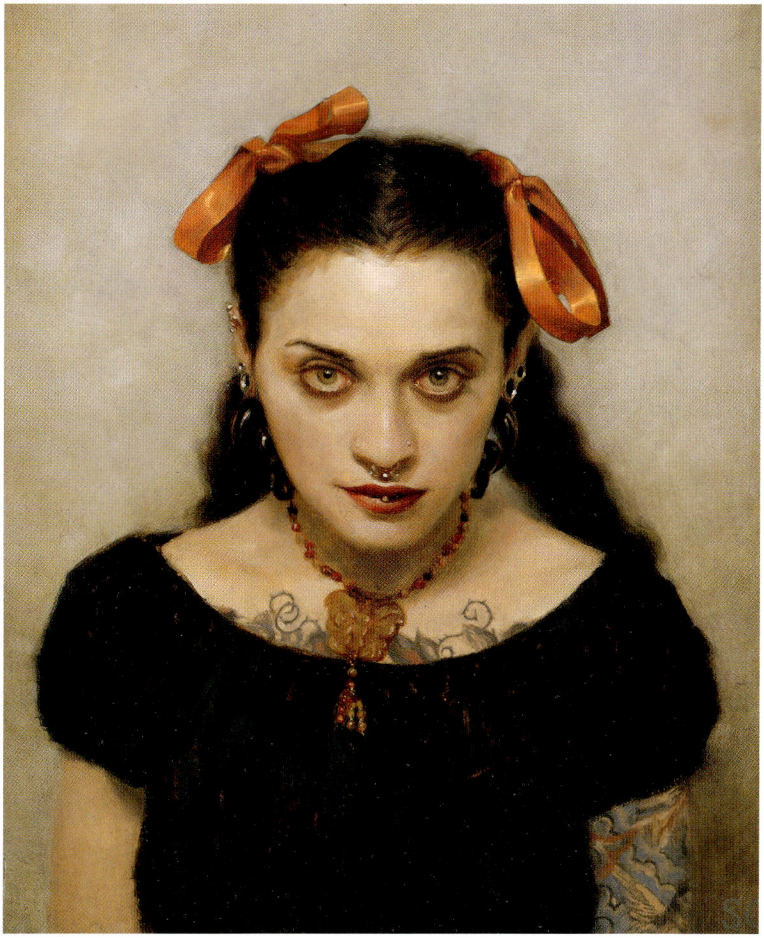

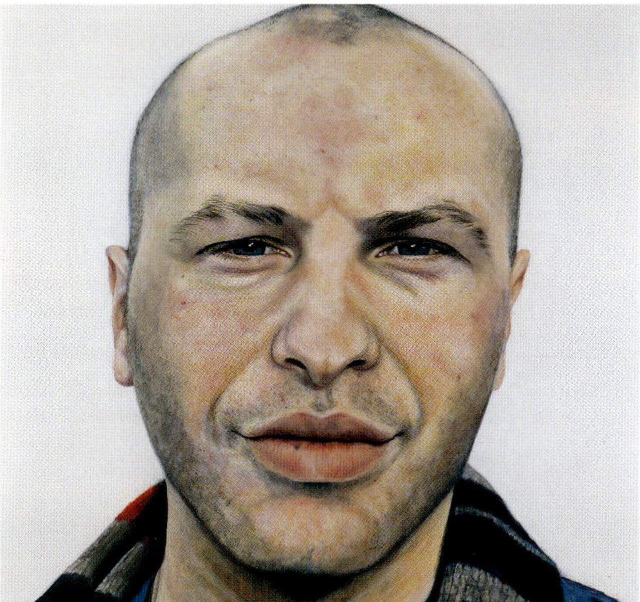

Gran Turismo
Megan Davies
Oil on canvas
1255 x 1718mm

Person 2004/5
Roy Eastland
Acrylic on board
280 x 255mm

Sebastien
Joel Ely
Oil on canvas
1220 x 915mm

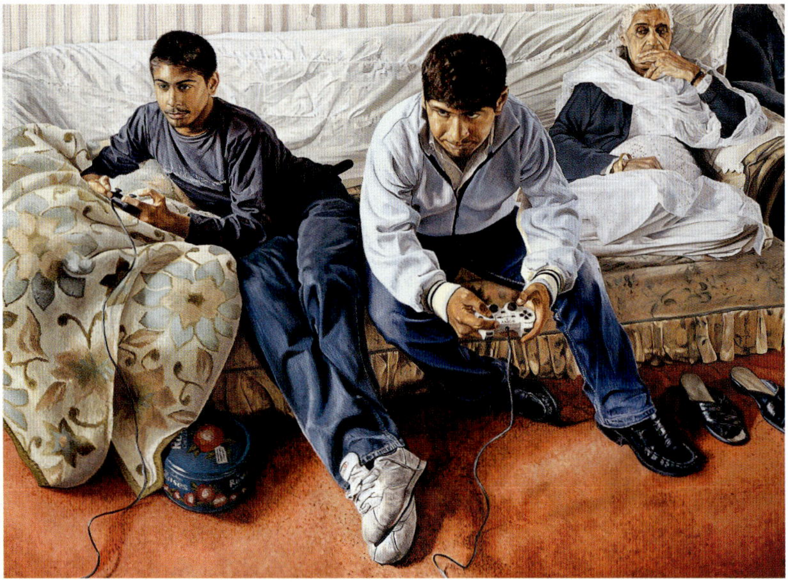

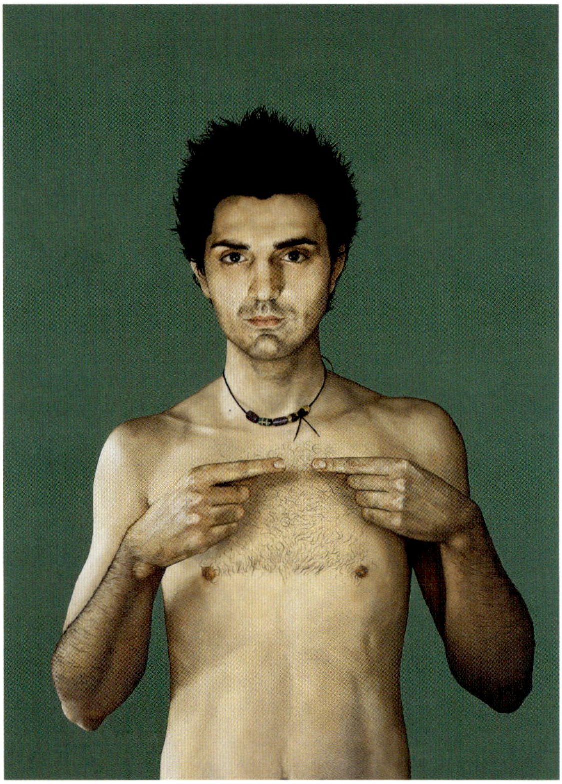

Portrait of Sally Esdaile & her Family or Tea-time
Eneko Fraile-Ugalde
Oil on canvas
800 x 890mm

Anna and Kiki
James Hart Dyke
Oil on canvas
1800 x 1540mm

Tibi Tibi
Daniel Hughes
Oil on board
510 x 410mm

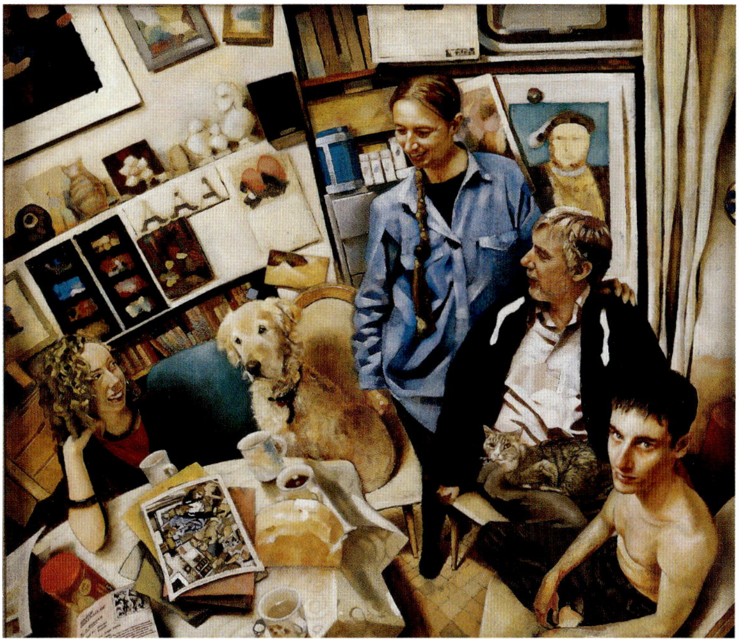

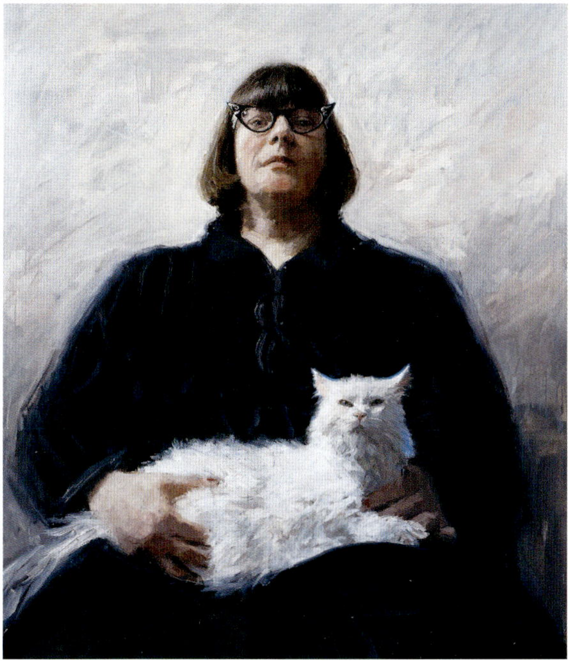

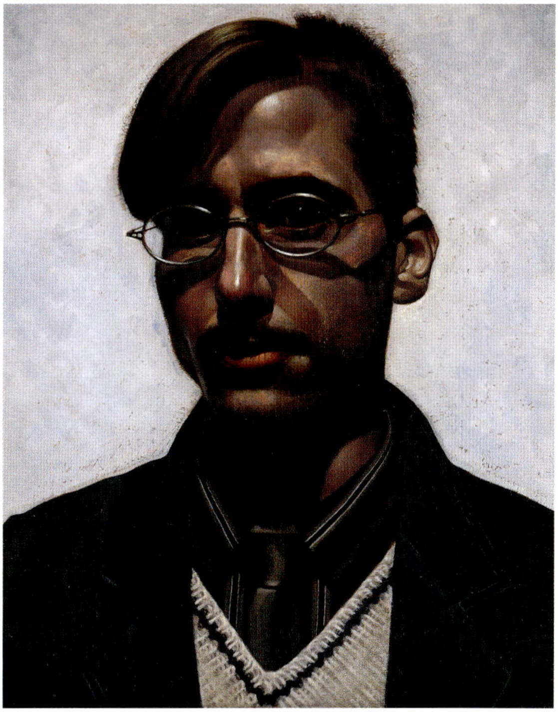

Tell Me
Helena Hugo
Oil on board
970 x 660mm

Five to Midnight
Sheldon Hutchinson
Oil on board
599 x 485mm

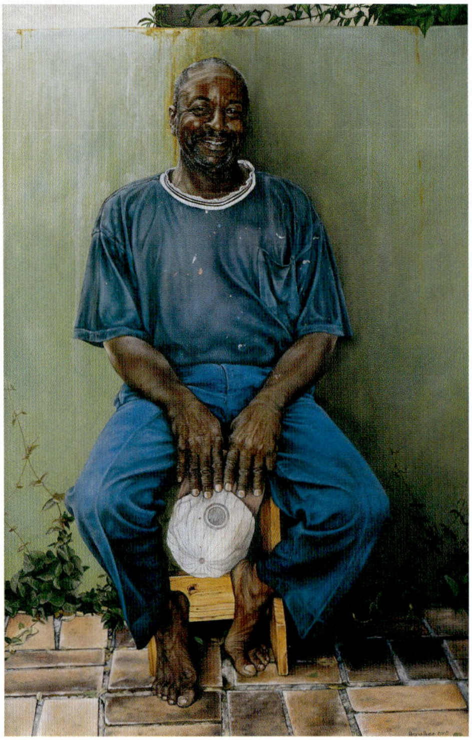

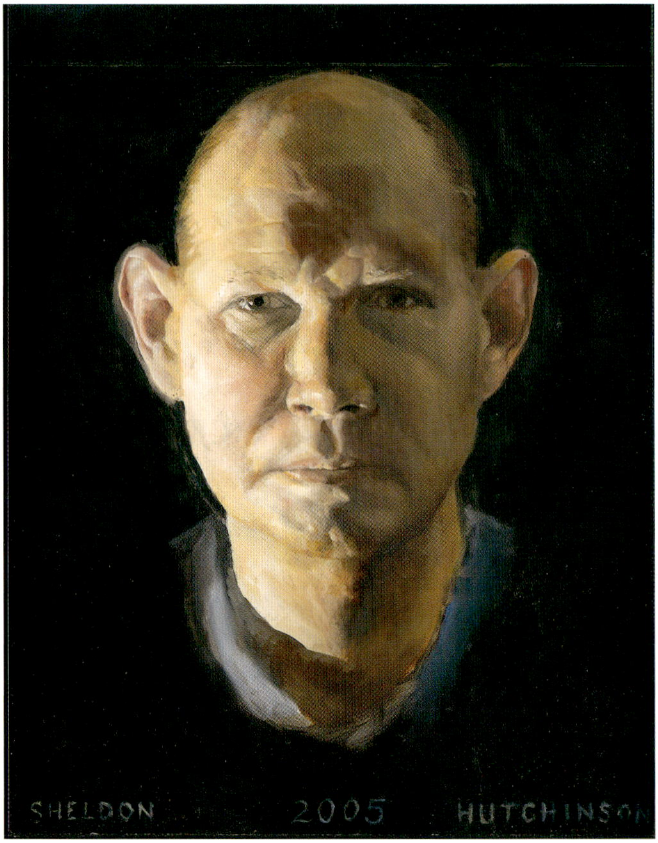

This is Me when I'm Painting (Self-portrait)
Shaun James Nielsen
Oil on board
570 x 570mm

Sir Duncan Joseph
Duncan Joseph
Oil on canvas
1940 x 1445mm

Morgan
Jack Kettlewell
Acrylic on canvas
1543 x 886mm

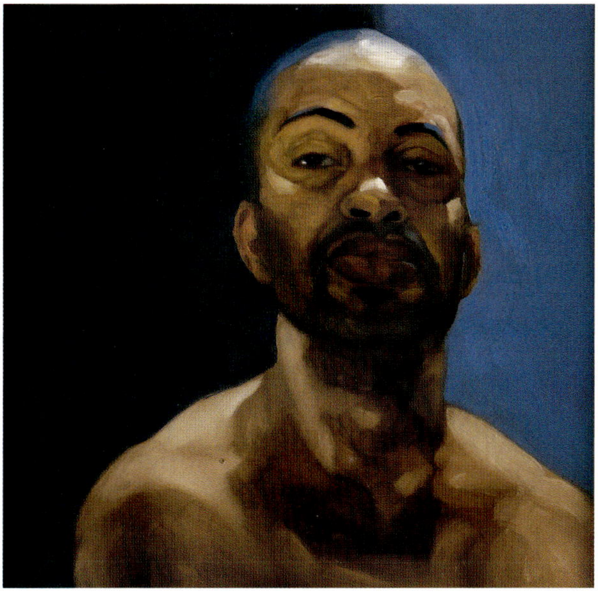

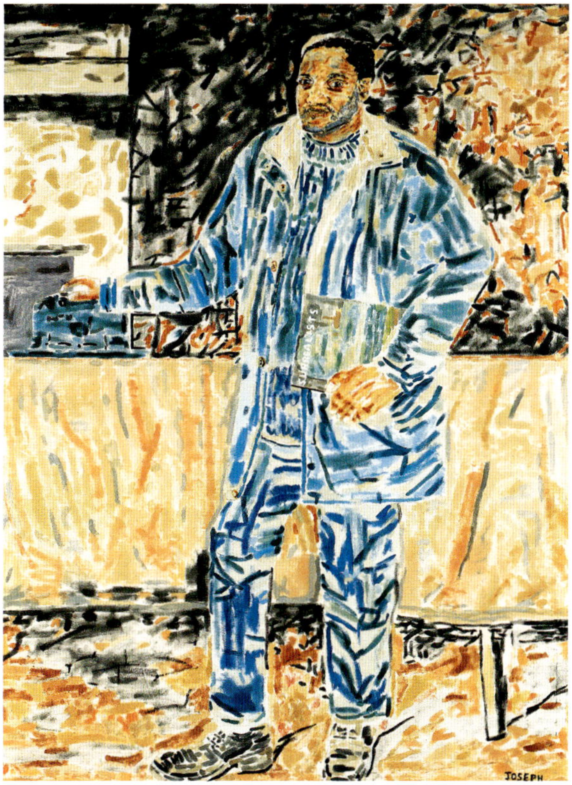

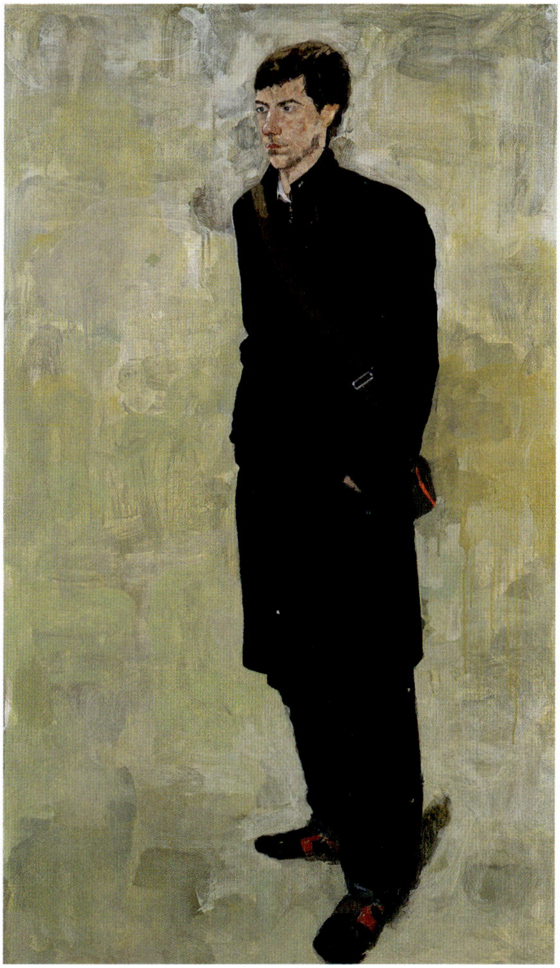

Self-portrait, Shaving 2 (Return of the Mach)
Ian Lamont
Oil on canvas on board
730 x 630mm

End of the Festival
David Martin
Oil on canvas
1290 x 1040mm

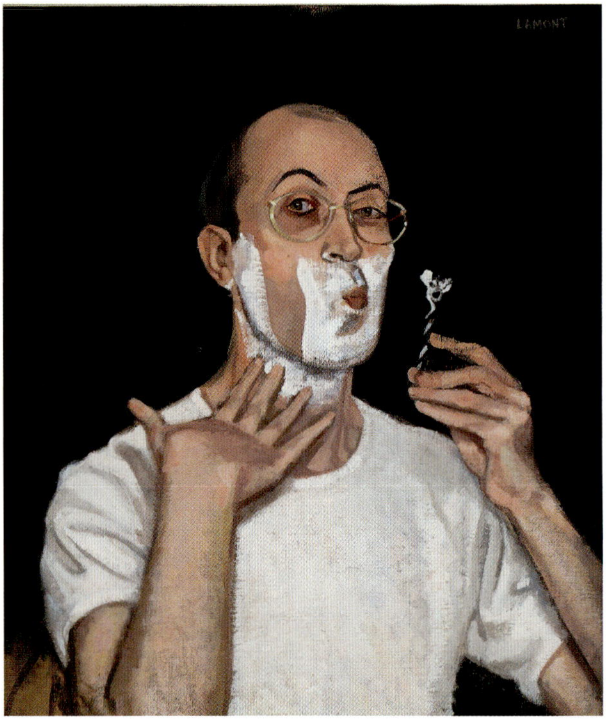

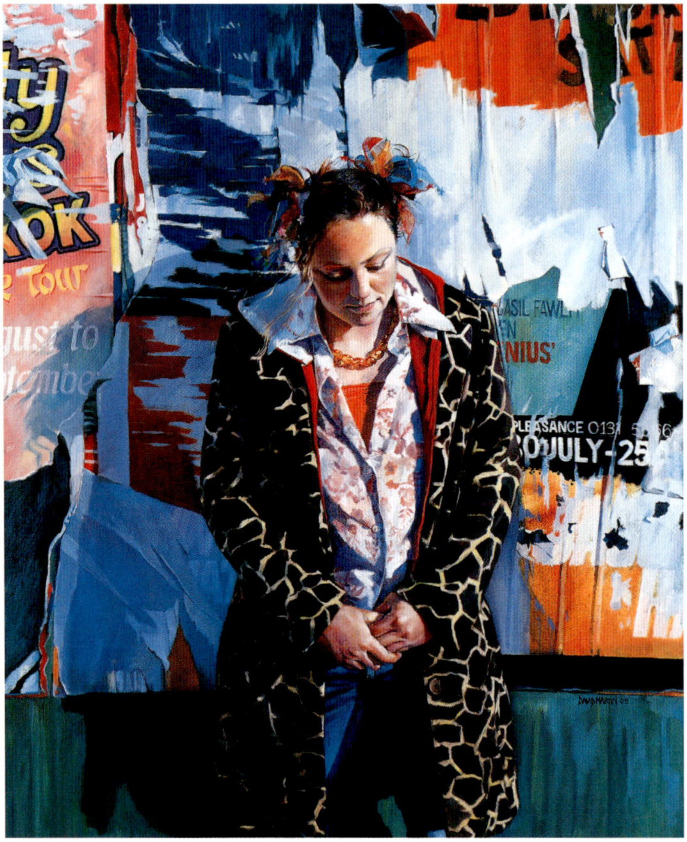

Portrait of Kevin Kiely – Writer
Maeve McCarthy
Oil on panel
1210 x 845mm

Self-portrait
Cian McLoughlin
Oil on canvas
690 x 580mm

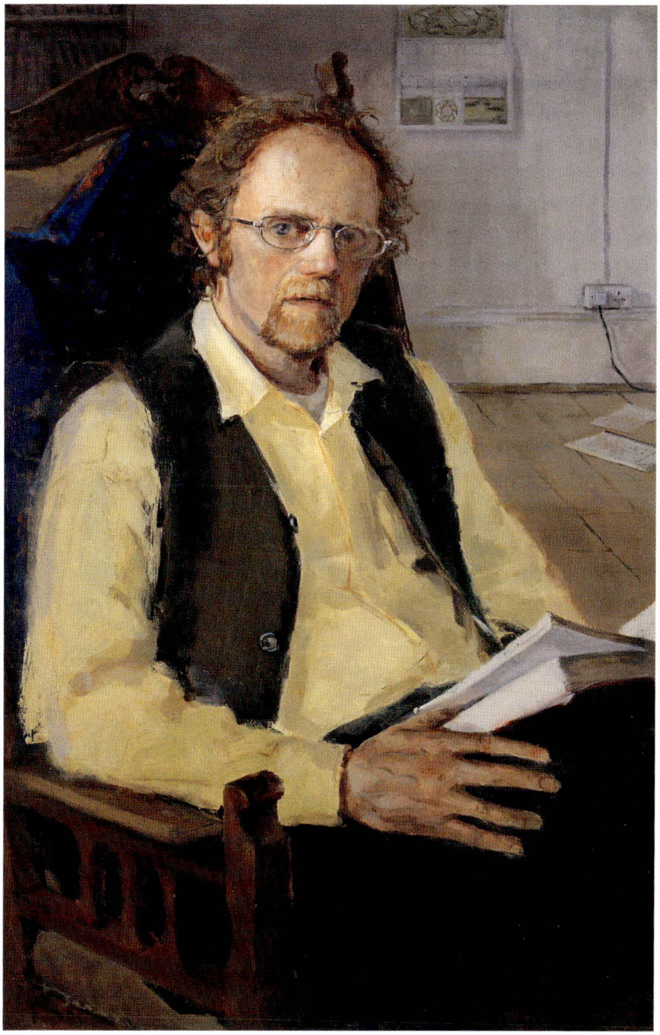

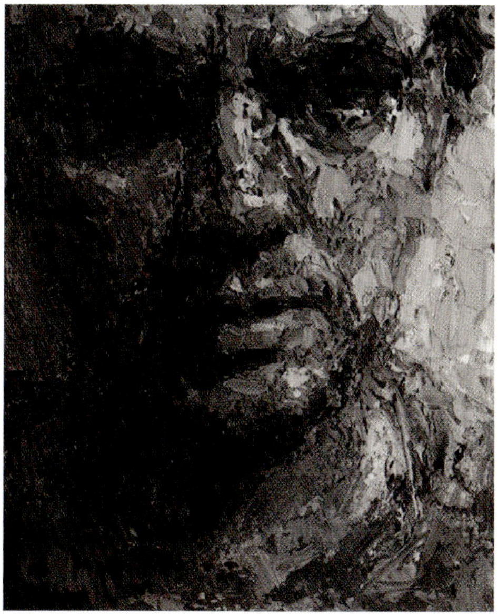

Beky Stoddart (Mural Painter)
Nicholas Middleton
Oil on canvas
910 x 910mm

Claire
Graham Milton
Oil on canvas
1003 x 503mm

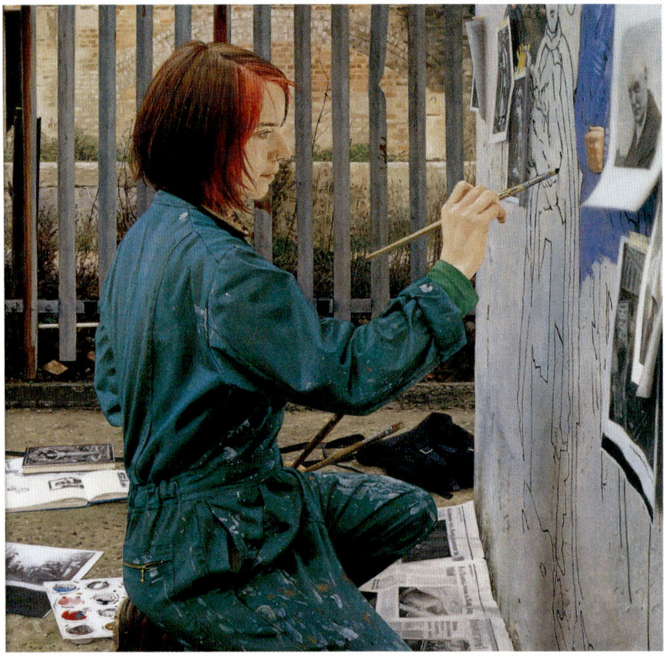

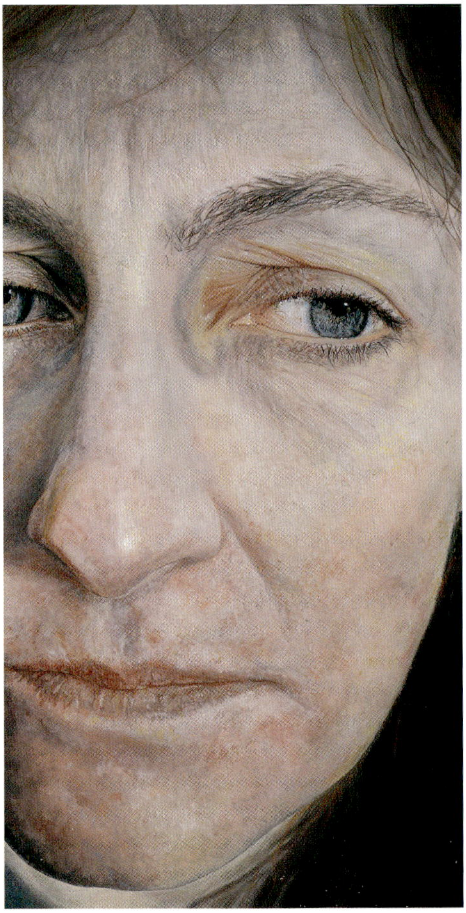

A Quiet Place
Jon Murphy-Woolford
Oil on board
558 x 680mm

Self-portrait
Daniel Munday
Oil on canvas
380 x 370mm

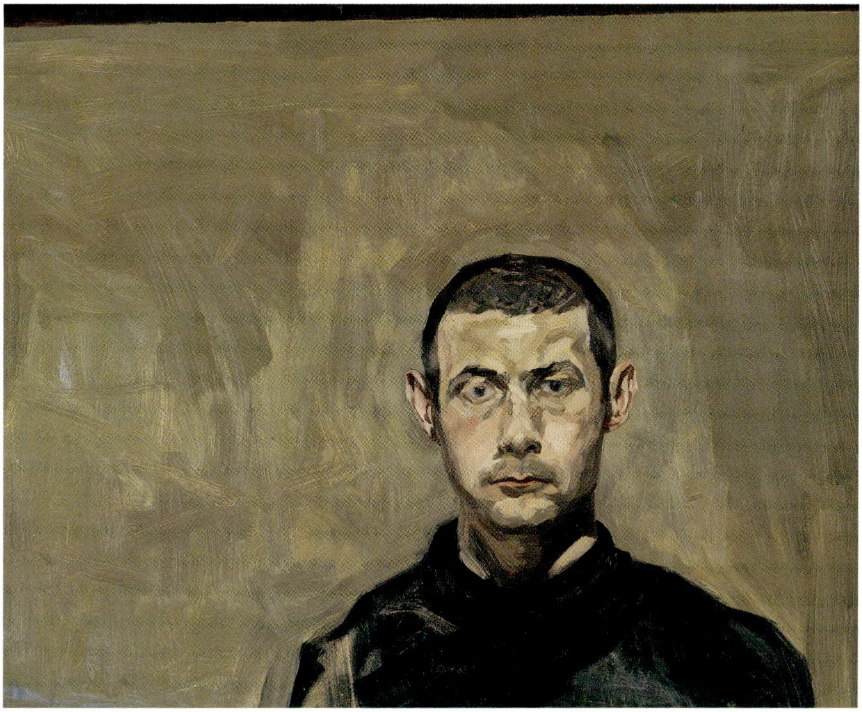

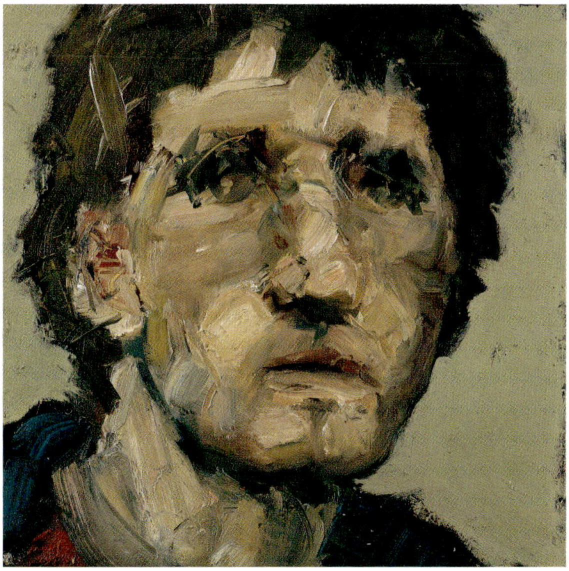

Javier
Paul Oxborough
Oil on linen
790 x 990mm

L as Miss Palmer
after Reynolds
Andy Pankhurst
Oil on canvas
920 x 790mm

Self-portrait in Front of
Red Dawn 2005
Nicky Philipps
Oil on canvas
1250 x 994mm

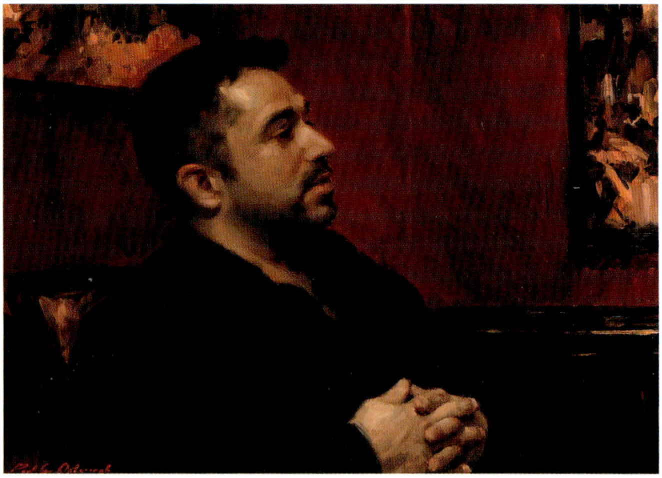

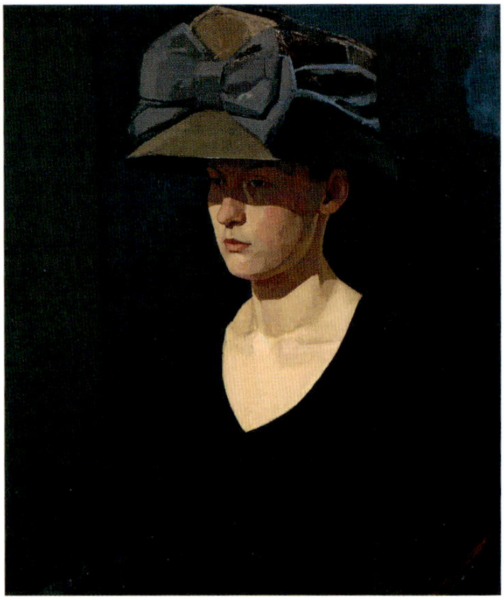

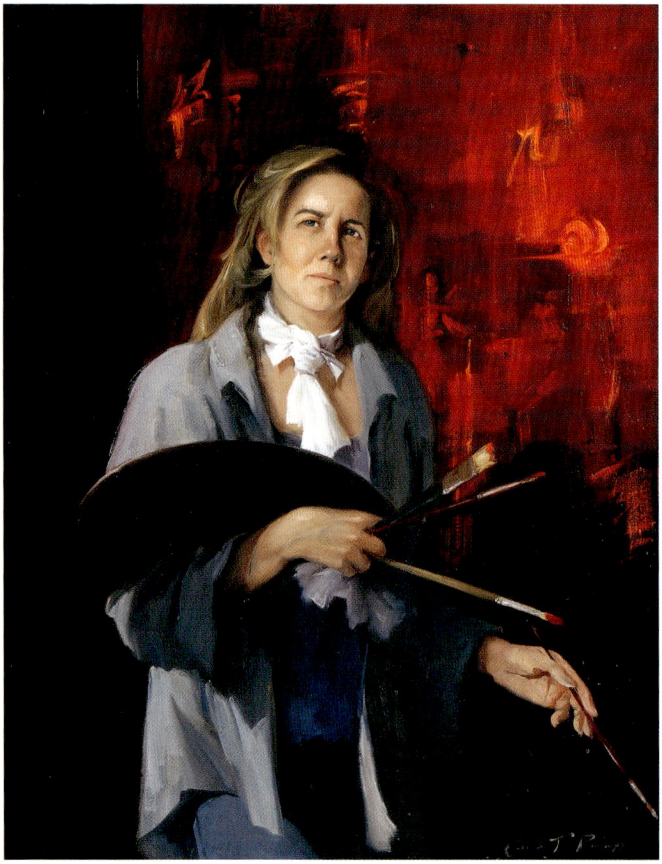

(Self-portrait)
With Knife and Meat
Alex Rennie
Oil on canvas
1220 x 870mm

Ailing Novelist
Konstantin Sheiko
Oil on canvas
610 x 455mm

Maria
Paul Smith
Oil on canvas
500 x 580mm

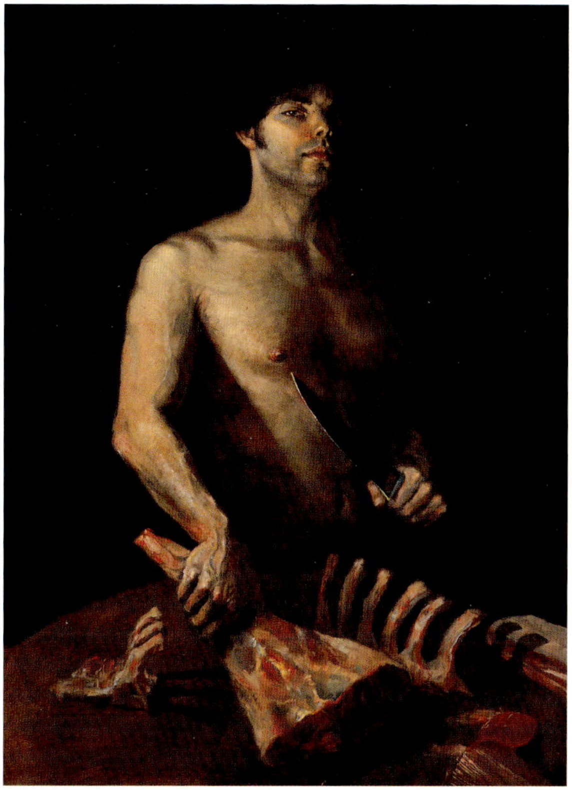

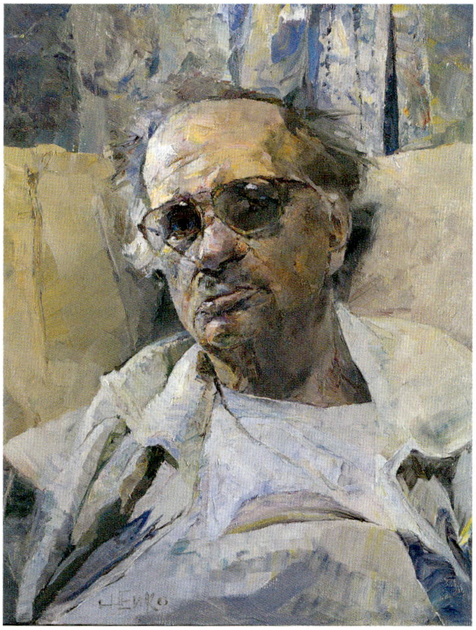

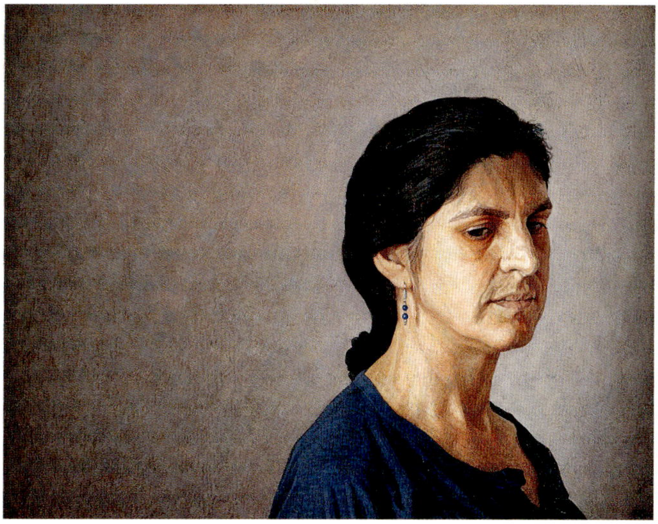

Older
Charlotte Steel
Oil on board
780 x 510mm

Self-portrait
Bonnie Thompson
Oil on board
440 x 330mm

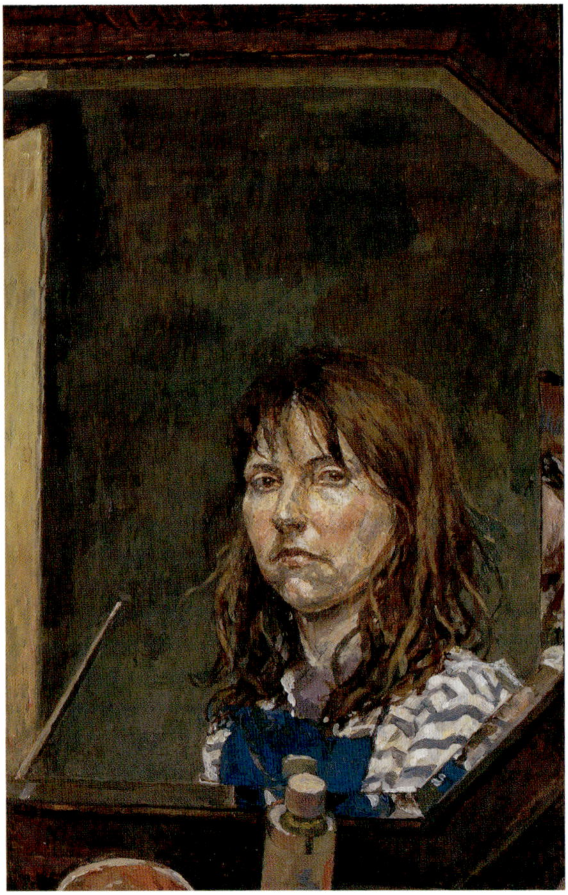

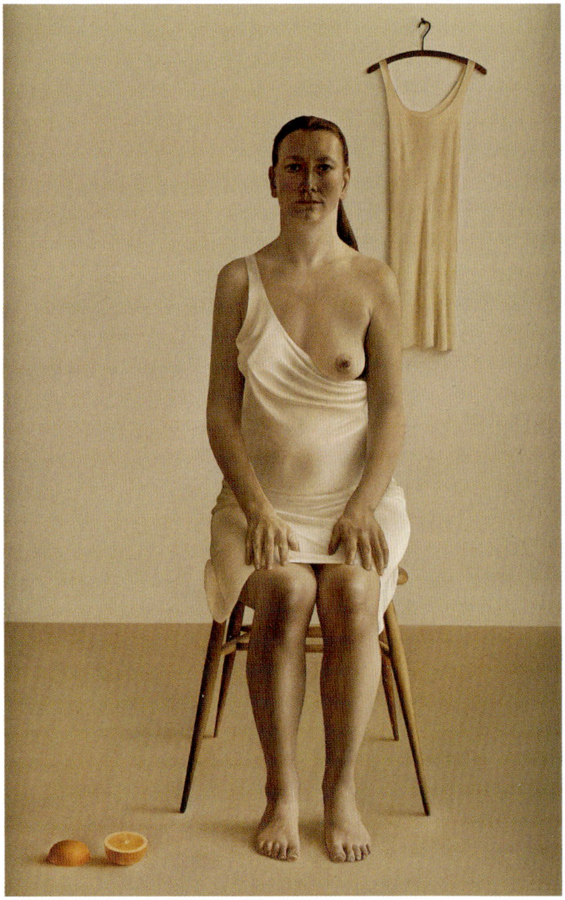

Arrival
Stefan Towler
Oil on board
529 x 415mm

Wife and Daughter
Thierry Louis Tremas
Oil on canvas
925 x 730mm

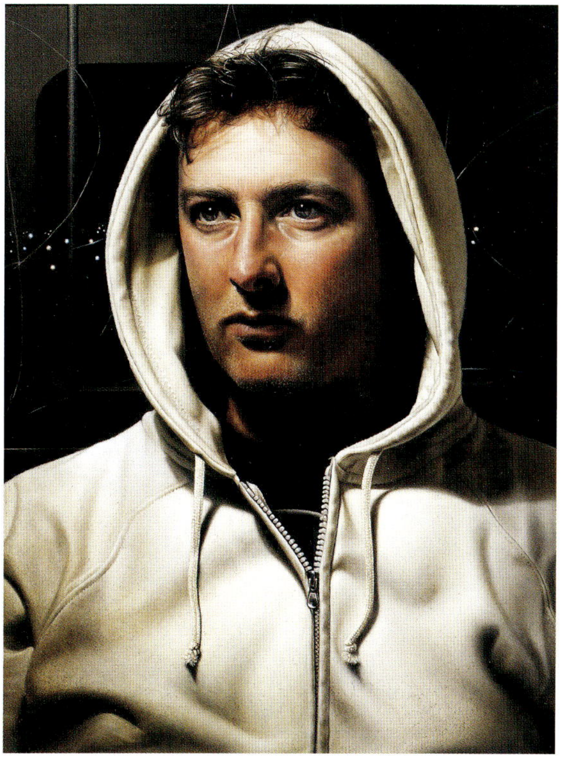

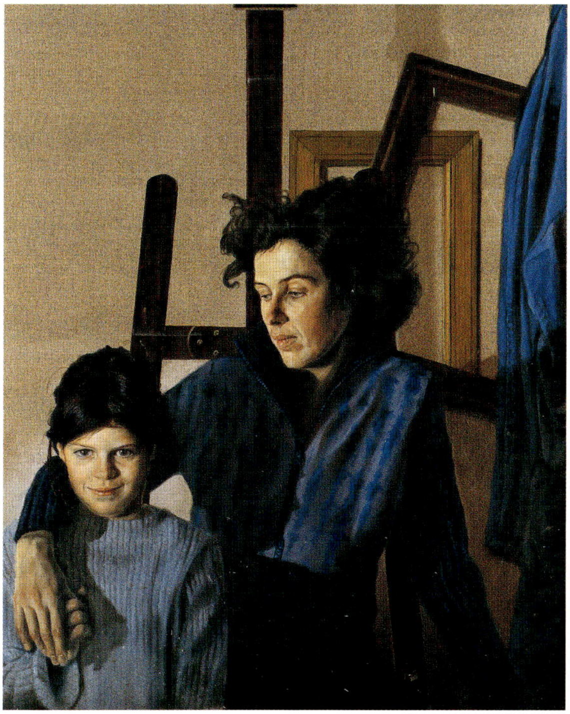

Orange Angel
David Webb
Acrylic on canvas
290 x 295mm

Ed
Antony Williams
Egg tempera on panel
548 x 500mm

Untitled
Hugo Wilson
Oil on canvas
778 x 680mm

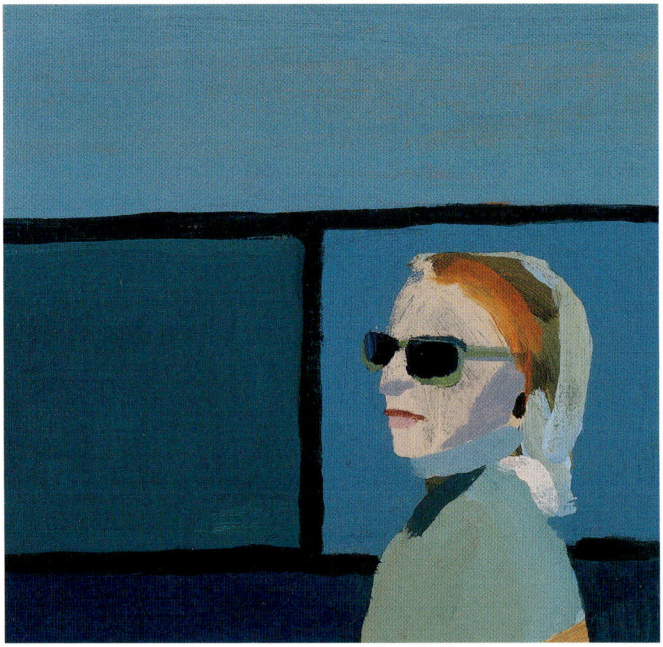

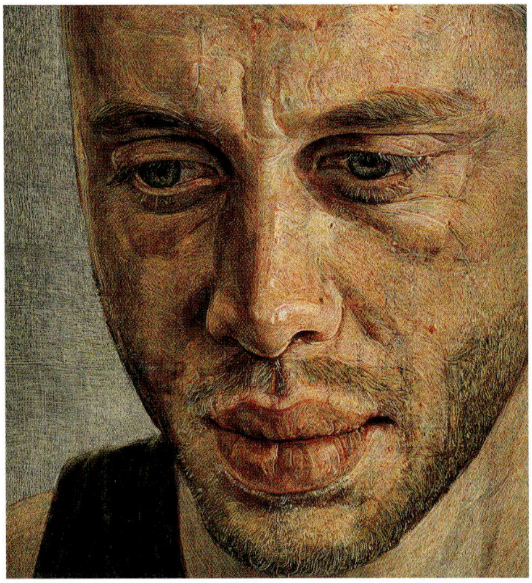

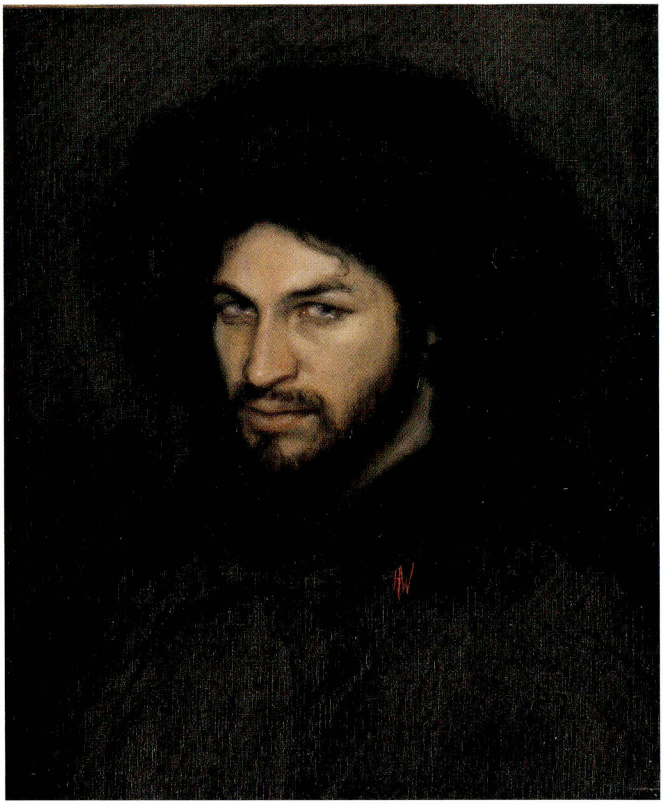

The Craftsman
Daniel Wray
Oil on board
650 x 1170mm

Erin
Jonathan Yeo
Oil on canvas
1100 x 720mm

Self-portrait
Gavin Young
Oil on board
385 x 360mm

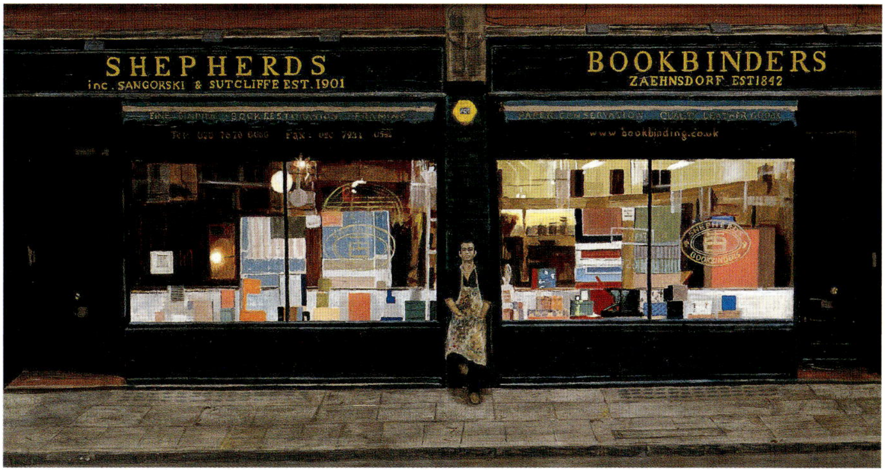

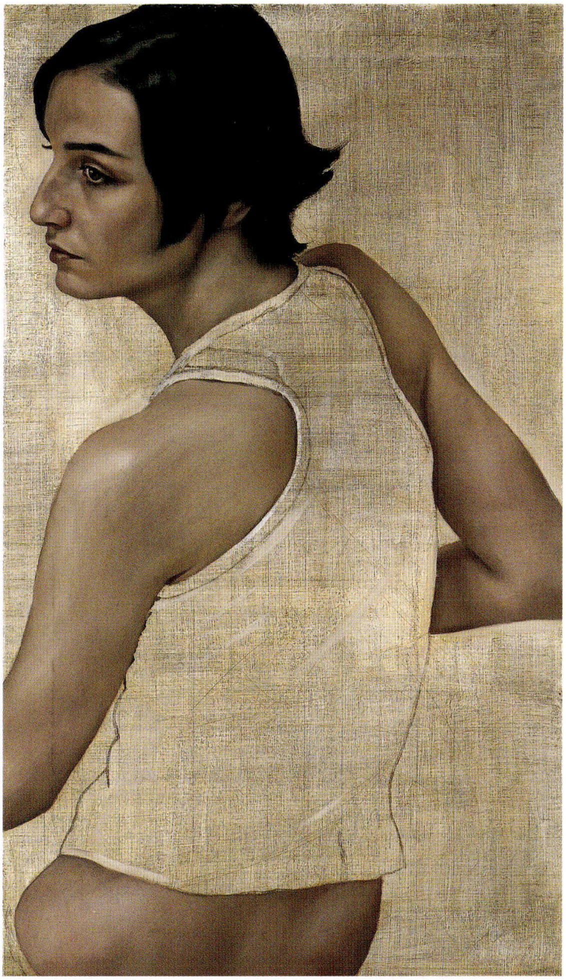

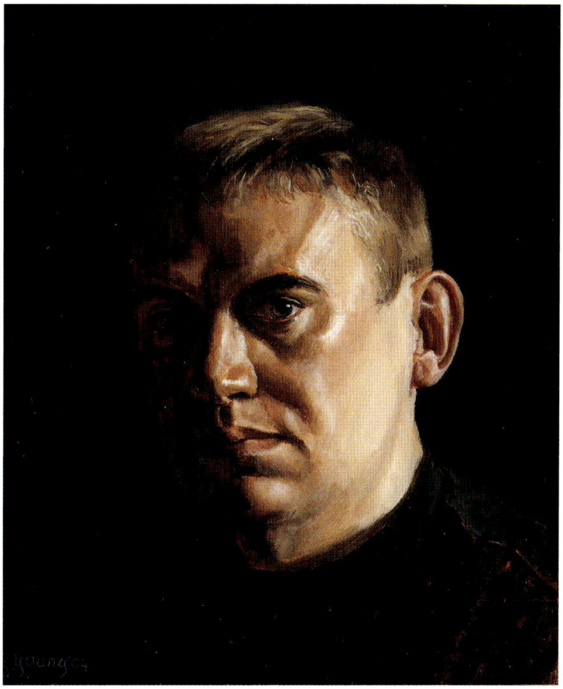

2006

ARTISTS WHOSE PORTRAITS WERE EXHIBITED

Joseph Avery / Mary Beale / Annemarie Busschers / Rafael Rodriguez Cruz / Gregory Cumins / Michael De Brito / Jeremy Delvine / Clara Drummond / Robert Dukes / Darvish Fakhr / Irene Ferguson / David Fulford / Iain Gardiner / Vanessa Garwood / Nicola Green / Barry Haines / Howard Craig Hanna / Andrew Hilling / Leo Holloway / Alexander Innes / Ben Jamie / Aleksandra Jarosz Laszlo / Jon Jones / Shi-Chi Lin / Norman Long / Gentian Lulanaj / Ana-Maria Micu / Graham Milton / Grace O'Conner / Tim Okamura / Geraldine O'Neill / Sergio Ostroverhy / Jekaterina Pertoft / Anastasia Pollard / Erin Raedeke / Angela Reilly / Stephen Earl Rogers / Patricia Rorie / Rebecca Smith / Jung-Im Song / Sarah Spencer / Emily Stainer / Benjamin Sullivan / Andrew Tift / Craig Tiley / Stefan Towler / William Tuck / Covadonga Valdes / Adele Wagstaff / Jason Walker / Emma Wesley / Monica Whalley / Toby Wiggins / Katie Wright / Paul Wright / Craig Wylie / Jonathan Yeo

SECOND PRIZE
FROM THE SERIES MODEL FOR A SELF-PORTRAIT 'MODEL 1 (LOLA)'
RAFAEL RODRIGUEZ CRUZ

Oil on canvas
300 x 400mm

Rafael Rodriguez Cruz lives and works in Mexico, where he studied architecture and fine art. He has been working as an artist since 1998 and has exhibited in Mexico, where his exhibition *Ansikte*, based on a journey around Mexico City, Queretaro and Monterrey, toured the country's national museums, and internationally. In 2004 he was artist in residence in the Swedish region of Vastra, based at the Nordic Watercolour Museum in Tjörn, Sweden.

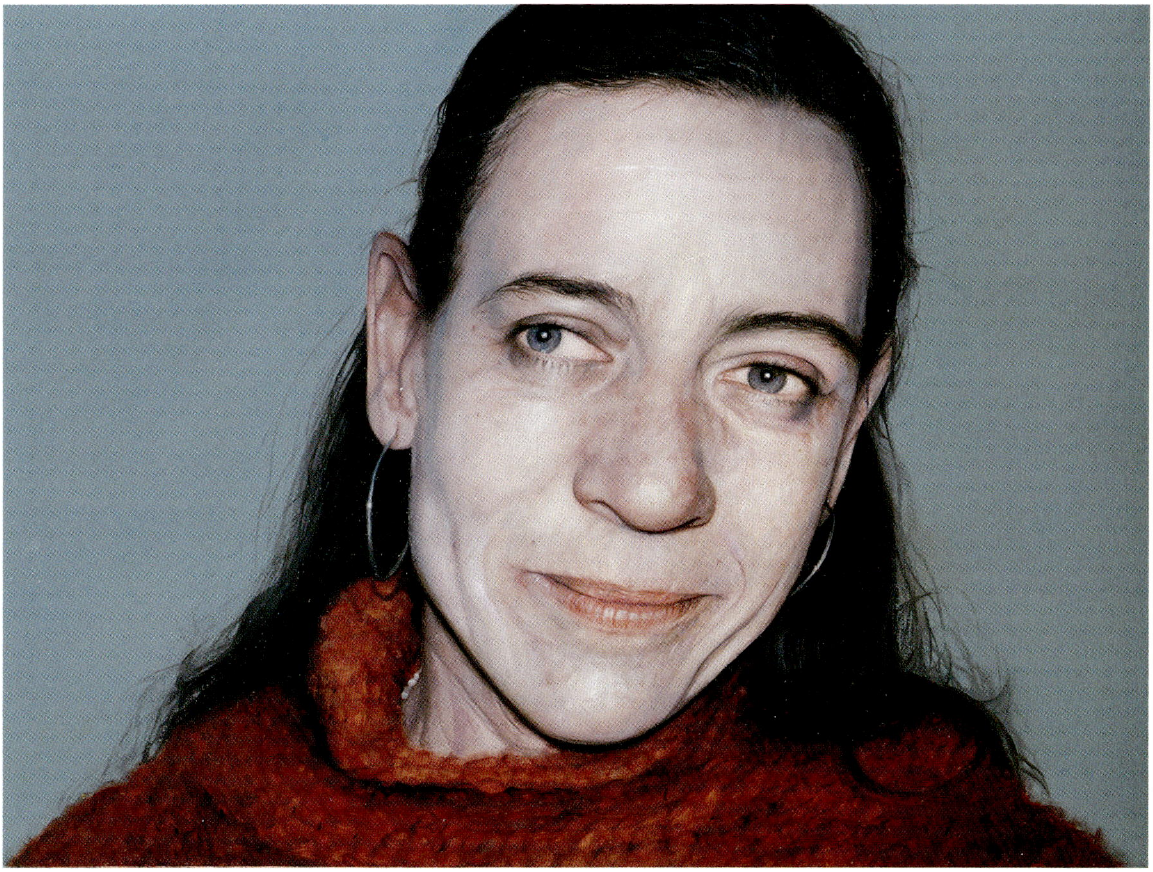

THIRD PRIZE
SELF-PORTRAIT
ANGELA REILLY

Oil on canvas
1230 x 925mm

Having studied Fine Art at Duncan of Jordanstone College of Art and Design, Dundee, in the 1980s, Angela Reilly worked as an illustrator in London. She has exhibited regularly in Scotland and London, and won the NS Macfarlane Award at the Royal Glasgow Institute of the Fine Arts in 2004. Now living and working in Glasgow, Reilly has described how she tries to create portraits that express the hidden depths of her subjects by focusing on their expressions and composure, with an emphasis on light and tone.

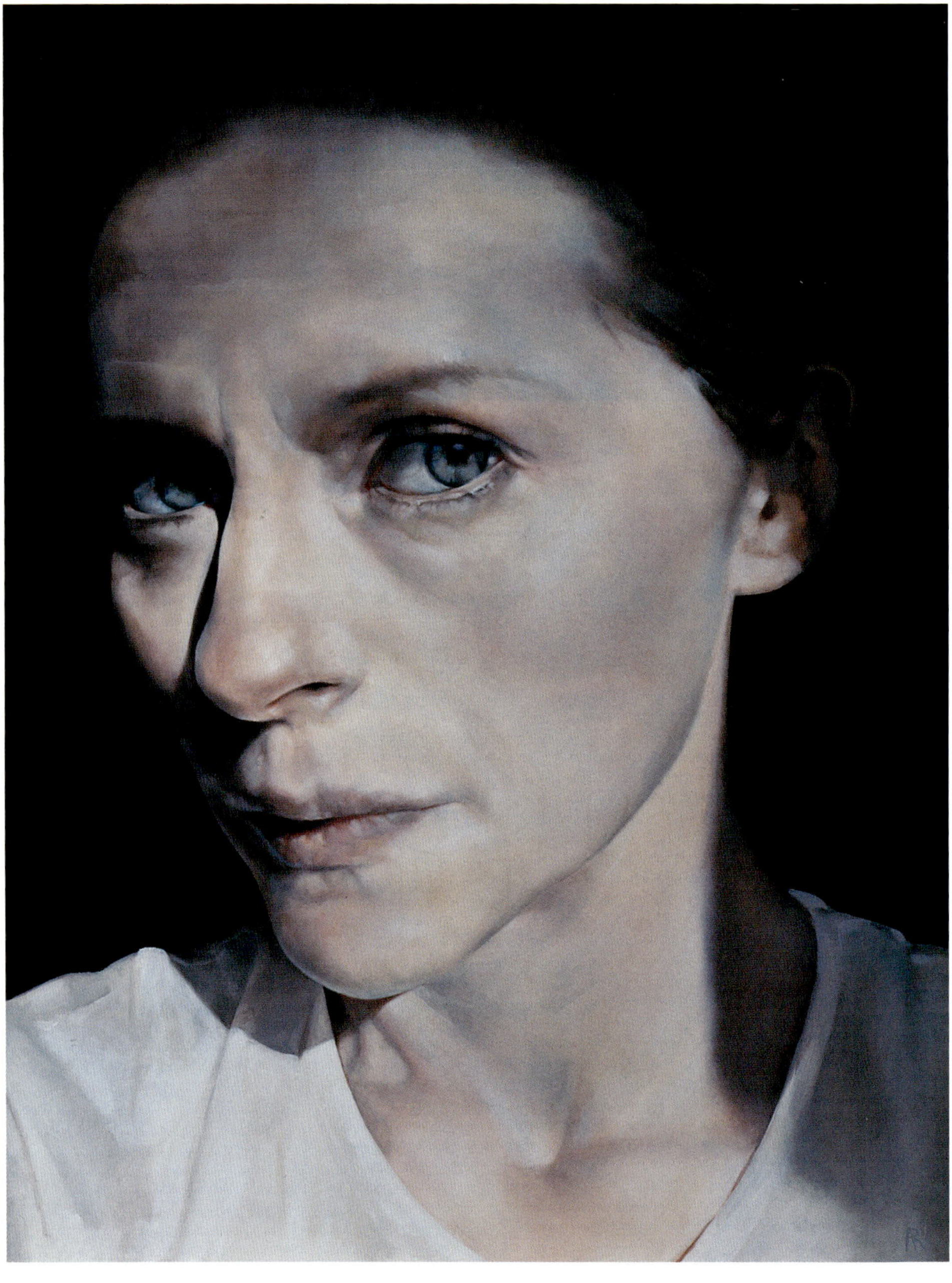

Self-portrait
Joseph Avery
Oil on board
300 x 250mm

Poet Laureate
Annemarie Busschers
Acrylic on canvas
2500 x 1600mm

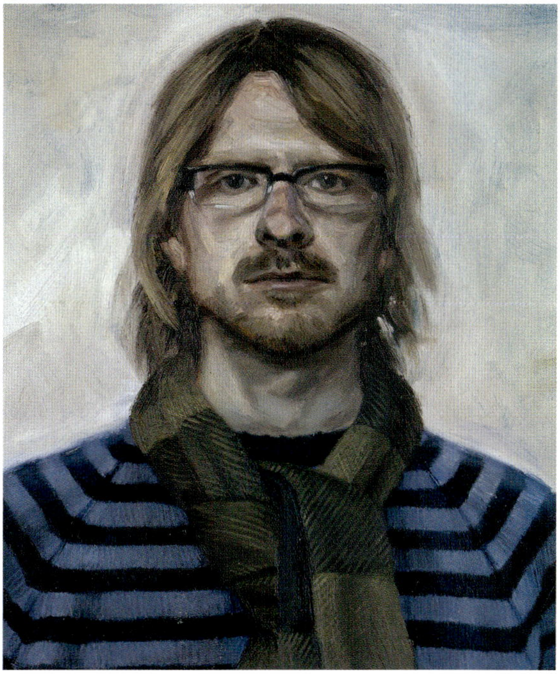

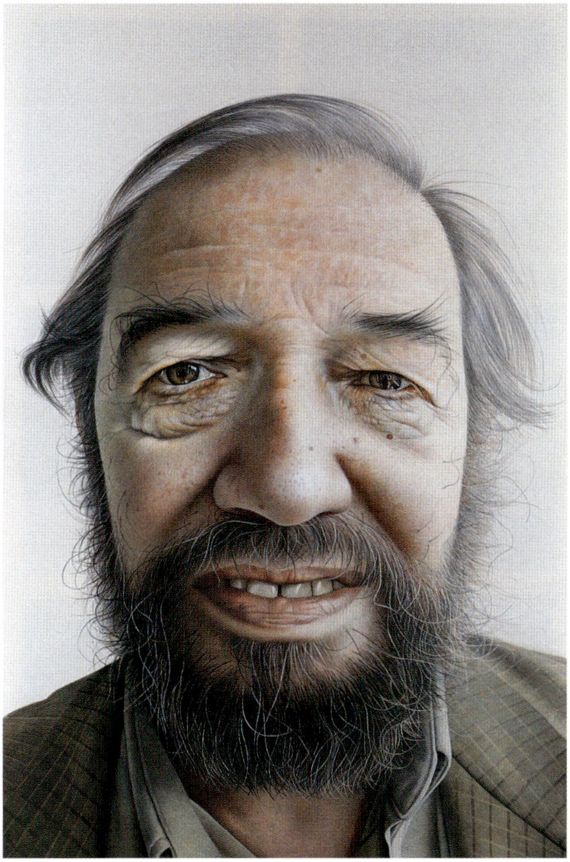

Napi
Gregory Cumins
Ink on canvas
1500 x 1500mm

Seated Man
Michael De Brito
Oil on canvas
555 x 400mm

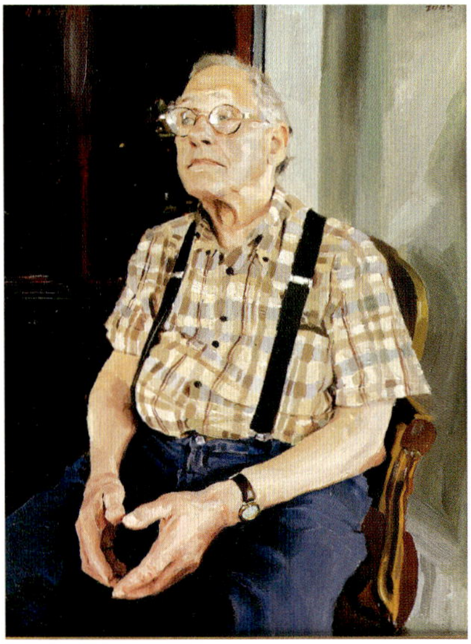

Portrait of the Artist's Wife
Jeremy Delvine
Acrylic on canvas
1440 x 1635mm

Jaemi
Clara Drummond
Oil on board
325 x 255mm

Rosie Sekers
Robert Dukes
Oil on board
350 x 275mm

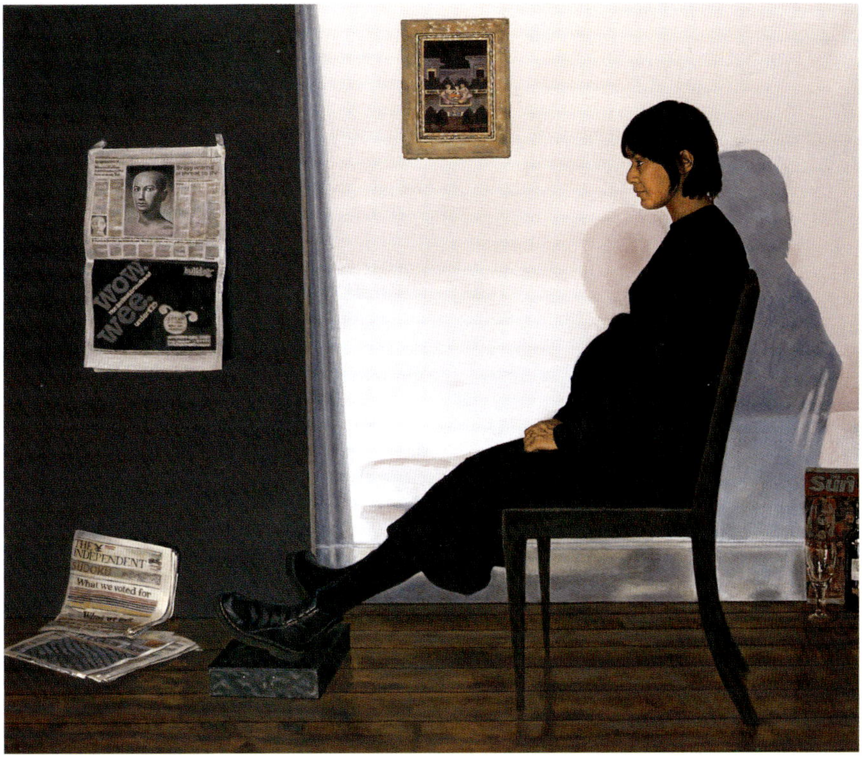

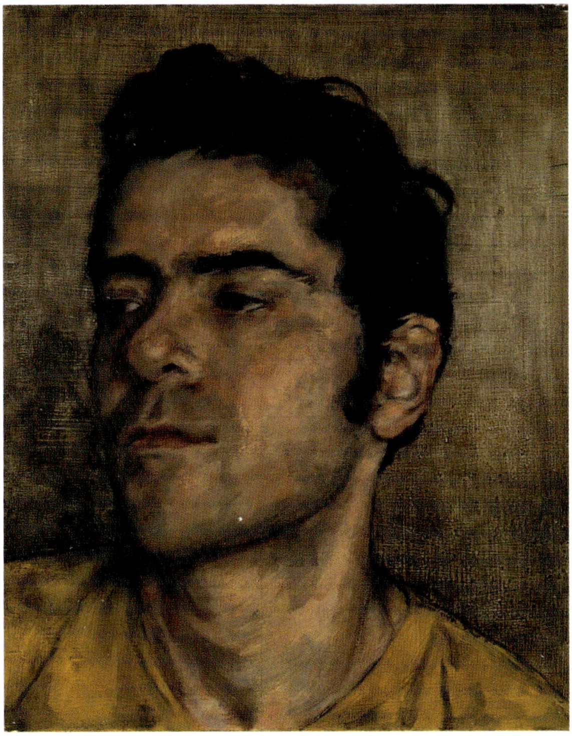

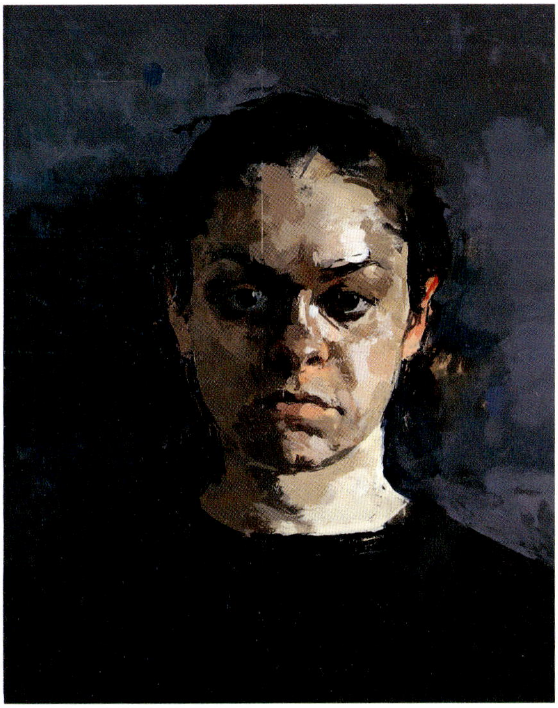

Sarah
Darvish Fakhr
Oil on canvas
3050 x 2040mm

No Title
Irene Ferguson
Oil on canvas
1320 x 715mm

Untitled
David Fulford
Oil on canvas
1200 x 850mm

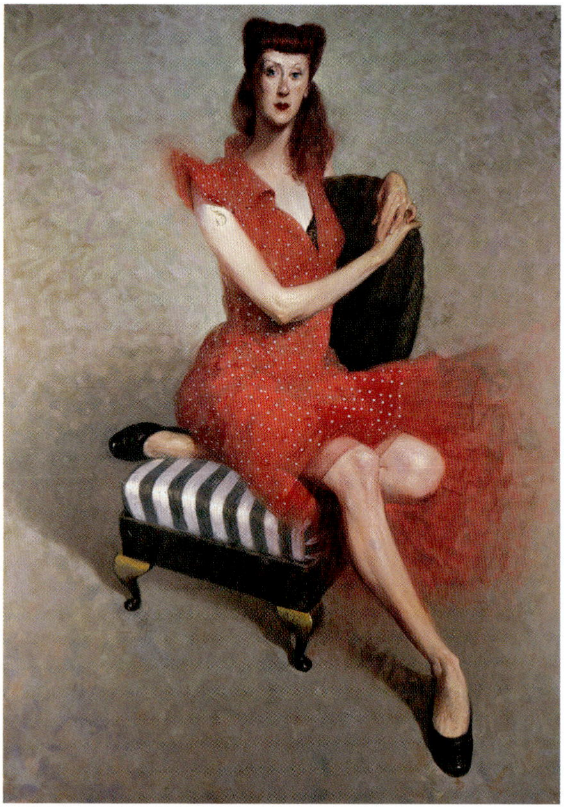

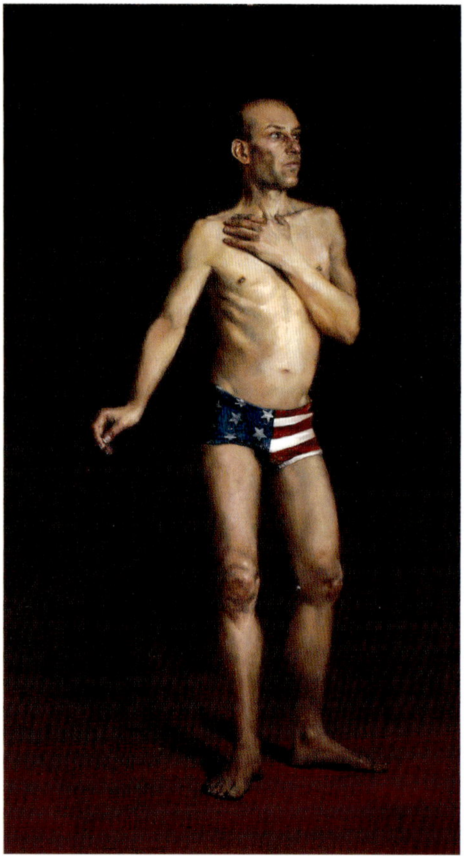

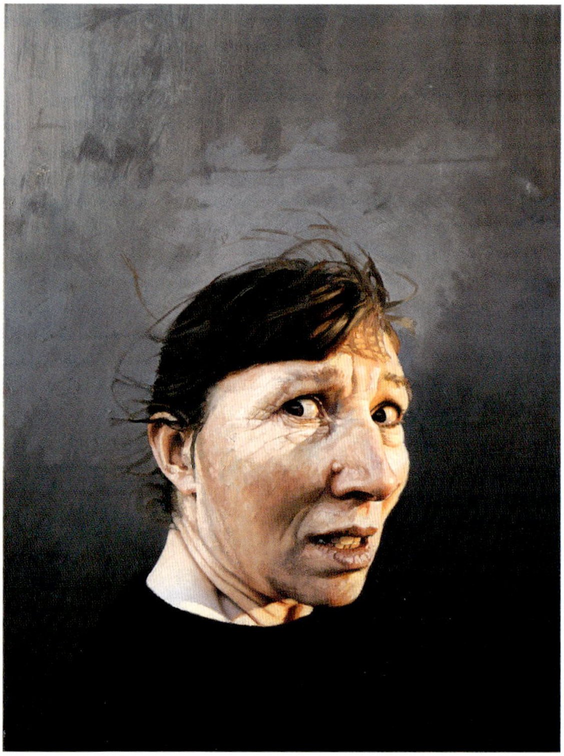

Mr & Mrs Gardiner
Iain Gardiner
Oil on canvas
565 x 460mm

Silvia
Vanessa Garwood
Oil on canvas
590 x 490mm

The Late Joshua Compston
Nicola Green
Oil on board
1830 x 760mm

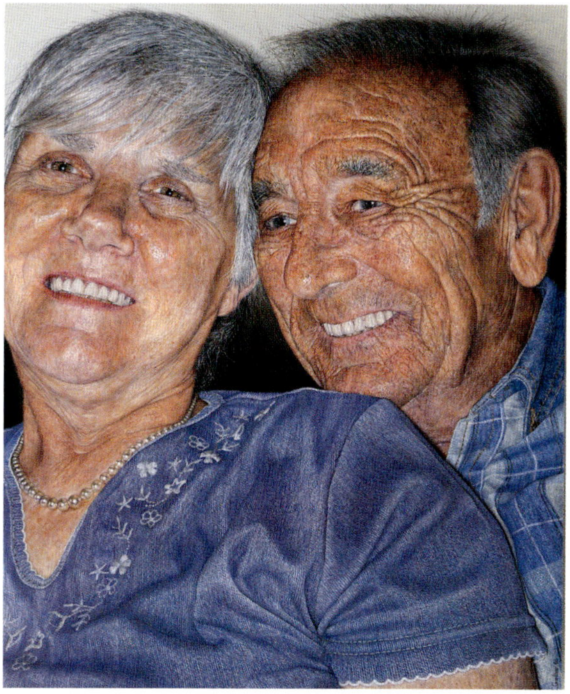

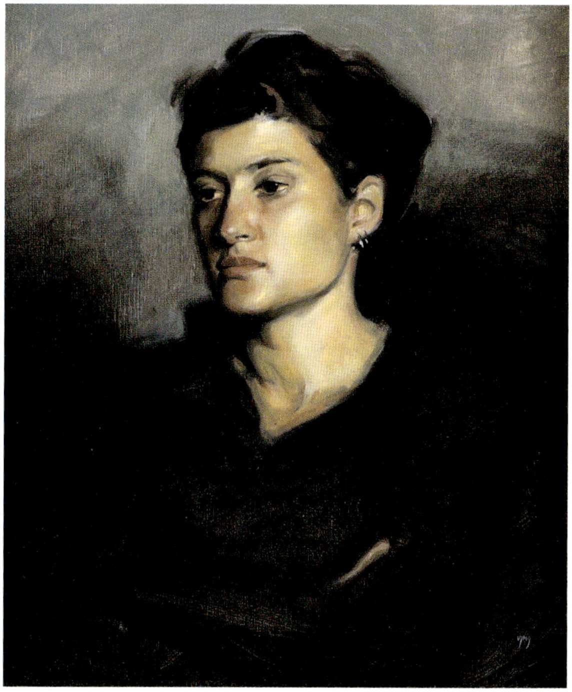

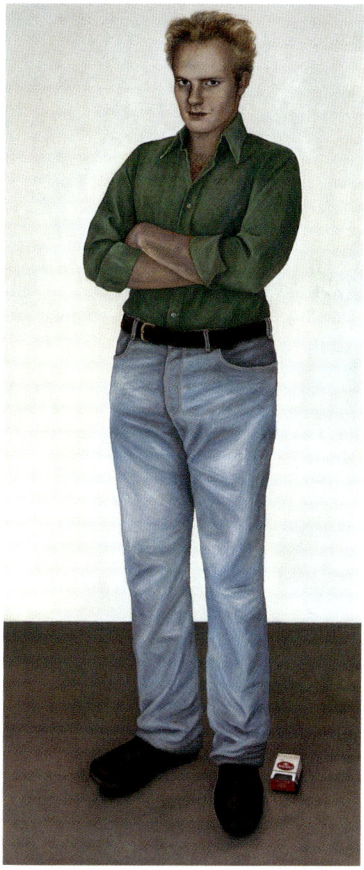

Worried
Barry Haines
Oil on linen
285 x 235mm

Hermes and George
Howard Craig Hanna
Oil on canvas
900 x 805mm

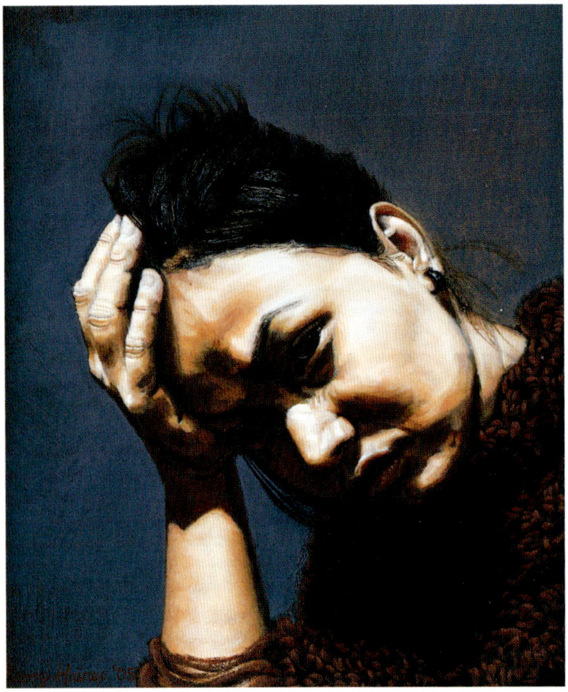

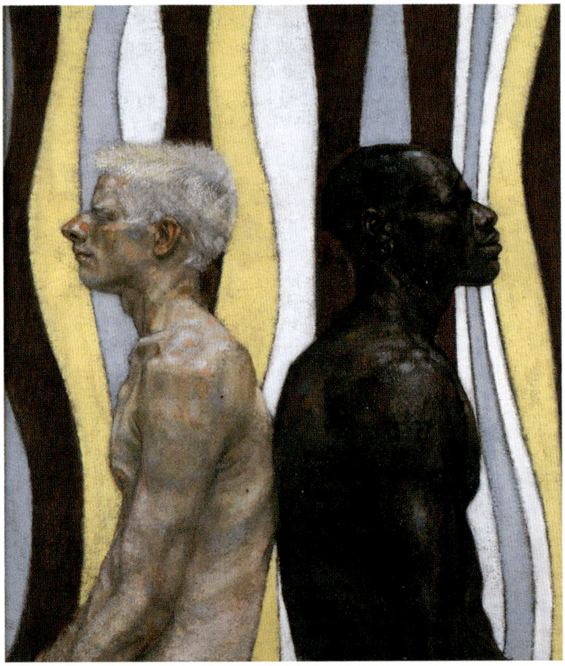

Watch Now
Andrew Hilling
Acrylic and mixed media on canvas
1220 x 970mm

Roger Holloway
Leo Holloway
Egg tempera on oak board
230 x 230mm

Beginning
Alexander Innes
Oil on canvas
395 x 295mm

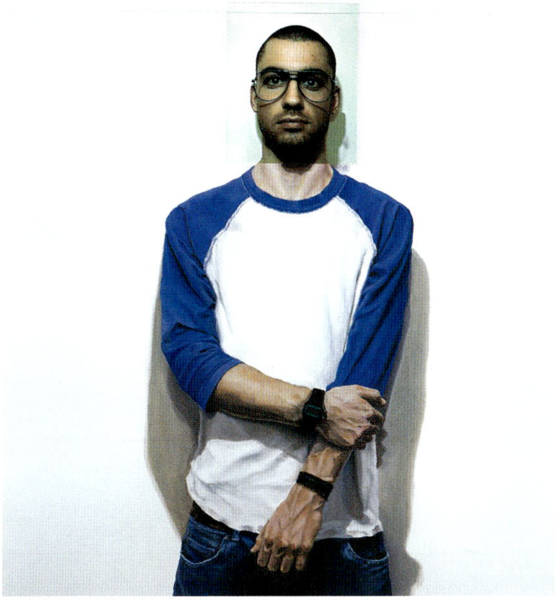

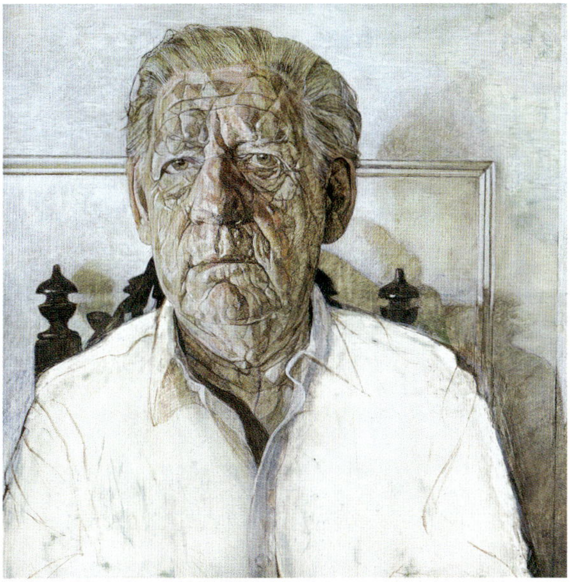

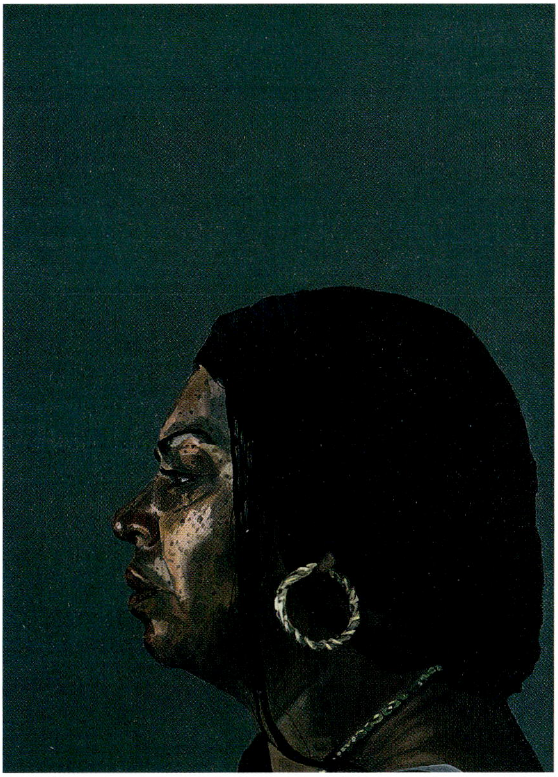

Matthew
Ben Jamie
Oil on linen
1020 x 864mm

Leon
Aleksandra Jarosz Laszlo
Acrylic on canvas
1000 x 810mm

Marlon
Jon Jones
Oil on board
380 x 380mm

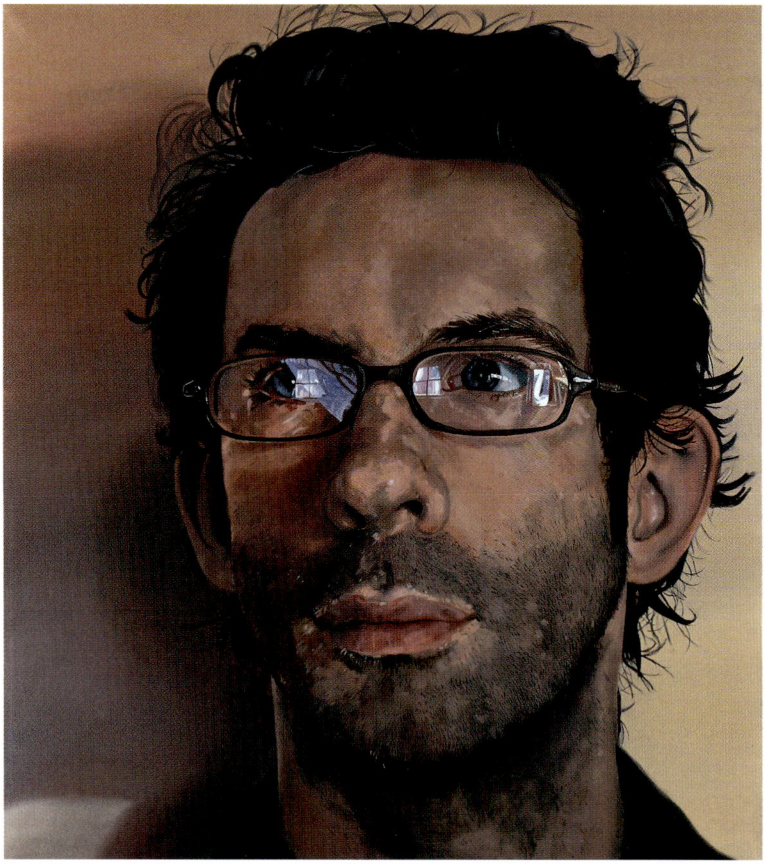

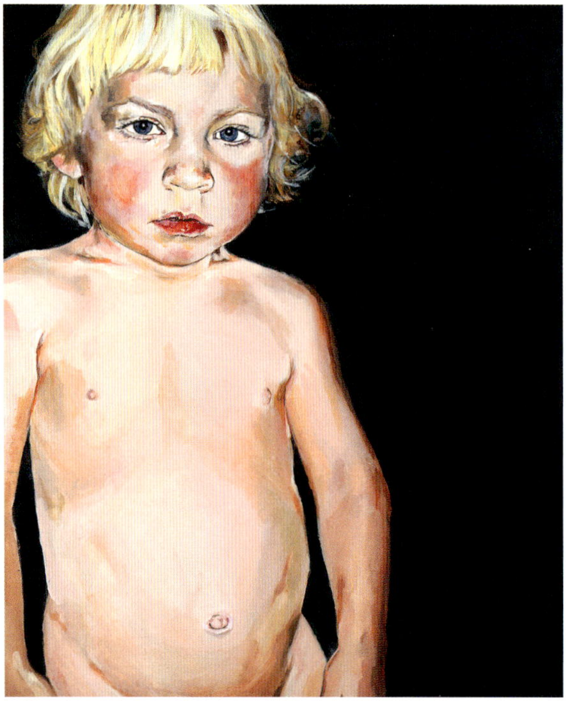

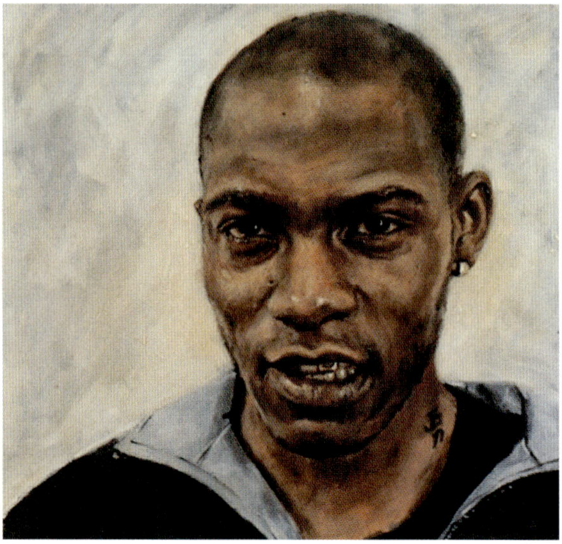

Will
Shi-Chi Lin
Oil on canvas
1220 x 915mm

Portrait of Matthew
Norman Long
Oil on board
410 x 355mm

British Ambassador
Gentian Lulanaj
Oil on board
510 x 430mm

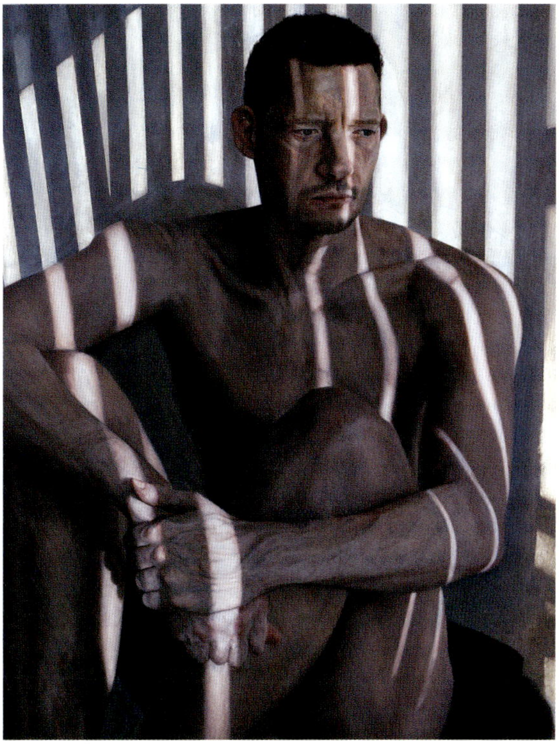

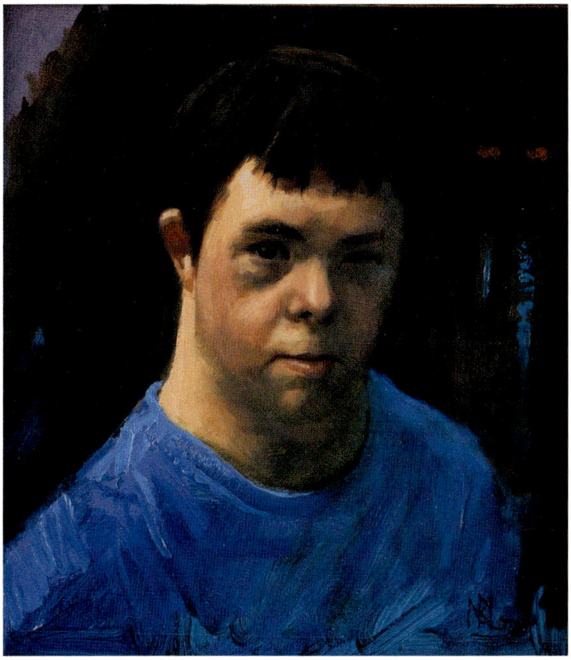

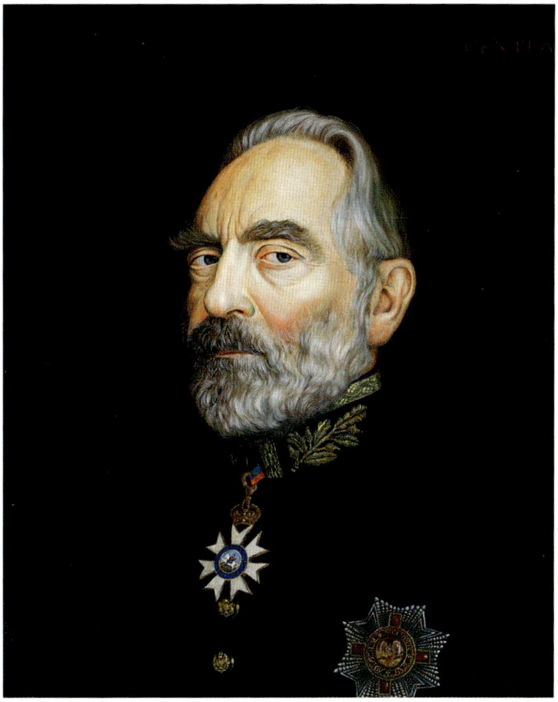

Self-portrait
Ana-Maria Micu
Oil on canvas
900 x 1200mm

Personal Space
Graham Milton
Oil on canvas
920 x 920mm

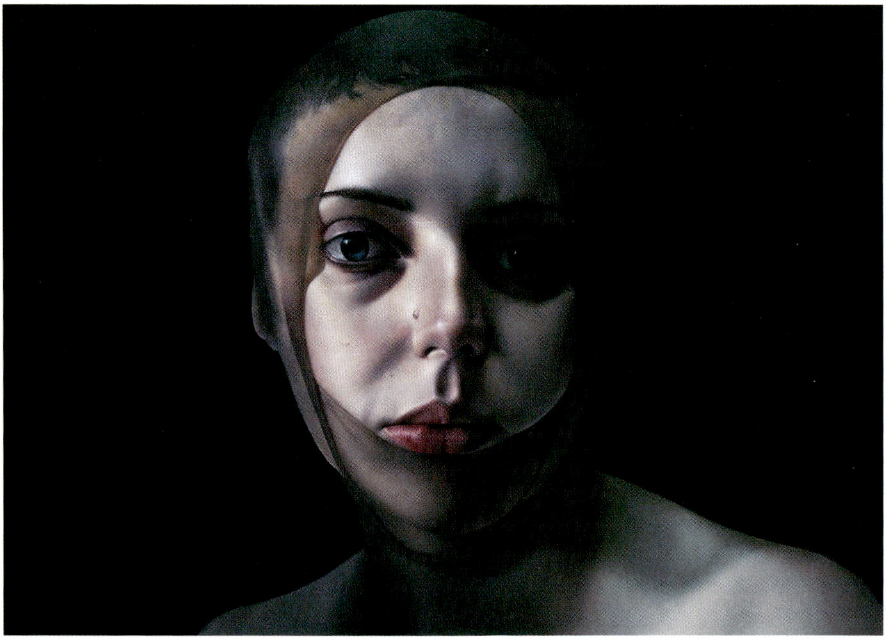

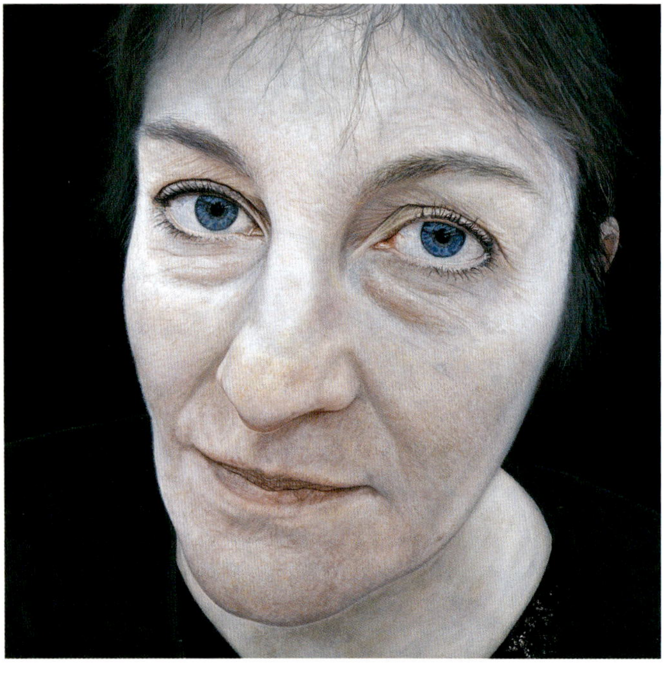

My Father Praying
Grace O'Conner
Oil on canvas
310 x 360mm

Gallery Man
Geraldine O'Neill
Oil on canvas
1055 x 670mm

When thou Walkest Through the Fire thou Shalt not be Burned, Neither Shall the Flame Kindle upon thee ... Isaiah 43:2
Sergio Ostroverhy
Oil on canvas
2424 x 2298mm

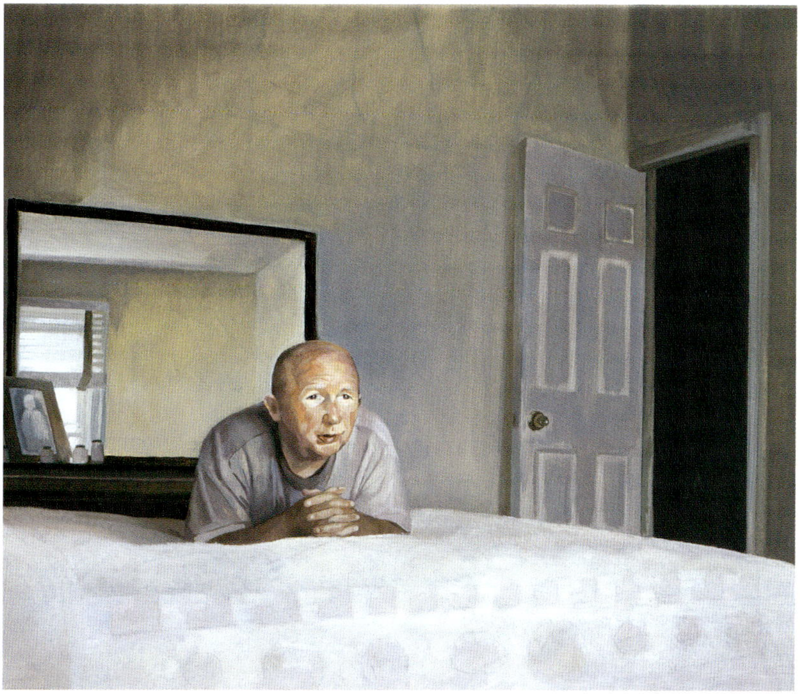

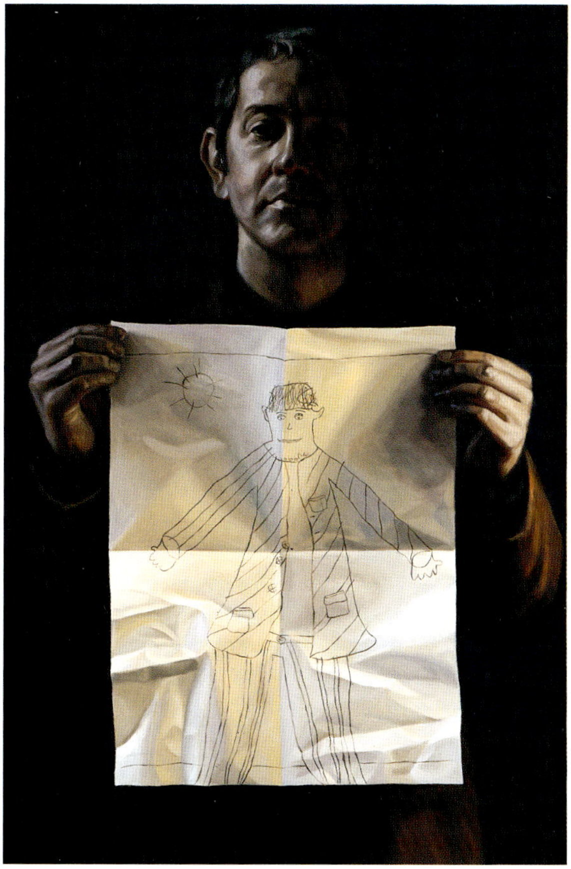

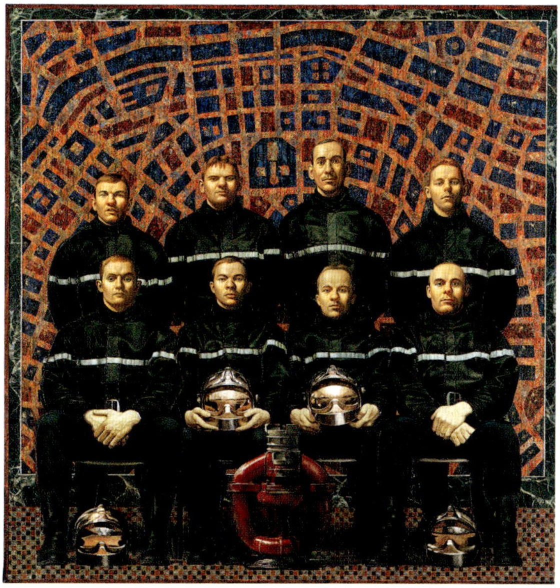

Dear Demented Mother
Jekaterina Pertoft
Oil on canvas
635 x 555mm

Ageing Clown
Anastasia Pollard
Oil on board
390 x 290mm

Self-portrait with Pink Roses
Erin Raedeke
Oil on canvas
345 x 345mm

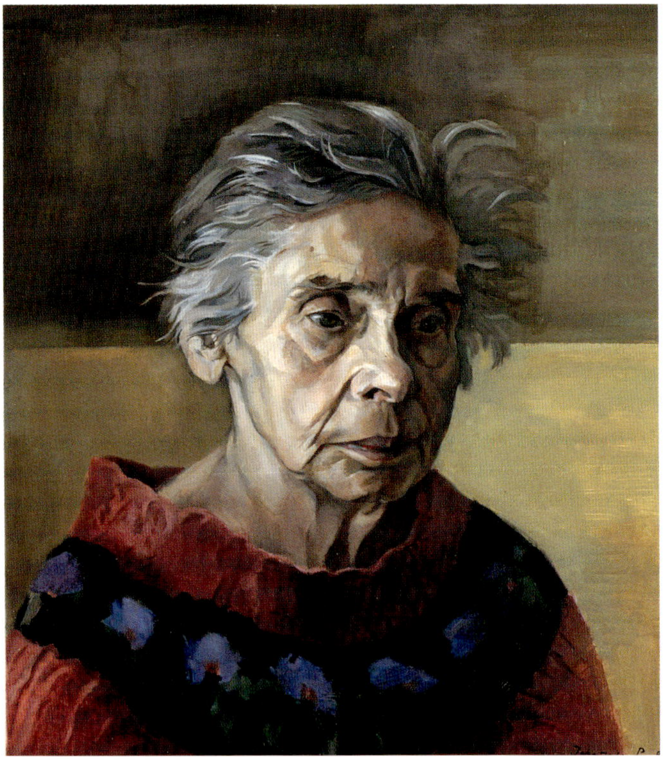

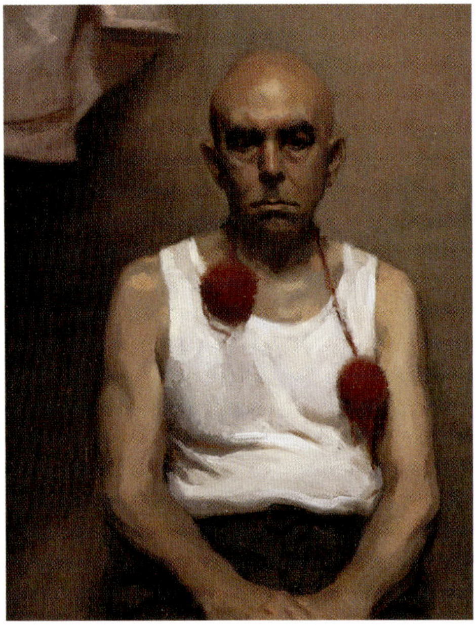

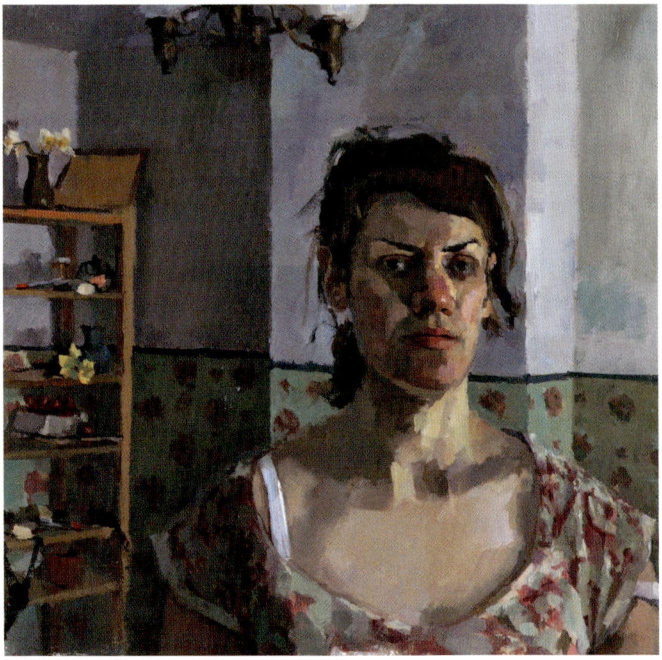

Illumine
Stephen Earl Rogers
Oil on board
420 x 290mm

Black Beads
Patricia Rorie
Oil on board
1219 x 915mm

Dr Wayper
Rebecca Smith
Acrylic on board
525 x 365mm

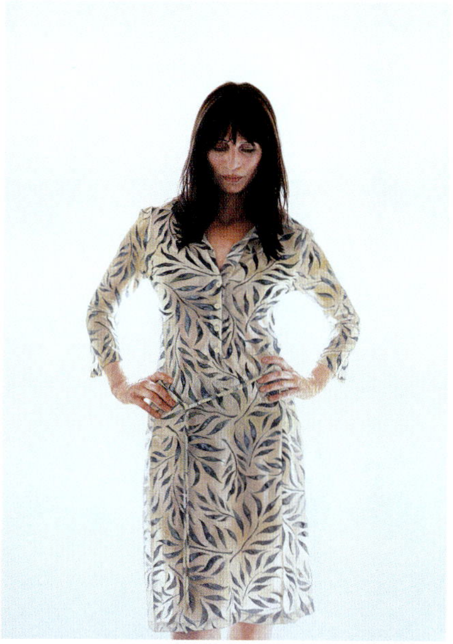

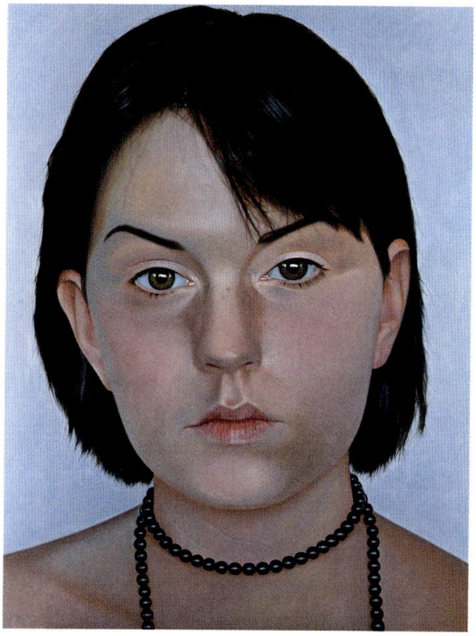

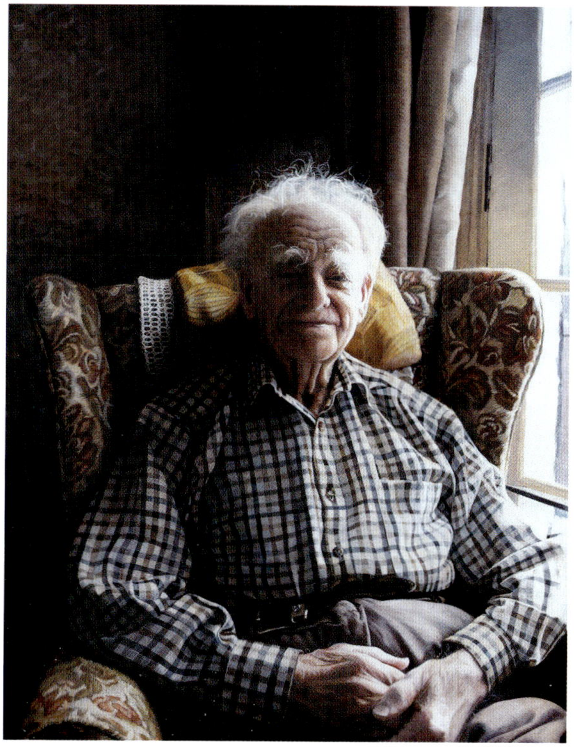

My Twins
Sarah Spencer
Oil on board
235 x 350mm

I am Sorry!
Jung-Im Song
Oil on canvas
800 x 400mm

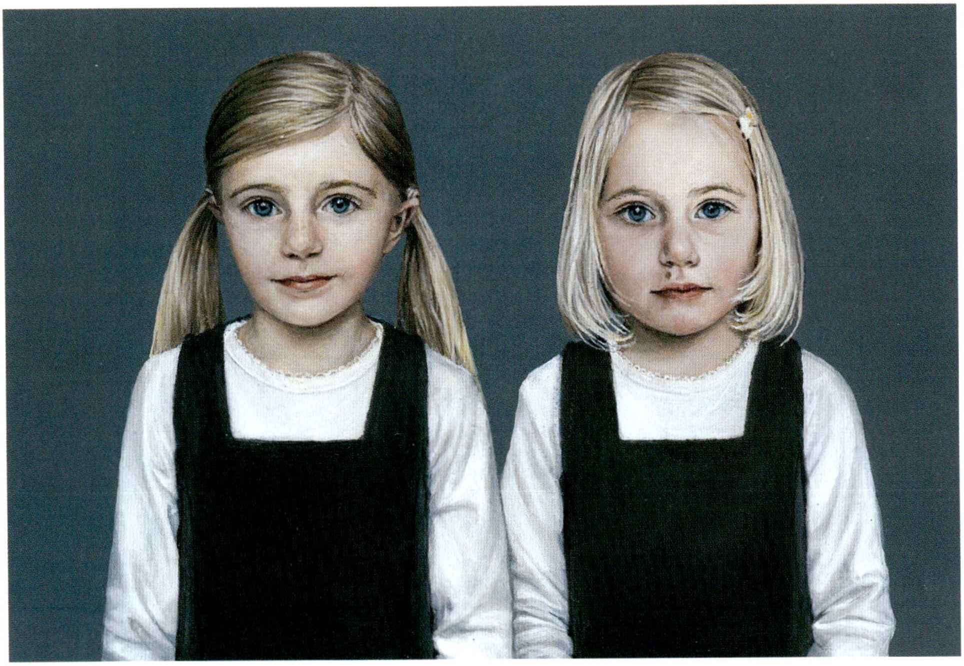

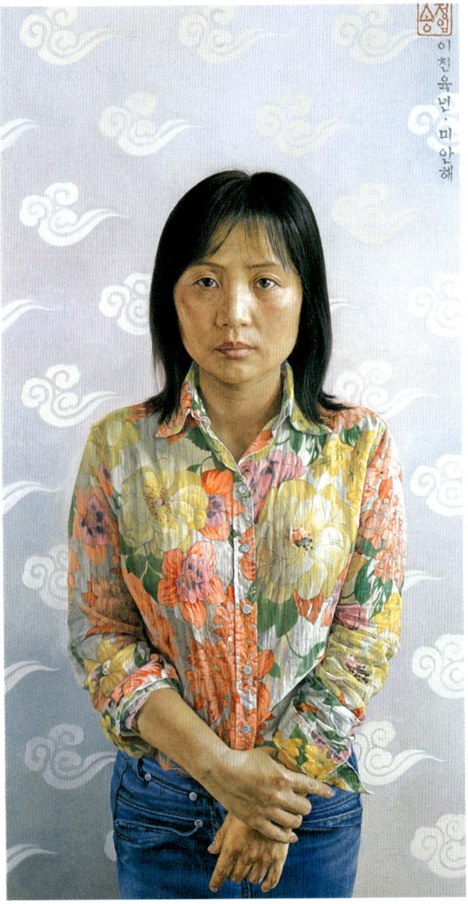

Gerry
Emily Stainer
Oil and acrylic on canvas
700 x 550mm

Mandy, Ginnie and Katie
Benjamin Sullivan
Oil on canvas
1110 x 760mm

My Tutor
Craig Tiley
Acrylic on canvas
1220 x 910mm

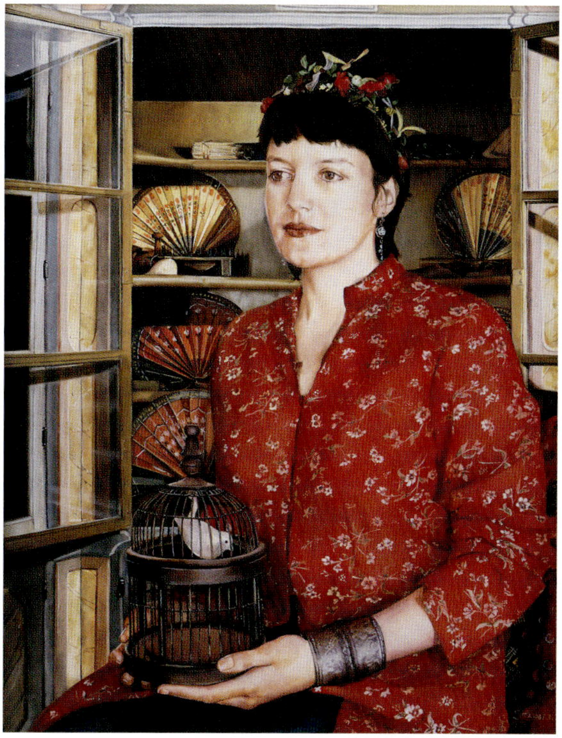

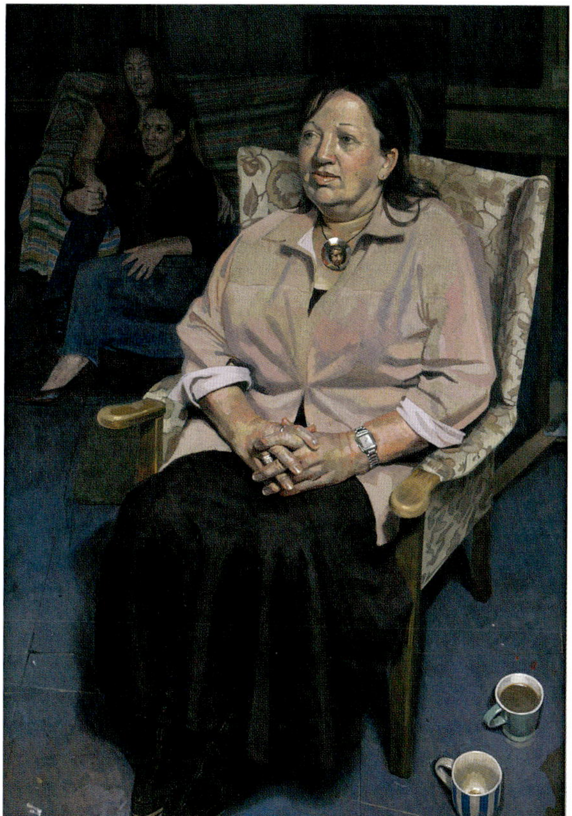

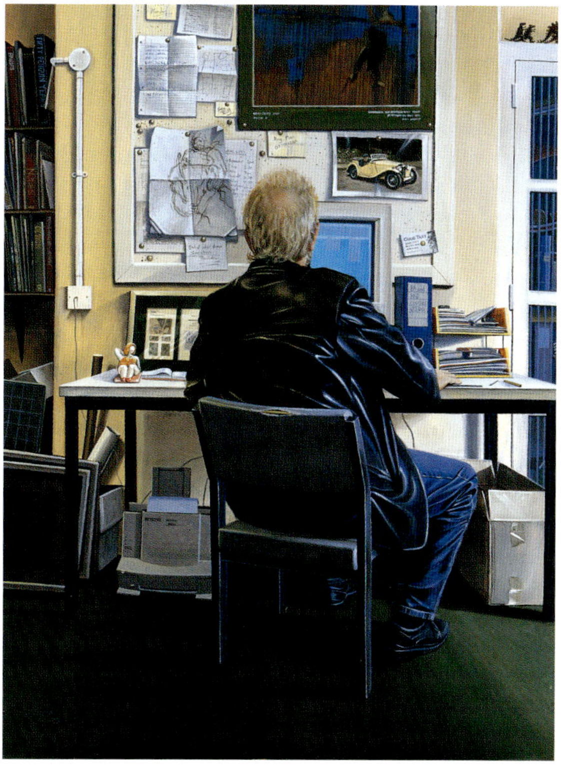

Strange Cargo
Stefan Towler
Oil on board
550 x 270mm

Yuan
William Tuck
Acrylic on canvas
810 x 555mm

Molly Jones
Covadonga Valdes
Oil on linen
940 x 690mm

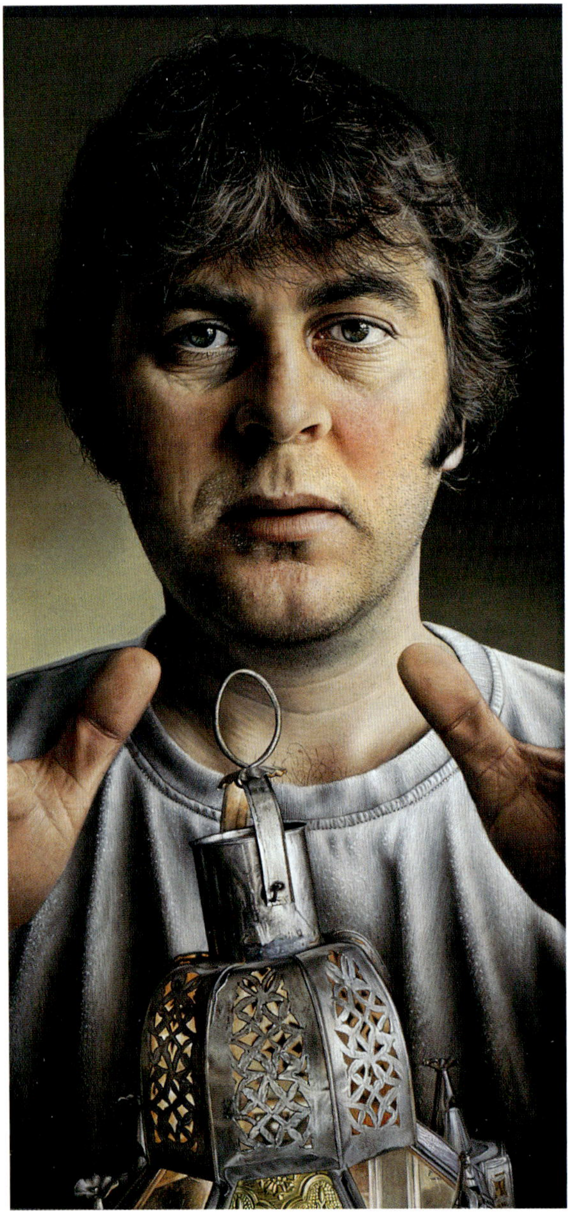

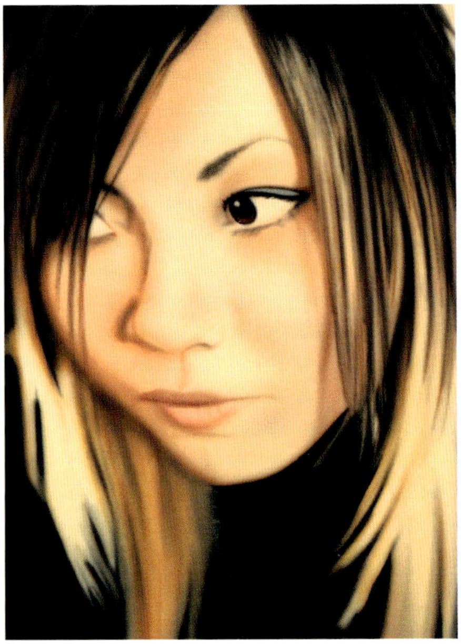

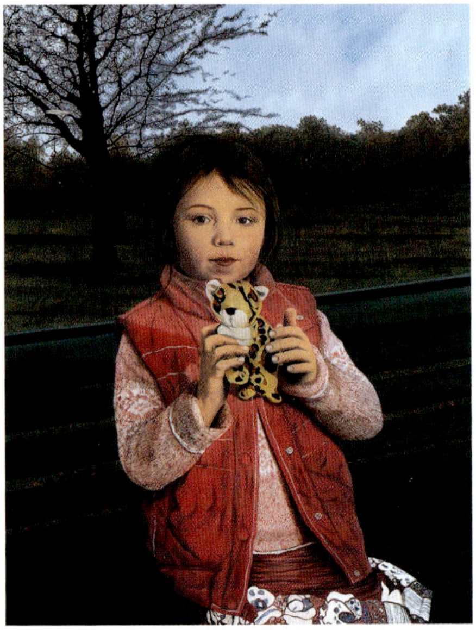

Contemplation
Adele Wagstaff
Oil on linen
460 x 355mm

Dawn
Monica Whalley
Oil on board
1530 x 1125mm

Catherine
Toby Wiggins
Oil on panel
910 x 580mm

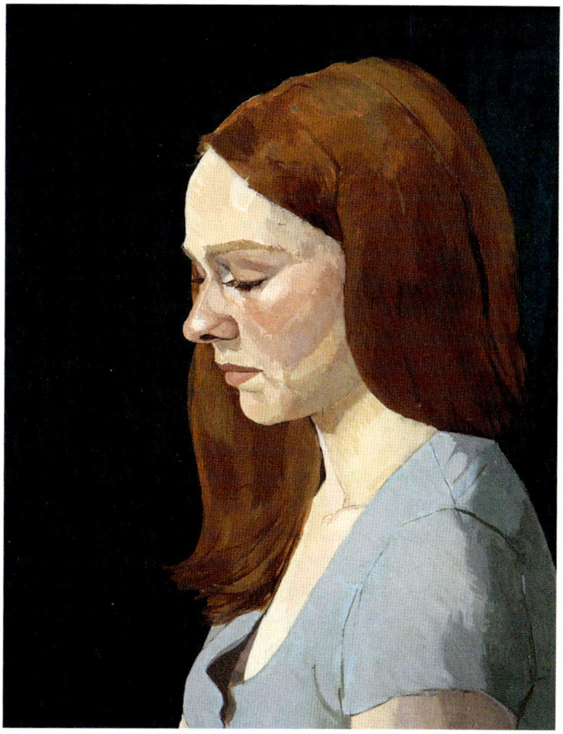

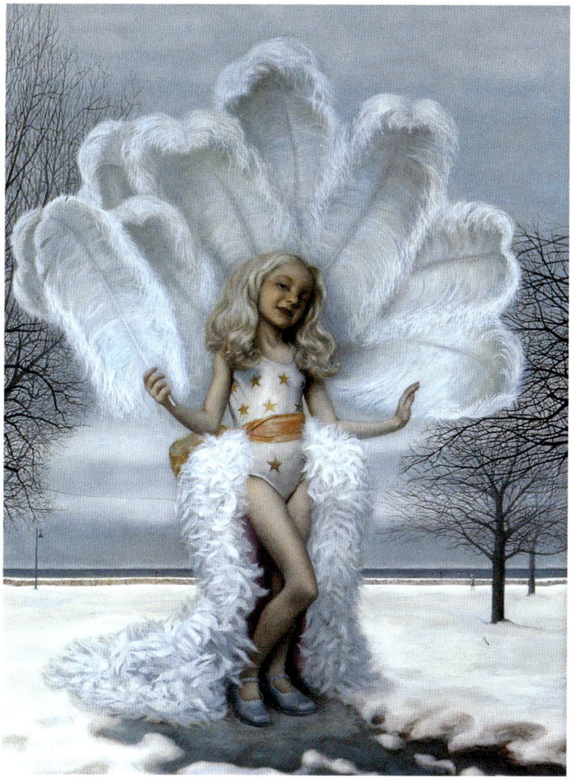

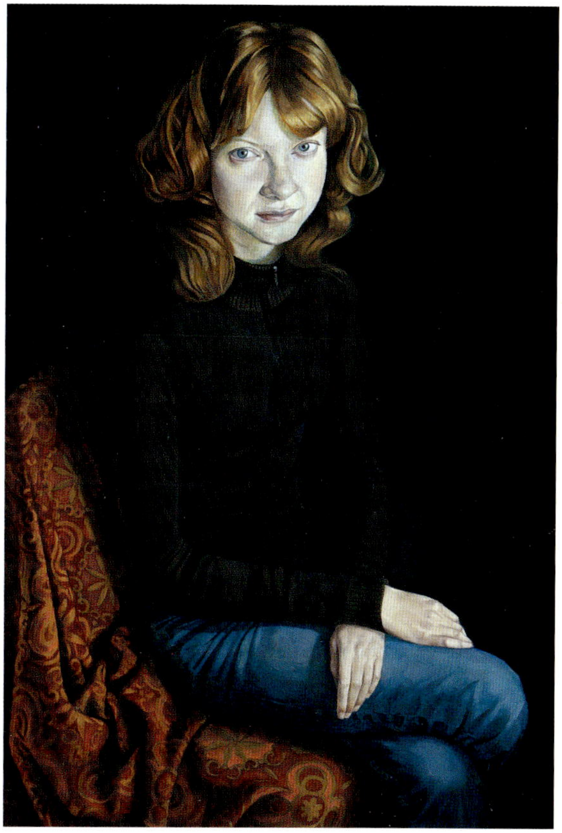

Smile
Katie Wright
Acrylic on board
450 x 660mm

Ian
Paul Wright
Oil on canvas
255 x 205mm

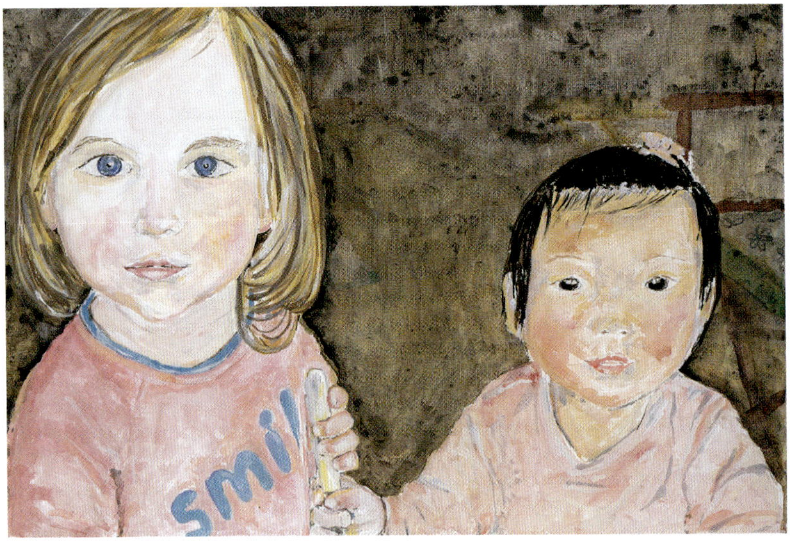

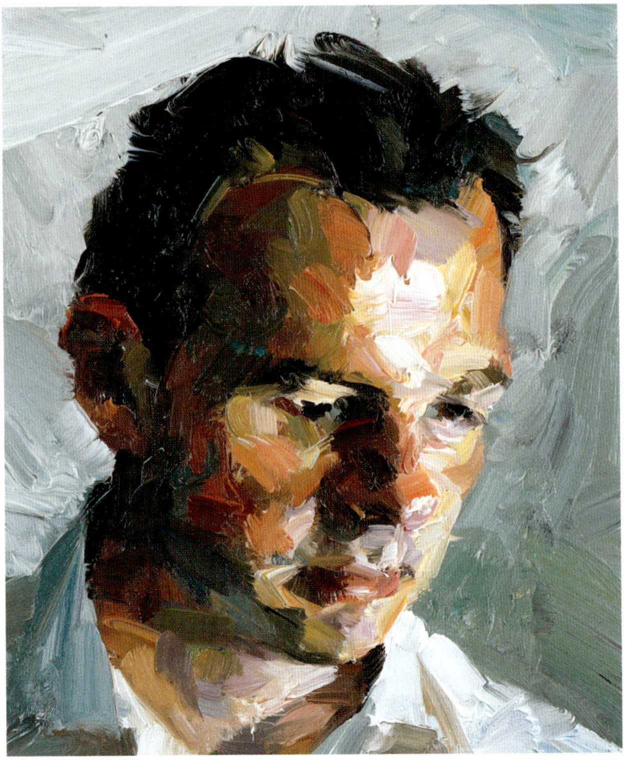

33
Craig Wylie
Oil on linen
2340 x 1675mm

Portrait
Jonathan Yeo
Oil on canvas
260 x 360mm

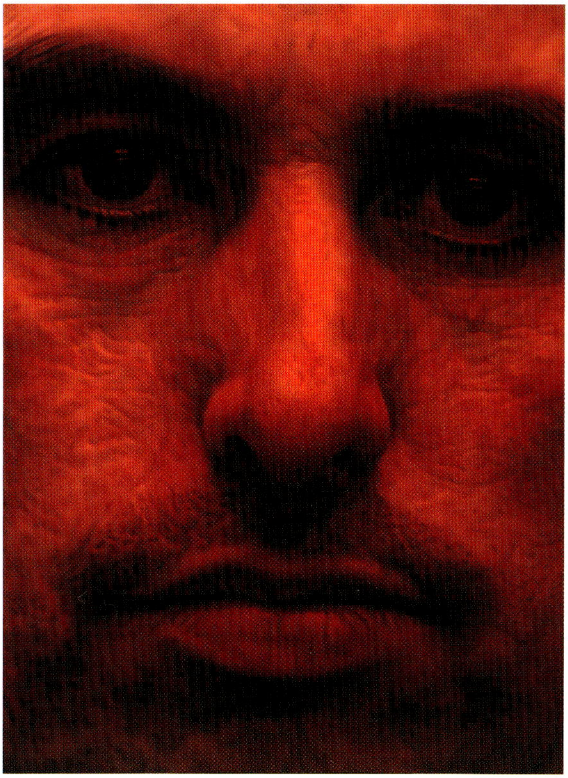

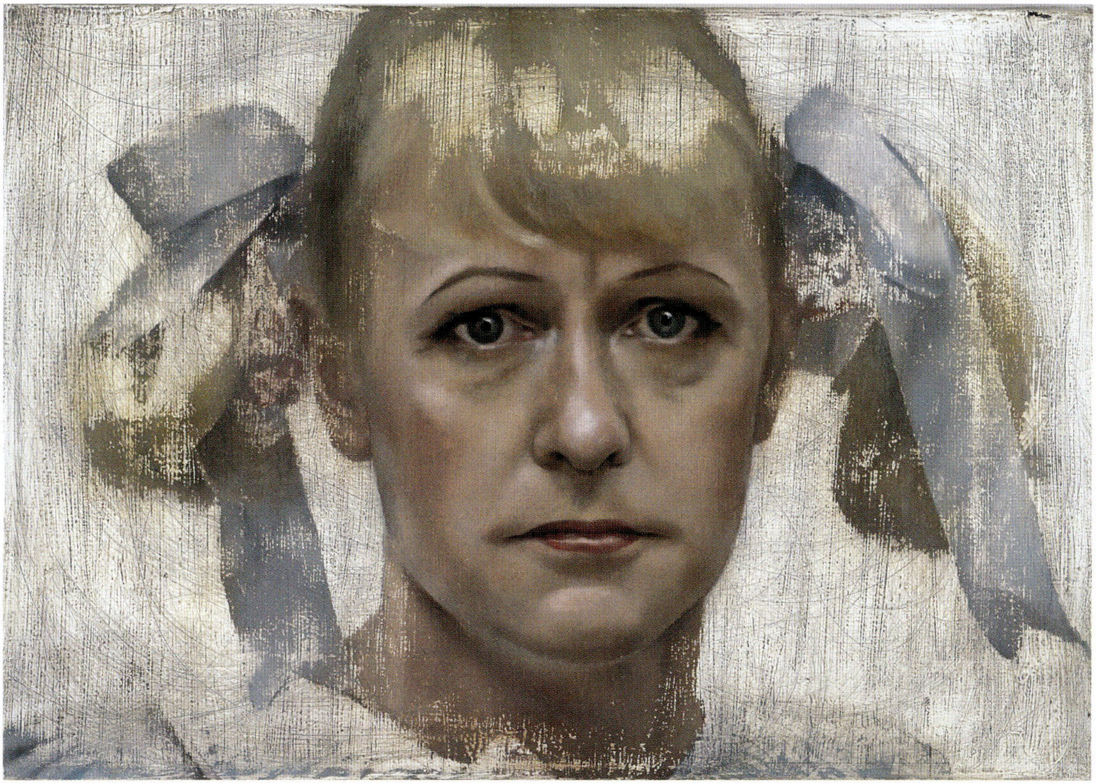

2007

ARTISTS WHOSE PORTRAITS WERE EXHIBITED

Lynn Ahrens / Rupert Alexander / Johan Andersson / Jeremy Andrews / Maryanne Aytoun-Ellis / John Ball / Robert Benchley / Polly Benford / Jim Bennett / Emmanouil Bitsakis / Richard Brazier / Vincent Brown / Francis Corsham / Tony Cottrell / Paul Emsley / Miriam Escofet / Darvish Fakhr / Maryam Foroozanfar / Aram Gershuni / Robin-Lee Hall / Jaemi Hardy / Ingolv Helland / Amanda Hext / Eileen Hogan / Jill Hooper / Timothy Hyman / Kwang-Sik Im / Diarmuid Kelley / Sandro Kopp / David Lawton / Thomas Leveritt / Dionis Macnair / Anna Madia / Hynek Martinec / Susannah Massey / Francesco Mernini / Nicholas Merton / Ana Maria Micu / Luis Morris / Neil Nelson / Paul Oxborough / Morgan Penn / Scott Pohlschmidt / Anastasia Pollard / Gareth Reid / Philip Renforth / Keith Robinson / Stephen Earl Rogers / Geert Schless / Perdita Sinclair / Benjamin Sullivan / Edward Sutcliffe / Cassandra Szekely / Ivan Tafrov / David Tebbs / Tom Tinknell / Daphne Todd / Jaime Valero Perandones / David Vincent / Jason Walker / Vicky White / Roger Wilkins / Antony Williams / Suzy Willis / Paula Wilson / Steve Wilson / William Wright

SECOND PRIZE
STEPHEN
DAVID LAWTON

Oil on canvas
270 x 200mm

David Lawton studied art in Chester, and English and Social Anthropology at Lancaster University. This portrait depicts his friend Stephen Player, a San Francisco-based illustrator whom Lawton had painted on a number of occasions, including an earlier nude study, which was selected for exhibition in the BP Portrait Award of 2000. Lawton has exhibited widely and currently lives in Chester.

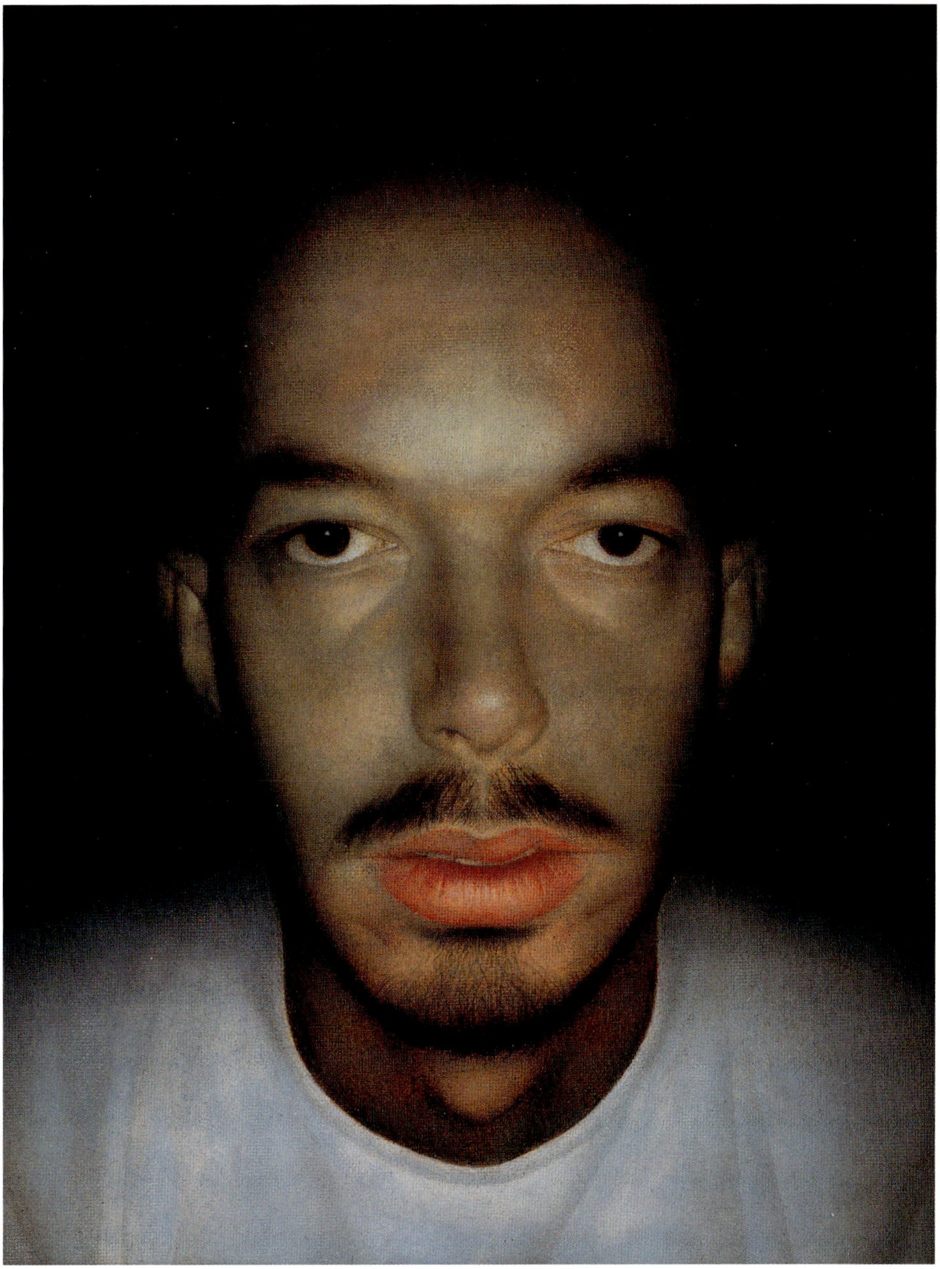

THIRD PRIZE
TAMARA
JOHAN ANDERSSON

Oil on canvas
1000 x 730mm

Swedish-born Johan Andersson moved to England at the age of eight and was still studying Fine Art at Central St Martin's College of Art and Design in London when he won Third Prize with this portrait of his friend, Tamara, posed in her sitting room. Tamara was just twenty-one at the time and hesitant about posing nude. Her insecurity in this is evident in the awkwardness of her posture in the portrait. In 2008, Andersson was awarded the Jerwood Contemporary Painters Prize.

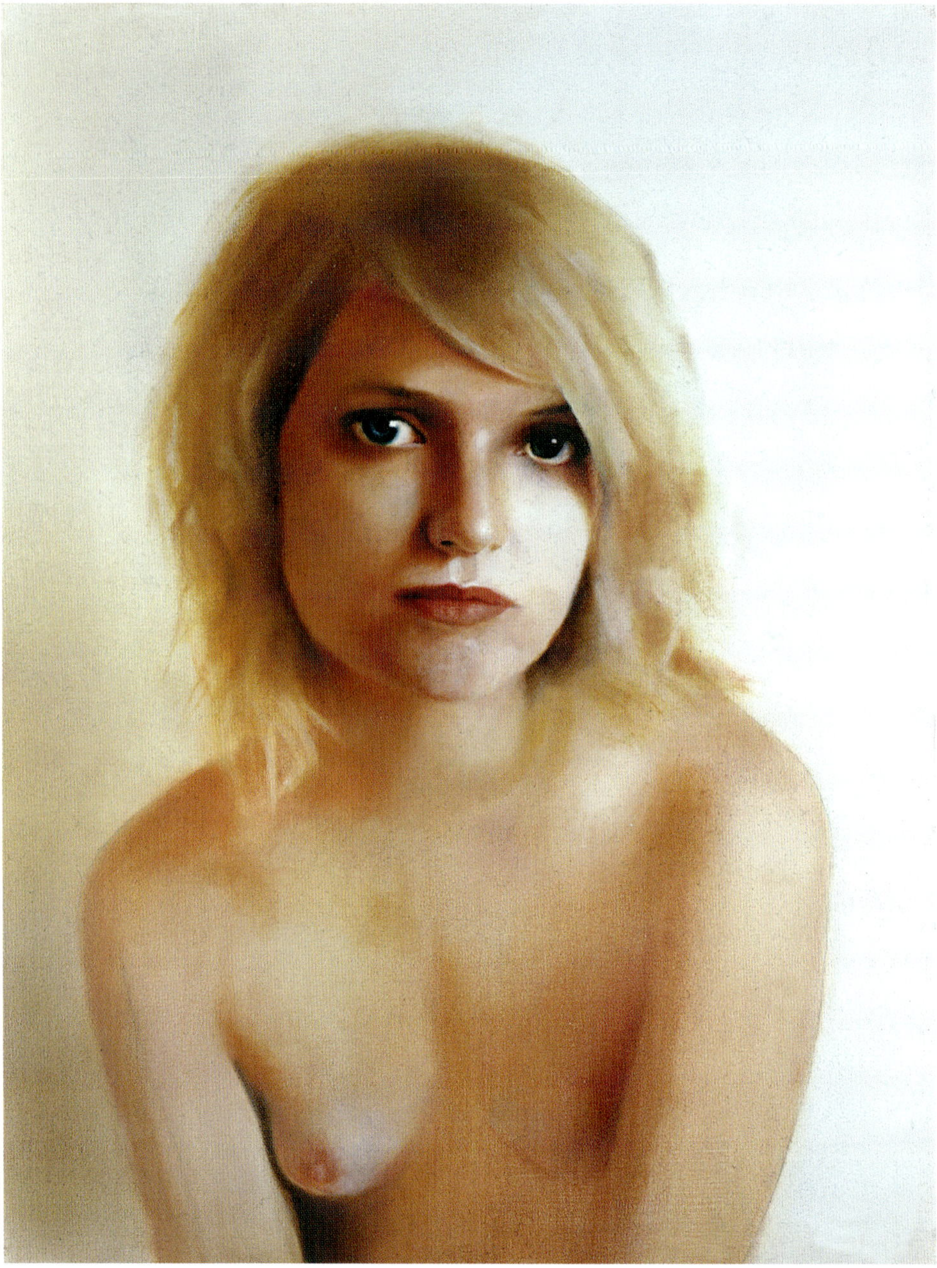

YOUNG ARTIST AWARD
ZUZANA IN THE PARIS STUDIO
HYNEK MARTINEC

Acrylic on canvas
1300 x 1100mm

Born in the Czech Republic, Hynek Martinec currently lives and works in London. He graduated from the Academy of Fine Art in Prague in 2005, where in 2003 he had won the Academy's Studio Prize. His works are featured in collections in Vienna, Miami and New York, as well as the National Gallery in Prague and the British Museum in London. Martinec painted this portrait of his friend Zuzana Jungmanova the previous summer, while they were caretaking an artist's studio in Paris. Striking and detailed, Martinec's work is painted with photographic precision.

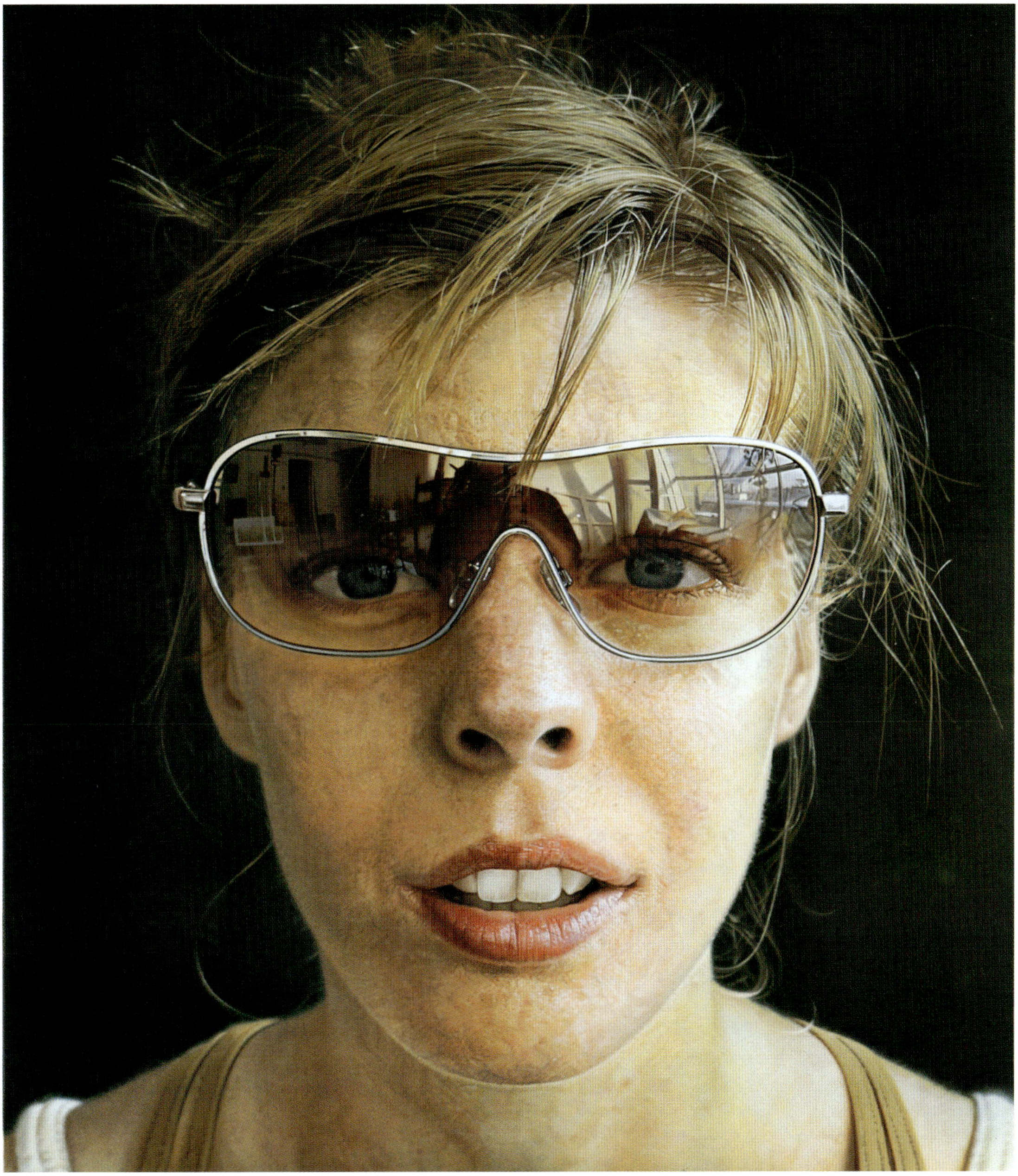

Time to Talk
Lynn Ahrens
Oil on canvas
720 x 590mm

Portrait of Christopher Darroux-Xavier
Rupert Alexander
Oil on canvas
600 x 440mm

Franko B
Jeremy Andrews
Oil on canvas
440 x 340mm

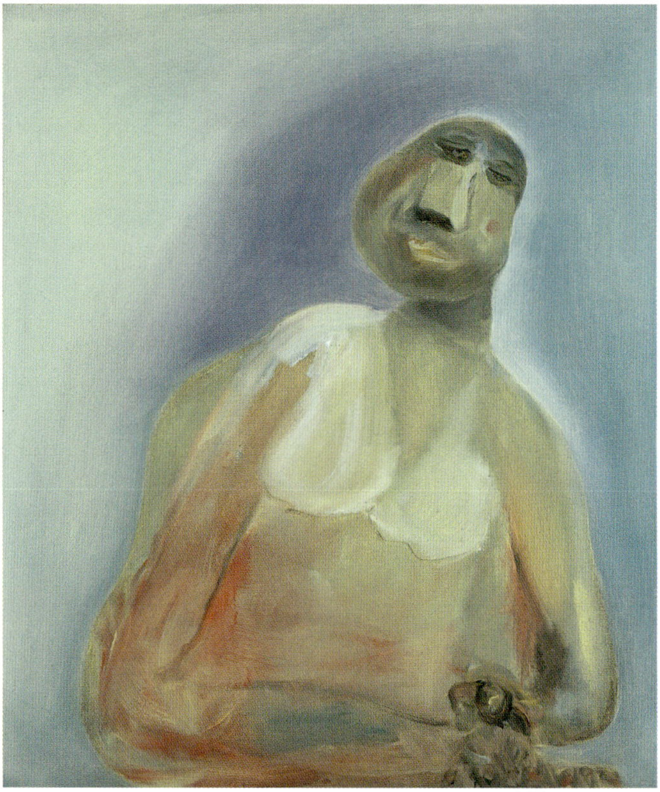

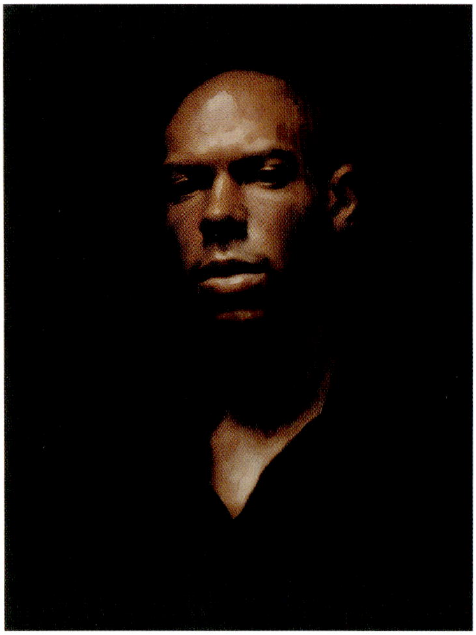

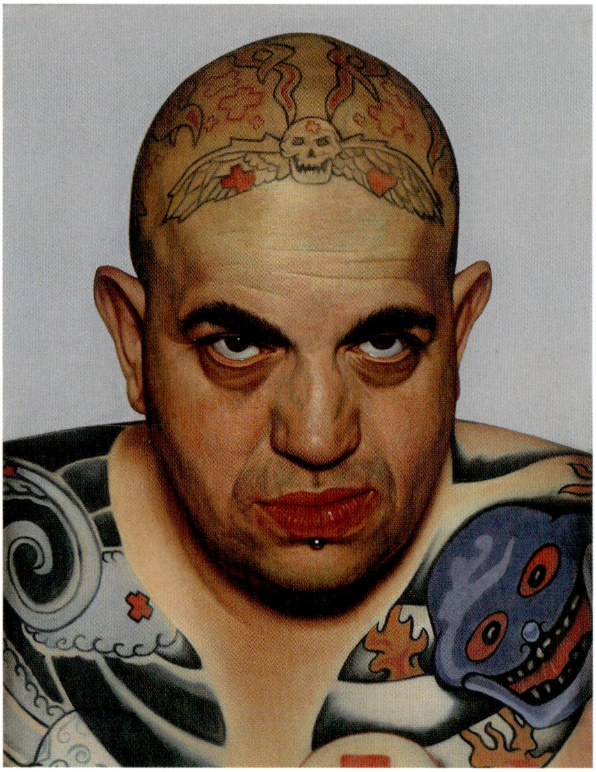

Man Staring
Maryanne Aytoun-Ellis
Egg tempera on board
410 x 350mm

Commuter
John Ball
Oil on canvas
505 x 405mm

Nicola
Polly Benford
Acrylic on board
300 x 210mm

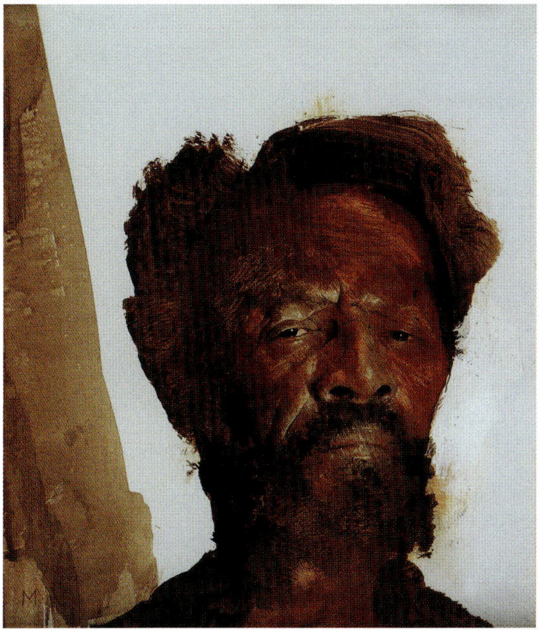

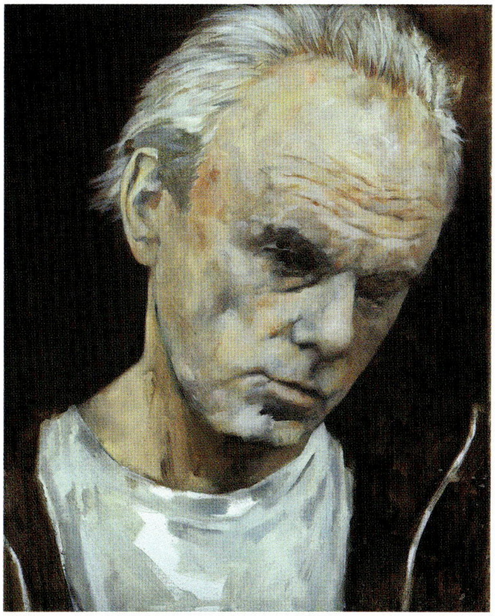

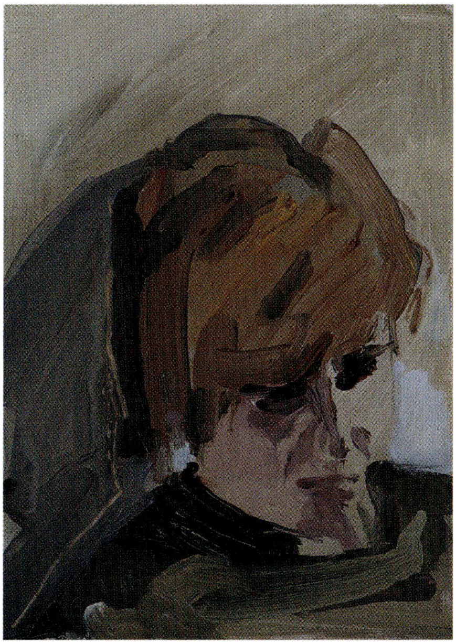

Portrait
Emmanouil Bitsakis
Oil on canvas
290 x 230mm

Johnny and Glory
Richard Brazier
Oil on canvas
1550 x 1190mm

Mr & Mrs Brown
Vincent Brown
Acrylic on linen
1000 x 900mm

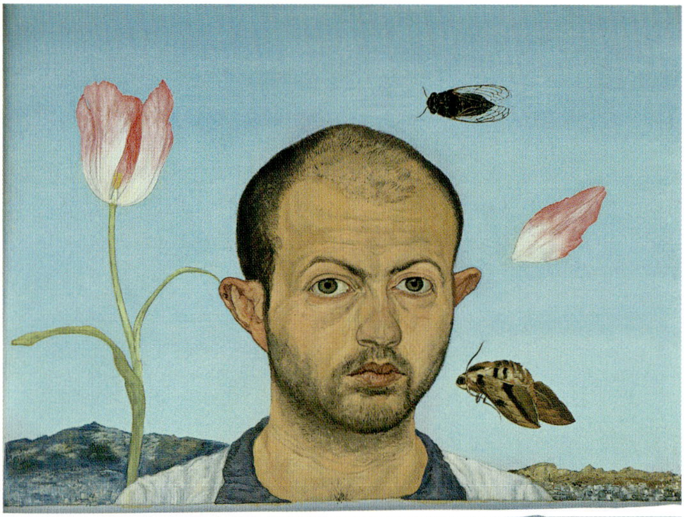

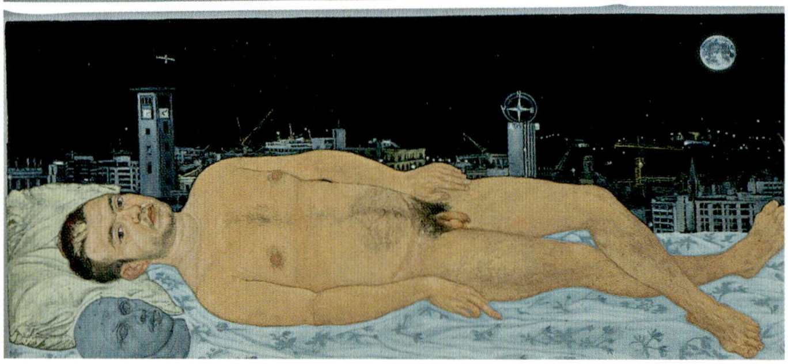

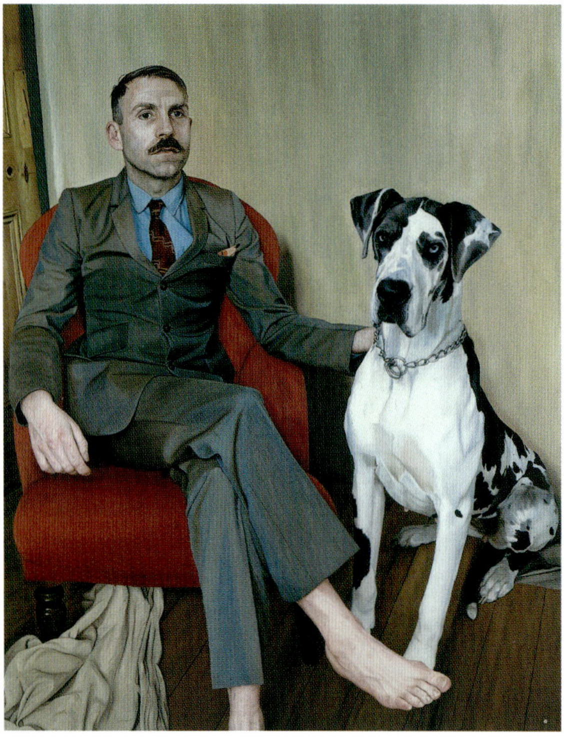

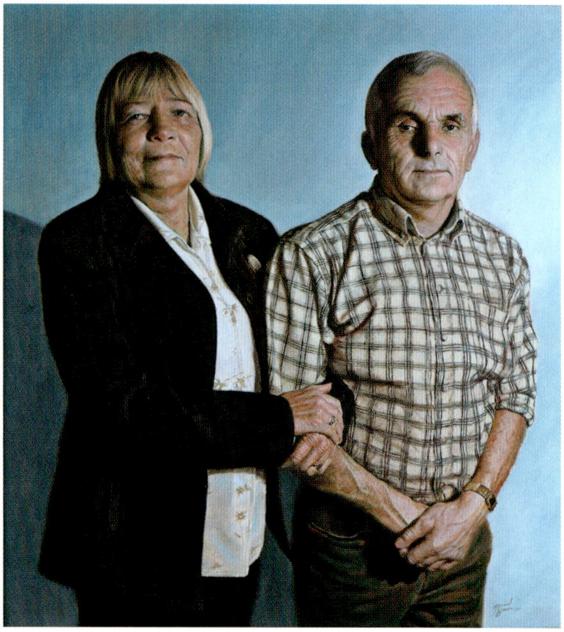

Irene (My Wife)
Francis Corsham
Acrylic and water oils on hardboard
265 x 215mm

Jose Escofet
Miriam Escofet
Oil on canvas on board
500 x 400mm

Kaveh, Age 31
Maryam Foroozanfar
Oil on canvas
250 x 200mm

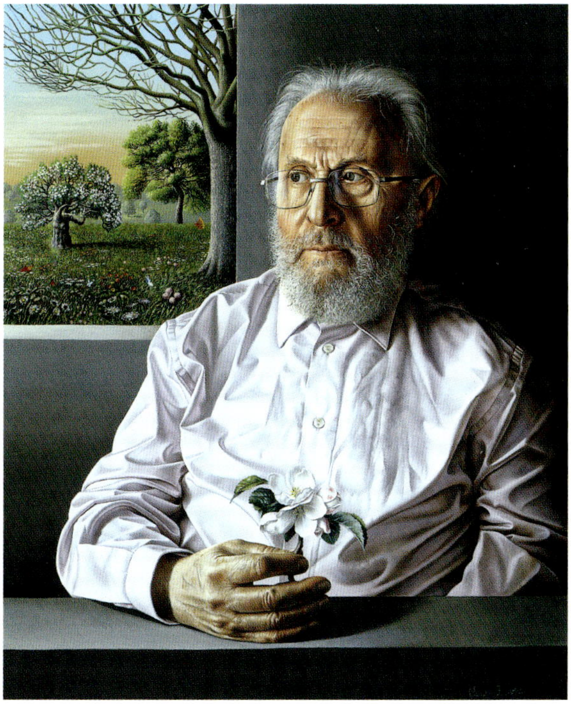

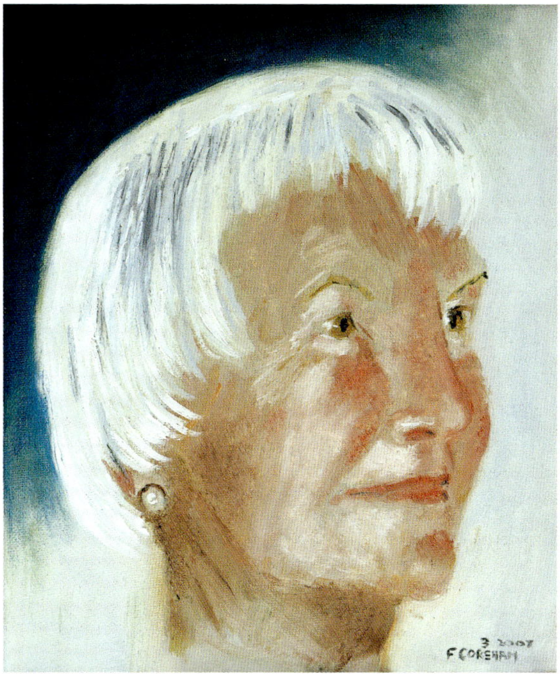

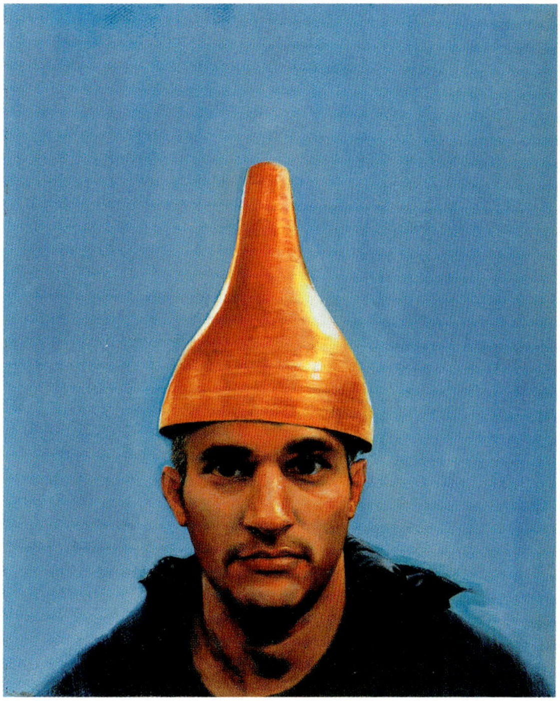

Looking Back
Aram Gershuni
Oil on board
440 x 330mm

Joy
Robin-Lee Hall
Egg tempera on board
700 x 600mm

Self-portrait
Jaemi Hardy
Oil on canvas on panel
250 x 200mm

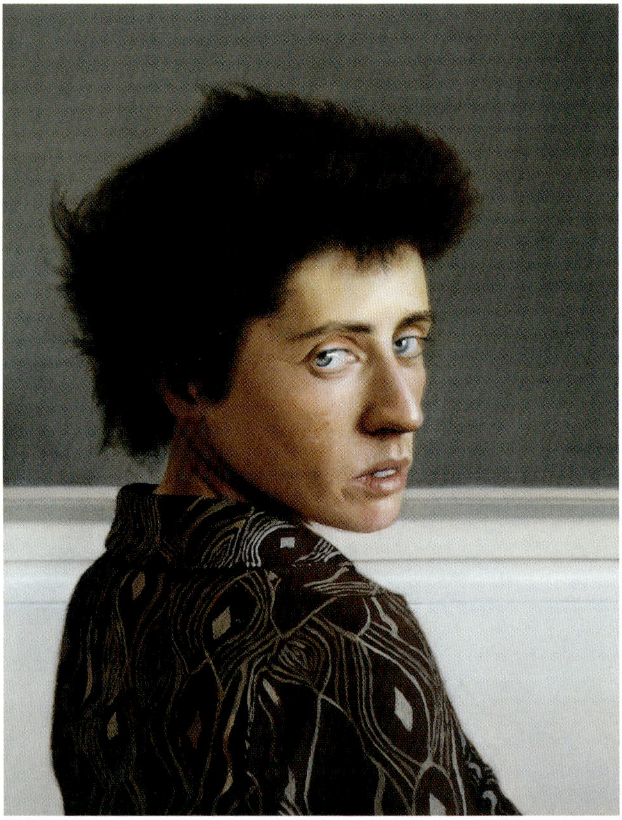

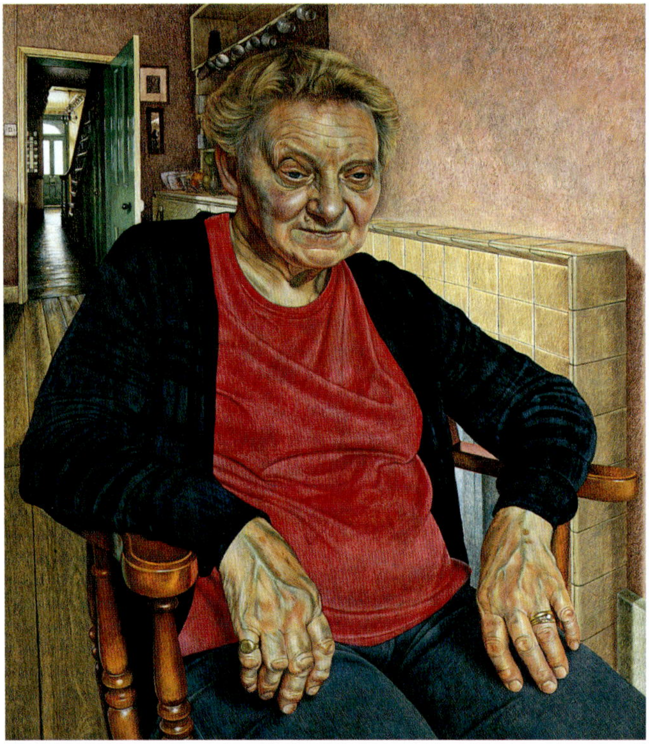

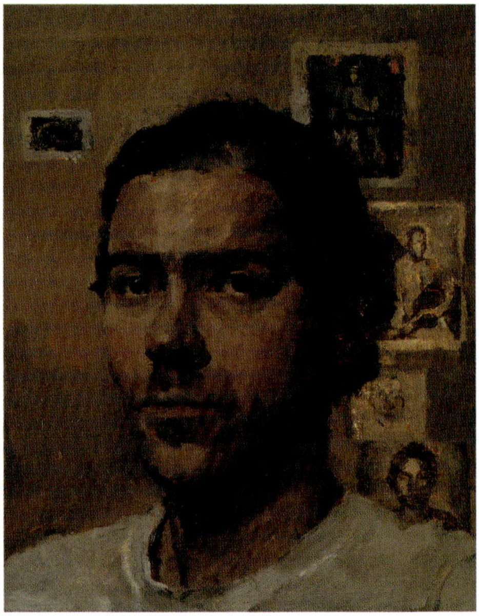

Winter Portrait
Ingolv Helland
Oil on canvas
545 x 395mm

Redhead (Self-portrait)
Amanda Hext
Oil on board
400 x 400mm

Ian Hamilton Finlay: Portraits Between 1997 and 2006
Eileen Hogan
Oil on board, triptych,
each 250 x 200mm

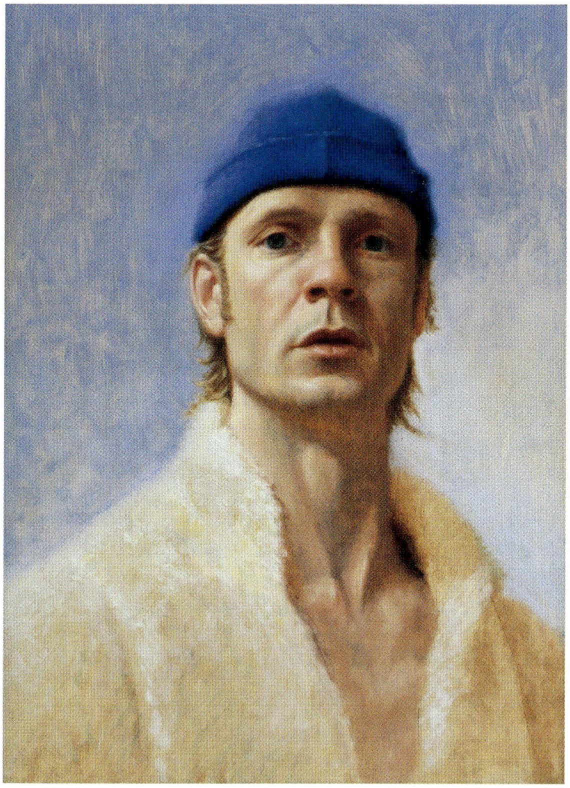

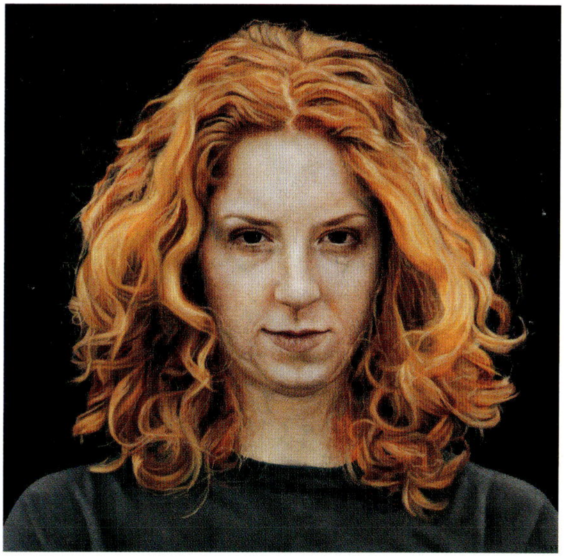

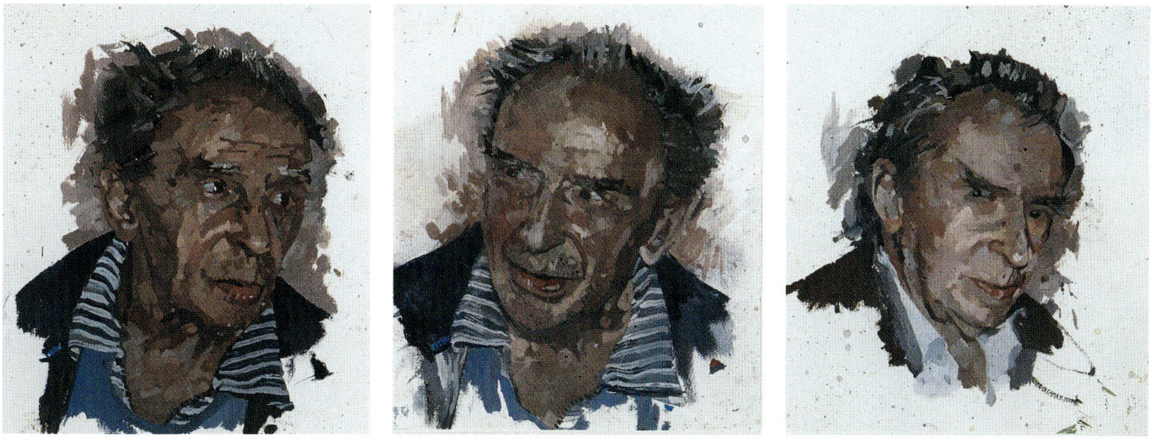

Pugnis et Calcibus
Jill Hooper
Oil on board
250 x 200mm

She and Me
Timothy Hyman
Oil on board
610 x 460mm

Self-portrait
Kwang-Sik Im
Oil on canvas
350 x 250mm

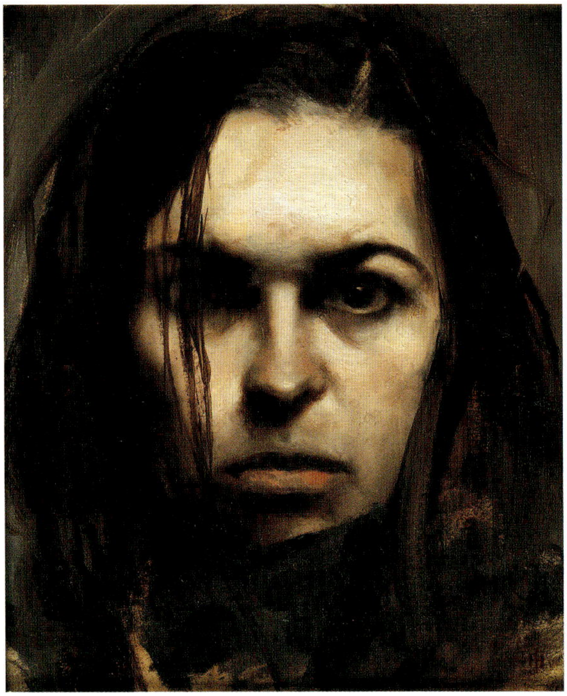

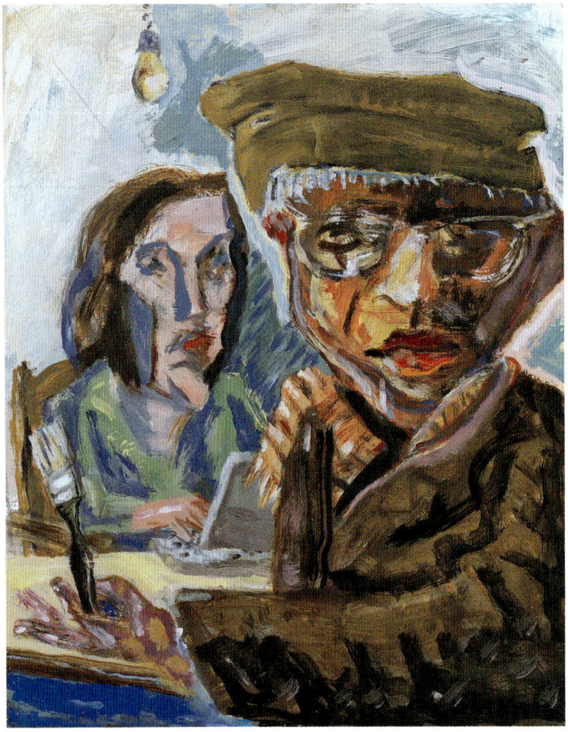

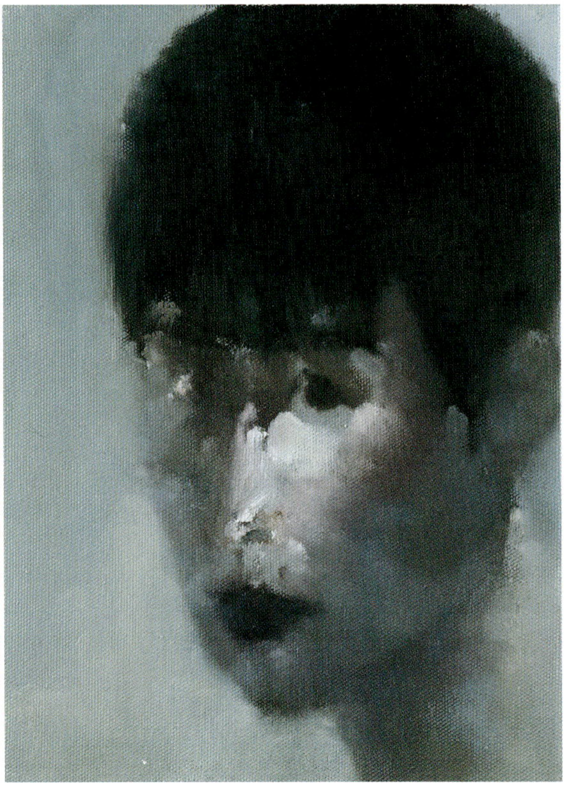

Painting of Waris
Sandro Kopp
Oil on canvas
535 x 725mm

A.C. Grayling
Thomas Leveritt
Oil on panel
1015 x 1015mm

Figura Onirica
Anna Madia
Acrylic on board
405 x 495mm

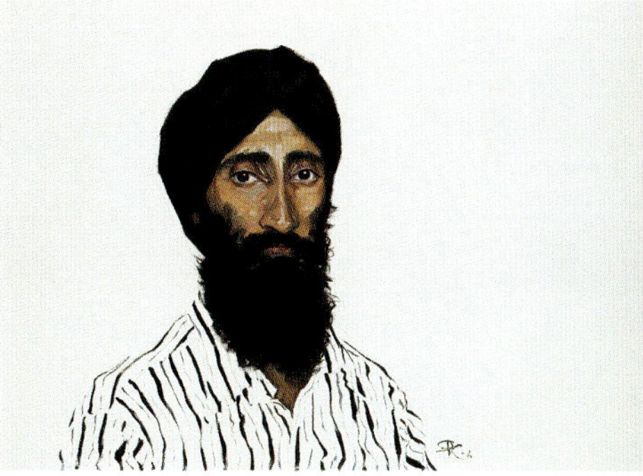

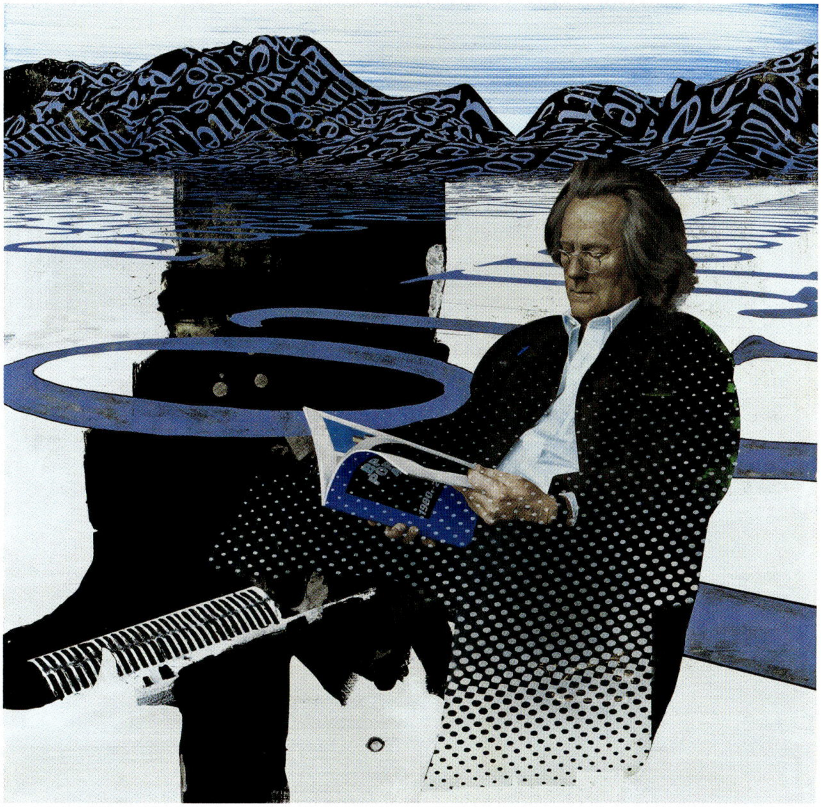

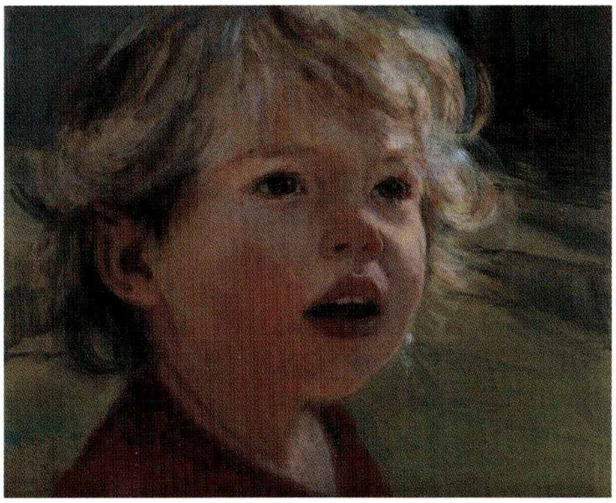

Novelty
Susannah Massey
Oil and acrylic on canvas
595 x 440mm

Camilla
Francesco Mernini
Oil on canvas on board
390 x 490mm

Alex
Nicholas Merton
Oil on board
460 x 320mm

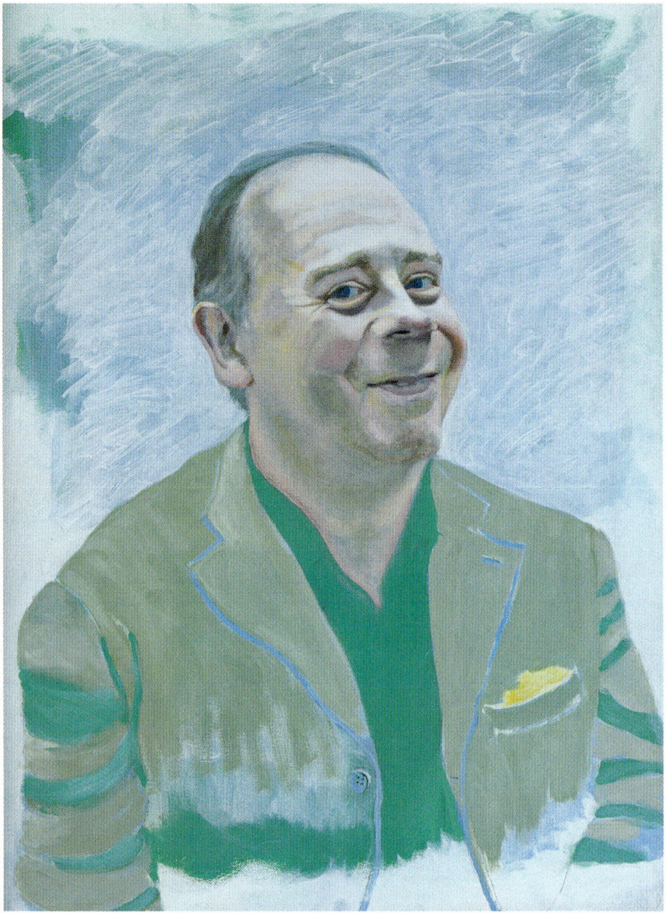

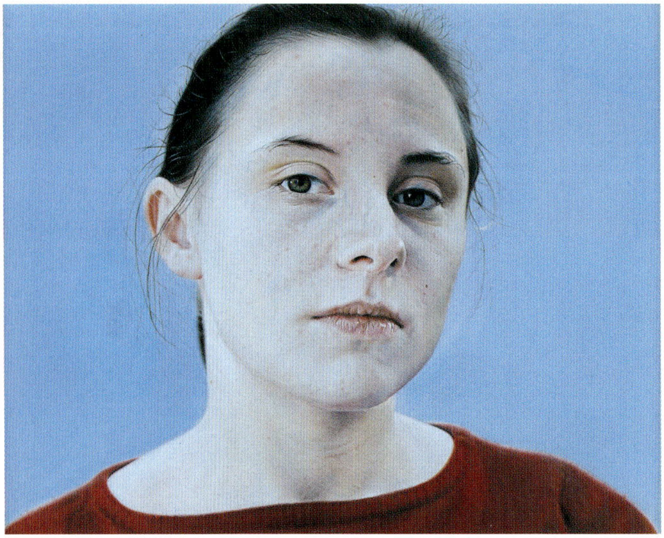

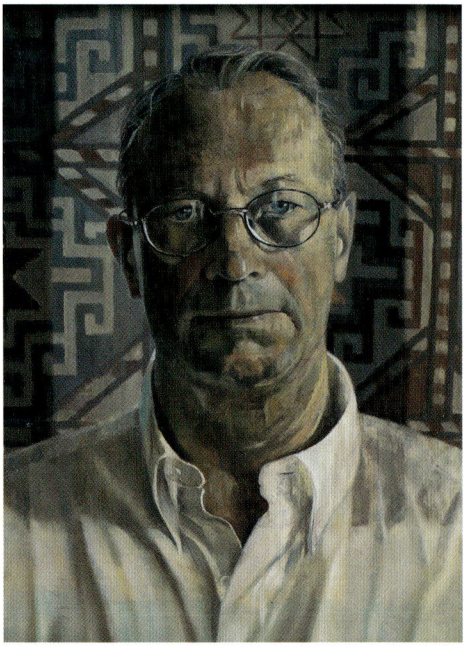

Self-portrait
Ana Maria Micu
Oil on canvas
500 x 500mm

Sally
Luis Morris
Oil on canvas
740 x 490mm

Georgia in Profile
Neil Nelson
Oil on canvas
290 x 290mm

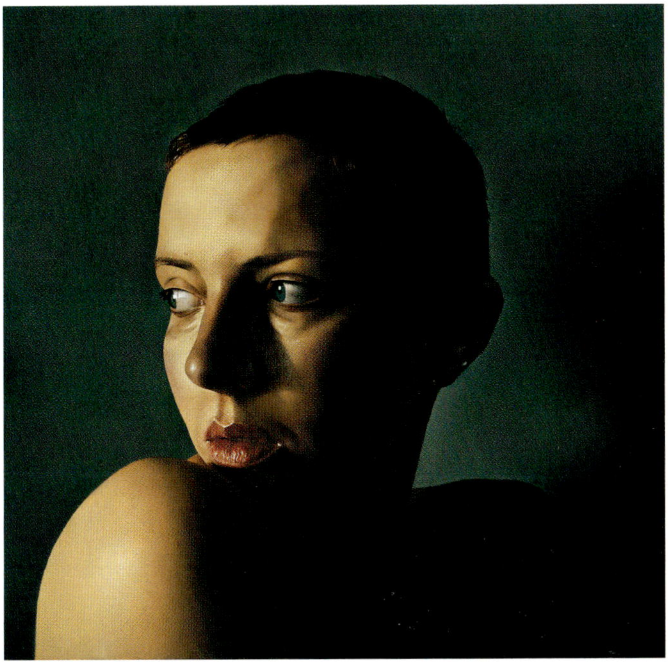

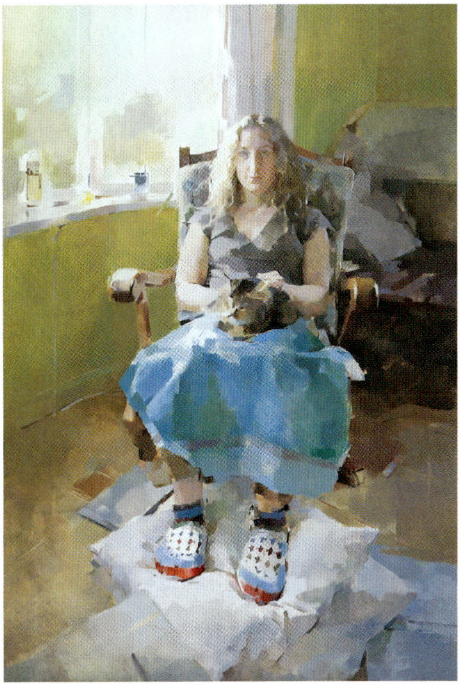

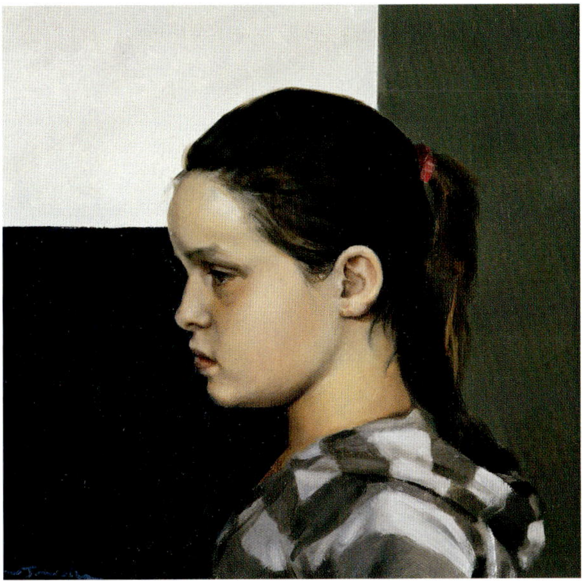

Katy Does it While Baking a Cake
Morgan Penn
Oil on canvas
710 x 560mm

Tim
Scott Pohlschmidt
Oil on canvas
385 x 285mm

Organia
Anastasia Pollard
Oil on board
700 x 380mm

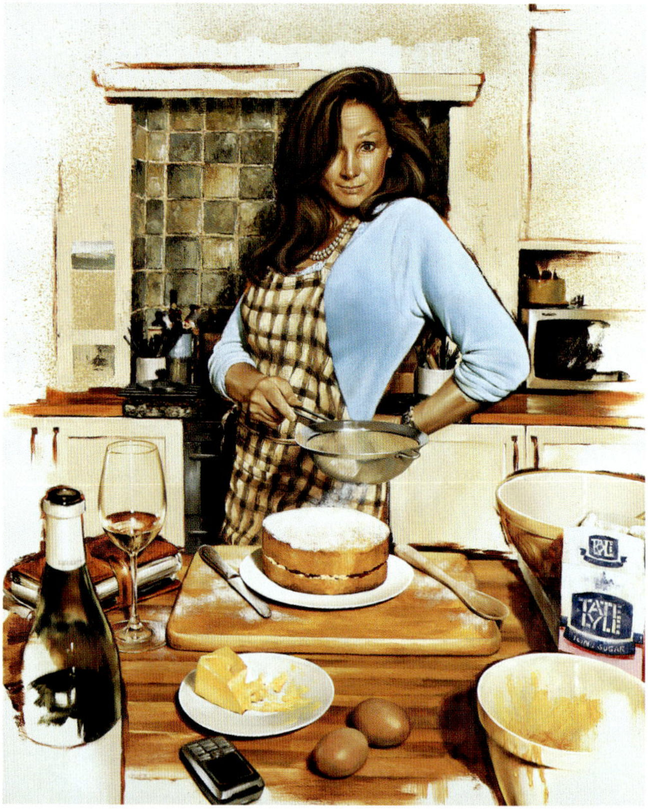

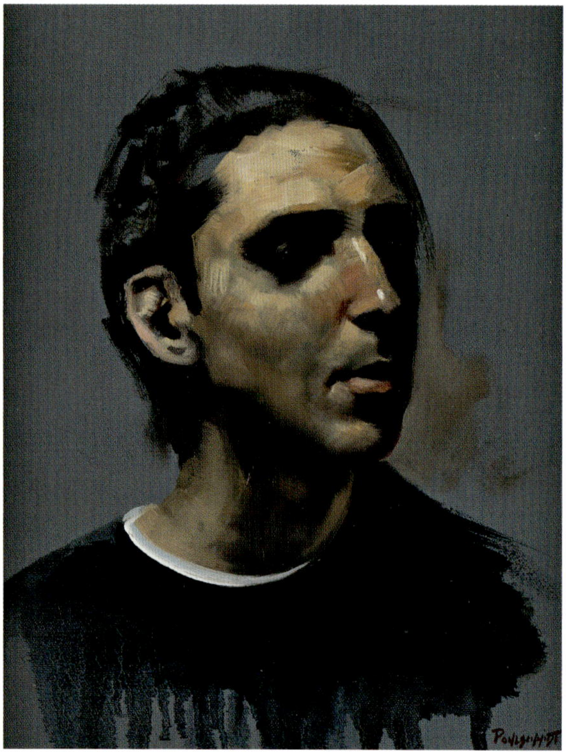

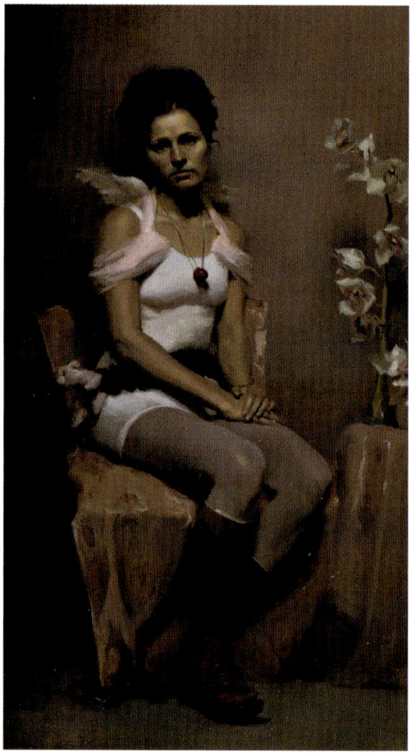

Lola
Gareth Reid
Acrylic on board
250 x 200mm

The Bevin Boy
Philip Renforth
Oil on board
545 x 330mm

Stanley
Keith Robinson
Oil on canvas
750 x 490mm

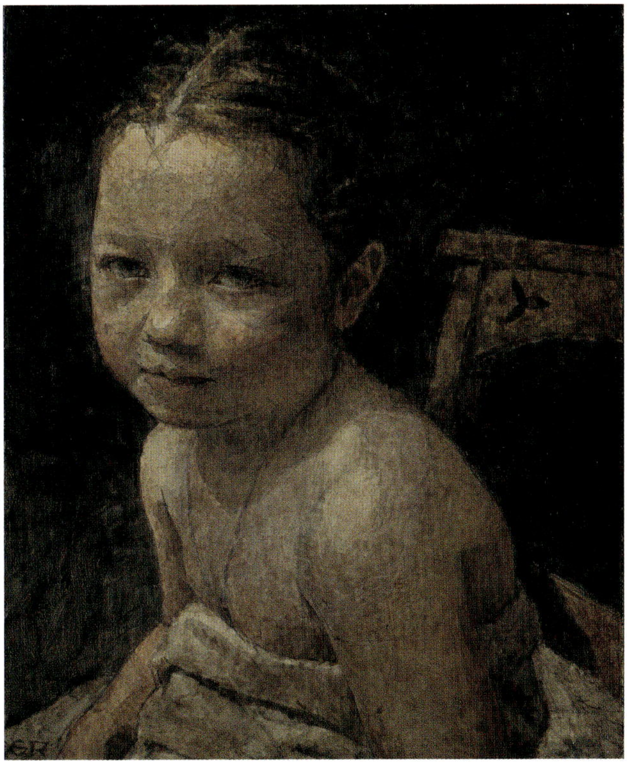

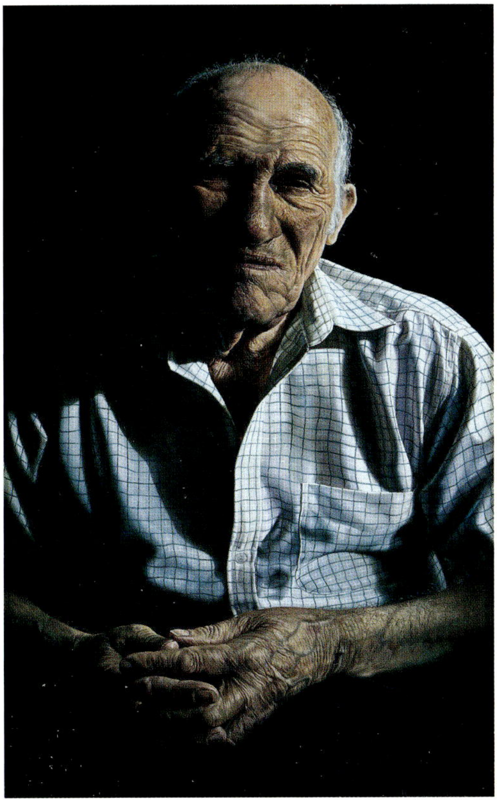

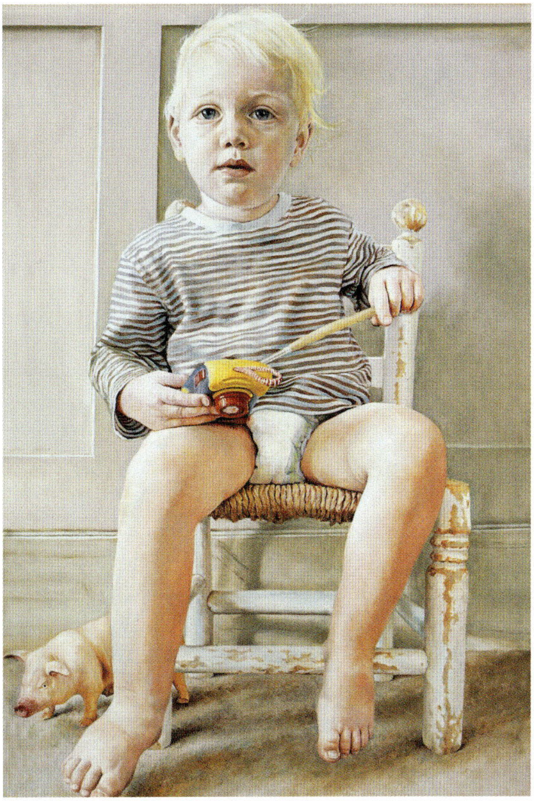

Tom, Jan, Mike, Choe and Lillie –
The Potters
Stephen Earl Rogers
Oil on board
780 x 1060mm

Ricardo
Geert Schless
Oil on board
1500 x 600mm

Aileen
Perdita Sinclair
Acrylic and oil on canvas
400 x 350mm

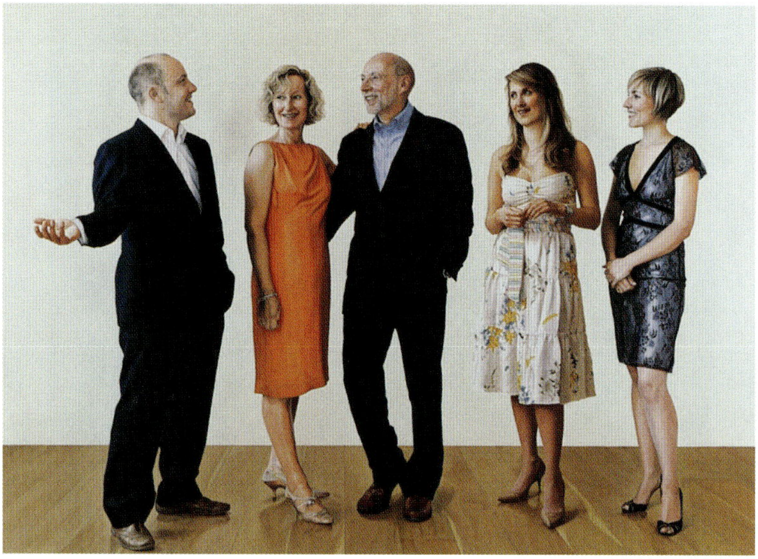

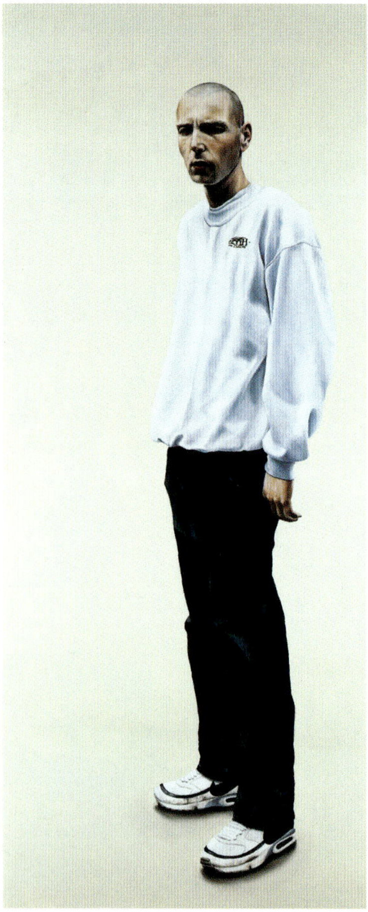

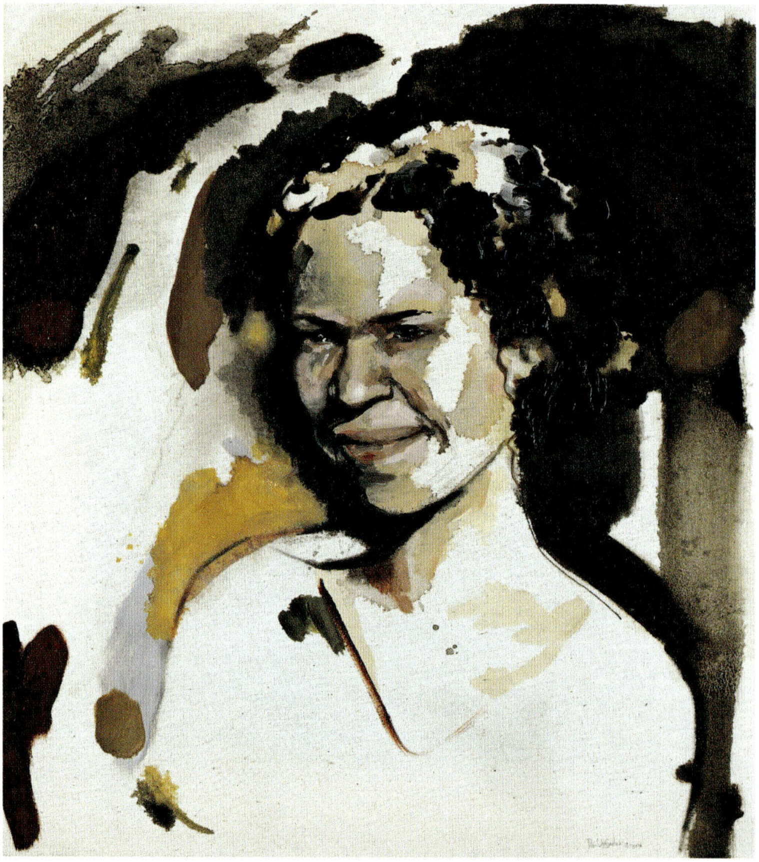

Only for a Fiver
Edward Sutcliffe
Oil on canvas
300 x 300mm

Amelie
Cassandra Szekely
Oil on panel
415 x 300mm

Portrait of Denitsa
Ivan Tafrov
Acrylic on canvas
920 x 615mm

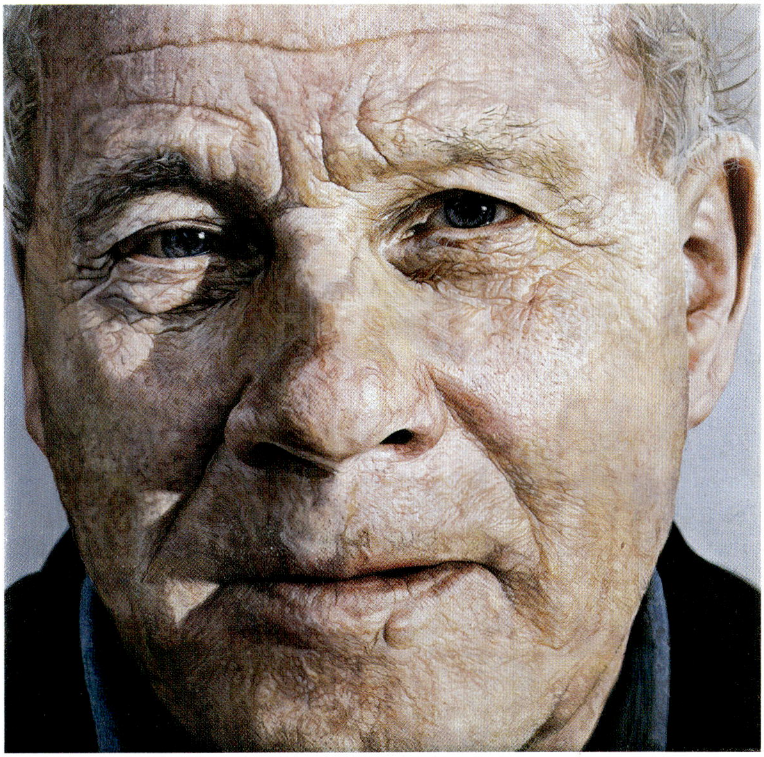

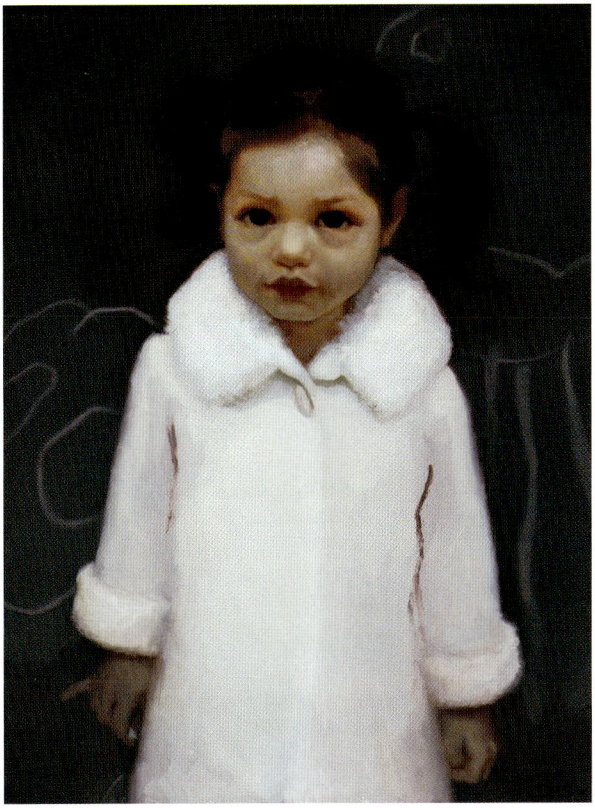

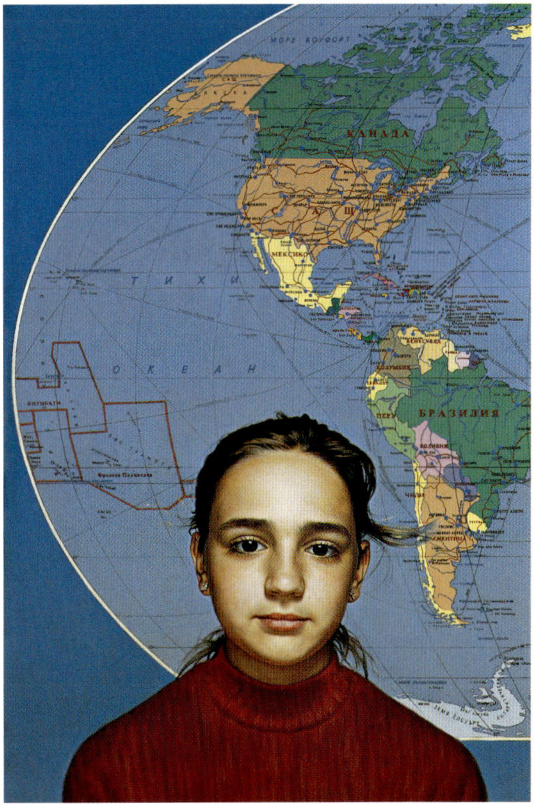

Annie
David Tebbs
Oil on canvas
400 x 300mm

William Packer
Daphne Todd
Oil on birch panels
735 x 545mm

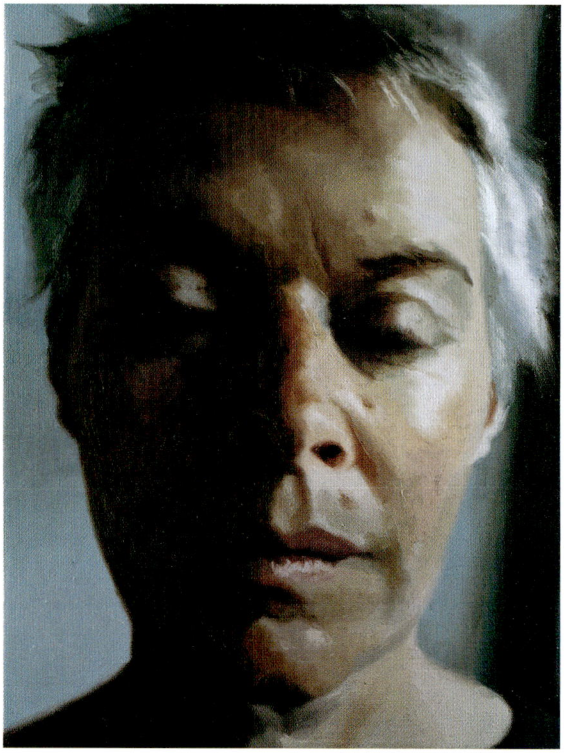

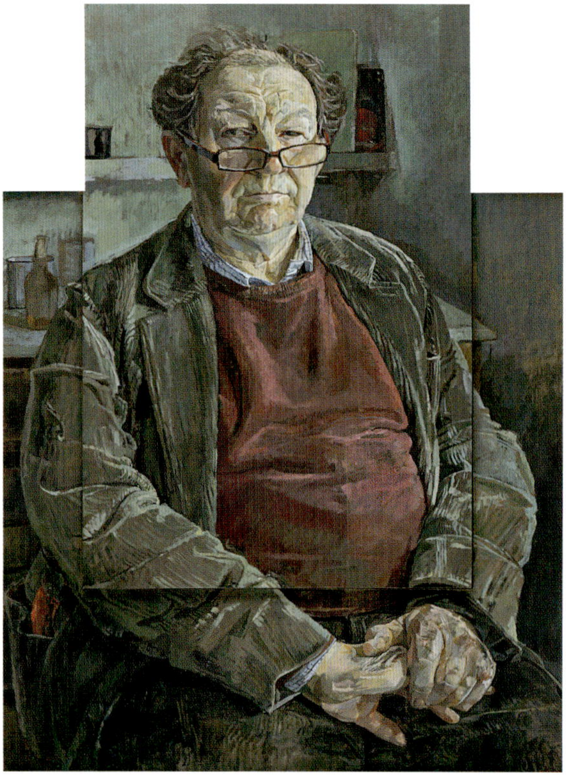

Chrisa
Jaime Valero Perandones
Oil on board
550 x 1005mm

Happy Thought – Self-portrait
Jason Walker
Oil on canvas
500 x 390mm

Kate
Vicky White
Oil on linen on board
605 x 400mm

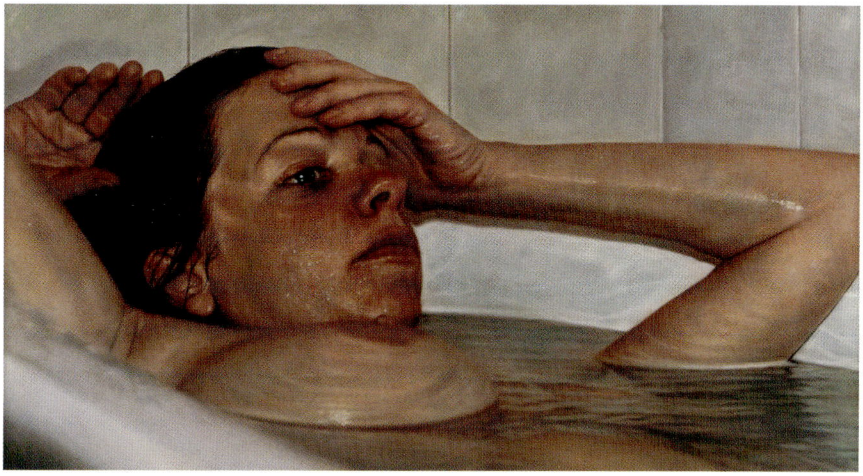

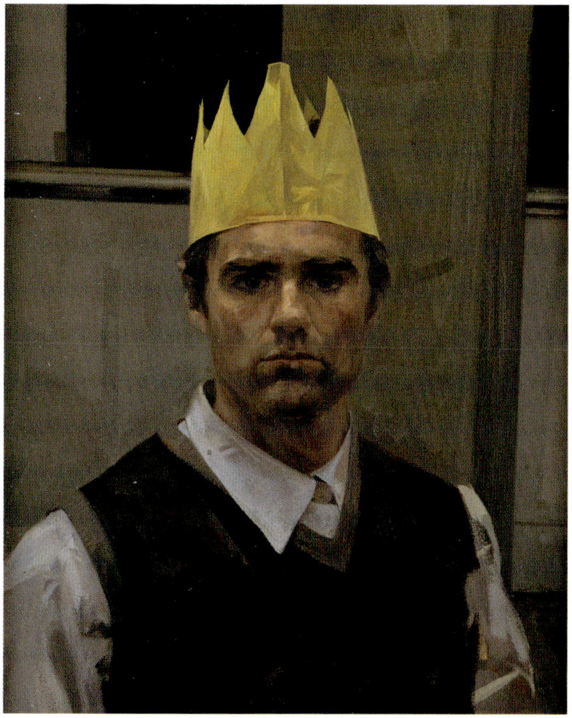

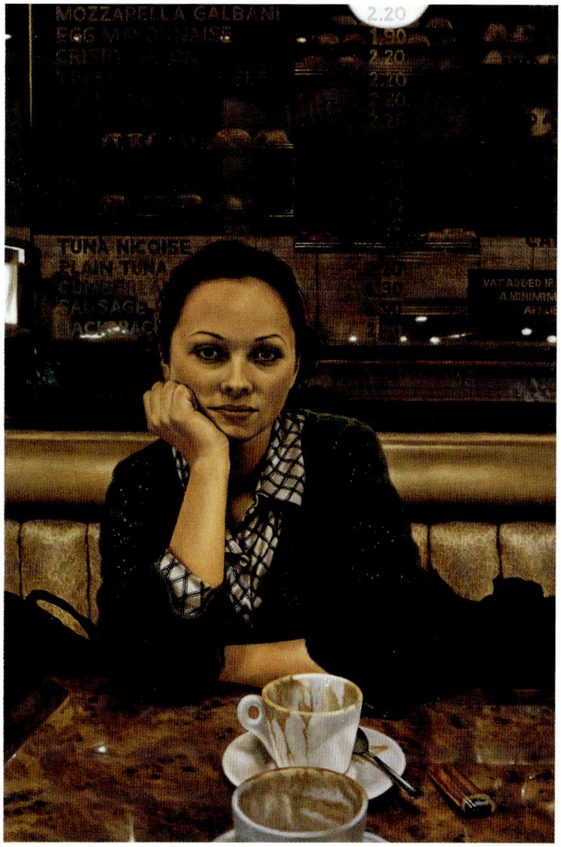

Father and Sons
Antony Williams
Egg tempera on board
1400 x 1900mm

Macular Me
Suzy Willis
Oil and wax on canvas
250 x 200mm

Self-portrait as Twins
Paula Wilson
Oil on board
335 x 335mm

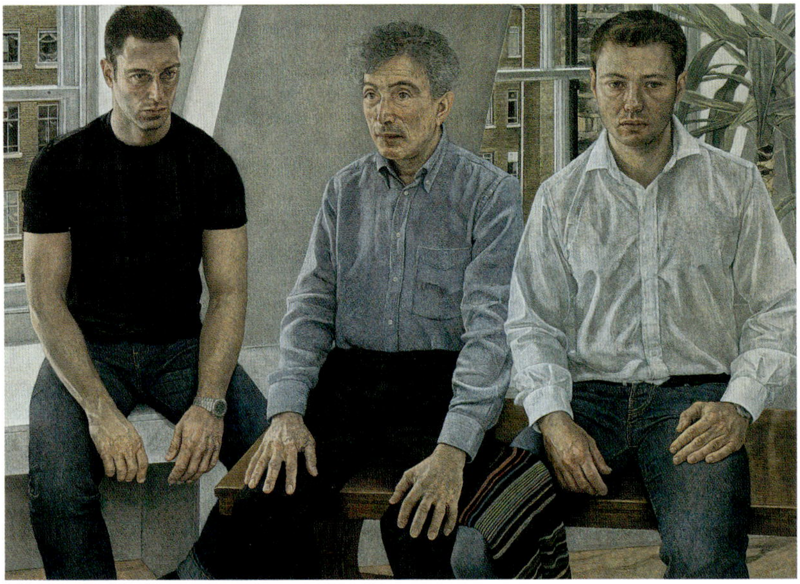

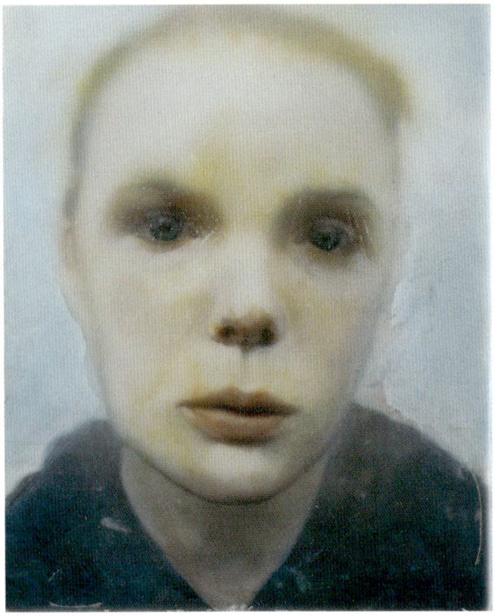

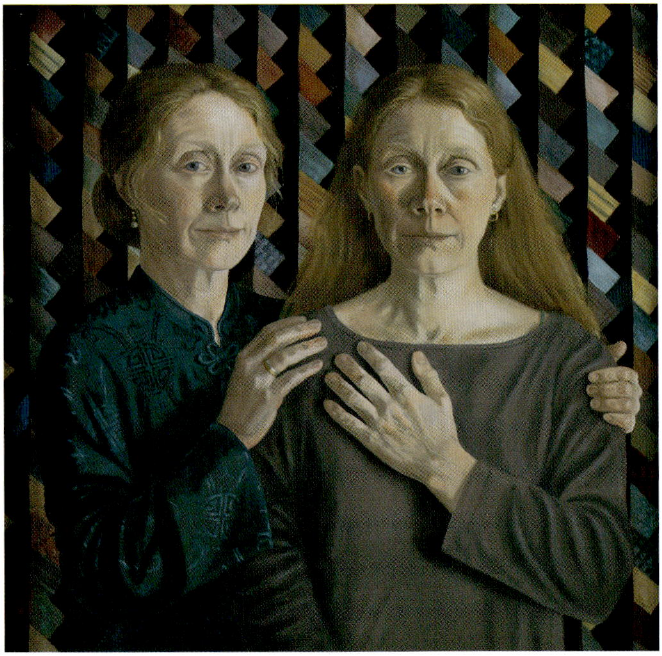

Cara
Steve Wilson
Oil on board
380 x 250mm

Self-portrait
William Wright
Oil on canvas
300 x 240mm

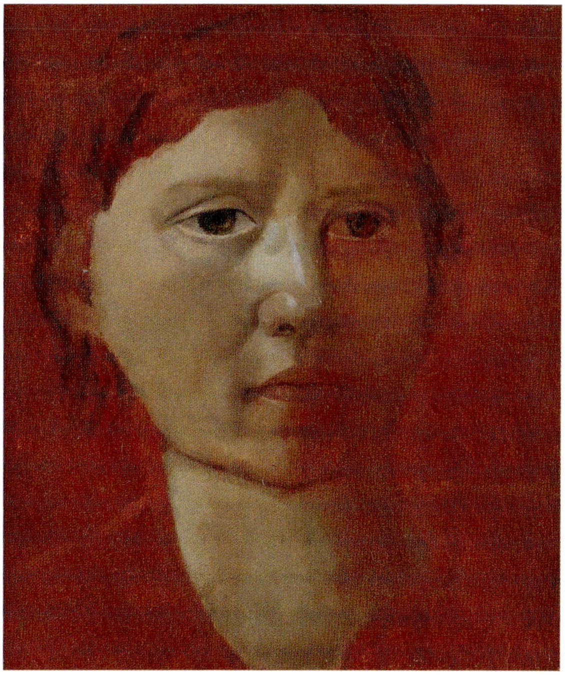

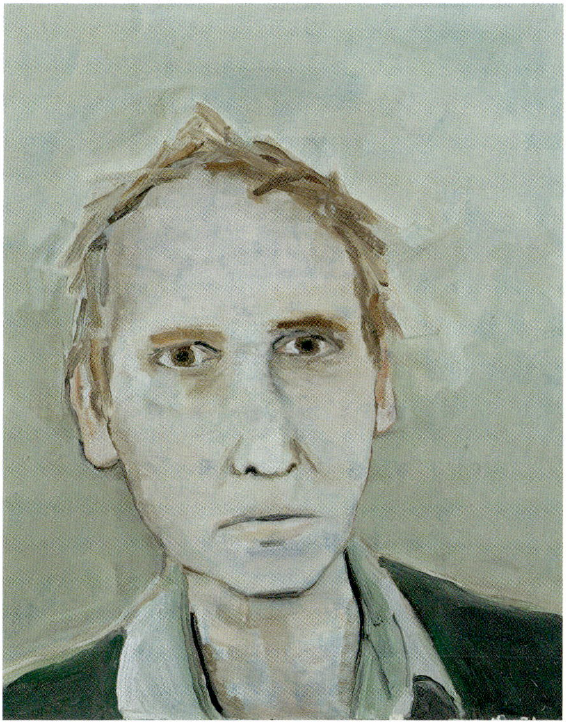

2008

ARTISTS WHOSE PORTRAITS WERE EXHIBITED

Jackie Anderson / Andres Basurto / John Beard / Celia Bennett / Paul Benney / Emmanouil Bitsakis / Sue Burns / Annemarie Busschers / Stephen Chappell / Brian Clements / Benjamin Cohen / Lucie Cookson / José Luis Corella García / Arth Daniels / Nerys Davies / Simon Davis / Tom Dewhurst / Atul Dodiya / Alejandro Domingo / Maryam Foroozanfar / Nina Mae Fowler / Nicola Green / Gabriele Grones / Pauline Hazelwood / Wim Heldens / Linda Hubbard / Andrew Hunt / Oliver Jeffers / Peiyuan Jiang / Krasimir Kolev / Alison Lee / Paul Lisak / Barry McGlashan / Alejandro Marco Montalvo / Tony Noble / Robert O'Brien / Tim Okamura / Tom Phillips CBE RA / Flavia Maria Pitis / Angela Reilly / Keith Robinson / Oisin Roche / Rafael Rodríguez Cruz / Josep Joachin Santilari Perarnau / Geert Schless / Fred Schley / Elie Shamir / Nathan Stell / Benita Stoney / Benjamin Sullivan / Jason Walker / Emma Wesley / Harriet White / Nigel Wood / Craig Wiley / Joanna Yates

SECOND PRIZE
PORTRAIT OF AMANDA SMITH AT VINCENT AVENUE
SIMON DAVIS

Oil on board
650 x 398mm

Simon Davis is a Worcestershire-based artist with a background in illustration and design. His work was exhibited by the Royal Society of Portrait Painters in London in 2006 and 2007, when he became a member. For his prizewinning portrait of his friend Amanda Smith, Davis was influenced by a study by Henri Toulouse-Lautrec of his mother. Davis remarked at the time that he had aimed to create a calm and contemplative composition, with the sitter surrounded by lots of space.

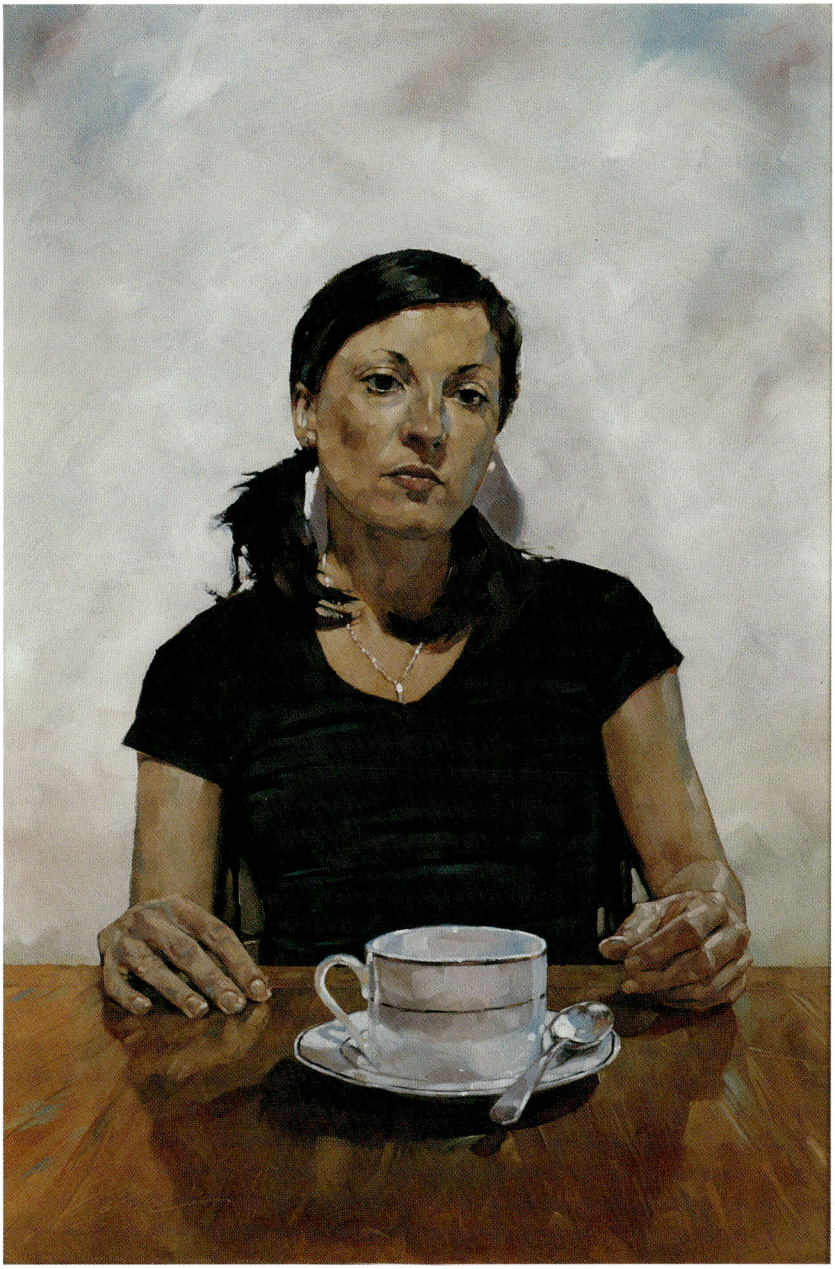

THIRD PRIZE
HANNAH O'BRIEN
ROBERT O'BRIEN

Oil on board
300 x 200mm

Figurative painter Robert O'Brien lives and works in London and Sweden. In 2000 he embarked on a degree course at Buckinghamshire Chilterns University College, spending his final year studying art and design in Sweden, where he graduated in 2003. This painting depicts O'Brien's grandmother, who had died in October 2007. Sittings took place at the care home where she lived in Hayes, Middlesex, and were kept short because of her poor health. O'Brien sought to convey his grandmother's strength and determination.

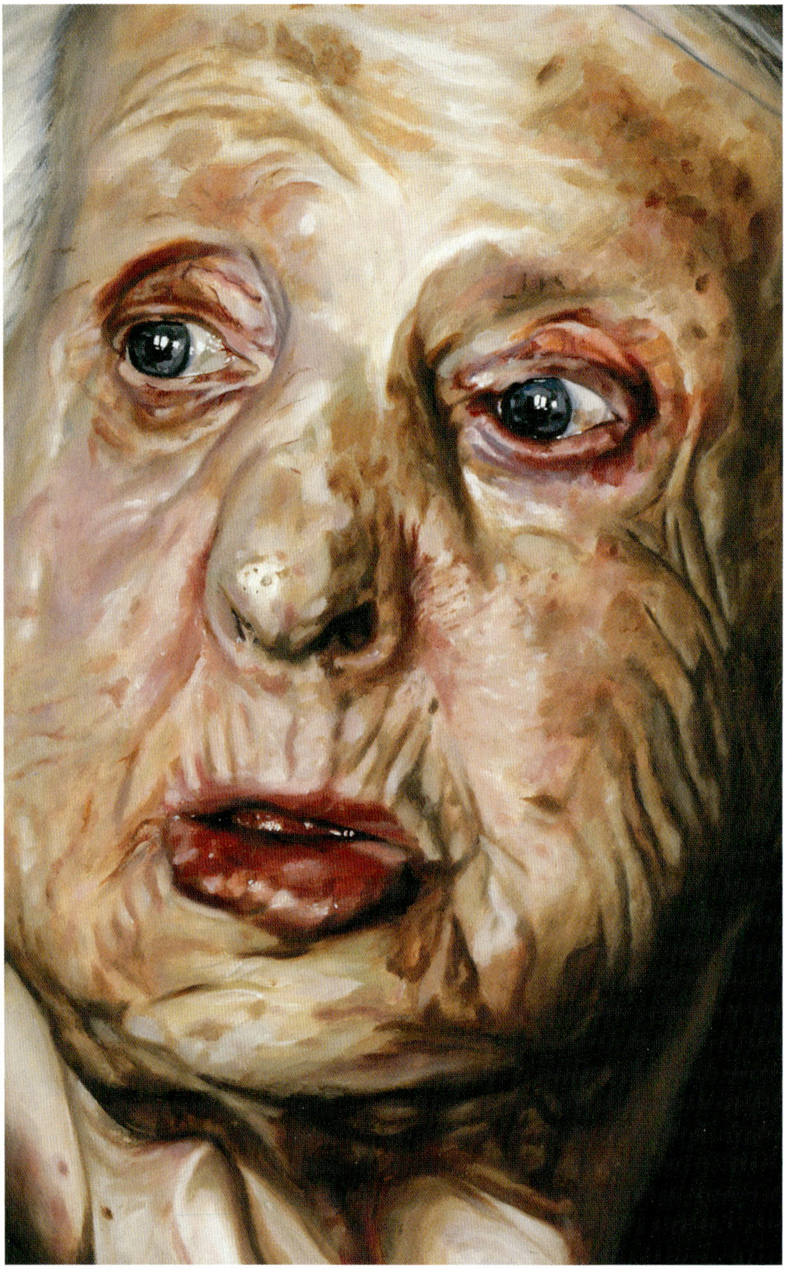

YOUNG ARTIST AWARD
UNTITLED
PEIYUAN JIANG

Oil and acrylic on canvas
700 x 800mm

Peiyuan Jiang was born in China and lives in London, where he studied for a Master of Arts in Fine Art at the Chelsea College of Art and Design. He has exhibited within the United Kingdom, at the Royal Institute of Painters in Watercolours Annual Exhibition at the Mall Galleries, London, in 2007, and the Royal Birmingham Society of Artists Friends Exhibition in 2006, among others, and internationally. Jiang has said that his work is influenced by the Pre-Raphaelites. This portrait of his flatmate, Malgosia, was painted just a week after meeting his sitter for the first time.

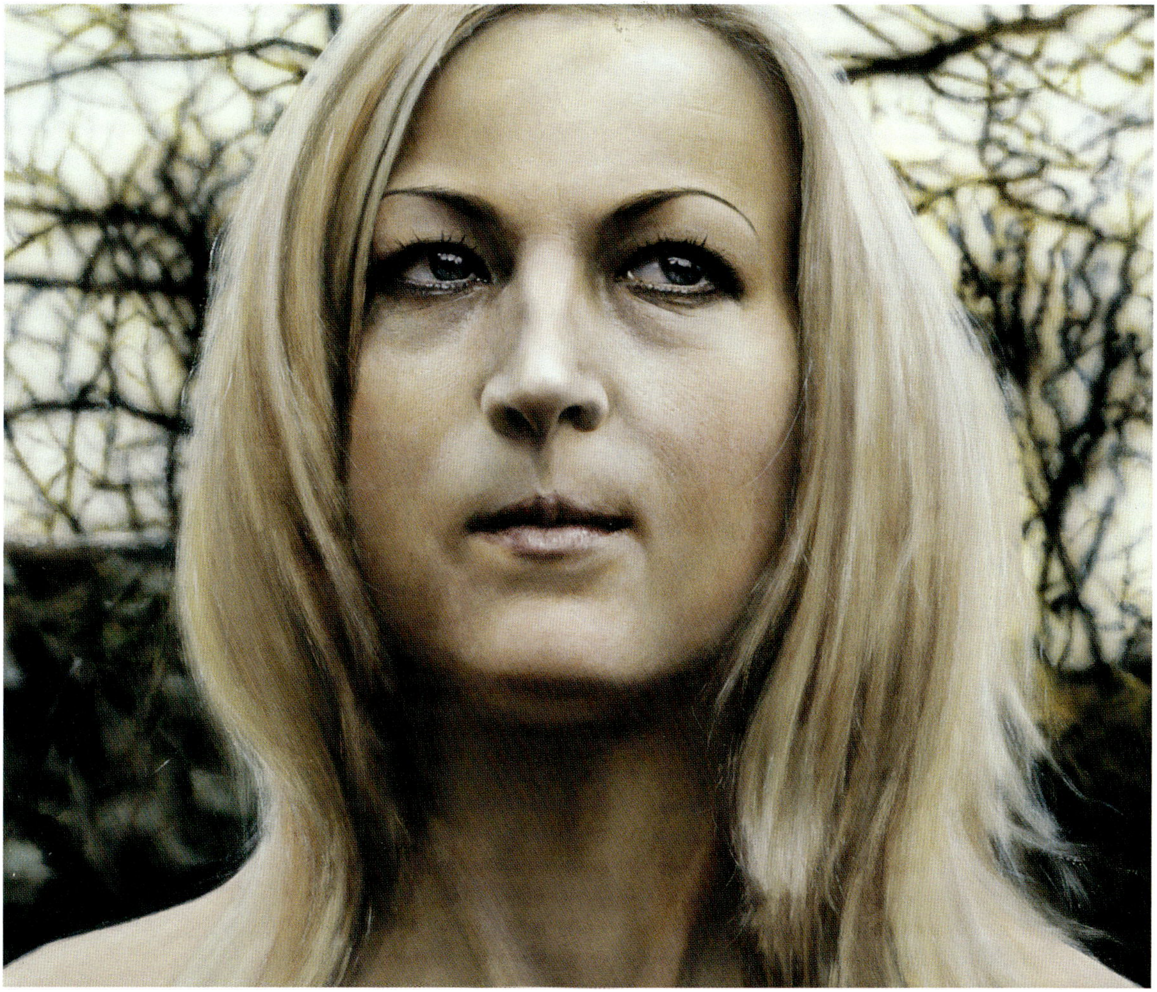

Laura
Andres Basurto
Oil on linen
360 x 280mm

Head-SP4
John Beard
Oil on linen
1800 x 1800mm

Seraph
Celia Bennett
Oil on canvas on board
380 x 300mm

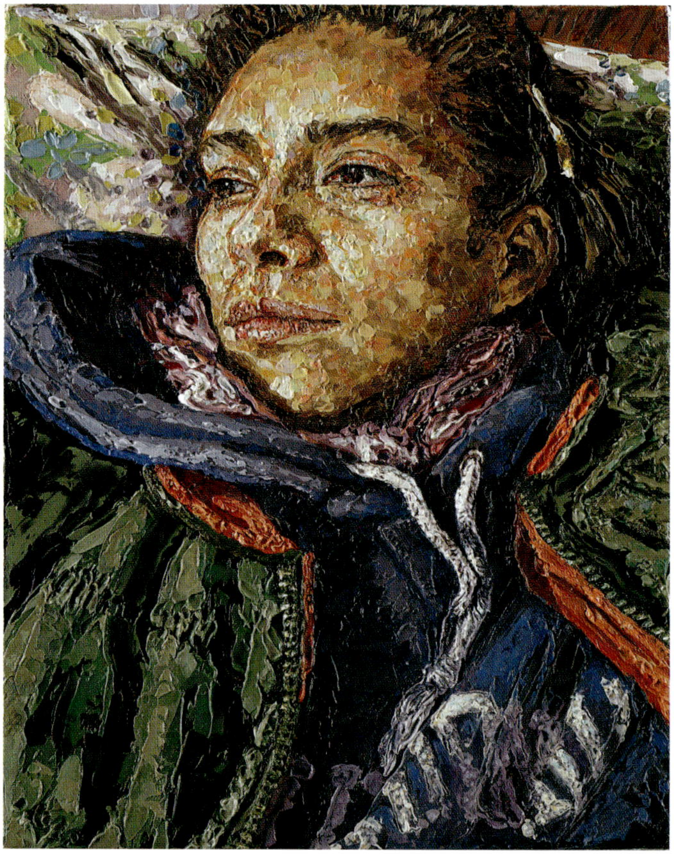

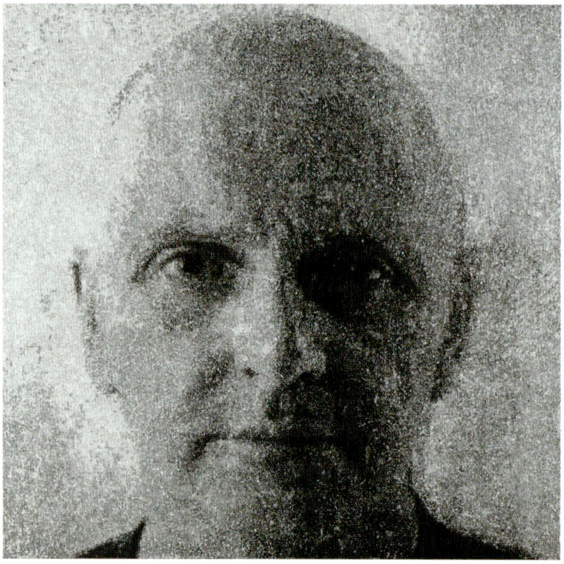

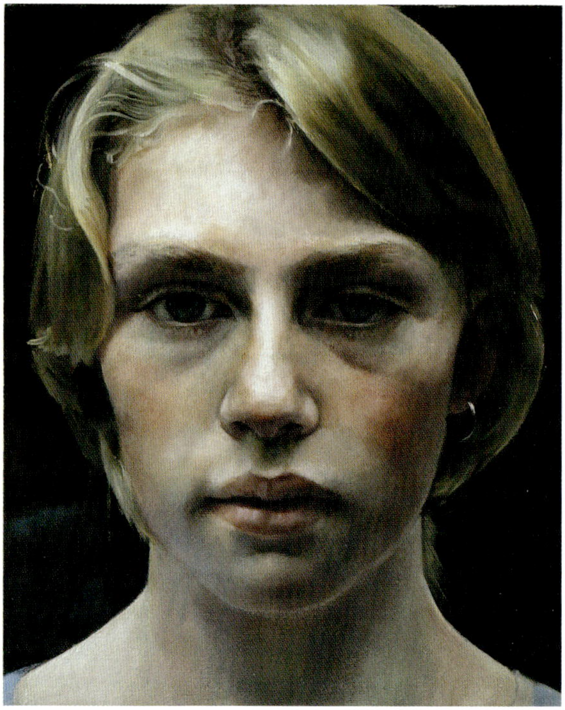

Portrait of a Serbian Student of Theology with Serbian Patriarch in Background
Emmanouil Bitsakis
Oil on canvas
330 x 210mm

Sunny Jim
Sue Burns
Oil on canvas
1420 x 1115mm

Ooh Err Mrs!
Stephen Chappell
Oil on canvas
760 x 610mm

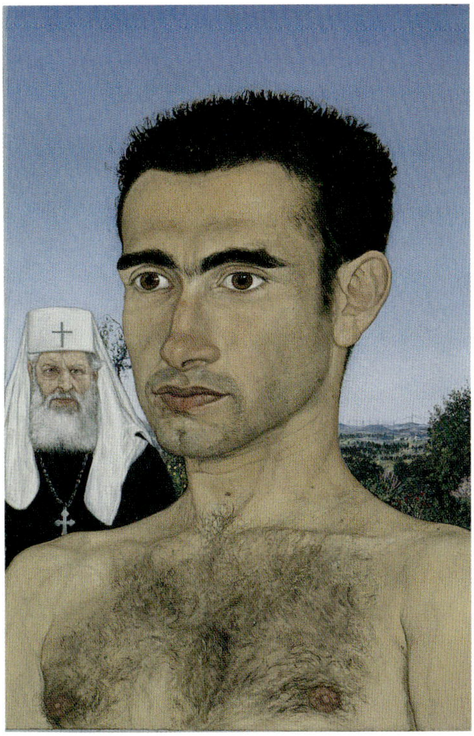

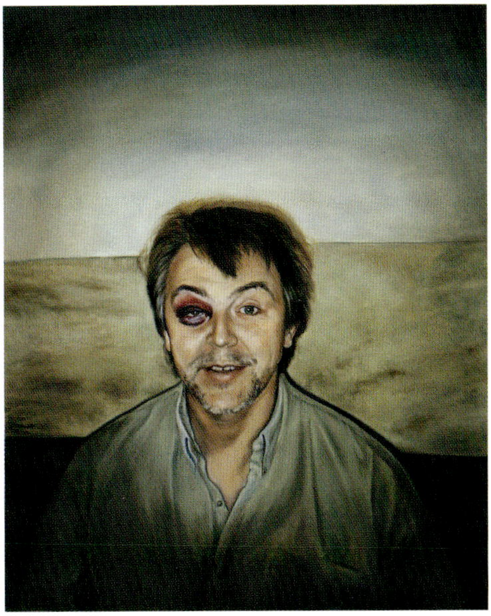

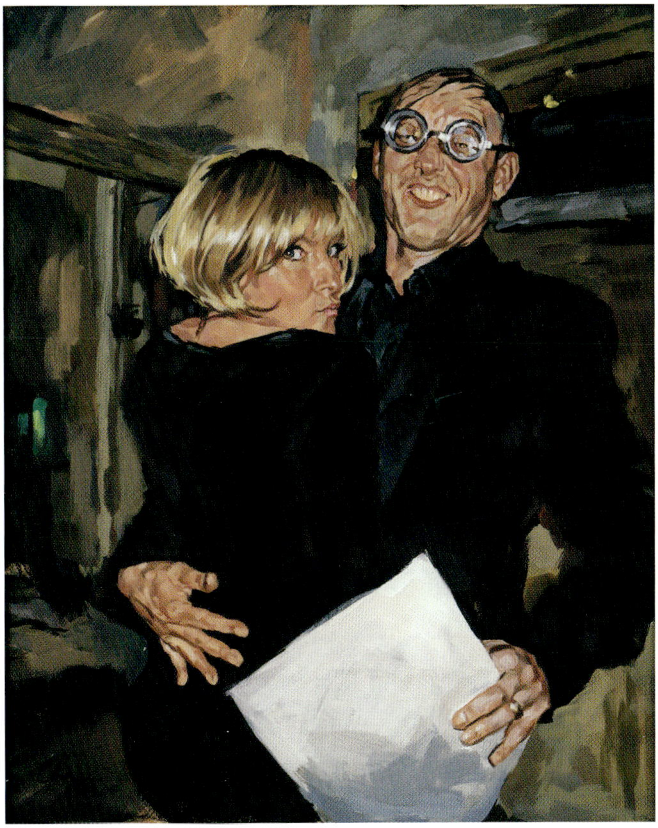

In the Bathroom Mirror
Brian Clements
Oil on board
460 x 360mm

John
Benjamin Cohen
Oil on canvas
2000 x 1490mm

Her Name is Rio
Lucie Cookson
Oil on canvas
700 x 1100mm

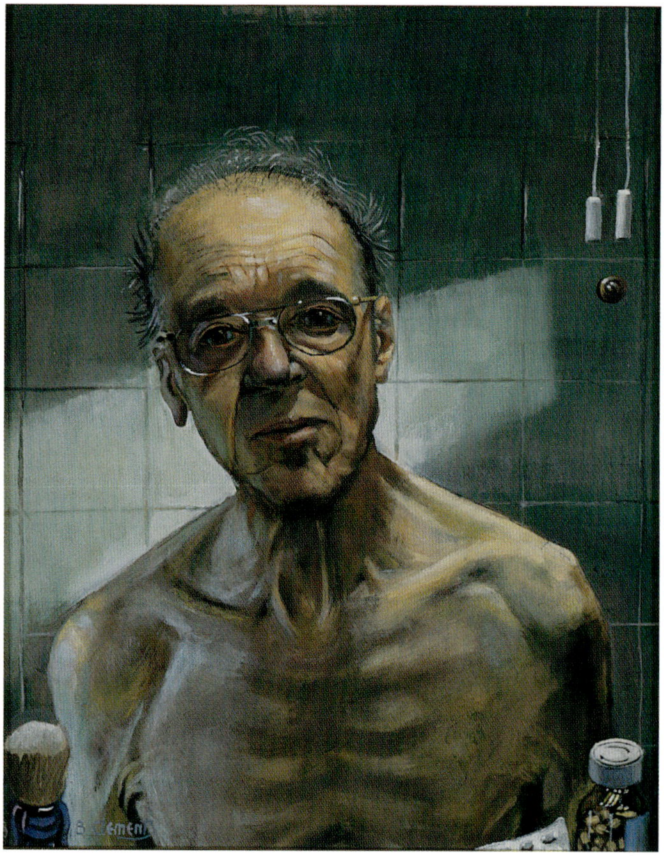

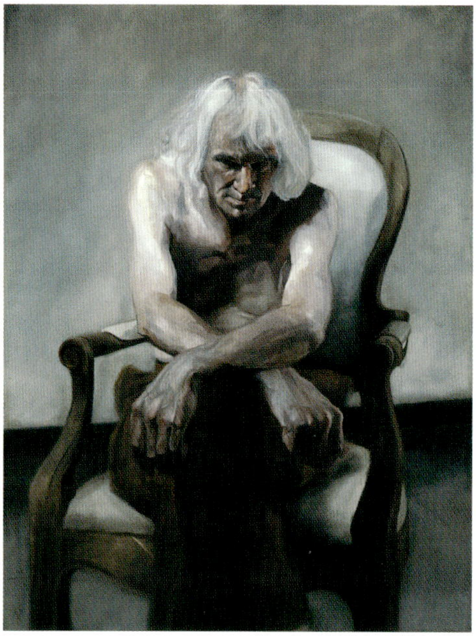

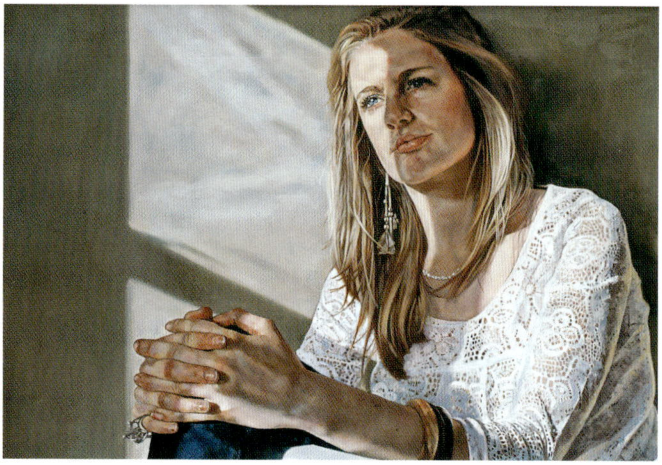

Metamorphosis
José Luis Corella García
Oil on wooden board
1000 x 1000mm

Wordtomother
Arth Daniels
Oil on canvas
970 x 1370mm

Mike Figgis
Nerys Davies
Oil on canvas
1524 x 1016mm

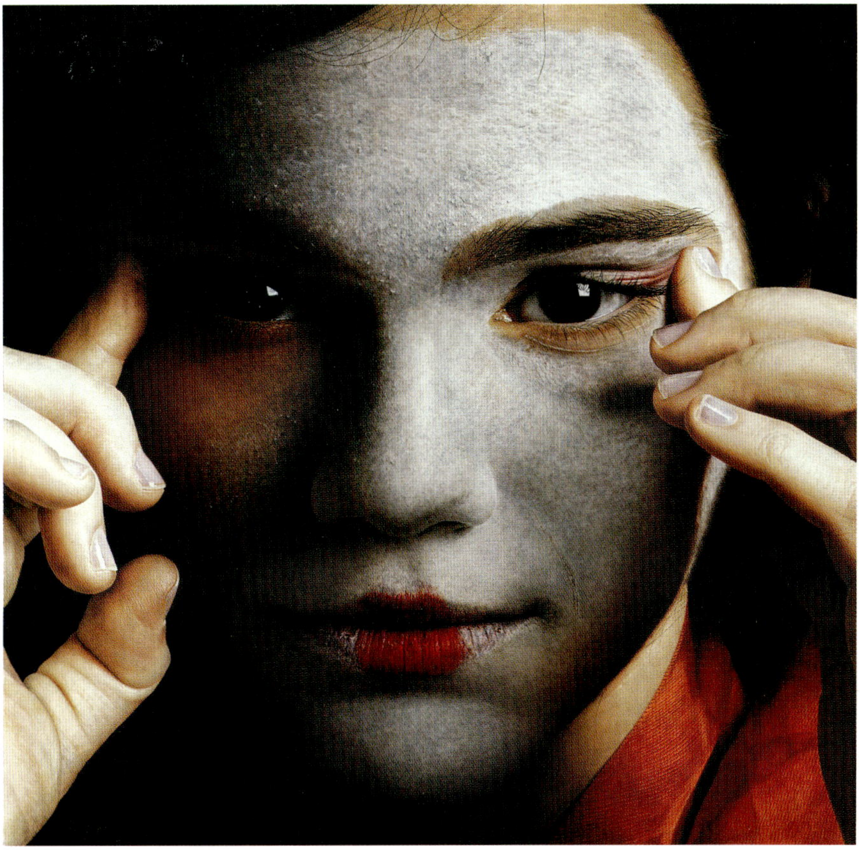

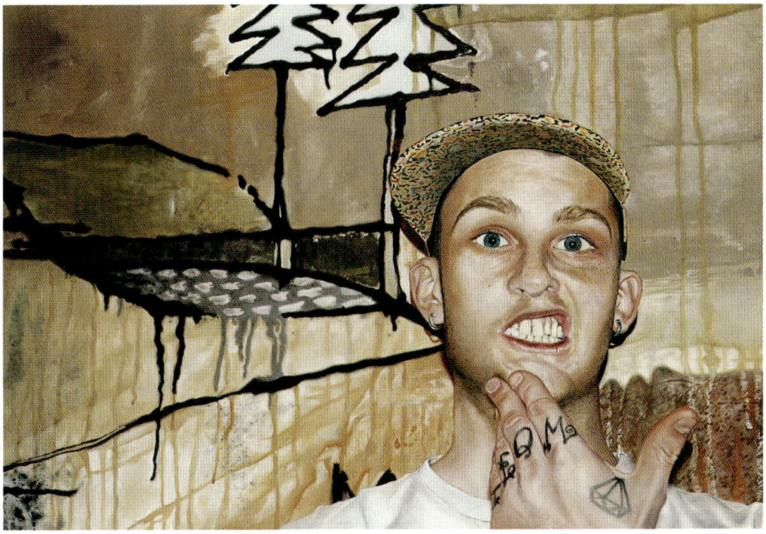

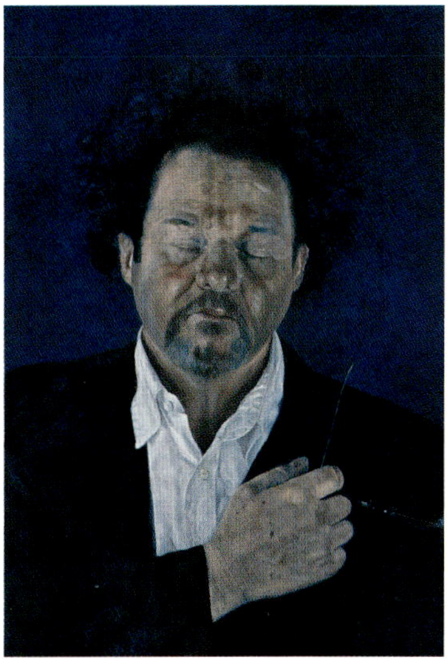

Dad and his Newspaper
Alejandro Domingo
Oil on board
400 x 400mm

Konjit
Maryam Foroozanfar
Acrylic on canvas
254 x 203mm

Carlos, 27 Years Later
Nina Mae Fowler
Oil on canvas
300 x 250mm

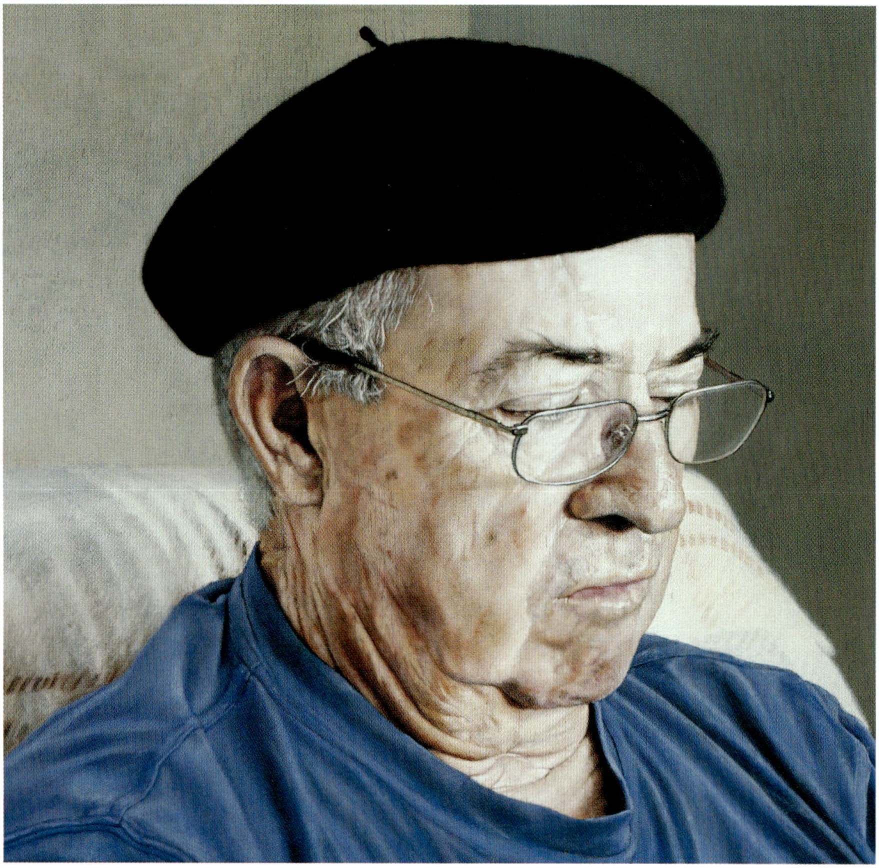

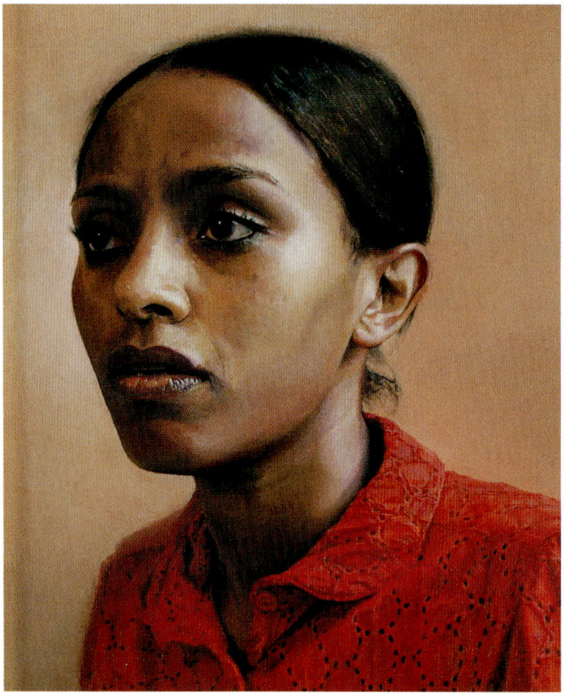

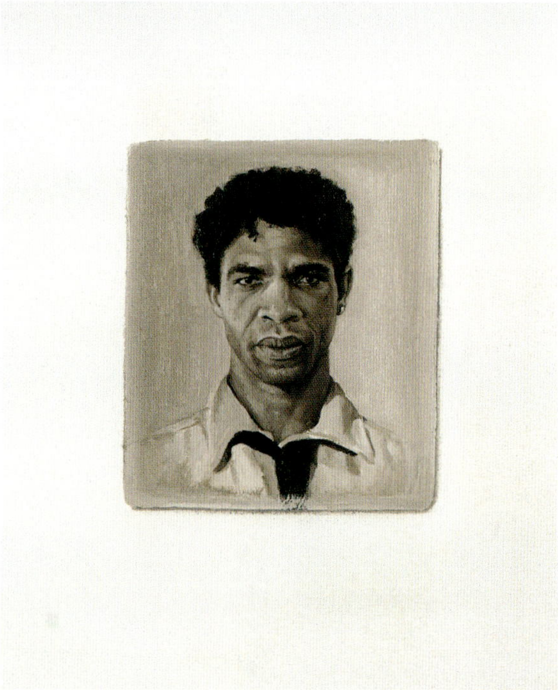

Manuel
Gabriele Grones
Oil on canvas
280 x 200mm

Camisa a Cuadros
(Chequered Shirt)
Pauline Hazelwood
Oil on canvas
610 x 457mm

La Bohème
Wim Heldens
Oil on canvas
540 x 660mm

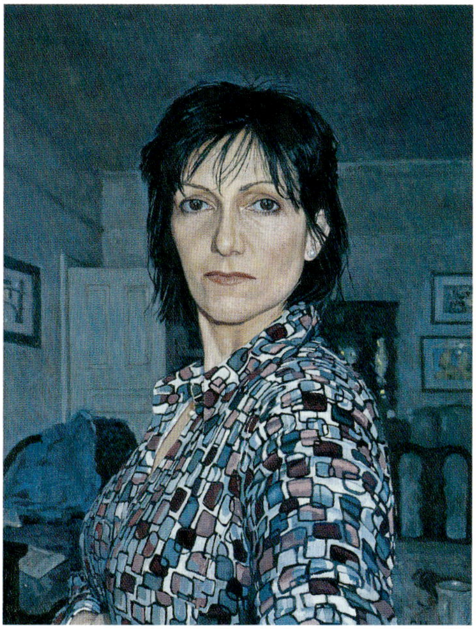

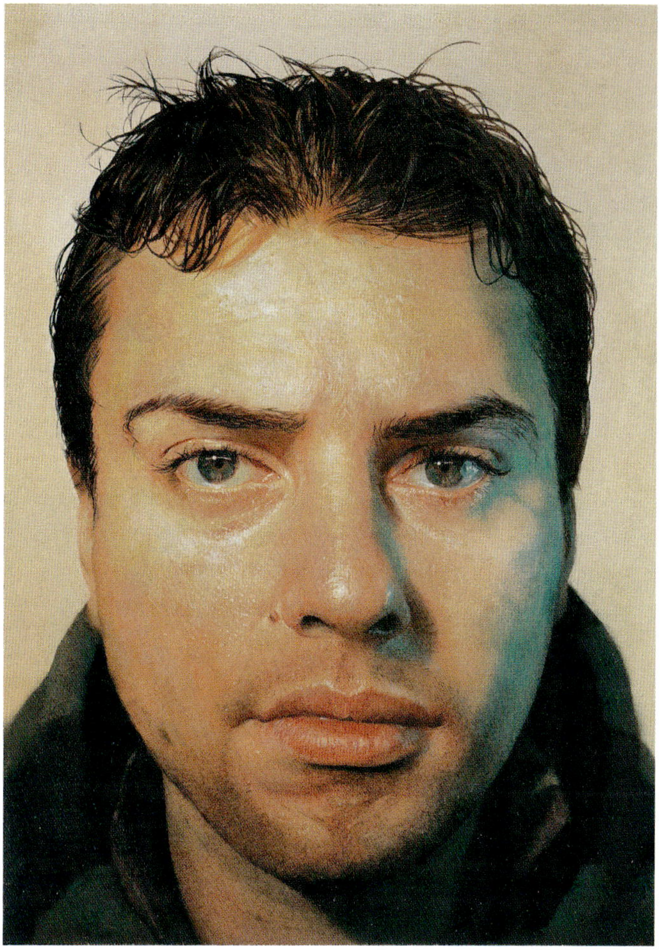

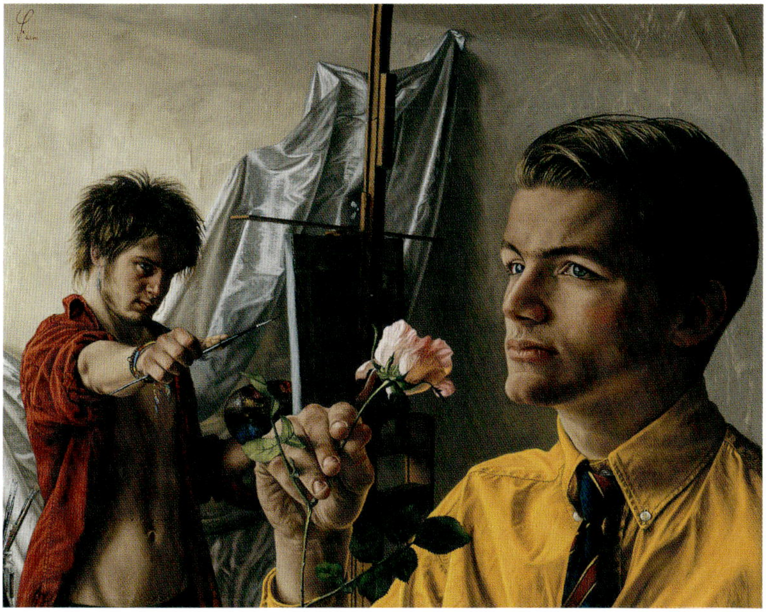

Made in Britain
Linda Hubbard
Oil on canvas
600 x 500mm

Self-portrait with Winnie
Andrew Hunt
Oil on board
828 x 587mm

Walter
Oliver Jeffers
Oil on canvas
1300 x 1000mm

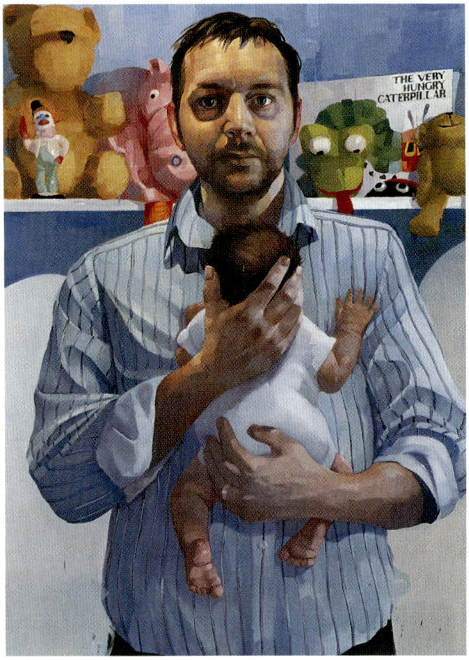

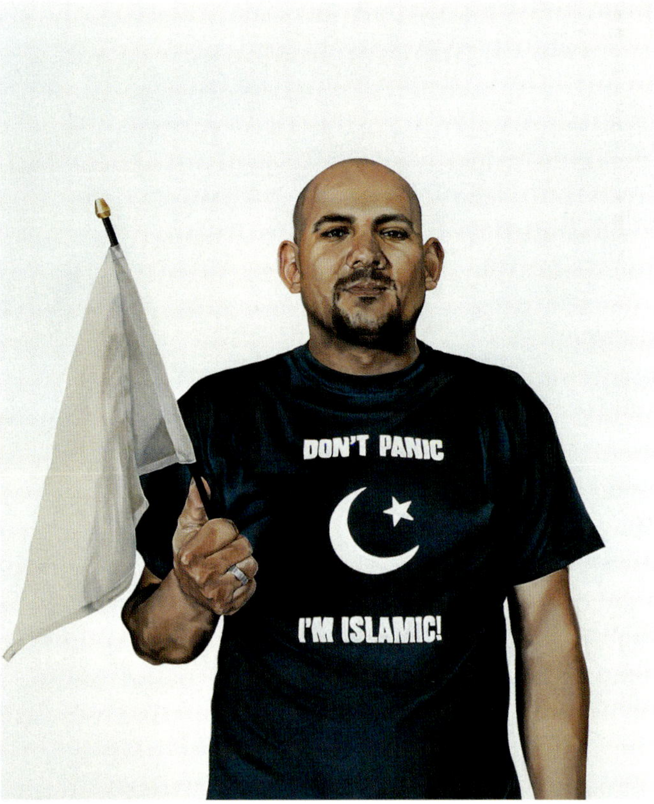

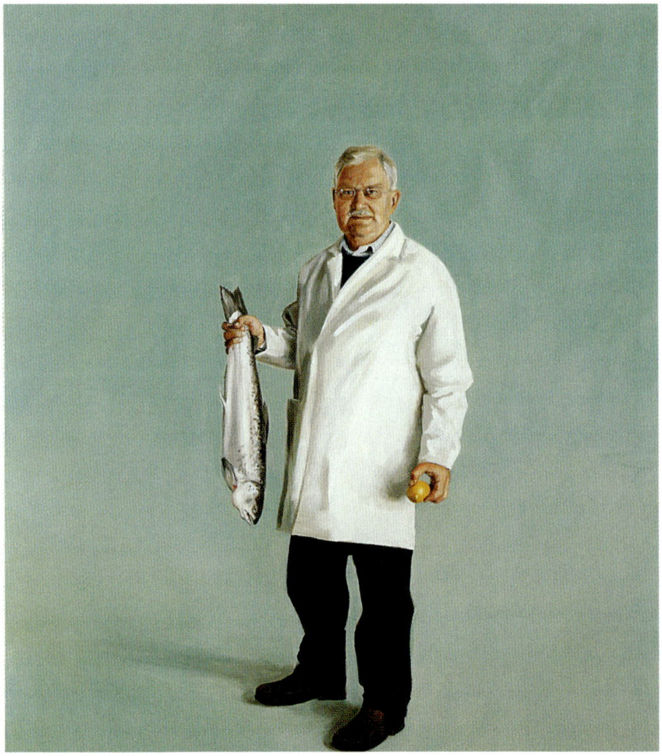

Lliana
Krasimir Kolev
Oil on canvas
540 x 930mm

Lola
Alison Lee
Oil on canvas
1020 x 765mm

Hamzah: The Silver Penny
Paul Lisak
Oil on canvas
1000 x 950mm

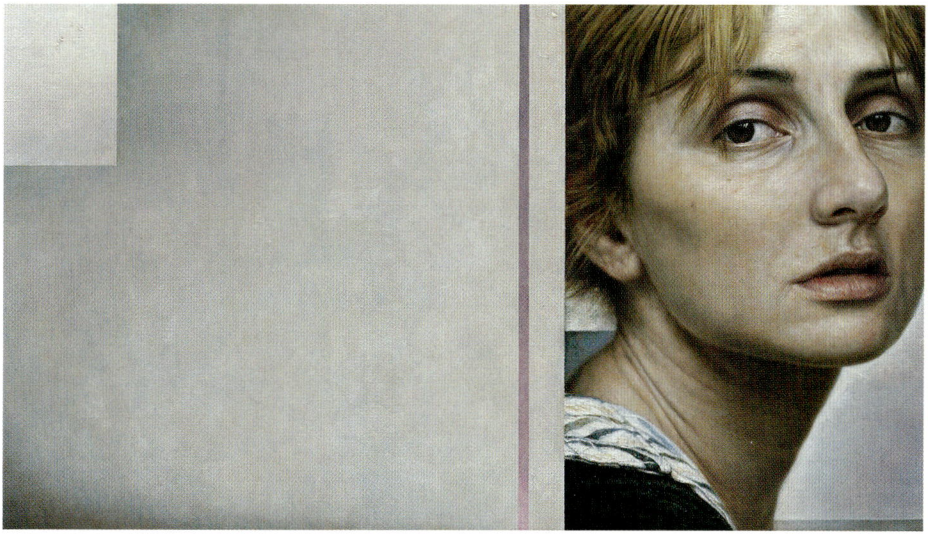

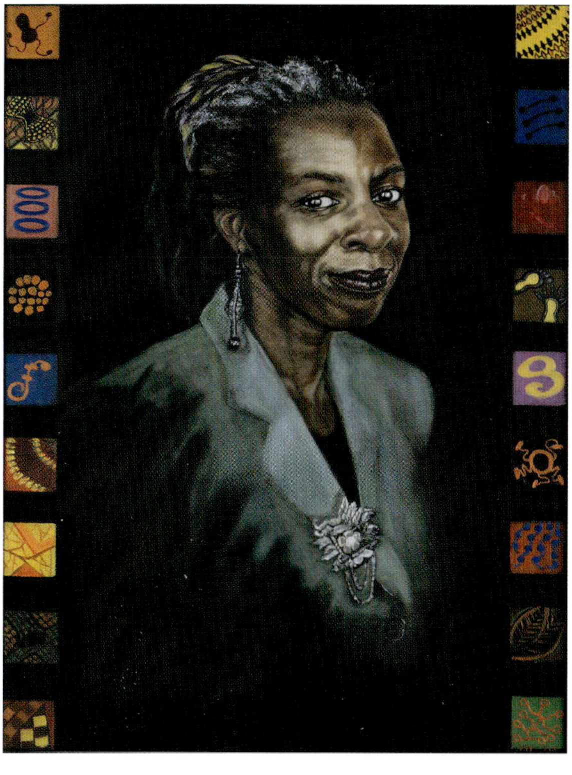

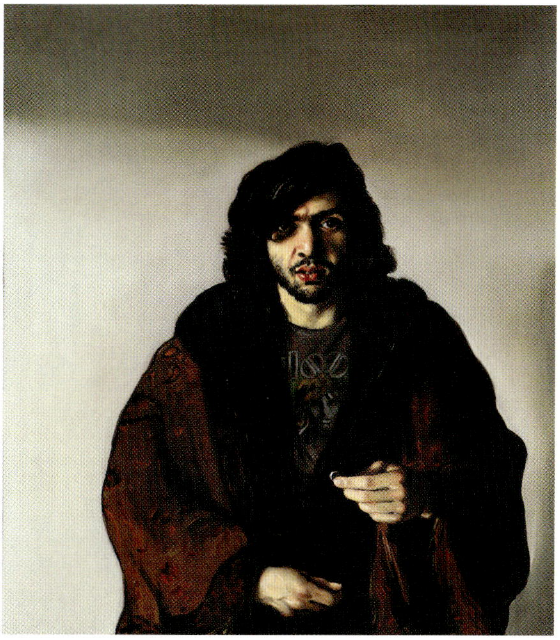

Retrato del Pintor Carlos Mondrià (Portrait of the Painter Carlos Mondrià)
Alejandro Marco Montalvo
Oil on wood
1200 x 900mm

Elixir
Barry McGlashan
Oil on wooden panel
1220 x 615mm

My Mother-in-law, Anne, and her Sister, Auntie Audrey
Tony Noble
Oil on canvas
1085 x 910mm

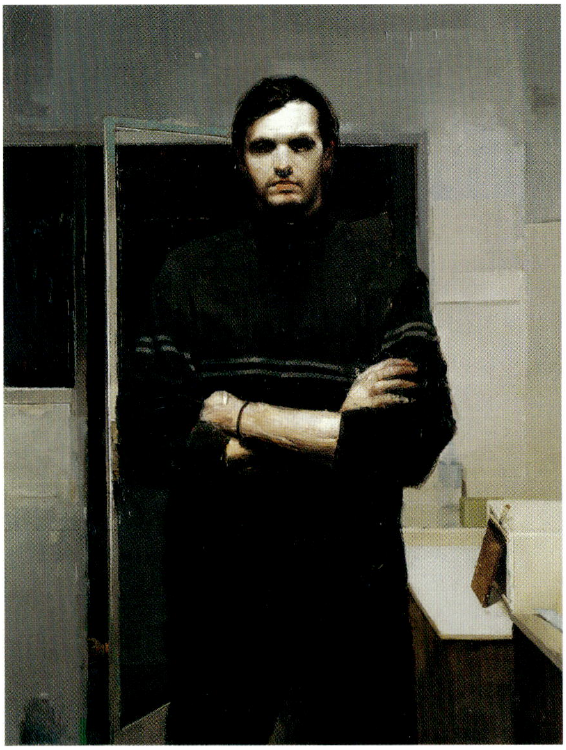

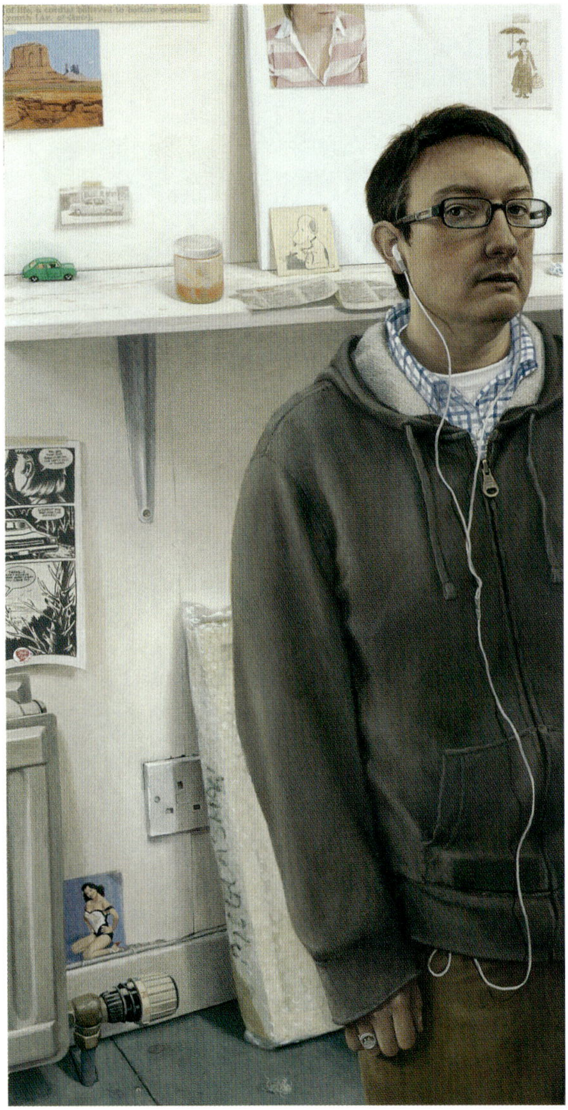

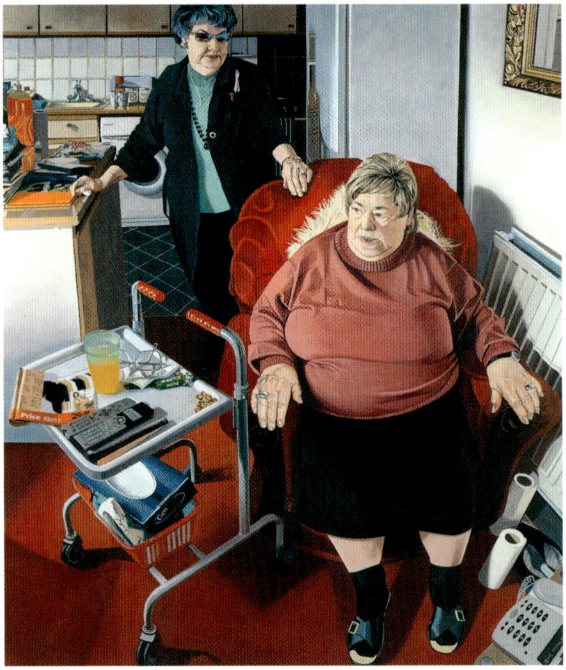

Taha (as Ronin)
Tim Okamura
Oil on canvas
1917 x 1371mm

Sir Jeremy Isaacs
Tom Phillips CBE RA
Oil on canvas
1215 x 910mm

Buti
Flavia Maria Pitis
Oil on canvas
800 x 600mm

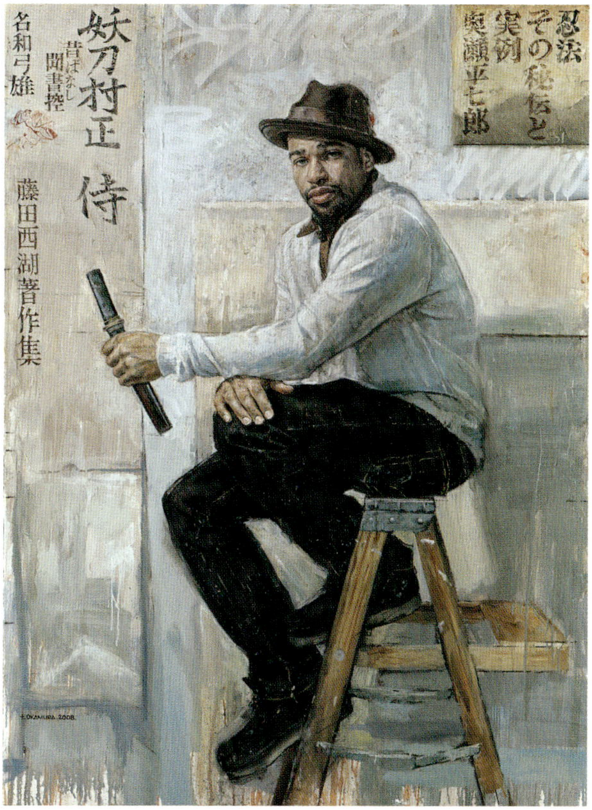

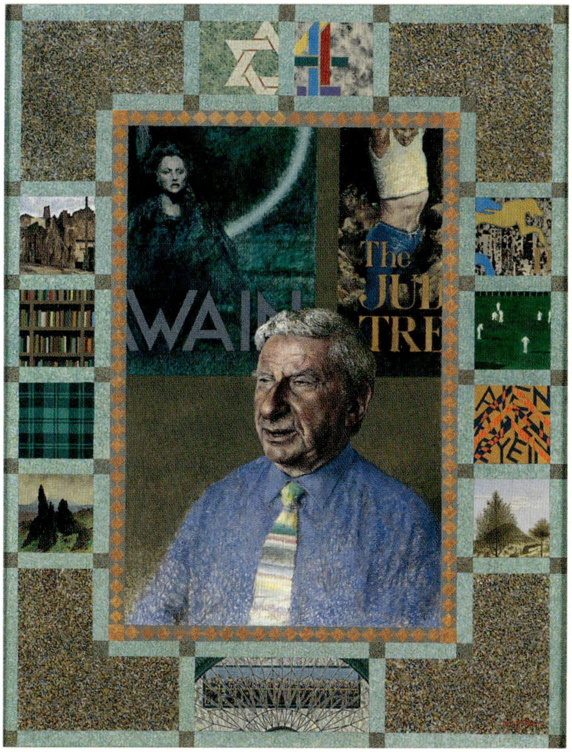

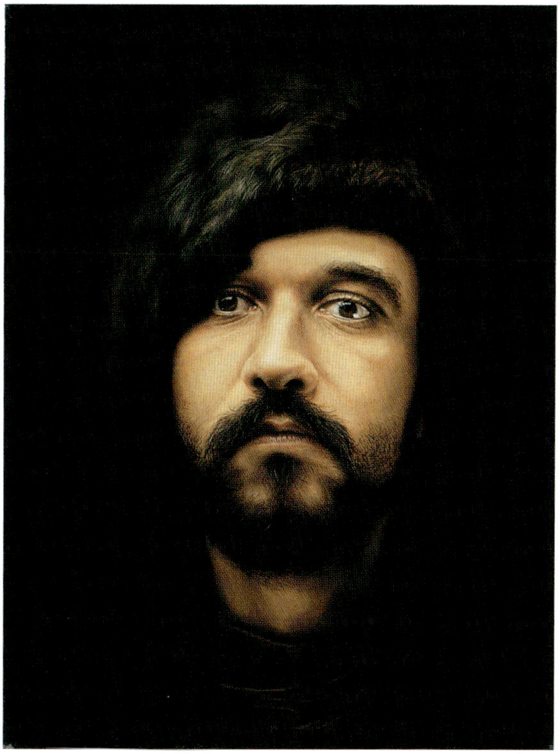

Portrait
Angela Reilly
Oil on canvas
1016 x 762mm

Kerry
Keith Robinson
Oil on canvas
1000 x 755mm

John Waters
(Journalist and Author)
Oisin Roche
Oil on canvas
1702 x 991mm

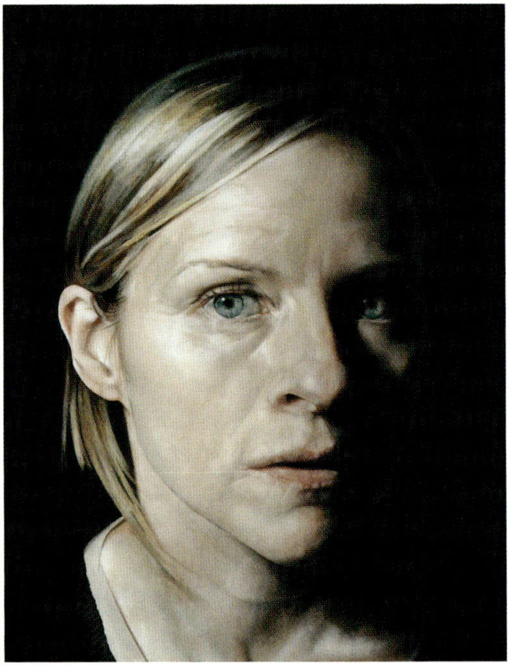

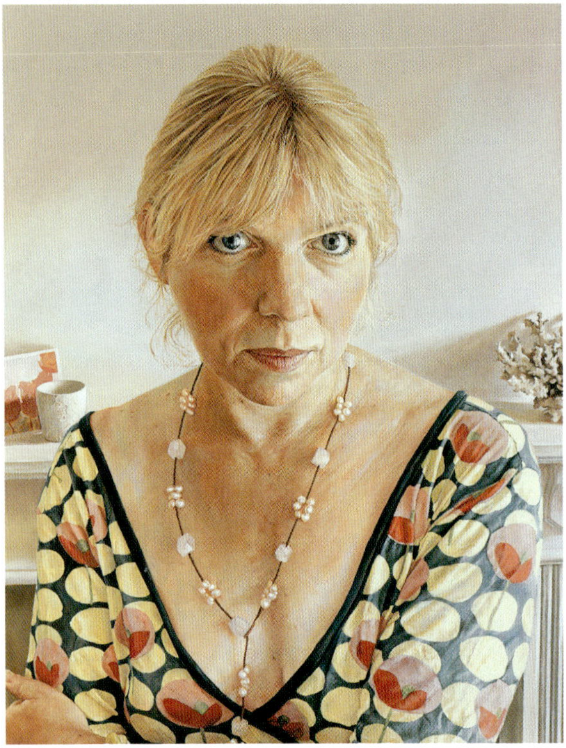

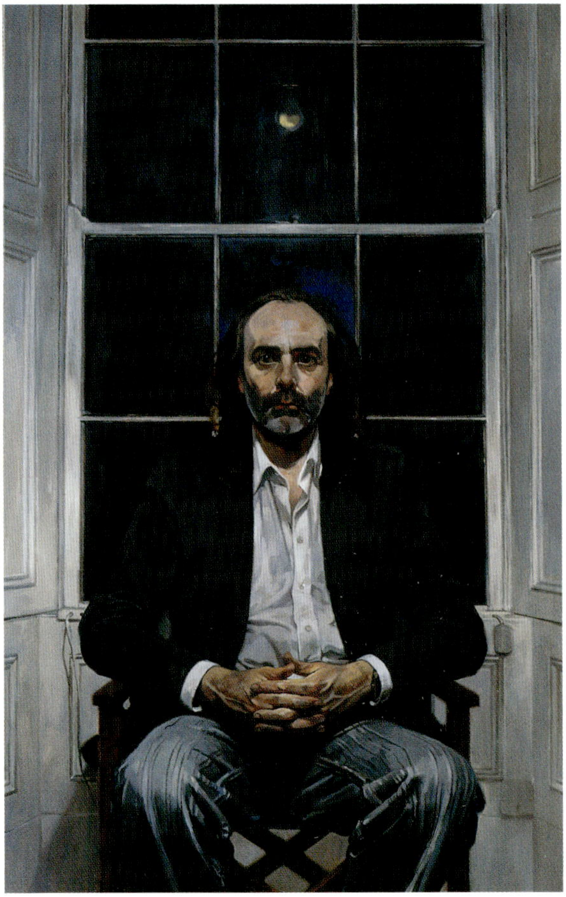

Marian Dormint (Marian Sleeping)
Josep Joaquim Santilari Perarnau
Oil on canvas
270 x 300mm

Kristy, 3rd Attempt
Geert Schless
Oil on wooden board
250 x 200mm

Tina
Fred Schley
Oil on canvas
240 x 350mm

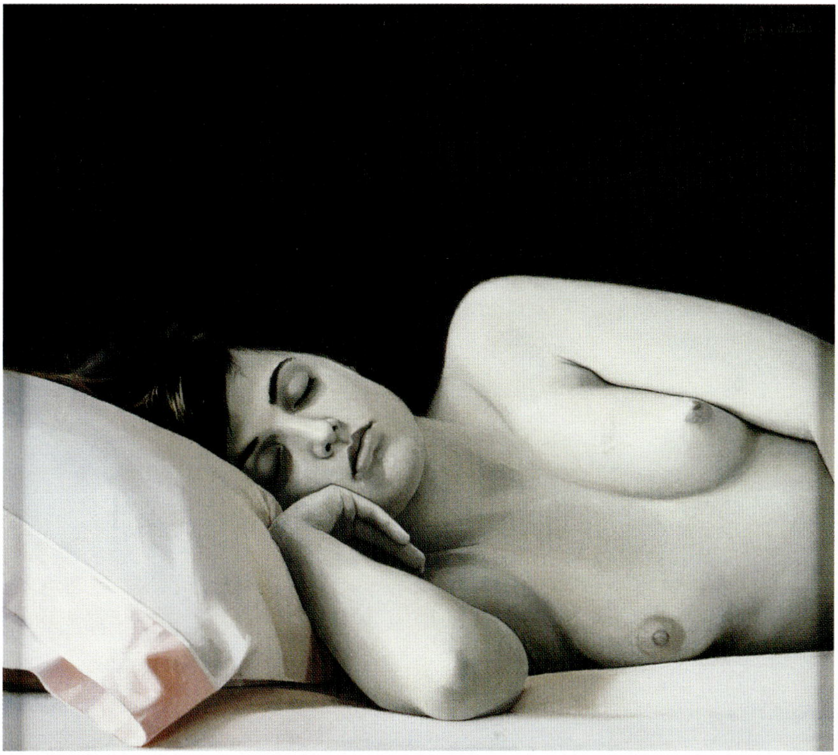

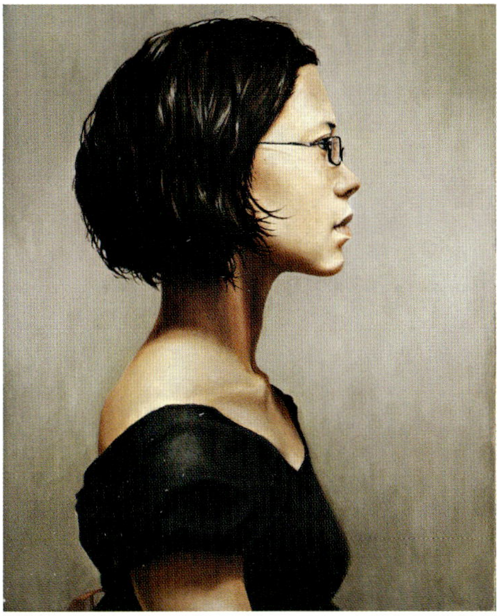

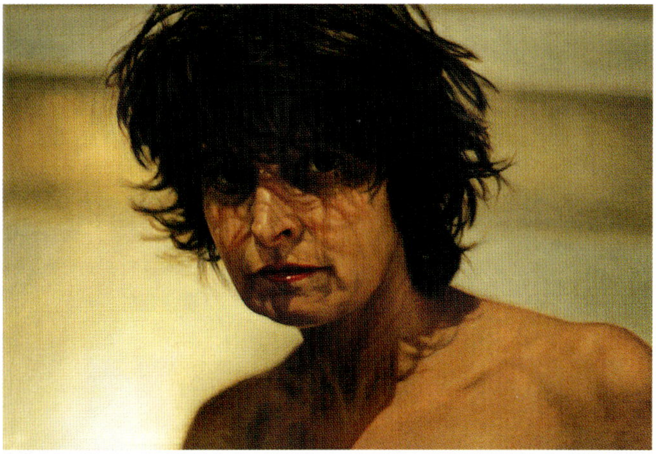

Rachel
Elie Shamir
Oil on canvas
600 x 500mm

Student Debt
Nathan Stell
Acrylic on canvas
615 x 810mm

Volker
Benita Stoney
Egg tempera on board
267 x 218mm

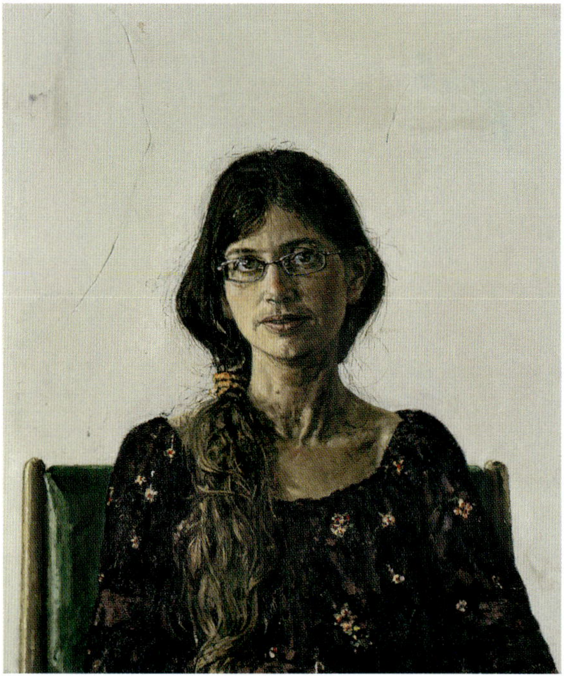

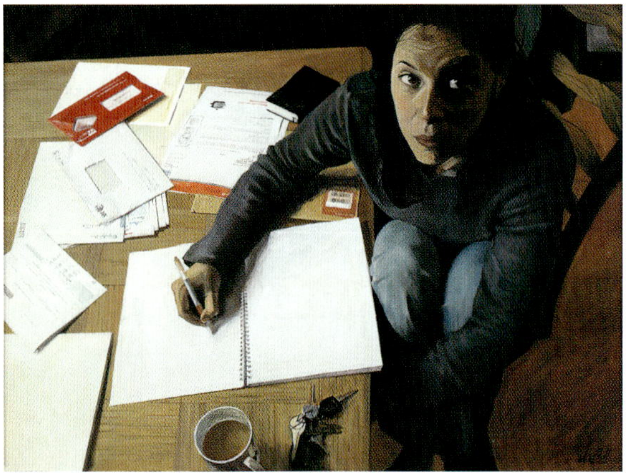

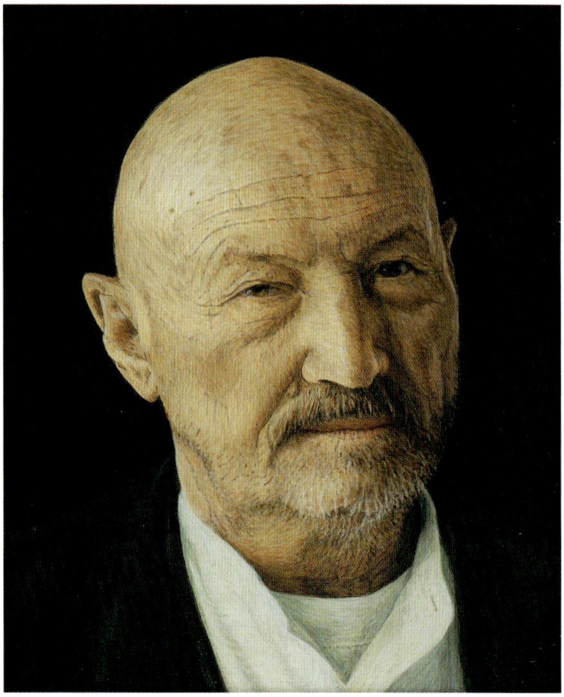

Boots No. 7 (2)
Harriet White
Oil on canvas
910 x 1220mm

Self
Nigel Wood
Oil on canvas
450 x 280mm

Meral
Joanna Yates
Oil on canvas
1000 x 1200mm

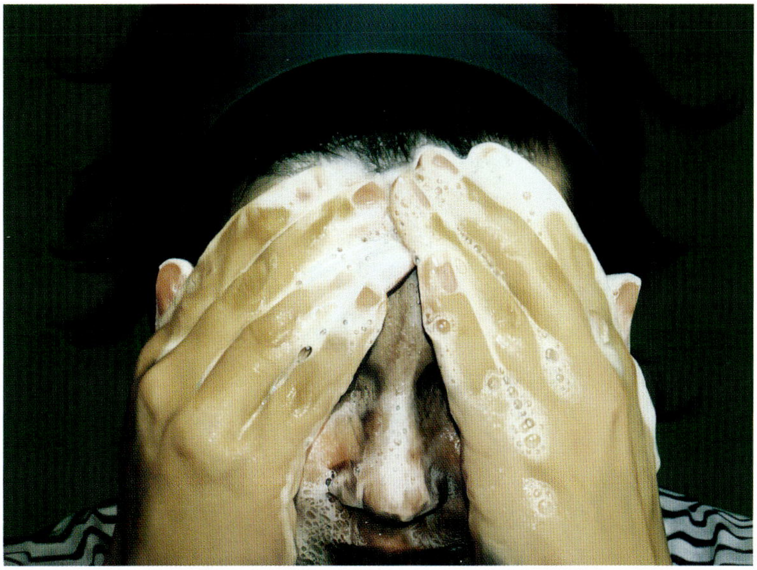

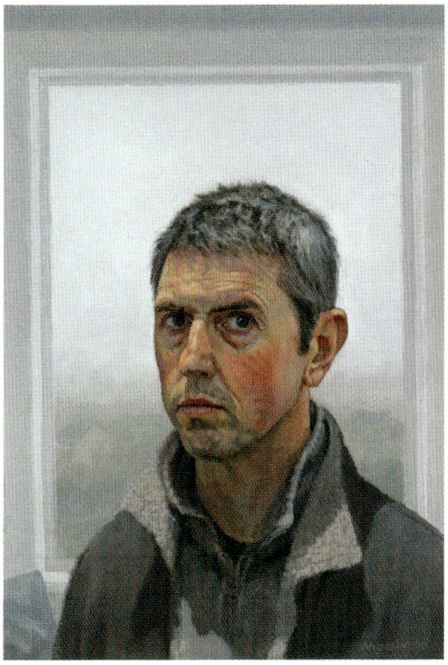

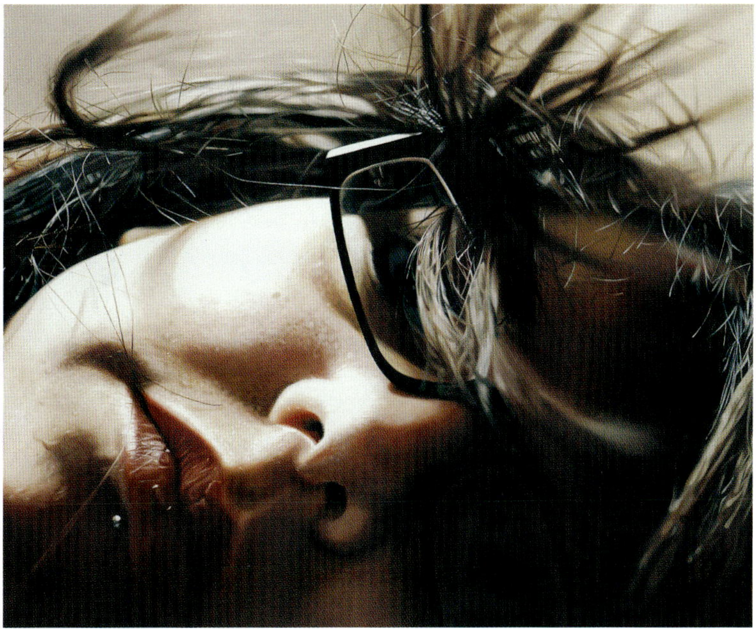

2009

ARTISTS WHOSE PORTRAITS WERE EXHIBITED

Jennifer Anderson / Mary Jane Ansell / Annalisa Avancini / Elena Baranoff / Matthew Batt / Celia Bennett / Shany van den Berg / Carey Clarke / Mark Clay / Jayne Cooper / José Luis Corella / Ian Cumberland / Clara Drummond / Ben Edge / Miriam Escofet / Lee Fether / Maryam Foroozanfar / Ismael Fuentes / Michael Gaskell / Marianne L.Gibson / June Glasson / Daniel González Coves / Hector M. Hernandez / Eileen Hogan / Natalie Holland / Peter Holt / Mark Jameson / Ho-Jun Lee / Susan Light / Dan Llywelyn Hall / Graeme Lothian / Eleanor McCaughey / Donald Macdonald / Jennifer McRae / Hynek Martinec / James Metcalfe / Peter Monkman / David Nipo / Tim Okamura / Paul Oxborough / Isobel Peachey / Natan Pernick / Anastasia Pollard / Philip Renforth / Stephen Earl Rogers / Sue Rubira / Karl Rudziak / SACRIS / Louis Smith / Jung-Im Song / Benjamin Sullivan / Edward Sutcliffe / Mieke Teirlinck / Daphne Todd / Erin Wozniak / William Wright

SECOND PRIZE
TOM
MICHAEL GASKELL

Egg tempera on board
270 x 210mm

Having won Second Prize in 2003, Michael Gaskell was again awarded Second Prize with this portrait of his son Tom, who was seventeen at the time of the first sitting. Gaskell sought to capture that fleeting period of suspension between boy and manhood during adolescence. While the work was primarily inspired by Botticelli's *Portrait of a Young Man* (c.1480–5), which is in the National Gallery's collection, the pose is reminiscent of a number of portraits by Holbein, whose work Gaskell also particularly admires.

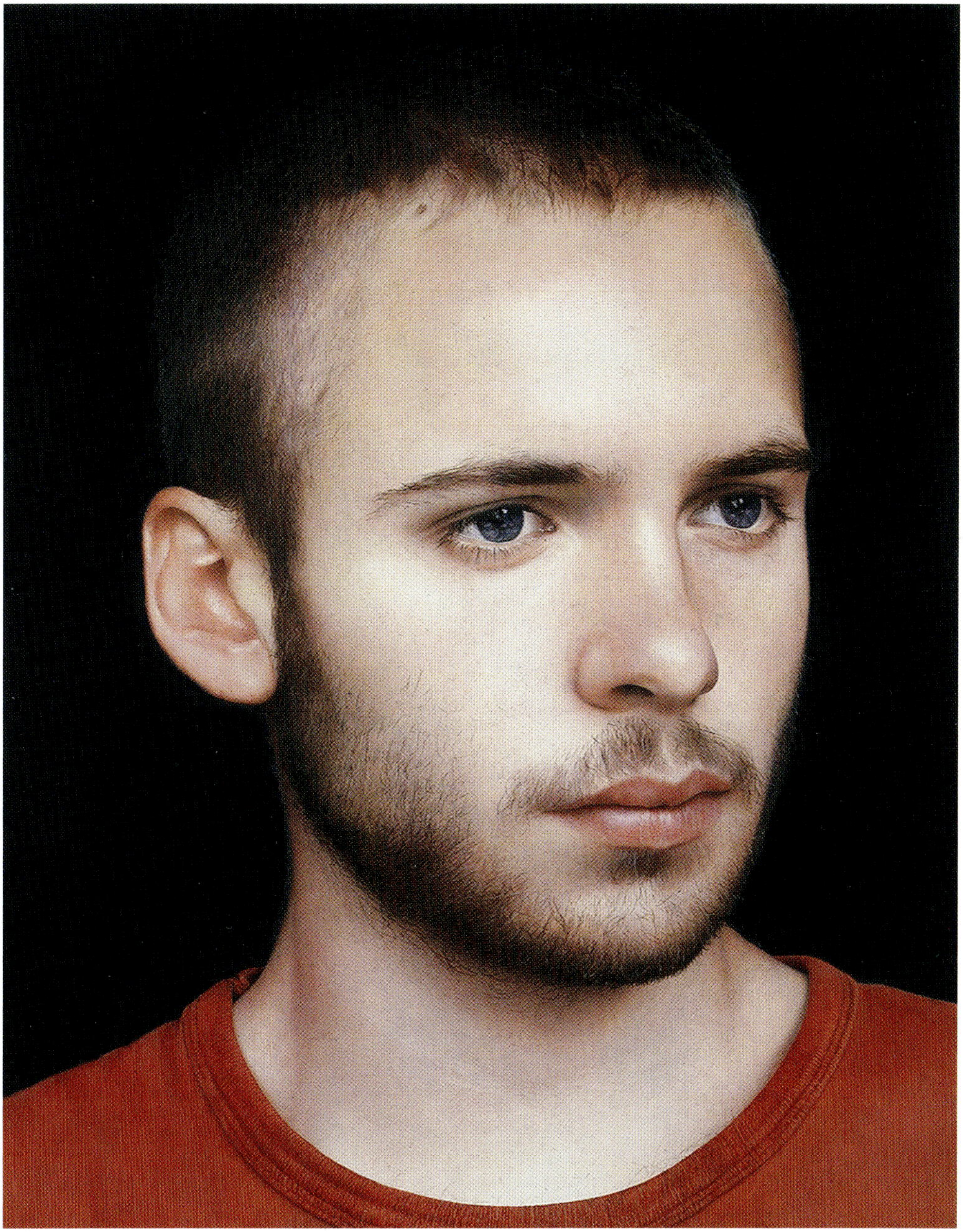

THIRD PRIZE
MANUEL
ANNALISA AVANCINI

Oil on canvas
1000 x 800mm

Italian-born Annalisa Avancini studied at the Arts High School of Trento and the Marangoni Institute of Milan. This painting was Avancini's third portrait of Manuel, who was aged thirty-one at the time that it was started in the summer of 2008. The artist was attracted by Manuel's eclectic personality and by the rich experience that seemed to shine through his face despite his relatively young age. Avancini's work has been exhibited throughout Europe and the United States, and she had previously won first prize in both the Contemporary Art Show at the Museum of the Americas, Miami (2006) and the Painting Prize for Young Artists at the Verona Fine Art Society (2007). She currently lives and works in Trento, Italy.

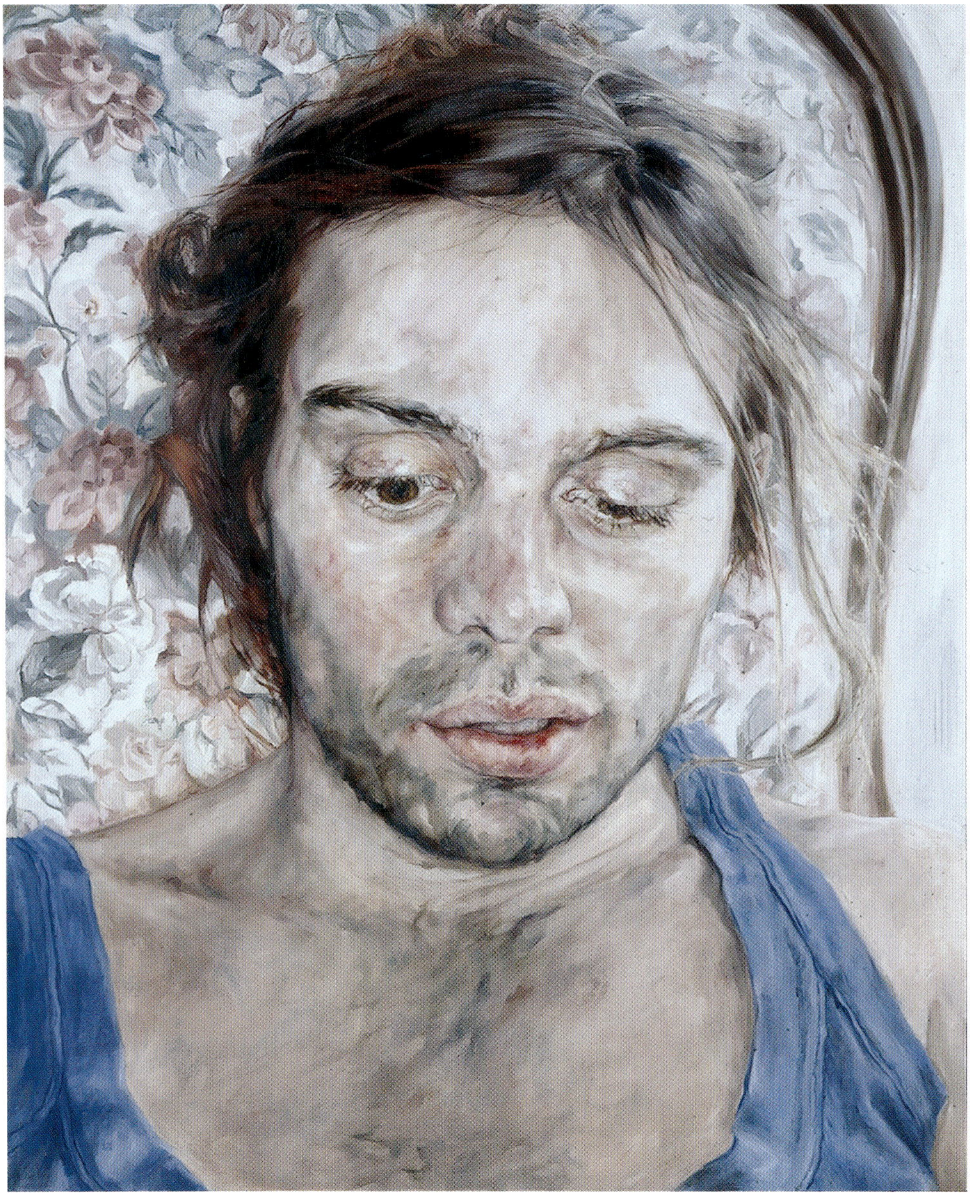

YOUNG ARTIST AWARD
BENFICA BLUE
MARK JAMESON

Oil and acrylic on linen
1220 x 762mm

Mark Jameson painted this portrait of his sister Lyndsey in less than a month. The sittings took place at their parents' house in County Durham. Jameson said that he had intended to capture aspects of his sitter's persona, conveyed in a modern and relevant way. Having graduated from the City of Sunderland University in 2003, Jameson has undertaken several commissions through local art dealers and appeared in various exhibitions, including the BP Portrait Award 2010.

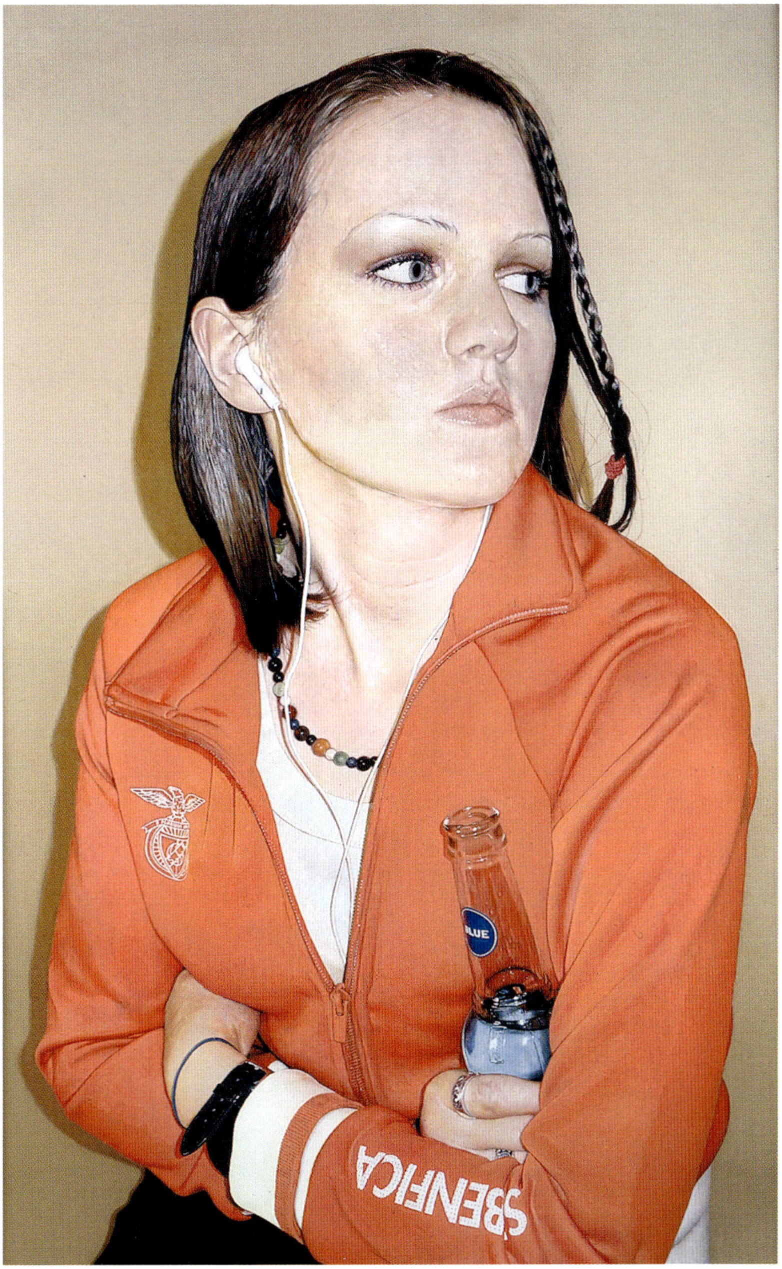

White Linen
Jennifer Anderson
Oil on canvas
900 x 700mm

Georgie
Mary Jane Ansell
Oil on wooden panel
344 x 216mm

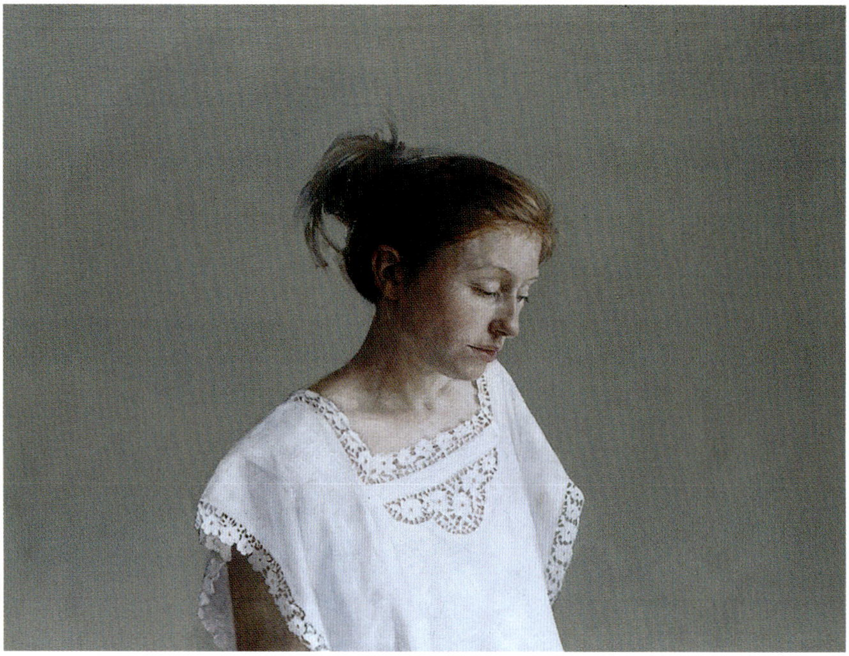

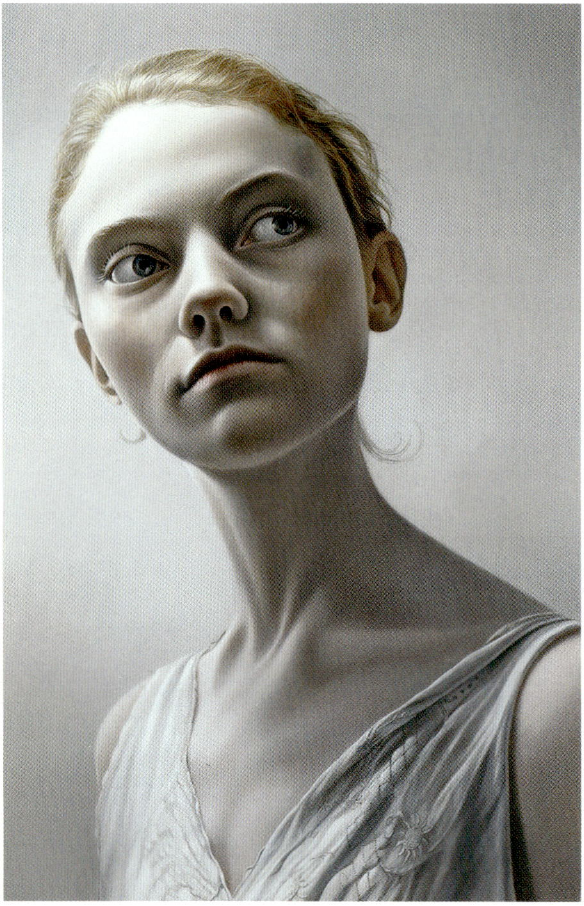

Debs
Matthew Batt
Acrylic on canvas board
457 x 356mm

Dik is ek Gladys
(It is me Gladys)
Shany van den Berg
Oil on wooden board
700 x 900mm

Robert
Mark Clay
Oil on wooden board
400 x 280mm

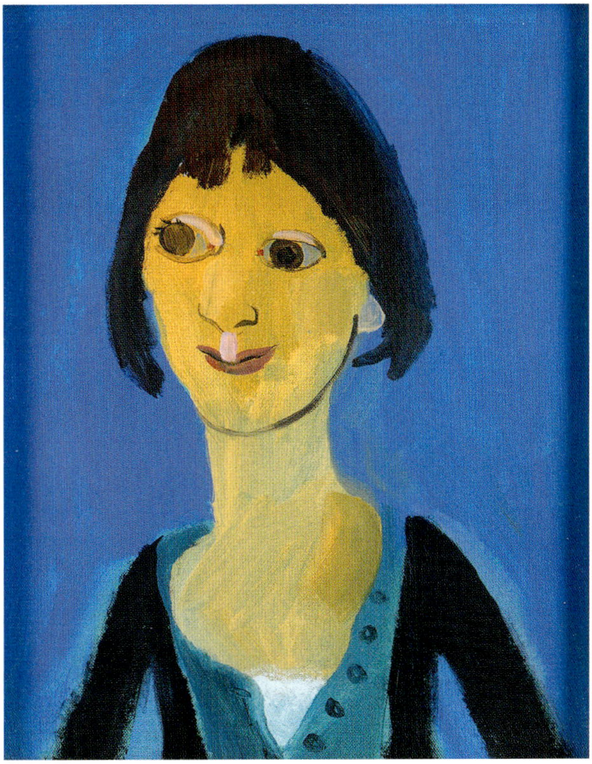

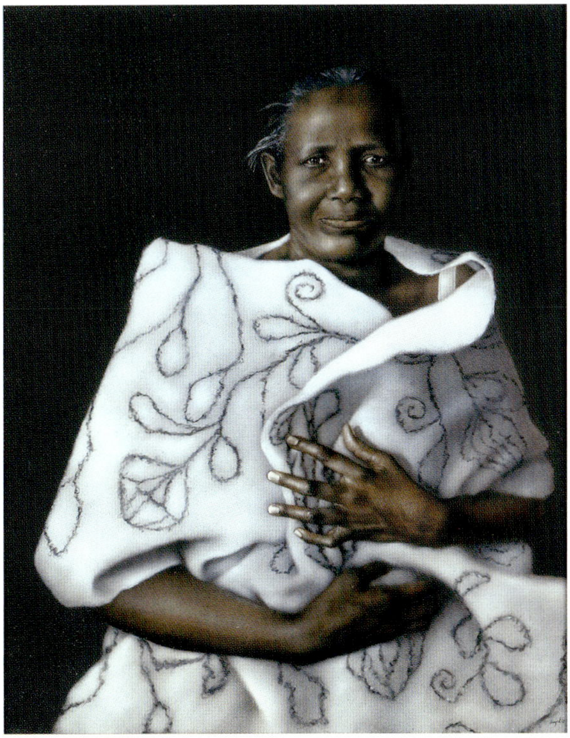

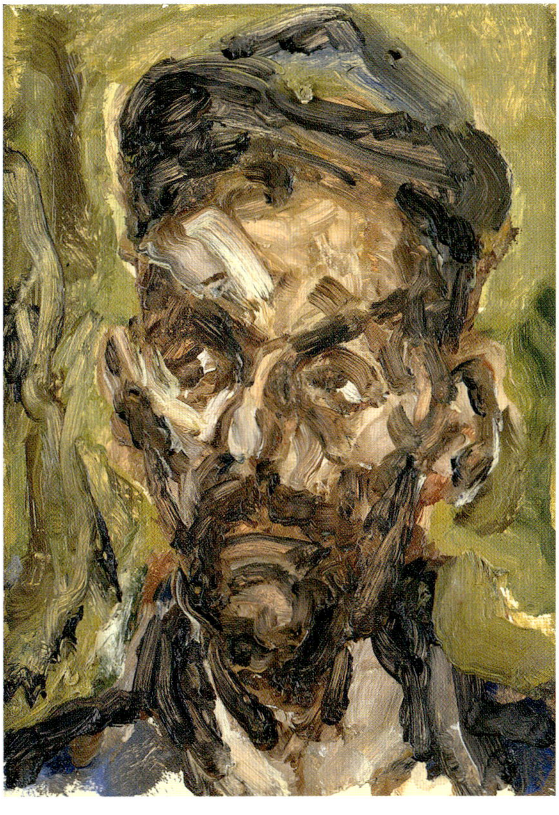

Imagine
José Luis Corella
Oil on wooden board
1000 x 1000mm

Guillem
Miriam Escofet
Oil on canvas on wooden board
500 x 400mm

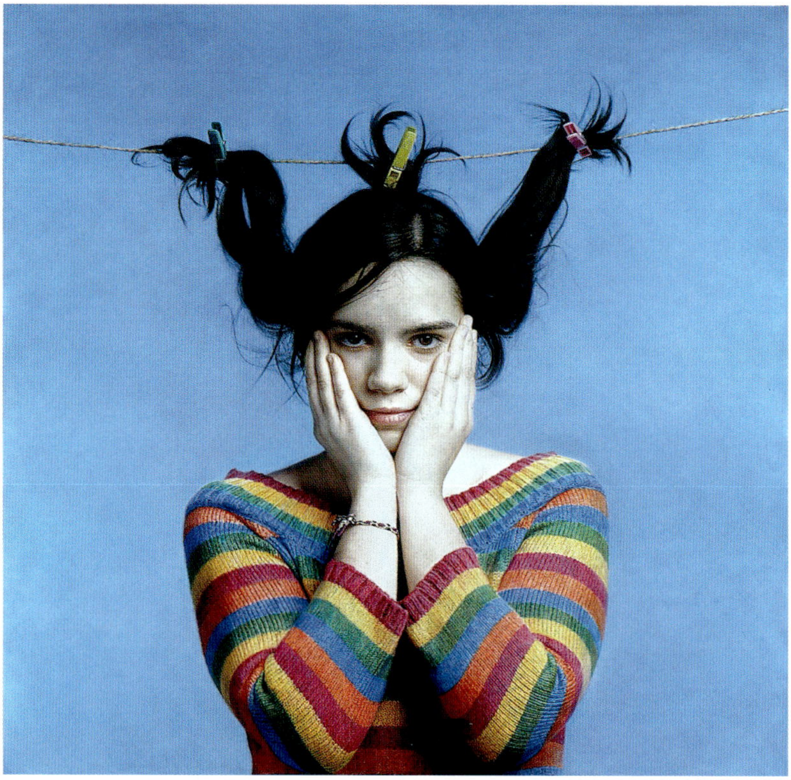

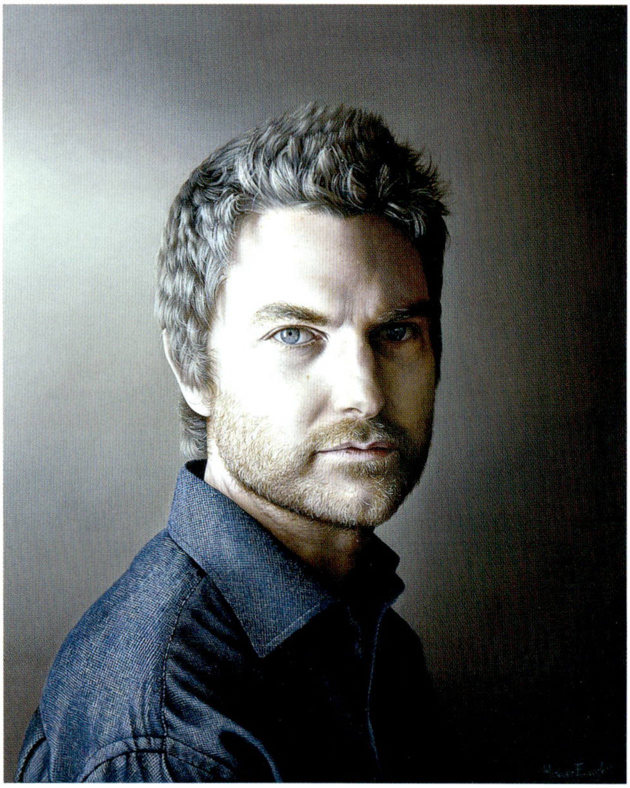

Gail Porter
Lee Fether
Oil on canvas
800 x 600mm

5am
Marianne L. Gibson
Oil on board
270 x 220mm

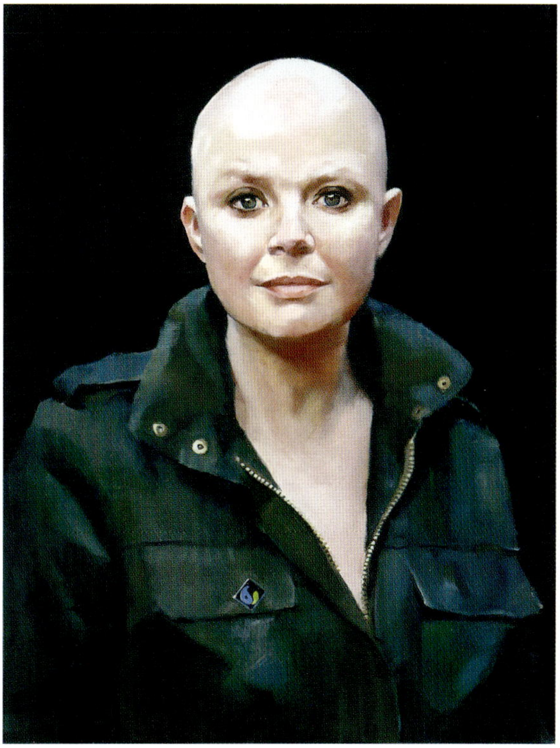

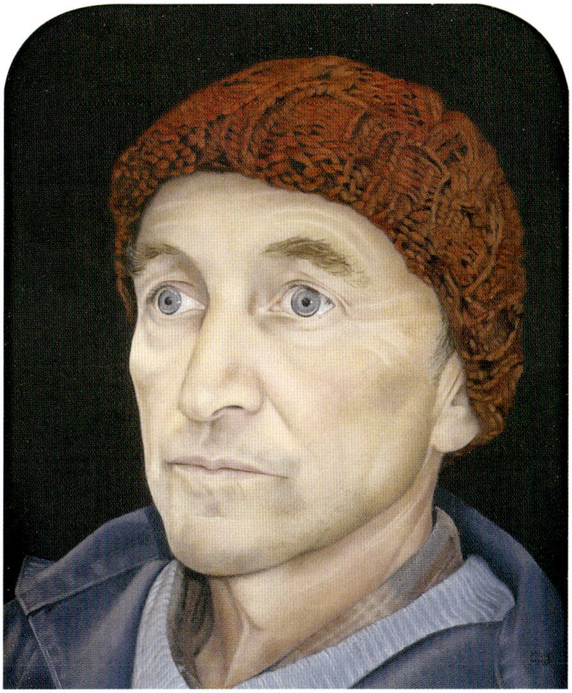

Brittani
June Glasson
Oil on wooden board
300 x 400mm

Agnes
Natalie Holland
Oil on canvas
600 x 450mm

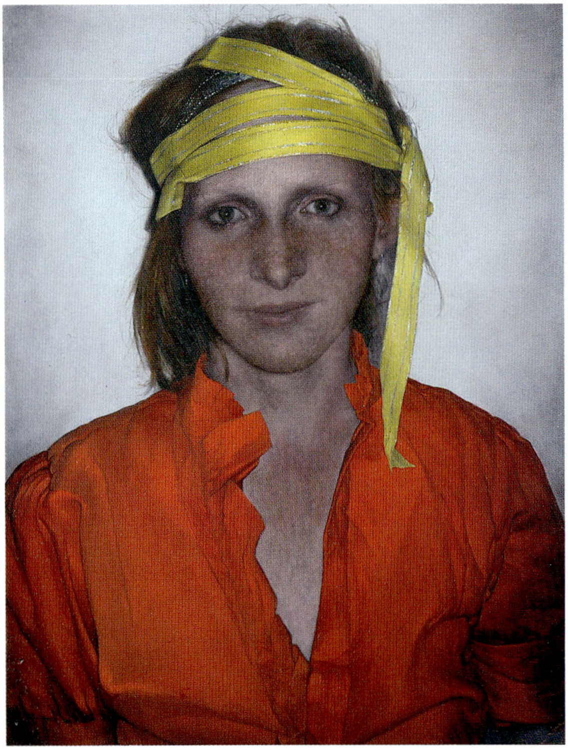

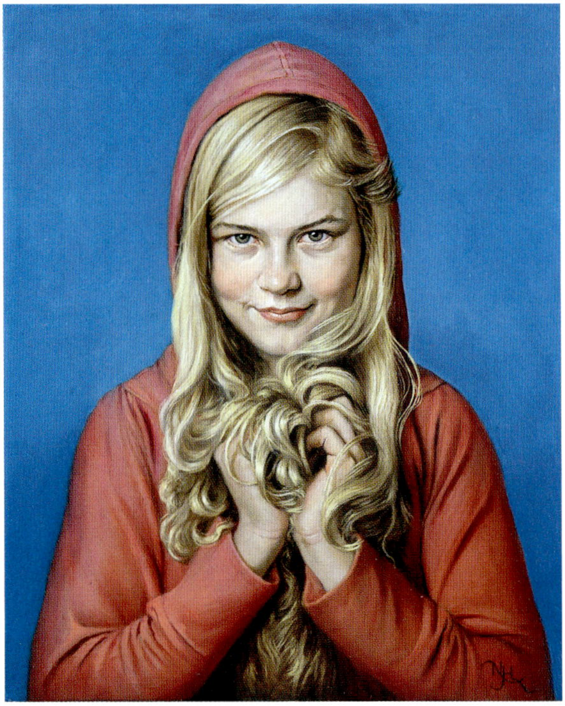

Tom
Peter Holt
Oil on canvas
460 x 360mm

Fatema
Susan Light
Oil on linen
1520 x 610mm

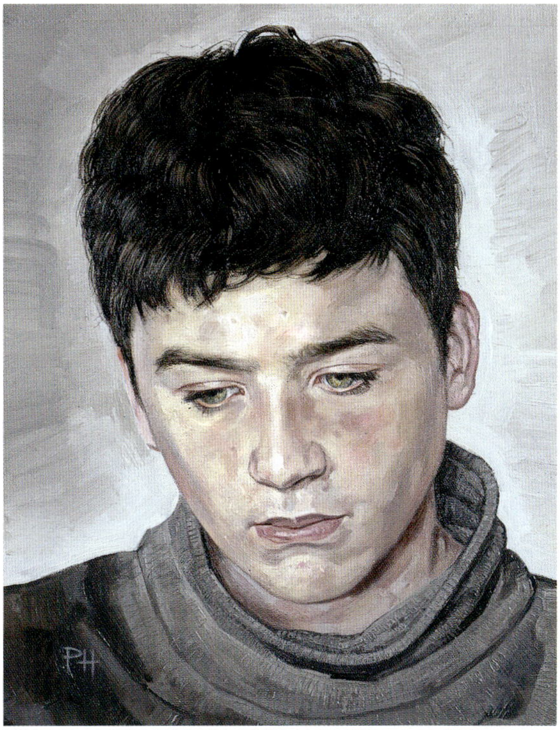

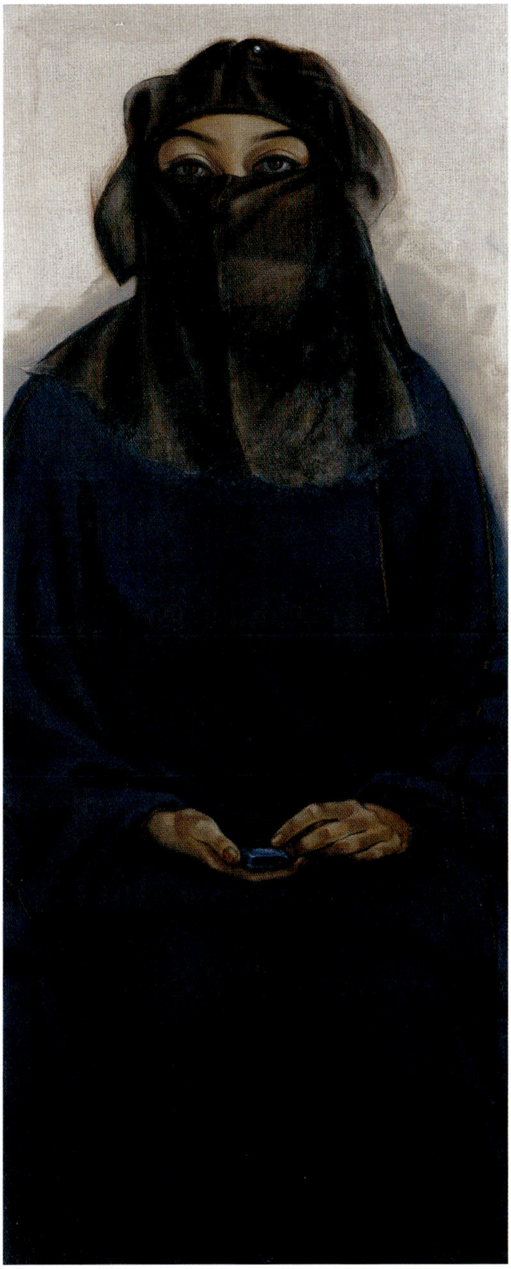

Eva
Natan Pernick
Oil on canvas
800 x 600mm

Maggie
Sue Rubira
Oil on canvas
1020 x 760mm

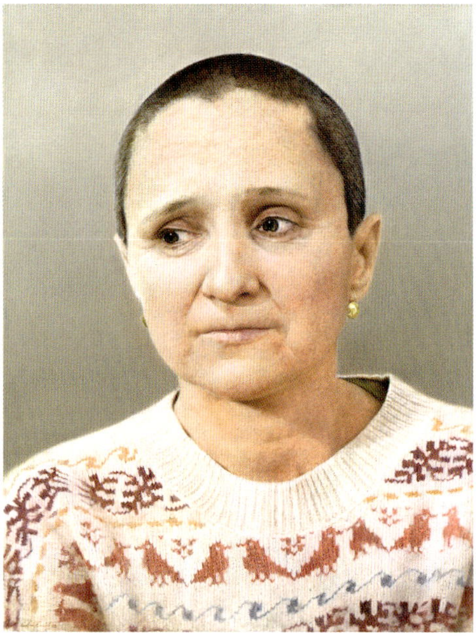

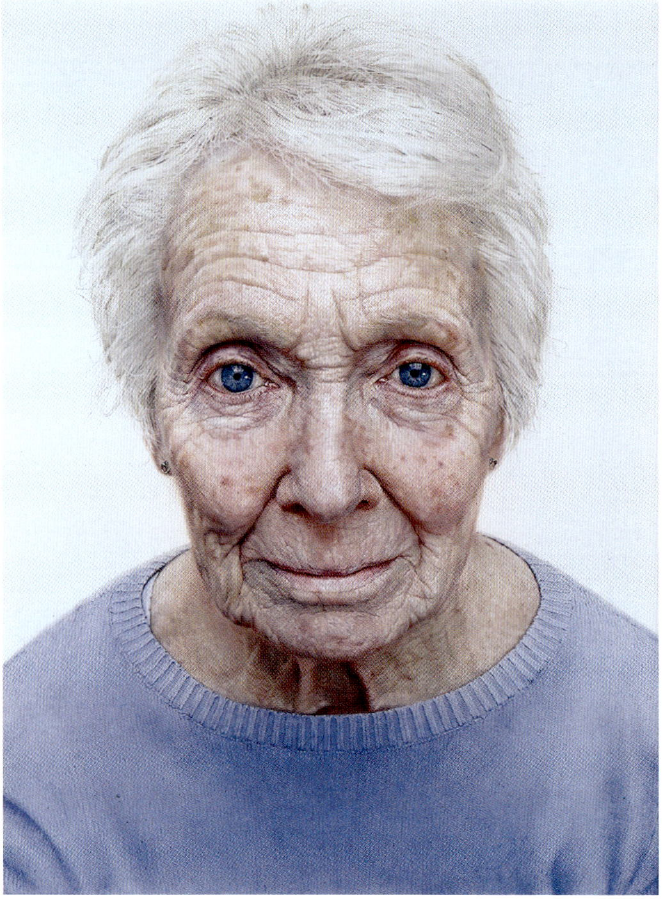

John Anthony, Portsmouth Football Club Westwood
Karl Rudziak
Oil on canvas
2000 x 1200mm

Grandmother
SACRIS
Oil on canvas
1980 x 1525mm

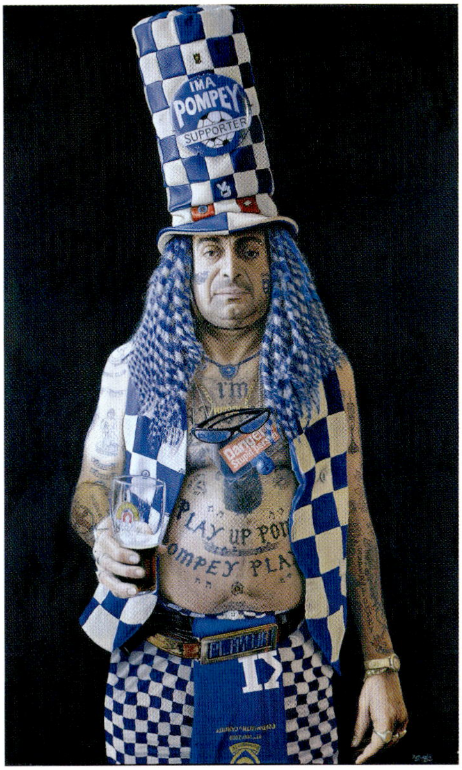

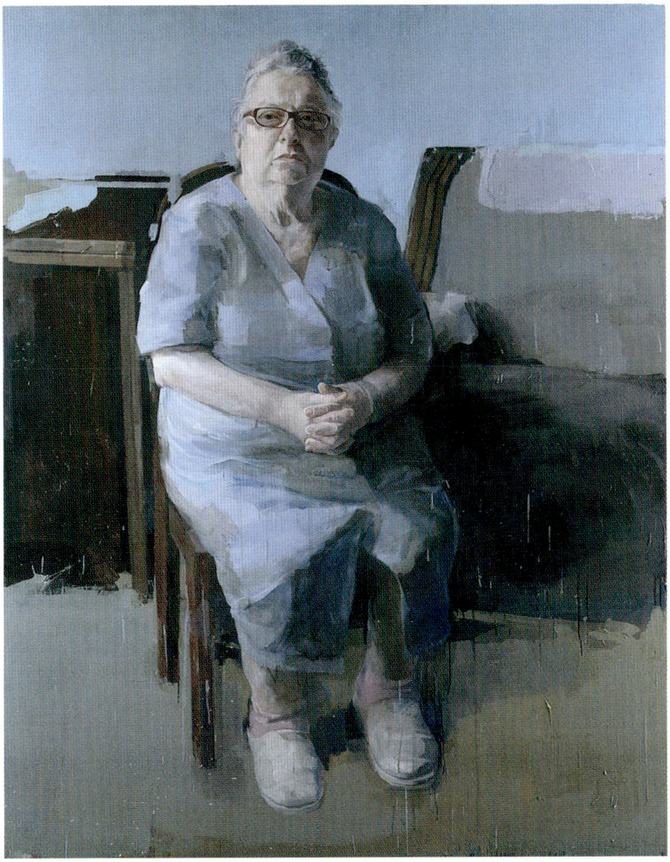

George
Louis Smith
Oil on canvas
700 x 550mm

My Song
Jung-Im Song
Oil on canvas
610 x 455mm

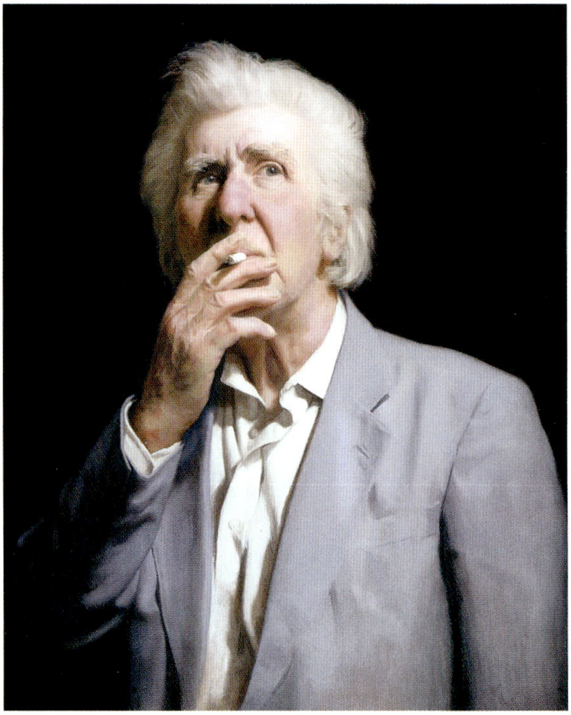

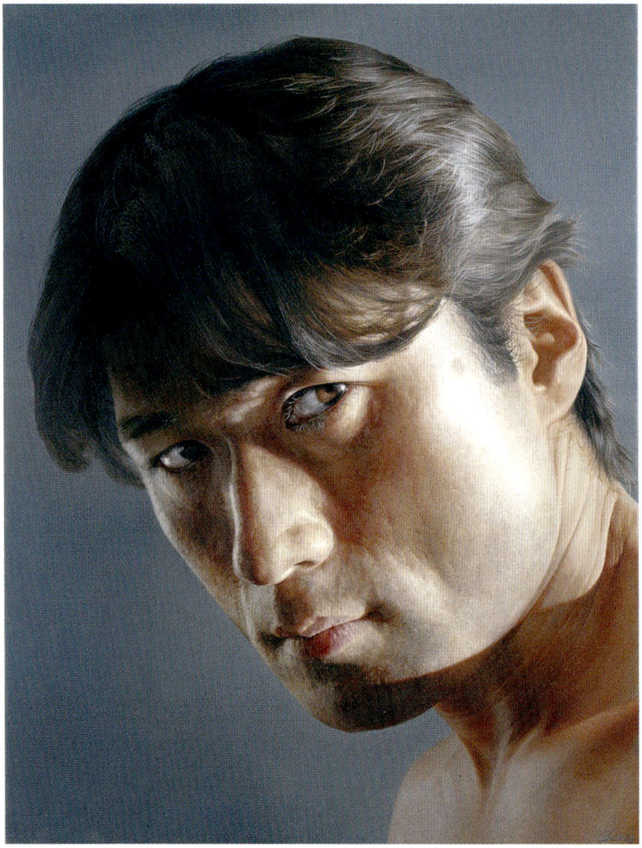

Francis
Mieke Teirlinck
Oil on canvas
400 x 400mm

Mother
William Wright
Oil on board
305 x 254mm

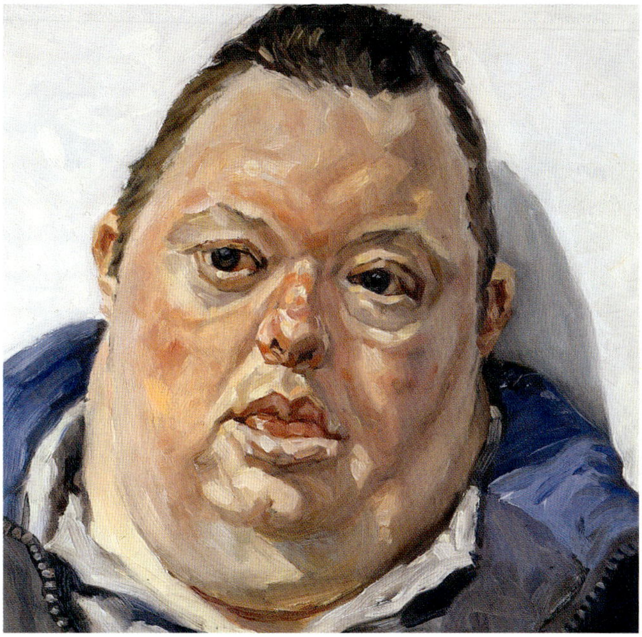

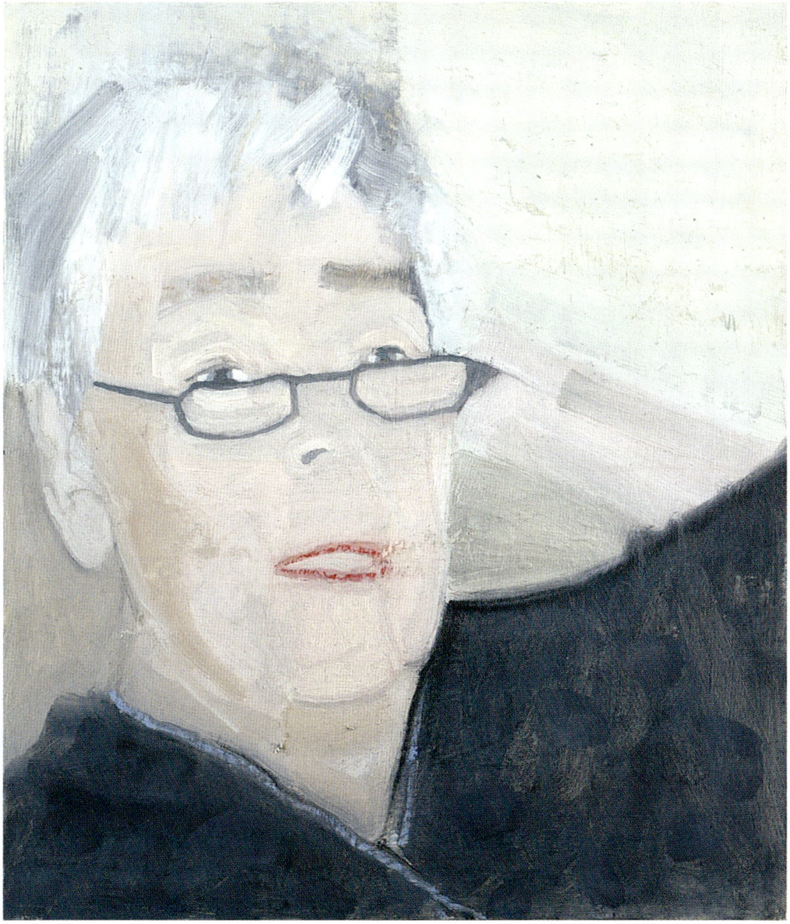

2010

ARTISTS WHOSE PORTRAITS WERE EXHIBITED

Mary Jane Ansell / Annalisa Avancini / Robin Bagnall / Paul Beel / Paul Benney / Shany van den Berg / Oscar Burnett / Jason Butler / Darren Coffield / Alan Coulson / Richard Cross / Tom Dewhurst / David Dipré / Anna Dougherty / Shaun Downey / David Eichenberg / Wendy Elia / Daniel Enkauoa / Miriam Escofet / Nathan Ford / Maryam Foroozanfar / Michael Gaskell / Eliot Haigh / Bruce Hanke / Alex Hanna / Jason Harper / Wim Heldens / Kaye Hodges / Lyndsey Jameson / Mark Jameson / Diarmuid Kelley / Rosy Lamb / Peter Layzell / Elizabeth McDonald / Raoul Martinez / Helen Masacz / George Melling / Miguel Angel Moya / Carlos Muro / David Nightingale / Tony Noble / Benjamin Ogbebor / Tim Okamura / Michal Ožibko / Thea Penna / Nicky Philipps / Philip Renforth / Rafael Rodríguez / Ilaria Rosselli del Turco / Giampaolo Russo / Fred Schley / Nathalie Beauvillain Scott / Brian Shields / Benjamin Sullivan / Edward Sutcliffe / Daphne Todd / Henry Ward / Antony Williams

SECOND PRIZE
HARRY
MICHAEL GASKELL

Egg tempera on wooden board
290 x 205mm

Having previously exhibited in the BP Portrait Award on five separate occasions, Michael Gaskell was awarded Second Prize for a third time with this portrait of Harry, whom he had first seen while out shopping with his family. Gaskell was persuaded by his wife to approach Harry and the resulting portrait was completed in a short burst of intense work over the winter of 2009 to 2010. In the painting, Gaskell tried to evoke a sense of what had drawn him to his sitter, but the image was also informed by what he learned about the sitter's experiences and aspirations as he got to know him during the sittings.

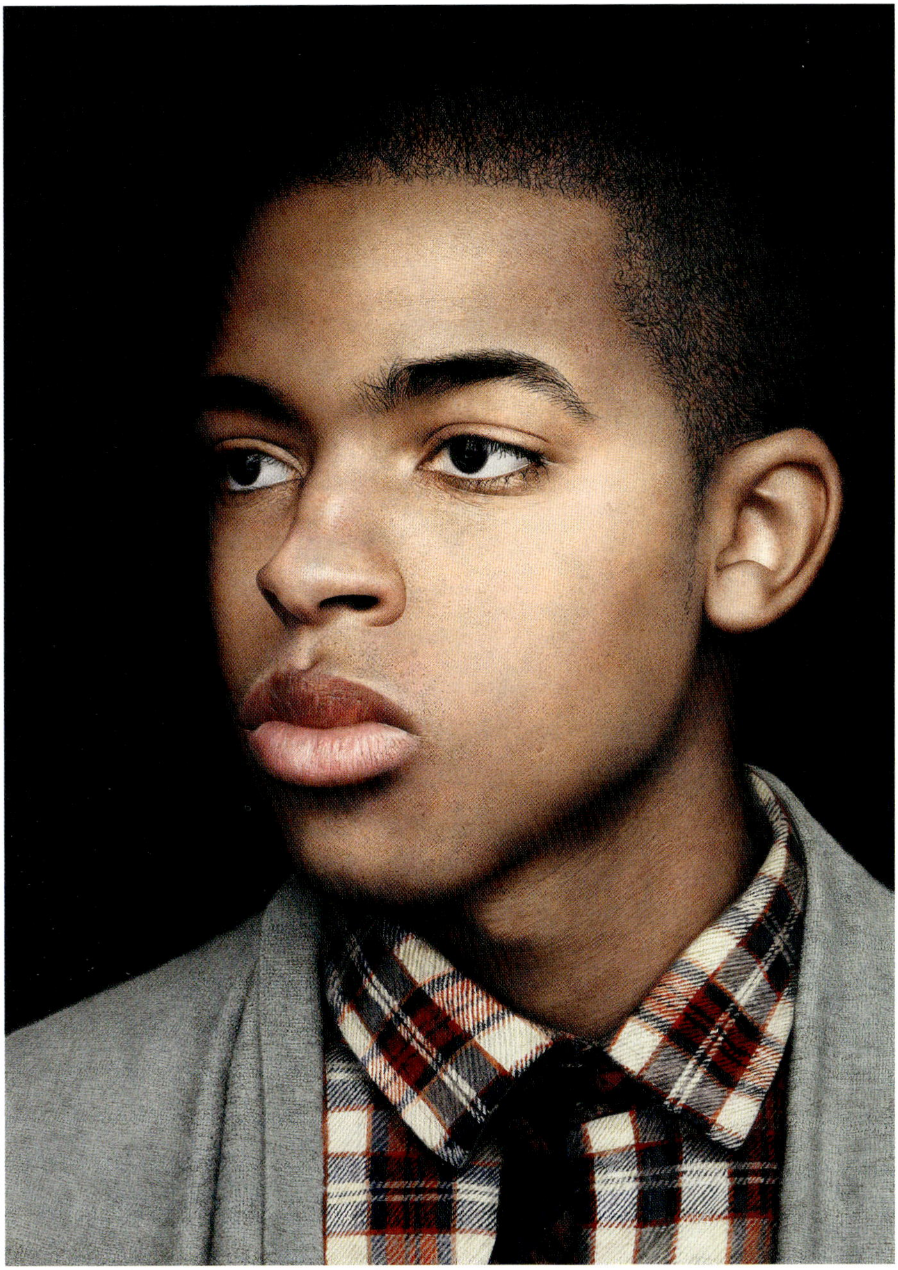

THIRD PRIZE
TIM II
DAVID EICHENBERG

Oil on panel
337 x 324mm

David Eichenberg studied painting and sculpture at the University of Toledo in Ohio. After graduating in 1998 his primary focus was sculpture, but in 2002 he began concentrating on painting. He has exhibited throughout the United States in both solo and group exhibitions. This portrait depicts Eichenberg's friend, the sculptor Timothy A. Stover. Eichenberg wanted the painting to read like a work by Holbein, where every item in the portrait is symbolic of a particular aspect of the sitter's life, such as the highlighted shape on the wall, representing a map of Ohio, where Stover was born and was living at the time of the sitting.

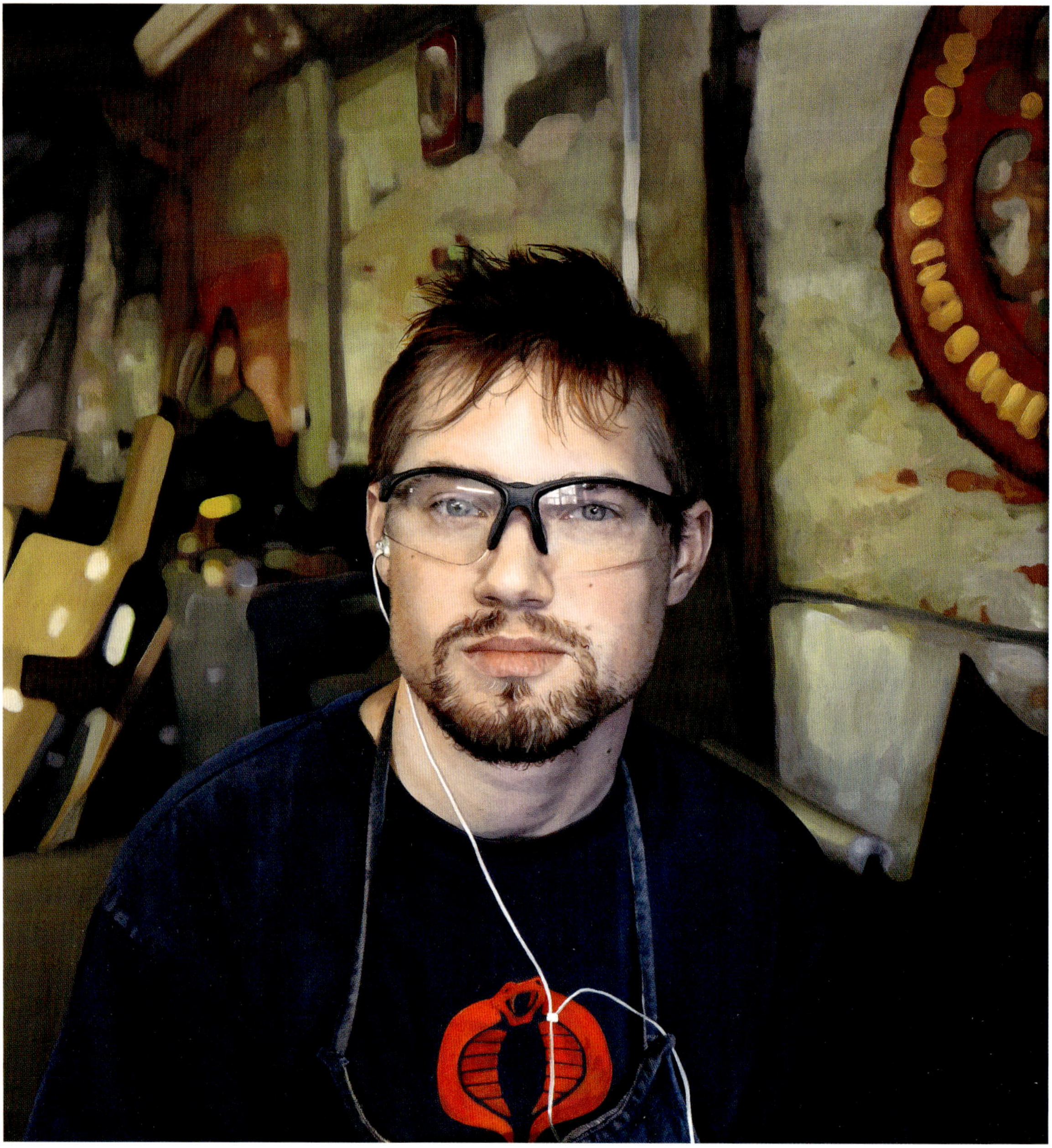

YOUNG ARTIST AWARD
DON'T BE TOO SERIOUS
ELIZABETH MCDONALD

Oil on canvas
635 x 432mm

Born in Texas, Elizabeth McDonald studied at the Southern Methodist University in Dallas and the University of North Texas. In the same year that she won the BP Young Artist Award, she was a finalist in the Hunting Art Prize, Texas, and shortlisted for the John Moores Contemporary Painting Prize. McDonald is currently working towards a Master of Arts in Fine Art at the Glasgow School of Art. This portrait depicts fellow artist Camillo Paravicini in his studio in Glasgow. Although the two artists worked in neighbouring studios, they hardly knew each other. While the clothing Paravicini wears in the portrait is similar to that which he would normally wear, his posture was staged to accentuate the tension between youth and maturity.

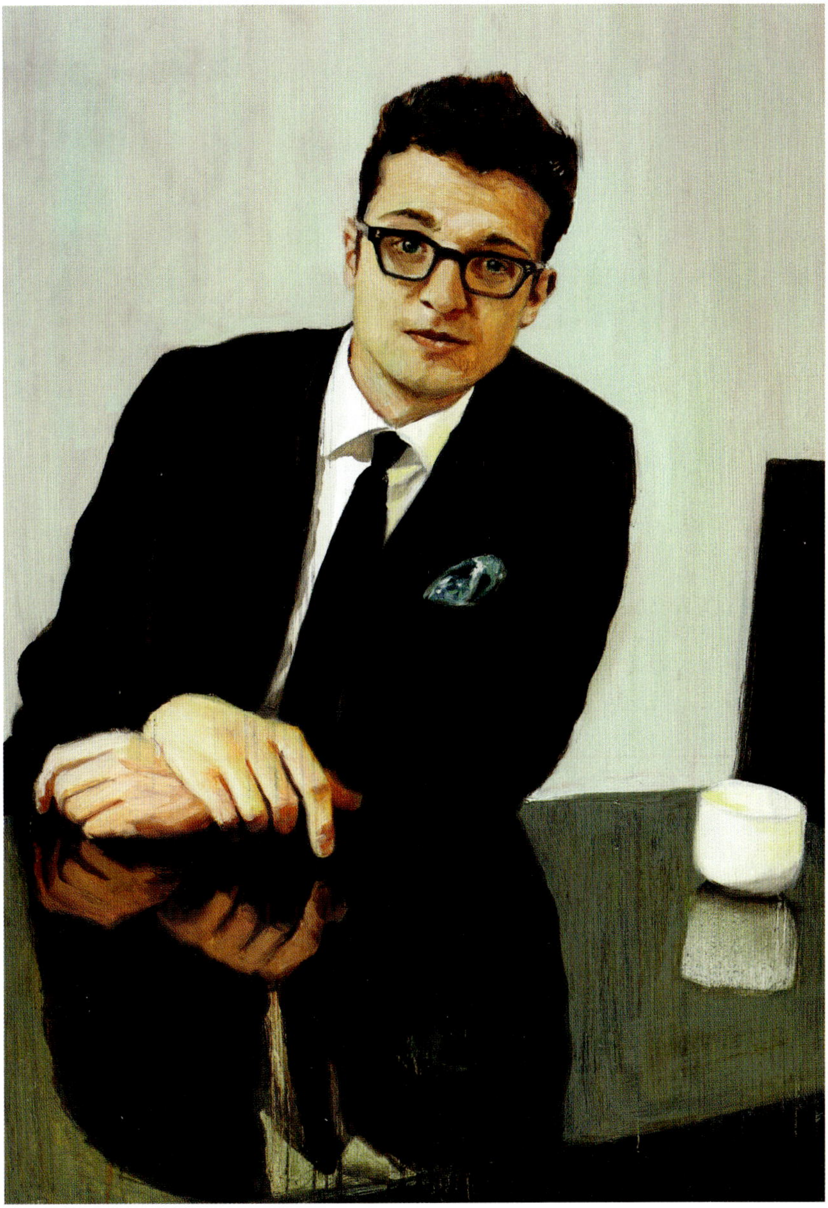

David
Annalisa Avancini
Oil on canvas
1200 x 1000mm

Self-portrait
Robin Bagnall
Oil on hardboard
725 x 540mm

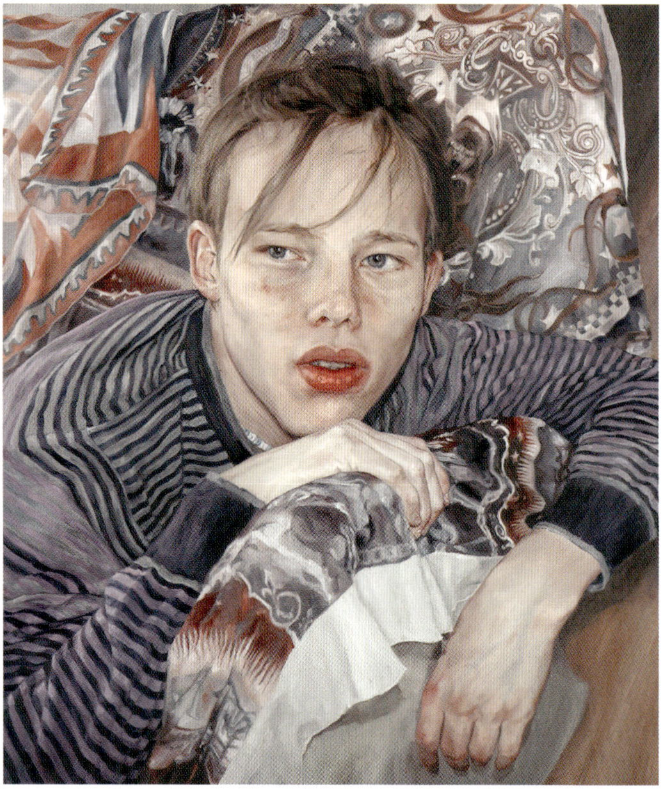

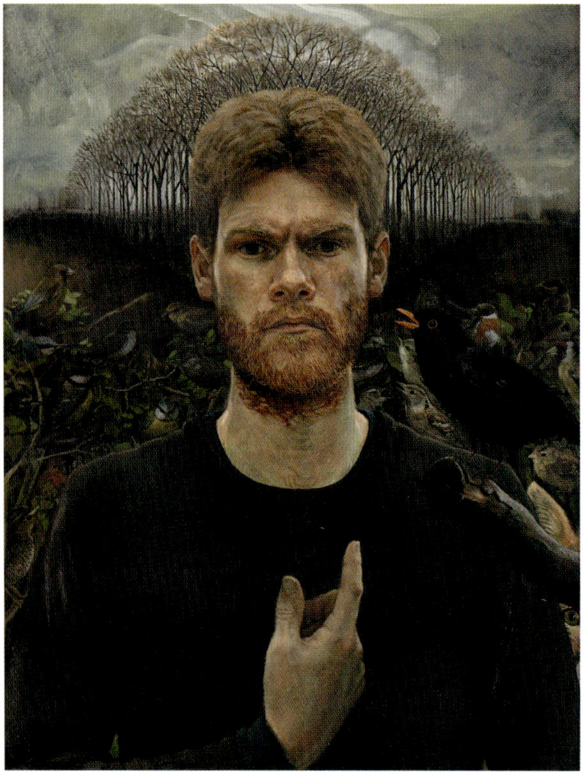

Free David
Paul Beel
Oil on linen
1500 x 1500mm

Paul Getty III
Paul Benney
Oil on canvas
1422 x 1270mm

Bloedlyn/Bloodline ...
Sannie en Leah
Shany van den Berg
Oil on wooden board
850 x 550mm

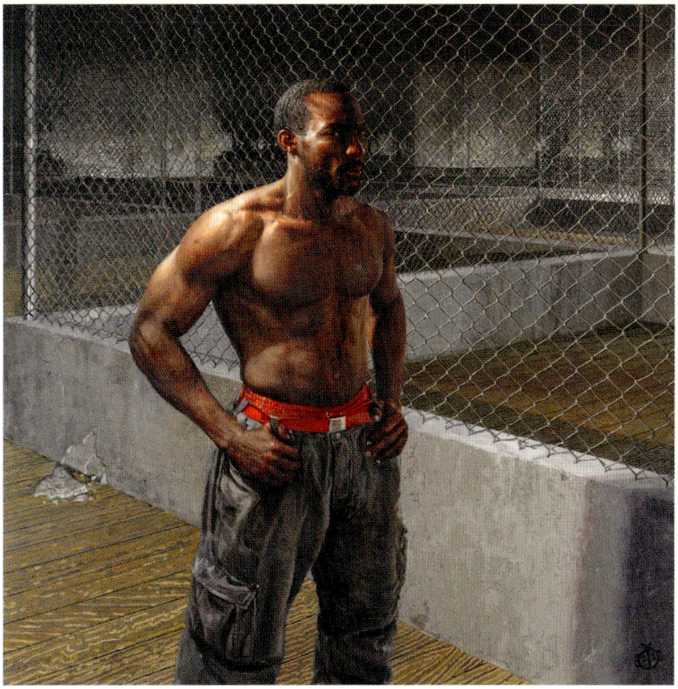

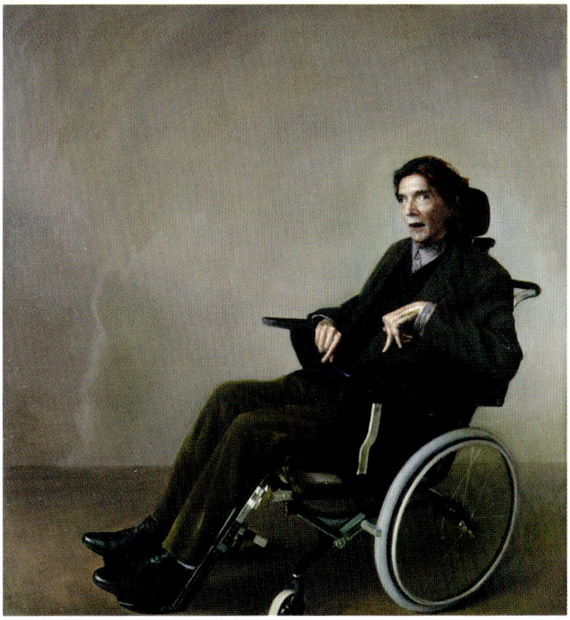

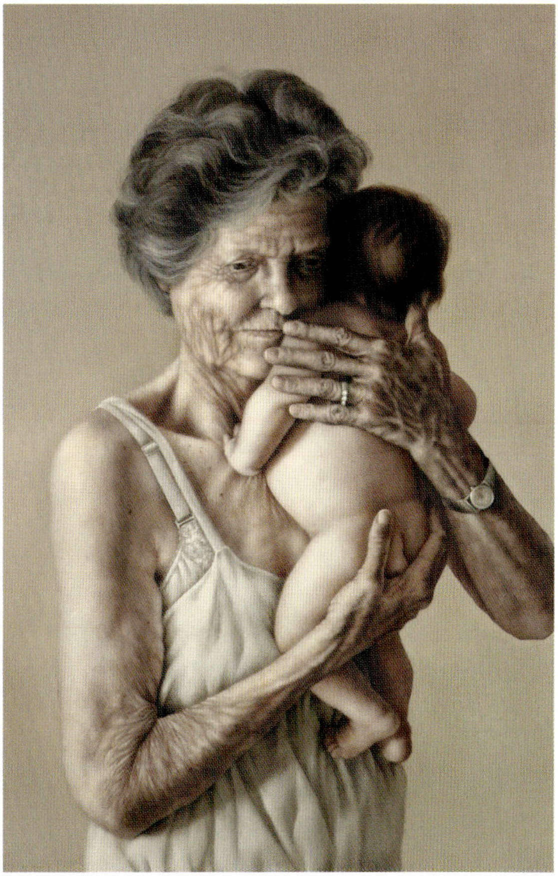

The Player?
Oscar Burnett
Oil on canvas
1270 x 610mm

Molly Parkin
Darren Coffield, a.k.a. Darcoff
Acrylic on canvas
1200 x 1030mm

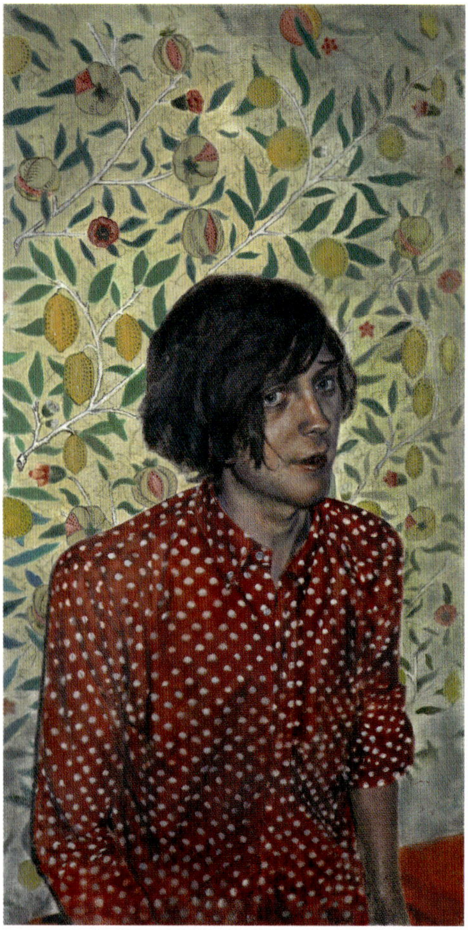

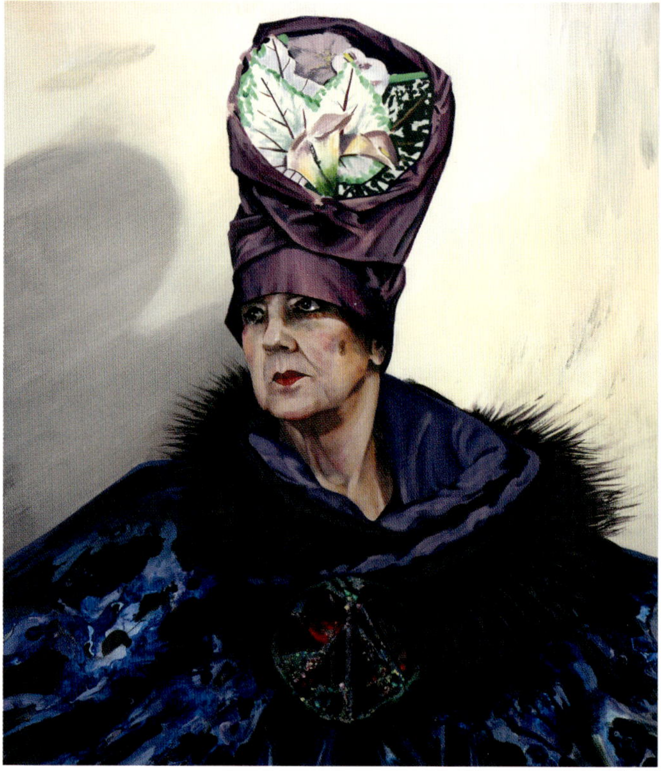

Ciara
Alan Coulson
Oil on panel
403 x 297mm

Then and Now
Richard Cross
Oil on hardboard
305 x 255mm

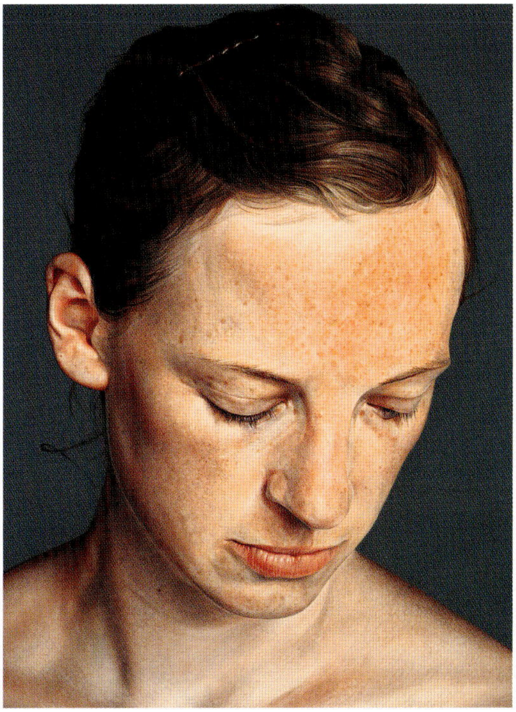

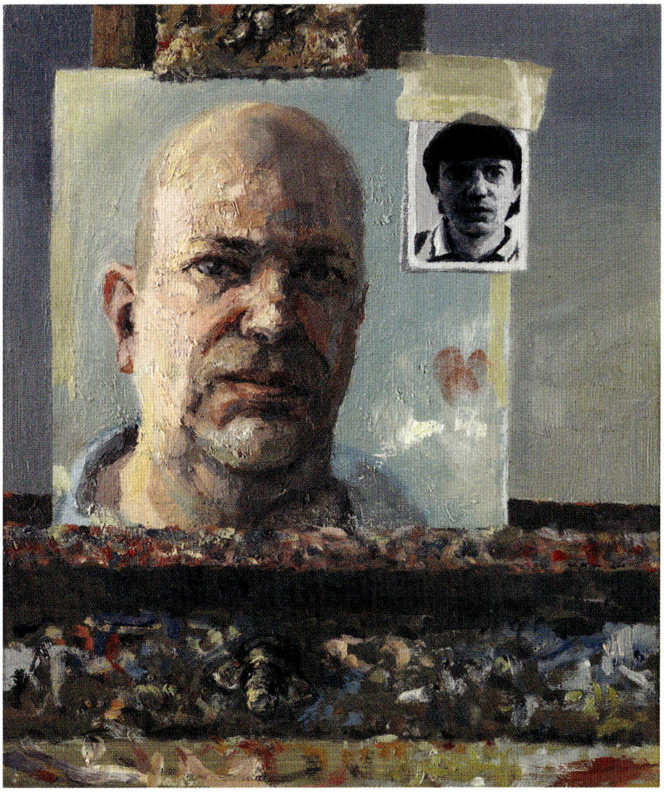

Laurie and the Shed
Tom Dewhurst
Oil on canvas
1020 x 760mm

Daytime Observations
David Dipré
Oil on board
250 x 200mm

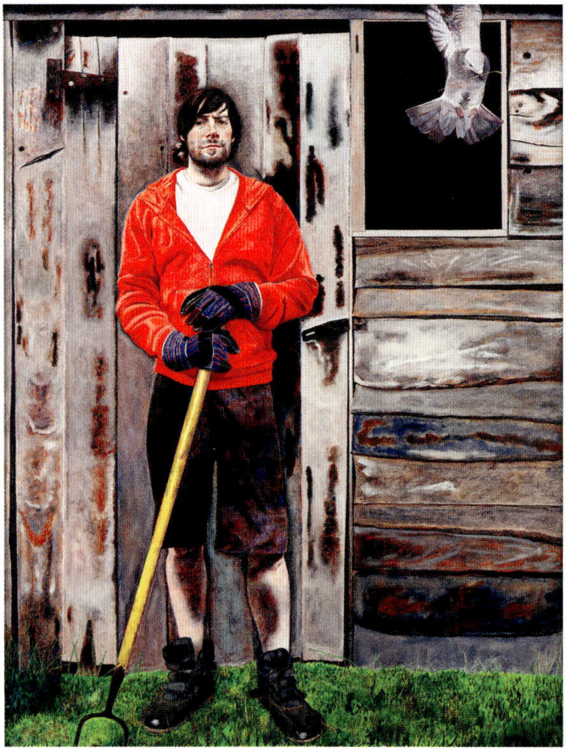

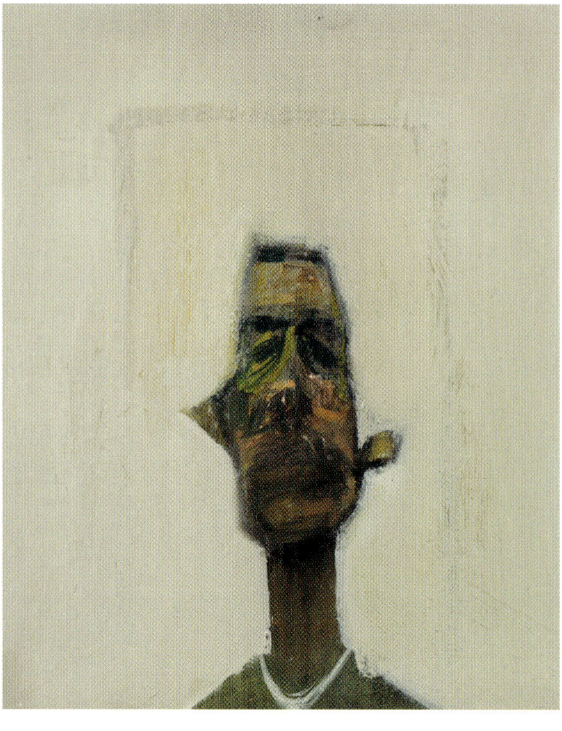

Self-portrait
(with Ribera's Club-footed Boy)
Anna Dougherty
Oil on board
250 x 200mm

Blue Coco
Shaun Downey
Oil on canvas
508 x 432mm

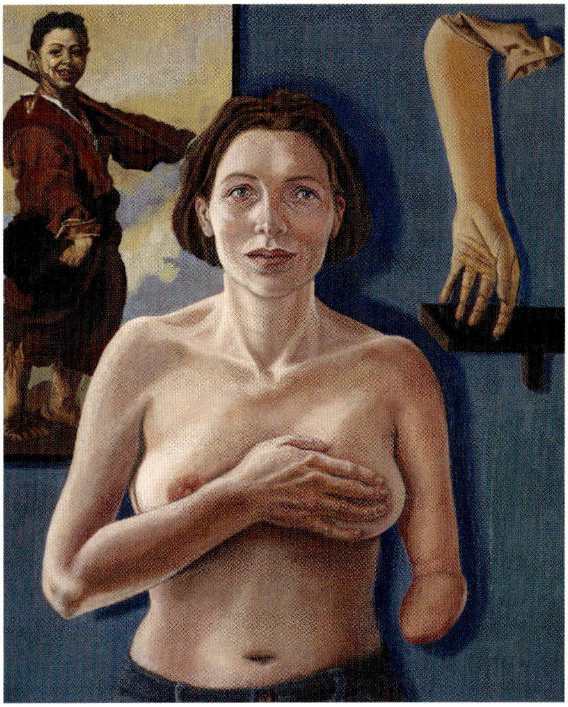

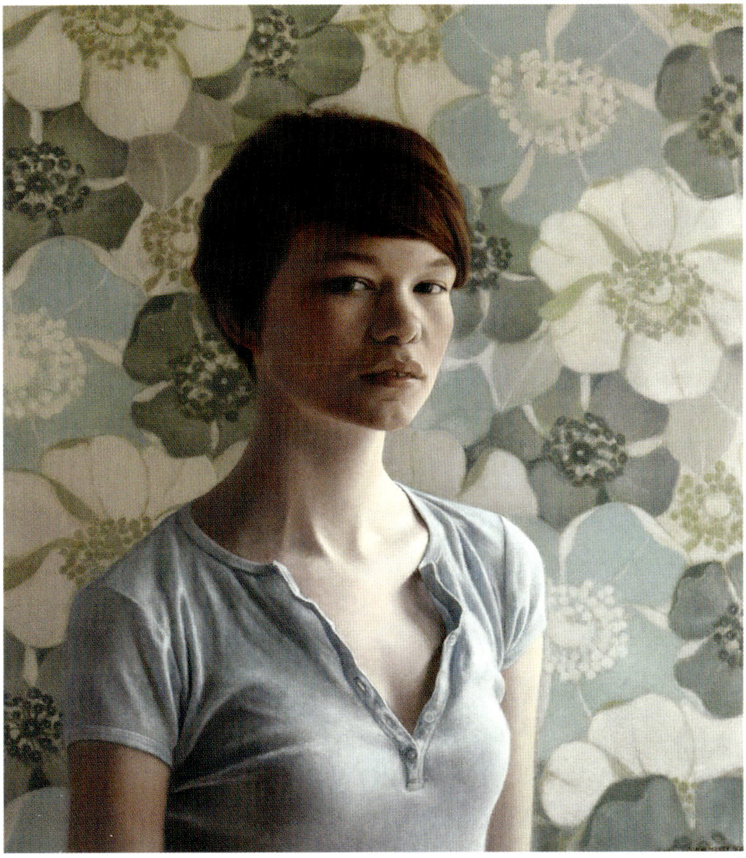

The Visit V (Mary)
Wendy Elia
Oil on canvas
1300 x 1700mm

Le Grand Natan
Daniel Enkaoua
Oil on canvas
2270 x 1825mm

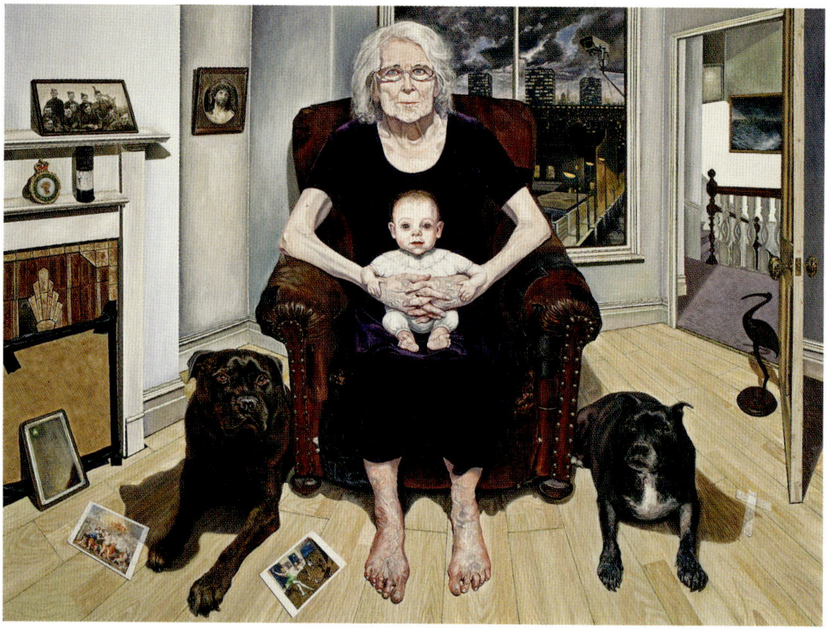

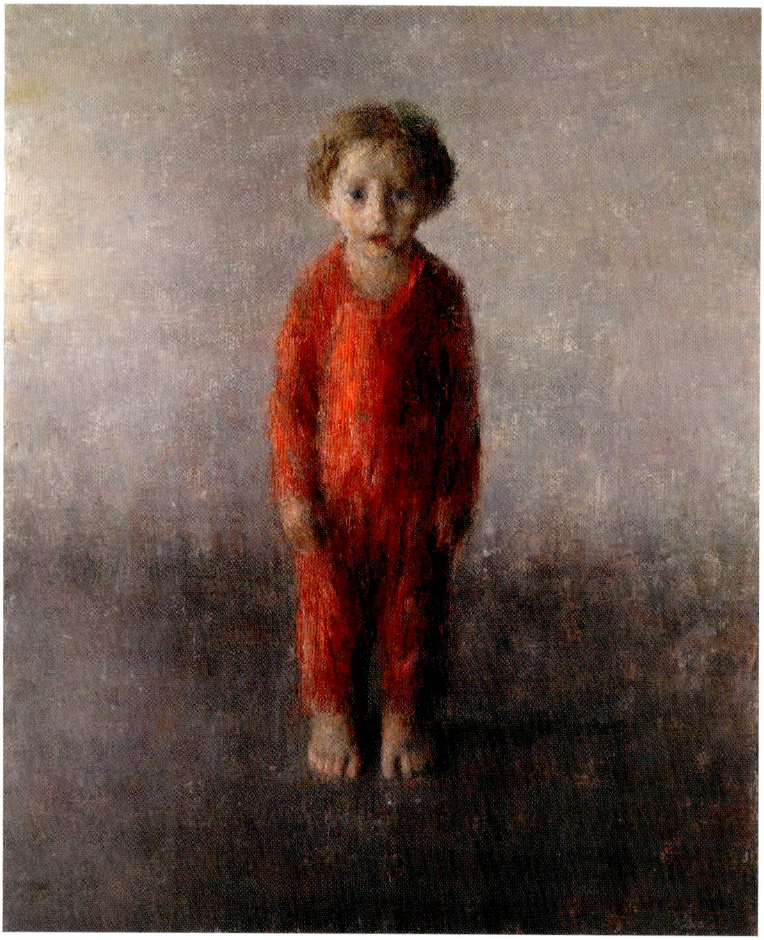

Paul
Nathan Ford
Oil on canvas
280 x 200mm

Quena
Eliot Haigh
Oil on canvas
600 x 500mm

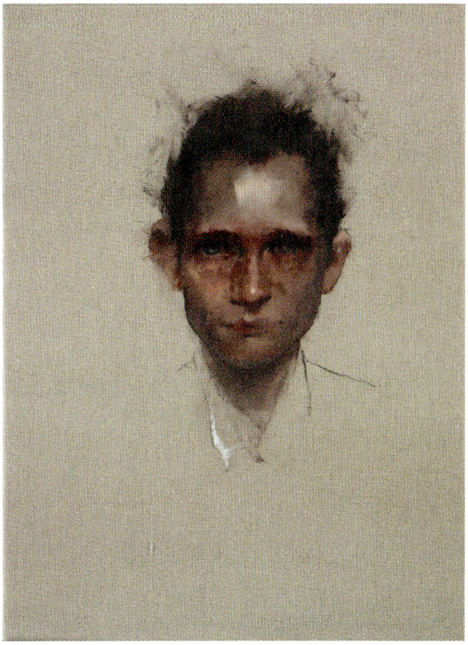

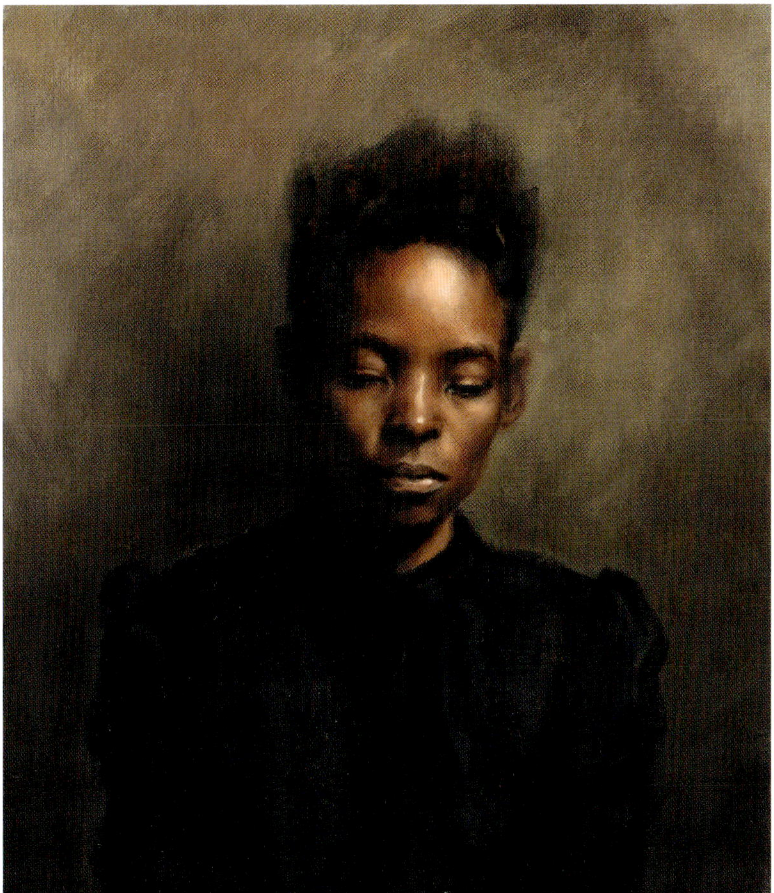

Like Father
Bruce Hanke
Oil on canvas
381 x 305mm

Sandy Watching
Alex Hanna
Oil on canvas
500 x 760mm

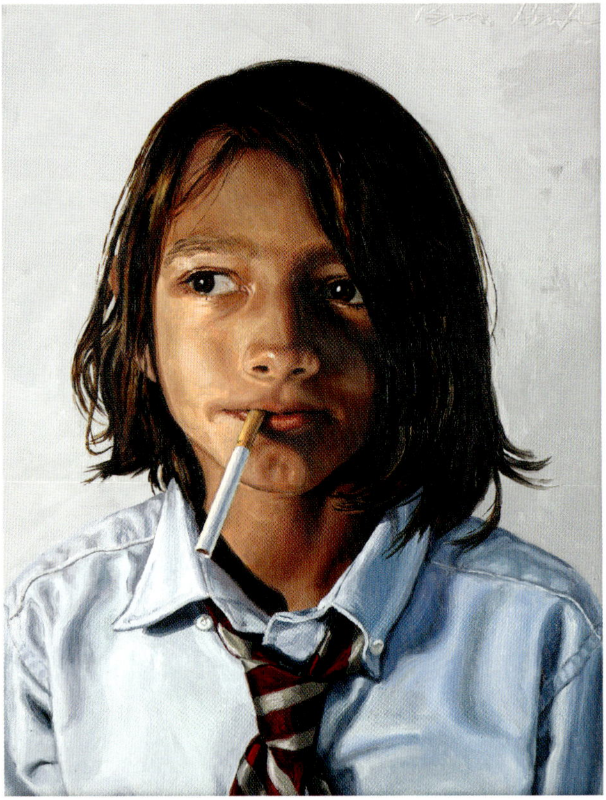

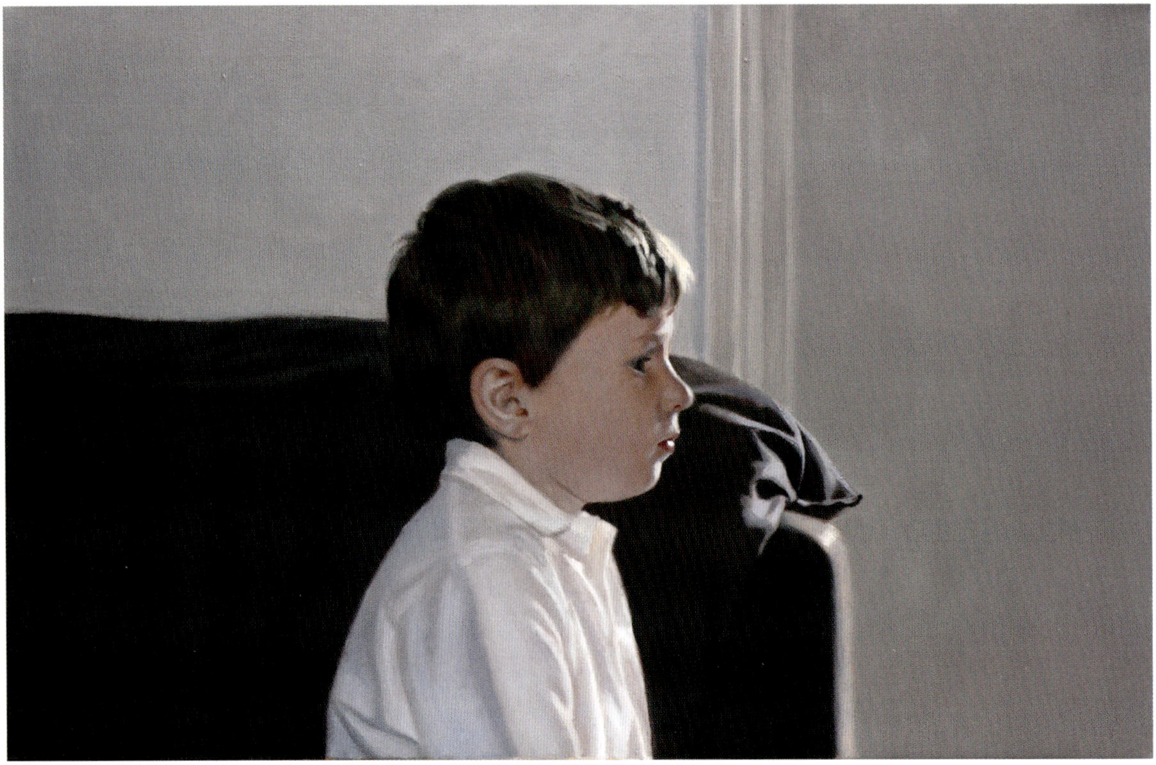

Stationed in Utah
Wim Heldens
Oil on canvas
305 x 406mm

Hoxton Youth
Jason Harper
Oil on canvas
250 x 250mm

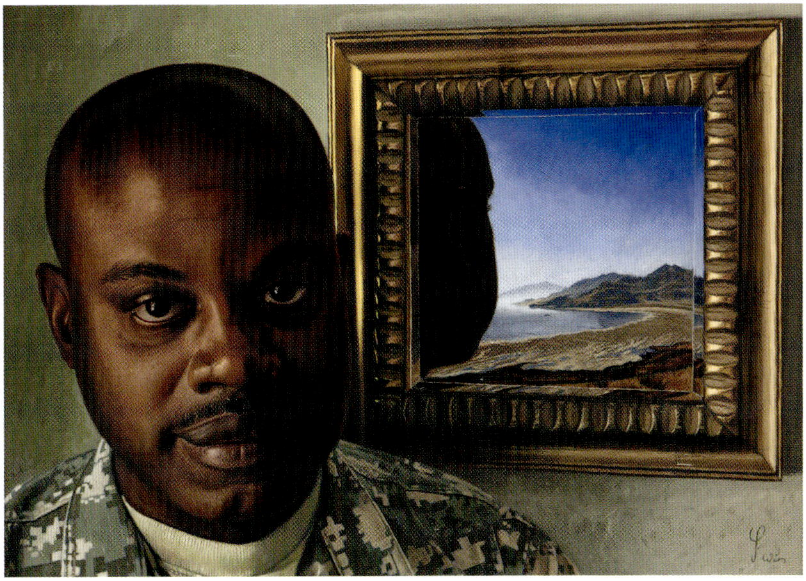

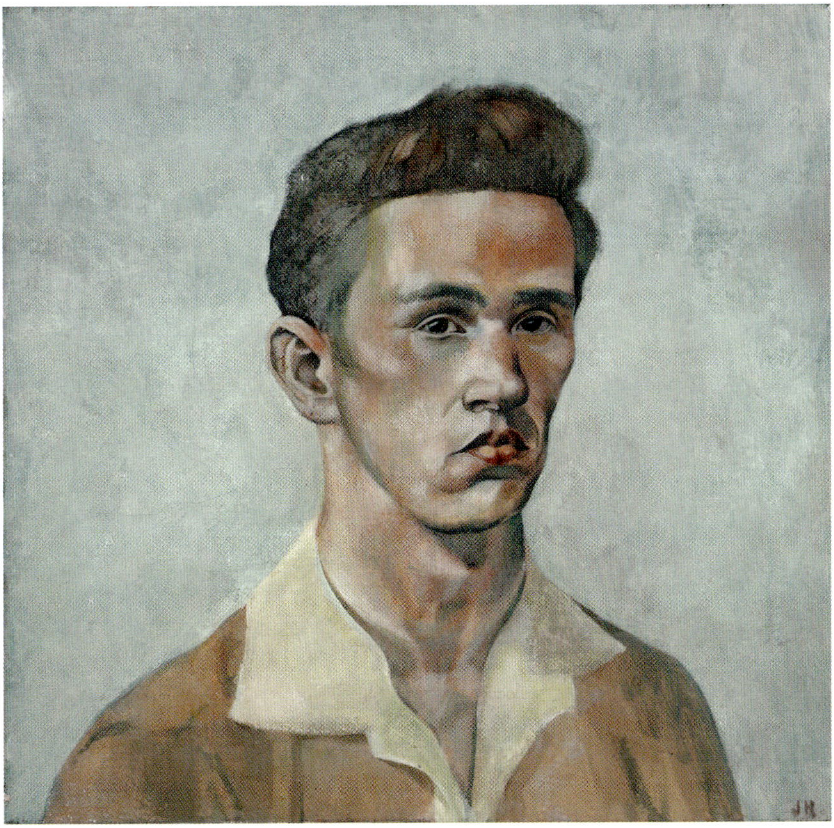

The Hockey Player, Marden Russets
Kaye Hodges
Acrylic on canvas
1360 x 500mm

Sentinel
Lyndsey Jameson
Oil on linen
1220 x 770mm

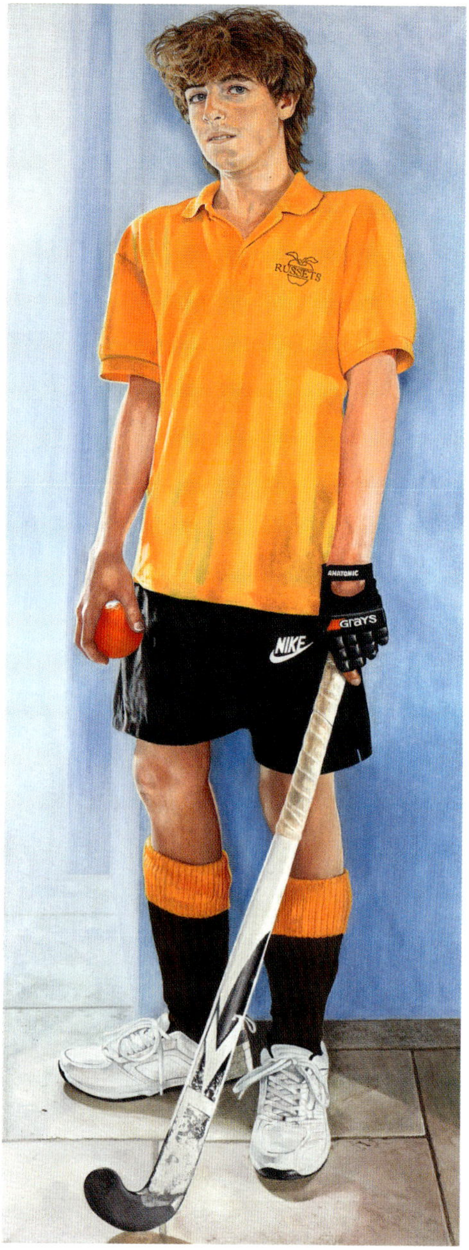

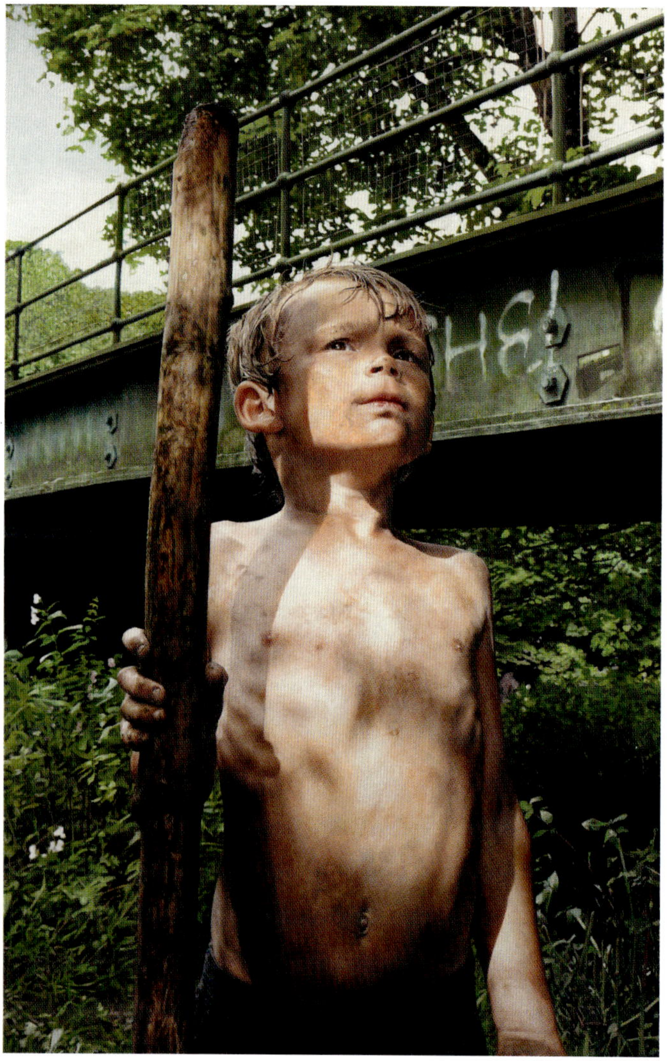

That Sinking Feeling
Mark Jameson
Oil on linen
1000 x 650mm

I Went to a Marvellous Party
Diarmuid Kelley
Oil on linen
1270 x 1016mm

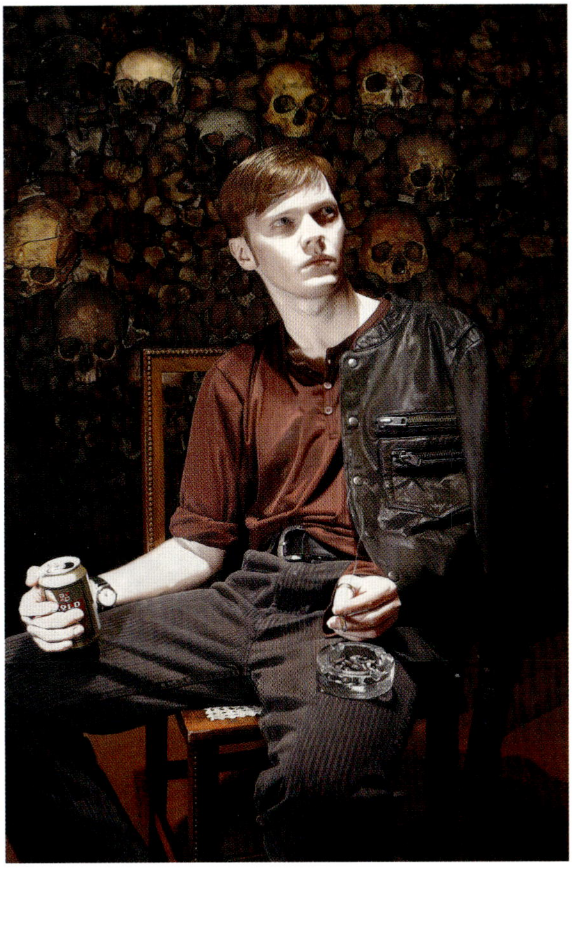

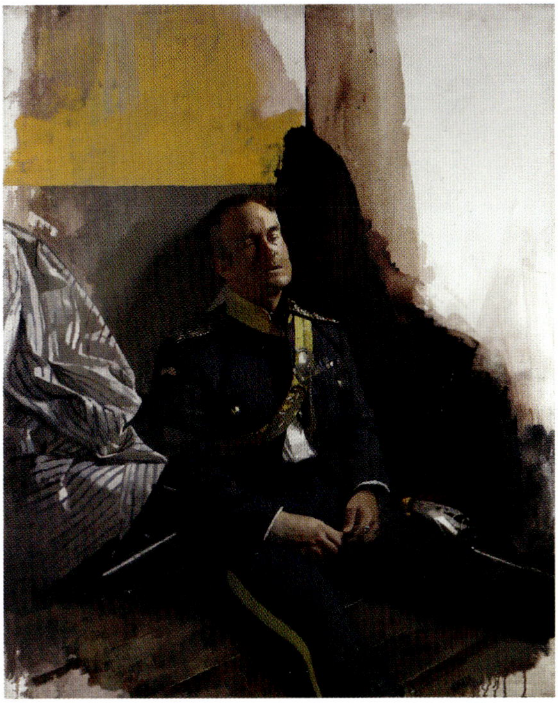

Put the Dog and the Cat in the Poster
Rosy Lamb
Oil on canvas
600 x 800mm

Fathers and Sons
Peter Layzell
Oil on panel
450 x 450mm

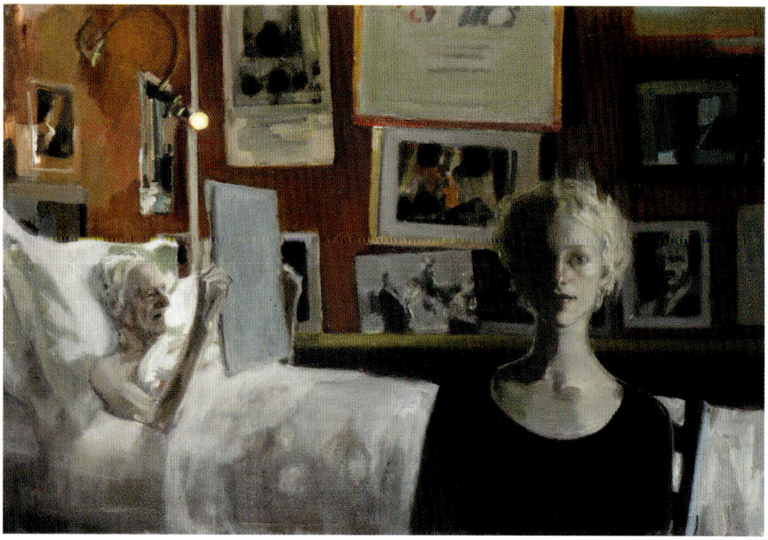

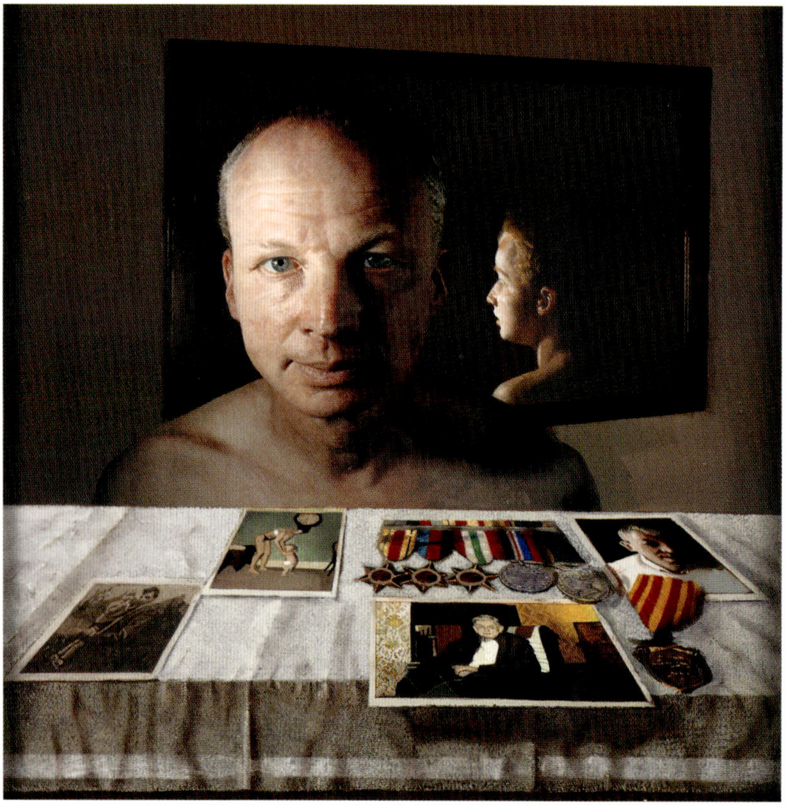

Alan Rickman
Raoul Martinez
Oil on canvas
978 x 878mm

Mayor Boris Johnson
Helen Masacz
Oil on board
1230 x 930mm

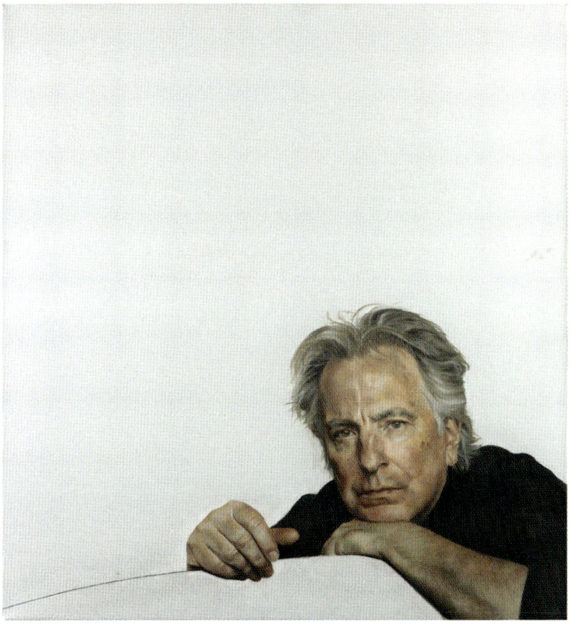

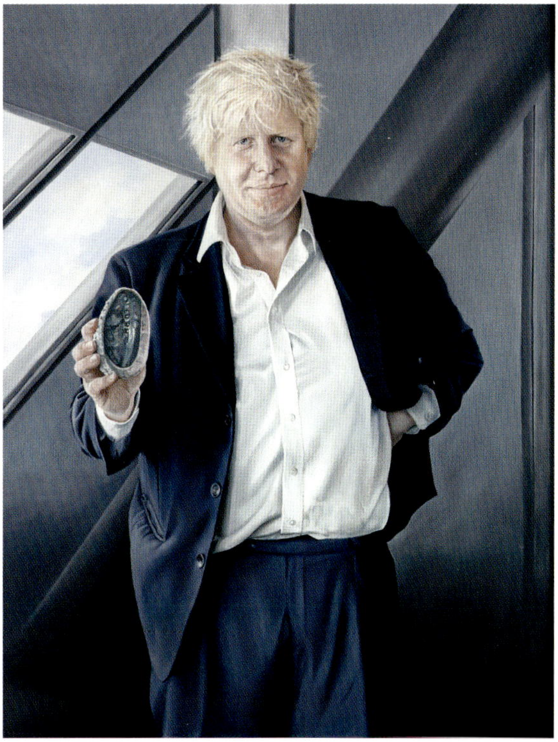

Almus Quartet
Miguel Angel Moya
Oil on canvas
1620 x 1620mm

The True Self-portrait
Carlos Muro
Acrylic on linen
1800 x 2000mm

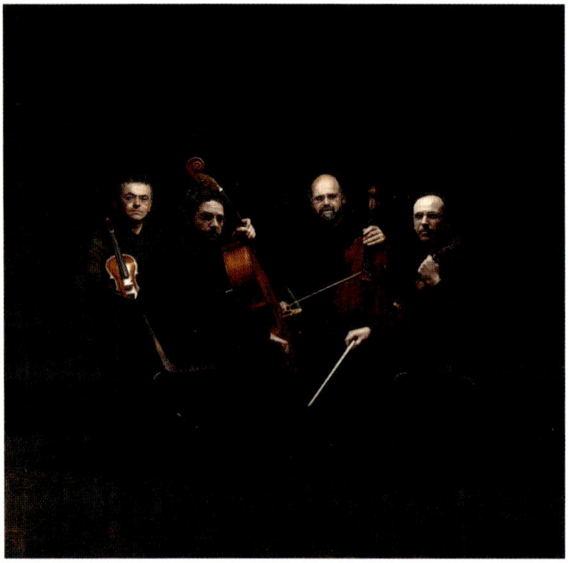

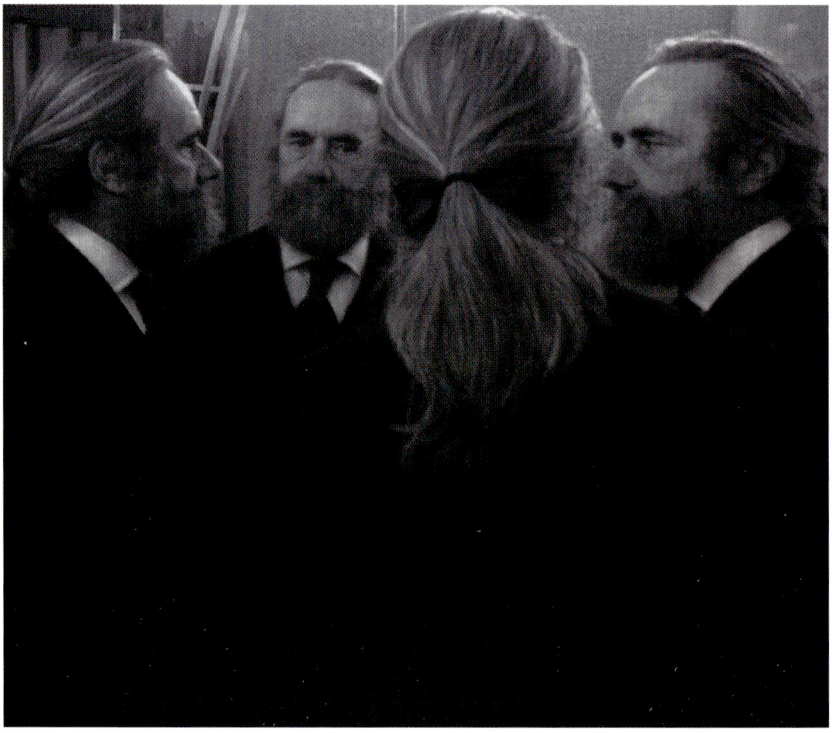

From my Soul I Cannot Hide
David Nightingale
Oil on linen
240 x 270mm

Love Painting –
Portrait of my Wife Jackie and our Cat Amy, Redbrick Mill Studio
Tony Noble
Acrylic on linen
1300 x 750mm

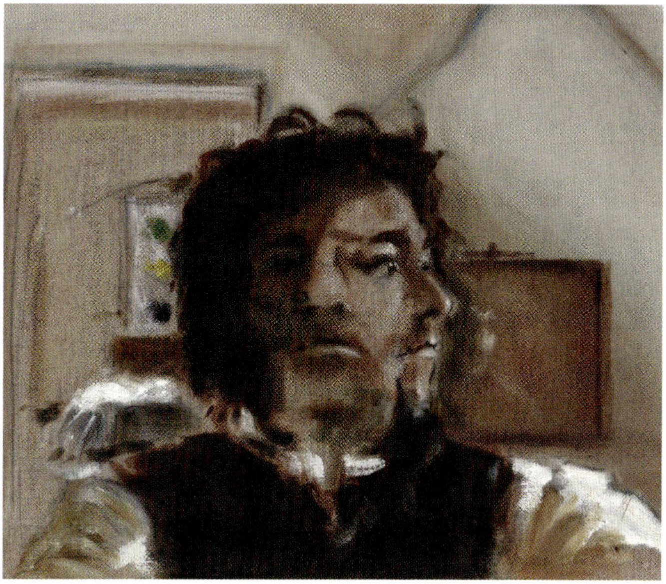

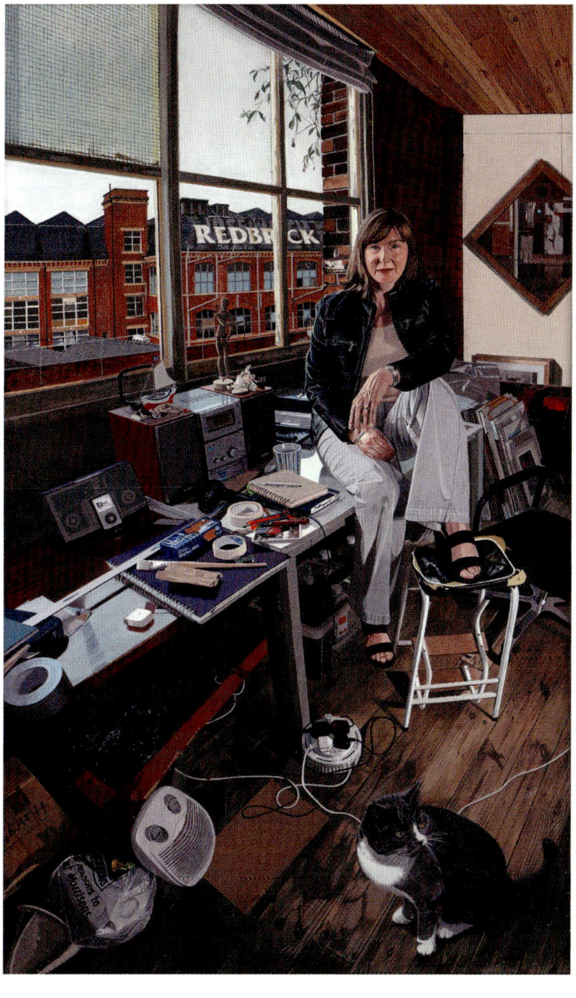

Benjamin Ogbebor
(Self-portrait)
Benjamin Ogbebor
Oil on canvas
300 x 240mm

iDeath
Michal Ožibko
Oil with acrylic background on canvas
2200 x 1700mm

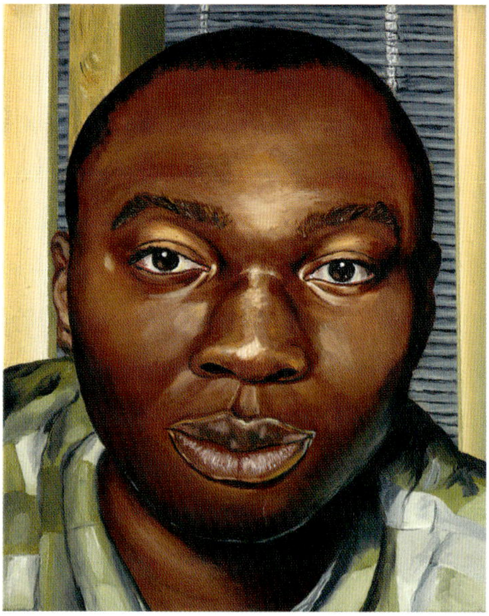

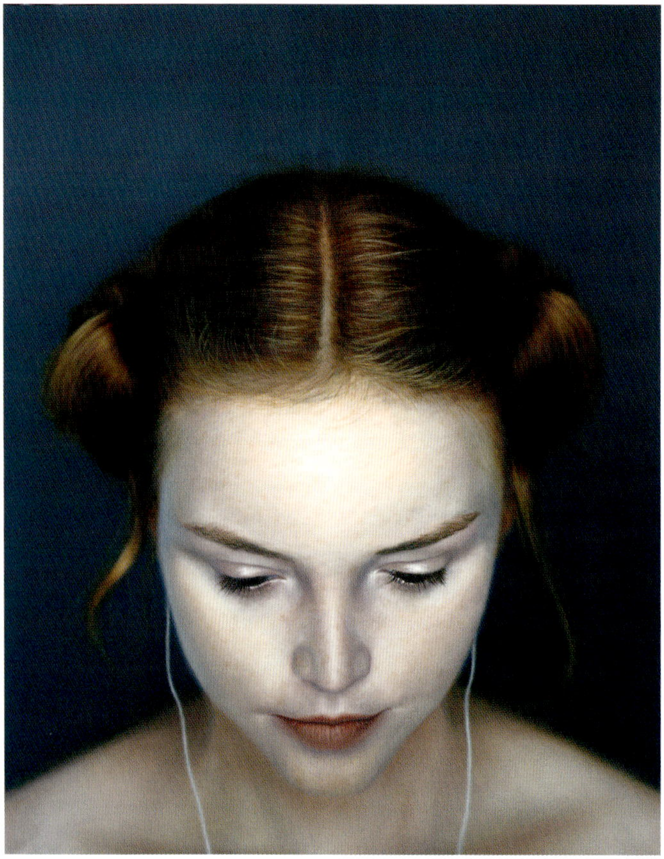

Lila Pearl
Thea Penna
Acrylic on canvas
505 x 505mm

Paddy (Le Flaneur)
Nicky Philipps
Oil on canvas
1016 x 762mm

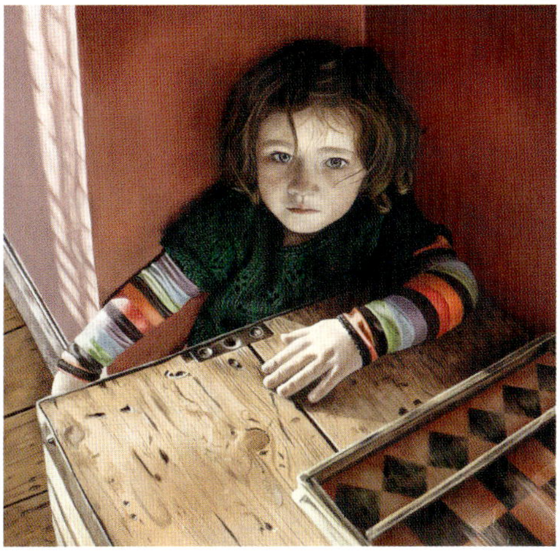

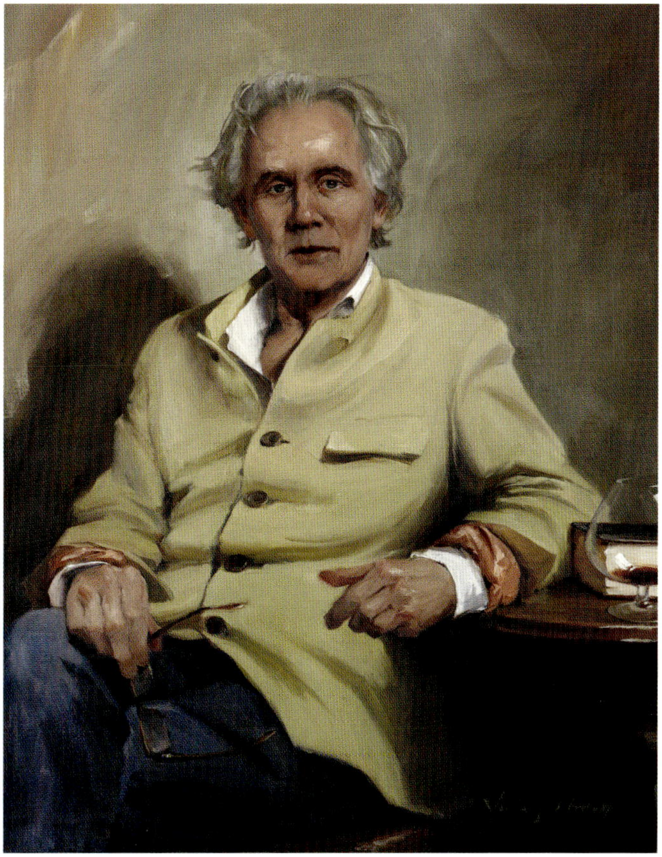

Debra
Philip Renforth
Oil on board
1380 x 980mm

Portrait of Giuseppe
Giampaolo Russo
Oil on canvas
850 x 800mm

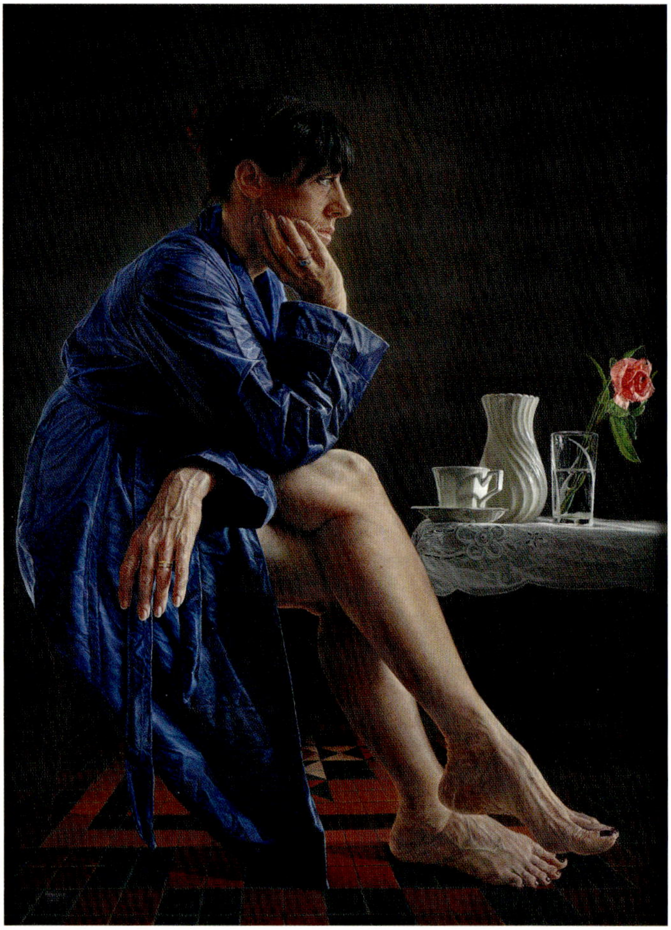

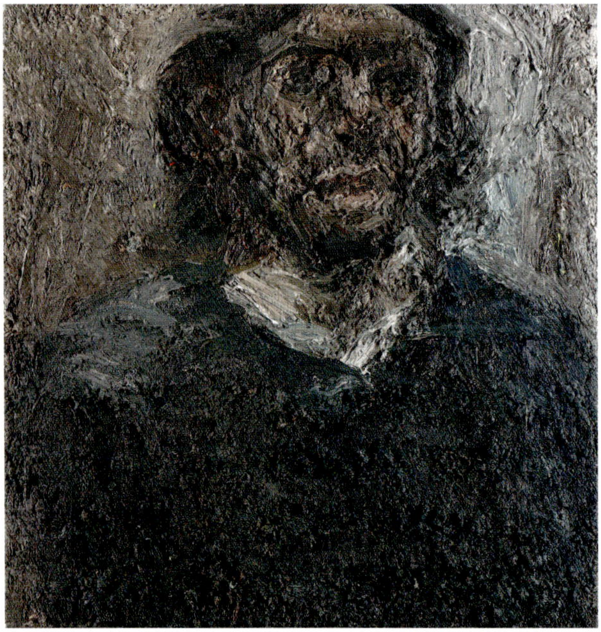

Geneva
Ilaria Rosselli Del Turco
Oil on wooden board
340 x 235mm

Chris, Art Critic
Fred Schley
Oil on canvas
500 x 600mm

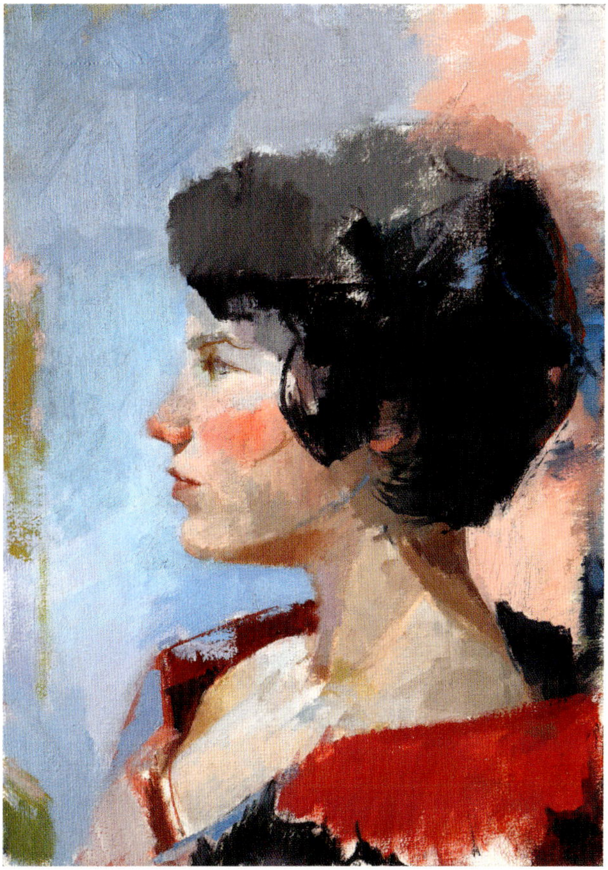

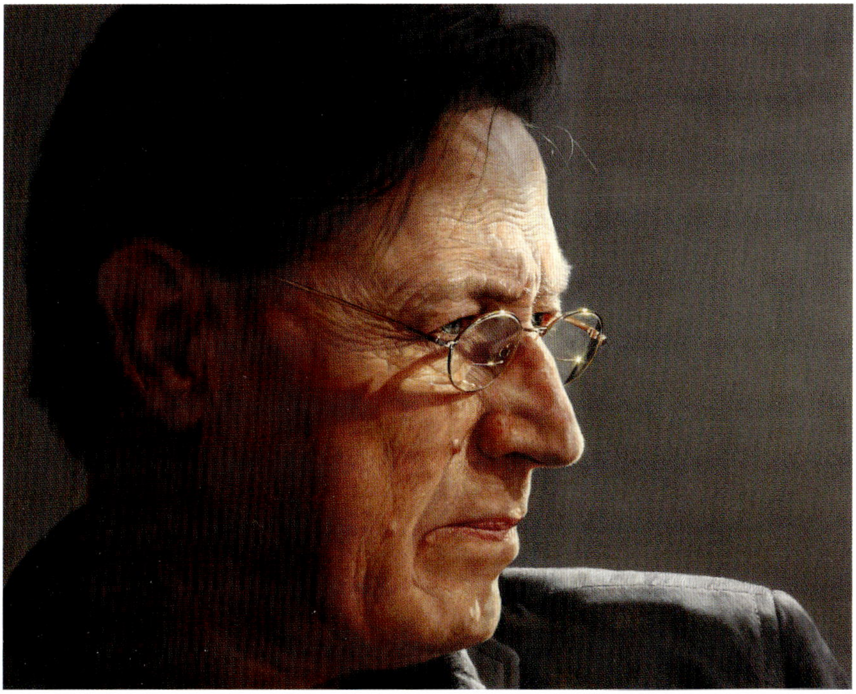

Theo
Nathalie Beauvillain Scott
Oil on canvas
405 x 305mm

Inside Outside (Clare with Claire)
Brian Shields
Acrylic on canvas
1180 x 730mm

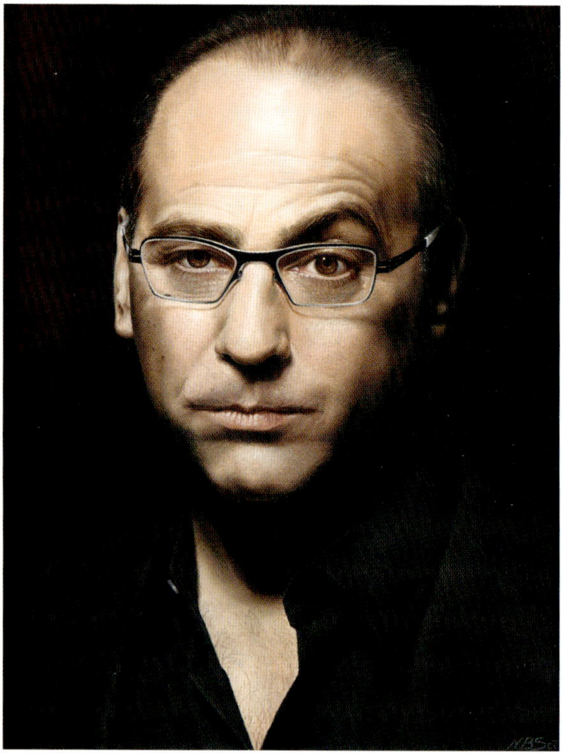

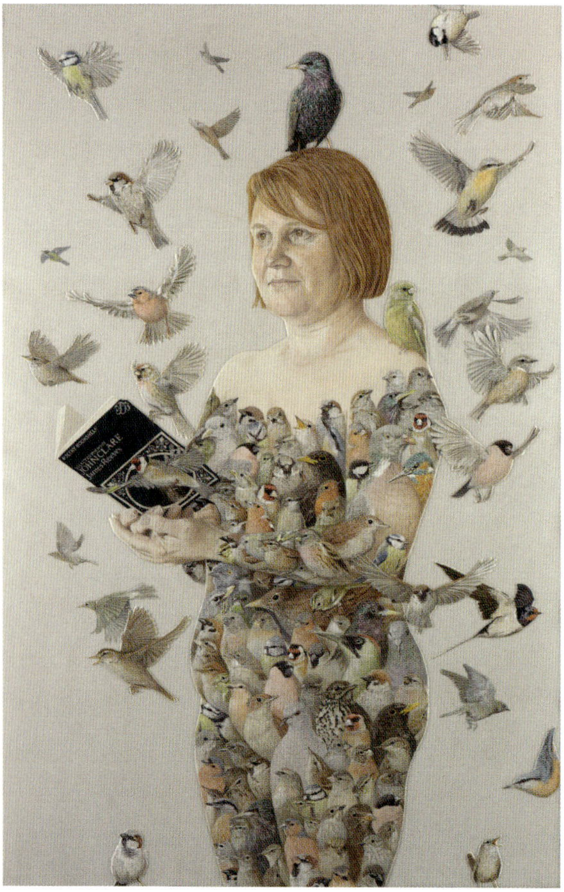

Nora
Edward Sutcliffe
Oil on canvas
450 x 300mm

The 'Finger-Assisted' Nephrectomy of Professor Nadey Hakim and the World Presidents of the International College of Surgeons in Chicago, or, The Wise in Examination of the Torn Contemporary State
Henry Ward
Oil on canvas
1676 x 3048mm

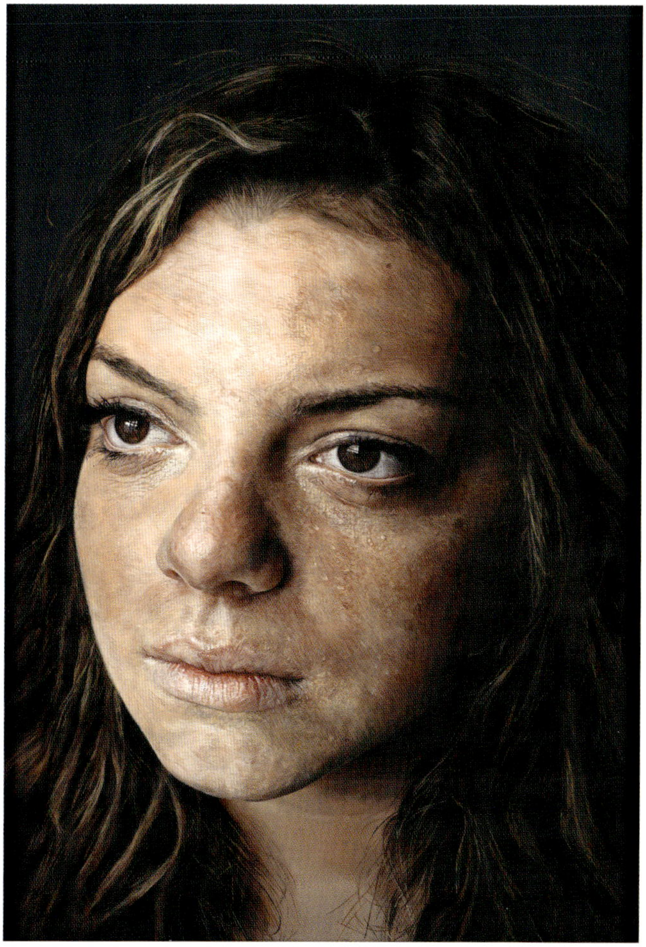

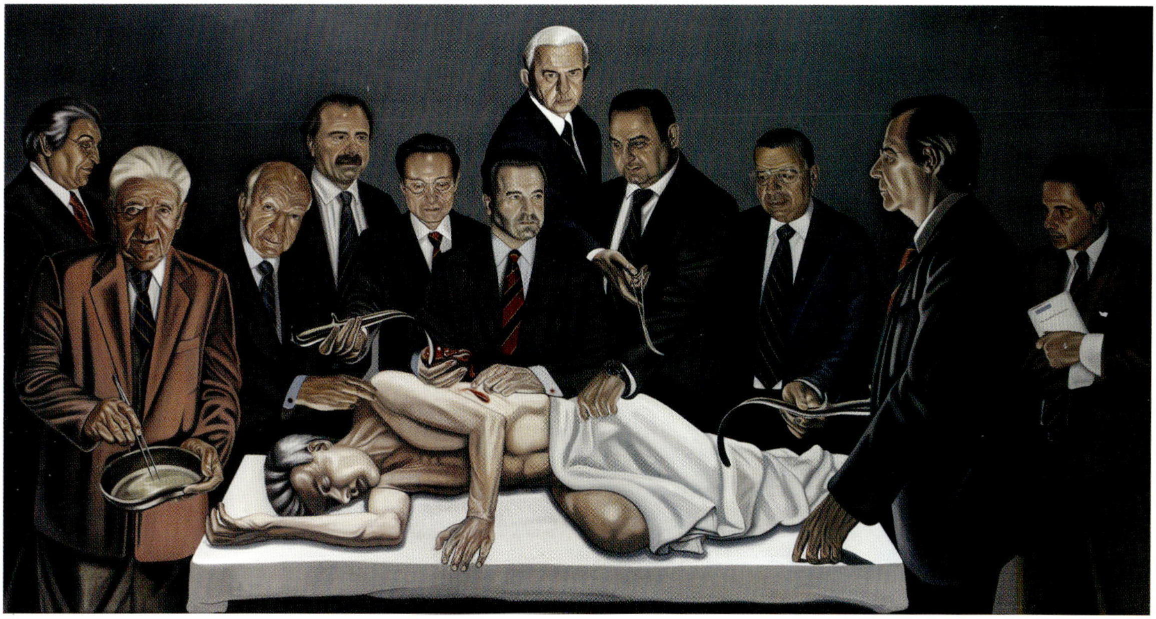

BP TRAVEL AWARD WINNERS

The Travel Award has been given annually since 1991, and the resulting work is shown as part of the subsequent year's exhibition.

Haydn Cottam / 1991
Alec Chanda / 1992
Susannah Fiennes / 1993
Andrew Tift / 1994
Christopher Stevens / 1995
Sadie Lee / 1996
Akash Bhatt / 1997
Stuart Pearson Wright / 1998
Jennifer McRae / 1999
Si Sapsford / 2000
Alan Parker / 2001
Daisy Richardson and
Jessica Wolfson / 2002
Ulyana Gumeniuk / 2003
Darvish Fakhr / 2004
Joel Ely / 2005
Toby Wiggins / 2006
Timothy Hyman and
Gareth Reid / 2007
Emmanouil Bitsakis / 2008
Isobel Peachey / 2009
Paul Beel / 2010

TRAVEL AWARD
SARAH HOWGATE

Curator of Contemporary Portraits,
National Portrait Gallery, London

Many young artists entering the BP Portrait Award choose subjects close to home: for practical and economic reasons, sitters are usually family, friends and the artists themselves. However, since 1991, the creation of the BP Travel Award has provided a winning artist with the opportunity to broaden their horizons through painting in a different environment, either in Britain or further afield.

To enter the Travel Award artists are invited to submit a proposal outlining their idea, itinerary and budget. The shortlisted artists are interviewed by a panel of judges and the following year the winner exhibits their resulting work at the Gallery during the BP Portrait Award exhibition.

Past projects have been diverse: Si Sapsford, who won in 2000, visited Salcombe, Devon, and Reykjavik, Iceland, to depict the rigorous lives of two lifeboat crews. The previous year, Jennifer McRae spent a month studying the staff and students of a Brussels art school, where the emphasis was on working from the life model. In 2001, the Award was won by police officer and artist Alan Parker, who hung up his policeman's hat for a month but continued to go to work, making a series of paintings of the officers and public on his Leicestershire beat. More recently, Isobel Peachey, winner of the 2009 Award, journeyed to Switzerland and Belgium to paint portraits of people engaged in historical re-enactment events.

PORTRAIT COMMISSIONS FOR THE COLLECTION

In commissioning portraits by a variety of artists working in a range of media, the Gallery hopes to encourage portraiture and to keep alive the representation of the human figure. The BP Portrait Award provides the opportunity for the Gallery to commission new works for the collection, not only by the First Prizewinners, but also by the other shortlisted artists. The works featured on the following pages are examples of these

Dame Muriel Spark
Bob Tulloch
Pencil and wash
1993
(BP Portrait Award, exhibited 1991)
282 x 282mm
NPG 6226

George Weidenfeld, Baron Weidenfeld of Chelsea
Paul Benney
Oil on canvas
1996
(BP Portrait Award, exhibited 1995–2000, 2008, 2010)
914 x 552mm
NPG 6360

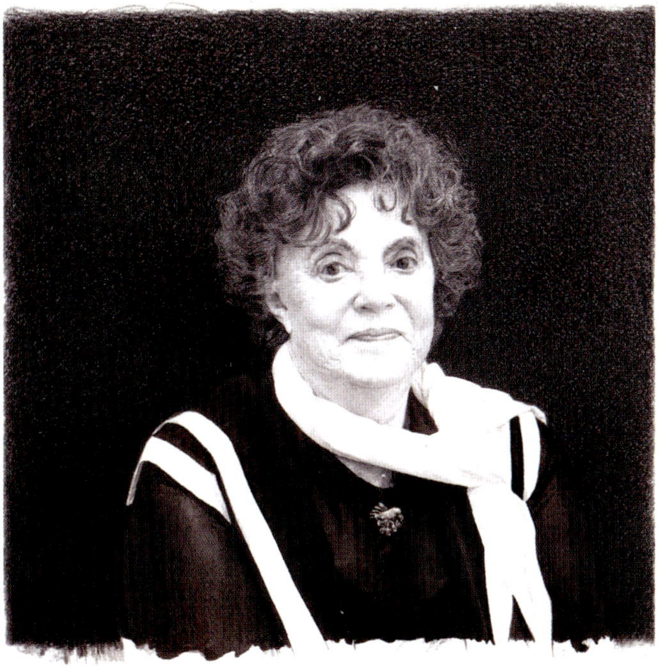

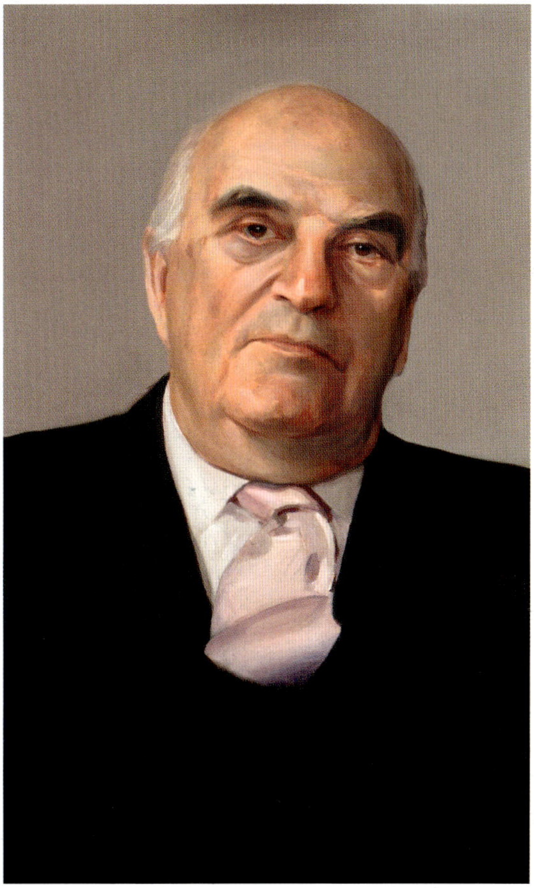

Thomas Adès
Phil Hale
Oil on canvas
Jerwood Commission
2002
(BP Portrait Award, exhibited 2000–2004)
2138 x 1073mm
NPG 6619

Amartya Sen
Antony Williams
Egg tempera on board
2003
(BP Portrait Award, exhibited 1995, 1998, 2005, 2007, 2010)
431 x 358mm
NPG 6640

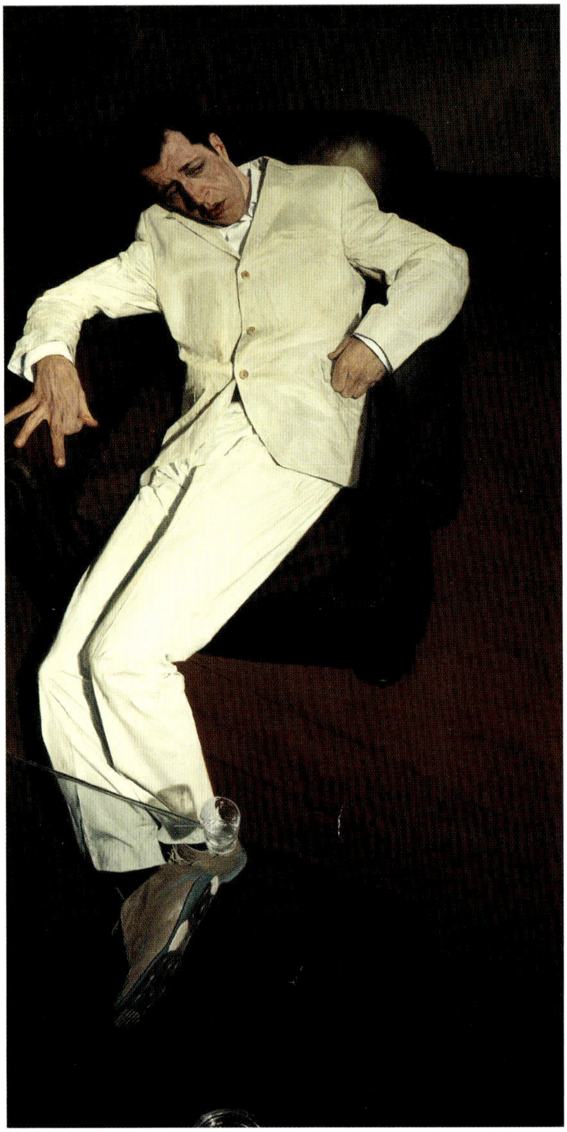

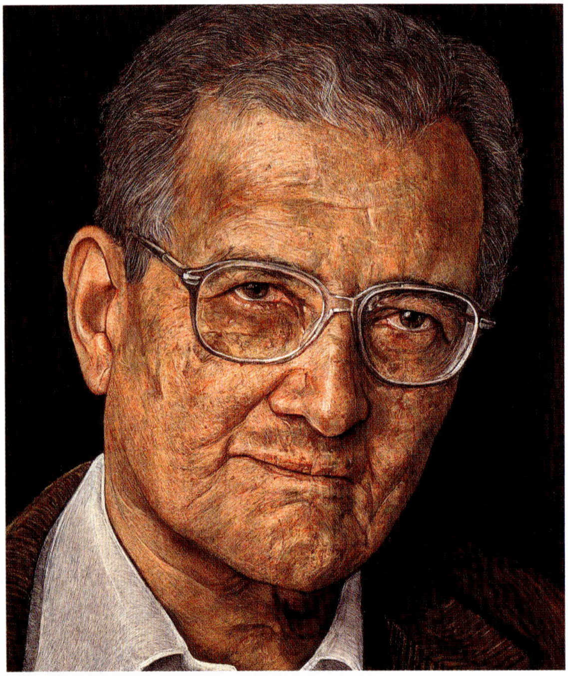

Sir Michael ('Mike') Jackson
Brendan Kelly
Oil on canvas
2009
(BP Portrait Award,
exhibited 1991–5, 2001,
2003, 2005)
1005 x 1005mm
NPG 6885

Martin Rees, Baron Rees of Ludlow
Benjamin Sullivan
Oil on panel
2008
(BP Portrait Award,
exhibited 2002, 2006–10)
561 x 301mm
NPG 6851

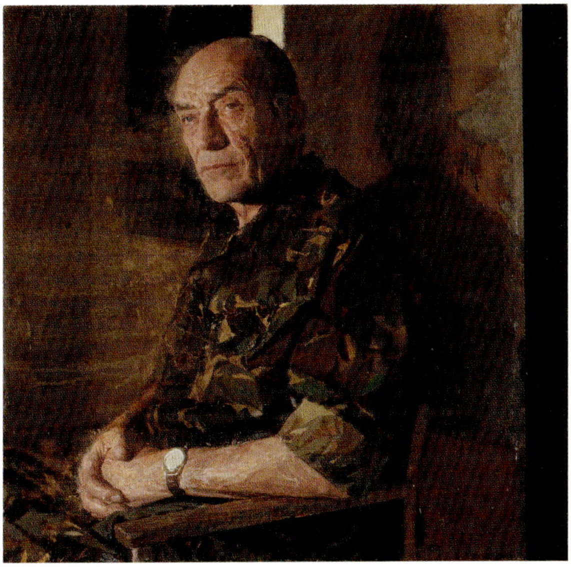

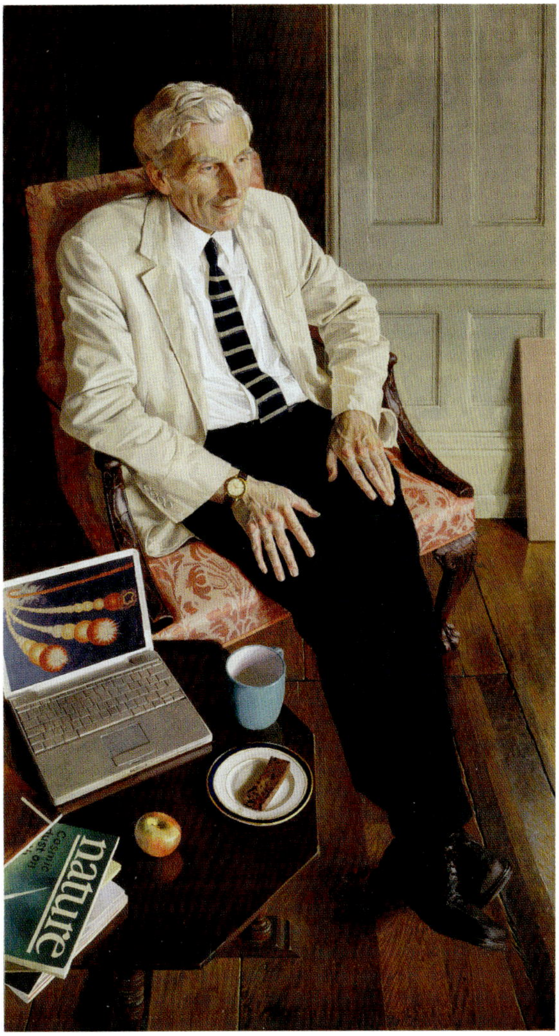

BP PORTRAIT AWARD: NEXT GENERATION

JUSTINE MCLISKY

*Head of Young People,
National Portrait Gallery, London*

BP Portrait Award: Next Generation is an innovative project to increase the engagement of young people aged fourteen to nineteen years old with painted portraiture through the BP Portrait Award. Inspired by the London 2012 Olympics and Paralympics, Next Generation links to the Cultural Olympiad themes of inspiration, challenge and 'having a go' at new cultural experiences.

Next Generation introduces young people to the BP Portrait Award and to the National Portrait Gallery by opening up creative responses and critical dialogue around painted portraiture. The project started in the summer of 2010 with short 'Taster Sessions' held at the Gallery during London's 2012 Open Weekend, and two intensive three-day Summer School workshops. These events engaged over 100 young people, including new visitors from the five 2012 Host Boroughs in East London. One participant commented, 'It was great to come into an environment where no-one has expectations about your way of working, which was really freeing for me.'

Next Generation provides the rare opportunity for participants to connect with artists, gaining insights into their practice, careers and their experience of being selected for the BP Portrait Award. Sixteen BP Portrait Award artists contributed in 2010, including former First Prizewinners Annabel Cullen, Philip Harris, Ishbel Myerscough and Victoria Russell, encouraging a new wave of young artists and potential future entrants.

Increasing access to portraiture through close consultation with young people is key to the success of Next Generation. Inspired by their experience, some of the 2010 participants have joined the Gallery's peer-led Youth Forum and will continue their involvement with the Gallery as the project unfolds, learning new skills and spreading the word to their friends.

Next Generation will evolve to include an interactive website, offering a bank of video interviews with BP Portrait Award artists, insights into the exhibition, and the ability for young people to upload their own portraits. Young people at regional museums and galleries will be able to participate through Next Generation programmes locally as part of the BP Portrait Award tour.

For further information on BP Portrait Award: Next Generation, please see www.npg.org.uk/bp